U0136513

THE
TAIWANESE YEAR BOOK OF
INTERNATIONAL LAW
2016

SECOND YEAR OF ISSUE

TAIWANESE SOCIETY OF INTERNATIONAL LAW

2017

PROFESSOR DR YAW-SHYANG CHEN
PROFESSOR MING-JUINN LI
PROFESSOR DR TING-HUI LIN
PROFESSOR DR SZU-WEI WANG

Editorial Communications should be addressed as follows:

Articles and Notes:

Professor Dr Ching-Chang Yen

14F-1, No 125, Nan-King East Road Section 2,

Taipei 10409,

Taiwan

Email: tsilorg@ms78.hinet.net

The Editors and members of the Editorial Committee do not make themselves in any way responsible for the views expressed by contributors.

The Taiwanese Yearbook of International Law is published by the Taiwanese Society of International Law, a scholarly organization devoted to the promotion of Taiwan in international legal community.

CONTENTS

Preface from the Founder

DR. MING-MIN PENG

As one of the co-founders of the Taiwanese Society of International Law (TSIL) in 2000, it gives me great pleasure to see the second issue of our yearbook in English. Last year's edition represented one kind of milestone, because it was our first. This year's publication is a different kind of achievement, marking the start of what we hope will be a long tradition of annual publications. This second issue gives us at TSIL confidence to paint a picture of our vision for the future. As was the case last year, we note our academic contribution to the discourse of topics on international law. We are providing an excellent platform for international scholars to exchange their views on international law topics pertaining to Taiwan.

I want to express once again my resolute goal: We all in Taiwan work together to further strengthen international visibility as a sovereign state. It has become ever clearer that Taiwan needs to engage other foreign governments to help us proclaim our reasonable and legitimate claim to be a sovereign nation. This fact must be recognized by the international community. I believe that broad acceptance of our sovereignty will be good not only for the people of Taiwan, but it will help provide regional balance and geopolitical stability.

I observe that Taiwan has successfully transformed itself into a living model of democracy for other nations in the Asia Pacific region. At the same time, Taiwan's economic and social attributes are ones that can and should be shared with the rest of the world. Taiwan continues to distinguish itself by ranking the 22nd largest economy in the world with a GDP per capita of 22,585 USD, according to 2016 International Monetary Fund statistics.

I once again offer sincere congratulations to Dr. Ching-Chang Yen, President of TSIL, for a job well done. Also, my appreciation to the contributors to this year's yearbook as well as to all those who have supported TSIL during the past year.

Acknowledgements

CHING-CHANG YEN

President of TSIL and Editor in Chief of TSIL Yearbook

As President of Taiwanese Society of International Law and Editor-in-Chief of the yearbook, I am thrilled to remind everyone of the milestone that we reached this past year of publishing the first-ever English yearbook. This year, I am honored to announce that we are repeating this achievement in what I hope will soon be seen as a tradition.

TSIL has accomplished much since 2000. Most importantly, TSIL has steadily continued to raise awareness to the general public and throughout the world about issues of importance regarding Taiwan. With great intellectual integrity, TSIL continues grappling with issues concerning international law.

We have an outstanding list of contributors to this year's publication. I wish to extend my sincerest thanks to them for their outstanding articles. In particular, I want to note specific contributions: Dr. Richard Bush, "A One-China Policy Primer"; Professor Charles Irish, who writes on "Trump, Trade and Taiwan"; Professor A. Asada, "The Intensity Element in the Concept of International Armed Conflict Under International Humanitarian Law: A Dissenting Opinion To The International Law Association's Use of Force Committee Report"; Professor Lutz-Christian Wolff, "Competition Advocacy and Competition Culture"; Dr. Wei-Ting Yen, "Reform without Transformation-Globalization and Financial Supervisory Reform in Taiwan"; and last but not least, Dr. Eric Hung, who has done an excellent job of editing this yearbook.

The Taiwanese Society of International Law (TSIL) was founded in 2000 as a result of the leadership of Dr. Ming-Min Peng, who has been unwavering in his commitment to promote Taiwan's international visibility as a sovereign state. I greatly appreciate his continued inspiration for TSIL.

10

His vision certainly guides us as we strive to strengthen TSIL's forward-looking mission.

I also would like to note my thanks to Dr. Eric Hung for his great help on all matters regarding the publication of this yearbook. More generally, I am grateful for his involvement in the operation of TSIL.

I wish also to thank the Wu Foundation as well as President Eric Wu specifically for their continued generous financial support of TSIL and, in particular, for financing the publication of this yearbook. As outlined last year, the Wu Foundation was established in honor of Dr. Eric Wu's late father, Mr. Ho-Su Wu, founder of the Shin Kong Group. The Wu Foundation continues to be well-recognized for its dedication to academic research in Taiwan. The Wu Foundation is a generous supporter of TSIL. I thankfully acknowledge the profound support from Dr. Eric T. Wu.

DR CHING-CHANG YEN

Dr. Yen is the current President of the Taiwanese Society of International law and a law professor at Soochow University.

Dr. Yen worked for twenty-eight years at the Ministry of Finance, beginning as a junior level official and completing his career as Finance Minister, 2000-2002. As Deputy Finance Minister, 1996-2000, Dr. Yen successfully assisted in introducing an integrated income tax system and helped to tackle the destructive influence arising from the Asian Financial Crisis. As Finance Minister, he continued his work to strengthen Taiwan's financial position by initiating the first-ever financial reform.

In 2002, Dr. Yen was appointed serve as Taiwan's first Ambassador to the WTO where he was able to utilize his expertise in interest in GATT/WTO law. His participation in this multilateral trading system was well recognized in Geneva and around the world.

Dr. Yen has published extensively in the areas of taxation and GATT/WTO law.

DR. RICHARD BUSH III

Richard Bush is a senior fellow at the Brookings Institution, holds the The Michael H. Armacost Chair and Chen-Fu and Cecilia Yen Koo Chair in Taiwan Studies, and is co-director, with Mireya Solís, of its *Center for East Asia Policy Studies* (CEAP). He also holds a joint appointment as a senior fellow in the Brookings John L. Thornton China Center. Bush came to the Brookings Institution in July 2002, after serving almost five years as the chairman and managing director of the American Institute in Taiwan.

Dr. Bush is the author of a number of articles on China's relations with its neighbors, particularly Taiwan. His latest book, *Hong Kong in the Shadow of China: Living with the Leviathan*, 2016, is a study of recent developments in Hong Kong and its political and economic future. Other publications include the following:

- *At Cross Purposes: U.S.-Taiwan Relations Since 1942*, 2004.

- *Untying the Knot: Making Peace in the Taiwan Strait*, 2005.

- *A War Like No Other: The Truth About China's Challenge to America* (Co-written with M. O'Hanlon), 2007.

- *Perils of Proximity: China-Japan Security Relations*, 2010.

- *Uncharted Strait: The Future of China-Taiwan Relations*, 2013.

Richard Bush received his undergraduate education at Lawrence University in Appleton, Wisconsin. He did his graduate work in political science at Columbia University, getting a master's in 1973 and his doctorate in 1978.

PROFESSOR CHARLES R. IRISH

Charles R. Irish is the Volkman-Bascom Professor of Law (emeritus) and Director of the East Asian Legal Studies Center (emeritus) from the University of Wisconsin Madison Law School. Professor Irish is a well-known scholar in the areas of tax law and international trade law.

In Asia, Professor Irish teaches courses in international tax and an introduction to US laws and legal institutions. Over the course of his career, Professor Irish has traveled to about 80 countries and done extensive advisory work on tax reform and trade policy for governments in Africa, Asia, Europe and the Caribbean. He also was of counsel with the Madison law firm of Stafford Rosenbaum LLP for over 20 year where he worked on domestic and international tax issues.

Professor Irish's research interests focus on international taxation, trade policies and U.S. laws affecting international business. He has written many articles and monographs on international taxation, and trade policies.

Professor Irish has a B.A. degree from Columbia University, with a major in economics, and a J.D. degree from Vanderbilt Law School, where he was Order of the Coif and a member of the Vanderbilt Law Review. He also has an honorary doctorate in law degree from Far Eastern National University in Vladivostok, Russia, has received special awards from Thammasat University in Bangkok and the Shanghai Municipal Government, and is an honorary citizen of Shanghai's Minhang District.

PROFESSOR MASAHIKO ASADA

Professor of International Law, Kyoto University, Japan

Masahiko Asada is Professor of international Law at the Graduate School of Law, Kyoto University. He served as Legal Adviser to many high-profile Japanese Delegations: Conference on Disarmament in 1991-1993; Biological Weapons Convention in 1995-2001; Preparatory Committees for the NPT Review Conference; and, on many occasions, to the Review Conferences. He was also a member of the UN Panel of Government Experts on Verification in 2006-2007, and served on the Panel of Experts for the DPRK Sanctions in 2009-2010.

Professor Asada was the Editor-in-Chief of the *Kokusaiho Gaiko Zasshi* in 2012-2014. He has been a long-standing member of the editorial boards of two Journals: *Japanese Yearbook of International Law* and *Journal of Conflict* and Security Law. His most recent book, published in Japanese in 2015, is entitled *Post-War Reparations between Japan and China under International Law*.

Professor Asada was a former Senior Associate at St. Anthony's College, Oxford. He holds executive board positions: Japanese Society of International Law; Japanese Association of World Law; Japan Branch of the International Law Association (ILA); and Japan Chapter of the Asian Society of International Law. In 2009-2011 Professor Asada served as the President of the Japan Association of International Security and Trade, and between 2013-2015 he was President of the Japan Association of Disarmament Studies.

PROFESSOR LUTZ-CHRISTIAN WOLFF

Professor Wolff specializes in International and Chinese Business Law, Comparative Law, and Private International Law. He has studied, worked and conducted research in a number of jurisdictions, including mainland China, Taiwan, and the USA. He is admitted to practice in England & Wales and in Germany. He is frequently invited to work with multi-national companies on investment projects in the Greater China region. Professor Wolff was a founding member of the Faculty of Law (then: School of Law). He has served amongst others as Associate Dean (Faculty Development) (9/2008 to 7/2010), as Director of the Master of Laws Programmes in International Economic Law, Common Law and Chinese Business Law (9/2008 to 7/2011) and as Associate Dean (Graduate Studies) & Head Graduate Division of Law (8/2010 to 8/2014). Professor Wolff has been appointed as Dean of the CUHK Graduate School as of 1 September 2014.

WEI-TING YEN (PH.D. CANDIDATE)

Wei-Ting Yen is a Ph.D. candidate (ABD) of Political Science at The Ohio State University, where her research interest centers on the intersection of comparative political economy, social policy, and political behavior in the developing countries, with the regional focus on Asia. She was selected as the Chiang Ching-Kuo Doctoral Dissertation Fellow in the North America region in the 2016-17 academic year. In the current 2017-2018 year, she serves as the program director for the North America Taiwan Studies Association.

Ms Yen's dissertation focuses on how income insecurity affects individual social policy participation and the subsequent implications for social policy design. She is also collaborating on several research projects that examine political attitudes and behaviors across Asian countries. Topics include trade preference and nationalism, labor market transformation and political attitudes. She has conducted field work research in Indonesia, Taiwan, and Cambodia. Her work has appeared in the Journal of Asian and African Studies.

Before joining The Ohio State University, she holds an MA in East Asia Studies from Yale University, an MA in Political Science from National Taiwan University, and BA degrees in Economics and Political Science (double major) from National Taiwan University. With the MA degree in Political Science from National Taiwan University, her master's thesis focused on the politics of financial regulatory reforms in Taiwan.

A ONE-CHINA POLICY PRIMER

BY RICHARD C. BUSH

The Brookings Institution

March 2017

KEY FINDINGS

The one-China policy of the United States is not the same thing as the one-China principle of the People's Republic of China (PRC). The one-China policy contains more elements, such as the U.S. interest in a peaceful process, and its interpretation of Taiwan's legal status is different from the Beijing's interpretation.

Today, the U.S. one-China policy is a distillation from key documents such as the three U.S.-China joint communiqués and the Taiwan Relations Act (TRA), and a series of policy statements made over the years, such as the "six assurances."

The United States had a one-China policy from 1900 to 1949 that was a response to the fragmentation of China into multiple power centers. Since 1949, the U.S. one-China policy has addressed the existence of two rival governments: the PRC in Beijing and the Republic of China (ROC) in Taipei. During the Cold War, Washington was forced to choose between the two governments, because each side rejected any idea that the United States could have diplomatic relations with both. Washington maintained diplomatic relations with Taipei until 1979, when it switched to Beijing. Beijing still imposes its forced choice on Washington.

At the time that the Carter established diplomatic relations with the PRC in 1979, it pledged to have unofficial relations with Taiwan. It created an organization—the American Institute in Taiwan (AIT)—that was non-governmental in its legal form, but carried out the substance of U.S. government policy in relations with Taiwan. More generally, Washington has found "work arounds" to the limitations imposed by unofficial relations.

The United States takes no position on the substance of a solution to the differences that divide Beijing and Taipei, whether it be the unification of Taiwan with China or any other scenario. But it does oppose either side unilaterally changing the status quo, and has consistently stated its "abiding interest" in a peaceful resolution of cross-Strait differences. More recently,

Washington has stated that any solution should have "the assent of the people of Taiwan."

Since 1979, there is at least an implicit linkage between Washington's implementation of the one-China policy, including unofficial ties with Taiwan, and Beijing's stated preference for a peaceful resolution of differences with Taiwan. The linkage also goes the other way: if Beijing chose to use force against Taiwan, it would likely trigger a sharp deterioration in U.S.-PRC relations.

RECOMMENDATIONS: DOS AND DON'TS FOR THE TRUMP ADMINISTRATION

1. DO NOT state as the position of the U.S. government that Taiwan is a part of China.
2. DO NOT use the phrase "one-China principle" (the PRC term). Instead, continue the practice of referring to "our one-China policy."
3. DO NOT take a position on the merits of one country, two systems as a substantive formula for resolving the Taiwan Strait dispute.
4. DO continue to restate the U.S. "abiding interest" in a resolution of the dispute that is peaceful and acceptable to the people of Taiwan.
5. DO urge both Beijing and Taipei to conduct cross-Strait relations with flexibility, patience, creativity, and restraint.
6. DO emphasize to Beijing that the principal obstacle to its achieving its goal of unification is not U.S. arms sales to Taiwan, but the opposition of the Taiwan public to its unification formula.
7. DO continue to provide weaponry to Taiwan that is tailored to the existing and likely future threat from the PRC.
8. DO continue interactions with Taiwan's defense establishment on how to strengthen deterrence.
9. DO deepen our substantive interaction with Taiwan on bilateral issues.
10. DO work with Taiwan to find ways to enhance its international role and participation in international governmental institutions where it is not a member.

11. If it is in the U.S. interests to take steps to improve bilateral relations with Taiwan, DO NOT implement those changes in ways that create a public challenge to Beijing.

12. DO consult in advance with leaders of Taiwan on any changes in U.S. policy towards the island—either positive or negative—before making them. Taiwan's leaders are the best judges of whether those steps will serve their interests.

INTRODUCTION

It was Donald J. Trump who inspired me to write this essay. On December 2, 2016, twenty-five days after his surprise election to the presidency, he took a congratulatory phone call from Taiwan's president Tsai Ing-wen. This was the first time to anyone's knowledge that a U.S. president or president-elect had spoken to his counterpart in Taiwan, and questions quickly arose whether Trump had violated the one-China policy governing U.S. relations with China and Taiwan. Most observers inferred that the president-elect had committed a diplomatic gaffe and so demonstrated that he was not ready for the office that he would soon occupy.

Two things quickly became clear. The first was that Trump believed he knew what he was doing, and that the phone call was part of a calculated strategy. He told *Fox News Sunday* on December 11 that, "I fully understand the one-China policy, but I don't know why we have to be bound by a one-China policy unless we make a deal with China having to do with other things, including trade." The second thing was that most pundits who commented on the one-China policy didn't really know what they were talking about. Perhaps Trump didn't either. With the encouragement of my friend and colleague, Jeffrey Bader, I was moved to join the discussion. I wrote "An Open Letter to Donald Trump on the One-China policy," which was posted on the Brookings website on December 13. The short essay was generally well received as a brief explainer on the nuances of the one-China policy.[1]

Trump's statement on one China alarmed the Chinese government, which feared that he might abandon what it regarded as the framework of the bilateral relationship, the basis on which all other cooperation was possible. Observers on Taiwan were also worried that the U.S. president intended to use them as leverage or a bargaining chip in negotiations with China. From within and outside the U.S. government, voices encouraged Trump to

---

[1] Richard C. Bush, "Open Letter to Donald J. Trump on the One-China Policy," The Brookings Institution, December 13, 2016 (https://www.brookings.edu/blog/order-from-chaos/2016/12/13/an-open-letter-to-donald-trump-on-the-one-china-policy/

avoid a fight on the one-China issue. Consequently, Trump walked back his position soon after his inauguration. On February 9, 2017, he told Chinese president Xi Jinping during a phone call that he would "honor our 'one China' policy." The issue seemed to blow over.

I remained worried, however, that the issue is not settled once and for all. The president could have used a stronger verb than "honor," and the White House statement about the phone call said that Trump made this commitment at Xi's request. Moreover, and much more than in previous administrations, Trump's personality dominates the policymaking process. Just because the president has set the issue aside does not mean that he will not re-open it at a moment's notice. Moreover, during the election campaign, he blamed China for America's economic malaise, with some success. Some of his advisers would like to reduce, if not end, American companies reliance on the global economic system in general and China in particular. So it may be politically difficult for him to do nothing on U.S.-China economic relations. Finally, as he approaches negotiations, he can be expected to try to accumulate bargaining leverage and then apply it in a tough-minded way. I for one cannot rule out the possibility that he personally might choose to use Taiwan as such a point of leverage in negotiating with China, or being willing to make Taiwan-related "side-payments" to Beijing that would damage the island's interests.

I decided, therefore, that I should expand on my quick and dirty blogpost from December 13 and provide a longer, yet still relatively short, explanation of the U.S. one-China policy: what it means; what it doesn't mean; how it came about; and why putting it in play in bargaining with China is actually quite reckless, if only because it puts Taiwan's interests at risk. Hence, this report, which draws considerably on my past work, particularly *At Cross Purposes: U.S.-Taiwan Relations Since 1942*, and *Untying the Knot: Making Peace in the Taiwan Strait*. I also draw heavily on the work and insights of Alan Romberg of the Stimson Center, particularly his *Rein In on the Brink of the Precipice*.[2]

2   Richard C. Bush, *At Cross Purposes: U.S.-Taiwan Relations Since 1942* (Armonk, N.Y.: M. E.

Many who write about the one-China policy rely in making their case on textual analysis, going back to the "sacred texts" of U.S.-China-Taiwan relations. I do so to an extent, because some of the principles in those documents remain highly relevant. But, I also place emphasis on how those tenets are interpreted and applied in the present. China, Taiwan, and the United States have all changed since Richard Nixon initiated a rapprochement with the People's Republic of China in 1971-72 and Jimmy Carter completed the process of normalization of relations in 1978-79 and the U.S. Congress passed the Taiwan Relations Act. Most important, China's turn to a basic policy of reform and opening up, initiated in late 1978, and Taiwan's democratic transition, which began in 1986 and was completed in 1996, altered the way each pole of this triangle interacted with the others. But that was a long time ago. The priesthood of Americans who first mastered the "sacred texts" of U.S. policy is small and getting smaller. New generations of political leaders cannot always figure out why they must take so seriously the principles accepted by Presidents Nixon, Carter, and Reagan, and their relevance to twenty-first century circumstances. It is not always possible to deduce from the principles in those old texts how they should be defined and applied today. Hence the value of exploring what the one-China policy means *and doesn't mean*, what it restricts and what it allows.

"We Have a One-China Policy"

In the United States' relations with both China and Taiwan, the verbal formulations used to describe policy for stating policy than perhaps any other foreign policy relationship. Words themselves become policy.

Sometime in the 1980s, U.S. officials began to refer to "our one-China policy" and to say "we have a one-China policy." This practice, which continues today, contrasts with the practice of Henry Kissinger, the National Security Adviser and then Secretary of State in the Nixon administration.

Sharpe, 2004); Richard C. Bush, *Untying the Knot: Making Peace in the Taiwan Strait* (Washington, D.C.: Brookings Institution Press, 2005); Richard C. Bush: *Uncharted Strait: The Future of China-Taiwan Relations* (Washington, D.C.: Brookings Institution Press, 2013); Alan D. Romberg, *Rein In at the Brink of the Precipice: American Policy Toward Taiwan and U.S.-PRC Relations* (Washington, D.C.: Henry L. Stimson Center, 2003).

He referred usually to "the one-China principle." The shift from "principle" to "policy" was welcome, if only because Beijing has its own version of the one-China principle, which differs from the U.S. approach in a couple of important respects.

The PRC definition of the one-China principle for international consumption is that, "there is only one China in the world, Taiwan is a part of China and the government of the PRC is the sole legal government representing the whole of China."[3] As we shall see, the United States has associated itself in various ways with the first of these points for over a century. It effectively accepted the third point in 1978 in the communiqué that established diplomatic relations with Beijing (hereafter the "normalization communiqué"). On the second point, and in the same document, Washington took a more ambiguous position. Moreover, over time successive administrations have found ways to "work around" a strict constructionist view of its normalization commitments.

The U.S. government does not have such a concise rendering of "its" one-China policy as Beijing does. When American officials say that "we have a one-China policy," they usually elaborate by listing several defining elements: adherence to the three U.S.-PRC communiqués of 1972, 1978, and 1982; implementation of the Taiwan Relations Act enacted in April 1979; an abiding interest in the peaceful resolution of the differences between the two sides; opposition to either side unilaterally changing the status quo and non-support for de jure independence of Taiwan; the "six assurances" conveyed to Taiwan in August 1982; a preference for continuing dialogue and cooperation between Beijing and Taipei; and so on. (More on all of these elements later.) Not all of these points is mentioned every time a U.S. official speaks about the one-China policy. Some are important for Taiwan and others important for China. Beijing wants to hear about the three communiqués and non-support for Taiwan independence. Taipei likes Washington to reaffirm the Taiwan Relations Act and the six assurances.

---

3   Taiwan Affairs Office and The Information Office of the State Council, "White Paper--The One-China Principle and the Taiwan Issue," issued February 21, 2000 (http://www.taiwandocuments.org/white.htm).

In his confirmation hearing to be secretary of state in January 2017, Rex Tillerson made only general statements about the one-China policy, mainly that there were no plans to revise it and that the new administration reaffirmed the U.S. commitment to Taiwan. In response to a written question from a Senator, however, the State Department provided a more detailed statement:

> The Three Communiques, Taiwan Relations Act, and Six Assurances provide the foundation for U.S. policy toward China and Taiwan. The United States should continue to uphold the One China policy and support a peaceful and mutually agreeable cross-Strait outcome. Under this policy, the United States recognizes the People's Republic of China as the sole legal government of China and acknowledges the Chinese position that Taiwan is part of China. As required by the Taiwan Relations Act, the United States continues to provide Taiwan with arms of a defensive character and maintains the capacity of the United States to resist any resort to force or other forms of coercion that would jeopardize the security, or the social or economic system, of the people of Taiwan. The United States also upholds the Six Assurances on U.S. policy toward Taiwan.

It may seem odd to readers unfamiliar with the theology of U.S.-China-Taiwan relations that the three governments place so much emphasis on verbal formulations and on their consistent repetition. Yet as American officials new to working on U.S. policy regarding China and Taiwan quickly learn, part of their on-the-job training is to master the vocabulary, syntax, and grammar of these verbal formulations and to repeat them earnestly and without hesitation whenever the situation demands. In my time serving in such a role, I was struck by how carefully Chinese and Taiwan readers examined my speeches to identify textual changes and assess what such changes might mean. This is set of relationships like no other.

One reason for this phenomenon is that diplomats from both sides of the Taiwan Strait are all culturally Chinese. Both in Beijing and Taipei, the governments place high priority on getting the words right and vigilantly watching how both friends and adversaries pick their words. In China especially, a key phase of both the internal policy process and diplomacy is precisely defining the words attached to any policy. Changing the terms used to refer to basically the same thing has policy significance, or so people in Beijing believe. In both Beijing and Taipei, officials and scholars have mastered the record of past diplomatic understandings, and they will correct Americans who do not use the proper formulations.

But this is not just a cultural phenomenon at work. Power asymmetries are also at play. Words can be the weapons of the weak, used to constrain a more powerful party whose behavior begins to differ from its past verbal commitments. At one time, both the PRC and the ROC were weak relative to the United States and each sought to use words for their respective advantage and protection. China is stronger today, but old habits die hard and its officials are unlikely to abandon a policy tool that they believe has served them well.

U.S. officials can and do adapt the elements of the U.S. one-China policy that they cite to the situation. For example, they stress the need for dialogue between Beijing and Taipei most of all when dialogue is not happening. The two sides initiated a dialogue in 1993 and Washington endorsed it. Then talks were suspended in 1995 after then-President Lee Teng-hui's visit to the United States that year, and so the need to resume dialogue became a more salient element in U.S. statements.

No element is ever dropped, and the way to shift rhetorical policy is to introduce a new element. In 1998, when I was serving as chairman of the American Institute in Taiwan, I concluded that U.S. statements should give attention to the fact that Taiwan was a democracy. That, I believed, was important for its own sake but also because this political transformation had given the Taiwan public a seat in any cross-Strait negotiations. That meant that if Beijing was to achieve its goal of unification of Taiwan, it would have to convince not just the Taiwan government but also the Taiwan people. I added a paragraph to that effect to the end of a speech I was to give at a Taiwan event in Arizona. I sent the draft text of my remarks to the

State Department for clearance, as I always did. I would have understood if that final paragraph had been excised, but to my delight it was approved basically unchanged. My initiative was rewarded eighteen months later when then-President Bill Clinton, in a speech on economic policy towards China, said that the United States should be "absolutely clear that the issues between Beijing and Taiwan must be resolved peacefully and with the assent of the people of Taiwan."[4] To my regret, the George W. Bush administration undercut my small achievement a couple of years later by changing the last part of the formulation to refer the assent of people on both sides of the Taiwan Strait. Of course, the people of the PRC have no way to register their assent, and the Chinese Communist Party arrogates to itself the right and power to speak for the Chinese people. As originally stated, the principle constituted rhetorical pressure on Beijing to creatively re-shape its policy in ways that Taiwan voters might find appealing. In the end, that value was diminished.

The United States' One-China Policy Before 1949

For the first half of the twentieth century, the division of China into different power centers was a central focus of U.S. policy. In its rhetoric, it emphasized the sovereignty and territorial integrity of China. Most of the time, however, Washington possessed neither the ability nor the will to back up its words.

The United States' one-China policy goes back at least to 1900, but its focus has varied according to circumstances. Indeed, the word "one" in the phrase "one-China policy" has a couple of different connotations, each of which contains within it one or more alternatives to "one." In recent decades, the alternative to "one China" is two Chinas, a subject to which I address in the next section. But the word "one" also can refer to both unity and its opposite, division and separation. That connotation is present today, of course. Chinese nationalists regard Taiwan's continued separate existence

---

4   "Full Text of Clinton's Speech on China Trade Bill," *New York Times*, March 9, 2000 (https://www.nytimes.com/library/world/asia/030900clinton-china-text.html).

as a continuing obstacle to their country's return to greatness (in this sense, unity also implies strength and division connotes weakness). Taiwan nationalists regard the very idea that Taiwan should be a part of Beijing's one China as an affront to their own political aspirations for independence. For the first half of the twentieth century, however, the focus was on the internal division of China, and, in an important sense, the subject of one China was as much about state- and nation-building and domestic politics as it is about international relations.

Two hundred and fifty years ago, the question of one China would not have come up. China—Imperial China—was a unified and imposing entity. It was the world's largest country, both in territory and the size of its economy. It was the dominant power in East Asia. To be sure, there had been times previously when the Chinese empire had broken up into competing power centers, but the last occasion was in the mid-to-late seventeenth century. And that division didn't last forever. As the beginning of a famous Chinese novel, *The Romance of the Three Kingdoms,* put it, "They say the momentum of history was ever thus: the empire long divided must unite; long united, must divide."[5]

The first part of twentieth century was a time of break-up in China. At the beginning of the century, the anti-foreign Boxer Rebellion swept over many parts of the country and almost brought the imperial regime to an end. By 1911, a constitutional movement worked alongside a modernizing military to force the abdication of the emperor. The Republic of China was declared on New Year's Day 1912 and hopes for a democratic system were high. Quickly, however, military leaders began competing for power, geographic spheres of influence, and the customs revenues that control of the capital provided. Diplomats did their best to conduct foreign relations, but the unity of China quickly became a thing of the past. Decentralized, political power flowed from the barrels of opposing guns.

With its Soviet-trained armies, the Kuomintang entered into this military

---

[5] Lo Kuan-chung, *Three Kingdoms: China's Epic Drama,* translated from the Chinese and edited by Moss Roberts (New York: Pantheon Books, 1976), p. 3

competition in the late 1920s and began a temporary process of unification. Chiang Kai-shek knocked off rival warlords in a series of campaigns, and his government, now recognized as the government of China with its capital in Nanjing, increased both its capacity and effective jurisdiction. All that was reversed in the 1930s as two new military adversaries emerged. The first was the communist Red Army in the mountains of southeastern China. The second was Imperial Japanese Army, which took over the three northeastern provinces of Manchuria in 1931 and then proceeded incrementally to expand its control into North China. Chiang was able to evict the communists from their mountain bases and then chase them into northwestern China. But the Red Army survived to fight another day. In 1937, war broke out in the area around Beiping (Beijing's name at that time) and spread through eastern China. After losing Shanghai and Nanjing late in the year, Chiang moved his government first to Wuhan and then to Chongqing (then called Chungking). At this time, China was both divided internally and partially occupied by a foreign power.

Like other outside powers, the United States had to base policy on the sober reality that China presented. Yet rhetorically at least, the United States favored the unity of the country and opposed division, as illustrated by its actions at several key historical junctures:

- As China descended into the chaos wrought by the Boxer Rebellion and as other foreign powers were competing for special privileges in different parts of the country, on July 3, 1900, Secretary of State John Hay called on those countries to respect China's "territorial and administrative integrity."[6] This was the second of his "Open Door" notes and became a sort of one-China policy. Yet it was driven by national self-interest, not a high-minded concern for China. The McKinley administration worried that its foreign competitors in China were "carving up the melon" to improve their competitive advantage, to the detriment of American companies (similarly, the first of the

---

[6] "Secretary of State John Hay and the Open Door in China, 1899-1900," Department of State, Office of the Historian (https://history.state.gov/milestones/1899-1913/hay-and-china).

Open Door notes called for equality of commercial advantage).

- At the Washington Naval Conference of 1921-22, which took place as Chinese militarist fought each other for territory and resources, Washington sponsored the Nine-Power Treaty. In this pact, the countries with the greatest stake in China pledged to respect its territorial integrity.[7]

- In the late 1920s, the United States looked with favor on the formation of the new ROC government led by Chiang Kai-shek and his Nationalist Party (Kuomintang; KMT). The new regime took some steps to unify China and improve its strength, but Washington did little to help China after the Japanese military occupied Manchuria in September 1931. It simply reaffirmed its principles and said it would not legally recognize this seizure of Chinese territory.[8] Japan later established a puppet government – Manchukuo or Manzhouguo – under its tight control, and Washington did not recognize that either.

During this period, the focus of U.S. policy towards China was practical and relatively modest: preserving adequate access to the Chinese economy for American business and protecting American citizens living in China. But each time Washington intervened rhetorically, it did not act on its pro-unity principles. It had neither the will nor the capability to make China whole.

Once Japan and China went to war in 1937, the Roosevelt administration took China's side rhetorically (FDR spoke of a "quarantine" against Japan), and it eventually provided financial and material aid. Yet it was not until 1940 that the United States began to impose economic sanctions against Japan, in an effort to get Tokyo to end its occupation of China. Those sanctions were one factor motivating Japan to attack Pearl Harbor in late 1941. Only then did the United States ally with China in a serious way. As early as the end of 1942, FDR had decided that not only Manchuria but also

---

[7]　"The Mukden Incident of 1931 and the Stimson Doctrine." Department of State, Office of the Historian (https://history.state.gov/milestones/1921-1936/naval-conference).

[8]　"The Mukden Incident of 1931 and the Stimson Doctrine." Department of State, Office of the Historian (https://history.state.gov/milestones/1921-1936/naval-conference).

Taiwan would be returned to China after the war, a decision that advanced Chiang Kai-shek's goal of putting China back together again after the war and restoring the country's territorial reach to what it had been during late imperial times.

Even so, the alliance was fraught with problems. The United States placed its focus and its resources on Europe and the Pacific, not on the mainland of Asia. While Washington's priority was the defeat of Japan, Chiang Kai-shek's priority increasingly was defending his regime against Mao Zedong's communists, who had emerged from their bases in the northwest to penetrate many areas of North China. Even the return of Taiwan reflected a difference in objectives. Chiang wanted it back so it could serve as a fortress for the forward defense of China; FDR saw it as a base for international security operations.

Still, even with the end of the war the unity of China was up for grabs. The ROC was the internationally recognized government, but war with Japan had degraded its military capabilities, and inflation had undermined public morale. The communists had used the war to good effect, expanding its military forces, penetrating new territory, and building its governing capacity. Soon after Japan's surrender, the Truman administration sought to mediate the postwar conflict between the KMT and Mao's Chinese Communist Party (CCP), and avoid a destructive internal war. General George Marshall spent a year trying to create a set of understandings that would contain the military conflict and create political structure in which the KMT and CCP would share power and together address China's many postwar problems. Marshall failed in this effort, but not for lack of trying. Ultimately, he decided that the mistrust between the two sides was too deep and that their goals were in irreconcilable conflict, so he returned to the United States in February 1947. Thirty months thereafter, the communists had gained control of most of mainland China and Mao declared the establishment of the People's Republic of China on October 1, 1949. The KMT government and armed forces retreated to Taiwan, where Chiang hoped in vain of resuming his fight with Mao at a later time and regaining control of the mainland.

The Truman administration chose not to challenge the looming communist victory. Although the "loss of China" and the PRC's alliance with the Soviet Union was a clear strategic setback for the United States, Truman and his secretary of state, Dean Acheson, believed that sooner or later a unified but nationalistic China would split with the Soviet Union, to America's benefit (which was what ultimately happened). And despite opposition from Republicans in Congress, the administration was even willing to let Taiwan fall to the communists and see the ROC disappear. But North Korea's invasion of South Korea in June 1950 caused the United States to quickly change course, and gradually it increased the protection it was willing to provide to Taiwan. After Chinese "volunteers" entered the war on North Korea's side in late 1950 and fought against American soldiers, there was no longer any political support in the United States for recognizing the PRC and letting it join the United Nations.

In sum, China was anything but unified—or "one"—for the first half of the twentieth century, and some observers had doubted whether the country would ever become one again. The CCP ended those doubts with its victory over the ROC government in 1949. But the ROC survived and thrived on Taiwan, and the issue of one China took on a new and different character.

Forced Choice: America's One China/Two-China Problem

From the victory of the Chinese Communist Party in 1949 until the 1990s, the PRC and the ROC each insisted that the United States and other countries had to choose between them regarding diplomatic relations and which of them would represent China in international organizations. Beijing still takes that position. Washington sided with the ROC until 1979 but then switched to the PRC. Yet Taiwan still existed in fact, and maintaining a substantive relationship with its government was still in the interests of the United States.

After 1949, the United States and other countries had to face competing claims over who was the government of China. On one side of the argument was the ROC government, which was founded in 1912 and under the control of Chiang Kai-shek's KMT after 1928. That regime had led China's fight in the destructive eight-year war with Japan, and it was the ROC government that helped found the United Nations in San Francisco in 1945. But by 1979 Chiang's government only controlled Taiwan and some other smaller islands. On the other side was the PRC government, which soon had control of the entire Chinese mainland and began a program of revolutionary social, economic, and political change. In the communist view, the ROC had ceased to exist and the PRC was its successor state. In the KMT view, the communists were bandits who had no right to rule nor a claim international legitimacy.

For the foreign powers, including the United States, this was a new situation. Throughout the decades of disunion, there had never been a long-term rivalry between any two Chinese entities each claiming internationally to be the government of China. From 1949 on, however, the PRC and the ROC competed in an intense, zero-sum rivalry over diplomatic relations with other countries and membership in international governmental organizations. These two Chinese governments did not give foreign governments the luxury of having diplomatic relations with each. Instead, all countries had to choose.

Framing this competition were the principles of international relations established in the Treaty of Westphalia in 1648, after a hundred years of religious wars. To simplify, these principles were sovereign states were the constituent members of the international system; each state had a clearly defined territory and no territory was shared by two or more states; and, each state had the right to rule in the territory under its jurisdiction (thus excluding the authority of the Church).

These principles have evolved over the centuries and they are not always applied in practice. For example, some states are members of the UN, where membership is open to sovereign states, but they lack the capacity to rule within their territory (the situation in China before 1949). The Republic of China today is not a UN member but its government is much more capable than what exists in most developing countries. In some states, there are arrangements to create dual, pooled, or shared sovereignty (for example, the United States and the European Union).[9] Still, these principles remain at the core of the international system, and they shaped the PRC-ROC competition after 1949.

Under this framework, the state called China has existed for centuries, even though its political unity has waxed and waned. In the first half of the twentieth century, the ROC was a member of the League of Nations and many other international organizations. The post-1949 competition between the PRC and the ROC was essentially to establish which government represented China in the international system, and at present, the PRC has basically won that contest. It has diplomatic relations with most countries around the world. It represents China in most international organizational organizations and has resisted Taipei's current effort to have some role in international governmental institutions, even if the desired participation is less than formal membership.

On the issue of territory, as noted, the Westphalian approach is that all geographic territory belongs to one state or another and that each state has its well-defined territory. Specific procedures exist to delineate and mark borders between states. States may disagree over which of them owns a specific piece of territory, and they sometimes go to war to end the disagreement, but the principle remains.

In the China case, the question is whether the geographic territories of Taiwan and the associated Penghu Islands are part of the sovereign territory of the state called China. The consistent answer of the PRC is that they do. Traditionally, the position of KMT governments was the same. But with Taiwan's democratization, the view has emerged among some on the island that Taiwan is not a part of China and that it should be its own state. That remains a minority view, but it exists. The more widespread view is that if Taiwan's belonging to China means that it belongs to the PRC and all that entails, then they want no part of it. As I have written elsewhere, *how*

---

[9]   Stephen D. Krasner, *Sovereignty: Organized Hypocrisy* (Princeton, N.J.: Princeton University Press, 1999).

Taiwan is to be part of China will determine the verdict of the Taiwan public on *whether* they are willing to agree that Taiwan is a part of China.[10]

Returning to the post-1949 period, the United States put up with the zero-sum competition between the ROC and the PRC, and the opposition by each to a two-China solution. Sooner or later, most American foreign policy professionals likely concluded that the best thing for U.S. diplomacy would have been for Washington to have diplomatic relations with both the PRC and the ROC, and for each to become members of the UN. But neither Beijing nor Taipei would allow that. So Washington accepted that it would have to choose which of the two governments represented China in the international system and to have which diplomatic relations with one or the other. In the early 1950s, Washington chose the ROC, and did so for both strategic and political reasons. Its basic Asia policy was the containment and isolation of the communist PRC, in part through alliances with and military forward deployment to friendly countries on the PRC's periphery. Politically, Chiang Kai-shek and the ROC retained strong political support in the U.S.

For the Truman administration, this was a reluctant default choice, because it had little confidence in the capacity of Chiang Kai-shek's regime to survive. Thus, it refused to appoint an ambassador from 1950 through 1952. In any event, the beginning of the Korean War negated any possibility of recognizing Beijing. But the Eisenhower administration was more forward leaning. Strategically, it regarded Taiwan as one link in the chain of containment against China and so normalized relations with the ROC. Washington upgraded diplomatic relations with Taipei and appointed an ambassador (the U.S. would have no diplomatic presence in Beijing until 1973). Taiwan became the leading recipient of American economic aid, and the U.S. military re-established its ties with Taiwan's armed forces and established a significant presence on the island. Washington supported the ROC's continued presence in the UN. This comprehensive rapprochement culminated in the U.S.-ROC mutual defense treaty, which was concluded in

---

[10] Bush, *Untying the Knot.*

late 1954 and ratified in 1955. U.S. domestic politics reinforced this strategic choice: Congress and the media strongly supported the ROC in general and Chiang Kai-shek in particular.

Washington's approach on the territory issue was more interesting. The Truman administration initially took the position that Taiwan was a part of China, but once the Korean War began, U.S. officials were afraid that an all-out communist offensive had begun in Asia. It therefore shifted its position to say that the status of Taiwan was yet to be determined. The rationale was that if Taiwan were legally deemed to be a part of China, then its conflict with Beijing was a civil war, into which neither the United States nor the United Nations could intervene. That created the ironic situation that Washington recognized the ROC as the government of China but reserved judgment on whether Chinese sovereign territory included Taiwan, the only territory the ROC controlled.[11] Both Beijing and Taipei rejected the U.S. position categorically.

Yet the Eisenhower administration realized that it could not totally ignore Beijing, even though it sided with the ROC when it came to diplomatic relations and membership in the United Nations and despite its strategy of containment against the PRC with Taiwan's help. The PRC existed and its actions affected U.S. interests. Even though Washington officially recognized one China (the ROC), in fact it accepted the reality of two Chinas.

A tense episode in the fall of 1954 and early 1955 brought home the imperative of dealing with the PRC. It began when the People's Liberation Army shelled the ROC-controlled island of Jinmen, just off the coast of Fujian province. Eisenhower and his secretary of state, John Foster Dulles, knew both that Jinmen and other off-shore islands had no military value, but that the their loss to the PRC would damage morale on Taiwan and the reliability of the U.S. defense commitment. Nonetheless, the islands were

---

[11] The only exceptions were some small islands just off the Chinese coast that the Nationalist military held and that were generally recognized to be part of Fujian province.

so vulnerable to communist attack that Washington might have to go to the extreme length of using nuclear weapons to protect them, which would likely trigger the Soviet Union's security commitment to the PRC.

So in the spring of 1955 the Eisenhower administration agreed to open a communications channel with the Beijing at the ambassadorial level in order to reduce tensions and manage crises. In effect, the United States took these and other steps in order to work around the forced choice that both Taipei and Beijing imposed. Chiang Kai-shek strenuously opposed these initiatives because he believed that they granted legitimacy to a "bandit" regime and had the unacceptable political effect of creating two Chinas. In a sense, he was correct: de jure, Washington had a one-China policy; de facto, a two-China policy.

Unfortunately for the ROC, the status quo of the 1950s could not be sustained. The world was changing, and in two ways in particular. First, a large number of African nations were gaining their independence and were more ideologically inclined to the PRC than the ROC. Forced to choose between the two, they picked Beijing. Second, a deep rift was emerging between the PRC and the Soviet Union over a wide range of ideological, foreign policy, and security issues. Sooner or later, it would occur to Washington decision-makers that the enemy of its enemy might be its friend.

The United Nations was the ROC's Achilles' Heel. During the 1950s the United States had been able to block any consideration of membership for the PRC, but with the change in the composition of the organization's membership, that was no longer possible. Together, Taipei and Washington had to fight an annual battle to prevent the ejection of the ROC from the UN. Washington devoted considerable time and political clout to preserving Taipei's membership, but the trend was clear. To prevent the ROC's expulsion, U.S. officials began in the late 1950s to proactively explore ways that Beijing and Taipei might both be UN members and in a manner consistent with international law. These efforts accelerated in the Kennedy and Johnson administrations. The most creative approach was to posit that there were two "successor states" to the ROC that had been present at the founding of the UN: the PRC and the ROC on Taiwan. Actually, officials were realistic enough to assume that Beijing at least would reject such approaches out of hand. But, they reasoned, if Taipei went along with what could be portrayed as a reasonable compromise, it would be harder for countries that had supported PRC membership so far to do so in the future. The immediate challenge was to convince Chiang Kai-shek. On that, U.S. diplomats failed. Ideologically opposed as he was to anything that hinted of two Chinas, Chiang rejected the proposal out of hand.

More important was the fundamental strategic shift occurring in international politics: the Sino-Soviet split. American China specialists and Democratic members of Congress had begun in the mid-1960s to argue for a new policy approach towards the PRC, and through skillful signaling during the Vietnam War, the United States and the PRC had managed to limit the possibility that their support for South and North Vietnam would lead to direct conflict, as had happened in Korea a decade before. But it was Richard Nixon who best understood the logic of cultivating Beijing in order to use it as a counterweight against Moscow. As soon as he became president in 1969, he took steps to initiate that cultivation. This effort culminated first in National Security Adviser Henry Kissinger's secret trip to Beijing in July 1971 and Nixon's own visit to China in February 1972. The Nixon opening both removed the last obstacle to the PRC's assuming China's membership in the UN in October 1971 and laid the foundation for Jimmy Carter's normalization of relations with the PRC in 1978-79.

Despite the strategic imperative of U.S.-PRC rapprochement, neither the Nixon nor Carter administrations could (or would) avoid the forced choice concerning one-China.[12] In Nixon's first meeting with Chinese Premier Zhou Enlai, he stated a set of principles relating to Taiwan. The first was "There is one China, and Taiwan is a part of China. There will be no more statements made . . . to the effect that the status of Taiwan is undetermined." The second was that the United States did not and would not support Taiwan

---

[12]   It is interesting to speculate what might have happened if Nixon and Carter had tried to avoid a forced choice. The premise would have been that a weak and threatened China needed the United States more than the U.S. needed China. Would Beijing have accepted a less rigid approach to Taiwan? It is impossible to know.

independence.[13] The text of the Shanghai Communiqué, which was issued at the end of Nixon's visit was more ambiguous on these issues. It said, "The United States acknowledges that all Chinese on either side of the Taiwan Strait maintain there is but one China and that Taiwan is a part of China. The United States does not challenge that position."[14] That is, the Nixon administration did not adopt for itself what "all Chinese" maintained. Leaving aside the issue of how Nixon and Kissinger could have known what people on Taiwan believed since it was still an authoritarian system, there is also the difficulty of interpreting what it means to acknowledge a position and then not challenge it. Yet privately at least, the Nixon administration had made a choice of one China instead of two, had associated itself with the view that the territory of Taiwan was a part of China, and had begun a shift towards regarding the PRC as the government of China.

The more important document was the communiqué on establishment of diplomatic relations, issued on December 16, 1978 in Beijing and the day before in Washington. It did not just state policy but it announced fundamental actions. The first sentence of the normalization communiqué read: "The United States of America recognizes the government of the People's Republic of China as the sole, legal government of China." Washington would continue to formulate a formal one-China policy, but it now viewed the PRC, not the ROC, as the government of China.

The rhetorical position of the United States on "one China, not two" was elaborated in the August 1982 communiqué on American arms sales to Taiwan. Therein, the Reagan administration stated that the United States "reiterates that it has no intention of . . . pursuing a policy of 'two China's or one China, one Taiwan." Bill Clinton elaborated further in June 1998, when he uttered the so-called "three nos," that the United States did not support two Chinas or one China/one Taiwan, Taiwan independence, and Taiwan's membership in international organizations for which statehood was

---

13 Romberg, *Rein In at the Brink*, pp. 42-43.
14 This discussion of the Shanghai Communiqué, the normalization communiqué, the arms sales communiqué, and the Taiwan Relations Act, including direct quotes, are drawn from Bush, *At Cross Purposes*, pp. 124-178.

a prerequisite. Yet all of these elements arguably reiterated past American policy.

The issue of territory–whether the geographic entity of Taiwan is a part of the state called China—is surrounded with confusion. General observers believe that through the normalization communiqué the United States recognized both that Taiwan was a part of China and that the PRC was the sole legal government of China. Therefore, in the eyes of the U.S. government, Taiwan was a part of the PRC.

In fact, the normalization communiqué and subsequent statements did not state a U.S. position that Taiwan was a part of China. During the negotiations in the fall of 1978, Chinese diplomats tried to attribute to the United States its own position that Taiwan was a "province of China," but President Carter gave strict instructions to reject this view.[15] In the end, the communiqué's second sentence said that the U.S. government "acknowledges *the Chinese position* that there is but one China and Taiwan is a part of China." Gone was the awkward formulation that "all Chinese on either side of the Taiwan Strait. . . ." In its place was a vague reference to "the Chinese position." Moreover, the sentence from the Shanghai Communiqué that the United States "did not challenge" the Chinese view was gone. By only acknowledging "the Chinese position," the United States did not adopt as its own. The one flaw in this interpretation is that U.S. diplomats allowed the PRC side to use the stronger verb, "recognize," in the Chinese text of the communiqué for the sentence stating the U.S. position on territory. The Carter administration claimed with justification that the English text was binding, but any PRC or Taiwan citizen who read the communiqué in their own language would believe that Washington had gone further than it said it did.[16] The Reagan administration reinforced the interpretation of the English version of the communique in 1982 when it stated to Congress that the United States took no position on Taiwan's sovereignty (i.e. whether the island belonged to China) and that this was an issue the two sides of the

---

15 Ibid., p. 93
16 Ibid., p. 99-101.

Strait should resolve.[17] This suggests that the previous U.S. position—that the status of Taiwan was undetermined—had not changed, Chinese views to the contrary notwithstanding.

Bilateral Relations and International Organizations

Recognizing the PRC as the government of China cleared the way for Beijing to enter most international organizations. Although Taiwan was excluded from membership in organizations in the UN system, Washington sought to preserve its place in others and secure its participation even in some UN institutions.

Several concrete steps flowed from the U.S.-PRC rapprochement. First of all, the United States terminated diplomatic relations with the ROC and established them with PRC. The American embassy in Taipei was closed and the liaison office that had opened in Beijing in 1973 was converted to an embassy. This shift by the United States accelerated the trend of other countries recognizing Beijing instead of Taipei. Second, the way was now clear for the PRC to take China's seat in a number of international organizations. The United States would no longer work to facilitate dual representation by both Beijing and Taipei in these organizations, as it had tried to do within the United Nations in 1971. The organizations most important for China's future economic development were the World Bank and the International Monetary Fund. The ROC was further isolated. (Changes in U.S. relations with Taiwan are covered in the next section.)

Yet in spite of Washington's official one-China position in favor of the PRC when it came to international organizations, U.S. officials saw a value in having Taiwan be a member of certain organizations, if possible, or at least participate in some way. So from time to time, the United States sought to find work-arounds that would allow Taiwan to participate wherever

---

[17] Bush, *At Cross Purposes*, p. 174. An international-law rationale for continuing to say that Taiwan's status has yet to be determined, a logic that goes back to the 1950s, says that as long as that is the case, Taiwan is a matter of international concern regarding which other states have the right to act (e.g. by selling arms or coming to the island's defense). Once the island is deemed to be a part of China and the United States recognizes the PRC as the government of China, it really is Beijing's internal affair.

possible. Thus, in 1983, under pressure from Congress and in spite of resistance from Beijing, the Reagan administration worked out a formula by which Taiwan could remain in the Asian Development Bank when the PRC entered. In 1990, the George H. W. Bush administration developed a formula under which the PRC, Taiwan, and Hong Kong *economies* all joined the Asia-Pacific Economic Cooperation grouping at the same time. The Clinton and George W. Bush administrations facilitated the entry of the PRC and Taiwan into the World Trade Organization at the same time. Different terms of art were created to refer to Taiwan—the most common being "Chinese Taipei"—but that was a small price to pay to ensure that Taiwan had a presence in the multilateral economic architecture.

But these three organizations were special cases. First of all, they were all economic organizations and so having Taiwan as a member made sense since even Beijing acknowledged that it was an economic entity. More importantly, the PRC was not already a member of these three organizations and thus could not exert leverage on other countries to block Taiwan's full membership. In organizations in the United Nations system, where the PRC had replaced the ROC from 1971 on, it did have that blocking advantage. In the 1990s, there was growing domestic pressure within Taiwan for some degree of participation in organizations like the United Nations and the World Health Organization. The Clinton administration was supportive, at least rhetorically, saying in 1994 that it supported Taiwan's "voice being heard" in organizations for which statehood was required for membership. The Bush administration worked harder to push for Taiwan participation, but the hard fact was that Beijing could mobilize its friends to oppose the consensus these organizations required to allow a role for Taiwan. In such multilateral settings, even significant U.S. efforts were unavailing. Beijing chose to regard Taipei's efforts during the Lee Teng-hui and Chen Shui-bian periods to expand "international space" as part of a separatist plot, and so requiring intense opposition. The only partial exception to this exclusionism occurred during the presidency of Ma Ying-jeou, whom the PRC trusted to stay within a one-China framework. Even here, the concessions were small and grudging.

Unofficial Ties with Taiwan

Although the Carter administration pledged that the United States would conduct ties with Taiwan on an unofficial basis, "unofficiality" was subject to a range of different interpretations by successive administration. Generally, the trend has been toward more flexible interpretation. Quiet implementation of the resulting changes usually avoided diplomatic opposition from Beijing.

When the United States recognized the PRC, there was one more practical consequence for the conduct of policy. The 1978 normalization communiqué stated: "Within this context [of recognizing the PRC government as the sole legal government of China], the people of the United States will maintain cultural, commercial, and other unofficial relations with the people of Taiwan." In making this pledge, the Carter administration was accepting Beijing's demand that it terminate relations with Taipei. It then had to create *de novo* a new structure through which substantive relations would be conducted.

The Carter administration went a long way in meeting Beijing's requirements, at least formally. Even the phrases "people of the United States" and "people of Taiwan" were diplomatic terms of art that were consistent with the principle of unofficiality. Legally, the American Institute in Taiwan, which Congress authorized in the Taiwan Relations Act, was a private, non-governmental organization. Taiwan had an analogous set of institutions, whose name initially was the Coordination Council on North American Affairs (note the absence of any reference to Taiwan)

Operations were adjusted to preserve the façade of unofficiality. For many years, AIT's employees had to formally separate from the government agencies where they worked (e.g. the Departments of State and Commerce) to serve in either AIT's small Washington office or in a much larger office in Taipei. Once their tours were over, they returned to their home agencies (but magically their time at AIT was counted as time-in-service for their government pensions). Meetings between AIT officers and their Taiwan counterparts took place outside of government offices. For example, I served as chairman and managing director of AIT from 1997 to 2002 headed its Washington office. There were certain places in Washington D.C. where State Department and White House officials met with Taiwan officials. My AIT colleagues or I attended those meetings, which, so the logic went, made them unofficial.

The U.S. government had not negotiated with Beijing over these rules of engagement, and it always reserved the right to define what was official and what was unofficial. Yet in the first years after the end of diplomatic relations, Washington's definition was strict, as if to demonstrate to Beijing that it was living up to its normalization commitment. These arrangements required the utmost forbearance on the part of Taiwan's officials, for whom the form of diplomacy still had (and has) substantive meaning. They had to live with the daily marginalization that Beijing had imposed on them by forcing Washington to make a choice. But because the United States was key to Taiwan's security, its government had no choice but to accept unofficiality and all that came with it.

As far as the substance of U.S.-Taiwan relations were concerned, AIT and its Taiwan counterparts became an effective work-around to cope with formal unofficiality. In fact, AIT was an arm of the U.S. government that conducted U.S. government business. From the inside, and in most respects, the Taipei office of AIT operates like an embassy.

There were, of course, no objective definitions of officiality and unofficiality. In some cases, American officials had an easy time deciding which was which. A clear-cut case of officiality was the visit of Lee Teng-hui to the United States in June 1995, to give a speech at Cornell University, his alma mater. It had long been within the ambit of unofficiality for Taiwan's president and other very senior officials to *transit* a U.S. city on the way to and from another country, assuming the two governments agreed on the length of the stay and what the official would due during brief stop. But a *visit*, coming to the United States and participating in public events was seen as another case entirely. How, the logic went, could we say with a straight face that a visit by Taiwan's president was not official? The Clinton administration therefore opposed Lee's proposed visit, but broad and strong congressional pressure forced it to reverse its stance. The Congress either did not appreciate the importance of unofficiality as a key element in U.S. China policy, or it did not care.

In between the clearly official and clearly unofficial, there are a lot of grey areas. For example, Taiwan's foreign minister may visit the United States but not the Washington, DC, area. The rationale is that the foreign minister is Taiwan's leading diplomatic official, and diplomacy is by definition official for purposes of U.S. policy. In fact, the U.S. definition of unofficiality changed over time, in the direction of looser interpretations. Practices that early on were regarded as official were now seen as being within the parameters of the unofficiality commitment. The most well-known liberalization occurred during the Clinton administration with the formal "Taiwan Policy Review" of 1994. Among the steps taken were the following:

- The name of the Taiwan government's office in Washington, DC, was changed from the Coordination Council for North American Affairs to the Taipei Economic and Cultural Representative Office (TECRO), thus signaling that the organization had something to do with Taiwan.

- Taiwan's diplomats in Washington and visiting Taiwan officials could visit U.S. officials in their offices, except for those working in the State Department, the Eisenhower Executive Office Building, and the White House. For example, as AIT chairman I, on several of occasions, accompanied Taiwan's minister of economic affairs to meetings with the Secretary of Commerce and the U.S. Trade Representative in their offices.

- U.S. employees of the Taipei office of the AIT could visit their counterparts in their offices no matter how high their level or jobs were.

- U.S. cabinet-level officials in economic and functional agencies were now permitted, when appropriate, to visit Taiwan.

- The transits of very senior Taiwan officials through the United States "for their convenience, safety, and comfort" was formalized.

- The United States would support Taiwan's "voice to be heard" in international organizations for which statehood was required for membership.

Because it was well known that the Clinton administration was conducting the Taiwan Policy Review, expectations and worries were higher than otherwise might have been the case. Beijing, Taipei, and the members of Congress who had pressured the administration to go through the exercise in the first place were all dissatisfied with the result, but for different reasons.

Subsequent improvements occurred, which caused less ruckus because they received less publicity. For example, after the Taiwan Strait crisis of 1995-96, the Clinton administration realized that it was in the American interest that senior U.S. national security officials meet with their Taiwan counterparts periodically in the United States to clarify and coordinate the two governments' respective policies. Similarly, meetings between defense officials began during that same period and over time expanded the security relationship well beyond arms sales. By 2016, a Pentagon official described the broad scope of those interactions:

> As part of our broad defense and security assistance agenda, we are constantly engaged with Taiwan in evaluating, assessing, and reviewing its defense needs. Together we have, and will continue to work with Taiwan, in areas that include: the development and implementation of joint doctrine, improving service interoperability, increasing overall readiness, making training more demanding and realistic, identifying measures of effectiveness, and developing a professional non-commissioned officer corps. These actions enable self-defense and force development.

> High-level talks with Taiwan represent another element of our comprehensive and durable partnership. From defense policy to

foreign policy, from senior-leader political-military dialogues to pilot training, these exchanges between the U.S. and Taiwan are strategic, professional, focused, and objectives based. Our common goal is to have a credible and visible deterrent to potential coercion and aggression against Taiwan.[18]

The George W. Bush administration decided, among other things, that the requirement in the Taiwan Relations Act that U.S. diplomats separate from the foreign service to work at the AIT office in Taipei wasted administrative resources and created a burden for the individuals concerned. So in 2003, working with the relevant congressional committees, the Department secured legislation that authorized it to detail diplomats to AIT, thus negating the original requirement. In 2011, the Obama administration changed its previous guidance on where TECRO, Taiwan's office in Washington, could hold its annual reception on the anniversary of China's October 1911, revolution, which the ROC has always celebrated as its national day. Previously the reception was held at a downtown hotel. Now, the reception could be held at Twin Oaks, the lovely estate in Northwest Washington that before 1979 was the residence of the ROC ambassador. Previous administrations had judged that using Twin Oaks for the reception would be "too official," but the Obama administration chose to interpret unofficiality in a more flexible way.

Four factors govern U.S. decisions on these matters. The first is an assessment of U.S. interests and whether improving existing practices would serve those interests. The late 1990s changes concerning high-level meetings and military-to-military contacts are examples. If there is even a small chance that the United States had to act on its stated concern for Taiwan's security, building prior relationships with the island's senior civilian leaders and military establishment would facilitate cooperation during a conflict.

Second is the likely PRC reaction. Beijing has its own definition of what

---

[18] David Helvey, "Remarks To The U.S.-Taiwan Business Council Defense Industry Conference," Oct. 3, 2016 (http://china.usc.edu/david-helvey-remarks-us-taiwan-business-council-defense-industry-conference-oct-3-2016).

constitutes officiality in U.S.-Taiwan, and not surprisingly it is stricter than Washington's interpretation. For example, it vociferously opposed the Lee Teng-hui visit to Cornell in 1995, and once it happened Beijing triggered a downturn in both U.S.-China relations and Beijing-Taipei relations. But the PRC government has adjusted its approach as well. What it might have opposed at one time was tolerated later on. Indeed, it may judge that closer contact between U.S. and Taiwan senior officials may constrain actions by Taipei that it regards as a challenge to its interests. The PRC is more likely to object an action carried out very publicly than one that is done more quietly, by both Washington and Taipei. The Lee visit and the Taiwan Policy Review of 1994 were too "in their face" to ignore. But Beijing accommodated to changes like the shift from separation to detailing regarding U.S. diplomats serving in Taipei, and it tolerated the use of Twin Oaks for TECRO's reception every October. Each event "just happened."

The third factor governing Washington's degree of flexibility on officiality is the policy approach by the Taiwan government. If Taipei's objectives overlap well with U.S. interests and if the two sides conduct relations professionally and follow the norm of "no surprises," then a looser interpretation of flexibility is possible. If U.S. officials perceive that there is a difference over goals that might undermine peace and stability in the Taiwan Strait, they will be reluctant to accommodate liberalizing changes. Washington grew increasingly reluctant to accommodate Taipei during the Lee Teng-hui and Chen Shui-bian administrations, but was more flexible during Ma Ying-jeou's presidency.

The fourth factor is political pressure in the United States. This can come from Congress, as in the Clinton administration, or from a new administration that believes that greater flexibility is both possible and necessary. That was true in the early George W. Bush administration and appears true of the Trump administration.

In short, the administrations that followed the Carter administration have interpreted its unofficiality commitment to Beijing with increasing flexibility. Most changes have come not as the result of a formal Taiwan Policy Review like that in the Clinton administration. Rather, each new administration weighs the aforementioned factors and, as appropriate, makes adjustment in the conduct of our relations with Taiwan. When they have usually done so quietly, the odds of avoiding problems with Beijing increase.

Resolution of the Fundamental Cross-Strait Dispute

The United States takes no position on how the two sides of the Strait should resolve their differences in a substantive sense. It does consistently state an "abiding interest" in peace and security in the Taiwan Strait. The Taiwan Relations Act conveys a political commitment to come to Taiwan's defense if the PRC attacked the island militarily. Taiwan's democratization complicated how the United States should act on its interest in preserving peace and security, and it has, at times, employed an approach of "dual deterrence."

Much of the one-China policy concerns how the U.S. and Taiwan governments interact in the absence of diplomatic relations. Yet a fundamental and consistent element of the policy is how the differences between the PRC and the ROC are resolved, if they are ever resolved. That is because unification, somehow combining the two sides of the Taiwan Strait into one, is one of the options for resolving the perennial dispute.

It is the PRC that sees unification as the only option for resolving the dispute, and its only formula for unification has been the approach it calls "one country, two systems." This is the same approach that Beijing has used for Hong Kong and Macau, which became special administrative regions of the PRC with fairly broad authority to manage their own affairs. Still, Beijing maintained control over which local people would be in charge. For example, Hong Kong kept the common law legal system it inherited from the British and its residents have enjoyed civil and political rights, but voters pick only half the members of the Legislative Council through free and fair elections. The chief executive is selected by a committee of 1,200 members, almost three-fourths of whom take Beijing's preferences into account as they make their choice.

The Taiwan public has opposed the one country, two systems formula ever since it was proffered in the early 1980s. For some it was defective because it did not accept that the ROC or Taiwan was a sovereign entity. A minority of citizens has no desire for the island to be unified with China on any terms, and their idealistic solution would be that Taiwan be an independent country (something Beijing resolutely opposes). At least hypothetically, there are other options for resolving the dispute besides these two. Some type of confederal arrangement would accommodate both Beijing's desire for a political union and acknowledge the claim that Taiwan is a sovereign entity. What Taiwan most fears is that the PRC would choose sometime in the future to end the dispute by the use of force. The possibility that it might try to intimidate Taiwan into submission without war cannot be ruled out. Because none of these options are feasible in the near term, the default for Taiwan people is to work within the context of a complex status quo.

The United States has always eschewed any discussion on the substance of the fundamental dispute resolution. It has dissociated itself from certain outcomes, saying that it does not pursue a policy of two Chinas and one China, one Taiwan, and that it does not support Taiwan independence. But if Beijing and Taipei were to mutually decide on their own to adopt any of these approaches, Washington would not object. At the same time, Washington has never associated itself with Beijing's reunification formula. Its key question has always been the process by which the two sides resolve their dispute.

Consistent with their goal of preserving peace and stability in the Taiwan Strait area, successive U.S. administrations have stated an "abiding interest" in the peaceful resolution of cross-Strait differences. As long ago as the late 1950s, the Eisenhower administration tried to get the PRC to renounce the use of force in handling the Taiwan issue but to no avail. Beijing has always taken the position that Taiwan is an internal affair, not subject to foreign interference, and that it can use any means it chooses to resolve the dispute.

This conflict between Washington's "abiding interest" and Beijing's refusal to renounce the use of force was played out in the three U.S.-PRC communiqués:

- In the Shanghai Communiqué of 1972, the Nixon administration was able to include the sentence, "It [the United States] reaffirms its interest in a peaceful settlement of the Taiwan question by the Chinese themselves." In the communique, the PRC reiterated in its own statement its position that Taiwan was its internal affair that brooked no external interference.

- There was no mention of the issue in the 1978 normalization communiqué, but by prior understanding, Jimmy Carter made this statement when announcing normalization: "The United States is confident that the people of Taiwan face a peaceful and prosperous future. The United States continues to have an interest in the peaceful resolution of the Taiwan issue and expects that the Taiwan issue will be settled peacefully by the Chinese themselves." Beijing did not directly challenge those sentences, but in its own statement did say, "As for the way of bringing Taiwan back to the embrace of the motherland and reunifying the country, that is entirely China's affair."

- In the arms sales communiqué from 1982, China reiterated that the Taiwan question was its internal affair but cited two official statements from 1979 that outlined "a fundamental policy of striving for peaceful unification of the Motherland." The United States expressed its understanding and appreciation of this policy, and said that it created "a new situation . . . with regard to the Taiwan question." Still, China's stated policy of peaceful reunification did not constitute a renunciation of the use of force.

Other documents and statements addressed the issue of how cross-Strait differences were to be resolved:

- The Taiwan Relations Act of 1979 stated that it was U.S. policy to consider that "any effort to determine the future of Taiwan by other than peaceful means, including boycotts and embargoes, a threat to the peace and security of the Western Pacific area and of grave concern to the United States." But this was a statement of policy only, and had no binding effect on the executive branch.

- The "six assurances," which the Reagan administration conveyed to Taiwan just before the release of the arms sales communiqué, included pledges that Washington would neither mediate the cross-Strait dispute nor pressure Taipei to negotiate with Beijing.

- In June 1996, in the wake of Lee Teng-hui's visit to the United States and the intimidating PRC military exercises that followed (including test firing of missiles in waters close to the island), Secretary of State Warren Christopher stated that, "We have emphasized to both sides the importance of avoiding provocative actions or unilateral measures that would alter the status quo or pose a threat to peaceful resolution of outstanding issues."[19] This statement was notable for specifying that both Taipei and Beijing had a responsibility to preserve peace and stability.

- As noted above, in March 2000, Bill Clinton stated that the United States should be "absolutely clear that the issues between Beijing and Taiwan must be resolved peacefully and with the assent of the people of Taiwan." Implied in this statement was the reality that Taiwan had a democratic system and that Beijing would have to satisfy Taiwan leaders as well as the public in any effort to resolve the dispute.

There is an implicit linkage that can be drawn from these key documents and statements that is relevant to the question of how the cross-Strait dispute should be resolved. The linkage is between the U.S. government's recognition of the PRC as the government of China and its commitment to unofficiality in its ties with Taiwan on the one hand, and between Beijing's policy commitment to using peaceful means in settling that dispute on the

---

[19] "American Interests and the U.S.-China Relationship," Address by Secretary of State Warren Christopher to the Asia Society, the Council on Foreign Relations and the National Committee on U.S. - China Relations, May 17, 1996 (http://dosfan.lib.uic.edu/ERC/briefing/dossec/1996/9605/960517dossec1.html).

other. This is in no way a legally binding undertaking between the United States and the PRC. Beijing regards the Taiwan issue as its internal affair and has been unwilling to renounce the use of force. Over the years, it has built up military capabilities relevant to Taiwan in order, it would say, to deter Taiwan's leaders from seeking de jure independence. In its 2005 anti-secession law, it stated three conditions under which it would be authorized to use "non-peaceful means" in response: "In the event that the 'Taiwan independence' secessionist forces should act under any name or by any means to cause the fact of Taiwan's secession from China, or that major incidents entailing Taiwan's secession from China should occur, or that possibilities for a peaceful reunification should be completely exhausted."[20] In the absence of such conditions, however, Beijing would likely prefer to achieve its goals concerning Taiwan by political means rather than by military ones. One factor strengthening that preference is the adherence of the United States to the one-China policy, plus the possibility that the United States would intervene to defend Taiwan in case of an attack. So even though this is linkage, not a binding commitment, and should be constantly evaluated, a probabilistic statement is possible: Beijing is more likely to stick to its peaceful policy as long as Washington adheres to its one-China policy.

But the linkage also goes the other way. If Beijing were to choose to resolve the dispute through a unilateral use of force, that would fundamentally affect U.S. policy towards both the PRC and Taiwan. How it would do so has always depended on the circumstances and will continue to do so. Yet a key reason for Beijing's restraint on the use of force has been fear of the U.S. reaction and the consequences for its interests.

The usual focus of discussion here is whether the United States would come to Taiwan's defense and how credible any commitment to do so would be. In late 1954, the United States and the ROC concluded a mutual defense treaty, in which Washington said that an armed attack against Taiwan "would

---

[20] "Anti-Secession Law (Full Text)," website of the embassy of the People's Republic of China in the United States, March 15, 2005 (http://www.china-embassy.org/eng/zt/999999999/t187406.htm).

be dangerous to its own peace and security" and that it "would act to meet the common danger in accordance with its constitutional procedures." As with all treaties, the United States still faced challenges in reassuring Taipei about the credibility of its commitment.

When, in 1978, the Carter administration announced that it would terminate the defense treaty (as Beijing had demanded), the U.S. Congress tried to use the Taiwan Relations Act to create a replacement security commitment. In the end, it didn't really succeed.[21]

Section 2 of the TRA created policy statements that are relevant. Subsection 4 said that any effort to determine the future of Taiwan by other than peaceful means would be considered "a threat to the peace and security of the Western Pacific area and of grave concern to the United States." Subsection 6 said that it was U.S. policy "to maintain the capacity of the United States to resist any resort of force or other forms of coercion that would jeopardize the security, or the social or economic system of the people on Taiwan." Yet such congressional statements have no binding effect on the executive and, after all, the president is commander in chief. Moreover, although these clauses illustrate how the United States should regard an attack and how it should be prepared to respond, it says nothing about *how* to respond.

That was the subject of section 3(c), which declared: "The President is directed to inform the Congress promptly of any threat to the security or the social or economic system of the people on Taiwan and any danger to the interests of the U.S. arising therefrom. The President and the Congress shall determine, in accordance with constitutional processes, appropriate action by the United States in response to any such danger." These sentences are written as binding statements, but actually do less than they seem. The action required in the first sentence is to inform the Congress. The action required in the second "shall determine . . . appropriate action" is what would happen in any threat to the peace, and the reference to "constitutional processes"

---

[21] The other security demand that Beijing made in return for normalization was the withdrawal of U.S. military personnel and installations from the island.

implicitly references the President's power as commander in chief. Nowhere in the TRA is there a statement analogous to the treaty's declaration to "act to meet the common danger." If there is a U.S. commitment to Taiwan's defense, it is more political than legal. Still, the belief in Taiwan, the PRC, and some quarters in the United States, is that the commitment is stronger legally than it is.

Taiwan's democratization in the 1990s complicated the U.S. commitment to Taiwan's security. The assumption all along had been that the PRC would be the one to create a conflict. But the emergence of Taiwan independence sentiment and its association with the Democratic Progressive Party now fostered fear in Beijing that a Taiwan leader might declare independence. Because the PRC regarded national unification as a fundamental regime goal, it deemed any outcome that negated the possibility of unification as a war and peace issue. Consequently, U.S. decision-makers had new reason to worry that that they might have to act on the political commitment embodied in the TRA. Both during the late Lee Teng-hui era and most of the Chen Shui-bian administration, they feared to some degree that Taiwan might actually take steps that would be considered a move toward Taiwan independence. Even more, they worried that Beijing would exaggerate the challenge presented from a Taiwan action and then overreact in a coercive way. At the same time, there was annoyance from U.S. policymakers that a Taiwan leader might appeal for domestic political support from Taiwanese nationalists that Beijing would interpret as evidence of an intention to change Taiwan's status.

The policy approach that was deployed during the Clinton and Bush administrations was what I call "dual deterrence." Washington had both warnings and reassurances for both sides of the Taiwan Strait. To Beijing, we warned against the use of force but stressed that we did not support Taiwan independence. To Taipei, we warned against political steps that objectively might provoke a coercive response from the PRC but offered assurance that the United States would not sacrifice its interests for the sake of good relations with Beijing. The balance of warning and reassurance shifted over time depending on the circumstances. The clearest U.S. policy statement of this approach was Warren Christopher's assertion about "both sides . . . avoiding provocative actions or unilateral measures that would alter the status quo or pose a threat to peaceful resolution of outstanding issues."[22] Dual deterrence was not necessary during the Ma Ying-jeou administration because he and his counterparts worked to stabilize the relationship and reduce the possibility of conflict to a low level. But circumstances could emerge in the future that necessitated reviving the approach, such as the growth in Chinese military power and Taiwan's attendant vulnerability.

The hope, of course, is that political restraint on the part of Taiwan's leaders, Taiwan's own military capabilities, U.S. forces deployed in the Western Pacific, and Washington's warnings to Beijing will together deter the PRC from taking military or coercive action against Taiwan. Among other things, such PRC restraint will help to maintain the floor under U.S.-China relations. If deterrence fails, however, and the PRC decides to use force to "make China one again," it is highly likely that U.S. policy towards China would change fundamentally. American public and congressional support for Taiwan and antipathy towards the PRC is too strong to permit a continuation of business as usual. A PRC attack on Taiwan would also be a fundamental test of U.S. credibility in Asia and the world. It is impossible to predict the scope and depth of the deterioration of relations that would occur. A reversal of the U.S.'s current one-China policy—recognizing the government in Taipei and re-establishing diplomatic relations—might not be the first action on Washington's list. If Beijing's attack was successful, it wouldn't be an option. But the deterioration of U.S.-China relations would still be profound.

PROCESS AND THE ONE-CHINA POLICY

Missing from this discussion of the Unites States' one-China policy has been the question of how American decision-makers formulated that policy.

---

[22] "American Interests and the U.S.-China Relationship," Address by Secretary of State Warren Christopher.

In fact, there were several occasions over the last seventy-five years when the United States made decisions concerning Taiwan and its relationship with China without much ROC consultation. This happened both before the ROC government lost the war with the communists and then again after it relocated to Taiwan. Moreover, the decisions were made with little or no regard to the opinions of the people of the island. To be sure, for most of that period it was not possible to gauge the opinion of Taiwan people because they lived under authoritarian governments. These historical cases include:

- FDR's wartime decision to return the island to China after the end of the war.

- The Truman administration's decision that it would accept the fall of the island to the communists, which it deemed likely until North Korea invaded South Korea in June 1950.

- Richard Nixon's opening to the PRC in 1971-72 and his private statements to Chinese leaders that it was his view that Taiwan was a part of China (the Shanghai Communiqué was vague on the matter).

- Jimmy Carter's decision to establish diplomatic relations with the PRC, put relations with Taiwan on an unofficial basis and terminate the mutual defense treaty with the ROC.

- Ronald Reagan's acceptance of the arms sales communiqué, which at least temporarily created concern in Taiwan that it increasingly would be vulnerable to a PRC attack.

In some of these cases, U.S. officials argued that Taiwan had the resilience to survive in spite of these changes to the bilateral relationship. These predictions turned out to be true, but not necessarily because these officials were so prescient at the time. It is very true that successive administrations improved Taiwan's prospects by working around the formal strictures of the one-China policy, and that Taiwan's leaders were generally willing to work within the remaining parameters. But the fact remains that several American presidents did negotiate over the heads of Taiwan's people and their government on successive occasions. President Chiang Ching-kuo's decision in 1986 to liberalize and democratize the Taiwan political system made it harder—if not impossible—for the United States to do that thereafter. Bill Clinton acknowledged that new reality when he said in March 2000 that any resolution of cross-Strait difference had to have the "assent of the people of Taiwan."

It is therefore politically—if not morally—imperative that no U.S. administration consider negotiating with Beijing concerning cross-Strait relations and Taiwan's future without taking into account the views of the Taiwan people. There is extensive polling on Taiwan that provides ample evidence about how people feel about the island's relationship with the PRC. Moreover, Taiwan's president and legislators are selected through elections and to some significant measure represent the popular will. Taiwan's president and its senior diplomats have the best-informed sense of the island's interests and deserve to be fully consulted on any significant changes in U.S. policy that will affect those interests.

ONE-CHINA POLICY DOS AND DON'TS

The U.S. one-China policy is difficult to navigate, and as explained in this report, both actions and words bear equal weight of importance for Beijing and Taipei. The Trump administration would be wise to adhere to the following guidelines to ensure the one-China policy encourages stability, consistency and peace across the Strait.

1. DO NOT state as the position of the U.S. government that Taiwan is a part of China.
2. DO NOT use the phrase "one-China principle" (the PRC term). Instead, continue the practice of referring to "our one-China policy."
3. DO NOT take a position on the merits of one country, two systems as a substantive formula for resolving the Taiwan Strait dispute.
4. DO continue to restate the U.S. "abiding interest" in a resolution of the dispute that is peaceful and acceptable to the people of Taiwan.
5. DO urge both Beijing and Taipei to conduct cross-Strait relations with

flexibility, patience, creativity, and restraint.

6. DO emphasize to Beijing that the principal obstacle to its achieving its goal of unification is not U.S. arms sales to Taiwan, but the opposition of the Taiwan public to its unification formula.

7. DO continue to provide weaponry to Taiwan that is tailored to the existing and likely future threat from the PRC.

8. DO continue interactions with Taiwan's defense establishment on how to strengthen deterrence.

9. DO deepen our substantive interaction with Taiwan on bilateral issues.

10. DO work with Taiwan to find ways to enhance its international role and participation in international governmental institutions where it is not a member.

11. If it is in the U.S. interests to take steps to improve bilateral relations with Taiwan, DO NOT implement those changes in ways that create a public challenge to Beijing.

12. DO consult in advance with leaders of Taiwan on any changes in U.S. policy towards the island—either positive or negative—before making them. Taiwan's leaders are the best judges of whether those steps will serve their interests.

TAIWAN, TRUMP AND TRADE:
EFFECTS OF US TRADE POLICIES ON THE
GLOBAL ORDER WITH SPECIAL ATTENTION
TO TAIWAN
BY CHARLES R. IRISH[1]

Director (Emeritus), East Asian Legal Studies Center

Volkman-Bascom Professor of Law (Emeritus)

University of Wisconsin

Madison, USA

May, 2017

[1] Tamon Nakaprawing provided excellent and timely assistance in the preparation of this essay. I am grateful for her help. In April, 2017, I was also had the good fortune to present this essay to students and faculty at Soochow University Law School, National Taipei University, and FuJen Catholic University and their comments and criticisms significantly influenced the ideas laid out here.

INTRODUCTION

Over the last 70 years, the United States has played a leading role in the liberalization of economic activity around the world. The globalized economy that has resulted has brought enormous improvements in health, education and economic prosperity to billions of people in almost all parts of the world. But the benefits of globalization have never been shared evenly and those missing out on the increased prosperity are finding their political voice. It now appears that globalization may have reached an historic apex and is threatened by a rise in nationalism and a retreat toward greater economic protectionism. There also are strong pressures for the US to turn inward and no longer take the lead in supporting economic liberalization and combatting trade protectionism.

For the last several years, there have been signs of growing opposition to the globalization process in many parts of the world. Among the more prominent examples are the British vote to leave the European Union in June, 2016 (Brexit) and the growing strength of hard right, anti-immigration parties in Poland, the Czech Republic, Slovakia, Hungary, Germany, and other parts of Europe. Even the electoral defeats of radical populist candidates in the Netherlands in March, 2017 and France in May, 2017 demonstrated that populism and the hard right groups have moved from the fringes of the political spectrum to become potent political forces in many parts of Europe.

Within the United States, an increasing number of Americans also have expressed unhappiness with the globalization process and the American Government's prominent role as a leading advocate for economic liberalization. There is a widespread feeling in the US that the political system has been corrupted by special interests and that globalization has only rewarded the rich and powerful at the expense of the poor and middle classes. The opponents of globalization have argued that the benefits of international economic integration have gone disproportionately to upper income individuals and large corporations, while the wages of the working middle class have stagnated and the job opportunities for unskilled labor have been shipped overseas. During the US presidential campaign in 2015 and 2016, none of the pro-trade candidates gained support from the voters, while the anti-trade, anti-globalization rhetoric of Bernie Sanders, Hillary Clinton, and Donald Trump was very popular. The popularity of their messages seemed to presage the election of Donald Trump as the 45th president of the US in November, 2016, which has given the opponents of globalization control of the executive branch of the US Government. When he was elected, it was widely expected that Trump would push for his "America First" policy and no longer be a strong advocate for economic liberalization. During his presidential campaign, Trump promised protectionist actions that would reverse the last 70 years of American led efforts to introduce economic liberalizations throughout the world. Since his inauguration on January 20, 2017, however, Trump's continuing messages of bluster and threats of protectionism have not been matched with actions – in fact, on a number of occasions the Trump Administration's trade policy pronouncements have been closer to those of this predecessors than to his campaign promises. This growing evidence of moderation in the Trump Administration's trade policies suggests that Trump's most extreme advisors are becoming less influential and that his protectionism is being tempered by the many forces supporting a continuing role for the US as a leader in the world economy.

This purpose of this essay is to consider the impact of the Trump Administration on international economic relations, especially on Taiwan. After this introduction, the essay continues with a section describing the actions Trump already has taken, including his trade related personnel appointments, tweets, telephone calls, public meetings, and executive orders. This is followed by a section on the reality of what Trump has the power to do under the US Constitution, various statutes dealing with international trade and national security, the US courts and Congress, and international organizations. The final section concludes with a discussion of the impact of Trump's presidency on America's international economic relations and then specifically its impact on Taiwan/US economic relations. The broader conclusions of the final section are that Trumpian policies could have effects that range from moderately disruptive to the current international order to severely destructive of the existing system of international trade and investment. Based on the first few months of the Trump Administration, there is good reason to expect that the most likely impact will be on the less disruptive end of the scale. It is true that Trump is a narcissistic bore, a bully, and a misogynist. He seems to have no moral grounding and his business partners and consumers of his products tell us that he is untrustworthy. There also are real questions about his ability to understand or deal with the complex world that extends beyond his penthouse apartment in Manhattan and Mar-a-Lago Resort in Palm Beach. But the people and institutions of the United States are much bigger and stronger than any single person, even somebody as disruptive as Trump with all of the powers of the US presidency. So, although Trump is bringing protectionist trade policies into the White House, the combined power of the US Government's trade and foreign policy bureaucracy, the US Congress, and the private sector should be able to soften many of Trump's more extreme positions. It is likely, however, that Trump's protectionist threats will cause foreign and American businesses to establish more manufacturing facilities in the US to insure continued access to US markets and avoid the ire of a vindictive Trump Administration. The new investments will be accompanied by great fanfare and paeans to President Trump, but unfortunately, because of productivity improvements in manufacturing processes, these investments will not have much impact on manufacturing jobs, so the malaise in manufacturing employment will continue even if corporate profits improve and the US economy expands at a healthy rate.

Trump's trade relations with China will have a profound impact on US relations throughout the world and they will bring some serious threats as well as unique opportunities to Taiwan. During the presidential campaign, Trump was harshly critical of China's trade policies and its impact on the US economy. It is becoming apparent, however, that Trump is a simple person with a transactional view of world affairs: According to the Trumpian philosophy, if you help him, he will help you and be your friend. As a consequence, it is not surprising that since his inauguration, Trump has softened his anti-China rhetoric as he has linked China's access to US markets to China's assistance in curbing the nuclear ambitions of North Korea's Kim Jun Un. When Xi Jinping met Trump in the US in April, 2017, China also played Trump very well by proposing the 100 day action plan on trade issues, thus giving Trump a press release that showed Trump in a good light. In addition, it is almost certainly not coincidental that Trump's dramatic reversals on China occurred just as China approved long pending trademark applications for Ivanka Trump's brand, covering jewelry, bags and spa services. It still is likely that the US will confront China with major trade issues, but since the US (and the EU) have a number of legitimate grievances with China's international economic policies, a major disruption in trade devolving into a China/US trade war is not inevitable. In fact, an intriguing possibility is that the US, perhaps with a push from Taiwan and America's other Asian allies, will engage China in negotiating a bilateral (or three party) free trade agreement that is similar in scope to the aborted Trans-Pacific Partnership Agreement (TPP).

Much to the dismay of many trade and foreign policy experts in the US and East Asia, the most significant trade related action of the Trump Administration (as of May, 2017) was the withdrawal from TPP shortly after Trump's inauguration in January, 2017. In lieu of regional or multilateral agreements, the newly stated policy of the Trump Administration is to pursue bilateral agreements and it is having discussions with the Japanese about a bilateral free trade agreement. The Trump Administration also will soon seek to renegotiate the North American Free Trade Agreement (Nafta) because, in Trump's words, it is "the worst deal ever;" and the Trump Administration has said it will seek an early renegotiation of Korea/US Free Trade Agreement (KORUS FTA) because of the US's growing trade deficit with Korea. The US has bilateral free trade agreements with two other countries in the region – Australia and Singapore, but since the Trump Administration is fixated on bilateral trade deficits and the US currently has trade surpluses with each of them, the administration is not likely to devote much attention to them.

On the future of Taiwan/US economic relations, there are four conclusions:

- First, as a general matter, Trump views Taiwan as an important element in securing more favorable political and economic relations with China. Unfortunately, this is both good news and bad news. On the positive side, the Trump Administration is not likely to intentionally harm Taiwan's economy or its economic relations with the US. Given Trump's transactional view of the world, his favorable opinion of Taiwan will be markedly enhanced if Hon Hai Precision Industry Co. (i.e., Foxconn) and other large Taiwanese enterprises carry through with plans to make major investments in the US, including Hon Hai's proposed $7 billion investment for manufacturing flat panels. The bad news is that Trump is likely to see Taiwan as an important chip in his bargaining with China. Trump learned quickly from Beijing's reaction to his telephone call with President Tsai Ing-wen that adherence to the One China Policy is of critical importance to the Chinese leadership. This (probably new) knowledge coupled with Trump's non-ideological core and his transactional view of world affairs mean that there is a high risk the Trump Administration may make Taiwan related concessions to the Chinese to secure a more favorable economic relationship with China or China's cooperation in dealing with North Korea. To prevent this outcome, Taiwan's Ministry of Foreign Affairs and the Taipei Economic and Cultural Representative Office in Washington, D.C. should pressure senior Republican congressional leaders and Trump's key aides not to negotiate away essential elements of the Taiwan/US relationship.

- The second conclusion involves TPP. As TPP was being finalized by the 12 member countries in 2015, Taiwan expressed considerable interest in being included in the second round of TPP participants.[2] Trump's withdrawal from TPP has dramatically changed the dynamics

---

[2] See https://www.brookings.edu/research/taiwan-and-the-trans-pacific-partnership-preparing-the-way/ (visited May 20, 2017).

and for a few months after the US withdrawal it appeared that TPP was going nowhere. Now, the 11 remaining members of TPP are actively engaged in resurrecting TPP in such a fashion that is not viewed as either anti-China or anti-Trump.[3] The Trump Administration also recognizes that parts of TPP may be useful in the upcoming Nafta and KOR US FTA renegotiations, just as TPP may be relevant to the new China/US Comprehensive Economic Dialogue. As a result, this may be an opportune time for Taiwan to take the lead in promoting a TPP style trade agreement between the US, China and Taiwan. A three party agreement would have very significant attractions for all sides.

- One area where Taiwan is vulnerable is with respect to exchange rate policies. During the presidential campaign, Trump harshly attacked China for currency manipulations. He also said that Japan and Germany are guilty of undervaluing their currencies to give their exporters improper competitive advantages. In the early months of his administration, Trump has soften his stance on currency manipulations – even explicitly saying that China is not manipulating its currency to gain a competitive advantage.[4] Under a newly enacted US trade law that treats currency manipulations as unfair trade practices,[5] however, Taiwan now is included on a watch list, along with China, Japan, Germany, Switzerland and Korea. The result is that in the months ahead the US Treasury will be more closely scrutinizing Taiwan's exchange rate policies to see if they warrant being characterized as an unfair trade subsidy; but if that happens, Taiwan is likely to be part of a broader attack on currency manipulations.

- An overarching problem is that the unfortunate combination of Trump's many personality disorders, the aggressive and/or inexperienced international affairs advisors Trump has brought into

---

3   See http://asia.nikkei.com/Politics-Economy/International-Relations/Japan-looks-to-revive-moribund-TPP-sans-US (visited May 21, 2017).
4   See http://www.nbcnews.com/politics/politics-news/major-reversal-trump-says-china-not-currency-manipulators-n745826 (visited May 17, 2017).
5   The Trade Facilitation and Trade Enforcement Act of 2015 at https://www.congress.gov/bill/114th-congress/house-bill/644 (visited May 17, 2017).

his administration and the growing assertiveness of China, Russia and North Korea create a much greater risk of a major foreign policy miscalculation than at any time in recent history. This risk seems to rise and fall each day as Trump stumbles from one self-created crisis to another and his aides can do little but shake their heads in bewilderment. Of course, a major foreign policy miscalculation would have disastrous consequences for Taiwan, but also for the entire world.

PRESIDENT TRUMP ON TRADE

Trump as president appears to be no different than Trump as the candidate: his rhetoric, his mendacity and the bombastic style of his orations as president are much the same as when he was campaigning. While many people had hoped that after this election Trump would evolve into a more mature and "presidential" persona, he has continued to demonstrate a hyper-sensitivity to criticism, an astonishing disregard for the truth, and an almost total lack of diplomatic skills. Still, apart from his serious personality disorders, it is notable and perhaps admirable that as president Trump is fixated on what he promised during the campaign. During that campaign, Trump expressed support for proposals aimed at reversing many years of trade liberalization embraced by both Democratic and Republican presidents with bi-partisan support from Congress. In several campaign speeches, in his early morning tweets and during the presidential debates, Trump said he would reduce the US trade deficit and bring manufacturing jobs back to America. To achieve these goals, he proclaimed that he would quit the TPP, renegotiate or leave Nafta, and renegotiate or "rip up" existing bilateral trade agreements, including the KORUS FTA. He also threatened to impose a 5 to 35 percent tariff on imports from Mexico and a 45 percent tariff on imports from China.[6] In addition, Trump has suggested that if necessary he might "pull out" of the World Trade Organization (WTO), which is the main pillar of international trade for the US and the WTO's 163 other

---

[6]   See Peterson Institute for International Economics, *Assessing Trade Agendas in the US Presidential Campaign* at p. 5, at https://piie.com/system/files/documents/piieb16-6.pdf (visited November 27, 2016).

member countries.[7] But Trump's rhetoric has not been matched with what his administration has done. Because of the realities of the American presidency and the broader environment in which the president operates, but also in large part because of Trump's inexperience and incompetence, Trump's trade related actions during the early days of his administration bear more resemblance to that of this predecessors than to the protectionist promises Trump made during the presidential campaign. It is true that Trump has brought meanness, a stunning disregard for diplomatic protocol, unimaginable chaos and much greater uncertainty into American trade policies, but with only a few important exceptions his actions so far have been more mainstream and much less protectionist than what he threatened during his campaign. With Trump in the White House, the future of US trade policy is likely to be chaotic and punctuated with considerable uncertainties, but there is growing evidence that the trade policies will be less disruptive and less protectionist than Trump promised during the presidential campaign.

The remainder of this section describes the principal people Trump has appointed to assist him with his trade agenda and the specific trade related actions of the Trump Administration during the early months of the administration.

1. Trade related personnel appointments.

The Trump Administration's three most prominent trade related appointments are a clear indication of Trump's pro-American, protectionist tone:

- Trump has appointed **Wilbur Ross** as the Secretary of Commerce. Traditionally, the Secretary of Commerce has been a weak and relatively minor position, but Trump has given Ross responsibility for overseeing the administration's trade policies. During the presidential campaign, Ross played a significant role in formulating the "America

---

[7] See Peterson Institute for International Economics, *Assessing Trade Agendas in the US Presidential Campaign* at p. 5, at https://piie.com/system/files/documents/piieb16-6.pdf (visited November 27, 2016).

first" policy that now is a central feature of the administration's trade policies.[8] During his confirmation hearings, Ross said that China is the most protectionist of the large economies in the world,[9] but he also said he would not start a trade war. In the early days of the Trump Administration, Ross has been the administration's most public voice for moderation in trade policy and he has spoken against the most extreme protectionist policies being advocated elsewhere in the Trump Administration.[10]

- **Peter Navarro** is a Trump advisor who is head of the White House's new National Trade Council and the director of trade and industrial policy. Navarro is no friend of China – in the last 10 years he has written three books warning about the dangers of China's increased economic and military powers.[11] Navarro's principal economic charges directed at China are (i) currency manipulations to keep the yuan undervalued, (ii) stringent requirements on intellectual property transfers for foreign enterprises entering China's markets, and (iii) the ability of Chinese firms to pollute the environment more freely and provide working conditions far worse than in the US and then produce exports that often benefit from government subsidies. Navarro's most contentious position, which apparently is shared by Trump, is that if China is forced to adopt fair trade rules it will reduce the US trade deficit with China and bring manufacturing jobs back to the US.[12] Navarro also is a strong opponent of Nafta and he has urged Trump to withdraw from Nafta rather than renegotiate it.[13] In the first few months of the Trump Administration, Trump's public pronouncements

---

[8]   Trump to give Wilbur Ross trade policy powers, Financial Times (December 9, 2016) at https://www. ft.com/content/29973b68-be68-11e6-8b45-b8b81dd5d080.

[9]   See http://money.cnn.com/2017/01/18/investing/wilbur-ross-hearing-trump-commerce-secretary/ (visited February 1, 2017).

[10]   See, e.g., https://insidetrade.com/daily-news/ross-downplays-administration-split-nafta-outlines-priority-areas-renegotiation (visited May 1, 2017).

[11]   "Peter Navarro: Free-trader turned game changer, The Economist (US edition, January 21, 2017) at p. 19.

[12]   Id.

[13]   See https://insidetrade.com/daily-news/ross-downplays-administration-split-nafta-outlines-priority-areas-renegotiation (visited May 1, 2017).

have often reflected Navarro's extreme positions on trade, but the actions taken by the Trump Administration have been much more consistent with traditional American trade policies.

• Trump appointed **Robert Lighthizer** as the US Trade Representative. Lighthizer led the Trump transition team's meetings on trade with the Obama administration and previously served as deputy US trade representative in the administration of Ronald Reagan at a time when the office was renowned for its battles with Japan. He has long represented the US steel industry in cases seeking protection from foreign competitors and in recent years has been a vocal advocate for a protectionist shift in the Republican Party. As US trade representative, it is expected that Lighthizer will play a key role in delivering on Trump's campaign promises to crack down on unfair trading practices by China and to renegotiate the Nafta with Canada and Mexico.[14] Traditionally, the USTR also would take a leading role in the negotiation of new free trade agreements, but Trump has indicated that responsibility will be shared with Ross and Navarro.

In addition, Trump's appointment of **Stephen Bannon** as the Chief White House Strategist has caused real concern in the US and Asia because of Bannon's extreme far-right positions. Of special concern is Bannon's assertion (made before he joined the Trump campaign team) that war with China is inevitable within the next few years.[15] In addition, when Trump's White House staff was initially announced, Bannon was given a permanent position on the very influential National Security Council, while the Chairman of the Joint Chiefs of Staff and the Director of National Intelligence were downgraded to occasional participants. In early April, 2017, however, Bannon was removed from his position on the National Security Council. At the same time, the Chairman of the Joint Chiefs of Staff and Director of National Intelligence were reinstated as permanent

[14] "Trump chooses protectionist leaning trade representative," **Financial Times** (January 3, 2017) at https://www.ft.com/content/e1487162-d170-11e6-9341-7393bb2e1b51 (visited February 1, 2017).
[15] See https://www.aol.com/article/news/2017/02/01/trumps-chief-strategist-steve-bannon-no-doubt-the-us-will-be/21704928/ (visited may 2, 2017).

members and the Secretary of Energy, the director of the CIA, and the UN Ambassador were added to the National Security Council.

Secretary Ross's prominent voice of moderation on trade issues and Bannon demotion are widely seen as evidence of the Trump Administration's shift towards less protectionist, less disruptive trade policies, but heated, protectionist rhetoric still emerges from Trump himself and some of the White House's pronouncements. Navarro, Lighthizer and Bannon also continue to occupy positions very close to the president, so their ability to influence future policy decisions should not be ignored.

2. Bringing jobs back to America.

Shortly after his election in November, 2016, Trump began efforts to persuade US and foreign companies to keep their production facilities in the US or to move their factories back to the US. In a blaze of publicity through a combination of tweets, telephone calls, and in person meetings with business leaders, Trump has offered incentives of deregulation and tax reforms and threats of taxes on imports to persuade companies to add manufacturing jobs in the US. According to the Trump, his efforts are responsible for Carrier's decision to keep its plant open in Indiana to save over a thousand jobs[16] and Ford's decision to invest US$700 million in its Flat Rock, Michigan assembly plant and cancel plans to build a US$1.6 billion plant in Mexico.[17] Shortly after Trump's inauguration, Terry Guo, the head of Taiwan's tech giant Hon Hai Precision Industry Co., also confirmed that he is considering a US$7 billion investment to make flat panels in the United States. In addition, Hon Hai is in the early stages of considering much larger investments in the US, possibly with Japan's SoftBank.[18] With the new attention to manufacturing job creation, several other US and foreign companies have joined in with announcements of increased investments in production facilities.[19]

---

[16] See https://www.washingtonpost.com/news/fact-checker/wp/2016/12/05/trumps-misleading-numbers-about-the-carrier-deal/?utm_term=.5aa48533d58d (visited February 2, 2017).

[17] See http://www.foxnews.com/politics/2017/01/03/ford-to-scrap-mexico-plant-invest-in-michigan-due-to-trump-policies.html (visited February 2, 2017).

[18] See http://chinapost.com.tw/taiwan/2017/04/30/496478/Terry-Gou.htm (visited April 30, 2017).

[19] See http://www.japantimes.co.jp/news/2017/01/23/business/corporate-business/hon-hai-chief-

The impression Trump is trying to create is that jobs are coming back to America because of his strong persuasiveness or the threats of taxes and tariffs on imports.[20] There are, however, many criticisms of Trump's approach. The critics argue that focusing on individual or small groups of companies is grossly inefficient because the American job market is so vast. They also argue that even assuming 100 percent accuracy of Trump's statements about job creation, which they strongly question,[21] the number of jobs created is on the margin of the large number of jobs destroyed and created each month in the US labor market. During the 2nd quarter of 2016, for example, there were 7,463,000 jobs created and 7,156,000 jobs lost, for net job creation of 307,000,[22] so Trump's effort are of little consequence when compared to the overall labor market. The critics also suggest that the motives for CEOs claiming new job creation may be more public relations gestures and avoiding the ire of a vindictive Trump Administration than the introduction of actual new investments. In many cases, the critics say, the investments were long planned and it just was fortuitous that the investment plans matured as announcements of new jobs would be excellent tactical moves. Finally, the critics have pointed out that all the new investment in manufacturing in America will not lead to much job creation because the new production processes have become so automated.

But the critics miss the point. In just the first few months of his presidency, Trump has given the impression of doing more for manufacturing employment than any president in recent memory. He has used the power of the presidency and his crude, overbearing manner to support people with modest job skills who feel left behind by the globalization process. It is true that Trump's efforts are not likely to have much impact on manufacturing employment in America, but at least he is trying to fulfill his campaign promises, which is much more than what has been done in the past.

confirms-7-billion-u-s-investment-works/#.WJIZyX9KUfQ (visited February 2, 2017).

[20]   See http://www.latimes.com/business/la-fi-agenda-trump-jobs-20170130-story.html (visited February 2, 2017).

[21]   See https://www.vox.com/the-big-idea/2017/1/24/14330472/jobs-layoffs-carrier-trump-manufacturing-hiring-firing (visited May 2, 2017).

[22]   See https://www.bls.gov/news.release/cewbd.t01.htm (visited February 2, 2017).

Whatever the critics say about the effectiveness of Trump's jawboning of the US and foreign manufacturing CEOs, his efforts are certain to be met with high applause among his supporters.[23] It also may have the effect of expanding the base of his supporters.

While Trump's "America First" policy and his threats of tariffs and other trade barriers on imports are good political gestures, they also will have a positive impact on direct investment in the US. The American markets are too attractive to ignore and the risk of being closed out of the markets warrant aggressive actions to protect access to them. Since the surest way to guarantee continued access to the American markets is to make the products in the US, foreign and American manufacturers are scaling up their investment plans in the US. The upsurge in new investment may even be similar to what occurred in the 1980s when the US also was threatening major protectionist measures. The principal difference between then and now is that the 1980s' trade demon was Japan and now it is China. The results are likely to be similar, however, with a major upsurge in foreign direct investment in the US. In the current environment, well publicized new investments by Carrier, Ford, Hon Hai and SoftBank are being joined by GM, Hyundai, WalMart, Amazon, Toyota and other foreign and American companies with new or expanded operations in the US.[24] The impact on American investment will be even greater if Trump and the Republican controlled Congress carry through with plans to improve the business climate in the American economy. The remarkable innovations in the oil and gas industry already have given American industries energy costs that are among the lowest in the world and are one third or one quarter the level of energy costs in many parts of Asia and Europe. Adding much needed corporate tax reform and infrastructure development along with some sensible deregulation could go a long way towards making the US attractive

---

[23]   Trump's overall approval rating at this point in his presidency is the lowest of any president since at least the 1940s. See https://projects.fivethirtyeight.com/trump-approval-ratings/ (visited May 2, 2017). But among his supporters, Trump has a 93 percent approval rating. See http://www.washingtonexaminer.com/poll-trump-the-lion-scores-93-percent-approval-among-2016-supporters/article/2621410 (visited May 2, 2017).

[24]   For a catalogue of announcement of major new investments in the US, see http://www.latimes.com/business/la-fi-agenda-trump-jobs-20170130-story.html (visited February 2, 2017).

as a production base for US and foreign industries even without the threats of greater protectionism.

The increases in new investment in the US should be good for the economy, but it will not bring back the manufacturing jobs lost over the last several decades. Although international trade is most often cited as the villain in American manufacturing job losses, the real problem is productivity improvements.[25] The continuing automation of manufacturing processes has meant that even as the US manufacturing sector produced more goods in 2016 than ever before, the number of workers needed to produce those goods remained stagnant or declined.[26] For the US manufacturing industry, the last several decades have been similar to what occurred in the agricultural sector in the late 19th and early 20th centuries when the mechanization of agriculture lead to a sharp decline in the farm labor force even as agricultural production increased and food costs declined.

Because of Trump's preoccupation with employment in the manufacturing sector, there is an intriguing possibility that if key advisors in the Trump Administration are able to steer Trump towards real solutions to the employment problems, he could actually do some good for those who feel they have been left on the sidelines in the globalization game. His personality is such that he probably needs to be seen cajoling business leaders to locate their manufacturing operations in the US, so that will continue. As to what really needs to be done, there is fairly widespread agreement although there is a continuing refusal to do anything serious about it. What is needed is a major program that offers expanded unemployment compensation, job retraining and relocations services for displaced workers, irrespective of the reason for their displacement. One program that focuses on job losses and business dislocations caused by increased imports already

---

[25] See https://www.washingtonpost.com/posteverything/wp/2015/08/03/donald-trumps-big-lie-about-the-global-economy/?tid=a_inl&utm_term=.1cbf495aea66 (visited February 4, 2017).

[26] See https://www.forbes.com/sites/timworstall/2016/11/16/youre-not-going-to-believe-this-but-us-manufacturing-is-now-bigger-than-ever-before/#1acd76d8578d (visited May 2, 2017).

does exist: Trade Adjustment Assistance (TAA);[27] but because TAA focuses only on job losses due to increased imports, while the great majority of job losses are caused by productivity improvement, TAA has never been effective nor adequately funded. TAA was introduced in 1963 by then President John Kennedy, but it has always been seriously underfunded and serves only a small portion of the unemployed, in part because of the difficulty of proving the job losses are due to international trade. In 2010, for example, when about 15 million people were officially unemployed, 228,000 received TAA benefits or services (about 0.015 percent of the unemployed) and the average benefit received was less than $5,000.[28] What is needed is a much more expansive and generous program that provides assistance to displaced workers irrespective of the reasons. A portion of the largesse from globalization that typically flows to higher income individuals and larger corporations needs to be diverted to those left behind in the globalization process. Although the need for such a program has long been recognized, both Democrats and Republicans in Congress and Democratic and Republican presidential administrations have repeatedly failed to act to pass the necessary legislation. By focusing on the need for such an expanded worker assistance program, the Trump Administration could move beyond populist slogans to real substance. Just as then President Richard Nixon was the perfect person to reopen an American dialogue with China in the early 1970s, Trump is uniquely positioned to bring substantial resources to where they will do some good in the labor market. Establishing a major worker assistance program also would make it more evident that international trade is much less the villain causing job losses and shift attention to where it belongs: productivity improvements in the domestic economy. At the same time, by moderating the employment bugaboo in American relations with China, Mexico, and any other countries that attract Trump's attention, it would remove a major irritant in American relations with China, make the renegotiation of Nafta much less contentious, and put US trade relations around the world on more stable footing.

---

[27] See https://www.doleta.gov/tradeact/factsheet.cfm (visited November 30, 2016).
[28] See https://www.doleta.gov/tradeact/factsheet.cfm (visited November 30, 2016).

3. Reducing the US trade deficit.

Trump views trade as a zero sum game: exports create winners, imports are for losers. The chronic American trade deficit, under Trump's view, shows that the US is losing in international trade, and the US is losing because other countries, especially China and Mexico, are taking advantage of the US through unfair trade practices.[29] In Trump's mind, the American bilateral and regional trade agreements are important enablers of the unfair trade practices. Hence the need to renegotiate or cancel the existing trade agreements with countries with which the US has major trade deficits.[30] Where the trade is not covered by a bilateral trade agreement, such as US trade with China, the US needs to counter the unfair trade practices through the imposition of tariffs or other non-tariff barriers on imports. In Trump's view, by eliminating the US trade deficits, manufacturing jobs will return to the US, just as he promised in his campaign.

Trump's views on the causes and effects of the US trade deficit generally are widely regarded as too simplistic and incorrect.[31] The mainstream view of trade balances is that they are part of complex savings and investment patterns.[32] In the case of US and China, the trade imbalance means that US consumers get greater access to low cost goods than would be the case with balanced trade. The trade imbalance also is responsible for China's sizeable investments in US government bonds and more recently in direct investments in US companies. It is true that the US trade deficit with China has been exacerbated at times by China's currency manipulations and improper subsidies to its exporters, but the size of a bilateral trade deficit does not measure these improper trade practices. The appropriate response,

---

[29] See http://www.japantimes.co.jp/news/2017/01/24/business/trump-scotches-tpp-hits-japan-china-unfair-trade-partners-freezes-federal-hiring/#.WJZTIX9KUfQ (visited February 4, 2017).

[30] See https://www.washingtonpost.com/posteverything/wp/2016/09/28/how-donald-trump-would-worsen-americas-trade-deficit/?utm_term=.4b66670f64c (visited February 4, 2017).

[31] See https://www.nytimes.com/2016/07/22/upshot/what-donald-trump-doesnt-understand-about-the-trade-deficit.html (visited February 4, 2017). The Economist has referred to Trump and Peter Navarro's views on the US trade deficit as "fantasy." "Peter Navarro: Free-trader turned game changer, The Economist (US edition, January 21, 2017) p. 18, at p. 19.

[32] See "Peter Navarro: Free-trader turned game changer, The Economist (US edition, January 21, 2017)p. 18, at p. 19.

many would argue, is to deal with unfair trade practices through the US and international trade law remedies that were introduced for just this purpose.

The US dollar's status as the world's reserve currency also contributes to the overall US trade deficit. The French have called the dollar's reserve status the "exorbitant privilege" because all Americans have to do to pay for imports is print more money.[33] The predominance of the dollar in international business and investment transactions does confer major economic and foreign policy benefits on the US government and American businesses. For example, the US Government's economic sanctions and threats of sanctions on Iran, North Korea and Russia are powerful precisely because of the US Government's ability to curtail dealings in US dollars. Similarly, the US Government's financing of its sizeable budget deficit is relatively easy because the Chinese, Japanese, Koreans, Taiwanese and many others are eager to buy US Government bonds with the dollars they have collected as a result of their running trade surpluses with the US. In US capital markets, interest rates also are lower in the US and stock prices are higher because of the US dollar's reserve status.

Being the global reserve currency does have costs to the US economy. The global demand for US dollars means that it is perpetually overvalued, which makes American exports less competitive and imports cheaper. So the cost to the American economy of having the US dollar as a reserve currency is that American trade deficits are higher and its exports are lower.[34]

If the Trump Administration is going to attack US trade deficits, Trump and his advisors should make certain they have some idea of the overall consequences of their actions. Unfortunately, the resumes of many of Trump's trade policy advisors are not grounds for optimism. On the other hand, during the first part of the Trump Administration, the trade actions taken by the Trump Administration have either been long on polemics and short on substance (notable exceptions are Trump's withdrawal from TPP

---

[33] See https://www.washingtonpost.com/opinions/the-dollars-stubborn-challenges/2015/05/06/7a87b388-f405-11e4-bcc4-e8141e5eb0c9_story.html?utm_term=.ab1cb4304de1 (visited February 4, 2017).

[34] See https://www.washingtonpost.com/opinions/the-dollars-stubborn-challenges/2015/05/06/7a87b388-f405-11e4-bcc4-e8141e5eb0c9_story.html?utm_term=.ab1cb4304de1 (visited February 4, 2017).

and the efforts to deal with oversupplies of steel and aluminum) or they have focused on trade issues where the US Government's attention is warranted. Apart from the withdrawal from TPP, none of Trump Administration's actions have been isolationist or radically protectionist. For example, in April, 2017, in celebration of the first 100 days of his administration, Trump signed two trade related executive orders. One directed the Department of Commerce and the USTR to undertake a study of US trade agreements to insure that the US is being treated fairly by its trading partners and the 164 member WTO. The second established the Office of Trade and Manufacturing Policy with the goal of strengthening US manufacturing and reducing the trade deficit.[35] At the same time, Commerce Secretary Ross outlined several issues that should be considered in the Nafta renegotiations, including trade in services, digital trade, rules of origin and dispute resolution – all issues that are not overtly protectionist and seem appropriate for a trade agreement that is 23 years old and badly in need of modernization. If Trump's more conventional advisors can shift the emphasis away from his preoccupation with the trade deficit, as Secretary Ross seems to be doing, Trump's trade policies as president may come to more closely resemble that of his predecessors than Trump the protectionist candidate.

4. Withdraw from TPP.[36]

As part of his platform to restore American manufacturing employment and reduce US trade deficits, Trump repeatedly called TPP a disaster for the country and stated that on his first day in office, he would quit TPP[37] and not send it to the US Congress for ratification. Here is what Trump said about TPP:

---

[35] See http://www.latimes.com/politics/la-pol-updates-everything-president-trump-highlights-executive-orders-on-1493672444-htmlstory.html (visited May 2, 2017).

[36] TPP's 12 member countries are Australia, Brunei, Canada, Chile, Japan, Malaysia, Mexico, New Zealand, Peru, Singapore, Vietnam, and the United States.

[37] For one of the instances when Trump said he would quit the TPP, see http://www.bbc.com/news/world-us-canada-38059623 (visited November 22, 2016). In fairness to Trump, Bernie Sanders and Hillary Clinton also said they were opposed to TPP, which in Clinton's case seemed hypocritical since she had supported TPP when she was the Secretary of State in the Obama Administration.

The TPP is a horrible deal. It is a deal that is going to lead to nothing but trouble. It's a deal that was designed for China to come in, as they always do, through the back door and totally take advantage of everyone. It's 5,600 pages long, so complex that nobody's read it. This is one of the worst trade deals. And I would, yes, rather not have it. We're losing now over $500 billion in terms of imbalance with China, $75 billion a year imbalance with Japan.[38]

Trump's six sentences quoted above contain an astonishing number of inaccuracies and contradictions and illustrate the incoherence of Trump's trade policies. Nonetheless, consistent with his campaign promise, one of Trump's first actions in office was to sign an executive order withdrawing the US from TPP's negotiating process.[39] Even though Trump suggests that his objection to TPP is partly because China, which is not one of the 12 members of TPP, somehow gains special benefits from TPP and that even though neither he nor anybody close to him has read the agreement, he somehow knows the agreement is bad for the US. It is unlikely, but possible that Trump does understand TPP's importance. If this is true, he may be calculating that by withdrawing from such an important component of American trade policy, he is enhancing his reputation as unpredictable, but generally protectionist. Trump may believe that he will be better able to achieve favorable concessions in other areas of international trade by taking this hardline approach on TPP. Trump also has said that he will emphasize negotiation of fair, high standard bilateral trade agreements in lieu of TPP, but increasingly Trump's aides are looking to the text of TPP for guidance on these agreements.[40]

For the last several years of the Obama Administration, TPP was the economic cornerstone of America's engagement with the Asia/Pacific region. It is an ambitious trade deal signed in February, 2016 after 10 years

---

[38] This is a direct quote from the Fox Business/WSJ First Tier debate, Nov 10, 2015 and is available at http://www.ontheissues.org/2016/Donald_Trump_Free_Trade.htm (visited November 27, 2016).

[39] See http://www.cnn.com/2017/01/23/politics/trans-pacific-partnership-trade-deal-withdrawal-trumps-first-executive-action-monday-sources-say/ (visited February 2, 2017).

[40] See https://www.wsj.com/articles/which-countries-will-trump-target-for-trade-deals-1485531848 (visited February 2, 2017).

of arduous negotiations that go back to the last years of George W. Bush (a Republican president). Until the US withdrawal from TPP, its membership included the US and 11 other countries in the Asia/Pacific region which account for 40 percent of the world's economy. Taiwan is not a member of TPP, although it has expressed interest in joining in the second round of accessions. To become effective, TPP has to be ratified by at least 6 countries that account for 85 percent of the group's economic output by February, 2018. Because of the 85 percent requirement, ratification by Japan and the US are preconditions for TPP becoming effective so the American withdrawal from TPP has killed the agreement, at least in its current form.

Measuring the effect of existing trade agreements is imprecise and contentious, so forecasting the impact of TPP on the American economy is very hard to estimate. It is generally agreed that TPP would have stimulated growth within the 12 member countries and several independent studies have concluded that the US would have had the biggest absolute gain because it is by far the biggest economy among the 12 members.[41] Given the size of the American economy, the overall effect of TPP would have been fairly modest, but the emerging markets, especially Vietnam, would have the most to gain relative to their size.[42] Of course, all trade agreements create both winners and losers and while gains usually exceed the losses, some individuals and businesses wind up being hurt by the trade agreements. This also would be true with TPP's impact on the American economy, just as it would be for the other 11 members of TPP. The losers from TPP are justified in opposing it, but the answer is to accommodate the legitimate grievances of the losers (generally job losses and business dislocations), not kill the whole deal which is in broad terms beneficial to the US and other TPP economy.[43]

---

[41]   The apolitical International Trade Commission's concluded that the US economy would be TPP's major beneficiary, but only because the US economy is so much larger than the other eleven members of TPP. The ITC's report is at https://www.usitc.gov/publications/332/pub4607.pdf (visited November 30, 2016).

[42]   See http://www.economist.com/blogs/economist-explains/2016/11/economist-explains-14?cid1=cust/ ddnew/n/n/n/20161124n/owned/n/n/nwl/n/n/NA/8207260/email&etear=dailydispatch (visited November 24, 2016)

[43]   Until the US presidential campaign in 2015-2016, this was the prevailing view in the US and the other TPP countries, although, as explained below, previous US efforts to assist those displaced by international trade have been almost totally ineffective.

As is true with most of America's free trade agreements, TPP was more an American foreign policy instrument than about improving American GDP. TPP's trade liberalizations are fairly important, but the agreement was ambitious because it extended rich world standards in many important areas that go well beyond trade. The most remarkable aspect of TPP is that any agreement was concluded at all given the very different approaches and standards within the member countries, including environmental protection, labor standards, and regulatory coherence as well as special provisions for state owned enterprises and other protected industries. Leaders in Japan, Vietnam and some other member countries expended considerable political capital to obtain support for TPP within their own governments.

By American design, China was not a member of TPP. The American position was that China's absence will enable the US and the other TPP member countries to write the rules governing future trade in the region in a fashion that guarantees rule based free and open trade and investment as well as up to date protections of intellectual property rights.[44] In other words, China's exclusion from the TPP negotiations allowed the US (with support from the other 11 members) to write comprehensive rules governing trade in the Asia Pacific region and to set a precedent for future trade agreements, including most specifically the Transatlantic Trade and Investment Partnership[45] and the Free Trade Area of the Asia Pacific, with the latter being a possible successor agreement to TPP. Members of TPP, including the US, did say that once TPP became effective, China and several other countries would be invited to join. But at that point, the rules would have been written, so China and the other countries joining in the second stage would have no little impact on the newest iteration of trade rules

In sum, from an American perspective, TPP was a central component

---

[44] The US Trade Representative, which is the office of the US Government responsible for negotiating international trade agreements argues that TPP's importance is largely because it will establish a modernized trading system largely consistent with US laws and regulations and very much supportive of US values. The USTR's website listing the benefits of TPP is at https://ustr.gov/tpp/#overall-us-benefits (visited November 22, 2016).

[45] TTIP was a proposed free trade agreement between the US and the EU. It is still in the early stages of negotiation, but will almost certainly suffer the same fate as TPP.

of US trade and foreign policy. TPP would have been the most important trade agreement concluded by the US since the establishment of the WTO in 1995. Although TPP's impact on the US economy probably would have been modest, its main attraction was that it would extend many American regulatory standards to a significant part of the world and create a precedent for even broader application in future trade agreements. TPP also was of critical importance to maintain any credibility with our allies in the Asia/ Pacific region.[46] The American Government had repeatedly said that TPP demonstrated the seriousness of America's tilt towards Asia. In addition, after the American Government had pushed and prodded the other member states to make the reforms necessary to accommodate TPP's ambitious agenda, and the other member states had done so even where the domestic political consequences were quite severe, US withdrawal from TPP at this late date is having a catastrophic impact on the US reputation as a trustworthy ally.

TPP's was so importance to sustaining America's credibility in Asia that six outgoing US ambassadors to Asian countries co-signed a letter to Trump urging him not to withdraw from TPP. The ambassadors said "Walking away from TPP may be seen by future generations as the moment America chose to cede leadership to others in this part of the world and accept a diminished role... Such an outcome would be cause for celebration among those who favor 'Asia for Asians' and 'state capitalism [i.e., China and Russia].'"[47]

It is not surprising given the amount of time, energy and political capital put into concluding TPP that the other 11 members of TPP were deeply dismayed by America's withdrawal. The general view of America's allies who watched the TPP's arduous 10 year negotiation process is that this is a prime example of the feckless Americans and a good reason why they cannot be trusted. China and Russia, on the other hand, see American withdrawal

---

[46]   Countries hostile to the US, such as North Korea, also may see the US position on TPP as evidence of the seriousness of any American threat directed towards them.

[47]   See https://www.bloomberg.com/politics/articles/2017-01-12/departing-u-s-ambassadors-urge-congress-to-revive-trade-deal (visited February 4, 2017).

from TPP as a major opening for them.[48] China in particular is expected to benefit from the increased importance of the Chinese led, but much less ambitious regional trade agreement, the Regional Comprehensive Economic Partnership Agreement. With TPP now dead, RCEP is the only regional trade agreement in the Asia Pacific under active development.[49]

2. Renegotiate or withdraw from Nafta .

The North American Free Trade Agreement is a comprehensive regional free trade agreement that has significantly integrated the economies of Canada, Mexico and the US. It was negotiated during the Republican presidency of George H.W. Bush in 1989 – 1993, and ratified by Congress with bi-partisan support in 1993, during Democratic President Bill Clinton's first term in office.

Since Nafta came into force, total US trade with Canada and Mexico has quadrupled to $1.3 trillion a year, but the combined deficit in trade in goods also has grown from $9.1 billion in 1993 to $76.2 billion in 2015. Canada is the number one export destination for US goods, while Mexico is second; and Canada and Mexico are the second and third largest importers of the US goods. Nafta's effect on US jobs is in dispute. Organized labor is hostile to Nafta because it claims that Nafta has cost 850,000 US manufacturing jobs; but the business oriented US Chamber of Commerce says that Nafta has added a net of 5 million jobs. The relatively objective Congressional Research Service has concluded that Nafta's effect on the US economy has been slightly positive, but it has helped US manufacturers become more competitive because of more efficient supply chains.[50]

Trump has long been a critic of Nafta as he claims that it is the "worst trade deal ever."[51] Now that he is president, he has repeated his campaign

---

[48]   Two articles that discuss how the US withdrawal from TPP will benefit China and Russia are available at *US change of guard offers Beijing whip hand on trade*, Financial Times (US edition) at p. 2 (18 November, 2016) and http://www.reuters.com/article/us-apec-summit-idUSKBN13F117 (visited November 27, 2016).

[49]   See https://sputniknews.com/politics/201611261047865042-china-us-tpp-rcep-asia-pacific/ (visited November 27, 2016).

[50]   See http://www.cnbc.com/2016/11/22/trumps-Nafta-revamp-would-require-concessions-may-borrow-from-tpp.html (visited November 22, 2016).

[51]   Trump has criticized NAFTA for many years. During the presidential campaign, he frequently called

promises to renegotiate Nafta or, if the renegotiations fail, withdraw from Nafta. In theory, getting to the renegotiating table should not be a problem, however, since Mexican President Enrique Pena Nieto and Canadian Prime Minister Justin Trudeau agree with Trump on the need for a Nafta renegotiation, which is not surprising given that the agreement is 23 years old and there have been many major changes in international trade since it came into force in 1994. The principal obstacle to renegotiation of Nafta is Trump's preoccupation with his campaign promise to build a wall along the US border with Mexico and make Mexico pay for it. At various times, Trump has characterized Mexican immigrants as rapists, drug dealers and other criminals and has said the wall is necessary to keep the border secure. Mexico is enormously insulted by the wall and Trump's disparaging description of Mexicans. On the American side, Trump's Secretary of Homeland Security, John Kelly, has said the wall will not make the US safe and that the best protections are working closely with the countries south of the border to limit cross border drug trafficking and other illegal immigration.[52] Congress also has pushed back against the wall by refusing to provide funding for it.[53] If Trump can be persuaded to look beyond his preoccupations with the wall, Mexico's US$60 billion trade surplus with the US, and the US manufacturing job losses, the presidents of Mexico and the US and the prime minister of Canada may be able to agree that the renegotiations should focus on modernizing Nafta. It is anomalous, however, that Nafta's modernization is likely to include updated trade provisions taken from TPP – specifically more rigorous provisions on environment, labor and digital economy standards.[54] TPP also contains detailed rules on e-commerce and cross-border data flows. These activities hardly existed when Nafta was negotiated in the early 1990s, but the new regulatory provisions now could

---

NAFTA the "worst deal ever." See, e.g., http://www.cnbc.com/2016/11/22/trumps-Nafta-revamp-would-require-concessions-may-borrow-from-tpp.html (visited November 22, 2016).

[52] See https://www.nytimes.com/2017/01/25/us/politics/homeland-security-john-kelly-border-wall.html (visited February 5, 2017).

[53] See https://www.buzzfeed.com/emmaloop/congress-wont-fund-trumps-border-wall-at-least-not-yet?utm_term=.rrvObw5NQ#.vu3RZdBP6 (visited May 17, 2017).

[54] See http://www.cnbc.com/2016/11/22/trumps-Nafta-revamp-would-require-concessions-may-borrow-from-tpp.html (visited November 22, 2016).

offer better protections for intellectual property rights, which is usually a priority in US international trade negotiations.

3. Renegotiate or withdraw from other bilateral trade agreements, including the KOR US FTA.

The US has free trade agreements with 20 countries, including Canada and Mexico through NAFTA.[55] All of these agreements provide for reciprocal tariff reductions and an easing of non-tariff barriers to trade.

The US's most significant bilateral trade agreement is the KOR US FTA. It was initially signed in 2007, but because of strong opposition within the US Congress and some Korean and US businesses and labor groups, ratification of the agreement could not proceed until a supplemental agreement was concluded in 2010. The supplemental agreement dealt mostly with agricultural trade issues and the disparity in trade in automobiles, with Korea exporting over 1 million automobiles to the US while importing about 13,000 units from the US in 2011.[56] The supplemental agreement added provisions aimed at giving US automakers easier access to the Korean market and additional protections from a surge in Korean auto imports.[57] As an indication of what the Trump Administration will face in its efforts to renegotiate unfavorable aspects of the US trade agreements, the office of the USTR reported that, in the negotiations involving the supplemental agreement, in order to obtain the concessions for US automakers the US had to agree to a longer phase-out of the steep Korean pork tariffs and allow Korea to retain its health care reimbursement system which favors domestic drug makers.[58] Following the conclusion of the supplemental agreement, the US Congress and the Korean National Assembly formally ratified the

---

[55] https://ustr.gov/trade-agreements/free-trade-agreements. The US also has bilateral investment treaties and other forms of economic cooperation, but the most significant are the free trade agreements.

[56] See https://www.statista.com/statistics/260899/number-of-vehicles-imported-into-the-united-states-by-country/ (visited November 27, 2016); http://www.trade.gov/td/otm/assets/auto/ExportPaper2015.pdf (visited November 27, 2016).

[57] See https://www.whitehouse.gov/sites/default/files/fact_sheet_increasing_us_auto_exports_us_korea_free_trade_ag-reement_v2_0.pdf (visited November 28, 2016).

[58] See See http://www.cnbc.com/2016/11/22/trumps-Nafta-revamp-would-require-concessions-may-borrow-from-tpp.html (visited November 22, 2016).

KORUS FTA and it went into effect on March 15, 2012.

Since the KOR US FTA became effective in 2012, bilateral trade has grown, but it has been largely with respect to Korean exports to the US. Korea's exports to the US have increased from $56.7 billion in 2011 to $71.8 billion in 2015, an increase of about 27 percent. Meanwhile, US exports to Korea have remained relatively flat at $43.4 billion in 2015. One consequence of the one sided growth in trade, already noted by the Trump Administration, is that from 2011 to 2015, the US bilateral trade deficit with Korea more than doubled as it grew from $13.2 billion in 2011 to $28.3 billion in 2015. Korea now is the 7th largest source of the US trade deficit, after China, Germany, Japan, Mexico, Vietnam, and Ireland.[59] Of course, the Korean Ministry of Trade, Industry and Energy would counter that under the KOR US FTA, US agricultural and auto exports were increasing at a remarkable rate and that the US generally runs a surplus with Korea on services trade. Between 2011 and 2014, for example, US auto exports increased from 12,500 to 32,200 automobiles, and in 2012 the US surplus in services trade was $8.7 billion, up 11.9 percent from 2011.[60] Based on the Trump Administration's expressed hostility to KOR US FTA, however, it seems that it will not be impressed by such an optimistic view of trade relations between Korea and the US. As a result, now that Robert Lighthizer has been confirmed by the US Senate as the USTR in May, 2017, renegotiation of the KOR US FTA is likely to be an importnat trade priority within the Trump Administration.

4. *Impose tariffs of 35 percent on Mexican goods and 45 percent on Chinese goods.*

The average US tariff on imported goods is 1.5 percent, which is roughly consistent with tariff rates in other industrialized countries.[61] Due to the successive rounds of multilateral trade negotiations, first under the General

[59] See https://www.census.gov/foreign-trade/statistics/highlights/top/top1512yr.html (visited November 27, 2016).
[60] See https://ustr.gov/countries-regions/japan-korea-apec/korea (visited November 27, 2016).
[61] See http://data.worldbank.org/indicator/TM.TAX.MRCH.WM.AR.ZS (visited November 25, 2016). Many other industrialized countries actually have tariff rates lower than the US rate of 1.5 percent.

Agreement on Tariffs and Trade and after 1994 under the World Trade Organization, tariffs in the US and most other countries in the world have been trending downward since the end of World War II in 1945. The current tariff levels stand in sharp contrast to the average tariff in the US in the early 1930s. At that time, tariffs averaged about 50 percent under the infamous Smoot Hawley Tariff Act of 1930. In fact, a great deal of America's support for economic liberalization over the last 80 years is in response to the effects of the Smoot Hawley Tariff Act,[62] which prompted swift tariff retaliations by America's major trading partners. The ensuing trade wars led to reductions in American imports, but an even greater reduction in American exports. Some contend that the Smoot Hawley Tariff Act made the Great Depression much worse than it would have been under less protectionist trade policies. It also may have contributed to the rise of Nazism in Germany and the Japanese ultra-nationalists that then led their countries into World War II.[63]

Although there is overwhelming evidence that job losses in the US are caused more by productivity improvements than international trade,[64] Trump (and Hillary Clinton and Bernie Sanders) has repeatedly ignored that evidence and accused other countries of stealing US manufacturing jobs. Trump has been especially aggressive in targeting Mexico and China as the causes for US manufacturing job losses. To counter the claimed job losses to Mexico and China and eliminate the US trade deficit, on several occasions during his presidential campaign Trump said he would impose a 35 percent tariff on Mexican goods and a 45 percent tariff on Chinese goods. Trump also has said that he would label China a "currency manipulator" under US trade laws, instruct the USTR to bring cases against China in the US and

[62]   The Smoot Hawley Tariff Act became effective in 1930. Four years later, President Franklin Roosevelt signed the Reciprocal Trade Agreement Act and began the move toward tariff reductions and international economic liberalization. See https://www.britannica.com/topic/Smoot-Hawley-Tariff-Act (visited November 27, 2016).

[63]   See https://www.britannica.com/topic/Smoot-Hawley-Tariff-Act (visited November 27, 2016).

[64]   The consensus among economists is that productivity improvements are by far more important causes of manufacturing job losses in the US. As reported by the Peterson Institute for International Economics, one study that examined the effects of productivity improvements, international trade, and changes in domestic demand on job losses during 2000 to 2010 concluded that productivity improvements caused 88 percent of the job losses. Discussion of the report is available at https://piie.com/publications/piie-briefings/assessing-trade-agendas-us-presidential-campaign at page 19.

before the WTO to challenge China's use of unfair subsidies, and use every lawful presidential power to remedy trade disputes if China does not stop its illegal activities, including its theft of American trade secrets.[65]

Effective in 2008, all goods moving within the NAFTA region were duty free. This means that Mexican and Canadian goods imported into the US are now duty free.[66] The average US tariff rate on imports from China and the other 162 countries in the WTO is about 3.5 percent.[67] As a result, if Trump imposes a tariff of 35 percent on Mexican goods and 45 percent on Chinese goods, the tariffs would have an enormous impact on trade flows from Mexico and China into the US market.[68] It would mean that Mexican and Chinese goods sold in the US would become much more expensive, which would disproportionately affect low and middle income households.[69] It also would significantly affect supply chains, which now account for about 80 percent of world trade. Of course, the high tariffs on Mexican and Chinese goods probably would lead to retaliation by the Mexican and Chinese governments. The trade retaliatory measures could be limited, such as boycotts of US aircraft and soybean exports or US business services, or they could be across the board, but in either case they would have a very harmful effect on the US economy, as well as the Mexican and Chinese economies.

Since becoming president, Trump's positions on Mexico and China are still somewhat uncertain, but the tone of his rhetoric and the actions he has taken are more moderate than his campaign promises of extreme protectionism. There is less and less talk of the wall along the US/Mexican border and even fewer suggestions that Trump will make Mexico pay for it. Instead, the emphasis is on how highly integrated the US, Canadian and Mexican economies are and the consequence that injury to one of the economies will have a major impact on the other two. The Trump

---

[65] See https://www.donaldjtrump.com/policies/trade (visited November 28, 2016).
[66] See http://www.Naftanow.org/faq_en.asp (visited November 27, 2016).
[67] See http://stat.wto.org/TariffProfiles/US_e.htm (visited November 28, 2016).
[68] As president, Trump has enormous powers to influence international trade, including the power to impose tariffs. The legality of Trump's proposed tariffs is discussed in more detail the next section.
[69] See http://www.nytimes.com/2016/04/08/upshot/how-a-tariff-on-chinese-imports-would-ripple-through-american-life.html?_r=0 (visited November 28, 2016).

Administration's list of 50 objectives in 19 areas in the Nafta renegotiations are notable for being relatively moderate and, with only a few exceptions, relatively non-controversial.[70] On China, Trump has explicitly stated that China is not manipulating its currency to gain a competitive advantage and there is little mention of threats to impose a 45 percent tariff on Chinese exports. On the other hand, the Trump Administration has begun investigations of the effects of steel and aluminum imports on US national security under US trade laws and Chinese exports are among the primary targets. These investigations could lead to significant tariffs or other restraints on Chinese steel and aluminum exports, similar to what occurred in 2001 when the Bush Administration used US trade laws to impose broad ranging protective tariffs on imported steel.[71] These new investigations make it apparent that there still are difficult issues facing trade relations between the US and China, but the Trump Administration seems to be moving away from threats of an all-out trade war with China.

5. Pull out of the World Trade Organization.

The WTO was established in 1995 as the successor to the General Agreement on Tariffs and Trade, which was formed just after the end of World War II. WTO has 164 member countries and is the heart of the current rules based system governing international trade and related issues. The US played a prominent role in the creation of GATT and then the WTO and it continues as WTO's dominant member. Under GATT and the WTO, tariffs worldwide have been reduced dramatically and many non-tariff barriers have been eliminated or lessened. The US also has had considerable success challenging many country specific unfair trade practices through the WTO's Dispute Settlement Mechanism, just as other countries have successfully challenged the US for its unfair trade practices.

Because of the successes of the multilateral trade negotiations in the

---

[70] See http://www.ghy.com/trade-compliance/trump-administration-outlines-nafta-negotiating-objectives/ (visited may 17, 2017).
[71] See http://www.lexology.com/library/detail.aspx?g=2b8f03a9-5e7b-41e2-99f7-15933d154450 (visited May 17, 2017).

70 years since GATT was formed, the trade issues that continue to hamper trade, such as agricultural subsidies, non-tariff barriers, and competition law policies, have a heightened sensitivity in member countries. It is largely for this reason that since its creation in 1995 the WTO has failed to adopt any additional significant trade liberalization measures. In fact, the one major effort at multilateral negotiations since the creation of the WTO, the Doha Round,[72] has floundered because of the sensitivity of the issues involved, the enormous differences in attitudes on these issues among the 164 member countries, and the requirement that decisions under the WTO have to be reached by consensus.

On a number of occasions, Trump or his aides have suggested that he would consider withdrawing from the WTO. Given the frail nature of WTO today, US withdrawal would likely be WTO's death knell. The immediate impact of the WTO's demise would be a return of high tariff levels around the world, followed by severe drops in international trade. Economies around the world would be thrown into recessions, unemployment would rise, and political instability would explode. The global impact of WTO's collapse would be cataclysmic. Unless Trump becomes suicidal, US withdrawal from WTO is not a realistic option.

DOES TRUMP HAVE THE POWER TO DO WHAT HE HAS PROMISED?

The short answer is yes, Trump could do all of things listed above at least in the short term. In the medium or long term, his actions would be vigorously challenged by business and labor groups adversely affected by his decisions, by a Congress that thinks Trump is usurping power reserved to it, and ultimately by the courts. For example, since trade agreements only become effective in the US after Congress passes legislation that incorporates the trade agreements, Congress could argue that Trump alone does not have the power to abrogate trade agreements, just as Trump alone cannot repeal any other legislative acts of Congress.[73] Trump's action also would invite

---

[72] As its name suggests, the Doha Round was begun in 2001 at a multilateral meeting in Doha, Qatar. See https://www.wto.org/english/tratop_e/dda_e/dda_e.htm (visited November 28, 2016).

[73] See *NAFTA isn't going anywhere, despite Trump's attacks*, Wis. State J. at p. A13 (December 1, 2016).

international responses, under the WTO or any of the regional or bilateral agreements to which the US is a party. But the domestic and international challenges are not guaranteed to succeed and they would take months or years to conclude, by which time the effects of Trump's actions would be felt throughout the world. The wisest course of action, therefore, is to mount whatever efforts are possible to keep Trump from taking these extreme actions in the first place.

Under Article I, Section 8 of the US Constitution, Congress is given the power "to regulate Commerce with foreign Nations, and among the several States, and with the Indian Tribes." In Article II, Section 2 of the US Constitution, the president is expressly given the authority to make treaties, subject to the approval of two thirds of the senators. In addition, over many years dating back to the founding of the country in the 18th Century, there has been recognition of an inherent power in the president to conduct foreign affairs.[74] It is through the exercise of this inherent power to conduct foreign affairs that Trump can withdraw from TPP, NAFTA, the KOR US FTA, and any other free trade agreements. The exercise of this power would be unprecedented, as historically presidents have used this power to lower tariffs, not raise them.[75] The specific agreements also all contain language that anticipate accessions and withdrawals and Trump's actions would seem to be legally permissible under them. For example, Article 24.5 of the KOR US FTA provides as follows:

ARTICLE 24.5: ENTRY INTO FORCE AND TERMINATION

1. This Agreement shall enter into force 60 days after the date the Parties exchange written notifications certifying that they have completed their respective applicable legal requirements and procedures or on such other date as the Parties may agree.

---

[74] See http://www.heritage.org/research/lecture/an-understanding-of-the-constitutions-foreign-affairs-power (visited November 29, 2016).

[75] See Peterson Institute for International Economics, *Assessing Trade Agendas in the US Presidential Campaign* at pp. 7 - 8 at https://piie.com/system/files/documents/piieb16-6.pdf (visited November 29, 2016).

2. This Agreement shall terminate 180 days after the date either Party notifies the other Party in writing that it wishes to terminate the Agreement.

Trump's withdrawal from any or all of the US trade agreements and the WTO would result in a barrage of criticism from the US Congress, swaths of the American public and the private sector. His withdrawal also would generate worldwide condemnation. The ability to effectively reverse Trump's action within the US courts, however, would take months or years and even then the challenges might not be successful. International legal actions also would be time consuming and may not be successful.[76] In either event, the damage from his actions would be widely felt in the US and around the world. As mentioned before, the better course of action is to take whatever efforts are possible to keep Trump from taking these extreme actions in the first place.

The president's inherent power to conduct foreign affairs also would be the basis for any attempts to renegotiate any bilateral or regional trade agreement, such as KOR US FTA and NAFTA. Once the renegotiations are completed, however, they would have to be ratified by Congress before becoming effective. Congress also closely guards its powers over trade issues. For example, although the renegotiation of Nafta is a high priority of the Trump Administration, the renegotiation process has been delayed because Congressional leaders required that Robert Lighthizer first be confirmed as the US Trade Representative.[77] In Lighthizer's confirmation hearings, Republican and Democratic senators made clear their opposition to Trump's threats to withdraw from Nafta if the renegotiations do not accommodate US demands. The senators also voiced great concerns about Trump's protectionist rhetoric and wanted Lighthizer and Trump to fully

---

[76] If China is faced with 45 percent tariffs on exports to the US, it will claim that the US is acting in violation of its commitments under the WTO. A similar case occurred when George Bush imposed tariffs on imports of Chinese (and other countries) steel in 2002. His actions were promptly challenged under the WTO's Dispute Settlement Mechanism. When the WTO ruled against the US in late 2003, however, 20 months had elapsed, and although Bush repealed the tariffs soon thereafter, by that time, he had largely achieved his political objectives, including securing trade promotion authority from Congress.

[77] See http://www.reuters.com/article/us-usa-trade-lighthizer-idUSKBN18727C (visited May 18, 2017).

understand the significant benefits Nafta offers to the US economy, as well as to the Canadian and Mexican economies.

Trump's legal support for imposing selective tariffs of 35 percent on Mexican goods and 45 percent on Chinese goods is more complex than with the relatively simple withdrawal from trade agreements. Congress has passed a number of laws dealing with trade abuses, such as dumping, export subsidies, and currency manipulations under which the president and the USTR are given the authority to enact tariffs and other measures aimed at counteracting the abuses. The president and the USTR also have authority to impose tariffs to prevent economic hardships resulting from import surges. In most cases, however, there are requirements that the abuses be quantified, as well as specific findings of injuries to US workers or industries and findings that the injuries were caused by the imported products being targeted. These trade remedies also involve the relatively independent International Trade Commission, which has been known to arrive at conclusions that are politically unpopular.[78] On the other hand, there are three statutes that do give Trump broad authority to impose tariffs or other restrictions without quantifying the abuse or findings of injury and causation:[79]

- Under section 232(b) of the Trade Expansion Act of 1962, the president (or some other party) can ask the director of the Office of Emergency Planning to investigate the impact on national security of specific imports and, if he finds an adverse impact, the president is empowered to impose import restrictions. The statute places no limit on the nature of restrictions or the height of tariffs. Presumably, Trump could impose the tariffs on Mexican and Chinese goods because they threaten the economic security of certain portions

[78] One of the most notable instances when the ITC's decision went against the political climate of the moment is the decision denying that US automakers were being injured by increased imports of Japanese and other foreign automobiles in November, 1980. See http://www.upi.com/Archives/1980/11/11/Automakers-look-to-White-House-and-Congress-for-import-relief/7804342766800/ (visited November 30, 2016).The ITC decision lead to pressure from the US automaker to impose restrictions on Japanese imports, which resulted in the Voluntary Restraint Agreement limiting Japanese auto imports to 1.86 million units per year.

[79] See Peterson Institute for International Economics, *Assessing Trade Agendas in the US Presidential Campaign* at pp. 9 – 10 at https://piie.com/system/files/documents/piieb16-6.pdf (visited November 29, 2016).

of the US economy where there has been significant economic displacement due to Mexican and Chinese imports. In April, 2017, the Trump Administration began section 232 investigations into steel and aluminum imports, which could lead to significant tariffs being imposed on Chinese exports of steel and aluminum into the US.[80] The tariffs also could affect steel and aluminum imports from other countries as well.

- Section 122 of the Trade Act of 1974 gives the president power to impose tariffs of up to 15 percent or quantitative restrictions for a maximum of 150 days in order to counteract large and serious balance of payments deficits. The restrictions can be imposed either across the board or targeted against specific countries contributing to the balance of payments deficit.

- If the USTR first determines that a country is denying the US rights under a trade agreement or is carrying out practices that are unjustifiable, unreasonable, or discriminatory and burden or restrict US commerce, under section 301 of the Trade Act of 1974, the president can take retaliatory actions, including the imposition of duties or other import restrictions. The statute does not specify a timetable for invoking or lifting Section 301 measures. Since Trump is attacking Mexico and the Chinese because of unfair trade practices of stealing US jobs and undervaluing the currency, he could impose the tariffs of 35 percent against Mexican goods and 45 percent against Chinese goods under section 301.

Trump's use of any of these three statutes, however, is likely to be challenged as a violation of the US obligations under the WTO. Of course, even if the challenge is successful, it will be several months or years after the initial imposition of the tariffs, so much of the damage from the tariffs would have been done to the US, Mexican and Chinese economies or Trump's political goals will have been achieved. Again, for those concerned

---

[80] See http://www.drinkerbiddle.com/insights/publications/2017/04/trump-admin-to-investigate-aluminum-imports (visited May 18, 2017).

with the maintenance of the current international trade system, the better course of action seems to forestall the imposition of the tariffs.

TRUMP'S TRADE POLICIES: FROM BLUSTER TO THE REALITIES OF THE AMERICAN PRESIDENCY

1. Trump's proposals in an historical perspective.

Trump's virulent, incoherent, contradictory trade rhetoric in the early days of his administration has caused a great deal of confusion and anxiety as foreign governments, international businesses and global investors look for indicators of what specific actions his administration will take on international economic issues. Although there are growing signs of moderation from within the Trump Administration, there still is a widespread feeling that we are teetering at the edge of an abyss and that the world's trading system, which has been 70 years in the making, may soon fall with cataclysmic consequences for the global economy. At this moment, it may be useful to recall that, while the US has played the leading role in the last 70 years' move towards international economic liberalization, there have been times in the last 7 decades when the US has turned away from its support for free trade and open markets. Four examples may add an historic perspective to Trump's threats on international trade and temper some of the angst dominating today's discussion on trade matters.

- *The International Trade Organization.* Shortly after the end of World War II, over 50 countries participated in negotiations to create an International Trade Organization (ITO) as a specialized agency of the United Nations. The draft ITO Charter was ambitious. It combined a significant effort to reduce tariffs and other traditional trade barriers with a rule based system that covering with investment, employment standards, development, business monopolies and commodity agreements. The ITO also introduced the concept that trade disputes should be settled by consultation and mediation rather than with economic or political power. Further it established an institutional linkage between trade and labor standards that would effect a major advance in global governance. Finally it embedded the full employment obligation, along with "a commitment to free markets" as the cornerstone of multilateralism.[81] The aim was to create the ITO at a UN Conference on Trade and Employment in Havana, Cuba in 1947. Even though the US was one of the leaders in developing the ITO, opposition from the US Congress effectively killed the ITO. That is why from 1947 – 1995 (when the World Trade Organization came into existence), the principal legal regime governing international trade was the General Agreement on Tariffs and Trade (1947), which originally had been intended as a temporary measure to be replaced by the ITO.[82]

- *The Nixon shock of 1971.* On August 15, 1971, President Richard M. Nixon announced his New Economic Policy, a program "to create a new prosperity without war." Known colloquially as the "Nixon shock," the initiative marked the beginning of the end for the Bretton Woods system of fixed exchange rates established at the end of World War II. Nixon identified a three-fold task: "We must create more and better jobs; we must stop the rise in the cost of living; we must protect the dollar from the attacks of international money speculators." To achieve the first two goals, he proposed tax cuts and a 90-day freeze on prices and wages; to achieve the third, Nixon directed the suspension of the dollar's convertibility into gold. He also ordered that an extra 10 percent tariff be levied on all dutiable imports; like the suspension of the dollar's gold convertibility, this measure was intended to induce the United States' major trading partners to adjust the value of their currencies upward and the level of their trade barriers downward so as to allow for more imports from the United States. Nixon's program was popular within the US, but it shocked many abroad, who saw it as an act of worrisome unilateralism.[83]

---

81 Drache, *The Short but Significant Life of the International Trade Organisation: Lessons for Our Time,* available at http://wrap.warwick.ac.uk/2063/1/WRAP_Drache_wp6200.pdf.

82 See https://www.wto.org/english/thewto_e/whatis_e/tif_e/fact4_e.htm (Visited November 28, 2016).

83 See https://history.state.gov/milestones/1969-1976/nixon-shock (visited November 28, 2016).

98

- *Reagan, Japanese auto imports and VER agreements.* In the late 1970s, early 1980s, America's foreign trade demon was Japan and particular attention was paid to Japanese imports of well designed, reliable and fuel efficient small cars. The Japanese automakers were killing the US "big three" of GM, Ford and Chrysler. In his campaign for the presidency, Ronald Reagan promised he would rein in Japanese auto imports. At the same time, the US automakers and organized labor filed a petition with the International Trade Commission asking for temporary tariffs on Japanese auto imports under US trade law. This would have cleared the way for Reagan to impose the tariffs in order to give the US automakers temporary protections from their Japanese competitors. But, to the surprise of many, the International Trade Commission denied the petition for relief in part because the ITC felt that the injuries being suffered by the US automakers were at least partly self-inflicted. The ITC decision created a political firestorm of anti-Japanese trade sentiment with the US Congress threatening major trade sanctions targeting the Japanese. At this point, the Reagan Administration stepped in and negotiated a Voluntary Export Restraint Agreement with the Japanese Government. Under the VER, Japanese automakers agreed to limit their exports to 1.68 million vehicles per year, but they did so principally to forestall more protectionist measures being enacted by an exceptionally hostile Congress.[84] The most significant effect of these threats of protectionism is that Japanese and other foreign manufacturers shifted large portions of their productive capacity into the US. During the 1980s, in part because of the congressional threats of protectionism, the US saw a boom in inbound foreign direct investment with new factories worth hundreds of billions of dollars being erected inside the US. The shift in production to the US was led by the Japanese automakers: 1982, Honda opened a plant in Marysville, Ohio; a Toyota joint venture with

---

[84] The tensions that led to the VER are described in *Carwars: Trying to Make Sense of U.S. Japan Trade Frictions in the Automobile and Automobile Parts Markets,* in **The Effects of U.S. Trade Protection and Promotion Policies** at p. 11 (1997).

GM was started in Fremont, California in 1984; Nissan opened a plant in Smyrna, Tennessee in 1985; Mazda's plant opened in Flat Rock, Michigan in 1987; Mitsubishi/Chrysler's joint venture was opened in 1988 in Bloomington – Normal, Illinois; Toyota opened another plant in Georgetown, Kentucky in 1988; and Fuji-Isuzu established a plant in Lafayette, Indiana in 1989.[85]

- *Bush and imported steel.* President George W. Bush imposed safeguard tariffs on a large volume of US steel imports in March 2002. At the time, the blatantly political decision was derided as "disgraceful" and "stupid."[86] In November 2003, some 20 months later, the WTO Appellate Body ruled that the Bush steel tariffs were inconsistent with US obligations under the WTO, and Bush lifted them in December 2003. By that time, Bush had achieved his political goals, in particular congressional passage of the Trade Promotion Authority Act of 2002, which was widely welcomed abroad. Once Bush had secured the Trade Promotion Authority, his administration reverted to being more supportive of free trade and concluded a series of free trade agreements, including in 2007 the KOR US FTA.

So, there are some grounds to think that increasing globalization and trade liberalization may survive the protectionist policies of a Trump Administration. Of course, this time may be different and international economic liberalism may be at the starting point of a retreat into protectionism. The threat of protectionism is made especially credible by the populist anti-trade forces that now extend beyond the US to many industrialized countries in Europe. But, at least in the US, as explained in the next subsection, there may be influences to limit the protectionist dogma of President Trump.

---

[85] The inbound FDI by Japanese automakers is catalogued in Nakaprawing, *Foreign Direct Investment in the U.S.A.* at pp. 4 – 5 (2016) (research paper on file with the author).
[86] See http://www.economist.com/node/1021395 (visited November 30, 2016).

2. Moderating influences.

Trump's blusterous, offensive speaking manner coupled with his willingness to make major pronouncements without regard for the truth and little understanding of the consequences cause many to discount Trump's rantings on international trade as a misguided recipe for trade protectionism. But after only a few months of Trumpian chaos with protectionist overtones, evidence of forces aimed at moderating Trump's most protectionist tendencies are appearing. This is doubly so as Trump continues to create so many self-destructive ethical controversies that people increasingly feel compelled to speak out. As a result, there now is a guarded optimism that there will be enough external influence to moderate Trump's proposals and perhaps even allow his administration to focus on those proposals that have merit. Trump is almost completely wrong in his opposition to TPP and any secret benefits China may obtain from TPP through a backdoor, he is also wrong about Mexico's 16 percent VAT being an impermissible export subsidy,[87] and he and Clinton and Sanders have greatly overstated the effects of international trade on American manufacturing job losses as most evidence suggests that productivity improvements account for the great majority of the job losses.[88] On the other hand, Trump seems on firm ground with his assertions that China engages in a number of unfair trade practices,[89] that NAFTA needs to be renegotiated, that the benefits of the KOR US FTA seem to flow disproportionately to Korea, and that other countries are not abiding by their commitments under free trade agreements and the WTO. What Trump needs is advice that separates the real problems from his mishmash of campaign promises. Of course, Trump also has to listen to this advice. Surprisingly, there may be reason for optimism in this regard.

Trump was elected US president in November, 2016, and his anti-trade rhetoric certainly contributed to his electoral success. But not everybody

---

[87] See http://www.forbes.com/sites/timworstall/2016/08/17/a-vat-is-not-a-subsidy-to-exports-nor-is-it-a-tax-on-imports/#2267f3311d87 (visited November 28, 2016).

[88] See https://piie.com/system/files/documents/piieb16-6.pdf at p. 19 (visited November 28, 2016).

[89] See https://piie.com/blogs/realtime-economic-issues-watch/new-us-currency-policy (visited November 28, 2016). China is not alone, however, as many other countries manipulate their currencies to gain a competitive advantage for their exports – among them as Japan, Korea, Taiwan and Thailand.

agrees with Trump's policies. In the presidential election, Trump lost the popular vote to Hillary Clinton, by 61.9 million votes to 63.6 million.[90] In addition, because Trump and Clinton were the two most unpopular candidates ever to appear on the same ballot for president, 95 million people or 42 percent of the eligible voters did not vote.[91] So, while Trump appeals to a significant portion of the American population, his supporters are a minority of Americans, albeit a sizeable minority. For a significant majority of Americans, the man himself and his views are anathemas. The American voting public, however, has lost most of its ability to influence the Trump Administration until the next presidential election in 2020, although the midterm congressional elections in 2018 may signal to Trump whether the public supports him or not.

Apart from the American voting public, the US Government's trade and foreign policy bureaucracy, the Republican dominated US Congress, and the private sector do have the power to moderate the Trump Administration's behavior on international economic issues. The US State Department, the Departments of Agriculture and Commerce, the office of the US Trade Representative, and the US Export Import Bank have a total of 185,000 employees.[92] A great many of these employees understand that international economic liberalization has been good for America, as well as for the rest of the world. Even if many of the appointees in key positions within the White House and the US trade bureaucracy support Trump's extreme protectionist positions, his appointees will be getting their information and their advice from many people who are not protectionist. Almost certainly there are enough strong willed free traders among the second and third tier of the US Government's trade bureaucracy to apply a filter to Trump's more extreme views. More significantly is the emergence of "grown-ups" in the White House staff and cabinet who have demonstrated an ability to promote moderate positions on trade. Trump's son-in-law and special advisor Jared

---

[90] Even though Trump lost the popular vote, because of the peculiarity of the American Electoral College, Trump had 290 electoral votes while Clinton obtained only 232, with 270 electoral votes needed to win the presidency.

[91] For the record, the author of this essay was part of the 58 percent who did vote.

[92] See US Government Manual 2016 (visited November 29, 2016).

Kushner, Gary Cohen, the director of the National Economic Council, and the secretaries of the Treasury and Commerce, Steve Mnuchin and Wilbur Ross have been effective in transforming Trump's protectionist rhetoric into less controversial, free market oriented proposals. On Nafta, for example, Trump initially said that he would give notice of an intention to withdraw from Nafta at the same time he began the renegotiation process. The threat of withdrawal, however, was quickly withdrawn and replaced with assurances that the Trump Administration would be proceeding with the renegotiations.[93] In mid-May, 2017, the USTR also sent Congress a formal notice of an intention to begin to Nafta renegotiation process.[94]

The Republican controlled US Congress also should have a moderating influence on Trump's trade policies. As the aborted effort to repeal Obamacare demonstrated, Trump's major non-trade initiatives, such as tax reform and infrastructure development, as well as the continuing efforts to repeal Obamacare, will require that he work closely with Congress. This will give the Republican controlled Congress leverage with the Trump Administration on trade matters where Trump's protectionism is very much at odds with the pro-trade positions of many of the Republicans (and a good many Democrats) in Congress. The list of pro-trade Republicans is long, but includes key members such as: the Senate Majority Leader, Mitch McConnell (whose wife, Elaine Chao has been named as the Secretary of Transportation in the Trump Administration); Chairman of the Senate Finance Committee, Orrin Hatch; the Chairman of the House Ways and Means Committee, Kevin Brady; and the Chairman of the House Subcommittee on Trade, Dave Reichert. All of them represent the Republican orthodoxy on international trade and generally support trade liberalization measures. Dave Reichert, for example, comes from the State of Washington where 40 percent of the State's employment is trade dependent.[95] These people know the enormous damage that protectionist measures can have on the American economy, as

---

[93]   See https://www.ft.com/content/6763a15c-2ad8-11e7-9ec8-168383da43b7 (visited May 18, 2017).

[94]   See https://www.ft.com/content/2f3667f3-dc8e-3b5c-92fa-b40fc7841fa9 (visited May 18, 2017).

[95]   See https://reichert.house.gov/press-release/rep-reichert-named-chairman-subcommittee-trade (visited November 29, 2016).

well as the massive economic disruptions and political instability they will cause in the rest of the world. Not all of the Republicans in Congress have Trump's ear, but some of them do and they should be able to soften Trump's actions on trade.

The American private sector also is likely to be a potent force for moderation on trade matters. The US Chamber of Commerce is one of the most powerful lobbyists in Washington, D.C. and it is strongly pro-trade. Listed below are some of top US exporters, each of which sees its continuing success dependent on free trade and open markets:

- Apple (<u>computer hardware</u>)
- Exxon Mobil (oil, gas)
- Johnson & Johnson (medical equipment, supplies)
- Chevron Corporation (oil, gas)
- Procter & Gamble (household, personal care items)
- Pfizer (pharmaceuticals)
- The Coca-Cola Company (beverages)
- Merck & Co (pharmaceuticals)
- Qualcomm (semiconductors)
- Philip Morris International (tobacco)
- Intel (semiconductors)
- Schlumberger (oil, gas)
- PepsiCo (beverages)
- Cisco Systems (communications equipment)
- Boeing (aerospace)
- ConocoPhillips (oil, gas)
- AbbVie (pharmaceuticals)
- Occidental Petroleum (oil, gas)

- Eli Lilly and Company (pharmaceuticals)[96]

These companies have the resources and political access to make their views known to the Trump Administration. It seems reasonable to expect that the trade dependent business community will be able to appeal to a president who takes pride in characterizing himself as an American businessman.

Another potent force favoring a rule based system supporting free trade are American service industries. In 2016, the US overall trade deficit for goods and services was $502.3 billion, but that included a deficit in goods trade of $750.1 billion and a surplus in services trade of $247.8 billion. 2016 was similar to prior years as the US traditionally has a surplus in services trade.[97] Travel (including education), charges for intellectual property, financial services, telecommunications, computer and information services, and maintenance and repair services are the major contributors to the US services trade surpluses.[98] Many of the American service companies are globally competitive and they strongly oppose any return to nationalistic policies that limit their export opportunities. These companies also have a strong voice in national politics.

3. Going Forward.[99]

Trump's trade related campaign promises focused on manufacturing job creation and reducing US bilateral trade deficits. His prescriptions for achieving these goals were to renegotiate or withdraw from Nafta, withdraw from TPP, impose high tariffs on imports from Mexico and China, and possibly leave the WTO. Although Trump did withdraw from TPP very quickly after becoming president, the realities of the global economy and the limits of the powers of the presidency (starkly evidenced by the initial failure of Congress to repeal ObamaCare and his difficulties with the courts

---

[96] See http://www.worldstopexports.com/united-states-top-10-exports/ (visited November 29, 2016).

[97] See https://www.bea.gov/newsreleases/international/trade/2017/trad1216.htm (visited May 18, 2017).

[98] See https://www.census.gov/foreign-trade/Press-Release/current_press_release/exh3.pdf (visited May 18, 2017).

[99] This was written on May 20, 2017. As there is growing uncertainty about Trump's ability to continue as president, the catastrophe that is the Trump Administration may render all of these forecasts wildly inaccurate or totally irrelevant.

over his travel bans directed at mostly Muslim countries) seem to have softened Trump's most protectionist positions. By mid-May, 2017, all of Trump's key trade appointees were in office, but now there is little talk of taking the US out of the WTO or imposing high tariffs on Mexican goods. Most of the Trump Administration's foreseeable trade agenda is likely to be centered on renegotiating Nafta and dealing with China's unfair trade practices. An additional agenda item may involve renegotiation of KOR US FTA, but the resurrection of TPP, if it occurs, could also catch the Trump Administration's attention.

Nafta. On May 11, 2017, the US Senate confirmed Robert Lighthizer's appointment as the USTR. Lighthizer was the last of Trump's cabinet appointments to be confirmed by the Senate and his confirmation cleared the way for the Trump Administration to begin the process of renegotiating Nafta. One week later, as required by US trade laws, Lighthizer wrote to Congress about the Trump Administration's intention to renegotiate Nafta.[100] The letter to Congress had the effect of officially beginning a 90 day consultation period before the formal Nafta renegotiations can begin.

In March, 2017, the Trump Administration sent a draft letter to Congress that broadly outlined the administration's objectives in the Nafta renegotiations. In a step back from Trump's fiercely anti-Nafta rhetoric, the letter describes objectives similar to those achieved in TPP, including digital trade and cross-border data flows, new limits on state-owned enterprises, and subjecting environmental and labor controversies to the same dispute settlement and remedies as with other enforceable obligations.[101] There are, however, several more contentious objectives, including:[102]

- Leveling "the playing field on tax treatment" could be the most controversial American objective from a Mexican perspective, although the exact meaning will depend on the outcome of the US

---

[100] See http://www.cbc.ca/news/politics/nafta-renegotiation-congress-1.4121341 (visited May 19, 2017).

[101] See https://piie.com/blogs/trade-investment-policy-watch/trump-administrations-potentially-constructive-objectives-nafta (visited May 19, 2017).

[102] For a Canadian perspective on the US negotiating objectives, see http://www.ghy.com/trade-compliance/trump-administration-outlines-nafta-negotiating-objectives/ (visited May 19, 2017).

Congress' tax reform proposals. If the reform proposals contain a "border adjustment tax", it would have the effect of increasing the cost of US imports from Canada and Mexico; but the language "level the playing field" also could refer to Trump's frequently voiced threat to impose tariffs on Mexican goods to counteract the effect of Mexico's value added tax, which Trump long has claimed is an impermissible export subsidy.[103]

- Introduction of a safeguard mechanism to allow for temporary tariffs when imports from a Nafta partner injure or threaten injury to a domestic industry.

- Revision of the Nafta rules of origin to insure that the revised Nafta supports production and jobs in the US.

- Reducing or eliminating non-tariff barriers to US agricultural exports, including permit and licensing barriers and restrictive administration of tariff rate quotas, which are objectives that seem to focus on Canada's agricultural supply management system that is currently at the heart of US complaints about Canadian restrictions on US dairy exports.[104]

- A revision of Nafta Chapter 11, the investment dispute settlement mechanism, to insure the efficient selection of arbitrators and the expeditious resolution of claims while promoting transparency and public participation in the dispute settlement proceedings.

Both Mexico and Canada understand the need to revise Nafta to meet current economic conditions, but they also have their own list of objectives, some of which will conflict sharply with American goals. Mexico will want increased US quotas for Mexican sugar and greater access to American markets for other Mexican agricultural products, which will be opposed by

[103] See https://piie.com/blogs/trade-investment-policy-watch/trump-administrations-potentially-constructive-objectives-nafta (visited May 19, 2017).

[104] See http://www.businessinsider.com/heres-whats-behind-the-us-canada-dairy-battle-that-trump-waded-into-2017-4 (visited May 19, 2017).

very potent agricultural lobbyists in Washington.[105] The Canadian also will insist that the long running dispute between the US and Canada involving Canadian softwood exports to the US be resolved, especially because of the Trump Administration recent imposition of tariffs on Canadian softwood imports.[106] And both the Mexicans and Canadians will seek greater access to US public sector procurements, which are now heavily protected by "Buy America" laws. Trump's large new infrastructure development program would make this access very attractive.

Because of the 90 day consultation period required under US trade laws, the earliest the Nafta renegotiations could begin is mid-August, 2017. The negotiations certainly will be tough and fraught with great uncertainties, especially because of the probable insertion of provocative Trumpian tweets at inopportune times. There is growing optimism, however, that a favorable outcome will be reached and that the newly revised Nafta will have many of the key components of TPP, which Trump spurned just a few months earlier.

In anticipation of the Nafta renegotiations, there are two Trumpian traits that seem especially relevant for the Canadian and Mexican negotiators. The first is uncertainty: the uncertainty surrounding Trump is not an accident. Trump intentionally creates uncertainty in order to strengthen his negotiating position as he seeks better deals for the US in various trade fora, including Nafta. If, for example, the Canadian and Mexican trade negotiators think Trump will cancel the entire agreement if he does not get the concessions he wants, they will take his demands very seriously. Of course, such erratic

---

[105] See http://www.cnbc.com/2016/11/22/trumps-Nafta-revamp-would-require-concessions-may-borrow-from-tpp.html (visited November 22, 2016).

[106] The Canada–US softwood lumber dispute is the largest and most enduring trade dispute between the two countries. The controversy began in its current form in 1982. The basic dispute centers on the US lumber industry's claim that Canadian softwood producers are improperly subsidized by the Canadian provincial and federal governments, which own most of the timber in Canada. The Americans charge that the Canadian governments undercharge the Canadian timber harvesters, which gives the Canadian timber producers an unfair competitive advantage. In April, 2017, the long simmering dispute was escalated when the Trump Administration imposed countervailing duties on Canadian softwoods of up to 24.1 percent. See https://www.bloomberg.com/politics/articles/2017-04-24/trump-said-to-plan-20-tariff-on-canadian-softwood-lumber-j1wq4tyg (visited May 20, 2017). For a detailed discussion of the softwood controversy, see Ikenson, *Tilting at Sawmills: America's Shameful Approach to the Softwood Lumber Dispute with Canada,* available at http://www.forbes.com/sites/danikenson/2016/11/29/tilting-at-sawmills-americas-shameful-approach-to-the-softwood-lumber-dispute-with-canada/#704b40cf57f4.

behavior on Trump's part carries considerable risks to all parties. It also does not build friendship and trust among our closest allies and it makes the negotiations harder and more acrimonious. Uncertainty, however, has become an unfortunate hallmark of dealing with the Trump Administration.

The second point is that Trump is not an ideologue. In fact, he seems to have very few firmly grounded principles other than doing what is good for him and those around him. But the absence of an ideological core gives Trump the freedom to vacillate according to the current circumstances. It suggests that on international trade issues, Trump will consider many options irrespective of their ideological hue and choose the one that is best suited for the current moment. This flexibility and pragmatism actually may serve American interests as Trump seeks to recalibrate America's position in global affairs. It also challenges the Canadian, Mexican and US negotiators to find innovative solutions to problems to accommodate all parties' interests.

China's Unfair Trade Practices. During the presidential campaign, Trump often was fiercely critical of China's trade practices. Trump now applies his transactional view of real estate development to world affairs, so when he met with Chinese President Xi Jinping in April, 2017, he made it clear that if China helped to curb the nuclear threats of North Korea the US would cut a better trade deal with China. The Chinese also played to Trump's transactional view of the US/Chinese relationship by proposing the major trade outcome of the meeting – the establishment of the China/US Economic Cooperation 100 Day Plan as part of the new Comprehensive Economic Dialogue, which was aimed at significantly improving trade relations. It also no doubt helped the relationship that since Trump's inauguration as president on January 20, 2017, five of the Chinese trademark applications for Ivanka Trump's brand have been approved – with three of them being approved as Xi Jinping was meeting with Trump in Florida (and dining with Ivanka and her husband, Jared Kushner).[107] Since the Florida meeting, Trump's rhetoric on China has turned from hostile to friendly. About the Florida meeting,

---

[107] See http://fortune.com/2017/04/20/china-ivanka-trump-trademark-application/ (visited may 20, 2017).

Trump said "we had very good chemistry, I think;" and he said Xi Jinping "is a good man, a very good man, and I got to know him very well."[108]

Just days after the Trump meeting with Xi Jinping, Trump announced that he would not label China a currency manipulator, which was a reversal of one of his biggest trade related campaign promises.[109] Trump said that he had changed his mind because China was no longer manipulating its currency and he wanted to secure Chinese assistance in reducing tensions with North Korea.[110]

Approximately one month after initiating the China/US Economic Cooperation 100 Day Plan, the first results of the bilateral negotiations were announced. They included allowing imports of US beef into China and imports of cooked poultry into the US, conducting in China science-based evaluations of all eight pending US biotechnology product applications to assess the safety of their products, giving China greater access to US exports of LNG, allowing foreign-owned financial service firms in China to provide credit rating services and to begin the process for credit investigation services, opening electronic payment services in China to US owned enterprises, and China's issuance of both bond underwriting and settlement licenses to two qualified US financial institutions.[111] In addition, the two sides have begun talks on a one-year plan to further promote China/US economic cooperation under the newly created Comprehensive Economic Dialogue.

Given the earlier threats that the Trump Administration would (intentionally or unintentionally) start a trade war with China, the much quieter and more thoughtful dialogue now dominating the relationship is most welcome. Even with the improved environment, however, China and

---

[108] See https://www.nytimes.com/2017/04/29/world/asia/trump-xi-jinping-china.html?_r=0 (visited May 20, 2017).

[109] See https://www.washingtonpost.com/news/wonk/wp/2017/04/12/trump-says-he-will-not-label-china-currency-manipulator-reversing-campaign-promise/?utm_term=.758061baa8f2 (visited May 20, 2017).

[110] See http://www.cnbc.com/2017/04/12/trump-backtracks-on-china-wont-label-it-a-currency-manipulator.html (visited May 20, 2017).

[111] See https://www.commerce.gov/news/press-releases/2017/05/joint-release-initial-results-100-day-action-plan-us-china-comprehensive (visited May 20, 2017).

the US are the two largest economies in the world with combined goods and services trade in excess of $648 billion, so it is not surprising that some significant trade issues remain, including burdensome Chinese restrictions on technology transfers, discriminatory treatment of US companies with operations in China, and cybertheft.[112] A very important dispute involves the global oversupplies of steel and aluminum and Chinese dumping of its surplus steel and aluminum in the US (and EU) markets. To address the oversupply problem, in April, 2017, the Trump Administration launched two "national security" investigations ("section232 investigations") into steel and aluminum imports. The investigations are considering overcapacity, dumping, impermissible subsidies and other factors to determine whether steel and aluminum imports constitute threats to US national security. If the US determines that steel and aluminum imports are a threat to US national security, Trump will be given broad powers to restrict the imports, including the imposition of punitive tariffs on Chinese (and other) steel and aluminum imports.[113]

The use of "national security" as the base for imposing import restrictions is a source of significant concern among international trade specialists. Because national security concerns are unlikely to be successfully challenged in the WTO settlement process, they have the potential to be very effective barriers to imports. But precisely due to their effectiveness, governments have been reluctant to use this is a base for their import restrictions because it invites retaliatory actions by trading partners. To have the US, the dominant actor in the WTO, use the national security exception to restrain imports could prompt its much wider use, with a very considerable erosion of the world trading regime.[114] To the extent Chinese steel and aluminum exports are targeted, the import restrictions also could reignite the trade tensions between China and the US, although the threat of

[112] See https://www.bloomberg.com/politics/articles/2017-05-12/u-s-reaches-deal-to-allow-exports-of-natural-gas-beef-to-china (visited May 20, 2017).

[113] See https://www.commerce.gov/page/section-232-investigation-effect-imports-steel-us-national-security and https://www.commerce.gov/news/press-releases/2017/04/president-donald-j-trump-signs-presidential-memo-prioritizing-department (visited May 20, 2017).

[114] See https://www.washingtonpost.com/news/wonk/wp/2017/04/20/trump-administration-launches-national-security-investigation-into-steel-imports/?utm_term=.f6e688078584 (visited May 20, 2017).

major tariffs or other barriers also might spur the Chinese to deal with the problems of their excess capacities in steel and aluminum.

One interesting possibility with the new Comprehensive Economic Dialogue would be to bundle many of the bilateral trade issues into a single agreement, which then could take the form of a comprehensive bilateral free trade agreement. Included as many of the key components would be the provisions of TPP dealing with digital trade and cross-border data flows, new limits on state owned enterprises, and subjecting environmental and labor controversies to the same dispute settlement and remedies as other enforceable obligations. China certainly understands the benefits to be obtained from participating in a rigorous trade agreement such as TPP. One of the reasons China joined the WTO in 2001 was that the WTO rules required much needed reforms in the Chinese economy. Now China is again at a juncture where major economic reforms are needed to sustain China's economic growth rates and membership in a TPP style trade agreement could provide the external impetus for some of the more troublesome economic reforms, such as reigning in the state owned enterprises and modernizing the financial services industry. Chinese domestic politics, most specifically the 19th Party Congress scheduled for the fall of 2017, suggest that major economic reforms will not be considered until the conclusion of that Congress, which is widely expected to consolidate Xi Jinping's power, but early 2018 may be an opportune time for Chinese and American negotiators to consider an ambitious bilateral free trade agreement or even broader coordination with the 11 members of a resurrected TPP. The new version of TPP also could bring in Korea and Taiwan as the other two major Northeast Asian trading economies not originally include in TPP.

KOR US FTA. In terms of the volume of trade, KOR US FTA is the US's most important bilateral trade agreement. During the presidential campaign, Trump spoke often about how bad the KOR US FTA was and the clear need to renegotiate it, or if the renegotiations failed, to withdraw from the agreement. Since his inauguration as president, however, Trump and his aides have concentrated less on KOR US FTA, with most of their trade related attention centered on the Nafta renegotiations and the new dialogue with China. When Vice President Mike Pence traveled to South Korea in April, 2017, however, he said that because the benefits from KOR US FTA flow disproportionately to the Korean economy the agreement was unfair to American workers and needed to be renegotiated.[115] Although KOR US FTA is only five years old, it principal effect has been to more than double the US's bilateral trade deficit to $28 billion.[116] In addition, some US companies have argued that parts of the KOR US FTA are not being properly implemented. They cite problems relating to rules of origin verification, express delivery shipments, data transfers, and pending auto regulations.[117]

The top two items on the US trade agenda will continue to be Nafta and greater engagement with China under the Comprehensive Economic Dialogue. As the Nafta renegotiations near completion and the discussions with China become more well established, the US Department of Commerce and the USTR will turn their attention to KOR US FTA. The substance of the KOR US FTA negotiations will be heavily influenced by the Nafta renegotiations, but the current text of TPP is still a good indicator of what the US considers best practices in trade agreements.

TPP. Amid considerable, albeit misguided fanfare, Trump withdrew from TPP very quickly after becoming president. Because TPP had not yet been ratified by Congress, withdrawing from it was easy and unquestionably within Trump's powers as president.

TPP was, however, a very important part of American involvement in the Asia Pacific region. In economic terms, TPP was the most important trade agreement concluded by the US since the establishment of the WTO in 1995, even though its impact on the US economy probably would have been modest. TPP's primary attraction was that it would extend many American regulatory standards to a large part of the world and create precedent for extending those standards even more broadly. Withdrawal from TPP has

---

[115] See https://www.ft.com/content/2697de84-23e1-11e7-8691-d5f7e0cd0a16 (visited May 20, 2017).

[116] See http://money.cnn.com/2017/04/18/news/economy/us-south-korea-trade-pence/ (visited May 20, 2017).

[117] See https://fas.org/sgp/crs/row/RL34330.pdf (visited November 30, 2016).

done enormous damage to American credibility in the region. It also is bolstering China's efforts to play a more dominant role in the region, which seems the very opposite of Trump's objectives in the Asia Pacific region.

In the immediate aftermath of Trump's withdrawal from TPP, some of the TPP member states suggested that the other 11 should go forward with the agreement without American participation, but Japanese Prime Minister Abe said that TPP without American involvement is meaningless.[118] More recently, the 11 remaining TPP member states have confounded the experts who declared TPP dead by meeting to discuss resurrecting TPP.[119] In at least one of the meetings, the 11 TPP members were joined by Korea and China, and even the US participated.[120] The future of TPP without US participation is still uncertain, but it is now under active discussion.

Since withdrawing from TPP, Trump and his aides have said that in lieu of TPP and similar regional agreements, the Trump Administration will seek to conclude bilateral trade agreements that will protect American workers. The United Kingdom and Japan have been mentioned as possible partners,[121] but the UK must first negotiate an exit from the EU (which is not likely to occur before 2019) and Japan has expressed a preference for regional or multilateral agreements, such as the trade agreement being negotiated between Japan and the EU.[122] Renegotiation of Nafta and the KOR US FTA also are likely to precede any new American bilateral agreements, but it is notable that TPP is increasingly mentioned by US trade officials as a useful guide for any new or renegotiated trade agreements.[123] If TPP is revived by the other 11 members, the Trump Administration also might be enticed to

---

[118] In a press conference in Buenos Aires on November 21, 2016, Prime Minister Shinzo Abe said that TPP without the US participation was totally useless. Abe's comments are available at http://fortune.com/2016/11/22/donald-trump-tpp-japan-trade/ (visited November 29, 2016).

[119] See http://www.huffingtonpost.ca/2017/05/02/tpp-talks-restart-toronto_n_16393512.html (visited May 17, 2017).

[120] See http://thediplomat.com/2017/03/tpp-signatories-to-meet-in-chile-to-explore-the-future-of-the-agreement/ (visited May 17, 2017).

[121] See http://www.vox.com/policy-and-politics/2017/1/23/14356398/trump-pull-out-tpp-nafta (visited February 5, 2017).

[122] See http://ec.europa.eu/trade/policy/countries-and-regions/countries/japan/ (visited May 17, 2017).

[123] See http://business.financialpost.com/news/economy/wilbur-ross-says-tpp-could-form-starting-point-for-u-s-on-revamped-nafta-talks (visited May 17, 2017).

rejoin if sufficient face saving measures were included. Something as simple as giving Trump credit for new rigor in the TPP agreement probably would be sufficient, whether Trump plays a role or not. Since Canada and Mexico are among the 11 other members of TPP, it could be put on the agenda as part of the Nafta renegotiations. Whatever happens, it seems fairly certain that the last chapter on TPP has not yet been written.

Taiwan, Trump and Trade. On the effects of Trump's trade policies on Taiwan, there are both significant concerns and attractive opportunities. First, as a general matter, Trump views Taiwan as an important element in securing more favorable political and economic relations with China. Unfortunately, this is both good news and bad news. On the positive side, the Trump Administration is not likely to intentionally harm Taiwan's economy or its economic relations with the US. Given Trump's transactional view of the world, his favorable opinion of Taiwan will be markedly enhanced if Hon Hai Precision Industry Co. (i.e., Foxconn) and other large Taiwanese enterprises carry through with plans to make major investments in the US, including Hon Hai's proposed $7 billion investment for manufacturing flat panels. The bad news is that Trump is likely to see Taiwan as an important chip in his bargaining with China. Trump learned quickly from Beijing's reaction to his telephone call with President Tsai Ing-wen that adherence to the One China Policy is of critical importance to the Chinese leadership. This (probably new) knowledge coupled with Trump's non-ideological core and his transactional view of world affairs mean that there is a high risk the Trump Administration may make Taiwan related concessions to the Chinese to secure a more favorable economic relationship with China or China's cooperation in dealing with North Korea. To prevent this outcome, Taiwan's Ministry of Foreign Affairs and the Taipei Economic and Cultural Representative Office in Washington, D.C. should pressure senior Republican congressional leaders and Trump's key aides not to negotiate away essential elements of the Taiwan/US relationship.

The second issue involves TPP. As TPP was being finalized by the 12 member countries in 2015, Taiwan expressed considerable interest in being included in the second round of TPP participants.[124] Trump's withdrawal from TPP has dramatically changed the dynamics and for a few months after the US withdrawal it appeared that TPP was going nowhere. Now, the 11 remaining members of TPP are actively engaged in resurrecting TPP in such a fashion that is not viewed as either anti-China or anti-Trump.[125] At the same time, the Trump Administration is pursuing Nafta renegotiations in which TPP is likely to have a significant role. The Nafta negotiations in all likelihood will be followed by renegotiation of KOR US FTA, in which TPP also will have a significant influence. And all during this time the US will be engaged with China in the Comprehensive Economic Dialogue where parts of TPP may have special relevance. As a result, this may be an opportune time for Taiwan to take the lead in promoting a TPP style trade agreement between the US, China and Taiwan. Of course, the Trump Administration has indicated it will pursue free and fair trade only through bilateral negotiations rather than in a regional or multilateral format,[126] but given the close economic interaction between Taiwan and China and the political reality that China has veto power over large sections of Taiwan's foreign and international economic affairs, a three party agreement could be very attractive for all sides. China and Taiwan's agreement with the US could make it relatively easy for them to join the other 11 members in a revived TPP. The US agreement combined with TPP membership would give Taiwan favored access to most of the other major economies in East Asia and set the stage for Taiwan's participation in the more comprehensive Free Trade Area of the Asia Pacific. For China, the US agreement and TPP could provide important external pressures that enable Xi Jinping to introduce badly needed economic and financial reforms into the Chinese economy. On the American side, a trade agreement with China and Taiwan would deal with a number of nettlesome trade issues and give the Trump Administration

---

[124] See https://www.brookings.edu/research/taiwan-and-the-trans-pacific-partnership-preparing-the-way/ (visited May 20, 2017).

[125] See http://asia.nikkei.com/Politics-Economy/International-Relations/Japan-looks-to-revive-moribund-TPP-sans-US (visited May 21, 2017).

[126] See http://asia.nikkei.com/Politics-Economy/International-Relations/US-trade-rep-says-no-return-to-TPP-deal-and-wants-bilateral-deals-in-Asia (visited May 21, 2017).

a much needed boost to its reputation, both within the US and on the global stage.

The third effect deals with an issue on which Taiwan is vulnerable: exchange rate policies. During the presidential campaign, Trump harshly attacked China for currency manipulations. He also said that Japan and Germany are guilty of undervaluing their currencies to give their exporters improper competitive advantages. In the early months of his administration, Trump has soften his stance on currency manipulations – even explicitly saying that China is not manipulating its currency to gain a competitive advantage.[127] Under a newly enacted US trade law that treats currency manipulations as unfair trade practices,[128] however, Taiwan now is included on a watch list, along with China, Japan, Germany, Switzerland and Korea.[129] The result is that in the months ahead the US Treasury will be more closely scrutinizing Taiwan's exchange rate policies to see if they warrant being characterized as an unfair trade subsidy; but if that happens, Taiwan is likely to be part of a broader attack on currency manipulations.

The final concern is that the unfortunate combination of Trump's many personality disorders, the aggressive and/or inexperienced international affairs advisors Trump has brought into his administration and the growing assertiveness of China, Russia and North Korea create a much greater risk of a major foreign policy miscalculation than at any time in recent history. This risk seems to rise and fall on a daily basis as Trump stumbles from one self-created crisis to another and his aides can do little but shake their heads in bewilderment. Of course, a major foreign policy miscalculation would have disastrous consequences for Taiwan, but also for the entire world.

---

[127] See http://www.nbcnews.com/politics/politics-news/major-reversal-trump-says-china-not-currency-manipulators-n745826 (visited May 17, 2017).

[128] The Trade Facilitation and Trade Enforcement Act of 2015 at https://www.congress.gov/bill/114th-congress/house-bill/644 (visited May 17, 2017).

[129] See http://www.zerohedge.com/news/2017-04-14/treasury-releases-fx-manipulation-report-says-china-must-allow-yuan-rise-market-forc (visited May 21, 2017).

*　　*　　*

As indicated in this essay, there are reasons to hope that a Trump Administration will not be as disastrous as the early evidence suggests. But there is an uncomfortable feeling that Trump's presence in the White House signals the beginning of a real, long term decline in America's preeminent position in the world. American leadership on trade liberalization and its sponsorship of open and democratic societies around the world both may become casualties of a new protectionist, less tolerant, anti-immigrant American society. Trump may join another rich Republican President, Herbert Hoover (president from 1929 – 1933), in moving the country backwards into a period of darkness and instability. There are good reasons for thinking this will not happen, but if it does, Americans will have only themselves to blame, although the consequences will be felt throughout the world.

THE INTENSITY ELEMENT IN THE CONCEPT OF INTERNATIONAL ARMED CONFLICT UNDER INTERNATIONAL HUMANITARIAN LAW: A DISSENTING OPINION TO THE INTERNATIONAL LAW ASSOCIATION'S USE OF FORCE COMMITTEE REPORT

MASAHIKO ASADA

TABLE OF CONTENTS

ABSTRACT

The International Law Association's (ILA) Committee on the Use of Force in 2010 produced a Final Report on the Meaning of Armed Conflict in International Law, which concludes that as a matter of customary international law, a situation of armed conflict depends on the satisfaction of certain essential minimum criteria, including the existence of fighting of some intensity. The author participated in the Committee throughout its deliberation on the meaning of armed conflict, and continued to hold and argue for a different view in relation to *international* armed conflict. This article is a sort of dissenting opinion to that part of the Final Report. As such, it attempts to show that the rules applicable in international armed conflicts apply even when only low-intensity fighting has occurred, and indicates that the ILA Report's above finding does not necessarily reflect the common understanding of the law. It will do so by examining legal texts, their commentaries, judicial decisions and state practice as well as legal doctrines.

KEY WORDS

International humanitarian law; Concept of armed conflict; Geneva Conventions; Additional Protocols; Intensity and duration of conflict; International Criminal Court; International Criminal Tribunal for Former Yugoslavia; Tadić decision; ILA Use of Force Committee.

I. INTRODUCTION

There are a number of treaties of quasi-universal application that govern the conduct of belligerents in armed conflicts. These include, *inter alia*, the 1949 Geneva Conventions and the 1977 Additional Protocols to the Geneva Conventions. In all these treaties, the concept of "armed conflict" is of vital importance for their actual application. With regard to *international* armed conflict, common article 2 of the Geneva Conventions stipulates that: "the present Convention shall apply to all cases of declared war or of any other *armed conflict* which may arise between two or more of the High Contracting Parties" (emphasis added).

Additional Protocol I to the Geneva Conventions (applicable to *international* armed conflict) in article 1(3) provides that: "this Protocol, which supplements the Geneva Conventions…, shall apply in the situations referred to in *Article 2 common to those Conventions*" (emphasis added). Thus, although there are some exceptions,[1] the Conventions and the Protocol apply in times of "armed conflict."

The same is also true of *non-international* armed conflict.[2] According to common article 3 of the Geneva Conventions, the provisions of the article apply to "*armed conflict* not of an international character occurring in the territory of one of the High Contracting Parties" (emphasis added). Additional Protocol II to the Geneva Conventions (applicable to *non-international* armed conflict) in article 1(1) provides that "[the] Protocol, which develops and supplements *Article 3 common to the Geneva Conventions…without modifying its existing conditions of application*, shall apply to all *armed conflicts*…which take place in the territory of a High Contracting Party" (emphasis added).

Hence, "armed conflict" is the concept that triggers the rules of

---

[1]　See, e.g., arts 47 and 49 of the First Geneva Convention, arts 48 and 50 of the Second Geneva Convention, arts 127 and 129 of the Third Geneva Convention, and arts 144 and 146 of the Fourth Geneva Convention.

[2]　In this article, the terms "internal armed conflict," "non-international armed conflict," and "civil war" are used interchangeably, although the first two terms are sometimes differentiated from each other. See *Hamdan v. Ramsfeld*, 126 S. Ct. 2749 (2006), at 2796.

international humanitarian law to operate and to override some of the peacetime rules of international law. As Professor Vaughan Lowe has said, "War—armed conflict—has a radical legal effect."[3]

However, the term "armed conflict" is not defined in the Geneva Conventions, the Additional Protocols, or any other international humanitarian law treaties.[4] The absence of a definition sometimes makes it difficult to determine which group of rules applies to a particular situation at a particular point in time.

Regarding this question, the International Law Association's (ILA) Committee on the Use of Force in its Final Report on the Meaning of Armed Conflict in International Law of 2010 (hereinafter cited as the "ILA Report") concludes that: "as a matter of customary international law, a situation of armed conflict depends on the satisfaction of two essential minimum criteria, namely: a. the existence of organized armed groups; b. engaged in fighting of some intensity."[5] This statement covers both international and non-international armed conflict. With regard to non-international armed conflict, there is no dissenting view; indeed, article 1 of Additional Protocol II provides that the Protocol shall apply to "all armed conflicts...which take place in the territory of a High Contracting Party between its *armed forces* and dissident *armed forces* or other *organized armed groups*" (para. 1, emphasis added), and that the Protocol shall *not* apply to "situations of internal disturbances and tensions, such as riots, isolated and sporadic acts of violence" as "not being armed conflicts" (para. 2). This seems to indicate that the two criteria of the ILA Report shown above are undoubtedly applicable to non-international armed conflicts.

International armed conflicts typically take place in the form of a fight

---

3   Professor Lowe goes on to write that: "Combatants in States' armed forces may kill and destroy property within the laws of war without fear of facing trial for murder or criminal damage." Vaughan Lowe, *International Law* (Oxford UP, 2007), pp. 282-283.

4   Christopher Greenwood, "The Development of International Humanitarian Law by the International Criminal Tribunal for the Former Yugoslavia," *Max Planck Yearbook of United Nations Law*, Vol. 2 (1998), p. 114. As we will discuss later, the Statute of the International Criminal Court (ICC) may be viewed as an exception if one considers it as an international humanitarian law treaty.

5   ILA Committee on the Use of Force, "Final Report on the Meaning of Armed Conflict in International Law," presented at The Hague Conference of the ILA (2010) (hereinafter cited as "ILA Report 2010"), p. 32.

between armed forces of states, although Additional Protocol I also applies to so-called national liberation war (art. 1(4)). It is reasonably assumed that armed forces of states are "organized" and satisfy the ILA Report's first criterion of "the existence of organized armed groups." The same should be true of the other party to a national liberation war, which must be so organised as to have the authority to represent a people engaged in the conflict and to apply the Geneva Conventions and Protocol I (art. 96(3) of Protocol I). Accordingly, it follows that the focus here should be placed on the ILA Report's second criterion of "fighting of some intensity" in the context of international armed conflict.

In this article, an attempt will be made to identify possible parameters with which to determine when the rules applicable in international armed conflicts apply, particularly whether they apply when only low-intensity fighting has occurred. By examining legal texts, their commentaries, judicial decisions, and state practice, as well as legal doctrines, this analysis will show that the ILA Report's above finding does not necessarily reflect the common understanding of the law.

Although the author participated in the ILA's Committee on the Use of Force throughout its deliberation on the meaning of armed conflict in international law, he continued to hold and argue for a view different from that of the Committee's Final Report on this issue, as articulated in this article. Thus, this article is a sort of dissenting opinion to the ILA Report, and for that reason, it mainly covers cases and materials that are relevant to the Report.

II. COMMENTARIES OF THE INTERNATIONAL COMMITTEE OF THE RED CROSS AND JUDICIAL DECISIONS

A. Two often-cited statements

Although no definition of "armed conflict" is provided in relevant international treaties, in a few instances what international armed conflict means has actually been discussed. For example, in its Commentary on the 1949 Geneva Convention (the First Convention), the International Committee of the Red Cross (ICRC) indicated what an armed conflict is, as follows:

> The Convention becomes applicable as from the actual opening of hostilities.[6] The existence of armed conflict between two or more Contracting Parties brings it automatically into operation.
>
> It remains to ascertain what is meant by "armed conflict." ...*Any difference arising between two States and leading to the intervention of armed forces is an armed conflict* within the meaning of Article 2, even if one of the Parties denies the existence of a state of war. *It makes no difference how long the conflict lasts, or how much slaughter takes place.* The respect due to human personality is not measured by the number of victims. ...If there is only a single wounded person as a result of the conflict, the Convention will have been applied as soon as he has been collected and tended....[7] (emphasis added)

The International Criminal Tribunal for the Former Yugoslavia (ICTY) looked into the definition of armed conflict in *The Prosecutor v. Tadić* (Jurisdiction, Appeals) in 1995. In that case, the issue in part was whether an armed conflict had existed, as the appellant asserted that "there did not exist a legally cognizable armed conflict—either internal or international—at the time and place that the alleged offences were committed."[8] The Appeals Chamber reached the following determination:

---

6   In the case of the Prisoners of War Convention (the Third Geneva Convention), the ICRC, in its Commentary on the Convention, further states that "[e]ven if there has been no fighting, the fact that persons covered by the Convention are detained is sufficient for its application." Jean S. Pictet (ed.), *Geneva Convention Relative to the Treatment of Prisoners of War: Commentary* (ICRC, 1960), p. 23.

7   Jean S. Pictet (ed.), *Geneva Convention for the Amelioration of the Condition of the Wounded and Sick in Armed Forces in the Field: Commentary* (ICRC, 1952), p. 32.

8   ICTY, Case No. IT-94-1-AR72 (*The Prosecutor v. Duško Tadić*), Decision on the Defence Motion for Interlocutory Appeal on Jurisdiction, Appeals Chamber, 2 October 1995 (hereinafter cited as "*The Prosecutor v. Tadić* (Jurisdiction, Appeals)"), *International Legal Materials*, Vol. 35, No. 1 (January 1996), p. 53, para. 66.

> [W]e find that an armed conflict exists whenever there is *a resort to armed force between States* or *protracted armed violence between governmental authorities and organized armed groups or between such groups within a State.*[9] (emphasis added)

With the contrasting descriptions in this so-called "*Tadić* test" of *international* armed conflict as being "a resort to armed force between States," and *internal* armed conflict as involving "*protracted* armed violence" (emphasis added), the ICTY seems to have differentiated between the two types of armed conflict, at least in terms of the duration of hostilities ("protracted"), and dismissed the importance of armed violence between states being protracted in the case of international conflict.

The correctness of this interpretation of the *Tadić* test was confirmed by the ICTY in *The Prosecutor v. Mucić* (Trial) in 1998. The Tribunal, after citing the above part of the *Tadić* decision, stated as follows:

> In the former situation [i.e., international conflict], the *existence of armed force between States is sufficient* of itself to trigger the application of international humanitarian law. In the latter situation [i.e., internal conflict], in order to distinguish from cases of civil unrest or terrorist activities, the emphasis is on the *protracted extent* of the

---

[9]   Ibid., para. 70. In the same paragraph, the decision further stated, in applying the concept of armed conflict quoted in the text to the hostilities in the former Yugoslavia: "These hostilities [i.e., fighting among the various entities within the former Yugoslavia] exceed the *intensity requirements applicable to both international and internal* armed conflicts. There has been protracted, large-scale violence between the armed forces of different States and between governmental forces and organized insurgent groups" (emphasis added). Ibid., para. 70. These sentences suggest that intensity requirements apply both to international and internal armed conflicts, notwithstanding the fact that the *concept* of armed conflict formulated by the ICTY a few sentences earlier (as quoted in the text) does not refer to intensity. Professor Mary Ellen O'Connell, after quoting paragraph 70 of the *Tadić* decision (including both the part shown in the text and the part cited just above), states that "the Court uses the qualifier 'protracted' for conflicts other than those between two states, but also refers to an 'intensity' standard for both internal and international armed conflicts." Mary Ellen O'Connell, *International Law and the Use of Force: Cases and Materials* (Foundation Press, 2005), p. 9; idem, *International Law and the Use of Force: Cases and Materials*, 2nd ed. (Foundation Press, 2009), pp. 8-9. There is no clear, immediate answer to the question of how one can interpret the whole paragraph (para. 70) in a consistent manner. Nevertheless, it should be emphasised that in the *Mucić* and other cases, the ICTY quotes from the *Tadić* decision only the part shown in the text and not the above-cited latter part of paragraph 70. Likewise, the ICC Statute does not refer to the intensity or duration requirement at all in relation to *international* armed conflict, while it does mention both requirements in relation to *non-international* armed conflict in one way or another (art 8(2)(f)).

armed violence and the *extent of organisation* of the parties involved.[10] (emphasis added)

From the above often-cited statements regarding when an international armed conflict exists and when international armed conflict rules are triggered, which seem to share essentially the same basis, we can identify two elements that are commonly mentioned. One is related to the duration (and intensity) of the conflict; the other concerns the participants who perform the relevant armed activities. This article will focus on the former element for the reason already stated.

B. Subsequent commentaries of the International Committee of the Red Cross

As mentioned earlier, the ICRC Commentary indicates that the Geneva Conventions are triggered regardless of the intensity or duration of hostilities by stating that "[i]t makes no difference how long the conflict lasts, or how much slaughter takes place." This interpretation of the law is maintained in the ICRC's Commentary on Additional Protocol I. On article 1(3) of the Protocol concerning the scope of application, the latter states that: "the [Geneva] Conventions are not applicable only in cases of declared war.... [A]s will most often be the case in practice, humanitarian law also covers any dispute between two States involving the use of their armed forces. *Neither the duration of the conflict, nor its intensity, play a role...*"[11] (emphasis added).

The ICRC's more recent opinion on this question is generally in accord. According to its opinion paper entitled "How is the Term 'Armed Conflict' Defined in International Humanitarian Law?," dated March 2008, it is said in the *concluding section* that: "International armed conflicts exist whenever there is *resort to armed force between two or more States*" (emphasis original).[12]

---

10   ICTY, Case No. IT-96-21-T (*The Prosecutor v. Zdravko Mucić* et al.), Judgement, Trial Chamber, 16 November 1998 (hereinafter cited as "*The Prosecutor v. Mucić* (Trial)"), para. 184.

11   Yves Sandoz et al. (eds.), *Commentary on the Additional Protocols of 8 June 1977 to the Geneva Conventions of 12 August 1949* (Nijhoff, 1987), p. 40, paras. 61-62.

12   International Committee of the Red Cross (ICRC), "How is the Term 'Armed Conflict' Defined in International Humanitarian Law?," ICRC Opinion Paper, March 2008, p. 5.

The phrase from the earlier Commentaries regarding the intensity and duration of hostilities is not repeated there. However, the ICRC's 2008 paper, which follows the wording of the ICTY's *Tadić* decision, does not seem to have deviated from its earlier position. This is confirmed by the ICRC's definition of "non-international armed conflicts" in the same paper, which reads as follows:

> Non-international armed conflicts are *protracted armed confrontations* occurring between governmental armed forces and the forces of one or more armed groups, or between such groups arising on the territory of a State [party to the Geneva Conventions]. The armed confrontation must reach *a minimum level of intensity* and the parties involved in the conflict must show *a minimum of organization.*[13] (emphasis and square brackets original)

The phrases as originally emphasised by the ICRC—protraction, intensity, and organisation—which are lacking in relation to international armed conflict, seem to support the interpretation here that the ICRC position remains unaltered.

What is more, the 2008 paper explicitly states in its *main body* (not in its *concluding section*, as quoted above) that: "An IAC [i.e., international armed conflict] occurs when one or more States have recourse to armed force against another State, *regardless of* the reasons or *the intensity of this confrontation*" (emphasis added). It even quotes the ICRC's Commentary on common article 2 of the Geneva Conventions in full, including the part: "It makes no difference how long the conflict lasts, or how much slaughter takes place."[14]

For unknown reasons, the ILA Report does not quote or refer to the part of the ICRC Commentary on Additional Protocol I, which states that "[n] either the duration of the conflict, nor its intensity, play a role."[15] Also,

---

[13]   Ibid., p. 5.

[14]   Ibid., pp. 1-2.

[15]   Instead, the ILA Report refers to a scholarly commentary on Additional Protocol I by Professor Karl Josef Partsch, which supports the ILA's idea. ILA Report 2010, *supra* note 5, p. 12.

with regard to the ICRC's 2008 paper, the ILA Report comments on it by saying that "[i]t omits the Commentary phrase 'regardless of duration or intensity'."[16] However, not only is there no such phrase as "regardless of duration or intensity" in the Commentary on the 1949 Conventions, but the 2008 paper could and should be read as not diverging from the earlier ICRC position, as was just discussed.

C. Subsequent judicial decisions and the meaning of "protracted armed violence"

In the *Tadić* case, the ICTY stated that "an armed conflict exists whenever there is a resort to armed force between States or protracted armed violence between governmental authorities and organized armed groups or between such groups within a State." This *Tadić* test for determining the existence of an armed conflict has been applied consistently by the same Tribunal.

In *The Prosecutor v. Slobodan Milosević* (2004), the ICTY stated that "the relevant portion of the *Tadić* test, which has been *consistently applied within the Tribunal*, is 'protracted armed violence between governmental authorities and organized armed groups'"[17] (emphasis added). "[T]he relevant portion" refers to non-international armed conflict part of the *Tadić* test. However, that the ICTY is consistent in applying the *Tadić* test as a whole was later confirmed by the Tribunal in *The Prosecutor v. Limaj* (2005), which said that "[t]he test for determining the existence of an armed conflict was set out in the *Tadić* Jurisdiction Decision and has been *applied consistently by the Tribunal*" (emphasis added) and quoted the whole test from the *Tadić* decision.[18]

---

[16]   Ibid., p. 19.

[17]   ICTY, Case No. IT-02-54-T (*The Prosecutor v. Slobodan Milosević*), Decision on Motion for Judgement of Acquittal, Trial Chamber, 16 June 2004 (hereinafter cited as "*The Prosecutor v. Slobodan Milosević* (Acquittal)"), para. 17.

[18]   ICTY, Case No. IT-03-66-T (*The Prosecutor v. Fatmir Limaj* et al.), Judgement, Trial Chamber II, 30 November 2005 (hereinafter cited as "*The Prosecutor v. Limaj* (Trial)"), para. 84. See also ICTY, Case No. IT-95-14-T (*The Prosecutor v. Tihomir Blaškić*), Judgement, Trial Chamber, 3 March 2000, paras. 63-64; ICTY, Case No. IT-98-33-T (*The Prosecutor v. Radislav Krstić*), Judgement, Trial Chamber, 2 August 2001, para. 481; ICTY, Case No. IT-96-23 & IT-96-23/1-A (*The Prosecutor v. Dragoljub Kunarac* et al.), Judgement, Appeals Chamber, 12 June 2002, para. 56.

The *Tadić* test has also been applied or adopted by other courts and tribunals or international fora, such as the International Criminal Tribunal for Rwanda (ICTR),[19] International Criminal Court (ICC) and the UN International Law Commission (ILC),[20] as we will see later. Thus, it is said that the *Tadić* test is "really beyond any debate."[21]

With regard to the content of the *Tadić* test, it is worth noting that the concept of "protracted armed violence" in the *Tadić* test, which apparently refers only to the duration of a conflict, in fact encompasses the element of *intensity* as well. It could even be said that more emphasis has been placed on the intensity of a conflict than its duration in subsequent decisions of the ICTY, including the *Tadić* case itself. The Tribunal held at the merits stage of the *Tadić* case that "[t]he test applied by the Appeals Chamber to the existence of an armed conflict for the purpose of the rules contained in Common Article 3 [on non-international armed conflict] focuses on two aspects of a conflict; the *intensity* of the conflict and the organization of the parties to the conflict" (emphasis added).[22] This was a statement under the heading of "*Protracted* armed violence between governmental forces and organized armed groups" (emphasis added).

This approach of referring especially to the *intensity* of a conflict in relation to the concept of "protracted armed violence" has been followed by the ICTY in subsequent cases. For instance, in the *Milosević* decision, the ICTY, commenting on the *Tadić* test of "protracted armed violence between governmental authorities and organized armed groups," stated that "[t]his calls for an examination of (1) the organisation of the parties to the conflict

---

19   See, e.g., ICTR, Case No. ICTR-96-4-T (*The Prosecutor v. Jean-Paul Akayesu*), Judgement, Trial Chamber I, 2 September 1998, para. 619. See also ICTR, Case No. ICTR-96-3 (*The Prosecutor v. Georges Anderson Nderubumwe Rutaganda*), Judgement and Sentence, Trial Chamber I, 6 December 1999, para. 92.

20   See art 2(b) of the UN International Law Commission's (ILC) Draft Articles on the Effects of Armed Conflicts on Treaties of 2011. *Report of the International Law Commission, 63rd Session*, UN Doc. A/66/10, 2011, p. 175. See also ibid., pp. 181-182.

21   William A. Schabas, *The UN International Criminal Tribunals: The Former Yugoslavia, Rwanda and Sierra Leone* (Cambridge UP, 2006), p. 229.

22   ICTY, Case No. IT-94-1-T (*The Prosecutor v. Tadić*), Opinion and Judgment, Trial Chamber, 7 May 1997, *International Legal Materials*, Vol. 36, No. 4 (July 1997), p. 920, para. 562.

and (2) the *intensity* of the conflict"[23] (emphasis added). It did the same in the *Limaj* judgement.[24]

Thus, it could be said that, in the above-cited contrasting definitions of international and non-international armed conflict, the ICTY dismissed the importance not only of the duration but also (and especially) of the intensity of conflict in the case of international armed conflict. This seems in harmony with how the ICRC sees the Geneva Conventions and Additional Protocol I.

Indeed, in the *Mucić* case, the ICTY explicitly indicated that it followed the views of the ICRC downplaying the importance of the intensity and duration of a conflict in the case of international armed conflict by saying that:

> In its adjudication of the nature of the armed conflict…*the Trial Chamber is guided by the Commentary to the Fourth Geneva Convention*, which considers that "[a]ny difference arising between two States and leading to the intervention of members of the armed forces" is an international armed conflict and "[i]t makes no difference how long the conflict lasts, or how much slaughter takes place."[25] (emphasis added)

Turning to an international court with more general jurisdiction in geographical and temporal terms, the Statute of the ICC in article 8(2)(f), provides that:

> Paragraph 2 (e) [on other serious violations of the laws and customs applicable in non-international armed conflicts] applies to armed conflicts not of an international character and thus does *not apply* to situations of *internal disturbances and tensions, such as riots, isolated and sporadic acts of violence or other acts of a similar nature.* It applies to armed conflicts that take place in the territory of a State when there is *protracted* armed conflict between governmental authorities and organized armed groups or between such groups. (emphasis added)

---

[23]   *The Prosecutor v. Slobodan Milosević* (Acquittal), *supra* note 17, para. 17.
[24]   *The Prosecutor v. Limaj* (Trial), *supra* note 18, paras. 84, 93.
[25]   *The Prosecutor v. Mucić* (Trial), *supra* note 10, para. 208.

The first sentence of this sub-paragraph copies almost *verbatim* the provision of article 1(2) of Additional Protocol II applicable to non-international armed conflicts;[26] the second sentence comes from the *Tadić* decision quoted above.[27] No comparable provision regarding intensity or duration is stipulated in relation to international armed conflict in article 8(2)(b) of the Statute. The ICC has thus adopted different thresholds of application for international and internal armed conflicts,[28] in line with what we have discussed above.

More notable from our perspective is that the ICC appears to have accepted in an actual case the definition of international armed conflict put forward by the ICRC. In its decision in *The Prosecutor v. Lubanga* (2007), the Court examined the term "international armed conflict" in article 8(2)(b) of the Statute. After pointing out that that term is not defined in the Statute or the Elements of Crimes, it quoted common article 2(1) and (2) of the Geneva Conventions and reproduced the main part of the ICRC Commentary on common article 2 in full.[29] In addition, it further observed that "the ICTY adopt[ed] the same interpretation of the expression 'international armed conflict'."[30] It did all this pursuant to article 21(1)(b) of the ICC Statute,[31]

---

[26] The first sentence of article 8(2)(f) of the ICC Statute has not incorporated article 1(1) of Additional Protocol II, which requires that the conflict take place between governmental forces and rebel forces, for the latter to control part of territory, and for there to be a responsible command. It is stated that this exclusion was intentional. See Anthony Cullen, "The Definition of Non-International Armed Conflict in the Rome Statute of the International Criminal Court: An Analysis of the Threshold of Application Contained in Article 8(2)(f)," *Journal of Conflict and Security Law*, Vol. 12, No. 3 (Winter 2007), pp. 436-437; Theodor Meron, "Crimes under the Jurisdiction of the International Criminal Court," in Herman A.M. von Hebel et al. (eds.), *Reflections on the International Criminal Court: Essays in Honour of Adriaan Bos* (T.M.C. Asser Press, 1999), p. 54. Professor Meron further points out that "[t]he reference to protracted armed conflict was designed to give some satisfaction to those delegations that insisted on the incorporation of the higher threshold of applicability of Article 1(1) of Additional Protocol II." Ibid., p. 54.

[27] The ICTY itself presents this view by saying that "Article 8 [of the ICC Statute] is not only consistent with the *Tadić* test, but also incorporates part of the *Tadić* Jurisdiction Appeals Decision into its own definition of 'war crimes'." *The Prosecutor v. Slobodan Milosević* (Acquittal), *supra* note 17, para. 20. See also Otto Triffterer and Kai Ambos (eds.), *Rome Statute of the International Criminal Court: A Commentary*, 3rd ed. (C.H. Beck, 2016), p. 575; Darryl Robinson and Herman von Hebel, "War Crimes in Internal Conflicts: Article 8 of the ICC Statute," *Yearbook of International Humanitarian Law*, Vol. 2 (1999), pp. 204-205.

[28] See Michael Bothe, "War Crimes," in Antonio Cassese, Paola Gaeta and John R.W.D. Jones (eds.), *The Rome Statute of the International Criminal Court: A Commentary* (Oxford UP, 2002), Vol. I, p. 418.

[29] ICC, Case No. ICC-01/04-01/06 (*The Prosecutor v. Thomas Lubanga Dylio*), Decision on the Confirmation of Charges, Pre-Trial Chamber I, 29 January 2007, paras. 206-207.

[30] Ibid., para. 208.

[31] Ibid., para. 205.

which on applicable law provides that "[t]he Court shall apply...where appropriate, applicable treaties and the principles and rules of international law, including the established principles of the international law of armed conflict." As ICRC Commentaries are not treaties, it would be safe to assume that the ICC has accepted the ICRC definition of international armed conflict as an (established) principle or rule of international law.

The ILA's Final Report on the Meaning of Armed Conflict in International Law of 2010, again for unknown reasons, does not refer to the above quoted or referred-to paragraphs of the *Lubanga* decision, although it does refer to the part of the decision concerning non-international armed conflict, which discusses the intensity and duration of the conflict.[32]

D. Interpretative declarations to Additional Protocol I

In this context, it is notable that a view has been expressed that may directly conflict with those of the ICRC, ICTY and the ICC regarding the requirement of intensity and/or duration of a conflict. That is the view of the United Kingdom (UK). In signing Additional Protocol I on 12 December 1977, the UK Government declared in relation to article 1 that:

> [T]he term "armed conflict" of itself and in its context implies *a certain level of intensity* of military operations which must be present before the Conventions or the Protocol are to apply to any given situation, and that this *level of intensity* cannot be less than that required for the application of Protocol II, by virtue of Article 1 of that Protocol, to internal conflicts.[33] (emphasis added)

In this declaration, the UK required a certain level of intensity of military operations for the Geneva Conventions and Protocol I to apply, and such level was, according to the UK, not less than that for the application of Protocol II. Is this UK view justifiable? And what was the background

---

[32] ILA Report 2010, *supra* note 5, p. 22.
[33] Dietrich Schindler and Jiri Toman (eds.), *The Laws of Armed Conflicts: A Collection of Conventions, Resolutions and Other Documents*, 4th ed. (Nijhoff, 2004), pp. 814-815.

of the UK making this declaration? There was a suggestive debate in the UK Parliament in 1977. In a written answer to the question asked in the Parliament the UK Government stated as follows:

[T]he Government have considered it desirable in this connection to place formally on record by means of an *interpretative declaration* their understanding of the meaning of the term "armed conflict," which implies *a high level of intensity* of military operations, and their understanding of the requirements to be fulfilled by any national liberation movement which sought to invoke the protocol. Neither in Northern Ireland nor in any other part of the United Kingdom is there a situation which meets the criteria laid down for the application of either protocol. Nor is there any terrorist organisation operating within the United Kingdom which fulfils the requirements which a national liberation movement must meet in order to be entitled to claim rights under Protocol I.[34] (emphasis added)

From this quotation, it appears that the UK Government, when making the declaration upon signature, had primarily in mind those conflicts involving national liberation movement or terrorist organisation such as the Irish Republican Army (IRA), which take place within a state, and not ordinary state-to-state conflicts. In that sense, the UK declaration had in mind, when discussing the intensity question, different situations than those borne in mind by the ICRC Commentaries and the decisions of the ICTY or ICC.

Although the UK declaration upon signature was made in relation to article 1 of Additional Protocol I and phrased in such a way as to allow it to apply to article 1 as a whole (including state-to-state conflicts), the UK did not repeat that declaration when it deposited its instrument of ratification of Additional Protocol I on 28 January 1998. Instead, it declared concerning the term of "armed conflict" in relation to article 1(4) (regarding national liberation conflict), as follows:

---

[34] *Parliamentary Debates (Hansard), House of Lords, Official Report*, Fifth Series, Vol. 387, pp. 2224-2225 [14 December 1977].

It is the understanding of the United Kingdom that the term "armed conflict" of itself and in its context denotes a situation of a kind which is not constituted by the commission of ordinary crimes including acts of terrorism whether concerted or in isolation.[35]

Although the precise scope of the declaration may not be clear from the above quotation itself, it was expressly stated in the declaration that that part was declared in regard to article 1(4) of Additional Protocol I.[36] Hence, in making the new declaration regarding the term "armed conflict," the UK bore national liberation type of conflicts *solely* in mind, unlike the declaration upon signature which had been made in relation to article 1 as a whole. In other words, it could be interpreted that the part of the original declaration that might have covered state-to-state conflicts, including its intensity argument, was abandoned in the new declaration.[37]

In the following year of ratification of Additional Protocol I (in 1999), the UK gave its consent to be bound by the 1996 amended Protocol II to the Certain Conventional Weapons (CCW) Convention, with the declaration that "[the declaration accompanying the UK *ratification* of Additional Protocol I of 1977], in so far as it is relevant, also applies to the provisions of Protocol II as amended."[38] The UK also made a similar declaration in ratifying the ICC Statute in 2001.[39]

These declarations refer only to the UK declaration made upon ratification of Additional Protocol I and not the one made upon signature. That being so, it is hard to understand why the UK Manual published in

---

[35] Schindler and Toman, *supra* note 33, p. 816; Adam Roberts and Richard Guelff (eds.), *Documents on the Laws of War*, 3rd ed. (Oxford UP, 2000), p. 510. The UK had already made the identical declaration when it ratified the Certain Conventional Weapons Convention on 13 February 1995. Schindler and Toman, *supra* note 33, p. 220; Roberts and Guelff, *supra*, p. 558. France made an almost identical declaration concerning article 1(4) of the same Protocol upon accession on 11 April 2001, available at https://www.icrc.org/applic/ihl/dih.nsf/NOTIF/470-FR?OpenDocument& (accessed 1 January 2017)

[36] Schindler and Toman, *supra* note 33, p. 816; Roberts and Guelff, *supra* note 35, p. 510.

[37] The new declaration made upon ratification supersedes and modifies the original declaration to the extent that the new one is different from the original one. This can be confirmed by the fact that in other parts of the UK declaration made upon ratification what had been declared upon signature was simply repeated.

[38] Schindler and Toman, *supra* note 33, p. 231; Roberts and Guelff, *supra* note 35, p. 559.

[39] Available at https://treaties.un.org/Pages/ViewDetails.aspx?src=TREATY&mtdsg_no=XVIII-10&chapter=18&lang=en#EndDec (accessed 22 December 2015)

2004 explicitly refers to the idea of threshold for the concept of "armed conflict" even for inter-state conflicts. The Manual states as follows:

> These definitions [of armed conflict given by the ICRC in its Commentary on the Geneva Conventions and by the ICTY in the *Tadić* Case] do not deal with the threshold for an armed conflict. Whether any particular intervention crosses the threshold so as to become an armed conflict will depend on all the surrounding circumstances. For example, the replacing of border police with soldiers or an accidental border incursion by members of the armed forces would not, in itself, amount to an armed conflict, nor would the accidental bombing of another country. At the other extreme, a full-scale invasion would amount to an armed conflict.[40]

This statement explicitly refers to the threshold requirement in a way apparently in conflict with the views of the ICRC, ICTY and ICC. What is the legal status of this and other military manuals under international law?

The preface of the UK Manual notes that: "the Manual represents the United Kingdom's interpretation of the law."[41] More generally, the ICTY in the *Tadić* Case referred to a few military manuals before reaching the conclusion that customary international law imposes criminal liability for serious violations of common article 3.[42] By doing so, the Tribunal seems to have treated the referenced military manuals as elements of state practice.

Whatever the content and legal status of the Manual may be, however, it is the declaration of the UK made upon ratification that constitutes its official position regarding the interpretation of Additional Protocol I vis-à-vis other parties to the Protocol. Should the UK become engaged in an international armed conflict, it is Additional Protocol I that would apply to

---

[40] UK Ministry of Defence, *The Manual of the Law of Armed Conflict* (Oxford UP, 2004), p. 29, para. 3.3.1. Some of the examples given in the quoted paragraph as not amounting to an armed conflict seem somewhat confusing. For instance, the first example of the replacing of border police with soldiers does not seem to involve any interaction, let alone armed violence, between states; thus, there could never be any chance for it to be an armed conflict in the first place.

[41] Ibid., p. ix.

[42] *The Prosecutor v. Tadić* (Jurisdiction, Appeals), *supra* note 8, paras. 131, 134.

it with its declaration made upon ratification having a certain legal effect.[43] The same is true of the UK position regarding the amended Protocol II to the CCW and the ICC Statute.

III. LEGAL SCHOLARSHIP

A. Single threshold school

Analysts differ as to whether intensity of conflict matters in triggering the application of rules of *international* armed conflict. There are two schools of thought in this regard. They can be termed the "single threshold" school (advocating the application of one and the same threshold for both international and non-international armed conflict) and the "separate threshold" school (advocating the application of separate thresholds for international and non-international armed conflict).

As a member of the former school,[44] Professor Karl Josef Partsch argues that certain situations mentioned in article 1 of Additional Protocol II (i.e., internal disturbances and tensions) "should also be excluded from the concept of armed conflict as this term is used in Art. 1 of the first Protocol."[45] At first sight, what he means by this statement is not entirely clear, because it is difficult to imagine that there exist such situations as "internal" disturbances and tensions in "international" conflict to which Additional Protocol I applies. He might have in mind national liberation war, to which Protocol I also applies; however, the reason he offers suggests

---

[43] For a possible legal effect of an interpretative declaration, see UN International Law Commission's Guide to Practice on Reservations to Treaties of 2011, para. 4.7.1, which provides that it "may, as appropriate, constitute an element to be taken into account in interpreting the treaty."

[44] Jelena Pejic somewhat ambiguously writes that "[i]nternational humanitarian law is the body of rules applicable when armed violence reaches the level of armed conflict, whether international or non-international." Jelena Pejic, "Terrorist Acts and Groups: A Role for International Law?," *British Year Book of International Law*, Vol. 75 (2004), p. 73. See also idem, "Status of Armed Conflicts," in Elizabeth Wilmshurst and Susan Breau (eds.), *Perspectives on the ICRC Study on Customary International Humanitarian Law* (Cambridge UP, 2007), p. 82.

[45] Michael Bothe, Karl Josef Partsch and Waldemar A. Solf, *New Rules for Victims of Armed Conflicts: Commentary on the Two 1977 Protocols Additional to the Geneva Conventions of 1949* (Nijhoff, 1982), p. 46; Michael Bothe, Karl Josef Partsch and Waldemar A. Solf, *New Rules for Victims of Armed Conflicts: Commentary on the Two 1977 Protocols Additional to the Geneva Conventions of 1949*, 2nd ed. (Nijhoff, 2013), p. 45. The 2013 edition is essentially a reprint of the 1982 edition, though necessary corrections are made reflecting new developments. Ibid., p. xv, note 1.

that he is asserting a more general application of his proposed exclusion, which also applies to inter-state conflicts. He states that "it can be supposed that the concepts used in both Protocols [i.e., armed conflict] have the same meaning."[46]

This reasoning is not very convincing, however. Although the same term, "armed conflict," is used in both Protocols, they are different treaties dealing with entirely different kinds of situations. Indeed, the situations to which the two Protocols apply are mutually exclusive. According to article 1(1) of Additional Protocol II, "[t]his Protocol...shall apply to all armed conflicts which are not covered by Article 1 of [Additional Protocol I]." In addition, it is important to note the conspicuous fact that Additional Protocol II excludes from its scope of application certain low-intensity violence (i.e., internal disturbances and tensions), while Additional Protocol I does not. This suggests that in the case of international armed conflict, there is no comparable requirement in terms of intensity of conflict.

There are others who appear to argue that an intensity requirement would also apply to international armed conflict. Commenting on international armed conflict, Professor Christopher Greenwood argues that "many isolated incidents, such as border clashes and naval incidents, are not treated as armed conflicts. It may well be, therefore, that only when fighting reaches a level of intensity which exceeds that of such isolated clashes will it be treated as an armed conflict to which the rules of international humanitarian law apply."[47] At the same time, he also points out elsewhere, after quoting a passage from the ICRC Commentary on the Geneva Conventions referred to above, that: "In humanitarian terms, this approach makes good sense. However, State practice is *more equivocal* and it is by no means clear that most States would regard an isolated incident or exchange of fire, however serious the consequences, as an armed conflict, bringing into operation the

---

[46] Bothe, Partsch and Solf (1982), *supra* note 45, p. 46; Bothe, Partsch and Solf (2013), *supra* note 45, pp. 44-45.

[47] Christopher Greenwood, "Scope of Application of Humanitarian Law," in Dieter Fleck (ed.), *The Handbook of Humanitarian Law in Armed Conflicts* (Oxford UP, 1995), p. 42, para. 202.3; idem, "Scope of Application of Humanitarian Law," in Dieter Fleck (ed.), *The Handbook of International Humanitarian Law*, 2nd ed. (Oxford UP, 2008), p. 48, para. 202.3.

full panoply of the Geneva Conventions"[48] (emphasis added). Thus, his position seems somewhat indeterminate and at least divergent from that of the pure single threshold school that advocates that the *same* intensity threshold applies both to international and non-international armed conflict for triggering the rules of international humanitarian law.

In order to support the idea of one and the same intensity requirement for both international and non-international armed conflicts, one may also point to the noticeable tendency among the post-Cold War armed conflicts to possess both international and internal characters, including the conflicts in the former Yugoslavia. In the *Tadić* case, the ITCY concluded that "the conflicts in the former Yugoslavia have both internal and international aspects."[49] If a conflict has both international and internal aspects, there may arise a question of which group of rules of armed conflict are to be applied, as the law of international armed conflict has traditionally been vastly different in content from the law of non-international armed conflict.

Moreover, given that the threshold for armed conflict has traditionally been different between international and internal armed conflict, a more fundamental question may further arise of whether the law of armed conflict or the law of peace (human rights law in particular) is to be applied. This is because, provided that the intensity of fighting in a given internal conflict is below the threshold for non-international armed conflict, the law of peace would apply; however, if the conflict has both an international and an internal character, the law of international armed conflict may apply to the extent that it can qualify as an international armed conflict, because there is no comparable threshold of intensity for international armed conflict—at least according to traditional law. What is more, the character of the conflict may evolve as time goes by, giving rise to an extremely complicated legal situation. It is, therefore, somewhat understandable if one advocates a

---

[48] Christopher Greenwood, "The Law of War (International Humanitarian Law)," in Malcolm D. Evans (ed.), *International Law* (Oxford UP, 2003), p. 792; idem, "The Law of War (International Humanitarian Law)," in Malcolm D. Evans (ed.), *International Law*, 2nd ed. (Oxford UP, 2006), p. 786.
[49] *The Prosecutor v. Tadić* (Jurisdiction, Appeals), *supra* note 8, para. 77.

single threshold applicable to both international and non-international armed conflicts as one of the easiest ways to resolve the problems.

However, these are not really new questions. More or less analogous questions have long been discussed in the context of internationalised civil wars.[50] Therefore, it is not really persuasive to argue that the intensity threshold should *now* be the same for international and non-international armed conflicts, relying solely on the above-mentioned tendency among post-Cold War armed conflicts.

Moreover, it is true that with the increase of such "hybrid" types of armed conflicts and internal armed conflicts in general, a growing number of writers are arguing that the rules of international and non-international armed conflict should converge (and indeed there is a certain trend in that direction),[51] and that a single body of rules should be applicable to all armed conflicts, be they international or internal. It is, however, to be noted that what they are primarily advocating or arguing for is to expand the scope of application of the rules governing conduct in international armed conflicts to non-international armed conflicts,[52] rather than to introduce the same threshold for the application of the law of armed conflict in relation to both

---

[50]   For legal questions arising from the internationalisation of civil wars, see Christine Byron, "Armed Conflicts: International or Non-International?," *Journal of Conflict and Security Law*, Vol. 6, No. 1 (June 2001), pp. 86-90.

[51]   See Dieter Fleck, "The Law of Non-International Armed Conflict," in Dieter Fleck (ed.), *The Handbook of International Humanitarian Law*, 3rd ed. (Oxford UP, 2013), p. 593, paras. 1204.2-1204.3. Such a trend can be seen particularly in terms of prohibited weapons and individual criminal responsibility in the context of international criminal courts and tribunals. See, e.g., ICC Statute, art 8(2)(c) and (e); Resolution RC/Res.5 (amendments to art 8 of the Rome Statute), adopted 10 June 2010, in ICC Doc. RC/11, 2010, p. 13.

[52]   See, e.g., Emily Crawford, "Unequal before the Law: The Case for the Elimination of the Distinction between International and Non-international Armed Conflicts," *Leiden Journal of International Law*, Vol. 20, No. 2 (June 2007), pp. 448-462; idem, *The Treatment of Combatants and Insurgents under the Law of Armed Conflict* (Oxford UP, 2010), pp. 168-169; James G. Stewart, "Towards a Single Definition of Armed Conflict in International Humanitarian Law: A Critique of Internationalized Armed Conflict," *International Review of the Red Cross*, Vol. 85, No. 850 (June 2003), pp. 344-349; Lindsay Moir, *The Law of Internal Armed Conflict* (Cambridge UP, 2002), p. 51; idem, "Towards the Unification of International Humanitarian Law?," in Richard Burchill et al. (eds.), *International Conflict and Security Law: Essays in Memory of Hilaire McCoubrey* (Cambridge UP, 2005), pp. 125-127; François Bugnion, "*Jus ad Bellum, Jus in Bello* and Non-International Armed Conflicts," *Yearbook of International Humanitarian Law*, Vol. 6 (2003), pp. 195-198; George H. Aldrich, "The Laws of War on Land," *American Journal of International Law*, Vol. 94, No. 1 (January 2000), pp. 62-63; Jean-Marie Henckaerts and Louise Doswald-Beck (ICRC), *Customary International Humanitarian Law*, Vol. I (Cambridge UP, 2005), p. xxix. See also *The Prosecutor v. Tadić* (Jurisdiction, Appeals), *supra* note 8, paras. 97, 119.

types of armed conflicts, so that the high threshold for the application of the law of non-international armed conflict would also be used to trigger the application of the law of international armed conflict. The former argument is designed to extend the protection of the law of international armed conflict to the victims of non-international armed conflict, particularly in terms of the prohibition of the use of certain weapons and protection of civilians, while the latter would deprive the victims of international armed conflicts below the "new" threshold of the protection of international humanitarian law, though human rights law might provide different kinds of protection to some of them.[53]

B. Separate threshold school

Professor Dietrich Schindler leads a second school of thought regarding the intensity requirement for international armed conflict.[54] He argues that:

> The existence of an armed conflict within the meaning of Article 2 common to the [Geneva] Conventions can always be assumed when parts of the armed forces of two States clash with each other. Even a minor frontier incident is sufficient. Any kind of use of arms between two States brings the Conventions into effect.[55]

---

[53] It has been pointed out that human rights accountability is one-sided in that it imposes responsibility on the government only. Christine Gray, "The Meaning of Armed Conflict: Non-International Armed Conflict," in Mary Ellen O'Connell (ed.), *What Is War?: An Investigation in the Wake of 9/11* (Nijhoff, 2012), p. 80. It may be added that the extraterritorial application of human rights treaties, which is usually the prerequisite for protecting the victims of an international armed conflict under human rights law, is not necessarily assured or at least debatable. For more on this question, see Marko Milanovic, *Extraterritorial Application of Human Rights Treaties: Law, Principles, and Policy* (Oxford UP, 2011), pp. 118-228; Dapo Akande, "UK Parliamentary Inquiry into UK Policy on the Use of Drones for Target Killing," *EJIL; Talk!*, 23 December 2015.

[54] Other writers belonging to this school include Has-Peter Gasser, who argues that according to state practice, "*any use of armed force* by one State against the territory of another triggers the applicability of the Geneva Conventions between the two States" (emphasis added). Hans-Peter Gasser, "International Humanitarian Law," in Hans Haug et al., *Humanity for All: The International Red Cross and Red Crescent Movement* (Paul Haupt Publishers, 1993), pp. 510-511.

[55] Dietrich Schindler, "The Different Types of Armed Conflicts according to the Geneva Conventions and Protocols," *Recueil des Cours*, tome 163 (1979-II), p. 131.

More recently, Professor Éric David maintains:

En ce qui concerne donc le droit des conflits armés *stricto sensu*, on constatera simplement que, pour la doctrine, et notamment pour les juristes du CICR, tout *affrontement armé* entre forces des Etats parties aux CG [Conventions de Genève] de 1949 (et éventuellement au 1er PA [Protocole additionnel] de 1977) relève de ces instruments, quelle que soit l'ampleur de cet affrontement: une escarmouche, une incident de frontière entre les forces armées des Parties suffisent à provoquer l'application des Conventions (et du 1er Protocole, s'il lie les Etats) à cette situation. ...Il suffit qu'il y ait un seul blessé ou un seul naufragé ou un seul prisonnier.[56] (emphasis original)

Similarly, Professor René Provost asserts that: "The threshold of applicability [of the Geneva Conventions] is clearly intended to be very low, and to include all situations where humanitarian law may provide some protection to the victims of military operations."[57] He presents a couple of cases that support his argument, which we will examine later.

Although these writers scarcely provide specific reasons for their different treatments of international and non-international armed conflicts in terms of the intensity requirement, article 1(2) of Additional Protocol II offers some illumination in this regard. It provides that the Protocol shall *not* apply to "situations of internal disturbances and tensions, such as riots, isolated and sporadic acts of violence and other acts of a similar nature." It thus excludes from the scope of application of Protocol II those situations that are to be regarded as the internal affairs of the state concerned.

Internal conflicts have long been treated as outside the scope of application of any international law of war or armed conflict unless the recognition of belligerency was granted to the insurgents. They were essentially viewed as the internal affairs of a state. Even today the same considerations seem to contribute to making the application of rules of

---

[56] Éric David, *Principes de droit des conflits armés* (Bruylant, 2002), p. 109.
[57] René Provost, *International Human Rights and Humanitarian Law* (Cambridge UP, 2002), p. 250.

humanitarian law for internal conflicts subject to certain conditions and limitations. Such measures can be seen as safeguards on the part of the states against the excessive intrusion of international law into their inherently domestic sphere and their freedom of action.[58]

Article 3(1) of Additional Protocol II confirms this by providing that no provision of the Protocol "shall be invoked for the purpose of affecting the sovereignty of a State or the responsibility of the government…to maintain or re-establish law and order." Furthermore, its article 3(2) more directly provides for the above point, as follows:

> Nothing in this Protocol shall be invoked as a justification for intervening, directly or indirectly, for any reason whatever, in the armed conflict or in the internal or external affairs of the High Contracting Party in the territory of which that conflict occurs.

Essentially the same provisions can be found in article 1(4) and (5) of Protocol II to the CCW Convention as amended in 1996, and article 1(4) and (5) of the CCW Convention as amended in 2001, as well as article 8(3) of the ICC Statute.

In contrast, no such considerations are required to play a role in the case of international armed conflicts. There is no comparable obstacle that would prevent the rules of humanitarian law from applying to those conflicts upon resorting to armed forces by states, irrespective of the intensity or duration of violence.

IV. STATE PRACTICE: RELEVANT AND IRRELEVANT CASES

A. Law enforcement or use of force/aggression

Recall that the ILA's Final Report on the Meaning of Armed Conflict in International Law as well as some authors argues that for an international conflict to constitute an "armed conflict" for the purpose of applying the

---

[58] See Yves Sandoz, "International Humanitarian Law in the Twenty-First Century," *Yearbook of International Humanitarian Law*, Vol. 6 (2003), p. 14.

law of armed conflict, it must satisfy certain criteria, including an intensity/ duration threshold similar to the one provided in Additional Protocol II applicable to non-international armed conflict. In fact, there are fairly numerous cases, mostly in the field of maritime operations, where despite the fact that shots were fired, the law of armed conflict was not applied, thus apparently supporting the above argument.

For instance, in 1929 the *I'm Alone,* a British schooner registered in Canada, was ordered to heave to by a US coast guard vessel on suspicion of smuggling liquor, which at the time was prohibited in the United States. When the *I'm Alone* refused to heave to, she was fired on by another coast guard vessel and sank more than 200 miles off the coast of the United States.[59] Similarly, in 1962, the *Red Crusader,* a Scottish trawler, was arrested by a Danish fisheries inspection vessel and ordered to proceed to the Faroe Islands (Danish territory) for trial for fishing in a prohibited area. After obeying for a while, the *Red Crusader* sought to escape. Because warnings to stop were not heeded, the ship was fired upon directly with solid shot and damaged (although it did not sink).[60]

In these cases, the law of armed conflict was not applied. The doctrinal arguments have centred on the question of whether the use of force was within reasonable and necessary limits, and not on the applicability of the law of armed conflict. This fact is referred to in the ILA Report to support the idea that a certain level of intensity is required for the law of armed conflict to apply in an international conflict.[61]

---

[59] *Reports of International Arbitral Awards*, Vol. 3 (1935), pp. 1609-1618.

[60] *International Law Reports*, Vol. 35, pp. 485-501.

[61] The ILA Report argues that, in the *Red Crusader* case, the Commission of Enquiry found that the Danes had used excessive force in arresting the trawler, but neither that fact nor the involvement of two parties to the Geneva Conventions led to treatment of the incident as an armed conflict. ILA Report 2010, *supra* note 5, p. 14. In the Report, after pointing out that a British Naval vessel escorted a Danish fishing enforcement vessel to a port, the ILA Committee also argues that this escort seems to fit the phrase "any engagement" used in the ICRC Commentary to define international armed conflict. Ibid., p. 14. Thus, the Committee tries to indicate that although the fact seems to fit the ICRC Commentary definition of international armed conflict, the incident was not treated as such. However, apart from the fact that there is no such phrase as "any engagement" used in the ICRC Commentary in the context of defining international armed conflict, it is doubtful whether an escort by a state vessel of a vessel of another state without resorting to force could ever be regarded as an "armed conflict" in the first place, even if the former vessel is armed.

However, the reason for not applying the law of armed conflict to these situations can be attributed to the following entirely different factor. In both cases, the use of force by the US coast guard and the Danish fisheries inspection vessels was directed against ships that were not owned or operated by a state, so there was no state-to-state use of force in these cases. If there is no actual state-to-state use of force, there is no possibility, basically,[62] for the law on the use of force in international relations or for the law of armed conflict to apply. The use of force in these cases should better be understood as police actions or domestic law enforcement measures. As Professor Howard Levie correctly points out, "police actions in conflicts such as fisheries conflicts [are] not matters involving armed conflict."[63]

There are a couple of International Court of Justice (ICJ) cases[64] in which one of the parties to an incident claimed that the other party had used force in contravention of article 2(4) of the UN Charter, thus potentially hinting at the applicability of the law of international armed conflict to the incident. In the 1974 Fisheries Jurisdiction case, Germany asserted that Icelandic patrol boats had violated article 2(4) of the UN Charter by using force against German trawlers (firing shots at them) outside Iceland's twelve-mile zone.[65] The Court did not address this issue, however, simply finding that the German request for compensation was too abstract and lacked any concrete indication of damages or detailed evidence.[66]

---

[62] Use of force between states may be deemed to exist without any actual state-to-state use of force, such as a use of force against a state by a *non-state actor* that is organized, instigated, or assisted by another state. Declaration on Principles of International Law Concerning Friendly Relations and Co-operation among States in Accordance with the Charter of the United Nations, UN Doc. A/RES/2625(XXV), 24 October 1970, Annex, first principle.

[63] "Neutrality, the Rights of Shipping and the Use of Force in the Persian Gulf War (Part II)" (hereinafter cited as "Neutrality (Part II)"), *Proceedings of the American Society of International Law 1988,* p. 609.

[64] In addition to the cases discussed in the text, the ICJ judgment in the Oil Platform case of 2003 may also be referred to as a relevant example. In that case, the United States invoked article 51 of the UN Charter in justifying its own use of force in response to the alleged Iranian attacks against US vessels. This claim was based on the premise that the preceding Iranian acts were an armed attack. The Court did not accept the United States' contention because of the lack of intention on the part of Iran to harm US vessels even if all attacks in the incidents were attributed to Iran. "Oil Platforms," *ICJ Reports 2003*, p. 185, para. 48, and pp. 191-192, para. 64.

[65] "Memorial on the Merits Submitted by the Government of the Federal Republic of Germany," *ICJ Pleadings, Fisheries Jurisdiction*, Vol. II, p. 277.

[66] "Fisheries Jurisdiction Case (Federal Republic of Germany v. Iceland)," *ICJ Reports 1974*, pp. 203-204, paras. 71-76.

Two decades later, the Court again dealt with a similar incident. In March 1995, Canadian government vessels seized a Spanish fishing vessel, the *Estai*, some 245 miles from the Canadian coast.[67] Spain argued before the Court that "the particular use of force directed against the *Estai*... amounted to a violation of Article 2, paragraph 4, of the [UN] Charter." To this argument, the Court held, speaking generally of the relevant Canadian legislation, that "the use of force authorized by the Canadian legislation and regulations falls within the ambit of what is commonly understood as *enforcement of conservation and management measures*" (emphasis added). Apparently rejecting Spain's arguments, it further stated that "[b] oarding, inspection, arrest and minimum use of force for those purposes are all contained within the concept of *enforcement of conservation and management measures* according to a 'natural and reasonable' interpretation of this concept" [68] (emphasis added).

Likewise, in the *Saiga* (No. 2) case of 1999, involving an oil tanker provisionally registered in Saint Vincent and conducting commercial activities (selling oil to fishing vessels) 22 miles from the Guinean island of Alcatraz, the International Tribunal for the Law of the Sea (ITLOS) described the Guinean patrol boat's use of force against the *Saiga* as "law enforcement operations."[69] Thus, there are a number of cases in which the relevant court or tribunal has (apparently) found that the use of force by a government vessel against a private vessel does not constitute a use of force envisaged by article 2(4) of the UN Charter, thus presumably rejecting any argument for the application of the law of international armed conflict even if such is claimed.

Yet, one cannot completely exclude the possibility that even a use of force by a government vessel against a merchant or other non-government ship might be held to be a use of force in international relations. The *Guyana/Suriname* case is one such rare example. In that case, the patrol

---

[67] "Fisheries Jurisdiction Case (Spain v. Canada)," *ICJ Reports 1998*, p. 443, para. 19.

[68] Ibid., pp. 465-466, paras. 78-84.

[69] "The M/V 'Saiga' (No. 2) Case," *International Legal Materials*, Vol. 38, No. 5 (September 1999), p. 1355, para. 156.

boats from the Surinamese navy approached the *C.E. Thornton*, an oil rig and drill ship of CGX (a Canadian oil exploration company licensed by Guyana under a concession), located in a disputed sea area, and ordered the ship and its service vessels to leave the area within twelve hours, warning that if they did not do so, the consequences would be theirs.[70] Suriname maintained that the measures taken were reasonable and proportionate law-enforcement measures to preclude unauthorised drilling in a disputed area of continental shelf, citing the ICJ's judgment in the *Estai* case and that of the ITLOS in the *Saiga* case. The Arbitral Tribunal, however, held that "the action mounted by Suriname…seemed more akin to a threat of military action rather than a mere law enforcement activity," and that it "constituted a threat of the use of force in breach of the [UN Convention on the Law of the Sea], the UN Charter, and general international law."[71]

It is not very clear exactly which aspects of the Surinamese action led the Tribunal to that conclusion, but the unique nature of this incident—that it took place in a disputed area (which means, for Guyana, that it took place in its own area of jurisdiction)—may have led the Tribunal to see the Surinamese naval measures as an action against Guyanese sovereignty (sovereign rights) rather than mere law enforcement.[72]

There is also an instrument which provides for the possibility that a use of force by a government vessel against merchant ships might be viewed as a use of force in international relations. The UN Definition of Aggression of 1974[73] provides in article 3 (d) that "[a]n attack by the armed forces of a State on the land, sea or air forces, or *marine and air fleets* of another State" (emphasis added) qualifies as an act of aggression. The "marine fleet" mentioned there must be a fleet of privately owned and operated (merchant

---

[70] "Arbitral Tribunal Constituted Pursuant to Article 287, and in Accordance with Annex VII, of the United Nations Convention on the Law of the Sea in the Matter of an Arbitration between Guyana and Suriname: Award of the Arbitral Tribunal," 17 September 2007, paras. 151, 436, 439.

[71] Ibid., paras. 441-443, 445.

[72] Cf. Patricia Jimenez Kwast, "Maritime Law Enforcement and the Use of Force: Reflections on the Categorisation of Forcible Action at Sea in the Light of the *Guyana/Suriname* Award," *Journal of Conflict and Security Law*, Vol. 13, No. 1 (Spring 2008), pp. 49-91.

[73] UN Doc. A/RES/3314(XXIX), 14 December 1974, Annex.

or fishing) ships because it is stipulated side-by-side with, and in addition to, the "sea forces" of a state in the same paragraph.[74]

It should, however, be borne in mind that an attack on a marine fleet referred to here must be, according to the drafting history,[75] on such a large scale that it could be equated with a blockade of the ports or coasts of a state, the latter being provided as another example of aggression in article 3(c) of the Definition. Hence, an attack on a marine fleet as an example of aggression should be viewed as an extreme case.[76] More importantly, all this does not conflict in any way with our analysis that the concept of *inter-state* armed conflict basically does not carry any particular threshold of intensity. Rather, the above-quoted provision of the Definition of Aggression should be seen as a good illustration that the use of force by a state against privately owned ships, as opposed to government-owned ships, has to reach a considerably high level of intensity in order to qualify as aggression and, arguably, as armed conflict.

Thus, it could be said that as far as the use of force between vessels is concerned, only the use of force between vessels of two or more governments could amount to an international armed conflict, barring the above-mentioned rare exceptions. In the latter case, a use of force against privately owned ships might be viewed as a use of force prohibited by article 2(4) of the UN Charter or even as an act of aggression, and thus possibly as constituting an international armed conflict, but that would be only where the intensity of the use of force reaches a considerably high level or in exceptional cases in which a use of force occurs in a disputed territory or area. Most importantly, this does not negate at all our concept

[74] Ships other than "sea forces" might include other state-owned or operated ships used for government non-commercial or commercial services. However, that the "marine fleet" mentioned in the Definition of Aggression is mainly intended to cover privately-owned and operated ships can be confirmed by the drafting history of the provision in question, as we will see below.

[75] See UN Doc. A/9619, 1974, pp. 15-16; A/9411, 10 December 1973, p. 10, para. 20, both reproduced in Benjamin B. Ferencz, *Defining International Aggression: The Search for World Peace*, Vol. 2 (Oceana Pub., 1975), pp. 549, 570-571. See also Bengt Broms, "The Definition of Aggression," *Recueil des Cours*, tome 154 (1977-I), pp. 350-352.

[76] During the drafting of the Definition of Aggression, it was said that "the words 'marine and air fleets' implied a massive attack and not isolated acts." UN Doc. A/9411, p. 10, para. 20, reproduced in Ferencz, *supra* note 75, p. 549.

that international law does not require a state-to-state conflict to reach a certain level of intensity for it to be an armed conflict to which international humanitarian law applies.

B. Low-intensity (and short-duration) armed conflicts

As discussed above, the ICTY explicitly accepted in the *Mucić* judgement that any conflict involving armed forces of two states is an international armed conflict, irrespective of its intensity or duration, and triggers the application of international humanitarian law. This is the standard that the ICTY has been applying in dealing with international armed conflict cases. The same is true of other international criminal courts and tribunals, including the ICC. These cases all constitute important international practice, which shows that international law does not require a certain level of intensity for a conflict to qualify as an international armed conflict.

In addition, there are some instances where one of the states concerned claimed the applicability of the law of international armed conflict to a very low-intensity (and short-duration) conflict. One such example is the "Lieutenant Goodman" incident. When Lieutenant Robert O. Goodman, flying regular, routine reconnaissance flights in a US plane, was shot down by Syria on 4 December 1983, he was held by the Syrians for about a month. The day following his downing, a US spokesman made a statement that Lieutenant Goodman was considered to be a prisoner of war.[77] This statement was based on a premise that the law of armed conflict was applicable to that incident. Moreover, the US Department of State prepared a press guidance on this point, as follows:

Question – Is the captured airman a "prisoner-of-war" under the Third Geneva Convention?

Answer – Yes. The Third Geneva Convention accords "prisoner-of-war" status to members of the armed forces who are captured during "armed conflict" between two or more parties to the Convention. "Armed

[77] "Neutrality (Part II)," *supra* note 63, p. 598.

conflict" includes *any situation* in which there is hostile action between the armed forces of two parties, *regardless of the duration, intensity or scope of the fighting* and irrespective of whether a state of war exists between the two parties.[78] (emphasis added)

This is one of the cases that Professor Provost cites when he asserts that: "The threshold of applicability [of the Geneva Conventions] is clearly intended to be very low."[79]

In an apparent contrast, Professor Levie questions if this particular incident was really a case of armed conflict. After pointing out that "[i]solated incidents can result in a state of armed conflict," but "usually nations don't elect to do that unless the intent of the incident was to create a basis for saying that there is an armed conflict," he states that he does not believe that that is how this incident can be interpreted.[80]

It is noteworthy that he is not advocating in this statement an intensity requirement for international armed conflict of the kind that the single threshold school advocates. In fact, he has admitted that international humanitarian law can be applied to isolated incidents; his criticism seems to be directed at the interpretation of the Goodman incident *per se*. What's more, commenting on the ICRC Commentary statement regarding the irrelevance of intensity and duration of conflict in international armed conflict, Professor Levie states that the ICRC statement does not necessarily apply in 100 percent of the cases but will in "99 percent of all cases."[81]

The ILA's Final Report on the Meaning of Armed Conflict in International Law of 2010, commenting on the Lieutenant Goodman incident, refers to the fact that President Ronald Reagan later called the US spokesman's statement into question by saying that "I don't know how you have a prisoner of war

---

[78] "Multinational Force in Lebanon: Captured U.S. Naval Airman," in Marian Nash, *Cumulative Digest of United States Practice in International Law 1981–1988*, Book III (Office of the Legal Adviser, Department of State, 1995), p. 3457.

[79] Provost, *supra* note 57, p. 250. The other case Professor Provost cites is a clash between Mexico and the United States in 1916 involving 250 soldiers and lasting for 30 minutes. Ibid., p. 250.

[80] "Neutrality (Part II)," *supra* note 63, p. 598.

[81] Ibid., p. 598.

when there is no declared war between nations. I don't think that makes you eligible for the Geneva Accords."[82]

This was a very dubious remark from an international legal perspective in that it made the application of Geneva Conventions conditional on the existence of a "declared war."[83] Moreover, the fact that the above-quoted press guidance was published in a volume compiled by the Office of the Legal Adviser of the US State Department as late as 1995 clearly indicates that the United States' official position is consistent with the US spokesman's statement, and that that position is that armed conflict includes "any situation in which there is hostile action between the armed forces of two parties, regardless of the duration, intensity or scope of the fighting."[84]

A more recent instance of low-intensity conflict in which one of the parties to the conflict claimed the application of international humanitarian law was that of the Iranian capture and detention of 15 UK navy personnel. On 24 March 2007, Iran captured at gunpoint the crew of a small British navy vessel, constituting part of the occupation forces in Iraq under UN auspices and having just completed their routine inspection activity. When the captives appeared on Iranian television, a spokesman for UK Prime Minister Tony Blair complained that doing so was a violation of the Third Geneva Convention relative to the Treatment of Prisoners of War.[85] This complaint was again premised on the application of the law of international armed conflict to the case, and apparently there is no official statement which retracts the above complaint. The ILA Report claims that the United Kingdom did not take an official position as to whether the Convention applied, based on an email message.[86] However, if a government in fact retracts its previous official statement, it is expected to do so equally officially.

---

82 ILA Report 2010, *supra* note 5, pp. 17-18.
83 "Neutrality (Part II)," *supra* note 63, p. 610.
84 See *supra* note 78 and accompanying text.
85 "An International Kidnapping," *Las Vegas Review-Journal*, 30 March 2007; "What Law Did Tehran Break?; Capture of British Sailors a Gray Area in Application of Geneva Conventions," *San Francisco Chronicle*, 1 April 2007.
86 ILA Report 2010, *supra* note 5, p. 27.

Thus, the fact is that there are indeed examples in which one of the states concerned claimed the application of the law of international armed conflict to situations of very-low-intensity (and short-duration) conflicts between states. In both cases, moreover, no effective counter-claim from the other side seems to have been made relying on the fact of the low intensity (and short duration) of the conflict. Although the number is small, the existence of these cases is important in itself, because they show that in the case of inter-state conflicts there is no such intensity (and duration) *requirement* as is applied in the case of non-international armed conflicts. As long as there are cases of low-intensity (and short-duration) conflicts where the application of the law of international armed conflict is made or claimed by the parties, and no effective counterargument has been made, we can hardly say that *opinion juris* exists to the effect that a certain degree of high intensity (or a certain length of duration) is *legally required* for the law of international armed conflict to be applied.

One might argue that the parties to the above cases simply sought to get better treatment for the captured persons and what they claimed was not necessarily reflective of existing international law. It seems, however, that in order for such an argument to gain backing, it would be necessary to show that such is the law despite the overwhelming support for the idea that there is no intensity requirement in the application of the law of international armed conflict, as reflected in the series of ICRC Commentaries and many judicial decisions.

Conversely, even if there is a low-intensity state-to-state conflict to which the law of international armed conflict is not actually applied, such should not necessarily be taken as an indication that the intensity requirement applies to international armed conflict. There are a couple of possible explanations for this. First, if no member of the opposing armed forces is captured in a low-intensity international conflict, it is inevitable that the law pertaining to prisoners of war will not actually be applied. This is for purely *factual* rather than legal reasons, namely that the facts are such that the preconditions for the operation of the law on prisoners of war are simply absent.[87] More generally speaking, if there is no factual need to extend the protection of international humanitarian law, the law is not required to operate and may appear inapplicable.

Another explanation might be that both parties to a low-intensity international conflict may have chosen not to treat it as an armed conflict, bearing in mind that choosing otherwise may prolong the hostilities and spur further military actions and escalation. Although there is a general agreement that the existence of an international armed conflict is a question of fact and independent of the substantive views of the parties to the conflict, as a matter of fact one cannot completely rule out that possibility.[88] One may not be able to show good examples indicating that this is indeed the case, but that may be because states do not usually assert openly that their inaction (non-application of the law of armed conflict) is based on a particular idea.

If these are indeed the reasons for non-application, the non-application of humanitarian law in low-intensity inter-state conflicts would have nothing to do with the threshold question.

V. CONCLUSION

This article has examined the question of intensity of conflict affecting the applicability of international humanitarian law. Whether or not a given conflict is an "armed conflict" determines the legal relationship between the parties involved. This is because with the passage from peace to armed conflict, the applicable rules dramatically change.

In addition, whether a given armed conflict is "international" or "non-international" makes no less substantive a difference[89] (though there is a certain trend toward convergence). The rules for international armed conflict have developed very much since the nineteenth century, while those for non-

---

87   See Jann K. Kleffner, "Scope of Application of International Humanitarian Law," in Fleck (ed.), *supra* note 51, p. 45, para. 202.1.

88   Professor Levie argues that: "Isolated incidents can result in a state of armed conflict. But usually nations don't *elect* to do that unless the *intent* of the incident was to create a basis for saying that there is an armed conflict" (emphasis added). "Neutrality (Part II)," *supra* note 63, p. 598.

89   Differences have mainly been related to the prisoners of war status, prohibited weapons, targeting (protection of civilians), and individual criminal responsibility.

international armed conflict have not evolved to the same degree. Until the mid-twentieth century, internal fighting lay outside the scope of international law, however severe the fighting was, unless the recognition of belligerency was granted to the insurgents, which was an extremely rare occurrence. It is only with common article 3 of the 1949 Geneva Conventions that the law of armed conflict started to regulate non-international armed conflict.[90]

Even now, if violence occurs within a state's territory, it will not be treated as "armed conflict" unless the violence reaches a certain level of intensity. Additional Protocol II, applicable to non-international armed conflict, stipulates in article 1(2) that the Protocol shall *not* apply to "situations of internal disturbances and tensions, such as riots, isolated and sporadic acts of violence." Thus, the intensity element is introduced in characterizing an internal conflict as "armed conflict." The reason for this is that low-intensity internal conflicts have always been regarded and treated as internal affairs of the state concerned, and thus should be blocked to international law by the sovereignty of the state.

In contrast, in the case of international conflict between states, any difference arising between states leading to the intervention of their armed forces could constitute an armed conflict to which international humanitarian law applies in principle. This is because in inter-state conflicts there is no room for the concept of sovereignty to play a role in order to exclude minor disturbances as "internal affairs of a state." Thus, in the case of international armed conflict, there are reasons for not invoking the intensity requirement that applies in the case of non-international armed conflict.

Additional Protocol I for international armed conflict contains no comparable provision excluding isolated and sporadic acts of violence such as that found in Additional Protocol II. The ICRC Commentaries on the Geneva Conventions and Additional Protocol I also affirm the different treatments of international and non-international armed conflict in this respect, as do a considerable number of judicial decisions. In state practice,

---

[90] Anthony Cullen, *The Concept of Non-International Armed Conflict in International Humanitarian Law* (Cambridge UP, 2010), pp. 7-23.

too, there are some very-low-intensity conflicts for which a state concerned claimed the application of the law of armed conflict with no apparent counter-claim from the other party.

All this seems to lead to the conclusion that the part of the conclusions in the ILA's Final Report on the Meaning of Armed Conflict in International Law of 2010 which disqualifies low-intensity state-to-state conflict from being international armed conflict does not reflect the current status of the international law of armed conflict.

During the discussions on the meaning of armed conflict in the ILA Committee on the Use of Force, the author consistently made the same points detailed in this article. However, his argument was not adequately reflected in the Committee's Final Report. In concluding this article, the author would like to draw readers' attention to the fact that many of the points made in this article are shared by most recent scholarly[91] and institutional commentaries[92] on the Geneva Conventions.

---

[91] Kleffner, *supra* note 87, p. 45, para. 202.1; Andrew Clapham, "The Concept of International Armed Conflict," in Andrew Clapham et al. (eds.), *The 1949 Geneva Conventions: A Commentary* (Oxford UP, 2015), pp. 10-17.

[92] ICRC, *Commentary on the First Geneva Convention: Convention (I) for the Amelioration of the Condition of the Wounded and Sick in Armed Forces in the Field,* 2nd edition, 2016, art 2 (Application of the Convention), paras. 236-238, 243, available at https://ihl-databases.icrc.org/ihl/full/GCI-commentary. However, there still are authors who argue that a certain degree of intensity is required for a state-to-state conflict to be an international armed conflict. Andrea Bianchi and Yasmin Naqvi, "Terrorism," in Andrew Clapham and Paola Gaeta (eds.), *The Oxford Handbook of International Law in Armed Conflict* (Oxford UP, 2014), p. 581.

COMPETITION ADVOCACY AND COMPETITION CULTURE

LUTZ-CHRISTIAN WOLFF*

ABSTRACT

Competition Advocacy is often understood as a "soft" alternative to "hard" regulation through legal norms. Competition Advocacy is amongst other things seen as preferable over regulation because regulation implies market intervention by the state which in itself can distort or even hinder competition. Furthermore, Competition Advocacy is regarded as a tool to reduce the exertion of influence by private interest groups on the use of regulatory measures, i.e. to counter the outgrowth of lobbying activities. In this context it is said to be one of the main tasks of Competition Advocacy to create a competition culture. This article aims to answer the question what this actually implies, i.e. which preconditions a competition culture must fulfil to ensure (perfect) competition. It also explores if the tools of Competition Advocacy are sufficient to affect market behaviour and thus to establish or at least support a particular competition culture so that regulatory measures will become fully or at least partly redundant.

Keywords: competition law, competition advocacy, competition culture, path dependence, inter-cultural management, organizational behaviour,

TABLE OF CONTENTS

  Wei Lun Professor of Law & Dean of the Graduate School, The Chinese University of Hong Kong – office address: Room 539, Faculty of Law, 5/F, Lee Shau Kee Building, The Chinese University of Hong Kong Shatin, NT, Hong Kong SAR; email: wolff@cuhk.edu.hk. I had presented some of the basic ideas underlying this article at the annual conferences of the Asian Competition Forum in Hong Kong in December 2007 and in December 2011 as well as at the international symposium "Reform of Monopoly Sectors: Competition and Regulation" in September 2015 in Nanjing. I wish to thank the audience for interesting and very helpful comments during the discussions following my presentations. Many thanks also to Jenny Chan for valuable research support. Online sources quoted in the following were last visited on 19 August 2016. Footnotes in the original text of word-for-word quotes are not reproduced in this article for the sake of user-friendliness. A Chinese version of this paper was published in Xiaomin Fang (ed.), Jahrbuch des Deutsch-Chinesischen Instituts für Rechtswissenschaften der Universitäten Göttingen und Nanjing (《中德法学论坛》)(Beijing: Law Press, 2016).

I. INTRODUCTION

Competition has been described as

> "the sum of all liberties to act within a market ..., which are constantly subject to new actions and reactions of the market participants ... Competition is therefore something like a constant 'Tour de France' of economic life, in which businessmen offer their performances to other market parties. ... Everybody may, everybody even shall try to challenge the position of others or even to grab the yellow jersey of the leader from him. Whoever does not manage the mountain stage, will be excluded without mercy. ... The formation of teams, which coordinate the pace or the 'winner' is as restriction of competition forbidden. ... (It) is the basic idea of our entire competition law to secure free and undistorted competition."[1]

Monopolies and other potentially anti-competitive behaviour which affects free competition are not compatible with this basic idea. It therefore seems plausible to create a rather strict regulatory framework to enforce perfect competition and to prevent anti-competitive practices. Despite its very fundamental significance it is, however, disputed until today what (perfect) competition really means and how competition can or should be promoted by using the tools of competition law.[2]

> "There are disagreements as to whether competition law should be a technocratic area of regulation that is purely based on economic analysis, or whether it should encompass other non-market or even non-economic goals. Some scholars have argued that there is an inherent political content in competition law that cannot be assumed away simply by incorporation of economic analysis. Disagreement is

---

[1] Axel Nordemann/Jan Bernd Nordemann/Anke Nordemann-Schiffel, Wettbewerbsrecht Markenrecht (Competition Law Trademark Law), 11th ed. (Baden-Baden: Nomos, 2012), pp. 34-35.

[2] Compare from a general point of view Thomas K. Cheng, Convergence and Its Discontents: A Reconsideration of the Merits of Convergence of Global Competition Law, 12 Chicago Journal of International Law No. 2 (Winter 2012), pp. 433-490 (436): "Competition law promotes free competition by prohibiting anti-competitive conduct by firms."

not confined to the goals pursued by competition law. It extends to the definition of some of the fundamental concepts that serve as guideposts for competition law analysis. These concepts include consumer welfare, total welfare and even competition itself."[3]

In light of these uncertainties it stands to reason to look for alternatives to strict regulatory approaches when it comes to protect the market and to foster competition. In this context the concept of Competition Advocacy has increasingly gained importance in recent years.

Competition Advocacy is often understood as a "soft" alternative to the "hard" regulation through legal norms. The argument is that Competition Advocacy can address the specifics of respective environments in a more flexible way and thus satisfy the requirements of the so-called "path dependence"[4] of legal norms and concepts. Competition Advocacy is also seen as preferable over regulation through legal norms because regulation implies market intervention by the state which in itself can distort or even hinder competition.[5] Furthermore, Competition Advocacy is regarded as a tool to reduce the exertion of influence by private interest groups on the use of regulatory measures, i.e. to counter the outgrowth of lobbying activities.[6] Finally, developing countries often lack the legislative know-how to develop and implement effective regulatory concepts.[7] Competition Advocacy is said to be able to fill this gap. In this context it is seen as one of the main tasks of Competition Advocacy to create a competition culture.

---

[3]   Cheng, ibid, pp. 465, 465-475; also compare Wolfgang Pape, Socio-Cultural Differences and International Competition Law, 5 European Law Journal (No. 4) (December 1999), pp. 438-460 (443).

[4]   Lutz-Christian Wolff, The Law of Cross-border Business Transactions – Principles, Concepts, Skills (Alphen aan den Rijn: Kluwer Law International, 2013), pp. 15, 320; compare Cheng, supra note 2, p. 441: "The law generally, and competition law specifically, must correspond to local norms to gain legitimacy."; A.E. Rodriguez/Malcolm B. Coate, Competition Policy in Transition Economies: The Role of Competition Advocacy, 23 Brooklyn Journal of International Law (1997-1998), pp. 367-401 (386, Note 37).

[5]   Simon J. Evenett, Competition Advocacy: Time for a Rethink?, 26 Northwestern Journal of International Law and Business (2006), pp. 495-514 (497); also compare Giuliano Amato/Laraine L. Laudati (eds.), The Anticompetitive Impact of Regulation (Cheltenham/Northampton: Edward Elgar, 2001).

[6]   Evenett, ibid, p. 498.

[7]   International Competition Network (ICN), Competition Advocacy in Regulated Sectors: Examples of Success (April 2004), http://www.internationalcompetitionnetwork.org/uploads/library/doc370.pdf, p. 48; Evenett, ibid, p. 499.

This article aims to answer the question what this implies, i.e. which preconditions a competition culture must fulfill to achieve these goals. It asks if the tools of Competition Advocacy as understood today are sufficient to affect market behaviour and thus to establish or at least support a particular competition culture so that regulatory measures will become fully or at least partly redundant. For this purpose this article relies on studies conducted in the area of intercultural management and organisational behaviour.

This article is structured as follows:

To set the scene, the first section summarizes the meaning of the term "Competition Advocacy", the goals of Competition Advocacy as well as the measures which are proposed to reach those goals. The subsequent section then contrasts the idea of regulatory measures with the tools of Competition Advocacy. This is followed by a discussion of the term "competition culture", which – as will be shown - much less clear than one might assume. The main part of this article then recalls the significance of culture for human behaviour followed by a discussion if and how it may be possible to develop and successfully implement a particular competition culture and which role Competition Advocacy can play in this regard. The last section summarizes the findings and draws attention to their relevance in a more general context.

II. COMPETITION ADVOCACY

Competition Advocacy is a relatively new concept which has gained much importance over the past 15 years.[8] While often discussed in particular in the Anglo-American world, it appears, however, that the term "Competition Advocacy" is not always used in the same way.

According to the apparently prevailing opinion Competition Advocacy comprises all activities of a competition authority which aim to foster

---

[8] Irina Knyazeva, Competition Advocacy: Soft Power in Competitive Policy, 6 Procedia Economics and Finance (2013), pp. 280-287 (282). The term was first introduced by Terry Murrissa, the former head of the U.P. Federal Trade Commission, during the annual ICN conference in 2002, ibid, p. 281.

competition[9] except for measures for the implementation of competition law in the widest sense.[10] The OECD has also made it clear in this regard, that Competition Advocacy and measures to implement competition law are not mutually exclusive, but rather complement each other.[11]

But what exactly is Competition Advocacy? The World Bank and the OECD have given the following explanation:

> "… private restrictive business practices are often facilitated by various government interventions in the marketplace. Thus, the mandate of the competition office extends beyond merely enforcing the competition law. It must also participate more broadly in the formulation of its country's economic policies, which may adversely affect competitive market structure, business conduct, and economic performance. It must assume the role of competition advocate, acting proactively to bring about government policies that lower barriers to entry, promote deregulation and trade liberalization, and otherwise minimize unnecessary government intervention in the marketplace."[12]

According to this explanation only government bodies seem to be the addressees of Competition Advocacy, i.e. not e.g. enterprises, judges, lawyers, interest groups and the general public as such. While this restriction

---

[9] For the difficulties to delineate the goal to promote competition compare Evenett, supra note 5, pp. 502-504.

[10] OECD Competition Advocacy: Challenges for Developing Countries, http://www.oecd.org/daf/competition/prosecutionandlawenforcement/32033710.pdf, p. 9; also compare the definition of the ICN Working Group Competition Culture Project Report (2015), http://www.internationalcompetitionnetwork.org/uploads/library/doc1035.pdf, p. 3: "Competition advocacy refers to those activities conducted by the competition authority related to the promotion of a competitive environment for economic activities by means of non-enforcement mechanisms, mainly through its relationship with other governmental entities and by increasing public awareness of the benefits of competition."; Knyazeva, supra note 8, p. 282; Evenett, supra note 5, p. 495-497 (514): "The conventional wisdom on competition advocacy was found to be wanting in a number of respects."; Pradeep P. Mehta, Competition Culture Key to Successful Competition Regime, http://www.cuts-ccier.org/pdf/competition_culture_key_to_successful_competition_regime.pdf , p. 4; Stanley M. Gorinson/Patrick P. Antrim/Theresa Fenelon, Competition Advocacy Before Regulatory Agencies, 5 Antitrust (1990-1991) (Summer 1991), pp. 24-27, understand Competition Advocacy as also including the activities of lawyers before government authorities, compare, ibid, pp. 500-502, 502: "(C)ompetition advocacy does not amount to blanket calls to either deregulate or promote a laissez-faire approach."

[11] OECD, ibid; compare Mehta, ibid, p. 2.

[12] The World Bank/OECD, A Framework for the Design and Implementation of Competition Law and Policy (1998), Chapter 6, p. 93, quoted by OECD, supra note 10.

can be found in many earlier statements regarding Competition Advocacy, in modern times a more inclusive understanding seems to be prevailing. This makes sense as competition is not only affected and controlled by government bodies, but rather collectively carried by all market participants.[13]

In its Report "Competition Advocacy: Challenges for Developing Countries"[14] the OECD has identified the following four core areas in which competition authorities can and even shall practice Competition Advocacy: (i) privatisation, (ii) law making, government policies and regulatory reforms, (iii) participation in law making and enforcement, and (iv) establishment of a competition culture. The first area concerns a special problem of developing countries[15] and is not of particular relevance for the purposes of this article. The second and the third area relate to topics which supplement regulatory activities and shall consequently also not be discussed further. The topic of this article is the relationship between Competition Advocacy and competition culture, i.e. the fourth area listed by the OECD. In fact, the development of a competition culture is understood as one of the core tasks of Competition Advocacy:

"A cornerstone of a successful market economy is the existence of a 'competition culture' within a country – an understanding by the public of the benefits of competition and broad-based support for a strong competition policy. An important focus for competition advocacy by the competition agency is the development of this competition culture. All parts of a society – consumers, business people, trade unions, educators, the legal community, government and regulatory officials and judges – should be addressed in this effort. This proposition is now widely accepted."[16]

---

[13] Compare infra, IV.

[14] The World Bank/OECD, ibid, p. 3; compare Evenett, supra note 5, p. 497.

[15] The World Bank/OECD, ibid; compare Evenett, ibid, p. 498, Cheng, supra note 2, p. 477-484; Marco Botta, Fostering Competition Culture in the Emerging Economies: The Brazilian Experience, 4 World Competition (2009), pp. 609-627.

[16] The World Bank/OECD, ibid, p. 8; John Clark, Competition Advocacy – Challenges for Developing Countries, 6 OECD Journal: Competition Law and Policy (No.4) (2005), pp. 69-80 (77); Mehta, supra note

Measures which can be adopted to develop a particular competition culture have been discussed extensively at national and international levels. Commentators mention in this context amongst others (i) the publication of decisions of competition authorities, (ii) the promulgation of implementation guidelines, (iii) the publication of brochures and other information materials, (iv) the publication of annual reports, (v) market surveys and other studies and their publication, (vi) regular interaction with the media, (vii) public presentations of representatives of competition authorities and other officials as well as (ix) trainings through conferences and seminars.[17]

The OECD has concluded that

> "(b)uilding a competition culture is important in every country, but once again it seems that it is especially critical in developing countries."[18]

III. COMPETITION REGULATION

Competition regulation in its traditional form means that mandatory legal norms are used to prohibit anti-competitive behaviour, to impose sanctions if prohibitions are violated and to promote pro-competition action. As already mentioned,[19] it is disputed until today if and how the state can and should contribute to the protection of the market and special market segments. In particular, there is no agreement in relation to the question if and in which form regulatory measures are adequate tools to guarantee to

---

10, p. 1; compare William J. Kolasky, A Culture of Competition for North America, Address at "Economic Competition Day: Shared Experiences" 2 (June 24, 2002), http://www.justice.gov/atr/file/519781/download, p. 2; Compare Maurice E. Stucke, Better Competition Advocacy, 82 S. John's Law Review (2008), p. 951-1036 (1027); ICN, Advocacy and Competition Policy – A Report Prepared by the Advocacy Working Group (presented at the ICN Annual Conference, Naples, Italy, 2002), http://www.internationalcompetitionnetwork. org/uploads/library/doc358.pdf, p. 3; Cheng, supra note 2, p. 488.

[17] The World Bank/OECD, ibid, p. 8; Clark, ibid, p. 78; compare Anatolie Caraganciu/Viorica Carare, Competition Advocacy: Challenge for Competition Policy, SEA Practical Application of Science Vol. II, Issue 3 (5) (2014), p. 185-188 (186-188); Mehta, supra note 10, p. 8.

[18] The World Bank/OECD, ibid; compare Susan Joekes/Phil Evans, Competition and Development (Ottawa: International Development Research Center, 2008).

[19] Supra, I.

promote competition and to ensure the functioning of the market. According to the Chicago School which seems to dominate the thinking in the USA state intervention to protect competition has to be reduced to an absolute minimum.

> "... the Chicago School's view of removing or minimizing governmental restraints on the free market. Competition is assumed to be 'a self-initiating process', which when left alone by government regulators, will generally allocate resources efficiently toward users who value them most. Any company's attempt to secure or maintain market power would likely be defeated by other well-informed profit maximizers, either new entrants or existing competitors. ... The government, under this theory, operates outside the free market, and must justify the necessity of its intervening and 'displacing' competition."[20]

In fact, it can be rather questionable which steps precisely promise success in this regard. Specifics of particular markets, the deliberate and intuitive competitive behaviour of market participants as well as the differing views of competition authorities and even within the same authorities[21] are difficult to assess and make the development implementation of competition policies through regulatory measures rather difficult. The so-called path dependence which was already mentioned above[22] requires competition laws and regulations to be catered to the specifics of the respective addressees as well as other applicable parameters in order to be successful.[23] In each individual case very diverse and sometimes fluctuating factors have to be taken into account and it is obvious that even the identification of these factors is a rather challenging task.

---

[20] Compare Stucke, supra note 16, p. 957.

[21] Gorinson/Antrim/Fenelon, supra note 10, p. 24, 26: "Each of the staffs within an agency may have different agendas. ... Changes in regulators can sometimes bring changes in policies and philosophies on competitive issues."

[22] Supra, I.

[23] Compare Ki Jong Lee, Culture and Competition: National and Regional Levels, 21 Loyola Consumer Law Review (2008), pp. 33-55 (48): "Nations often adopt competition laws that are inconsistent with their citizens' cultural values, and therefore have difficulty implementing them."

In addition, regulatory measures are not based on voluntariness. This can imply a particular psychological impact on all addressees and other related parties thus leading to anti-competitive consequences.[24] Moreover, the implementation of regulatory tools also requires the allocation of substantial resources, e.g. to control and – if necessary – enforce laws and regulations.[25]

In light of all the above it is not surprising that it has been suggested to establish a competition culture which makes the use of regulatory measures fully or partly redundant. As explained above,[26] this is seen as one of the main goals of Competition Advocacy.

IV. COMPETITION CULTURE

If it is the declared goal of Competition Advocacy to establish a particular competition culture, then it is necessary to achieve this goal to clarify what "competition culture" really means. Unfortunately, while often used the term "competition culture" is normally taken for granted and remains often undefined.[27] This is problematic as the reference to the lack or the existence of any particular competition culture without any further explanation can be used as a rhetoric silver bullet when it comes to justify or to criticize particular regulatory steps. Furthermore, it is nowadays commonly accepted that cultures can be rather different depending on the particular environment and the determining factors and one has to assume that the same is true for competition cultures.[28] The reference to a "competition culture" without filling this term with content therefore seems to be rather counter-productive.

In the year 2002 the Advocacy Working Group of the International Competition Network (ICN) had defined "competition culture" as

[24] Compare Amato/Laudati, supra note 5.
[25] Compare Kolasky, supra note 16, P. 8; Stucke, supra note 16, p. 955.
[26] Compare supra, II.
[27] Compare e.g. Timothy J. Muris, Creating a Culture of Competition: The Essential Role of Competition Advocacy (28 February 2002), https://www.ftc.gov/public-statements/2002/09/creating-culture-competition-essential-role-competition-advocacy; Botta, supra note 15, pp. 612, 627.
[28] Compare infra, D.

"the awareness of economic agents and the public at large about competition rules."[29]

This definition is rather surprising as it is not in line with the general understanding of culture as such,[30] which covers much more than just the awareness of certain legal norms. In addition, the reference to the awareness of competition rules seems to make sense only if such awareness also implies that rules will be observed. This, however, is certainly not the case. Finally, markets and competition within markets are of course not just guided by legal rules. This is precisely the idea of Competition Advocacy.

In the year 2015 the ICN then has added the following explanation:

"Competition culture comprises a diverse set of factors that determine individual and/or group behavior in the sphere of market competition and competition enforcement. These include knowledge, experience and perception. In defining competition culture, it is worth reflecting on the instrumental goals that make competition desirable. These include freedoms inherent in a competitive free market economy that allow individuals and firms to harness creativity, passions and ambitions in pursuit of bettering their welfare and the welfare of others.

…

Our working definition of competition culture for the purposes of this report is:

A set of institutions that determine individual and/or group behavior and attitudes in the sphere of market competition. These are influenced by wider social institutions and public policy choices and include customs impacting the degree of business competition and cooperation within a jurisdiction.

---

[29]   ICN 2002, supra note 16, p. iii.; also see the somewhat broader definition by Knyazeva, supra note 8, p. 283: "The concept of competition culture involves awareness by the various societal groups of the advantages and benefits associated with the safeguarding and the development of competition embodied in a values system of informal rules."; similar Mehta, supra note 10, p. 1.

[30]   Compare the discussion in the following.

Collectively these institutions determine the extent to which the behavior and attitudes of relevant public and private stakeholders are consistent with the promotion of competition, efficiency and consumer welfare."[31]

This "working definition" of the ICN is in fact broader than what had been published in 2002. However, it excludes the historical dimension of culture and thus ignores one of the core elements of the generally accepted meaning of culture thus provoking questions which will be discussed in a later part of this article.[32]

Moreover, the 2015 ICN explanation refers in sentence one to factors which are said to determine individual or group behaviour in the market. At the same time it remains open if these factors are comprehensively explained in sentence two with reference to "knowledge, experience and perception". In fact, knowledge, experience and perception may cause market participants to develop certain values, ideas and meanings which can form the basis of a particular competition behaviour and therefore lead to a particular individual or collective competition culture.[33] However, as already mentioned, this does not have to be the case if other factors are stronger or have contributed to the formation of a competition culture at a more influential point of time.

Finally, it is interesting to note that the 2015 ICN explanation in sentence three and four of paragraph one as well as in the last sentence of paragraph two adopt an obviously goal-oriented interpretation of the otherwise neutral "working definition".[34] This shows which kind of competition culture the ICN regards as preferable. However, it also deprives the term "competition culture" of its neutrality. Considering the differing views of what competition is and what competition should achieve,[35] this appears an unfortunate move.

---

[31] ICN 2015, supra note 10, pp. 8, 9; compare also Caraganciu/Carare, supra note 17, p. 186: "To promote a culture of competition …".

[32] Infra, D.

[33] Discussed in the following.

[34] Compare similar Ki Jong Lee, supra note 23, p. 33: "The lack of a competition culture has often been considered the central impediment to promoting competition.".

[35] Compare supra, I; Rodriguez/Coate, supra note 4, p. 371; Cheng, supra note 2, pp. 465, 489: " … myriad divergences among jurisdictions, or even within individual jurisdictions, on some of the fundamental aspects of competition law …".

A qualitative understanding of the term "competition culture" is also adopted by others. Commentators talk for example about "weakness of competition culture",[36] "relatively weak competition culture",[37] "weak competition culture among government officials",[38] "strong competition culture",[39] "stronger competition culture",[40] "new culture of competition",[41] "cultural textures which are not so competition friendly",[42] "competition friendly cultures"[43] and "competition-friendly traditions".[44] However, all these statements normally fail to clarify which criteria they have adopted in each case to make such assessments.

This article aims to explore the relationship between competition culture and Competition Advocacy. The focus is on the question if the instruments of Competition Advocacy [45] are really appropriate to promote or even develop a particular competition culture. For this purpose it seems crucial to adopt a neutral definition of the term "competition culture" which is based on an understanding of "culture" as such.

The term "culture" is rather disputed and publications discussing the question what culture is and what it means fill rows of bookshelves in many libraries. However, it appears that as the smallest common denominator culture can be defined as the entirety of historically developed values, attitudes and meanings which are adopted and shared by the members of a particular society and which govern their material and immaterial way of life.[46] Taking this basic understanding as a starting point in the following

---

[36] Ki Jong Lee, supra note 23, p. 34; compare Mehta, supra note 10, p. 3.
[37] Ki Jong Lee, ibid, p. 39.
[38] ICN 2015, supra note 10, p. 10.
[39] Ibid, p. 9; compare Mehta, supra note 10, p. 3.
[40] Ki Jong Lee, supra note 23, p. 39.
[41] Ibid, p. 34.
[42] Ibid, p. 49.
[43] Ibid, p. 51.
[44] Ibid, p. 53.
[45] Supra, II.
[46] Monir Tayeb, Cultural Differences across the World, in Monir Tayeb (ed.), International Management (Harlow et. al., 2003), p. 8-27 (10); compare Geert H. Hofstede, Cultures' Consequences: Comparing Values, Behaviours, Institutions and Organizations Across Nations – 2nd ed. (Thousand Oaks: Sage Publications, 2001), p. 46; Geert Hofstede/ Gert Jan Hofstede/Michael Minkov, Cultures and Organizations – Software of the Mind (New York et.al.: McGraw Hill, 2010), p. 4-7; Wolff 2013, supra note 4, p. 10.

competition culture shall be understood as the entirety of the historically developed values, attitudes and meanings in relation to competition and competition rules, which are adopted and shared by the members of a particular society and which determine their competitive behaviour. It is important in this regard, that the meaning of "members of a particular society" should not be restricted to a particular group such as entrepreneurs, managers or government officials. As explained above in the context of the discussion of the term "Competition Advocacy",[47] a particular competition culture is rather the culture of all members of a society which are directly or indirectly involved in market activities.

V. CAN COMPETITION ADVOCACY CREATE A (PERFECT) COMPETITION CULTURE?

A. General

The previous sections have explained how "Competition Advocacy", "Competition Regulation", "Culture" and "Competition Culture" shall be understood for the purposes of this article. This section now explores, if and how Competition Advocacy can promote or even develop a certain, ideally a perfect competition culture. As indicated at the outset, to achieve this study this section shall rely on studies conducted in the area of inter-cultural management and organisational behaviour which have gained major importance since the seventies of the last century.

In the legal area comprehensive studies to generate reliable data regarding the significance of culture are not yet very common. This is rather surprising as discussions of the impact of different and similar "legal cultures"[48] in times of globalisation are very common and one should on the one hand assume that related comments, statements and discussions are

---

[47] Compare supra, II.; from the viewpoint of Competition Advocacy see The World Bank/OECD, supra note 12, p. 8.

[48] Mark Edwin Burge, To Clever by Half: Reflections on Perception, Legitimacy, and Choice of Law Under Revised Article 1 of the Uniform Commercial Code, 6 William & Mary Business Law Review (2015), p. 357 ff.

conducted on a solid basis. It has on the other hand been correctly concluded that it is already very difficult to define the term "legal culture".[49] It appears even more difficult to comment on the significance of particular legal cultures in different societies and on the relationship between legal culture and competition behaviour.

In light of these difficulties this article therefore tries to take a different approach by using relying on the mentioned studies in the areas of inter-cultural management and organisational behaviour to allow a parallel assessment. As will be shown in the following this parallel assessment suggests that the effects of Competition Advocacy in relation to the creation of particular competition culture(s) are much more limited than generally assumed.

B. Excursus I: Culture and Management Approach

It is commonly accepted that culture determines human behaviour. It is one of the main achievements of research in the area of inter-cultural management to have drawn attention to the fact that this also has important implications for the business world. Business is ultimately conducted by people and people are determined by culture. Details are discussed controversially until today, but have led to some commonly acknowledged basic understanding. With the goal to exemplify this basic understanding excerpts of one of the related studies are introduced in the following.[50]

The study was conducted by André Laurent in the beginning of the 1990s. Laurent, now an Emeritus Professor, had taught organisational behaviour at the INSEAD Business School in Fontainebleu, France. In the context of executive trainings he worked with mid- and top-level managers

---

[49] Pitman B. Potter, The Chinese Legal System – Globalization and local legal culture (Abingdon/New York, 2001), p. 6; Alice Erh-Soon Tay, Legal Culture and Legal Pluralism in Common Law, Customary Law and Chinese Law, 26 Hong Kong Law Journal (1996), pp. 206-209; also compare Thomas M. Franck, The Legal Culture and the Culture, 93 American Society of International Law Proceedings (1999), pp. 271-278 (271): "The legal culture is a culture of generality. It is expressed by its commitment to equal and universal application of rights and duties."

[50] For the following also compare Lutz-Christian Wolff, Making Perfect Corporate Governance Rules: Mission Impossible?, Corporate Governance International (Hong Kong), Vol. 7, Issue 3 (September 2004), pp. 6-21.

from all over the world. For his research on inter-cultural management issues he asked these managers to complete a questionnaire which contained more than 50 statements with the request to indicate whether they agree or not.[51] Here are two examples of these statements and the percentages of agreement:[52]

(1) The main reason for having a hierarchical structure is so everybody knows who has authority over whom.

Percentage of agreement per country

1. USA	18 %
2. Germany	24 %
3. Switzerland	25%
4. Sweden	25 %
5. Denmark	35 %
6. Great Britain	38 %
7. Netherlands	38 %
8. France	45 %
9. Italy	69 %

(2) In order to have efficient work relationships, it is often necessary to bypass the hierarchical line.

Percentage of agreement per country

1. Sweden	22 %
2. Great Britain	31 %
3. USA	32 %
4. Denmark	37 %
5. Netherlands	39 %
6. Switzerland	41 %
7. France	42 %
8. Germany	46 %
9. Italy	75 %

---

[51] André Laurent, The Cross-Cultural Puzzle of Global Human Resources, in Vladimir Pucik/Noel M. Tichy/Carole K. Barett (Hsg.), Globalizing Management – Creating and Leading the Competitive Organization (New York: John Wiley & Sons Inc., 1992), pp. 174-184.

[52] Ibid.

As already mentioned, these data represent only a very small part of the findings of Laurent's comprehensive research project. Laurent concluded on the basis of his studies that of all the factors which influence management decisions and -approaches the cultural background of managers is two times more important than any other factor. This means that e.g. age, educational background, current or former management positions or the type of enterprise a manager is currently working for or has worked for in the past are relatively less important for a particular management approach and -style.[53]

Other researchers have questioned if the cultural background is really as important as suggested by Laurent.[54] However, the importance of culture for the management of enterprises has been confirmed by other studies and is nowadays generally acknowledged.[55]

C. Excursus II: Creation of a Successful Organisational Culture

Research projects concerned with organisational behaviour and the significance of culture in this regard have also explored the question, if and how a particular organisational culture can be developed to ensure the success of an enterprise. Such an endeavour would first of all have to define, what amounts to the success of an enterprise. Furthermore, a relationship between the success of an enterprise and management culture must be

---

[53] Ibid, p. 175.

[54] The probably most influential study was the one conducted by Hofstede 2001, supra note 46. Hofstede had worked on data collected between 1967 and 1973 from more than 116,000 employees of different IBM enterprises in 72 countries and the results later on supplemented by his own studies; also compare Geert H. Hofstede/Michael Harris Bond, The Confucius Connection: From Cultural Roots to Economic Growth, 16 Organizational Dynamics (1988), pp. 5-21 (9); Ki Jong Lee, supra note 23, pp. 35 ff.; Hofstede 2001, ibid, had identified the following culture-specific criteria to categorise organisational cultures in different countries": "power distance", "uncertainty avoidance", "individualism/collectivism", "masculinity/femininity", "long-term/short-term orientation"; compare Geert H. Hofstede, National Cultures in Four Dimensions: A Research-based Theory of Cultural Differences Among Nations, 13 International Studies of Management & Organisations (1983), pp. 46- 72; Hofstede/Bond, ibid, pp. 10-14; for the perceived correlation between these criteria and competition regulation see Ki Jong Lee, ibid, p. 39; Ki Jong Lee, Cultures and Cartels: Cross-Cultural Psychology for Antitrust Policies (undated), http://www.luc.edu/media/lucedu/law/centers/antitrust/pdfs/publications/workingpapers/culturep.pdf, p. 3.

[55] Compare, however, Barbara Senior/Stephen Swailes, Organizational Change, 4th ed. (Halow, 2000), p. 147; Reinhard Meckl, Internationales Management (München: Verlag Franz Vahlen, 2006), p. 265; Wolff 2013, supra note 4, p. 11.

established, i.e. it must be asked which organisational culture is most suitable to ensure the success of an enterprise.

Many research projects have identified different types of organisational cultures and their characteristics.[56] These studies also show that particular characteristics of organisational cultures may be regarded from different viewpoints and can also affect the success of an enterprise in different ways. For example, an organisational culture which is characterised by a clear organisational structure with a detailed future business strategy can be inflexible, de-motivating and "uncreative". In contrast, very loose organisational structures, which should not carry these negative connotations, may be regarded as disoriented and leading to chaos. Finally, it must again be considered that the impact of a particular organisational culture depends on the respective environment. In other words, the concept of path dependence is of major importance in this regard.[57] A particular organisational culture may be successful within one particular environment, but fail in another. All this means that it is rather difficult if not impossible, to determine what a "perfect" organisational culture is.

Another, probably even more important aspect in this regard is, that managerial attitudes, approaches and behaviour are to a very large extent determined by the respective managers' cultural background. Studies supporting this conclusion were introduced above.[58] This also means that any artificially created organisational culture can only have a very limited impact on the behaviour of individual managers. Management behaviour is predominantly guided by the individual managers' ideas, values and viewpoints which they have developed during the time of their socialisation, i.e. by their culture.[59] It is consequently widely acknowledged that cultural changes are only possible over a very long period of time.[60]

---

[56] Compare e.g. Meckl, ibid, pointing to the categorisation of organisational cultures into the Germanic type, the Lationo type, the Anglo-Nordic type and the Asian type; Stucke, supra note 16, p. 976.

[57] Supra, I; also compare ICN 2015, supra note 10, p. 9: "What may be considered as a 'strong competition culture' in one jurisdiction may not be feasible or appropriate in another."

[58] Supra, B.

[59] Compare Wolff 2013 supra note 4, pp. 14-15.

[60] Compare Hofstede 2001, supra note 46, p. 36; Ronald F. Inglehart/Wayne E. Baker, Modernization, Cultural Change, and the Persistence of Traditional Values, 65 American Sociological Review (2000), pp. 19-51 (40-42).

"Culture change ... will need either a much longer time period – say, 50 to 100 years – or extremely dramatic outside events."[61]

D. Culture and Competitive Conduct

What does this mean for the relationship between Competition Advocacy and competition culture? As already explained,[62] the creation of a particular competition culture is regarded as one of the main goals of competition advocacy. If the meaning of "competition culture" is not restricted to the pure awareness of competition related facts, but rather understood in a broader, culture-specific sense, then it appears rather questionable if this goal can really be achieved in light of the output of the above-quoted studies.[63]

For the creation of a particular competition culture it must be determined how this competition culture shall look like. It appears that it is commonly assumed that a "perfect" competition culture promotes "perfect" competition and prevents anti-competitive behaviour and related negative consequences.[64] However, a precise definition of a competition culture which is able to achieve exactly this will be very difficult.[65] This is not only because it is disputed what amounts to perfect competition.[66] Furthermore, as in relation to the question determination which organisational culture should be aspired,[67] it is rather questionable which cultural elements can ensure a perfect competition culture.

Competitive behaviour of enterprises is driven by managers and other entrepreneurial actors within particular markets. Competitive behaviour is

---

[61] Hofstede, ibid, p. 36.

[62] Supra, II.

[63] Compare Ki Jong Lee, supra note 23, p. 36-40.

[64] Compare ICN 2015, supra note 10, p. 19: "Competition culture within the business community is important to ensuring anti-competitive conduct and associated harm is avoided in the first place.", p. 23: "Public awareness of competition principles can help discourage anti-competitive conduct by stigmatizing the behavior and creating a pro-competitive social norm. It can also help ensure long-term political support for competition policy and the continued funding of competition agencies."

[65] Compare supra, IV.

[66] Compare supra, I.

[67] Compare supra, D.

therefore a result of the management approaches of individuals which again depends on ideas, attitudes and values of these individuals in relation to competition and competitive behaviour.

The competition culture of a particular society is broader than the competition culture of an enterprise and thus not only determined by managers. In contrast, also the competition related views, attitudes and values of other parties, such as members of competition authorities and other government bodies, of the legislature, judges as well as other legal practitioners and members of the general public as such are important in this regard and form collectively the prevailing competition culture.[68]

As the studies in the area of inter-cultural management imply, competition cultures can be rather different.[69] These differences can relate to specific, but also to in rather basic questions when it comes to determine

"elementary competition policy characteristics, for example, the goal(s) of competition policy, its relation to other political and social goals, the borderline between fair and unfair (legitimate and illegitimate) means of competitive interaction and business behavior, the extent of competition of a coordination device (for instance, with regard to the inclusion of markets for health and education), the degree of intervention and the weight of individual freedom, and so on."[70]

Moreover, the studies in the area of inter-cultural management also reveal the difficulties of attempts to install with success an artificial competition culture. Cultural norms and values are resistant to change.[71] Managers and other parties, whose competition related ideas, attitudes and values collectively form a particular competition culture, will not automatically give up their own cultural identity to adopt another, externally developed culture, even if this is promoted by Competition Advocacy.[72]

[68]   Ibid.
[69]   Compare Cheng, supra note 2, p. 440, 468-470; 484-489; Pape, supra note 3, p. 443.
[70]   Oliver Budzinski, The Governance of Global Competition: Competence Allocation in International Competition Policy (Cheltenham/Northampton: Edward Elgar, 2008), pp. 70-71.
[71]   Cheng, supra note 2, p. 488.
[72]   Compare e.g. Ki Jong Lee, supra note 23, p. 33-34: "In Japan, for example, the influence of the

All this implies that Competition Advocacy is unsuitable to develop a particular competition culture.[73] Anti-competitive behaviour cannot be countered with the tools of Competition Advocacy.

VI. FINAL REMARKS

Compared with tools of competition regulation, Competition Advocacy seems to offer a gentler way to ensure the functioning of markets. A critical assessment of the possible impact of Competition Advocacy on competition culture reveals, however, that the means of Competition Advocacy are rather limited. Competition Advocacy can therefore not replace regulatory measures, i.e. the enactment and implementation of competition laws and regulations, to counter anti-competitive behaviour. Competition Advocacy can of course assume a very important supplementary role in this regard. In particular, Competition Advocacy can make regulation transparent, create awareness and thus a sustainable basis for broad acceptance. However, it is important that this role of Competition Advocacy should not at the same time also be seen as determining the meaning of competition culture.[74]

It has to be acknowledged in this regard that also regulatory measures have certain cultural limits. To be effective regulatory measures must be catered to all potential addressees. This also means that the cultural determination of these potential addressees has to be considered. As in the context of Competition Advocacy it is a rather difficult task what this actually entails.[75] Moreover, in times of globalisation mono-cultural societies do hardly exist while multi-cultural societies become the norm. In multi-cultural societies "perfect" competition regulation means that competition

---

traditional harmonization culture, the preference for stability, and the past memory of economic success hinder people from accepting the new culture of competition."; Akinori Uesugi, How Japan is Tackling Enforcement Activities Against Cartels, 13 George Mason Law Review (2005), pp. 349 -365 (353-356); see, however, Stucke, supra note 16, p. 996: "Some competition agencies attribute their country's weak competition culture in part to inexperienced generalist courts and authorities' and economic agents' lack of acceptance of competition principles."; for the difficulties of generating culture specific data see Cheng, supra note 2, p. 440 ("the most elusive"); Ki Jong Lee, supra note 23, p. 1; Hofstede/Bond, supra note 54, p. 8-9.

[73] Compare Ki Jong Lee, ibid, p. 50: "A nation could maximize citizens' receptiveness to competition policy in the short term by aligning it with its culture."

[74] Supra, IV.

[75] Compare supra, D.

law should address all the different cultural dimensions. In light of the possible diversity this is an impossible task.[76] Regulatory steps either have to be based on the smallest common denominator or they have to ignore certain cultural specifics e.g. by building upon (only) the prevailing culture.[77]

The problems arising out of the different cultural determination of the addressees of regulatory measures are, however, less significant than in the context of Competition Advocacy. This is because Competition Advocacy is based on voluntariness and culture-specific resistance requires much less efforts than in regard to rules and regulations. Ironically this also means that what is normally regarded as the main strength of Competition Advocacy, namely the fact that it is based on voluntariness, now turns out to be its major weak point.

---

[76] Compare Wolff 2004, supra note 50.
[77] Ibid.

REFORM WITHOUT TRANSFORMATION –GLOBALIZATION AND FINANCIAL SUPERVISORY REFORM IN TAIWAN

WEI-TING YEN

ABSTRACT

The primary focus of this paper is to explore how the financial supervisory system in Taiwan has been reformed through the interaction between the international financial community and domestic institutions. The dependent variable in this study is "The Organizational Law of the Financial Supervisory Commission of the Executive Yuan" (FSC).

This paper argues that financial supervisory reform was initiated by the pressure of financial globalization; however, as our field research in policy network has shown, the pressure to reform was not imposed from the outside. Rather, the government began to reform first, anticipating the shocks that globalization might bring. This pre-emptive move represented the government's determination to be well-prepared to join the international financial community. The result of governmental efforts was to push supervisory reform into the political agenda and get support to build a single supervisory agency (the FSC).

While political elites initiated the reform, state bureaucrats were the main agents executing the reform. Financial bureaucrats did not feel the urge to prioritize the reform. Moreover, the main political cleavage in Taiwan did not rest on economic or financial ideology, so neither party viewed financial supervisory reform as a driving issue. There was a lack of political momentum during the reform process, leading to "reform without transformation." The financial supervisory reform remained stuck in the legislative process for eight years before it finally passed due to electoral considerations. In short, even though the reform resulted in the formation of a new organization, in reality little has changed.

I. INTRODUCTION

The New York branch of Mega International Commercial Bank, one of Taiwan's biggest banks, was fined $180 million US dollars by the New York State's financial regulators in August 2016. The wrongdoing was the bank's insufficient regulatory compliance of New York's anti-money laundering laws. The news was shocking to people in Taiwan. For one thing, the fine was large. For another thing, the fine reflected the failure to monitor what were considered high-risk banking behaviors by the international financial community as well as an obvious financial regulatory lapse within the Mega International Commercial Bank. The scandal exposed how insufficient the financial supervisory system is in Taiwan. However, to achieve better financial supervision, a single-bodied Financial Supervisory Commission (FSC) was already established in 2004 that merged all the financial regulatory power into a single agency. In principle, financial supervision should have become more efficient. Yet, in reality, banking scandals and poor compliance with financial regulation still persisted. Significantly, there still remained a gap between domestic and international regulatory standards. The Mega International Commercial Bank compliance violation was just one example of the lack of regulatory integrity.

Why is financial supervision not as effective as it should be in Taiwan? And why is there a gap between domestic and international financial regulatory standards? This article intends to untangle the puzzles behind regulatory reform in Taiwan. This paper attempts to answer the following questions: First, what motivated the financial supervisory reform in Taiwan? More specifically, what motivated Taiwan to set up a single financial supervisory agency? Second, what has changed as a result of the supervisory reform?

I argue that the development of the financial supervisory system in Taiwan was affected by the pressure of financial globalization; however, the pressure to make changes was not facilitated by an outside-in route (Coleman, 1996; Laurence, 2001; Moran, 1991; Vogel, 1996). Rather, Taiwan began reforming in anticipation of the shocks that globalization might bring, especially the shock to financial services resulting from joining the World Trade Organization (WTO). Financial reform for Taiwan, which had long been excluded from the international financial community, was a declaration that it was aligned with international standards. As a result of making this "declaration" to join the international community supervisory reform was pushed on to the political agenda, and the target of this agreed upon reform was to build a single supervisory agency known as the FSC.

However, even though political elites were able to initiate the reform, financial bureaucrats were reluctant to make it a priority agenda item because their regulatory power would be cut once the FSC is established. Moreover, the two largest political parties in Taiwan were largely indifferent toward reform; their primary political divide did not stem from economic or financial issues. Also, importantly, there were no pressure groups in society to oversee the reform. These factors resulted in a lack of political momentum during the reform process. Consequently, the financial supervisory reform was stuck in the legislative process for eight years. The bill finally passed in 2003 due to electoral considerations and a new single organization emerged out of the reform. In reality, however, little has changed since then.

My argument comes after collecting information from two primary sources. First, I conducted in-depth interviews with the policy network involved in the FSC Act, from former senior officials in the Ministry of Finance to legislators. I developed my understanding of the policymaking process as well as perspectives from different political actors. I interviewed twelve individuals: three from Legislative Yuan, who had interests related to FSC business; three from the financial community; two former senior officials in MOF; three current bureaucrats from FSC; and one professor specializing in finance. My second source of information came from printed material; I relied heavily on official government documents and other second-hand materials.

I structured my paper as follows. In Section II, I briefly put Taiwan's financial regulatory reform in the global context. In Section III, I review literature concerning financial regulation in the era of financial globalization;

I outline the contending frameworks that help explain the emerging financial reforms around the world. In Section IV, I explain regulatory reform in Taiwan. Taiwan advanced its reform efforts from the level of financial examination to the level of financial supervision; even so, there are still problems in the process of financial examination. I will demonstrate how the "declaration" of reform assisted in making progress in the area of financial reform. In section V, I assess each alternative explanation mentioned in section II, thereby strengthening my argument. Section VI is the conclusion.

II. TAIWAN'S FINANCIAL REGULATORY REFORM IN CONTEXT

In May 1997, the UK surprised the financial community by announcing the establishment of the Financial Services Authority (FSA), merging nine financial regulatory bodies of the UK into one single entity. Financial supervision would now be independent from the Bank of England (BoE), which had taken charge of this duty for a long time. This transformation was a result of deregulation of the financial markets (Briault, 1999). A distinction in financial markets between the banking, security and insurance industries had become blurred since 1980 as a result of rapid innovation of financial instruments and changing telecommunication technology. In some cases, financial conglomerates had been allowed to emerge without restrictions on their entry into the market; fixed commission on deals had been lifted. The regulatory regime was modified in order to catch up with the changing market, yielding to the rise of another trend called "regulatory reform"(Vogel, 1996) or "regulatory capitalism" (Jordana & Levi-Faru, 2005; 2004). The FSA in the UK exemplified regulatory reform on an institutional level.

Although the UK was not the first country to adopt a single financial regulatory agency, it was indeed the first leading economy to transform its supervisory agency from multiple agencies into one single agency.[1] After the

---

[1] Prior to the UK, three Scandinavian countries, including Sweden, Denmark and Norway, introduced single financial supervisory agency as a response to the increasing integration of financial institutions.

UK adopted a single financial regulatory regime, several countries followed it by implementing the same institutional arrangement. Even when other countries did not adopt a single regulatory agency, they had, to some extent, integrated their institutional base.[2]

Similarly, financial reform in Taiwan paralleled the process in other countries. In 1997, the same year in which the UK transformed its regulatory regime, Taiwan put forth into its policy agenda the idea of single financial regulator. Prior to reform, Taiwan had multiple agencies responsible for financial supervision. Since 1961, the financial regulatory regime had been divided into two parts,[3] with supervisory and administrative power centralized in the Ministry of Finance (MOF),[4] and the examination authority in the Central Bank.[5] Taiwan's new Financial Supervisory Commission (FSC) closely emulated UK's FSC; in both cases financial supervision was consolidated in one agency (The Ministry of Finance & Central Bank, 1997). In addition to Taiwan, both Japan and South Korea undertook similar reforms about the same time. However, compared to other countries which passed reforms rapidly,[6] it took Taiwan seven years (from 1997 to 2003) to finally pass the FSC Act.

III. FINANCIAL GLOBALIZATION AND FINANCIAL REGULATION

Existing literature provides different explanations for the world-wide trend to enact financial regulatory reforms. In this section, I review the existing scholarship on financial globalization and financial regulatory reforms.

---

[2] In 2008, there has been over two-third OECD countries integrating their supervisory systems to some extent, and most of which happened after 1999 (Courtis, 2008).

[3] Due to political reasons, the Central Bank resumed its business in Taiwan after 1961.

[4] Originally, MOF did not supervise securities industry because there was barely a capital market under the state's strict restriction. However, after capital markets grew bigger, MOF took over the responsibility of securities supervision from Ministry of Economic Affairs in 1981, and built the Securities and Exchange Commission (SEC).

[5] The power of Central Bank was actually authorized by MOF, for MOF was short of adequate professionals at that time to conduct the examination business on its own.

[6] Japan passed the Financial Supervisory Agency Act in 1997; and South Korea passed the Act for the Establishment of Financial Supervisory Organizations in 1997 too.

Regulatory Convergence or Divergence

Karl Polanyi (1944) argued half a century ago in *Great Transformation* that the rise of market society, an economic system that exchanges goods through price mechanisms, destroyed the basic social order that had existed throughout all earlier history. Since the 19th century, the self-regulating market has dominated the social order and demanded the expansion of market forces. Polanyi's delineation seems to fit the world after the Bretton Woods System was established. With financial globalization underway, a thread of literature has emerged arguing that globalization has constrained policy makers (Cerny, 1994; Rosenau, 2003; Strange, 1996).

Two arguments differ in the extent to which they put forth that the state has been constrained. Philip Cerny (1994) argues that technological innovation has brought about a reduction in transaction costs while amplifying price sensitivity; in this way, technological innovation has severely undermined the capacity of the state due to the possibility of "regulatory arbitrage." Unlike Cerny, who points to structural change in order to explain the limitation of a state, Susan Strange (1996) argues that the constraints facing some states can best be explained by uneven power distribution in international relations. The U.S. is still the biggest voice in policy arena due to its a power to issue credit in the international system.

Those who agree with the argument that states are being constrained under globalization usually agree that regulatory efforts would tend to conform. When speaking of technological innovation, Cerny (1994) pointed out that financial regulation would converge to the same standard because regulatory arbitrage tends to the encourage similar price sensitivity. The "Unholy Trinity" between exchange rate, interest rate and capital flow, a theory by Robert Mundell, also underscores the impossibility for central banks to make individualized policies. Market forces drive regulatory convergence; thus, international pressure, as well as the tendency of states to similarly pursue efficiencies, both would tend to explain and support the notion of regulatory convergence.

However, Karl Polanyi's argument in *Great Transformation* contains not only the idea of a self-regulating market force, but also the notion of a spontaneous impulse by society to protect itself, defending against the destruction brought by market forces. History is shaped by these interwoven forces. The sometimes-destructive result of market forces justifies a state's intervention into the market and also explains the potentially divergent path of regulation. This thread of literature can be traced back to Theda Skocpol (1985), who emphasizes the existence of state autonomy and state capacity, and argues that the state should be excluded from the society (Weiss, 1998; Evans, 1992, 1995). In the context of East Asia, the developmental state is at the focus of state-center researchers. They argue that pilot agencies in East Asian countries lead the region to rapidly develop their economies (Wong, 2004). State intervention, as opposed to a lassie-faire approach, is regarded as key to developing East Asia.

Regarding financial regulation, Elizabeth Thurbon (2001) argues that financial liberalization can be carried out in such a way so as both to enhance the capacity of the state to effectively intervene in the economy, as well as to promote financial stability and economic growth. In other words, the role of the state cannot be neglected. William Coleman (1996) also studies how a state transforms itself under financial globalization. He concludes that a state's past experience would affect its later transformation. Rosenbluth and Schaap (2003) explore financial regulation through an electoral system. They find that governments in centripetal systems are more likely to force banks, rather than consumers of banking services, to pay for financial system stability.

In summary, it remains a contentious issue whether or not financial regulations of various states tend to follow a similar converging direction. There is also much disagreement about whether or not there tends to be a convergence with respect to financial supervision. In the next part, I introduce some of the latest arguments on the adoption of single financial supervisory agency.

Contending Frameworks for Single Supervisory Agency

The existing frameworks for supervision integration can be separated into four categories: *pursuit for efficiency, international pressure, partisan politics,* and *politics of ideas.* These four explanations can be divided into two broader groups: functionalism and instrumentalism. Functionalism views financial reforms as a result of substantial needs, such as the need to improve of supervisory efficiency or a necessary response to market transformation; Instrumentalism, on the other hand, is the idea that reforms, while necessary, need not come about for financial reasons. Rather, reforms can be "instruments" for achieving non-financial goals, such as the consolidation of the legitimacy of a ruling party. Arguments for the need for efficiency and influence of international pressure are functionalist, whereas instrumentalist arguments would point to partisan politics and politics of ideas.

Functionalism

Pursuit of Efficiency. When proposing a single regulatory agency the most common argument centers around the pursuit of economic efficiency. (Abrams & Taylor, 1999; Briault, 1999; Padoa-Schioppa, 2004; Quaglia, 2008). The proponents of a single regulatory agency argue that the integration of the financial markets has resulted in a structural change in the ability to carry out financial supervision. The regulatory structure should be unified, they argue, because financial integration has resulted in blurring the distinction between bank, securities and insurance. A unified regulatory structure is required in order to maintain the ability to supervise. Unifying supervision will not only reduce supervisory costs, but it will also lead to the avoidance of potential conflict that may result from different agencies supervising the same financial business(Abrams & Taylor, 1999; Briault, 1999).

International Pressure. Another functionalist argument focuses on outside-in pressure. Three external pressures can be brought up easily when explaining the workings of the financial regulatory institution:

Americanization, Europeanization[7] and the Basel agreement from the Bank of International Settlement (Basel I & II). Though different in name and appearance, they all exert external pressure on a national political community. As Moran (1991, 1994) described clearly, the U.S., because it dominated the financial sector over other countries, demanded regulatory hegemony around the world, thereby motivating other countries to reform in order to be in compliance. Henry Laurence (2001) proposed four possible ways in which international pressure would be transmitted to domestic economies. Lucia Quaglia (2008) looks at how two international factors, "Internationalization of financial activities" and "EU financial integration", were antecedent variables influencing institutional reform of financial supervision in Europe. In short, these external pressures are activated by changing payoff structures. Governments start to initiate reforms under international competitive pressure because they understand the new potential benefit of financial regulation (Simmons & Elkins, 2004) .

Instrumentalism

Partisan Politics. Westrup (2007) sheds a light on the preferences of domestic elites and their influence on changes in financial supervision. Westrup argues that the underlying logic of creating a single powerful regulator lies in partisan politics; external factors served as catalysts to activate reform. By comparing the change in regulatory regimes in the UK and Germany, he points out the main reason for the creating a single financial regulatory agency was that politicians hoped to enhance the accountability of financial businesses. Due to the increasing financial risk, politicians demanded a single agency that would be accountable for all financial issues: In this way, financial regulation became a hot policy issue. Thus, reformers sought to achieve political accountability rather than financial goals.

---

[7] I put Europeanization here because it has been widely mentioned as an important factor accounting for the financial transformation in Europe. However, it is a context Taiwan does not fit in.

Symbolic Declaration. The relationship between ideas and institutions has been examined extensively in the area of economic or financial policy (Hall, 1993; McNamara, 1998). Vivien and Westrup (2008) use discursive institutionalism as they focus on the financial regulatory in particular. They want to understand, through ideas or discourses, financial regulatory reform in the U.S. and the UK in order to explain policy change. They show that there are two dominant discourses relating to financial regulation: the neoliberal discourse and the populist discourse. Vivien and Westrup show how these two sets of ideas compete with each other. In this way, they explain how ideas are the fundamental factor that separate the U.S and UK with respect to financial regulatory reform. McNamara's (2002) research on the independence of central bank demonstrates a similar causal mechanism. She argues that delegation has important legitimizing and symbolic properties for political leaders, especially in times of economic uncertainty; the diffusion of central bank independence is the result of institutional isomorphism.

IV. FINANCIAL SUPERVISORY REFORM IN TAIWAN

This section focuses on financial reform specifically in Taiwan. I first summarize the regulatory structure existent before the reform, and then I point out what is the main problem inside our system. Next, I examine the reform and I pay particular attention to the question of why the reform took hold. Lastly, I will investigate what has changed since reform.

Multiple Regulatory Bodies and the Problem of Financial Examination

Financial supervision consists of two parts: daily financial administration and financial examination. Financial administration refers to prudential regulation and the conduct of business regulation on daily base; financial examination refers to the occasional investigation of financial institutions to make sure that prudential regulation has, in fact, been implemented. Both parts complement each other in completing financial supervision. Before the supervisory reform, one of the main characteristics of Taiwan's financial supervision was its division of labor among multiple regulatory agencies. The division of labor happened in three aspects: between financial administration and financial examination; within financial examination; and within financial administration.

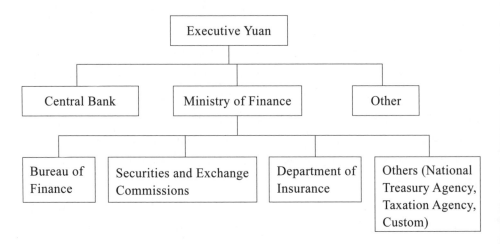

Briefly speaking, the structure of financial supervision in Taiwan before the reform is illustrated in figure 1, with the MOF responsible for financial administration and the Central Bank in charge of financial examination. This was the division of labor at the first level. Moreover, within the MOF, there were three sub agencies corresponding to different aspects of financial administration. The division was institutional-based, meaning that supervision was conducted in line with financial sectors. As for financial examination, even though the Central Bank was accountable, its examination power was later partitioned into more organizations due to the expansion of financial markets,[8] dividing the process of financial examination as well. The division within the MOF, and that within the financial examination,

---

[8]   From 1962 to 1971, only the Central Bank had the power to conduct financial examination. From 1971 to 1985, Central Bank delegated Taiwan Cooperative Bank (TCB) to do the examination of local financial institutions while it retained examination power over the rest of the financial institutions. Because Central Deposit Insurance Corporation (CDIC) was set up in 1985 to prevent systemic panic in financial market, it was assigned some degree of examination power too (Though according to Article 21 of the Deposit Insurance Act, it power cannot be activated without the approval of the Central Bank). In 1991, MOF's Department of Monetary Affairs was upgraded to Bureau of Monetary Affairs, and started taking responsibility of financial examination. As a result, from 1991 to 1995, there were four organizations in total responsible for financial examination. By the time FSA was established in 2004, there are still three organizations separately responsible for examination duty — namely Central Bank, CDIC and the Bureau of Monetary Affairs.

constitute the second level. The multiple-level regulatory structure had not changed at all from 1961 until the eve of financial reform.

In Taiwan, financial examination had always been the core of problem because of the long-term inadequate resources. Every time a financial crisis or a scandal erupted, concern for more prudential regulation would follow. For example, after several Trust and Investment Companies (TIC) scandals erupted in early 1980,[9] the government started to limit the business scope of TICs and to tighten financial examination of this type of financial institution. In another instance, the Tenth Credit Co-op (TCC) scandal in 1985 led directly to the establishment of Central Deposit Insurance Corporation (CDIC); the purpose this time was to strengthen financial examination and to prevent systemic panic when future scandals occurred (Cheng, 1993, p. 88; Lin, 2007, p. 189). In other words, regulatory improvements usually followed financial turmoil.

The fundamental reason for inadequate resources dedicated to financial examination was the speedy expansion of financial institutions, especially after the admission of new private banks in 1991. When we look at the statistics regarding financial examinations in 2000 (Table 1), we can see how insufficient were the financial examination. First of all, with the exception of the CDIC and the Central Bank, the number of examination remains low. Moreover, the low number of penalties also stands out as a sign of ineffectiveness of financial examination. As a result of rapid expansion without stringent financial examination, there have been a number of bank runs.

---

[9] Under the fact that entry into financial market in Taiwan was severely limited, TIC was a special permission operated by private financiers. Originally, it was permitted to provide long-term credit and to facilitate economy. However, private financiers, after being repressed for so long, took this chance to expand their financial powers by over investing on real estate and manufacturing sector, thus causing bank runs because of lack of liquidity.

Institutions	Number of Institutions that Should Be Examined (A)	Number of Institutions that is Examined (B)	The Ration of Examination (B/A)	Number of Cases Getting Penalties	Ration of Penalties (C/B)
Bureau of Finance	1005	149	0.15	103	0.04
Central Deposit Insurance Corporation (CDIC)	2369	1821	0.77		
Central Bank	1434	750	0.52		
Securities and Exchanges Commission	1752	8	0.004	154	19.25
Department of Insurance	59	14	0.24	14	1

The latest regulatory reform also stemmed from a major financial crisis, following the pattern that remedies always follow crises. Starting from 1995, financial scandals have erupted in several local financial institutions partly due to a lack of examination. While scandals caused systemic bank runs and a sense of distrust in the financial market, the ruling party (KMT government) initiated a financial examination reform in 1995. The reform targeted the need to centralize examination authority in order to make financial examinations more effective. The committee reached the consensus quickly after a crisis.

A Progression of Reform from Financial Examination to Financial Supervision

Clearly, Taiwan's financial reforms did not encompass the entirety of financial supervision; rather, they focused only on financial examination. The focus of this part is how the reform was implemented. First, I will describe the transition as well as identify the main political actors, and then I will analyze the underlying political logic behind the transition.

The establishment of the Financial Supervisory Agency (FSA) in the UK certainly influenced Taiwan's decision to broaden the scope of its reform; the idea of establishing a Financial Supervisory Commission (FSC) was on the table in 1997, the same year that the UK adopted its single financial regulatory agency. The former director general of banking bureau at MOF mentioned the effect of UK's reform on reshaping the policy agenda in Taiwan, and it is clear that UK motivated Taiwan to enlarge the extent of its own plans:

During the reform process, before completing the idea of the unification of financial examination, there was this speech by Gordon Brown, chancellor at that time, in the Parliament in the UK, hoping to promote the unification of financial supervision.....the UK can be taken as the starting point....several countries promote this trend following the UK....It was about this time when the UK started selling financial supervision unification that some people in the country began to promote this trend as well....after people promote for the unification of financial supervision, the policy issue was switched from financial examination to the broader financial supervision. (Interview)

UK's reform aroused the attention of political elites not only inside the MOF but also inside the broader bureaucracy loop. Both the Council for Economic Planning and Development (CEPD), a pilot agency guiding long-term economic development in Taiwan (Wade, 2004; Weiss, 1998), as well as Taiwan's Premier, noticed this seeming irreversible trend. As CEPD sensed this on-going trend, they asked the MOF to reconsider the scope of their planned reform. In a report that the CEPD sent to the MOF, the CEPD pointed out the importance of the trend:

The research outcome should refer to the financial supervisory development that is under way worldwide. In order to enhance the supervisory efficiency, we should not only consider the unification

of financial examination but also the supervisory system overall.
(Weiyuanhui, 1997b)

Moreover, the attitude of Vincent Hsiao, Premier of the Executive Yuan at that time, demonstrated a similar tone. Particularly when he discovered that Japan and South Korea were undergoing similar reforms, he found it not only appealing but also necessary to review the whole supervisory system. His concerns were vividly displayed in a talk Hsiao gave during a weekly meeting:

The establishment of financial regulatory system is vital for financial reform, so MOF should fit our regulatory norms for the international community. It is worth consulting that the international community has developed their regulatory regimes toward supervisory unification, including banking, securities and insurance in one agency. Referring to our financial supervisory unification scheme, we have put it as our priority project this year. As a result, MOF and Central Bank should cooperate together and have your proposal ready on assigned timing(Xingzhengyuan, 1997.11.06)

In summary, UK's reform along with the push from CEPD and Taiwan's Premier changed the scope of reform, expanding it from financial examination to financial supervision.

In order to account for the progression of regulatory reform from examination to supervision, we must consider the preference of political elites. However, we should separate the views of daily regulators from those of other bureaucrats in the government, because the two groups held different preferences at the time. Apparently, before the UK's reform the bureaucrats in the MOF focused on the issue of financial examination. The FSC Act in Taiwan emerged only after the top level political elites were made aware of international trend

Let's first examine the preference of the regulators in the MOF. For regulators supervising the market on daily basis, their main concern was the lack of financial examination and the situation of over-banking. For one thing, banking failures that had began in 1995 posed a need for them to review the flaws in financial examination system; for another thing, the regulators confronted a real challenge to control the over-banking situation, which was the consequence of hasty financial liberalization.[10] For the regulators, the integrity of the financial markets was much more urgent than was the need to unify financial examinations; they saw the immediate systemic risk that could explode anytime. This concern was evident when the former director general of banking bureau in MOF brought up the policy priority at that time:

> *From MOF's perspective, the priority we have in mind at that time was to pass "Resolution Trust Corporation (RTC) Act", which was a vital fund for dealing with troubled financial institutions. After that, "Financial Institution Merger Act and Financial Holding Company Act" was our second priority, for these two Acts were also important in resolving the over-banking environment. "Financial Supervisory Commission Act" was not on my list at that time.*

For the high level political elites in the MOF as well as those in the CEPD, their ideas about reform were different. They were not in a position of regulating the daily market; furthermore, those political elites were proposing a greater blueprint of the financial market reform. Following President Li Teng-Hui's policy, Paul Chu, the minister of the MOF at that time, once talked about the MOF's proposal for promoting Taiwan as the Asia-Pacific Financial Center, and how the financial supervision reform should be incorporated into this larger picture. From his talk, it is clear that the financial supervisory reform was the first step to joining the international community:

---

[10] The over-banking situation was a result of the political decision that permitted new private banks in 1991. The KMT government permitted too many banks at one time, yielding fierce competition between banks. After the domestic financial crisis hit Taiwan in 1998, officials in MOF were urged to tackle this "over-banking" problem and improve the financial environment.

The current policy focus of the Ministry of Finance (MOF)......in on building Taiwan as the Asia-Pacific Financial Center as well as the Asset Management Center...therefore, MOF initiated a lot of reforms – such as the modification of Banking Law to broaden and deepen the business of domestic banks, the privatization of state-owned banks, the setup of mid-term and long-term capital market, the maintaining of financial order and the unification of financial examination – and these are the prerequisites before internationalization. We have to build all these necessary conditions before the full openness of our financial market in 2000 to avoid troubles. (Li Xue Wen, 1997)

The preferences of high level political elites accounted for the rapid embrace of financial reform, and their collective preferences resulted in a general excitement about promoting Taiwan as the regional financial center. Another urgent challenge facing Taiwan at that time was joining the World Trade Organization (WTO) in 2000. The financial service sector would, after operating under the "commanding height" of the state for so many years (Cheng, 1993), suddenly after joining the WTO be confronted with an open market with large foreign competitors. This aroused an even more pressing desire for Taiwan to follow the international trend. As a result, once the upper political elites found that the UK had initiated a reform that was then followed by Taiwan's neighboring countries, they decided that Taiwan should emulate the reform as well. It was their desire to be with the trend that was a catalyst for supervisory reform efforts.

In this case, we see that state is not a monolithic entity, as those who put-forth the state-center argument would like you to believe. Even when people belong to the same organization, such as the MOF, they may hold differing opinions. More specifically, while the top political elites were in favor of the supervisory reform, it is likely that the daily regulators did not feel the same sense of urgency. This was the case in Taiwan and explains why and how financial reform was carried out.

FSC as Policy Issue and the Creation of FSC

Once a higher level of reform was initiated, the MOF proposed that there would be a new organization called Financial Supervisory Commission (FSC), which would take charge of all financial issues. This new agency would be under the MOF, reporting to the minister of finance. The daily regulators, however, designed the scheme so as to retain their day-to-day power. First of all, they put FSC under the MOF's governance, allowing the MOF to retain its higher governmental authority, while at the same time establishing its control of financial matters. Moreover, setting up a new administrator inside the MOF meant that they had implemented an organizational change rather than real institutional reform;[11] there was "reform" with manifest alternation, but little substantial change.

Before going into the political process, one question worth answering is how other political actors responded to these changes. Here, I will introduce several more political stakeholders, illustrating, first, how each of them reacted to this reform; then, I will discuss how their attitudes would end up affecting the implementation efforts. I will start with the Central Bank, and then move into political parties including KMT and DPP.

Surprisingly, there was no conflict between the Central Bank and the MOF during the financial supervision reform in Taiwan. In some European countries, because central banks take part of the responsibility (sometimes all of the responsibility) for bank supervision, the integration of supervision inevitably curtails Central Bank's power. This usually results in the resistance on the part the Central Banks. However, unlike the Central Banks in those countries, the Central Bank in Taiwan remained detached from the political process while setting up the FSC. One possible explanation is that although some of the Central Bank's examination power was curtailed after establishing the FSC, Taiwan's Central Bank still retained supervisory power

---

[11] Following Douglas North's (North, 1990)definition, institution refers to the "rule of game", and organization refers to the player in the game. When I said the reform was limited to organizational level, it meant that the rule of supervision stays the same, only players under the rule change.

in the name of monetary stability, which would be referred to as "project examination power."

Nevertheless, even if the Central Bank did not have any incentive to thwart the reform, one wonders why it did not choose, instead, to augment its own power. The underlying answer could be traced back to the duties the Central Bank as defined under the authoritarian regime. Because financial stability was one of the most important goals at that time, the KMT government separated monetary policy from other financial tasks and assigned its stability as the main duty of Central Bank. As a result, the Central Banks was not responsible for financial supervision. This separation of power was a critical aspect of the government. The Central Bank had accumulated its reputation for independence and retained its power because of this separation from financial policies. Therefore, even though Central Bank worked together with the MOF to design from the scratch the new FSC, it never intended to obtain political authority of any kind.

The major political parties in Taiwan also did not show much interest in the direction of financial regulatory reform. There are two explanations for this apathy. First of all, the social cleavage in Taiwan is traditionally not cut along economic lines, but rather has mostly to do with national identity. KMT and DPP have distinguished themselves on the basis of national identity, not by class or religion. As a result, there is no major difference in economic ideology between the two political parties. Both parties pursue economic development and generally support big business. That is why they showed no distinct inclination or interest in policy around the creation of the FSC.

The second explanation emerged through the comparison with European countries. European countries had an urgent need to make finance more accountable because they are facing a risk in financial markets as a result of privatization. A single accountable agency was essential (Westrup, 2007) in order to protect consumers and the public pension fund from fluctuations in the financial market, However, the financial market in Taiwan has never been as open as that in Europe, thus the risk resulting from privatization has not been as large either. In short, the political parties were not compelled to demand a single agency responsible for all financial tasks because neither felt great risk of the market or fear that they might be held accountable in the event of financial loss.

After the FSC became a policy issue, there were still several disputes before the law was passed; all of these disputes centered around how the FSC might be structured. At first, a disagreement centered on whether the FSC should be under the authority of the MOF or whether it should be parallel. Premier Hsiao settled the dispute by deciding that the FSC ought to be parallel to MOF in organizational structure. The second dispute involved the nature of the FSC; specifically, whether or not it should be an independent agency. This dispute has still not been solved even after the establishment of the FSC. The third disagreement was about how to generate the commissioners for the FSC. Each party preferred different methods according to their own political orientation. For the ruling party, they preferred that the commissioners be appointed by the president; for the opposition party, they preferred the commissioners be decided by the parliament.

There were two implications associated with the disputes about organizational structure. First of all, disagreement about organizational structure revealed the reality that reform did not relate to any major shift in the rules of the game. Government documents (Gazette, 2001-05-30) show that legislators fought over issues that had nothing to do with the transformation of supervisory goals or methods. Rather all sides were concerned, because these new positions possessed a great deal of power, namely about how to appoint commissioners who might push forward their own political agenda.

In addition, political actors on both sides were generally quite ignorant about the bigger issue at hand, and therefore they were satisfied arguing about organizational structure. None of the political actors really cared about the progress of reform because there were no real ideological conflicts of interest between them. Nobody disagreed about the idea of setting up the FSC. As a result of their lack of disagreement, no substantive change was made in financial supervision and the reforms were pushed off again for several years.

The FSC Act was finally passed in 2003, seven years after it was first brought up. It was a time, just before the presidential election of 2004, when both the KMT and the DPP suddenly had incentives to pass the FSC Act. For some in charge in the ruling DPP, the formation of a new agency would represent an achievement for President Chen's reelection campaign. The KMT, the opposition party at that time, was hopeful about winning the upcoming election and therefore saw an incentive of being able to nominate the commissioners of this new agency. In other words, there was a electoral logic for championing the Act.

The Outcome: What has changed?

There are three prevailing perspectives about what has changed as a result of the reform. First of all, in terms of the original goal of unifying the financial examination--—it appears to have been achieved. Both financial supervision and financial examination were integrated into the new FSA. However, unification guaranteed nothing about the effectiveness of financial examination. The inefficiency financial examination was due in part to the lack of experts in financial examination; so, we should also evaluate the reform in this respect. Yang (2009) found that even though there are 1056 official positions in the FSA, there are only 819 people working for this new organization. The FSA is having trouble in recruiting new experts, because most of the government officials prefer joining the Central Bank, which has a better reputation. This explains the concern about the possibility for real improvement in the area of financial examination.

Secondly, if we view the FSA from the organizational perspective, we would find that little has been changed even with regard to organizational structure. Figure 2 illustrates the new structure of financial supervision. If we compare this figure with figure 1, we can find mostly similarity. Put another way, it seems that we only gave the MOF a new title, while we kept everything else the same. When the UK merged their regulatory agencies, they soon thereafter transformed modes of regulation into function-based modes. Taiwan still conducted financial supervision with a functionalist approach, as opposed to the UK that was institutional. This raises doubts about how effectively FSC can reduce costs and avoid business redundancy. In fact, throughout all the interviews from former senior officer to current workers in the FSC, none of the interviewees sensed any real change in practices after the establishment of FSC. A senior bureaucrat even said that "the only change that took place was the signboard outside the door". In this respect, it is questionable if there has been any substantial change at all.

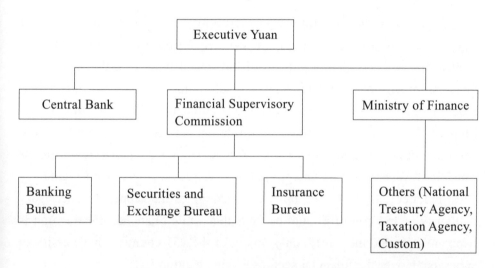

Finally, in the UK's experience, what followed the FSA Act was the Financial Services and Markets Act (FSMA), which required a broader transformation in the laws that govern financial tasks. The organizational change of FSA along with the fundamental transformation of FSMA led the UK to convert their supervision completely from an institutional-based method to risk/functional-based method. However, a similar Act in Taiwan still lies in the draft stage, even after five years the establishment of the FSA.

Laws concerning the transaction of financial activity, therefore, are vital catalyzing components that made financial regulatory reform complete. This is what is missing in Taiwan. Barth (2006) clearly points out how important a step like the FSMA is, *"even though there may be an integrated financial supervisor, there still may be separate laws governing the activities of different financial institutions."* If we have to evaluate the efficacy of this policy, Taiwan created a structure with no subsequent law to support it.

V. ALTERNATIVE EXPLANATIONS

In this section, I will examine some possible alternative explanations for the movement for supervisory integration of the financial sector. I aim to validate my argument through rejecting other alternative explanations.

I begin with the argument of efficiency, which emphasizes that supervisory integration is a necessary response to financial market transformation. The main argument of those who point to efficiency is that financial integration would necessarily result in unified financial supervision. Examining more closely, we can find this argument is still a contentious one. Empirically, there is no definite causal relation between financial integration and the unified financial supervision. Various studies demonstrate dissimilar causality (Westrup, 2007; Quaglia, 2008). Moreover, there is no regulatory "best practice". Barth (2006, pp. 92-96) examines the scope of Supervisory Authority in 151 countries, and he finds that while financial globalization is happening around the world, only 46 out of the 151 countries have assigned supervision over the financial sector to a single authority.[12]

If we consider Taiwan's case again, we would note that even after the establishment of the FSC, it was far from close to reaching its claimed goal of supervisory efficiency. Even though Taiwan set up the FSC as a new agency, there has not been much change in supervision because the supervisory mode remained institutional-based, meaning that supervision was conducted in line with financial sectors. However, the definition of unification of financial supervision is a functional-based supervision, because such a supervision requires that it be conducted in line with financial

---

[12] The specific number might even lower because the author considered that the answer of a few countries might be questionable. To fully capture the scope of a supervisory authority, one must consult the laws of individual country as well (Barth, et al., 2006).

products or activities. This better counteracts the blurred boundaries in the financial market.

A second contending argument, also a functionalist one, is that international pressure has forced countries to adopt unified financial supervision. Possible pressures are Americanization, Europeanization[13] and Basel I & II. However international pressure alone cannot fully explain why Taiwan set up the FSC; in fact, Taiwan actually followed opposite trends in the financial sector. While Taiwan embraces the single supervisory system following the UK's lead, Taiwan also passed the "Financial Conglomerate Act" that permited cross-selling in banking, securities and insurance soon after USA abolished the "Glass-Steagall Act". In other words, we cannot single out one international factor that accounted for Taiwan's reform.

The only international pressure that may have effected Taiwan is the Basel Accord. Taiwan does follow the Basel I & II whenever there are new regulations passed in the Basel committee. Moreover, Basel is the model to follow by several government-initiated financial committees. How this outside pressure would have been transmitted to Taiwan is an interesting question, because Taiwan was not a member country and there has no legal obligation to follow the Accord. Chey (2007) argues that the adoption of the Basel Accord by these non-member countries came as a result of regulatory authorities' concern about the potential risk to foreign markets by closure of noncompliant banks. That is to say, the concern of political elites explains the compliance with the Basel Accord and points to the logic underlying the move to financial supervisory reform in Taiwan.

Finally, I want to examine the argument of partisan politics. According to Westrup (2007), he argues that partisan politics accounts for the creation of single financial regulator, and he points out that the main reason lies in the fact that politicians hope to enhance the accountability of the financial business, especially in an era of great financial risk. Westrup uses the UK's experience as evidence for his argument, contending that the Labour party

---

[13] I put Europeanization here because it has been widely mentioned as an important factor accounting for the financial transformation in Europe. However, it is a context Taiwan does not fit in.

and the Conservative party proposed different institutional designs for financial regulation because of their distinct party preferences. As a result, the FSA Act passed only when a Labour government was in office.

Taiwan's story cannot be explained by such a partisan narrative. Major political parties in Taiwan showed no difference in their preference toward the design of financial regulatory agencies. Moreover, both parties even ignored the reform, which resulted as a key factor in the lagging the reform process. I have already demonstrated why partisan politics cannot explain the process of financial reform in Taiwan.

VI. CONCLUSION

The aim of this article is to explain the determinant that drove Taiwan to reform its supervisory framework, by setting up a new Financial Supervisory Commission aimed to govern financial tasks. From empirical evidence collected through in-depth interviews, we now know that political elites responded to the pressure of financial globalization, thereby initiating interest in financial regulatory reform. As noted above, the underlying impetus to reform was to "declare" that Taiwan was ready to globalize.

I have tried to untangle a number of problems in this paper. As I investigated what motivated financial reform in Taiwan and what caused the reform to follow the UK's experience, I found that concerns of Taiwan's political elites were critical: They desired a more solid financial environment and believed that financial reform was the way to ensure that stability. How the political elites perceived international trends was a key factor in setting up the FSC Act and forcing it into the policy agenda. Both Japan and South Korea had adopted regulatory reform in 1997; therefore, there was an atmosphere of acceptance of regulatory reform—that a new supervisory agency was desirable. Political elites understood the possible shocks that globalization might bring. Shocks might have come also from the pressure of joining WTO as well as from the reforms Taiwan's neighboring countries were undertaking. The influence of cultural peers definitely affected Taiwan's economic policy, initiating the process of financial reform in Taiwan (Simmons and Elkins's 2004)

After establishment of the FSC, the remaining puzzle was what had actually changed as a result of the financial reform? Empirical evidence shows that there was not much change at all. Because the MOF did not view the regulatory reform as their priority, they chose to limit the change to the organizational level. This decision affected the extent and the scope of reform; it also reflected the attitude of both political parties. There were no serious conflicts of interest among domestic political actors due to the inherently restrictive extent of the reform. As a result, the financial supervisory reform was stuck in the legislative process for eight years before finally passing due to electoral considerations. In appearance, a new single organization emerged out of the reform; but there is no substantive change. It had become a reform without any transformation.

Reference

Abrams, R. K., & Taylor, M. M. (1999). *Issues in the Unification of Financial Sector Supervision*, International Monetary Fund.

Barth, J. R., Gerard Caprio, J., & Levine, R. (2006). *Rethinking Bank Regulation: Till Angels Govern*. New York: Cambridge University Press.

Briault, C. (1999) *The Rationale for a Single National Financial Services Regulator*. Occasional Paper Series No2: Financial Service Authority.

Cerny, Philip. 1994. "The dynamics of financial globalization: Technology, market structure, and policy response." *Policy Sciences* 27(4): 319-342.

Cheng, T.-J. (1993). "Guarding the Commanding Heights: The State as Banker in Taiwan." In S. Haggard, C. H. Lee & S. Maxfield (Eds.), *The Politics of Finance in Developing Countries* (pp. 55-92). Ithaca: Cornell University Press.

Chey, H.-K. (2007). "Do markets enhance convergence on international standards? The case of financial regulation." *Regulation & Governance*, 1, 295-311.

Coleman, William D. (1996). *Financial Services, Globalization and Domestic Policy Change*. New York: St. Martin's Press.

Courtis, Neil. 2008. *How Countries Supervise Their Banks, Insurers and Securities Markets*. London: Central Banking Publications.

Evans, Peter. 1992. "The State as Problem and Solution: Predation, Embedded Autonomy, and Structural Change." In The Politics of Economic Adjustment, eds. Stephan Haggard and Robert Kaufman. Princeton, NJ: princeton University Press, 139-181.

Evans, Peter. 1995. Embedded Autonomy: States and Industrial Transformation. Princeton, NJ: Princeton University Press.

Finance, T. M. o., & Bank, C. (1997). *Jinrong Jiandu Guanli Zhidu Kaijin Fang'an* (Improvement Project of Financial Supervision).

Gazette, L. Y. (2001-05-30). "LiFaYuan DiSiJie DiWuHuiQi FaZhi、CaiZheng LiangWeiYuanHui DiErCi LianXi HuiYi JiLu" (The Second Minutes of Joint Meeting of Finance and Law Commission). *Legislative Yuan Gazette* (), 90(41).

Hall, P. (1993). Policy Paradigm, Social Learning, and the State: The Case of Economic Policymaking in Britain. *Comparative Politics*, 25(3), 275-296.

Jordana, J., & Levi-Faru, D. (2005). The ANNALS of the American Academy of Political and Social Science 598.

Jordana, J., & Levi-Faur, D. (Eds.). (2004). *The Politics of Regulation: an institutions and regulatory reform for the age of governance.* MA: Edward Elgar.

Laurence, H. (2001). *Money Rules: The New Politics of Finance in Britain and Japan.* Ithaca: Cornell University Press.

Lin, W.-P. (2007). *Riben, Hanguo, Taiwan Jinrong Tizhi Gaige de Bijiao Zhengzhi Jingji Fenxi* (The Politics of Finance: Japan, South Korea, and Taiwan). National Taiwan University, Taipei.

McNamara, K. R. (1998). *The currency of ideas.* Ithaca, N.Y.: Cornell University Press.

McNamara, Kathleen R. (2002). "Rational Fictions: Central Bank Independence and the Social Logic of Delegation." *West European Politics*, 25(1), 47-76.

Moran, M. (1991). *The Politics of the Financial Services Revolution: The USA, the UK, and Japan.* UK: MacMillan Publishing Company.

Moran, M. (1994). "The State and the Financial Service Revolution: The USA, THE THE UK and Japan." *West European Politics*, 17(3), 158-177.

Moran, M. (2002). "Understanding the Regulatory State." *British Journal of Political Science*, 32(2), 391-413.

North, D. (1990). *Institution, Institutional Change and Ecnomic Performance.* New York: Cambridge University Press.

Padoa-Schioppa, Tommaso. 2004. Regulating Finance : Balancing Freedom and Risk. New York: Oxford University Press.

Quaglia, L. (2008). "Explaining the Reform of Banking Supervision in Europe: An Integrative Approach." *Governance: An International Journal of Policy, Administration, and Institutions*, 21(3), 439-463.

Rosenbluth, F, & Schaap, R. (2003). The domestic politics of banking regulation. *International Organization*, 57(02), 307-336.

Rosenau, James. 2003. "Governance in a New Global Order." In *The Great Transformations Reader: An Introduction to the Globalization Debate*, eds. David Held and Anthony McGrew. Cambridge: Polity Press, 223-233.

Schmidt, V. A., & Westrup, J. (2008). "Taking the State Seriously: Policy, Polity, and the Politics of Ideas and Discourse in Political Economy". Paper presented at the American Political Science Association. Retrieved 2009.10.20, Simmons, B., & Elkins, Z. (2004)." The Globalization of Liberalization: Policy Diffusion in the International Political Economy." *American Political Science Review*, 98(1), 171-190.

Strange, Susan. 1996. *The Retreat of the State: The Diffusion of Power in the World Economy*. New York: Cambridge University Press.

Thurbon, Elizabeth. (2001). Two Paths to Financial Liberalization: South Korea and Taiwan. The Pacific Review, 14(2), 241-267.

Vogel, S. K. (1996). *Free markets, More Rules: Regulatory Reform in Advanced Industrial Countries.* Ithaca: Cornell University Press.

Wade, R. (2004). *Governing the Market: Economic Theory and the Role of Government in East Asian Industrialization* (2 ed.).NJ: Princeton University Press

Weiss, L. (1998). *The Myth of The Powerless State.* Ithaca: Cornell University Press.

Weiyuanhui, X. J. J. (1997a). Fengjiaoyi, Caizhengbu, Zhougyang Yinhand Hyitian Chenbao Jinrong Jiancha Zhidu Yiyuanhua Zhi Xiangguan Yanjiu Chengguo Yian. (The Result of the Unification of Financial Examination)

Weiyuanhui, X. J. J. (1997b). Tai86Tsai77791how (The Document of No. 8607791).

Westrup, J. (2007). "The Politics of Financial Reform in Britain and Germany." *West European Politics*, 30(5), 1096-1119.

Xiao, W.-S. (2000). *Zhongyan Yinhand Yu Jinrong Jianli* (Central Bank and Financial Supervision) .Taipei: YuanZhao.

Xingzhengyuan (1997.11.06). *Yi Ban Hui Yi Jian Yi*, Di 2552 Huiyi Tishi (The Suggestion of the Regular Meeting No. 2552).

Xingzhengyuan (1999). *Xingzhengyuan Di 2629 Ciyuanhui Jueyi* (The Decision of Meeting No. 2629 of Executive Yuan). from http://www.ey.gov.tw/ct.asp?xItem=21354&ctNode=1229&mp=1.

DFS MEGA Consent Order
The Department's Findings
After Examination and Additional Investigation

Mega International

1.   Mega International is based in Taipei, Taiwan. As of year-end 2015, Mega International had 107 domestic branches, and 22 branches,S sub-branches, and 4 representative offices internationally abroad. Mega International also has wholly-owned subsidiaries in Thailand and Canada, bringing the total number of overseas branches and offices to 39 in total.[1]

2.   Mega International has branches located in major U.S. cities, including New York, Chicago, Los Angeles and Silicon Valley. Mega International also has two branches in Panama, one located in the Colon Free Trade Zone ("FTZ") and the other in Panama City.

3.   Mega International has approximately 5,400 employees worldwide. At present, Mega International holds total assets of approximately $103 billion; assets held at Mega-New York are approximately $9 billion. In other words, Mega International is an important institution in the world financial system.

The New York Branch's Poor Internal Controls

4.   From January through March 2015, examiners from DFS conducted an examination of Mega-New York as of September 2014. The examination focused on the New York Branch's risk management, operational controls, compliance, and asset quality. The examiners also evaluated any corrective actions undertaken by management to address the issues from a prior examination conducted as of 20 13.

5.   The Department issued its Report of Examination in February 2016. The Bank submitted its response on March 24, 2016.

6.   What the examiners found was extremely troubling. They discovered numerous deficiencies in Mega-New York's compliance function.

---

[1]   See https:llwww.megabank.com.tw/enJabout.asp.

7. The examination found that the position ofBSAIAML Officer[2] in the New York Branch was held by a person from the Mega International Head Office who posse~sed little familiarity with U.S. regulatory requirements. Similarly, the Chief Compliance Officer ("CCO") for the New York Branch lacked adequate knowledge of U.S. BSAIAML and the Office of Foreign Assets Control of the United States Department of Treasury ("OFAC") requirements, as well as the supervisory expectations relating to these requirements.

8. The examiners also found that the compliance structure at Mega-New York was significantly flawed because the compliance and operational functions were coming led as a result of the dual conflicting responsibilities of certain compliance personnel. For example, the Branch's Vice President and Deputy General Manager also served as the Branch's CCO. The CCO provided support to all Branch operations, including its funding division, the business division, the correspondent banking division, the loan division, and also served as the Information Technology Security Officer.

9. Thus, the New York CCO devoted insufficient time and effort to important compliance responsibilities and, in any event, was conflicted in these responsibilities, since the CCO had a key business and operational role, along with the compliance role.

10. Similarly, the Branch's BSAIAML Officer also served as operations manager of the Business Division; this presented a clear conflict of interest between his compliance and business responsibilities.

11. A clear conflict of interest also existed with respect to the Branch's OFAC Officer, because that person also served as the Operations Manager for the Foreign Correspondent Banking Division.

12. To compound these structural deficiencies, the examination also

---

[2] "BSA" stands for the Bank Secrecy Act, 31 U.S.C. §§ 5311 et seq. "AML" stands for "anti-money laundering."The Bank Secrecy Act, the rules and regulations issued thereunder by the U.S. Department ofthe Treasury, 31 C.F.R. Chap. X; and the requirements of Regulation K ofthe Board of Governors of the Federal Reserve System to report suspicious activity and to maintain an adequate BSAlAML compliance program, 12 C.F.R. §§ 211.24 (f) and 0), all require a robust compliance structure in the New York and other branches of each regulated institution.

discovered that both the BSAIAML Officer and the CCO received inadequate training subsequent to their assignment to Mega-New York.

13.   The examination also uncovered serious deficiencies in the New York Branch's transaction monitoring systems and policies. For example, compliance personnel -- either at the Branch level or the Head Office - failed to periodically review surveillance monitoring filter criteria, required to evaluate the appropriateness of filter criteria and thresholds. Moreover, for a number of the criteria or key words purportedly used to detect suspicious transactions, branch management was unable to explain the validation process or justification of the selection of the criteria being used. And a number of documents relied upon in the transaction monitoring

process remained un-translated from the Chinese language, precluding effective examination by regulators.

14.   The examination discovered that the New York Branch had inadequate policies and procedures governing the processing of suspicious activity alerts and its case management system. Although compliance staff researched alerts, it failed to adequately maintain the documentation necessary to support decisions made by compliance personnel during the investigation of alerts - in many cases the only documentation maintained was in the case of an actual determination to file a Suspicious Activity Report ("SAR").

15.   Similarly, Branch procedures provided little guidance concerning the requirements for reporting continuing suspicious activity, and the notation of the latter in the Branch's SAR log book.

16.   The examination also concluded that the New York Branch's BSAIAML policies and procedures lacked consistency and unity of purpose. Deficiencies included, without limitation, (a) substantial inconsistencies between policies and procedures for the Business Division and the Correspondent Banking Division; (b) inconsistent policies and procedures concerning transaction monitoring, customer on-boarding and OFAC compliance; and (c) that written guidelines failed to properly incorporate federal regulatory guidance for reviews of Customer Due Diligence,

Enhanced Due Diligence, and diligence concerning Politically Exposed Persons.

17. The New York Branch did not perform adequate reviews of the Bank's affiliates' correspondent banking activities at the Branch. For example, New York Branch officials failed to (a) determine whether foreign affiliates had in place adequate AML compliance processes and controls; (b) ensure the New York Branch has an understanding of the effectiveness of the AML regime of the foreign jurisdictions in which its foreign correspondent banking customers operate;and (c) follow up on account activity and transactions that did not fit the foreign affiliates' customers' strategic profile.

Suspicious Activity Involving Mega International's Panama Branches

18. The compliance failures found at the New York Branch are serious. They indicate a lack of understanding by both Mega International and the New York Branch of the need for a vigorous compliance infrastructure.

19. These deficiencies make it all the more concerning given that Mega International operates branches in Panama City and the Colon FTZ. Panama has historically been recognized as a high-risk jurisdiction for money laundering, and only earlier in this year was it announced that Panama is no longer subject to the Financial Action Task Force's monitoring process.[3]

Moreover, the publication ofthe "Panama Papers" and information about the Mossack Fonseca Law firm emphasize Panama as a high-risk jurisdiction. Accordingly, Mega International is obligated to treat transactions running between its New York and Panama Branches with the highest level of diligence and scrutiny, yet compliance failures occurring at the New York Branch demonstrated that this did not occur.

20. This failure was serious in light of the significant amount of financial activity running between Mega International's New York and Panama Branches. For example, according to the Bank's records, the dollar value of credit transactions between the New York Branch and the Colon FTZ totaled

---

[3] See, e.g., http://www .state.govljlinl/rls/nrcrptl20 13/vol2/204062.htm; http://www.fatf-gan.org/ countries/ac/ afghan istan/documentsltiltf-compl !ance-february-_0 16.html.

$3.5 billion and $2.4 billion in 2013 and 2014, respectively. Corresponding figures for the Panama City branch were $1.1 billion and $4.5 billion.

21. Mega's International's Head Office has acted with indifference towards the risks associated with such transactions. The DFS examination found a number of concerning issues related to Mega International transactions involving its Panama Branches indicative of possible money laundering and other suspicious activity. For example:

  a. Mega-New York rated its Panama Colon FTZ Branch at high risk for AML purposes. It purports to conduct a quarterly enhanced due diligence ("EDD"), yet the Branch's responses to the DFS examination team indicated that this has not been implemented effectively.

  b. Despite repeated requests, the Bank has not provided an adequate explanation about the nature of its correspondent banking activities on behalf of its Panama City and Colon FTZ branches, as requested in DFS's Report of Examination and at the regulatory close-out meeting held with the Bank in February 2016.

  c. Mega-New York acted as an intermediary paying bank in connection with suspicious and unusual "debit authorizations" (or payment reversals) received from its Panamanian branches that reversed wire payments processed on behalf of various remitters (the "Suspicious Payment Reversals"). When asked about this in connection with the examination, New York Branch personnel provided explanations that did not address the examiners' concerns.

  d. A significant number of reported debit authorizations processed by Mega-New York between 2010 and 2014 occurred when the Panamanian beneficiary accounts identified in the underlying transactions were closed by the Colon FTZ Branch because of inadequate Know-Your-Customer ("KYC")documentation received by that Branch - a highly suspicious level of activity. Moreover, most of these accounts were open for less than two years; a number were open even less than one year - further evidence of very questionable activity. The suspicious nature of this activity is compounded by the fact that the remitters and beneficiaries associated with many of the Suspicious

Payment Reversals were identical parties; in some cases, the original payment instructions were sent months after the beneficiary accounts already had been closed. Moreover, the Suspicious Payment Reversals continued at least into 2015.

e. Examiners also noted that many of the Colon FTZ Branch accounts involved with the Suspicious Payment Reversals were opened with closely ranged account numbers - another compelling indicator of suspicious activity.

22.   Further, an account held in the name of a corporate customer of the Colon FTZ Branch that received funds remitted by Mega-New York and its reported beneficial owner have been the subject of significant adverse comment in the media. Among other things, the beneficial owner apparently has been linked to violations of U.S. law concerning the transfer of technology. Despite numerous requests by DFS, Mega International has failed to provide any meaningful explanation of its due diligence regarding this customer's account.

Failure to Conduct Adequate Customer Due Diligence

23.   The DFS examination also found that Mega-New York Branch personnel failed to follow established policies and procedures for enhanced due diligence, an increased level of scrutiny for high-risk customers. For example, the New York Branch failed to conduct a comprehensive review of such customers on a quarterly basis, as required by its own policies and procedures. Nor did New York Branch personnel regularly engage in periodic vetting of medium and low-risk customers in a timely manner to identify any increase in the risk profile of such customers.

24.   Similarly, the examination found that the New York Branch failed to perform adequate customer due diligence when taking in a correspondent account for a foreign financial institution.

25.   Furthermore, a review of 30 customer files indicated that approximately one-third of them lacked adequate information on beneficial ownership. The lack of such information seriously compromises the New York Branch's

Know-Your-Customer ("KYC") processes. Inadequate Risk Assessment
Policies and Procedures

26.   The examination also found serious flaws in the New York Branch's
overall risk assessments. For example, the New York Branch's risk
assessment for BSAIAML issues lacked a thorough review of Branch
customers, products, services, and geographic locations served. It likewise
was insufficient in its methodology, for, among other reasons, having
been conducted for a six month period, and not a year-long period as
recommended.

27.   The New York Branch's risk assessment for OFAC concerns was
found to be flawed for similar reasons.

Lack of Diligent Oversight by the Head Office

28.   In addition, with respect to the New York Branch's reporting to the
Head Office about the compliance function, DFS examiners found that
quarterly compliance meeting minutes were not forwarded to Head Office
compliance; and that the New York Branch regularly substituted a meeting
agenda in lieu of proper meeting minutes. Additionally, the New York
Branch's report on quarterly compliance meetings provided insufficient
information on the compliance environment, and critical information
concerning SARs filed during prior periods were omitted. These failings
prevented Head Office compliance from properly evaluating the compliance
adequacy of the New York Branch.

29.   Additionally, Head Office compliance did not ensure that numerous
documents employed and stored by the New York Branch were translated
from Chinese to English, thereby preventing effective examination by
regulators.

Mega-New York Branch's Troubling and
Dismissive Response to the DFS Examination

30.   In its March 24,2016 response to the February 2016 DFS examination
report, the Bank has refuted a number of the examination findings.

31. Perhaps most egregious, Mega International and the New York Branch, in its March 2016 response to the examination, declared that certain types of activity were not suspicious. As justification, the Bank's March 2016 examination response claimed that there is "no AML regulatory guidance related to filing [Suspicious Activity Reports] on these types of transactions" and that therefore such "transactions do not constitute suspicious activity."

32. This is a complete misstatement of well-established BSA law.

33. Moreover, the Bank did not act quickly to remedy the acute shortcomings as directed in the February 2016 Report of Examination. For example, despite communications between the Department and the New York Branch in the Spring of 2016, the Bank has not taken sufficient steps to demonstrate material improvement in the quality of its compliance program.

NOW THEREFORE, to resolve this matter without further proceedings pursuant to the Superintendent's authority under Sections 39 and 44 of the Banking Law, the Department and the Bank hereby stipulate and agree to the terms and conditions listed below requiring further review of the Bank's activities, for remediation, and for imposition of a penalty:

Violations of Law and Regulation

34. Mega International and Mega-New York failed to maintain an effective and compliant anti-money laundering program and OF AC compliance program, in violation of 3N.Y.C.R.R. § 116.2.

35. Mega International and Mega-New York failed to maintain and make available at its New York Branch true and accurate books, accounts and records reflecting all transactions and actions, in violation of New York Banking Law § 200-c.

36. Mega International and Mega-New York failed to submit a report to the Superintendent immediately upon discovering fraud, dishonesty, making of false entries and omission of true entries, and other misconduct, in violation of 3 N.Y.C.R.R. § 300.1.

Settlement Provisions

Monetary Payment

37.   Mega International shall pay a penalty pursuant to Banking Law § 44 to the Department in the amount of$180,000,000.00 as a result of having an inadequate and deficient compliance program as set forth above. The Bank shall pay the entire amount within ten (10) days of executing this Consent Order. Mega International agrees that it will not claim, assert, or apply for a tax deduction or tax credit with regard to any U.S. federal, state, or local tax, directly or indirectly, for any portion of the penalty paid pursuant to this Consent Order.

Immediate Compliance Consultant and Independent Monitor

38.   **Compliance Consultant**: Mega International and the New York Branch shall engage an independent third party of the Department's choosing, within ten (10) days of the Department's selection of such third party, to immediately consult about, oversee and address deficiencies in Mega-New York's compliance function, including, without limitation, compliance with BSAIAML requirements, compliance with federal sanctions laws, and compliance with New York laws and regulations (the "Compliance Consultant").

39.   The Compliance Consultant shall work with the Department, Mega International and Mega-New York to implement changes or modifications to policies, procedures or personnel that may be made immediately to address any identified deficiencies in the New York Branch's compliance function.

40.   The term ofthe Compliance Consultant's engagement shall extend for a period of up to six months, at the sole discretion of the Department, to be extended in the sole discretion of the Department should Mega International fail to cooperate as required.

41.   **Independent Monitor:** Within thirty (30) days of the Department's selection thereof, Mega International and Mega-New York shall retain an independent monitor (the "Independent Monitor") to: (i) conduct a

comprehensive review of the effectiveness of the Branch's program for compliance with BSAIAML requirements, laws and regulations (the "Compliance Review"); and (ii) prepare a written report of findings, conclusions, and recommendations (the "Compliance Report").

42.   The Independent Monitor will be selected by the Department in the exercise of its sole discretion, and will report directly to the Department.

43.   Within ten (10) days of the selection of the Independent Monitor, but prior to the Compliance Review, Mega International and Mega-New York shall jointly submit to the Department for approval an engagement letter that provides, at a minimum, for the Independent Monitor to:

    a. identify all of the Branch's business lines, activities, and products to ensure that such business lines, activities, and products are appropriately risk-rated and included in the Branch's BSAIAML compliance program, policies, and procedures;

    b. conduct a comprehensive assessment of the Branch's BSAIAML compliance program, policies, and procedures;

    c. complete the Compliance Review within 60 days of the Department's approval of the engagement letter;

    d. provide to the Department a copy of the Compliance Report at the same time that the report is provided to the Bank and the Branch; and

    e. commit that any and all interim reports, drafts, workpapers, or other supporting materials associated with the Compliance Review will be made available to the Department.

44.   The Independent Monitor shall also conduct a review of Mega-New York's U.S. dollar clearing transaction activity from January 1, 2012 through December 31, 2014, to determine whether transactions inconsistent with or in violation of the OFAC Regulations, or suspicious activity involving high risk customers or transactions or possible money laundering at, by, or through the Branch were properly identified and reported in accordance with the OF AC Regulations and suspicious activity reporting regulations and New York law (the "Transaction and OF AC Sanctions Review") and to prepare a written report detailing the Independent Monitor's party's findings (the "Transaction and OFAC Sanctions Review Report") for the Department.

45.   Within ten (10) days of the engagement of the Independent Monitor, but prior to the commencement of the Transaction and OFAC Sanctions Review, Mega International and Mega-New York shall jointly submit to the Department for approval additional terms in the engagement letter that set forth:

    a. the methodology for conducting the Transaction and OF AC Sanctions Review, including any sampling procedures to be followed;

    b. the expertise and resources to be dedicated to the Transaction and OF AC Sanctions Review;

    c. the anticipated date of completion of the Transaction and OFAC Sanctions Review and the Transaction and OF AC Sanctions Review Report; and

    d. a commitment that supporting material and drafts associated with the Transaction and OF AC Sanctions Review will be made available to the Department upon request.

46.   The Independent Monitor shall provide to the Department a copy of the Transaction and OF AC Sanctions Review Report at the same time that the report is provided to Mega International and Mega-New York.

47.   Throughout the Transaction and OFAC Sanctions Review, Mega International and Mega-New York shall ensure that all matters or transactions required to be reported that have not previously been reported are reported in accordance with applicable rules and regulations.

BSA/AML Compliance Program

48.   Within sixty (60) days of the submission of the Compliance Report, Mega Bank and Mega-New York shall jointly submit a written revised BSA/AML compliance program for the Branch acceptable to the Department. At a minimum, the program shall provide for:

    a. a system of internal controls designed to ensure compliance with the BSA/AML Requirements and the State Laws and Regulations;

    b. controls designed to ensure compliance with all requirements relating to correspondent accounts for foreign financial institutions;

    c. a comprehensive BSA/AML risk assessment that identifies and considers all products and services of the New York Branch, customer types, geographic locations, and transaction volumes, as appropriate, in determining inherent and residual risks;

d. management of the New York Branch's BSA/AML compliance program by a qualified compliance officer, who is given full autonomy, independence, and responsibility for implementing and maintaining an effective BSA/AML compliance program that is cO!llmensurate with the New York Branch's size and risk profile, and is supported by adequate staffing levels and resources;

e. identification of management information systems used to achieve compliance with the BSA/AML Requirements and the State Laws and Regulations and a time line to review key systems to ensure they are configured to mitigate BSAI AML risks;

f. comprehensive and timely independent testing for the New York Branch's compliance with applicable BSAI AML Requirements and the State Laws and Regulations; and

g. effective training for all appropriate Branch personnel and appropriate Mega International personnel that perform BSAIAML compliance-related functions for the New York Branch in all aspects of the BSA/ AML requirements, state laws and regulations, and internal policies and procedures.

Suspicious Activity Monitoring and Reporting

49. Within sixty (60) days of the submission of the Compliance Report, Mega International and Mega-New York shall jointly submit a written program to reasonably ensure the identification and timely, accurate, and complete reporting by the New York Branch of all known or suspected violations of law or suspicious transactions to law enforcement and supervisory authorities, as required by applicable suspicious activity reporting laws and regulations acceptable to the Department. At a minimum, the program shall include:

a. a well-documented methodology for establishing monitoring rules and thresholds appropriate for the New York Branch's profile which considers factors such as type of customer, type of product or service, geographic location, and foreign correspondent banking activities, including U.S. dollar clearing activities;

b. policies and procedures for analyzing, testing, and documenting changes to monitoring rules and thresholds;

c. enhanced monitoring and investigation criteria and procedures to ensure the timely detection, investigation, and reporting of all known or suspected violations oflaw and suspicious transactions, including, but not limited to:

    i. effective monitoring of customer accounts and transactions, including but not limited to, transactions conducted through foreign correspondent accounts;

    ii. appropriate allocation of resources to manage alert and case inventory;

    iii. adequate escalation of information about potentially suspicious activity through appropriate levels of management;

    iv. maintenance of sufficient documentation with respect to the investigation and analysis of potentially suspiciolls activity, including the resolution and escalation of concerns; and

    v. maintenance of accurate and comprehensive customer and transactional data and ensuring that it is utilized by the New Yark Branch's compliance program.

Customer Due Diligence

50.   Within sixty (60) days ofthe submission of the Compliance Report, Mega International and Mega-New York shall jointly submit a written enhanced customer due diligence program acceptable to the Department. At a minimum, the program shall include:

a. policies, procedures, and controls to ensure that the New York Branch collects, analyzes, and retains complete and accurate customer information for all account holders, including, but not limited to, affiliates;

b. a plan to remediate deficient due diligence for existing customers accounts;

c. a revised methodology for assigning risk ratings to account holders that considers factors such as type of customer, type of products and services, geographic locations, and transaction volume;

d. for each customer whose transactions require enhanced due diligence procedures to:

    i. determine the appropriate documentation necessary to verify the identity and business activities of the customer; and

    ii. understand the normal and expected transactions of the customer.

e. policies, procedures, and controls to ensure that foreign correspondent accounts are accorded the appropriate due diligence and, where necessary, enhanced due diligence; and

f. periodic reviews and evaluations of customer and account information for the entire customer base to ensure that information is current, complete, and that the risk rating reflects the current information, and if applicable, documenting rationales for any revisions made to the customer risk rating.

Corporate Governance and Management Oversight

51.   Within sixty (60) days of the submission of the Compliance Report, Mega International's board of directors and the management of Mega-New York shall jointly submit to the Department a written plan to enhance oversight, by the management of the Bank and New York Branch, of the New York Branch's compliance with the BSA/AML Requirements, the State Laws and Regulations, and the regulations issued by OF AC acceptable to the Department. The plan shall provide for a sustainable governance framework that, at a minimum, addresses, considers, and includes:

a. actions the board of directors will take to maintain effective control over, and oversight of, Branch management's compliance with the BSAI AML Requirements, the State Laws and Regulations, and the OF AC Regulations;

b. measures to improve the management information systems reporting of the Branch's compliance with the BSAIAML Requirements, the State Laws and Regulations, and the OFAC Regulations to senior management of the Bank and the Branch;

c. clearly defined roles, responsibilities, and accountability regarding compliance with the BSAIAML Requirements, the State Laws and Regulations, and the OF AC Regulations for the Bank's and the Branch's respective management, compliance personnel, and internal audit staff;

d. measures to ensure BSAIAML issues are appropriately tracked, escalated, and reviewed by the Branch's senior management;

e. measures to ensure that the person or groups at the Bank and the Branch charged with the responsibility of overseeing the Branch's compliance with the BSAIAML Requirements, the State Laws and Regulations, and the OFAC Regulations possess appropriate subject matter expertise and are actively involved in carrying out such responsibilities;

f. adequate resources to ensure the New York Branch's compliance with this Order, the BSAIAML Requirements, the State Laws and Regulations, and the OF AC Regulations; and

g. a direct reporting line between the Branch's BSAIAML compliance officer and the board of directors or committee thereof.

Full and Complete Cooperation of Mega International

52. Mega International and Mega-New York each agrees that it will fully cooperate with the Immediate Compliance Consultant and the Independent Monitor and support the work of each by, among other things, providing each with access to all relevant personnel, consultants and third-party service providers, files, reports, or records, whether located in New York, Taiwan, Panama, or any other location sought, consistent with applicable law.

53. The Independent Monitor will thereafter oversee the implementation of any corrective measures undertaken pursuant to the Action Plan and Management Oversight Plan.

54. The Independent Monitor will assess the Bank's compliance with its corrective measures and will submit subsequent progress reports and a final report to the Department and the Bank, at intervals to be determined by the Department. The Department may, in its sole discretion, extend any reporting deadline set forth in this Order.

55.   The term of the Independent Monitor's engagement will extend for two years from the date of its formal engagement by the Bank, to be extended in the Department's sole discretion if Mega International fails to cooperate. Any dispute as to the scope of the Independent Monitor's authority or mandate will be resolved by the Department in the exercise of its sole discretion, after appropriate consultation with the Bank and the Monitor.

Interaction with the Department

56.   Within 30 days ofthe submission of the Compliance Report, the Bank and the Branch shall jointly submit written policies and procedures that govern the conduct of the Branch's personnel in all supervisory and regulatory matters, including, but not limited to, interaction with and requests for information by examiners for the Branch, acceptable to the Department. The policies and procedures shall, at a minimum, ensure that all Branch personnel provide prompt, complete, and accurate information to examiners and provide for employee training that emphasizes the importance of full cooperation with banking regulators by all employees.

Breach of Consent Order

57.   In the event that the Department believes the Bank to be in material breach of the Consent Order, the Department will provide written notice to the Bank and the Bank must, within ten (10) business days of receiving such notice, or on a later date ifso determined in the Department's sole discretion, appear before the Department to demonstrate that no material breach has occurred or, to the extent pertinent, that the breach is not material or has been cured.

58.   The parties understand and agree that the Bank's failure to make the required showing within the designated time period shall be presumptive evidence of the Bank's breach. Upon a finding that the Bank has breached this Consent Order, the Department has all the remedies available to it under New York Banking and Financial Services Law and may use any evidence available to the Department in any ensuing hearings, notices, or orders.

Waiver of Rights

59.   The parties understand and agree that no provision of this Consent Order is subject to review in any court or tribunal outside the Department.

Parties Bound by the Consent Order

60.   This Consent Order is binding on the Department and the Bank, as well as any successors and assigns that are under the Department's supervisory authority. This Consent Order does not bind any federal or other state agency or law enforcement authority.

61.   No further action will be taken by the Department against the Bank for the conduct set forth in this Order, provided that the Bank complies with the terms of the Order. Notwithstanding any other provision in this Consent Order, however, the Department may undertake additional action against the Bank for transactions or conduct that comes to the attention ofthe Department, either as a result of the Transaction and OFAC Sanctions Review, or in some other manner.

Notices

62.   All notices or communications regarding this Consent Order shall be sent to:

For the Department:
Jeffrey Waddle
Elizabeth Nochlin
Megan Prendergast
New York State Department of Financial Services
One State Street
New York, NY 10004

For Mega International and Mega-New York:
Jui-Chung Chuang
Mega International Commercial Bank Co., Ltd.
10F, No. 123, Sec. 2 Jhongsiao E. Rd.
Taipei 10058, Taiwan, R.O.C.

Vincent S.M. Huang
Mega International Commercial Bank Co., Ltd - New York Branch
65 Liberty Street
New York, NY 10005

Miscellaneous

63.   Each provision of this Consent Order shall remain effective and enforceable until stayed, modified, suspended, or terminated by the Department.

64.   No promise, assurance, representation, or understanding other than those contained in this Consent Order has been made to induce any party to agree to the provisions of the Consent Order.

IN WITNESS WHEREOF, the parties have caused this Consent Order to be signed this 19th day of August, 2016.

MEGA INTERNATIONAL COMMERCIAL BANK CO., LTD.

By: _____

HANN-CHING WU

President, Mega International Commercial Bank Co., Ltd.

NEW YORK STATE DEPARTMENT OF FINANCIAL SERVICES

By: _____

MARIA T. VULLO

Superintendent of Financial Services

MEGA INTERNATIONAL COMMERCIAL BANK CO. LTD. - NEW YORK BRANCH

By:_____

VINCENT S.M. HUANG

Senior Vice President & General Manager,

Mega International Com mercial Bank Co., Ltd. - New York Branch

In re B & M KINGSTONE, LLC, Petitioner–Respondent, v. MEGA INTERNATIONAL COMMERCIAL BANK CO., LTD., Respondent–Appellant.

Decided: August 11, 2015

ROLANDO T. ACOSTA, J.P., DAVID B. SAXE, ROSALYN H. RICHTER, JUDITH J. GISCHE, BARBARA R. KAPNICK, JJ.Satterlee Stephens Burke & Burke LLP, New York (Alun W. Griffiths of counsel), for appellant. The Law Firm of Elias C. Schwartz, PLLC, Great Neck (Elias C. Schwartz of counsel), for respondent.

Petitioner, B & M Kingstone, LLC (B & M), served an information subpoena on the New York branch of respondent, Mega International Commercial Bank, Co., Ltd. (Mega), in order to enforce a money judgment obtained against a group of judgment debtors more than 10 years ago. Although it complied with demands for information pertaining to its New York branch, Mega refused to produce similar information regarding accounts and records at its branches outside New York State. It argued, among other things, that New York courts lack personal jurisdiction over it with respect to that information. We hold that Mega›s New York branch is subject to jurisdiction requiring it to comply with the appropriate information subpoenas, because it consented to the necessary regulatory oversight in return for permission to operate in New York. Moreover, Mega does not contend that compliance with the information subpoena would be onerous or unduly expensive or that the requested information is not available in New York.

Background

In 2003, a court in Florida entered judgment in excess of $39 million in favor of Super Vision International, Inc. (Super Vision) and against individual and corporate entities (the judgment debtors) in the matter of Super Vision Intl., Inc. v. Caruso (Fla. Cir. Ct., June 16, 2003, W. Thomas Spencer, Case No. CI–99–9392). Super Vision claimed that the judgment debtors had engaged in counterfeiting, civil theft, and misappropriation of its proprietary information. Judgment debtor Samson Wu subsequently executed a Consent to Disclosure of Bank Account Information (Consent) authorizing the disclosure of any account information for all accounts belonging to him and upon which he was authorized to draw.[1]

On March 24, 2009, Super Vision assigned its rights against the judgment debtors to B & M. Approximately five years later, the Florida judgment was entered and recorded in Nassau County in the State of New York in favor of B & M.

Mega is an international banking corporation, organized under the laws of Taiwan, with a principal place of business in Taipei City. It has 128 branches worldwide, 107 of which are located in Taiwan. The remaining branches are located in 14 other countries. Mega operates one branch in New York.

Believing that Mega maintains bank accounts for the judgment debtors and is in possession of assets belonging to the judgment debtors, B & M served Mega with a subpoena duces tecum and an information subpoena, with restraining notice and questionnaire, on August 7, 2014. The questionnaire asked, among other things, whether Mega had a record of any account in which each judgment debtor may have an interest and whether the judgment debtor was indebted to Mega in any manner.

On August 11, 2014, a representative of Mega called B & M's counsel and said that Mega could not and would not access accounts maintained outside the State of New York. By letter dated August 14, 2014, Mega served its responses to the questionnaire, together with responsive documents. In response to the information subpoena, Mega stated that its New York branch was not in possession of any judgment debtor's assets. It also stated that its New York branch was not holding any account or other property for the judgment debtors and that the judgment debtors were not indebted to it.

On August 19, 2014, B & M told Mega that the responses to the subpoenas were inadequate, in that they pertained only to one branch of Mega, and not Mega worldwide.

On August 27, 2014, B & M's counsel received Mega's response to the subpoena duces tecum, which addressed Mega's New York branch only. Mega stated that its New York branch was not in possession of assets belonging to any judgment debtor, and objected to the subpoena to the extent it sought records located in Mega branches outside New York.

On September 10, 2014, B & M commenced this proceeding by filing a petition signed by Brett Kingstone, the founder of Super Vision. Kingstone alleges that the judgment debtors have been deliberately evading enforcement of the judgment, including by filing Chapter 11 bankruptcy petitions, destroying material evidence, relocating inventory from Florida to Shanghai, China, and continuing to make use of Super Vision's proprietary equipment in Shanghai. Judgment debtor Wu had been found in criminal contempt of court in Florida in 2004 for attempting to avoid an order through a sham transaction. Kingstone set forth information that had been learned by a private investigator allegedly showing that Mega was intimately involved with the judgment debtors, especially Wu, and was involved in efforts to conceal the judgment debtors' assets, including through transactions in Panama, where the manager of the Free Zone branch of Mega was an officer of companies owned by Wu.

The petition seeks an order compelling compliance with the subpoena duces tecum and the information subpoena and questionnaire, and restraining any accounts held by judgment debtors.

B & M also moved for an order restraining bank accounts pursuant to CPLR 5222(b) and compliance with the subpoena duces tecum and the information subpoena restraining notice and questionnaire pursuant to CPLR 5224, and finding Mega in contempt for its failure to fully respond to the subpoenas pursuant to CPLR 5251.

B & M argued that Mega had failed to respond properly to the subpoenas when it limited its responses to its New York branch, and sought a preliminary injunction to prevent Mega from transferring or otherwise disposing of the assets of the judgment debtors. In the alternative, it requested an order compelling Mega's compliance or holding Mega in contempt. B & M argued that, pursuant to CPLR 5223 and 5224, Mega was required to fully comply with the subpoenas, regardless of where in the world the assets of the judgment debtors were held.

Citing Daimler AG v. Bauman (—— U.S. ——, ——, 134 S Ct 746, 760 [2014]), Mega argued that B & M had no jurisdiction over Mega as a whole. It argued that pursuant to Daimler, a court could not exercise general jurisdiction over an entity unless the entity could fairly be regarded as at home in the forum jurisdiction. Thus, merely operating a branch office in the forum jurisdiction was insufficient to establish general jurisdiction. Mega argued that, in this case, it was incorporated and had its principal place of business in Taiwan, and its operations in New York were so narrow and limited that it could not fairly be regarded as at home in New York.

Mega also argued that the "separate entity" rule precluded enforcement of subpoenas and restraining notices as to Mega branches outside New York. The separate entity rule provides that postjudgment subpoenas served on branches of banks in New York are operative only as to branches within New York State (see Matter of National Union Fire Ins. Co. of Pittsburgh, Pa. v. Advanced Empl. Concepts, 269 A.D.2d 101 [1st Dept 2000]).

Finally, Mega argued that principles of international comity precluded compelling international compliance with the subpoenas. It contended that compliance with the subpoenas could require Mega to violate banking regulations in multiple jurisdictions, and cited Panama and Taiwan as two jurisdictions that could impose fines on it if it were to comply with the subpoenas.

In support, Mega submitted a declaration by Huei–Ying Chen, a Vice President and Deputy General Manager of its New York branch. Chen stated that New York branch personnel were primarily responsible for banking operations pertaining to the New York branch; that New York branch personnel did not have decision-making authority for Mega as a whole or any other branches, and that no senior Mega executives were located in New York.

Mega also submitted declarations by two foreign legal experts. Hsiao–Ling Fan, an attorney in Taiwan, stated that it was his professional opinion that compelling Mega to comply with the subpoenas would place Mega in violation of portions of Taiwanese banking laws, specifically, Article 28.2 of Taiwan's Banking Act. He further asserted that disclosing personal information related to customer accounts would expose Mega to criminal liability in Taiwan. Fan argued that any subpoena seeking information about assets held in Taiwan should be delivered and served in accordance with the Taiwanese Law in Supporting Foreign Courts on Consigned Cases.

Luis Guinard, an attorney licensed to practice law in the Republic of Panama, stated that it was his professional opinion that compelling Mega to comply with the subpoenas as to accounts and assets of judgment debtors located in Panama would place Mega in violation of Article 111 of Executive Decree No. 52 of the Panamanian Banking Law. Guinard further stated that Wu's consent did not warrant disclosure of any accounts of assets that Wu may have had in Mega branches in Panama.

The IAS court found that it did not have jurisdiction over Mega, and the turnover aspect of the petition was therefore denied. However, since Mega had the ability to access information concerning accounts around the world, the court ordered it to comply with the information subpoena. The court also relied upon CPLR 5223, which permits a judgment creditor to demand information from any person. The court found that foreign laws were not cited with sufficient specificity to invoke the doctrine of international comity and furthermore that Wu had agreed in writing to the disclosure of any accounts that he may have owned or used.

Analysis

In Daimler AG v. Bauman (—— U.S. ——, 134 S Ct 746), the Supreme Court held that general, or all-purpose, jurisdiction allowed a court to hear any and all claims against a foreign corporation "only when the corporation's affiliations with the State in which suit is brought are so constant and pervasive as to render [it] essentially at home in the forum state" (134 S Ct at 751).

Applying Daimler in Gucci Am., Inc. v. Bank of China (768 F3d 122 [2d Cir2014]), the Second Circuit concluded that the District Court did not have general jurisdiction over the Bank of China to enforce a prejudgment asset freeze injunction. The bank had branch offices in New York, but it was incorporated and headquartered elsewhere, and its contacts were not so continuous and systematic as to render it essentially at home in New York. The bank had only four branch offices in the United States, and only a small portion of its worldwide business was conducted in New York.

Thus, under Daimler, New York does not have general jurisdiction over Mega's worldwide operations. However, that does not end the inquiry. Like Banco Bilboa Vizcaya Argentina (BBVA) in Vera v. Cuba (—— F Supp 3d ——, 2015 WL 1244050, 2015 U.S. Dist LEXIS 32846 [SD N.Y.2015]), Mega "consented to the necessary regulatory oversight in return for permission to operate in New York, and therefore is subject to jurisdiction requiring it to comply with the appropriate Information Subpoenas" (—— F Supp 3d at ——, 2015 WL 1244050 at *8, 2015 U.S. Dist LEXIS 32846 at *26). As the Vera court explained in finding that BBVA was subject to jurisdictiion:

"The state of New York in general, and New York City in particular, is a leading world financial center. In order to benefit from the advantages of transacting business in this forum, a foreign bank must register with and obtain a license from the Superintendent of the Department of Financial Services ('DFS'), and file a written instrument 'appointing the superintendent and his or her successors its true and lawful attorney, upon whom all process in any action or proceeding against it on a cause of action arising out of a transaction with its New York agency or agencies or branch or branches.' N.Y. Bnk. Law § 200(a). BBVA is registered with the DFS as a foreign branch. The Second Circuit recognized that the privileges and benefits associated with a foreign bank operating a branch in New York give rise to commensurate, reciprocal obligations. Foreign corporations which do business in New York are bound by the laws of both the state of New York and the United States, and are bound by the same judicial constraints as domestic corporations. Under New York Banking Law, foreign banks operating local branches in New York can both sue and be sued (see, e.g., Greenbaum v. Svenska Handlesbanken, 26 F.Supp.2d 649 [S.D. N.Y.1998]). This legal status also confers obligations to participate as third-parties in lawsuits which involve assets under their management" (—— F Supp 3d at ——, 2015 WL 1244050 at *7, 2015 U.S. Dist LEXIS 32846 at *24–25; but see Gliklad v. Bank Hapoalim B.M., 2014 N.Y. Slip Op 32117[U] [Sup Ct, N.Y. County 2014] [Banking Law § 200(a) only provides specific jurisdiction for a cause of action arising out of a transaction with its New York agency or agencies or branch or branches]).

The issue is whether the separate entity rule bars New York courts from compelling Mega's New York branch to produce information pertaining to Mega's foreign branches.

The separate entity rule is that "each branch of a bank is a separate entity, in no way concerned with accounts maintained by depositors in other branches or at the home office" (Cronan v. Schilling, 100 N.Y.S.2d 474, 476 [Sup Ct, N.Y. County 1950]; see also Matter of National Union Fire Ins. Co. of Pittsburgh, Pa. v. Advanced Empl. Concepts, 269 A.D.2d 101 [1st Dept 2000]; Therm–X–Chem. & Oil Corp. v. Extebank, 84 A.D.2d 787 [2d Dept 1981]). The continuing validity of this arcane rule was recently upheld by the Court of Appeals in Motorola Credit Corp. v. Standard Chartered Bank (24 NY3d 149 [2014]), solely with respect to restraining notices and turnover orders affecting assets located in foreign branch accounts (id. at 159 n 2 ["(t)he narrow question before us is whether the rule prevents the restraint of assets held in foreign branch accounts, and we limit our analysis to that inquiry"]). "In other words, a restraining notice or turnover order on a New York Branch will be effective for assets held in accounts at that branch but will have no impact on assets in other branches" (id. at 159). Thus, Motorola's expressly limited affirmation of the separate entity rule does not apply to the instant case, and the rule does not bar the court's exercise of jurisdiction over Mega to compel a full response to the information subpoena.

Moreover, public policy interests and innovations in technology support such an exercise of jurisdiction. As the Vera court noted, "[B]road post-judgment discovery in aid of execution is the norm in federal and New York state courts" (—— F Supp 3d at ——, 2015 WL 1244050 at *6, 2015 U.S. Dist LEXIS 32846 at *21 [internal quotation marks omitted]), and "New York law entitles judgment creditors to discover all matters relevant to the satisfaction of a judgment" (—— F Supp 3d at ——, 2015 WL 1244050 at *6, 2015 U.S. Dist LEXIS 32846 at *23 [internal quotation marks omitted]).

The court reasoned that

"Daimler and Gucci should not be read so broadly as to eliminate the necessary regulatory oversight into foreign entities that operate within the boundaries of the United States. There is no reason to give advantage to a foreign bank with a branch in New York, over a domestic bank□ When corporations receive the benefits of operating in this forum, it is critical that regulators and courts continue to have the power to compel information concerning their activities" (—— F Supp 3d at ——, 2015 WL 1244050 at *8, 2015 U.S. Dist LEXIS 32846 at *25).

As the Vera court concluded, "The information requested by the Information Subpoena can be found via electronic searches performed in BBVA's New York office, and [is] within this jurisdiction" (id .).

Mega does not claim that compliance with the information subpoena would be onerous or unduly expensive or that the requested information is not available in New York. Thus, the court's general personal jurisdiction over the bank's New York branch permits it to compel that branch to produce any requested information that can be found through electronic searches performed there (compare Ayyash v. Koleilat, 115 AD3d 495, 495 [1st Dept 2014] [affirming denial of motion to compel where, among other things, it "would likely cause great annoyance and expense" to the New York branch of the financial institution]; see also CPLR 5223).

The court properly determined that Mega did not show that principles of international comity preclude enforcement of the subpoena (see Morgenthau v. Avion Resources Ltd., 11 NY3d 383, 389–390 [2008]). In particular, Mega's submissions were insufficient to show that the bank could face liability for violating Taiwanese or Panamanian law if it were required to comply with the subpoena. Nor did Mega show that the interest of any other state or country is greater than New York's interest in enforcing its judgments and regulating banks operating within its jurisdiction (see Gucci Am., Inc. v. Bank of China, 768 F3d at 139 and n 20). In any event, at least with respect to Wu, any concerns about comity are overcome by the terms of the Consent.

Accordingly, the order of the Supreme Court, New York County (Geoffrey D. Wright, J.), entered September 19, 2014, which, to the extent appealed from, granted petitioner's motion to direct respondent to fully respond to an information subpoena, should be affirmed, with costs.

FOOTNOTES

1. The Consent, signed and notarized on January 7, 2004, contains the notarized signature of Samson Wu, and states that he directs any bank at which he may have an account of any kind to disclose and deliver copies of all documents that relate to those accounts to the law firm of Fisher, Rushmer, Werrenrath, Dickson, Talley & Dunlap, P .A., "for the period of January 2002 to the present date." The Consent states, "Such disclosures are authorized in connection with any request to enforce the Judgment" in the Super Vision case.

ACOSTA, J.P.
All concur.

28 June 2017

PRESS SUMMARY

Lord Advocate (representing the Taiwanese Judicial Authorities) (Appellant) v Dean (Respondent) (Scotland) [2017] UKSC 44

On appeal from [2016] HCJAC 83 and 117

JUSTICES: Lord Mance, Lord Sumption, Lord Reed, Lord Hughes, Lord Hodge

BACKGROUND TO THE APPEAL

The respondent was born in the United Kingdom. He had lived in Taiwan for about 19 years when he was involved in road traffic accident there which killed a man in 2010. He was convicted by the District Court of Taipei of driving under the influence of alcohol, negligent manslaughter and leaving the scene of an accident. He was sentenced to four years' imprisonment. While his appeal was pending, he fled Taiwan and came to Scotland. In his absence his conviction was confirmed and the Taiwanese authorities applied for his extradition.

The Ministry of Justice of Taiwan obtained a provisional arrest warrant for the respondent under the Extradition Act 2003 ("the 2003 Act"). The respondent was arrested in Scotland on 17 October 2013 and remained in custody for almost three years. An extradition hearing commenced in January 2014, following which the sheriff decided that the respondent's extradition would be compatible with his Convention rights and refused the respondent's devolution minutes. The Scottish Ministers made an extradition order on 1 August 2014.

The respondent appealed against the sheriff's decision and against the extradition order of the Scottish Ministers. The Appeal Court of the High Court of Justiciary ("the Appeal Court"), ordered an evidential hearing to determine whether prison conditions in Taiwan were such that to extradite the respondent would breach his right under article 3 of the European Convention for the Protection of Human Rights and Fundamental Freedoms ("ECHR") not to be subjected to torture or to inhuman or degrading treatment or punishment. It reserved its opinion on the extradition order appeal until it had dealt with the article 3 challenge. The Appeal Court, by majority, found that even if the written assurances given by the Taiwanese authorities to the Lord Advocate in respect of the conditions in which the respondent would be held were fulfilled, a real risk of ill treatment would remain and thus the respondent's extradition to Taiwan would be incompatible with article 3 ECHR.

The Lord Advocate appeals the judgment of the Appeal Court, on the ground that it had not applied the correct legal test in assessing the risk of harm which the respondent might face in Taiwan from non-state actors. The respondent raises a separate issue: whether the Appeal Court determined a devolution issue and, therefore, whether the Supreme Court has jurisdiction to hear the Lord Advocate's appeal. The respondent also advanced challenges under articles 5 and 8 ECHR.

JUDGMENT

The Supreme Court unanimously rejects the respondent's challenge to the competency of the appeal and allows the Lord Advocate's appeal on the devolution issue. The Court remits the case to the Appeal Court to deal with the respondent's appeal against the extradition order of the Scottish Ministers and his devolution minute in that appeal. Lord Hodge gives the judgment, with which the other Justices agree.

REASONS FOR THE JUDGMENT

The competency of the appeal to the Supreme Court

The challenge to the competency of the appeal is misconceived **[14]**.

An appeal from the sheriff's decision under section 87(1) of the 2003 Act as to whether extradition would be compatible with the respondent's Convention rights raises a question of the legal competence of the Scottish Government **[15]**. Schedule 6 to the Scotland Act 1998 paragraph 1(d) includes within the definition of a "devolution issue" "a question whether a [...] proposed exercise of a function of the Scottish Executive [...] would be, incompatible with any of the Convention rights" **[18]**. Therefore, the question whether the Scottish Government's acts in seeking to extradite the respondent are compatible with Convention rights is a devolution issue which was determined by the Appeal Court **[19, 22]**. Neither party to the appeal intimated the devolution issue to the Advocate General for Scotland thus depriving him of his right to take part in the Appeal Court proceedings. That omission, however, does not affect the competence of any appeal of the determination of the devolution issue to this court **[21]**.

The correct legal test

The Appeal Court, in assessing the compatibility of the extradition with article 3 ECHR, applied the wrong legal test **[9]**. The correct legal test when the threat comes from the acts of third parties is whether the state has failed to provide reasonable protection against harm inflicted by non-state agents. The Appeal Court did not address that test and no clear distinction was drawn between the threat from other prisoners, and the conduct for which the state was responsible. The court must assess, first, whether the Taiwanese authorities are undertaking to provide the respondent with reasonable protection against violence by third parties while in prison, and, secondly, if they are, whether the conditions in which he is to have such protection would infringe article 3 **[24]**.

There is no evidence that the Taiwanese authorities will not give the respondent reasonable protection against harm at the hands of other prisoners: the undertakings would allow him to elect to remain in his cell and exercise outdoors alone **[39]**. As to whether the confinement which such a regime would entail would risk a breach of article 3, the relative isolation which the respondent may elect for his own protection does not come close to a breach of article 3. Further, the other factors which influenced the majority of the Appeal Court, including the ratio of medical staff to prisoners and the monitoring of the assurances by UK consular staff, do not outweigh the other factors which point towards accepting the assurances [40-47]. The assurances offer the respondent reasonable protection against violence by non-state actors and the circumstances of his confinement, should he be unable to mix with the wider prison population, do not entail a real risk of his being subject to treatment that infringes article 3 [48].

Article 5 and Article 8

The article 5 and article 8 challenges are without substance [49]. There is nothing arbitrary for the purposes of article 5 in the respondent serving two-thirds of the remainder of his sentence in Taiwan before he would be eligible for parole. The respondent's inability to obtain credit toward parole in Taiwan for the time spent in custody in Scotland is the result of his flight from justice in Taiwan. This involves no injustice [50]. The interference with the respondent's article 8 right to private life which arises from his extradition and imprisonment in Taiwan is justified because it is necessary for both the prevention of crime and for the protection of the rights and freedoms of others [51].

References in square brackets are to paragraphs in the judgment

NOTE: This summary is provided to assist in understanding the Court's decision. It does not form part of the reasons for the decision. The full judgment of the Court is the only authoritative document. Judgments are public documents and are available at:

http://supremecourt.uk/decided-cases/index.html

Trinity Term
[2017] UKSC 44
On appeals from: [2016] HCJAC 83 and [2016] HCJAC 117

JUDGMENT

Lord Advocate (representing the Taiwanese Judicial Authorities) (Appellant) v Dean (Respondent) (Scotland)

before

Lord Mance

Lord Sumption

Lord Reed

Lord Hughes

Lord Hodge

JUDGMENT GIVEN ON

28 June 2017

Heard on 6 March 2017

Appellant	*Respondent*
Lord Advocate	Mungo Bovey QC
David J Dickson	Graeme R Brown
(Instructed by Crown Office)	(Instructed by GR Brown Solicitors)

LORD HODGE: (with whom Lord Mance, Lord Sumption, Lord Reed and Lord Hughes agree)

1.   This is an appeal about an extradition order. The Lord Advocate appeals under paragraph 13 of Schedule 6 to the Scotland Act 1998 against the determination of a devolution issue by the Appeal Court of the High Court of Justiciary ("the Appeal Court") on 23 September 2016. That court, by majority, quashed an order for the extradition of the respondent ("Mr Dean") to Taiwan. The underlying question is whether his extradition to serve the residue of a prison sentence there would be compatible with his right under article 3 of the European Convention for the Protection of Human Rights and Fundamental Freedoms ("the Convention"), which, as is well known, provides: "No one shall be subjected to torture or to inhuman or degrading treatment or punishment". The Appeal Court held that his extradition would not be compatible with that article of the Convention.

2.   The appeal raises two principal questions, namely (a) the competence of the appeal and (b) whether the Appeal Court applied the correct legal test

in assessing the risk of harm which Mr Dean might face in the requesting state from non-state actors. If the Appeal Court did not apply the correct legal test, it is for this court to apply that test to the factual findings of the Appeal Court.

3.   It is important to make clear at the outset that the Lord Advocate argued the Crown's case in a way in which the solicitor advocate who appeared for him in the courts below had not. The Lord Advocate frankly conceded that his argument on what was the correct legal test had not been presented before the Appeal Court. It therefore involved criticising the judges of the Appeal Court for not giving effect to an argument which they did not hear.

Background facts

4.   Mr Dean, a citizen of the United Kingdom, was born in Manchester. He grew up in Edinburgh but had lived and worked in Taiwan for about 19 years before he was involved in a road traffic accident on 25 March 2010. Following that accident, he was convicted after trial in the District Court of Taipei on 15 March 2011 of driving while under the influence of alcohol, negligent manslaughter and leaving the scene of an accident. The basis of his conviction was that, while under the influence of alcohol, he drove into and killed a man who was driving a motorcycle on a newspaper delivery round, that he did not stop, and that he did not report the accident. He was sentenced to imprisonment for two years and six months.

5.   He appealed against his conviction and sentence to the High Court in Taipei, which, having heard further evidence, refused his appeal and increased his sentence of imprisonment to four years. He then appealed to the Supreme Court of Taiwan. He remained on bail before and during his trial and while his appeals were pending. Before the Supreme Court of Taiwan had heard his appeal, he fled Taiwan, using a friend's passport, and came to Scotland. The Supreme Court of Taiwan confirmed his conviction and sentence in his absence.

6.   The authorities in Taiwan then applied for his extradition. On 9 October 2013 the Ministry of Justice of Taiwan sought a provisional arrest warrant under section 73 of the Extradition Act 2003 ("the 2003 Act"), which is available if a person is accused in a category 2 territory of the commission of an offence and he is alleged to be unlawfully at large after his conviction. Because there is no extradition treaty between the UK and Taiwan, the Home Office on behalf of the United Kingdom and the judicial authorities in Taiwan entered into a memorandum of understanding in relation to Mr Dean under section 194 of the 2003 Act dated 16 October 2013. This had the result that a certificate by the Scottish Ministers enabled the 2003 Act to apply in relation to Mr Dean's extradition as if Taiwan were a category 2 territory under that Act.

7.   Mr Dean was arrested in Scotland on 17 October 2013 and remained in custody for almost three years. On 28 October 2013 the Ministry of Justice of Taiwan delivered a written request for Mr Dean's extradition to the Secretary of State for the Home Department. The Cabinet Secretary for Justice, Mr Kenny MacAskill, certified the request under section 70(1) of 2003 Act on 18 November 2013 and sent the request to Edinburgh Sheriff Court. An extradition hearing before Sheriff Kenneth Maciver was scheduled to commence in January 2014. Mr Dean mounted numerous challenges and lodged two devolution minutes. The completion of the hearing was delayed by his withdrawal of instructions from his legal representatives, the obtaining of an expert report and the engagement of replacement legal representatives. By Note of Decision dated 11 June 2014, the sheriff decided under section 87(1) of the 2003 Act that Mr Dean's extradition would be compatible with his Convention rights within the meaning of Human Rights Act 1998, and refused the two devolution minutes. The Scottish Ministers made the extradition order on 1 August 2014.

8.   Mr Dean appealed under section 103 of the 2003 Act against Sheriff Maciver's decision and under section 108 of that Act against the extradition order of the Scottish Ministers. The Appeal Court (Lady Paton, Lord Drummond Young and Lady Clark of Calton) heard challenges as to whether

Taiwan was a "territory" within the meaning of the 2003 Act, whether Mr Dean's article 6 right to a fair trial had been infringed, and whether, under section 81 of the 2003 Act, extraneous considerations barred extradition - in this case whether there was a serious possibility that the request to extradite was for the purpose of punishing him by reason of his race or nationality. In its unanimous opinion dated 24 June 2015, the Appeal Court rejected those challenges. This appeal is not concerned with those issues. On the issue with which this court is concerned, namely the challenge under article 3 of the Convention concerning prison conditions in Taiwan, the Appeal Court ordered an evidential hearing. It reserved its opinion on the section 108 appeal until it had dealt with the article 3 challenge.

9.   After hearing evidence on the article 3 challenge, the Appeal Court on 23 September 2016 by a majority (Lord Drummond Young dissenting) held that Mr Dean's extradition to Taiwan would not be compatible with his article 3 right and ordered his discharge. The Appeal Court, in assessing the compatibility of the extradition, applied the test set out in *Saadi v Italy*(2009) 49 EHRR 30, namely "whether substantial grounds have been shown for believing that there is a real risk of treatment incompatible with article 3". The majority (Lady Paton and Lady Clark of Calton) concluded that there was such a risk. Because I am satisfied that the Appeal Court applied the wrong legal test and that this court must therefore make its own assessment of the facts found by the Appeal Court, I mean no discourtesy in summarising the majority's reasoning briefly.

10.   The Appeal Court heard evidence from Mr Dean and also two legal academics, Professor Mong Hwa Chin and Dr James McManus, who had been instructed on behalf of the Lord Advocate. That evidence vouched the conclusion that Taiwanese prisons were seriously overcrowded and that Taipei prison, where the Taiwanese authorities proposed to keep Mr Dean, was both overcrowded and understaffed. The Taiwanese authorities had given written assurances to the Lord Advocate in which they undertook that Mr Dean would not be housed in the overcrowded cells in the main prison block but would be housed in a separate building in an adequately sized cell,

which had a lavatory and a shower and which he would share with only one other foreign prisoner. The majority of the Appeal Court held that, if the Taiwanese authorities fulfilled their undertakings to the letter, there was still a real risk of ill treatment in accordance with the *Saadi* test because (a) Mr Dean suffered from some notoriety in Taiwan, the other inmates and prison staff would view the arrangements made for him as wholly exceptional, and this would give rise to animosity from other prisoners, (b) the staffing levels were not sufficient to protect Mr Dean if he were to mix with other prisoners, (c) therefore he was likely to choose to stay in his cell for most of the time and would not be able to work to earn parole, (d) he would also have only limited opportunity for outdoor exercise or interaction with others and solitary confinement was generally harmful to health, (e) the ratio of medical and pharmaceutical staff to prisoners was too low and prisoners had to pay for non-emergency medical treatment and non-standard drugs, (f) there was no formal system for a UK body or an international body to inspect the prison, (g) United Kingdom consular staff, who visited UK prisoners in Taiwanese prisons, did not assess prison standards, and (h) there were no established procedures by which prisoners could enforce their rights in the Taiwanese courts. Lady Clark also commented on the ad hoc nature of the assurances which the Taiwanese authorities had given and doubted the ability of the British consular staff to monitor those assurances.

11. Lord Drummond Young in his dissenting opinion emphasised the contribution which extradition makes to the rule of law both nationally and internationally. He pointed out that the European Court of Human Rights ("ECtHR") had held that article 3 was not a means by which contracting states might impose their own standards on other states: *Ahmad v United Kingdom* (2012) 56 EHRR 1, para 177. He argued that the court must proceed on the assumption that the Taiwanese authorities would observe in good faith the assurances they had given and he assessed the quality of those assurances against the criteria which the ECtHR set out in *Othman v United Kingdom* (2012) 55 EHRR 1, paras 177-190. Having assessed the evidence, Lord Drummond Young concluded that Mr Dean had failed to establish that

there was any real risk of his being subject to treatment that would infringe article 3 of the Convention.

12.　After the Appeal Court (again by majority) refused to give leave to appeal, a panel of this court granted the Lord Advocate permission to appeal on 21 December 2016.

Discussion

13.　I consider, first, the challenge to the competency of this appeal before discussing the correct legal test for compatibility with article 3 of the ECHR when the threat comes from the acts of third parties and applying that test to the findings of the Appeal Court.

The competence of this appeal

14.　Mr Bovey, who appears for Mr Dean, challenges the competence of this appeal on the ground that the Appeal Court has not determined a devolution issue. For the reasons set out below I consider that challenge to be misconceived.

15.　The decision of the Appeal Court which the Lord Advocate has appealed is a decision "whether the person's extradition would be compatible with the Convention rights within the meaning of the Human Rights Act 1998 (c 42)": section 87(1) of the 2003 Act. The decision was made in the context of an appeal under section 103 of the 2003 Act. There is no appeal to this court from a decision of a Scottish court under section 103 because the provision authorising an appeal to this court from decisions made under sections 103 and 108 (among others) does not apply to Scotland: section 114(13) of the 2003 Act. But that is not the end of the matter because an appeal from a decision under section 87(1) of the 2003 Act, which was the subject of this part of Mr Dean's section 103 appeal, raises a question of the legal competence of the Scottish Government.

16.   Section 57(2) of the Scotland Act 1998 provides

"A member of the Scottish Government has no power to make any subordinate legislation, or to do any other act, so far as the legislation or act is incompatible with any of the Convention rights …"

17.   The functions carried out by the Lord Advocate and the Scottish Ministers under Part 2 of the 2003 Act are acts that they perform as members of the Scottish Government: *BH v Lord Advocate* 2012 SC (UKSC) 308, paras 33-34 per Lord Hope, and *Kapri v Lord Advocate* 2013 SC (UKSC) 311, paras 18-23 per Lord Hope.

18.   In Schedule 6 to the Scotland Act 1998 paragraph 1(d) includes within the definition of a "devolution issue":

"a question whether a purported or proposed exercise of a function by a member of the Scottish Executive is, or would be, incompatible with any of the Convention rights …"

19.   The question as to whether the Scottish Government's acts in seeking to extradite Mr Dean to Taiwan are compatible with Convention rights is thus a devolution issue: *BH* (above), para 34, *Kapri* (above), para 22. Section 116(1) of the 2003 Act provides the general rule that a decision under Part 2 of the Act by a judge or the Scottish Ministers may be questioned in legal proceedings only by means of an appeal under that Part, but subsection (2) to that section excludes from that limitation an appeal against the determination of a devolution issue.

20.   When pursuing his appeal before the Appeal Court to challenge the sheriff's decision under section 87 of the 2003 Act Mr Dean had the option of proceeding either under section 103 of the 2003 Act or by means of raising a devolution issue under the Scotland Act 1998: *BH* (above), para 26; *Kapri* (above), para 19. He chose to proceed under section 103 of the 2003 Act and did not raise a devolution minute in relation to his challenge concerning prison conditions in the Appeal Court. The Lord Advocate was the respondent to Mr Dean's appeal before the Appeal Court. He therefore

did not need to exercise his right under paragraph 4 of Schedule 6 to the Scotland Act 1998 to institute proceedings to determine the devolution issue raised by Mr Dean's appeal.

21.   Where a devolution issue arises in proceedings, intimation of the issue should be given to the Advocate General for Scotland and the Lord Advocate, unless they are already parties to the proceedings: paragraph 5 of Schedule 6 to the Scotland Act 1998. Neither Mr Dean's legal advisers nor the Lord Advocate intimated the issue to the Advocate General for Scotland in relation to the proceedings before the Appeal Court. The Advocate General was thus deprived of his right under paragraph 6 of Schedule 6 to take part in the proceedings in the Appeal Court. That omission, however, does not affect the competence of any appeal to this court.

22.   Paragraph 13(a) of Schedule 6 to the Scotland Act 1998 confers a right of appeal to the Supreme Court against a determination of a devolution issue by a court of two or more judges of the High Court of Justiciary. The decision of the Appeal Court is such a determination. The Lord Advocate has informed this court that he had intimated the devolution issue, which he seeks to argue in this court, to the Advocate General for Scotland, who has indicated that he does not intend to take part in the proceedings. There is therefore no bar to this appeal.

23.   It may be that the Appeal Court would have determined the other devolution issues, which Mr Dean has raised, if it had been aware that the Lord Advocate might seek to appeal its determination of the article 3 devolution issue to this court. It did not do so. That is unfortunate because it may cause further delay, but that cannot affect the competence of this appeal.

The merits of the appeal

Article 3 of the Convention: summary

24.   The Lord Advocate concedes that, on the findings of fact by the Appeal Court, there are substantial grounds for believing that there is

a risk that Mr Dean would suffer harm from other prisoners in Taipei prison if protective measures were not put in place. But, he submits, the ECtHR laid down the appropriate legal test in such a circumstance in *HLR v France* (1998) 26 EHRR 29, which the House of Lords applied in *R (Bagdanavicius) v Secretary of State for the Home Department* [2005] 2 AC 668 ("*Bagdanavicius*"). As I set out below, the test is whether the state has failed to provide reasonable protection against harm inflicted by non-state agents. Mr Bovey acknowledges that test but submits that in substance the Appeal Court has addressed it. I do not accept that submission. In my view, the Appeal Court did not address that test. This is unsurprising, because, as Lady Paton recorded at para 8 of her opinion, counsel were agreed that the correct test was set out in *Saadi*, to which I have referred in para 9 above. As a result no clear distinction was drawn in her opinion (paras 8, 45, and 50-58) between the underlying threat from other prisoners, which the Appeal Court found to exist, and conduct for which the state was responsible. It is therefore incumbent on this court to apply the correct legal test to the findings of fact of the Appeal Court. In short, the court must assess, first, whether the Taiwanese authorities are undertaking to provide Mr Dean with reasonable protection against violence by third parties while he is in prison, and, secondly, if they are, whether the conditions in which he is to have such protection themselves entail an infringement of article 3.

The correct legal test

25.   Article 3 of the Convention enshrines one of the fundamental values of a democratic society. It is therefore incumbent on the court to be assiduous in its assessment of a challenge on this ground. A person asserting a breach of this article must show that there are substantial grounds for believing that he faces a real risk of being subjected to treatment contrary to article 3 if he is extradited: *Saadi v Italy* (above), para 125. In addressing that challenge, the court can have regard to assurances given by the receiving state: *Othman v United Kingdom* (above), paras 187-189. In particular, the court must assess not only the quality of the assurances given but also whether they can be relied on, having regard to the general situation in that country with

regard to respect for human rights. In *Othman* (para 189) the ECtHR set out eleven factors which, among others, a court could take into account in making that assessment. I discuss several of those factors in para 38 below.

26.   In *Bagdanavicius*, Lord Brown of Eaton-under-Heywood, who gave the leading speech in the House of Lords, observed (para 7) that it has long been established that article 3 imposes an obligation on the part of a contracting state not to expel someone from its territory where substantial grounds are shown for believing that he will face in the receiving country a real risk of being subjected to treatment contrary to that article. He cited *Soering v United Kingdom* (1989) 11 EHRR 439 as the initial authority for the principle that the act of expulsion in such a circumstance constitutes the proscribed ill-treatment. The expulsion itself breaches article 3 if such risk in the receiving country emanates either from acts of the public authorities of that state or from persons or groups of persons who are not public officials. In the latter circumstance, it is not sufficient to show that there is a real risk of suffering serious harm at the hands of non-state agents. In para 24 Lord Brown deprecated a failure in such cases to distinguish between the risk of serious harm on the one hand and the risk of treatment contrary to article 3 on the other. He said:

"In cases where the risk 'emanates from intentionally inflicted acts of the public authorities in the receiving country' (the language of *D v United Kingdom* (1997) 24 EHRR 423, 447, para 49) one can use those terms interchangeably: the intentionally inflicted acts would without more constitute the proscribed treatment. Where, however, the risk emanates from non-state bodies, that is not so: any harm inflicted by non-state agents will not constitute article 3 ill-treatment unless in addition the state has failed to provide reasonable protection. ... Non-state agents do not subject people to torture or to the other proscribed forms of ill-treatment, however violently they treat them: what, however, would transform such violent treatment into article 3 ill-treatment would be the state's failure to provide reasonable protection against it."

27.   It is this test that the court must apply to the facts of this case in relation to the harm which non-state actors might inflict, before asking whether the circumstances of such protection are themselves compatible with article 3.

Applying the tests

28.   The Appeal Court made findings that there were problems of over-crowding and under-staffing in the main detention building in Taipei prison which gave rise to uncontrolled bullying of weaker prisoners. There was also evidence, which the Appeal Court accepted, of inadequate ventilation and lavatory facilities which exacerbated the discomfort caused by the over-crowding, and inadequate opportunities for the prisoners to exercise in the open air (para 44). There was also a finding that Mr Dean was at particular risk of being the focus of hostility from prisoners within the prison (para 47). As against those findings, it is necessary to assess the undertakings which the Taiwanese authorities have made in support of their application for Mr Dean's extradition.

29.   Lady Paton in para 10 of her opinion recorded in summary the various undertakings which the Taiwanese authorities have given. I summarise those which are most relevant to prison conditions.

30.   First, in a letter dated 25 February 2014, Mrs Chen Wen-chi, the Director General of the Department of International and Cross-Strait Legal Affairs in the Ministry of Justice of Taiwan and signatory of the memorandum of understanding (para 6 above), undertook that Mr Dean would be supervised by English-speaking officers and that he would be housed in an appropriate cell with persons selected from among non-violent foreign inmates, to avoid bullying. The authorities would treat Mr Dean as a special assignment, take account of his concerns for his safety, and assess the level of protection which he needed. They would pre-screen inmates with ill intent towards him to prevent them having contact with him. If necessary, they would separate Mr Dean from group activities and restrict his interaction with other inmates. By letter dated 14 November 2014, Mr Luo Ying-shay, the Minister of Justice of Taiwan, confirmed Mrs Chen

Wen-chi's authority to give undertakings on behalf of his ministry, which supervised the Agency of Corrections which was responsible for managing prisons in Taiwan.

31.   Secondly, on 19 August 2015 Mrs Chen Wen-chi described and sent photographs of the cell which she undertook to prepare for Mr Dean and which he would share with one other foreign prisoner. The cell was located on the second floor of the 11th disciplinary area in Taipei prison and had an area of 13.76 square metres. The cell was equipped with a desk, a chair, a four-shelf cupboard, a bunk bed, and a bathroom with a toilet, a sink, a shower and a shower curtain. There was good natural lighting through a large window, electric lighting, an exhaust fan and an electric fan on the ceiling. Prisoners had the opportunity to spend about nine hours per day out of their cells, which included working, exercise time, rests and meals. Assurances were also given about the quality of drinking water and diet. By letter of the same date Mr Wu Man-Ying, the Director General of the Agency of Corrections, confirmed that his agency would abide by those assurances. He confirmed this a second time in a letter dated 2 June 2016.

32.   Thirdly, Mrs Chen Wen-chi by letter dated 25 December 2015 confirmed that if the United Kingdom consular staff raised an issue concerning a breach of an assurance about prison conditions, the Taiwanese authorities would respond to remedy any breach.

33.   Finally, on 31 May 2016, the new Minister of Justice, Mr Chui Tai-san, re-affirmed Mrs Chen Wen-chi's authority to provide the assurances and to undertake to put them into practice.

34.   Dr McManus's visit to Taipei prison in August 2015 provided further insight into the undertakings. The proposed cell measured 11.05 square metres, excluding the toilet and shower annex, giving 5.5 square metres to each of the proposed occupants. It was on the second floor of a reception area, where there were classrooms for the assessment of new arrivals. On the same floor there was an observation office and a 50-bed convalescent cell. The cell, which was proposed for Mr Dean, had been created in 2013

as a protected cell but had never been used. The proposed exercise area for Mr Dean was a tarmac basketball court adjacent to the building. The basketball court offered ample space for exercise and could be cleared of other prisoners when Mr Dean was using it. Dr McManus concluded that the accommodation met all the standards set by the Committee for the Prevention of Torture ("CPT") and the ECtHR in terms of space per prisoner, light, ventilation and toilet facilities. He also recorded that assurances had been given that Mr Dean could have a minimum of one hour's outdoor exercise per day and that he would be entitled to access to newspapers, radio and television. There was a work regime in the prison which, if Mr Dean engaged with it, would allow him to mix with other prisoners and to be out of his cell from 8.30 am to 5.30 pm.

35.   Understandably, it was not suggested on Mr Dean's behalf that the cell accommodation was inadequate or exposed him to overcrowding if he were to share it with one non-violent foreign prisoner. Nor was it suggested that he would not be reasonably safe when in that cell.

36.   In agreement with the judges of the Appeal Court, I proceed on the basis that the judicial authorities of Taiwan are acting in good faith in entering into the memorandum of understanding and in giving the assurances which they have. I also agree with the judges of the Appeal Court in so far as they proceeded on the assumption that the Taiwanese authorities responsible for the management of Taipei prison would make every effort to fulfil those undertakings. As Lord Drummond Young observed in his dissenting opinion, extradition assists in maintaining the rule of law both nationally and internationally. The United Kingdom Government has chosen to enter into extradition treaties with friendly foreign states or territories giving rise to mutual obligations in international law. In *Gomes v Government of Trinidad and Tobago* [2009] 1 WLR 1038, Lord Brown stated (para 36):

"The extradition process, it must be remembered, is only available for returning suspects to friendly foreign states with whom this country has entered into multilateral or bilateral treaty obligations involving mutually agreed and reciprocal commitments. The arrangements are founded on mutual trust and respect. There is a strong public interest in respecting such treaty obligations."

The Lord Advocate acknowledges that the memorandum of understanding does not have the status of a treaty enforceable in international law. That notwithstanding, there remains a strong public interest in promoting and maintaining the rule of law by means of extradition.

37.   But that strong public interest, while carrying great weight, has no paramountcy in the face of an article 3 challenge. In *Othman v United Kingdom* (above) the ECtHR stated how it would assess the quality of the assurances given by a receiving country in the context of deportation. The existence of an extradition agreement - whether a treaty or a memorandum of understanding - does not obviate the need for such an assessment in the context of a human rights challenge. It is possible, for example, that adverse political developments in a friendly foreign state might reduce the confidence which our courts could reasonably have about an extradited person's treatment in that country, notwithstanding the continued existence of an extradition treaty. In my view, it is incumbent on a court, which is addressing an article 3 challenge, to make such an assessment in the context of an extradition; and the existence of the extradition agreement is a factor in that assessment. This is consistent with the ECtHR's guidance in *Othman* which identified as relevant the length and strength of bilateral relations between the sending and receiving states.

38.   In this case the assurances are given on behalf of the central government of Taiwan, which is a developed society with a tradition of respect for the rule of law. There is no suggestion that the Taiwanese authorities ill-treated Mr Dean before he fled the country. The assurances are given by a senior responsible official and have been confirmed by two Ministers of Justice and by the Director General of the agency with responsibility for managing prisons. The assurances, and in particular those about his accommodation and separating him from group activities with other prisoners if that is necessary for his safety, are specific rather than general. The assurances envisage that United Kingdom consular staff will

have access to Mr Dean in prison and include an undertaking to remedy any breach of the assurances which the consular staff raise with the prison authorities. The memorandum of understanding and the assurances have given a role to the consular staff which they have not had in the past in relation to United Kingdom citizens imprisoned in Taiwan. There is no reason to think that the consular staff would not perform their obligations to monitor the assurances if Mr Dean were to request their help. While there appears to have been no examination of the access which Mr Dean might have to legal advice, Dr McManus recorded the apparently successful operation of a complaints system in the prison and that some prisoners had obtained access to the domestic courts. This is the first occasion on which Taiwan has sought to extradite a United Kingdom citizen and the memorandum of understanding and the assurances are therefore untested; but that novelty is significantly outweighed by the other factors which I have mentioned in this paragraph.

39.   Mr Dean's case is both that he has gained notoriety in Taiwan as a foreign businessman who was convicted of killing a local man through driving while drunk and also that other prisoners would resent his privileged status in the prison and wish to harm him. As a result, he may not be able to mix with other prisoners and work to earn parole, which in Taiwan depends in part upon a prisoner's taking part in work activities in the prison. I cannot judge in advance the extent to which Mr Dean's fear of being harmed by other prisoners will prevent him from mixing with them. But there is no evidence to support an inference that the Taiwanese authorities will not give him reasonable protection against harm at the hands of other prisoners: the undertakings would allow him to elect to remain in his cell and exercise outdoors by himself. There is nothing to suggest that such a regime would fail to prevent third parties from harming him.

40.   I turn then to the second question, which is whether the confinement which such a regime would entail would risk a breach of article 3. There is no issue about the quality of the cell accommodation or the fact that Mr Dean would share the cell with a non-violent foreign prisoner. But

the majority of the Appeal Court expressed concern that Mr Dean might have to elect to stay in his cell and thus be subjected to a form of solitary confinement, which might be harmful to his health.

41.   In Mr Dean's case we are not concerned with complete sensory isolation and total social isolation which the ECtHR has recognised as constituting a form of inhuman treatment. But the Convention looks beyond such isolation. In *Ahmad* at paras 207-210 the ECtHR stated:

"207. Other forms of solitary confinement which fall short of complete sensory isolation may violate article 3. Solitary confinement is one of the most serious measures which can be imposed within a prison and, as the Committee for the Prevention of Torture has stated, all forms of solitary confinement without appropriate mental and physical stimulation are likely, in the long term, to have damaging effects, resulting in deterioration of mental faculties and social abilities. Indeed, as the Committee's most recent report makes clear, the damaging effect of solitary confinement can be immediate and increases the longer the measure lasts and the more indeterminate it is.

208.   At the same time, however, the Court has found that the prohibition of contact with other prisoners for security, disciplinary or protective reasons does not itself amount to inhuman treatment or punishment. In many states parties to the Convention more stringent security measures, which are intended to prevent the risk of escape, attack or disturbance of the prison community, exist for dangerous prisoners.

209.   Thus, whilst prolonged removal from association with others is undesirable, whether such a measure falls within the ambit of article 3 of the Convention depends on the particular conditions, the stringency of the measure, its duration, the objective pursued and its effects on the person concerned.

210.   In applying these criteria, the Court has never laid down precise rules governing the operation of solitary confinement. For example, it

has never specified a period of time, beyond which solitary confinement will attain the minimum level of severity required for article 3. The Court has, however, emphasised that solitary confinement, even in cases entailing relative isolation, cannot be imposed on a prisoner indefinitely."

42.   In Mr Dean's case, we are concerned with what the ECtHR has described as "relative isolation" as he would share his cell with a non-violent foreign prisoner and would have access to newspapers, radio and television. There would also be opportunities for people to visit him. That relative isolation would not be imposed on him by the prison authorities but would be at his option, if he were to take the view that the risk of harm at the hands of other prisoners required him to dissociate himself from contact with them. Thus, the objective which might give rise to his relative isolation would be his own protection.

43.   Further, the period of Mr Dean's imprisonment resulting from his conviction is unlikely to exceed approximately 13 months because the Taiwanese authorities have undertaken to give him credit towards his four-year sentence for the period of almost three years which he has spent in prison in Scotland.

44.   When one has regard to the decisions of the ECtHR in other cases concerning solitary confinement, such as *Öcalan v Turkey* (2005) 41 EHRR 45, *Ramirez Sanchez v France* (2007) 45 EHRR 49 and *Ahmad v United Kingdom* (above), and the decision of this court in *Shahid v Scottish Ministers* [2015] UKSC 58; 2016 SC (UKSC) 1; [2016] AC 429, the circumstances of Mr Dean's possible relative isolation do not come close to a breach of article 3 of the Convention and do not contribute significantly to his assertion of such a breach when other circumstances are considered. It is necessary, of course, to take a holistic view of the circumstances of his detention in reaching a view as to whether there is a real risk of his being subject to treatment that infringes article 3 of the Convention. But the other factors which influenced the majority of the Appeal Court do not materially advance his case.

45. First, the ratio of medical staff to prisoners, to which Lady Paton referred in para 33 of her opinion, was well below the standard advocated by the CPT, which is one doctor per 350 prisoners. But, as she also recorded, Dr McManus concluded that there appeared to be "no great problem for prisoners obtaining medical attention when needed". The fact that prisoners have to pay for non-emergency medical and dental treatment and also for non-generic drugs is of little significance. It is important to recall that the ECtHR has repeatedly stated that the Convention does not purport to be a means of requiring the Contracting States to impose Convention standards on other states: *Al-Skeini v United Kingdom* (2011) 53 EHRR 18, para 141; *Ahmad v United Kingdom* (above), para 177.

46. Secondly, I do not infer from the past practice of United Kingdom consular staff of not pressing for the improvement of prison conditions for United Kingdom prisoners that they would not act to protect Mr Dean. As I have said, the existence of the memorandum of understanding and also the assurances by which the Taiwanese authorities have recognised the role of the consular staff in protecting Mr Dean's interests have given the consular staff a role which to date they have not had.

47. Thirdly, the majority of the Appeal Court was concerned both by the absence of an international system by which prison conditions in Taiwan were monitored and that "there is no established route within the Taiwanese courts whereby a prisoner can seek a remedy in respect of prison conditions" (paras 56 and 57). Those are among the factors which the ECtHR has identified as relevant considerations in assessing the quality of the assurances of the receiving state: *Othman v United Kingdom* (above) para 189. But in my view, those considerations do not outweigh the other factors which point towards accepting the assurances (para 38 above) and the role which the United Kingdom consular staff will undertake in monitoring the assurances.

48. I am therefore satisfied (a) that the assurances of the Taiwanese authorities offer Mr Dean reasonable protection against violence by non-state actors and (b) that the circumstances of his confinement, should he be

unable to mix with the wider prison population, do not entail a real risk of his being subject to treatment that infringes article 3 of the Convention.

Articles 5 and 8 of the Convention

49.   Mr Bovey also advances separate challenges under articles 5 and 8 of the Convention, which the Appeal Court did not need to decide. I am satisfied that those challenges are without substance and can deal with them briefly.

50.   *Article 5*: Mr Bovey submits that Mr Dean's detention in prison would involve arbitrariness because the Taiwanese authorities would not give him credit for the time spent in custody in Scotland in the calculation of his entitlement to parole. One of the assurances which Mrs Chen Wen-chi gave (in a letter dated 23 December 2013) was that all periods of detention in Scotland arising from the extradition request would be deducted from the total period which he would have to serve in Taiwan. That undertaking did not include any reference to entitlement to parole and, contrary to counsel's submission, I detect nothing in it that was objectively misleading. In a later letter, dated 1 June 2016, Mrs Chen Wen-chi explained that only periods of imprisonment in Taiwan would count towards the service of a minimum part of the sentence for entitlement to parole. It appears therefore that Mr Dean would have to serve two-thirds of the residue of his sentence in Taiwan before he would be eligible to be considered for parole. I detect nothing arbitrary in this regime. The Convention does not require United Kingdom courts to expect foreign states to have similar sentencing practices to ours or a particular form of parole system. Article 3 would be breached by extradition to serve a sentence, which the receiving state imposed, only if the sentence was grossly disproportionate: *Willcox v United Kingdom* (2013) 57 EHRR SE 16, para 74. Mr Dean's inability to obtain credit towards parole for the time he has spent in custody in Scotland is the result of his flight from justice in Taiwan. This involves no injustice.

51.   *Article 8*: Counsel also argues that Mr Dean's extradition to and imprisonment in Taiwan would interfere with his right to respect for his

private life. I agree that there would be such interference but am satisfied that it is justified because it is necessary in a democratic society both for the prevention of crime and for the protection of the rights and freedoms of others (article 8(2)). This court has recognised the strength of the public interest in extradition in the context of an article 8 challenge: *Norris v Government of the United States of America (No 2)* [2010] 2 AC 487; *H (H) v Deputy Prosecutor of the Italian Republic (Official Solicitor intervening)* [2013] 1 AC 338. Mr Dean has been convicted of a serious offence committed in Taiwan where he had resided for 19 years. A term of imprisonment for such an offence was clearly justified both as a punishment and to deter such behaviour by others. It may be that the special protective measures which are proposed will prevent Mr Dean from earning credit towards parole while serving the residue of his sentence. But that does not undermine the justification of the extradition.

Conclusion

52. I would allow the appeal on the devolution issue and remit the case to the Appeal Court to deal with Mr Dean's appeal under section 108 of the 2003 Act and his devolution minute in that appeal.

APPEALS UNDER SECTIONS 103 AND 108 OF THE EXTRADITION ACT 2003 BY ZAIN TAJ DEAN AGAINST (FIRST) THE LORD ADVOCATE AND (SECOND) THE SCOTTISH MINISTERS

Submitted: 24 June 2015

APPEAL COURT, HIGH COURT OF JUSTICIARY

[2015] HCJAC 52

HCA2014/3518/XM &

HCA2014/3519/XM

Lady Paton

Lord Drummond Young

Lady Clark of Calton

OPINION OF THE COURT

delivered by LADY PATON

in the APPEALS UNDER SECTIONS 103 AND 108 OF THE EXTRADITION

ACT 2003

by

ZAIN TAJ DEAN

Appellant;

against

(FIRST) THE LORD ADVOCATE; and (SECOND) THE SCOTTISH MINISTERS

Respondents:

Appellant: Bovey QC, Devlin; V Good & Co

First respondent: D Dickson, Solicitor Advocate; Crown Office

Second respondent: Moynihan QC, Charteris; Scottish Government Legal Directorate

24 June 2015

Extradition to Taiwan

[1]   This is the opinion of the court, to which each member of the bench has contributed.

[2]   The appellant is a businessman and a British citizen. His date of birth is 16 November 1971. He is currently in prison in Scotland. For many years, he lived and worked in Taiwan (the Republic of China). On 25 March 2010 he was involved in a road traffic accident there. He was prosecuted. In 2011 he was tried by three judges in the District Court of Taipei, Taiwan. He was convicted of drink driving, negligent manslaughter, and leaving the scene of the accident. He was sentenced to two and a half years imprisonment. He appealed against conviction and sentence, and was granted bail. In 2012, after an unsuccessful appeal to Taiwan High Court and while his appeal to the Taiwan Supreme Court was still pending, he left Taiwan (using a friend's passport) and came to Scotland. He was arrested in Scotland on 17 October 2013, and has been in custody since then. Following extradition proceedings, the Scottish Ministers made an extradition order returning him to Taiwan. He appeals first, under section 103 of the Extradition Act 2003, against the decision of Sheriff Maciver dated 11 June 2014 sending his case to the Scottish Ministers for their decision whether he should be extradited; and secondly, under section 108 of the 2003 Act, against the Scottish Ministers' decision dated 1 August 2014 to extradite him. If the appeal under section 103 were to succeed, the appeal under section 108 would become unnecessary.

[3]   There is no extradition treaty between the UK and Taiwan. There has never previously been an extradition of someone from the UK to Taiwan. A special memorandum of understanding relating to the appellant was entered into on 16 October 2013, as a result of which Taiwan is to be treated (so far as the appellant is concerned) as a category 2 territory in terms of the 2003 Act.

Events leading to the decision to extradite

[4]   The events leading to the decision to extradite the appellant were as follows:

2010

25 March 2010: The appellant had been drinking in a club in Taiwan. In the early hours of the morning, he left the club under the influence of drink. Initially he was being driven home in his own car by a club driver, and CCTV footage from outside the club showed the appellant in the passenger seat (although the driver could not be seen). Subsequently, it was less clear who was driving. A witness who was a club driver gave evidence at the trial that he had been the driver, and after a few minutes the appellant ordered him out of the car and took over the driving. That witness was seen on further CCTV footage, walking back to the club. However the appellant gave conflicting evidence, namely that the witness was lying, and a different man had been driving, although the appellant could not say who the driver was (sheriff's note of decision pages 17 and 26). At all events, the appellant's car struck a motorcyclist on a newspaper round. The appellant's car did not stop, nor did the appellant report the accident. No CCTV footage of the actual collision was produced or shown at the trial. The motorcyclist subsequently died.

19 April 2010: The appellant was prosecuted and charged with driving under the influence of alcohol, negligent manslaughter, and escaping after having caused a traffic casualty.

2011

March 2011: The appellant stood trial in the District Court of Taipei. As the sheriff explains (at page 25 of his note)

"The trial… hinged on the straightforward issue of identification of the driver of the offending motor vehicle which was owned by Mr Dean, and the court concluded that, on the evidence presented to it, Mr Dean was proved to be the driver at the time of the fatal impact with the motorcyclist".

The appellant appealed to Taiwan High Court.

2012

26 July 2012: In the course of the appeal, some evidence was re-heard, and some fresh evidence introduced (pages 26 and 30 of the sheriff's note). The appeal was refused, and the sentence increased to four years. The appellant appealed to the Taiwan Supreme Court.

14 August 2012: While his appeal was still pending, the appellant left Taiwan, using a friend's passport. He came to the UK.

20 December 2012: The Taiwan Supreme Court confirmed the conviction and the four year sentence.

2013

March 2013: Criminal proceedings in Taiwan were raised against the appellant in respect of his absconding from Taiwan. Those proceedings are currently suspended.

9 October 2013: The judicial authorities of Taiwan sought a provisional arrest warrant in respect of the appellant in terms of sections 73 and 74 of the 2003 Act.

16 October 2013: In terms of section 194 of the 2003 Act, a memorandum of understanding concerning the extradition of the appellant was entered into between the Home Office and the judicial authorities of Taiwan. Sheriff Maciver granted a warrant for the arrest of the appellant under sections 73 and 74 of the 2003 Act.

17 October 2013: The appellant was arrested. Since then he has been in custody in Saughton Prison, Edinburgh.

28 October 2013: A written request (dated *per incuriam* "October 28, 2014", in fact signed on October 28, 2013) for the extradition of the appellant was sent by Chen Wen-Chi, Director General, Department of International and Cross-Strait Legal Affairs, Ministry of Justice, Taiwan, to Theresa May, the Secretary of State for the Home Department.

18 November 2013: The Scottish Ministers certified the request in terms of section 70(1) of the Extradition Act 2003. The request was sent to Edinburgh Sheriff Court.

19 November 2013: The request for extradition was served on the appellant in Saughton.

23 December 2013: By letters dated 23 December 2013 Chen Wen-Chi, Director General, certified that time spent in custody in Scotland would be deducted from the total period of detention to be served in Taiwan as a result of the appellant's conviction of the extradition offence; the current four year sentence would not be subject to further review; and the death penalty would not be imposed.

2014

8 January – 9 June 2014: Extradition proceedings took place with several hearings in Edinburgh Sheriff Court. There were some unavoidable delays (for example, when the appellant sought a change of legal representation).

11 June 2014: Sheriff Maciver issued his decision, refused two devolution minutes relating to human rights, and sent the appellant's case to the Scottish Ministers for their decision whether the appellant should be extradited in accordance with Part 2 of the 2003 Act.

25 July 2014: A letter of assurance from Chen Wen-Chi,

Director General of the Department of International and Cross-Strait Legal Affairs, confirmed that, in the context of speciality, if the appellant were to be extradited in terms of the request of 28 October 2013, the Taiwan authorities would not prosecute the appellant for an offence not included in that request (in particular for the offence of absconding from Taiwan) without first seeking and obtaining the necessary consent from the Home Secretary in terms of section 129 of the 2003 Act.

1 August 2014: The Scottish Ministers made an extradition order returning the appellant to Taiwan. The appellant appealed to the High Court

The grounds of appeal

A. Appeal in terms of section 103

[5]   The appellant's grounds of appeal (read short, and not in the same order as in the amended note of appeal) are as follows:

(1) *Territory*: The sheriff erred in law in holding that Taiwan was a "territory" for the purposes of the 2003 Act.

(2) *Article 6 of the European Convention on Human Rights (ECHR)*: The sheriff erred in concluding that the appellant had received a fair trial in Taiwan. The sheriff should have ordered the appellant's discharge in terms of section 87(2) of the 2003 Act.

(3) *Extraneous considerations (section 81 of the 2003 Act)*: The sheriff erred in that he applied the wrong test when considering the evidence in the light of section 81. Applying the correct test, the evidence established that there was a "reasonable chance" or a "serious possibility" that the appellant, if extradited, might be punished, detained, or restricted in his personal liberty by reason of his nationality and/or race (namely British, of Indian origin), and therefore his extradition was barred on that ground.

(4) *Article 3 of the ECHR:* The sheriff erred in his decision that article 3 was not violated by the prison conditions in Taipei prison. The sheriff should have ordered the appellant's discharge in terms of section 87(2) of the 2003 Act.

A further ground of appeal alleging that the sheriff showed bias in favour of the Taiwanese judiciary in the course of the extradition proceedings was not insisted upon. The appellant also contends that the sheriff erred in his refusal of the two devolution minutes concerning human rights issues.

B. *Appeal in terms of section 108*

[6]　The appellant's amended note of appeal under section 108, read short, challenges the decision to extradite as an abuse of process, and in breach of his ECHR rights.

The effect of *Kapri* v *Lord Advocate*

[7]　On 25 April 2014 , in the course of the extradition proceedings in the sheriff court, the judgment of the appeal court in *Kapri* v *Lord Advocate* 2015 JC 30, 2014 SLT 557, 2014 SCCR 310, became available. In *Kapri*, Lord Justice Clerk Carloway gave guidance as to the law of evidence in extradition proceedings. In particular, he explained:

> "[125] the rules of criminal evidence and procedure are, in the absence of some special circumstance, normally applicable (*HM Advocate v Havrilova* 2012 SCCR 361) … If a fact, including a substantial ground, requires to be established, the normal rules must apply …

> [126] The ECtHR [may feel free] … to look at 'all the material placed before it, or, if necessary, material obtained *proprio motu*' … This may be entirely sensible for a court which operates across several jurisdictions …[but] the stark position is that it is not the law of evidence in criminal cases, which… applies in extradition proceedings such as these.

[127] There are specific provisions regarding the proof of documents emanating from extraditing states under the 2003 Act (s.202). However there is no general provision which allows the court to hold as proof of fact, merely by their production, the contents of reports or other papers emanating from foreign governments, international governmental or non-governmental bodies, or academic or research institutions.

[128] The approach of both parties was to put selected passages of reports and papers to one or other or both of the two witnesses, even if they had never seen the documents before, and ask them to confirm what was written in the document ... this left the court in a quandary about just what to do with the mass of material lodged, insofar as a part of it may have been put to the witnesses. In particular ... it is not at all clear what status ought to be afforded to the work of [certain] organisations ... [and the court] has difficulty with the concept that a judicial body should simply accept as true, and thus as proof of fact, the statements of officials in the executive of governments ... or in international institutions ... far less those in NGOs or groups with a particular human rights or other agenda ...

[129] Whether, and to what extent, there is corruption in the judiciary in Albania is not a matter of opinion. It is a matter of fact. It is for the court (and not an expert) to decide that matter based upon competent and relevant evidence placed before it. The role of the expert may be to interpret that evidence, where his or her special skills are required to do this. However, in relation to the content of the documents, that was not the role played by the witnesses. Rather, they were used almost as commentators to introduce material, most of which was never proved as fact, contained in the large range of documents lodged. The witnesses were not using their expertise as lawyers to assist the court's understanding of the material. The court was essentially just as capable of reading and understanding the documents as they were..."

[8]   The sheriff was, of course, bound by the guidance in *Kapri*. Never-theless he was placed in a difficult position, as he explains at page 42 of his note of decision:

"... this hearing began before the High Court decision in *Fatjon Kapri* (2013) HCJAC 33, and the position which I adopted in relation to admitting productions was very much more flexible than is recommended by the High Court in that case. However, I also have to be clear that, having started the hearing with a particular line in relation to acceptance of productions, I considered that it was necessary to maintain that position to the conclusion, and the line which I did adopt was one which favoured the position of Mr Dean. I did however make it clear from the outset that allowing productions to be lodged did not necessarily mean that these productions would automatically be considered relevant, nor did it mean that I would not feel free to examine the provenance and origin of the items in order to decide whether I would in fact properly include them in my consideration. As will be seen below, a number of items produced in this case had no provenance at all, and were simply extracts from internet discussions on topics such as prison overcrowding, and as such were clearly matters that cannot carry any weight in formal proceedings such as extradition hearings ... [Parties] were in complete agreement that issues such as ... judicial corruption and the integrity of a country's justice system are matters which, in the context of an extradition hearing, cannot be decided by reference to the speculative uninformed and inexpert view or opinion of interested parties, nor on the commentary of contributors to the media or internet discussion ..."

[9]   Senior counsel for the appellant submitted that the Lord Justice Clerk's observations in paragraph [125] *et seq* of *Kapri* were *obiter*. The more flexible approach outlined in paragraph [13] of *HM Advocate v Havrilova* 2012 SCCR 361, (namely bringing into play the evidential rules of criminal summary cause procedure "wherever circumstances allow") was to be preferred, certainly in extradition cases concerning human rights, abuse of process and extraneous considerations (cf *dicta* of

Lord Mance in *R(B)* v*Westminster Magistrates' Court* [2014] 3 WLR 1336, paragraphs 22 - 23). Section 77(2) of the Extradition Act 2003 did not say in terms that criminal evidential rules were to apply. If Scotland were to adopt a stricter approach than England to evidential rules in extradition cases, that would put the Scottish courts at risk of breaching the ECHR: cf *Mamazhonov* v *Russia* [2014] ECHR 1135 paragraphs 156 - 158. The practical difficulties of finding, instructing, and funding an appropriate expert and reports, all within the extradition timescales, should be borne in mind. The terms of section 202 of the 2003 Act (which assisted the requesting state) together with the more nuanced approach in *Havrilova* suggested a less rigorous approach to evidence than that set out in *Kapri*. But when dealing, for example, with article 3 of the ECHR (prison conditions) the sheriff had not made clear whether he was rejecting certain documents lodged as not complying with the guidance in *Kapri*, or whether he was taking them into account despite *Kapri*. But on any view, it would be unfair to apply the more rigorous approach set out in *Kapri* (and to find, for example, that insufficient evidence had been led relating to prison conditions) when the case had initially been conducted on the basis described in *R(B)* v *Westminster Magistrates' Court cit sup*. Senior counsel accordingly invited this court, when assessing extraneous considerations, human rights, and abuse of process in the context of extradition, to take into account all the information contained in documents which had been lodged in process, even if their provenance was unknown or doubtful, and even if no relevant witness had spoken to them.

[10] The solicitor advocate for the Lord Advocate referred to practice pre-*Kapri*. The courts had, in the context of human rights, taken into account reports from international organisations such as the Committee for the Prevention of Torture. But the weight given to such productions might vary. Section 202 of the 2003 Act permitted "a document issued in a category 2 territory" to be "received in evidence in proceedings under [the 2003 Act] if it is duly authenticated". It was accepted that the sheriff did not appear to state expressly in his note how ultimately he had reconciled practice to date, section 202, and the guidance in *Kapri*.

[11]   In our opinion, we are bound by the guidance given in *Kapri* v *Lord Advocate, cit sup*.   While section 202 of the 2003 Act permits duly authenticated documents emanating from the requesting state to be "received in evidence in proceedings under [the 2003 Act] if … duly authenticated", that provision applies only to documents "issued in a category 2 country" (i.e. the requesting state), and in any event, a document may be "received" but its contents are not necessarily thereby proved.   Accordingly it seems to us that section 202 does not elide the guidance in *Kapri*.   We do not therefore consider that a court in Scotland is entitled, in extradition proceedings, to hold facts proved by the methods disapproved of in paragraph [127] *et seq* of *Kapri*.   We acknowledge that the present extradition proceedings commenced prior to the issuing of the judgment in *Kapri*, but in our view that does not detract from the need to comply with *Kapri*.   As it happens, we consider that the only chapter in this case affected by the ruling in *Kapri* concerns prison conditions and article 3 of the ECHR, in relation to which, see paragraph [58] *et seq* below.

[12]   Against that background we turn to the grounds of appeal.

A. Appeal in terms of section 103

(1) Territory

[13]   The request by the Taiwanese authorities for the appellant's extradition is based on special extradition arrangements between the United Kingdom and Taiwan. Special extradition arrangements are authorised by section 194 of the Extradition Act 2003; this section permits the Home Secretary to make such arrangements with any territory provided that certain conditions are met. So far as material, the section is in the following terms:

"Special extradition arrangements

(1) This section applies if the Secretary of State believes that-

(a) arrangements have been made between the United Kingdom and another territory for the extradition of a person to the territory, and

(b) the territory is not a category 1 territory or a category 2 territory.

(2) The Secretary of State may certify that the conditions in paragraphs (a) and (b) of subsection (1) are satisfied in relation to the extradition of the person.

(3) If the Secretary of State issues a certificate under subsection (2) this Act applies in respect of the person's extradition to the territory as if the territory were a category 2 territory.

...

(5) A certificate under subsection (2) in relation to a person is conclusive evidence that the conditions in paragraphs (a) and (b) of subsection (1) are satisfied in relation to the person's extradition".

[14]   It is apparent from section 194 that special extradition arrangements can only be concluded between the United Kingdom and another "territory". For the appellant it was contended that Taiwan is not a "territory" for the purposes of this section; consequently the Home Secretary had no power to conclude any arrangements for the appellant's extradition. That argument was rejected by the sheriff. He held that the word "territory" was not defined, but was used throughout the Act without explanation. It was the only word used by the Act to refer to political entities, countries, states and the like. The sheriff thought that the lack of a definition was not accidental; the word was used deliberately, avoiding terminology such as nation, country, state and the like, and avoiding any reference to borders or geographical clarity. It meant a recognisable legal jurisdiction in a viable and settled area of populated land with a level of judicial authority stable and organised enough to be recognised and accepted by the United Kingdom. On that basis the sheriff held that Taiwan was a territory.

[15]   Counsel for the appellant submitted that the sheriff erred in so holding. While the sheriff's description of a territory was accepted, it was contended that he had failed to make findings in fact that justified the conclusion that Taiwan was a territory. The findings that he made went beyond the limits

of judicial knowledge. Moreover, Taiwan, or the Republic of China, was in dispute with the mainland of China, the People's Republic of China, over a number of important matters. The People's Republic of China denied the Republic of China's right to exist as a separate state, and disputes existed as to the ownership of certain islands lying between Taiwan and the mainland. Taiwan was not a member of the United Nations, and was not recognised by the United Kingdom.

[16] In our opinion, Taiwan, or the Republic of China, is a "territory" for the purposes of the 2003 Act; consequently the foregoing submission for the appellant must be rejected. We consider that the terms of section 194 make it clear that, if the Home Secretary issues a certificate under subsection (5), that is conclusive that the authority with which arrangements had been made in accordance with subsection (1)(a) is a "territory" for the purposes of the Act. Subsection (1)(a) authorises arrangements between the United Kingdom and "another territory" for extradition to that territory. Subsection (2) then permits the Home Secretary to certify that such arrangements have been made, and that in itself clearly involves recognition that the other party to the arrangements is a "territory" for the purposes of the Act. If such a certificate is granted, subsection (5) provides that it is "conclusive evidence that the conditions in paragraphs (a) and (b) of subsection (1) are satisfied" in relation to the particular extradition. The result of that in our opinion is that the certificate issued under subsection (2) is conclusive in determining that the entity to which extradition is to take place is a "territory". In the present case the Home Secretary issued a certificate in terms of section 194(2) on 16 October 2013. We are of opinion that that document is conclusive evidence that arrangements had been made between the United Kingdom and another "territory" as required by subsection (1)(a), and it follows from that that Taiwan must be treated as a "territory" for the purposes of the Act.

[17] In any event, we are of opinion that the court is entitled to hold as a matter of judicial knowledge that Taiwan is a "territory" for the purposes of the 2003 Act. Judicial knowledge was defined by Lord Nimmo Smith

in *McTear* v *Imperial Tobacco Ltd*, 2005 2 SC 1; [2005] CSOH 69, as follows:

"The judge will take notice of the matters... which can be immediately ascertained from sources of indisputable accuracy, which are so notorious as to be indisputable...".

The critical question is whether Taiwan is a "territory" for the purposes of the Act. As the sheriff observes, that word is not defined in the Act. In our view this is deliberate; while most of the world's land area is divided into states, parts are administered in other ways, including dependent territories, colonies and the like, and the intention underlying section 194 was to permit extradition to any such entity. The essential features of a "territory" are in our opinion threefold: there must be an area of land; that land must contain some population; and the land and population must be subject to effective government, including a functioning legal system. We note that as to the last of these requirements, it is difficult to understand how the United Kingdom could make extradition arrangements with any area where effective government was lacking.

[18]   In the case of Taiwan, a cursory examination of a world atlas discloses that it consists principally of a large island off the south-east coast of China. Reference books indicate that it has a population of approximately 25 million. They further disclose that it has a settled government. These are matters that cannot seriously be in dispute, and indeed they were not disputed by the appellant's counsel. The sheriff made findings in fact to that effect, and in our opinion he was clearly entitled to do so. That is sufficient to conclude that Taiwan is a "territory" for the purposes of the 2003 Act.

[19]   The sheriff made certain further findings which were challenged by counsel. He held that Taiwan had no boundary issues or disputes, but it was submitted that in reality there are disputes with the People's Republic of China as to the ownership of certain islands lying between the main island of Taiwan and the Chinese mainland. That in our view is irrelevant. Many countries around the world have disputes with neighbours over the precise

location of their boundaries, and the existence of such dispute could not possibly have the result that a country could not be considered a "territory". The sheriff further held that Taiwan has good international relationships, a flourishing export market and an internationally accepted democracy. None of these, however, is essential for the existence of a territory; apart from land and population, effective government is all that is required. Finally, the sheriff held that there were historic and long-standing political difficulties with the People's Republic of China, which had taken the seat in the United Nations previously occupied by Taiwan. That falls in our opinion within the category of judicial knowledge. Indeed, matters go further: the People's Republic of China denies the right of Taiwan to exist as an independent state. Nevertheless these factors are, in our opinion, irrelevant to the question of whether it is a "territory" for the purposes of the 2003 Act; while effective government is essential, it does not matter whether that government is recognised by others, or even whether its right to govern is denied by others. For this purpose "others" includes other states or territories or other parts of the same state or territory. Recognition is irrelevant to the existence of a territory. We accordingly reject the argument that Taiwan is not to be considered a "territory" for the purposes of the 2003 Act.

(2) Article 6 of the ECHR: the right to a fair trial

[20] It is convenient to consider the appellant's article 6 submission (right to a fair trial) before his section 81 submission (extraneous circumstances, viz race and/or nationality).

[21] Section 87 of the Extradition Act 2003 provides:

"**Human rights**

(1)   If the judge is required to proceed under this section (by virtue of ... section 85 [i.e. where the requested person has been convicted]) he must decide whether the person's extradition would be compatible with the Convention rights within the meaning of the Human Rights Act 1998 (c 42).

(2)   If the judge decides the question in subsection (1) in the negative he must order the person's discharge.

(3)   If the judge decides that question in the affirmative he must send the case to the Secretary of State for his decision whether the person is to be extradited."

[22] In this context, we note that it is for the appellant to prove a contravention of article 6 by establishing that his conviction was the result of a flagrant denial of justice: *Soering* v *UK* (1989) 11EHRR 439 at paragraph 113; *R (Ullah)* v *Special Adjudicator* [2004] 2 AC 323 at paragraphs 17 and 24, where Lord Bingham of Cornhill observed:

"24. While the Strasbourg jurisprudence does not preclude reliance on articles other than article 3 as a ground for resisting extradition or expulsion, it makes it quite clear that successful reliance demands presentation of a very strong case ... Where reliance is placed on article 6, it must be shown that a person has suffered or risks suffering a flagrant denial of a fair trial in the receiving state ... The lack of success of applicants relying on [article 6] before the Strasbourg court highlights the difficulty of meeting the stringent test which that court imposes ..."

[23] At the extradition hearing, the following material was available to the sheriff:

- the appellant's oral evidence (3 days), summarised at page 25 *et seq* of the sheriff's note of decision dated 11 June 2014.

- Mr Chen's oral evidence by video-link (Mr Chen being the lawyer who represented the appellant in the Taiwan trial), page 34 *et seq* of the note.

- the appellant's girlfriend's oral evidence by video-link, page 39 *et seq* of the note.

- newspaper cuttings described as showing media hostility towards the appellant (sheriff's note page 27).

- a DVD production 22, including pieces of footage of the appellant's various appearances in public in Taiwan before he left, all as described by the sheriff at page 46 of the note.

- the judgments attached to the request for extradition, in particular (but not in this order) a translation of the judgment of Taiwan Taipei District Court dated 15 March 2011;a translation of the judgment of the Taiwan High Court (which re-hears the trial evidence) dated 26 July 2012;and a translation of the judgment of the Taiwan Supreme Court dated 20 December 2012.

[24] The appellant did not lodge an expert report relating to the Taiwanese justice system, and led no evidence from an expert witness on that matter. Thus the sheriff records at pages 43 and 44 of his note:

"... the Crown had produced an expert report on the Taiwanese justice system ...its full content was never required because there is no argument before me in this hearing that the justice system in Taiwan is flawed to any extent which would permit an argument under extradition law, although there is an argument that Mr Dean claims that he did not receive a fair trial in his individual case.

... It is ... the position that the closest that I came in this hearing to hearing or seeing anything which could be argued as being an expert view on trial related issues was contained within the evidence of Billy Chen, Mr Dean's lawyer ..."

[25] What follows is a brief summary of the evidence referred to above.

[26] *The appellant's evidence:* According to the appellant, there was hostile media coverage with a "massively biased characterisation of him as a 'rich foreigner' who was showing disrespect to Taiwan and who was refusing to accept his guilt" (pages 27 *et seq* of the sheriff's note). The appellant described being exposed to physical abuse from a mob outside the police station, in particular being pushed and poked with an umbrella, because he was "black" (a Taiwanese reference to Indian). The appellant

explained that the adverse publicity was responsible for his conviction, as

> "the judges were bound to have read the press reports of his case and
> to be adversely influenced by these reports because the media can ...
> have an effect on the judge's career and 'if they do the wrong thing the
> media can put them out of office' ... (page 28 of the note)".

Thus, as his senior counsel explained to this court, the appellant's complaint
was not that the judges themselves were prejudiced against a foreigner,
nor that they had been influenced by organised crime such as the mafia,
but that the judges had been afraid to deliver a true verdict because of the
strength and vitriolic nature of the media coverage due to the fact that the
appellant was a foreigner. The media pressure had been particularly intense
at the district court level. The appellant also gave evidence that there had
been a lack of continuity in the judges who heard his case; a failure to
disclose certain evidence, although by the conclusion of the proceedings
all the evidence requested had been provided (pages 29-30); incomplete
CCTV coverage (attributed by the appellant to neglect by police officers
and/or the suppression of evidence, rather than the non - availability, for one
reason or another, of tapes from particular cameras); corruption within the
legal process generally (page 31); a failure to provide an interpreter; and
a judge falling asleep (page 33), although those latter two matters were not
included in the submissions to the sheriff.

[27] *Mr Chen's evidence:* Mr Chen stated that the press had portrayed the
appellant in a hostile manner as a rich foreigner who deserved all he got
(page 34 of the sheriff's note). The adverse publicity had caused the judges
to deliver an unfair decision, as it was inevitable that the judges read the
hostile media reports and felt under such pressure from the public reaction
that they "lost their confidence to give a fair verdict"(page 37). Further,
during the trial there had been preliminary difficulties about disclosure,
although ultimately all the material was available. The rejection of the
defence case demonstrated the media pressure, unfairness and bias. The
longer sentence also reflected xenophobia. There was "an anti-foreigner

mentality in Taiwan" which might affect the appellant if he were to be returned there. However Mr Chen confirmed in cross-examination that in his view, the trial in the District Court had proceeded entirely properly and in accordance with Taiwanese law. He had no complaint except in relation to the late provision of one area of evidence. He gave no indication that he was even threatened or placed under any pressure by outside influences of any sort (page 38 of the sheriff's note).

[28] *The appellant's girlfriend's evidence:* The sheriff summarises the appellant's girlfriend's evidence at pages 39 to 40 of his note. In particular he records:

" ... Her evidence at this hearing was confined to what happened when they were both arrested in relation to the fatal accident and were taken to the (Da-an) Police Station. She said that the manager of the KTV club arrived at the police station and that after he arrived the focus on Mr Dean as the offender hardened, and that shortly after that they were both charged. Concerning Mr Dean's evidence about what happened outside the police station she did not give the same account as he had about assault by a violent mob but she did confirm that when they went outside to go from the police station to the court they were 'surrounded by all the media and they all rushed towards [them]'. She did not suggest that the police had deliberately exposed them to that."

[29] *Media excerpts:* Media excerpts, to which senior counsel did not specifically refer during the appeal, but which we understand were available in the sheriff court extradition hearing, can be found in the appellant's productions at *inter alia* numbers 1 to 3, 16 to 18, 20 to 21, and 96 to 97. There are references to "British businessman", "chief executive officer of the Taiwan branch of NCL Media UK", "British passport holder", and "fugitive British merchant".

[30] In the appeal before us, senior counsel for the appellant lodged an additional inventory of excerpts from media coverage as number 17 of process. Counsel advised that these excerpts had not been placed before

the sheriff. They are therefore, strictly speaking, irrelevant to the appeal. However even if we were to take the new material into account, we note that the excerpts from the Taiwan media referred to the appellant as "Indian businessman", "British businessman", "businessman of British nationality", "British businessman of Indian origin", "a British businessman and CEO of Indian nationality", "a man of Indian nationality", "a foreign businessman" and similar terminology. The media also referred to the allegation against him, namely that he had killed a newspaper delivery man while driving under the influence of drink in a hit-and-run incident; the grief of the bereaved family; the prosecutor's submission that the appellant lacked the proper attitude and showed no remorse; a reporter's view that the sentence imposed on him was "lenient", and similar matters.

[31]   At pages 20 and 57 of his note, the sheriff deals with the newspaper articles and television programmes as follows:

"... [page 20] As detailed later, there were some newspaper articles and television programmes in Taiwan before his trial which could be seen as focusing on the fact that he was not a citizen of the country, but rather a rich foreigner who was responsible for the death of an innocent paper delivery man. That type of publicity is not restricted to Taiwan: it is very similar to what is seen here on occasions, and was not at a level which I considered was in any sense likely to influence professional judges in relation to either conviction or sentence. Taiwan does not have a jury trial system, so there was no issue of prejudice against him by a jury as a result of pre-trial publicity. [The appellant's] own evidence was that during the 20 years or so that he lived in Taiwan he had no impression of it being a country where there was a particular problem in relation to racial prejudice, and he had not previously experienced such prejudice in his encounters with other races including local Taiwanese ...

[page 57] ... Mr Dean was himself a resident of Taiwan for many years, and conceded that [he] had no reason to believe that xenophobia there was a significant issue. He had complete faith in the justice

system which, on his own evidence, he was supportive of in his public relations work on behalf of the government, and which he had no reason to doubt until his own conviction ... the press coverage was in any event not xenophobic ... and did not mention his colour, referring mainly to his wealth and to him being foreign to Taiwan ..."

[32] *The DVD*: At page 46 of his note, the sheriff refers to the media coverage contained in the DVD as follows:

" ... the third clip on production 22 [the DVD] was a compilation video of various pieces of footage surrounding Mr Dean's various appearances in public in Taiwan before he left. The part of this which he wanted me to see was the footage of him in custody presumably going to or from the court building and he asked me to note that these pieces of video were part of a TV programme which was broadcast to the public on 28 March 2010 (i.e. before his trial and soon after the event). The commentary did not appear to me to be particularly significant in any respect other than that it made it very clear that he was accused of causing the death of the motorcyclist and displayed a crude reconstruction which was almost cartoon-like in its presentation showing a car hitting a motorbike. There was however nothing in the translated version of this clip which suggested any language that was inflammatory or racially prejudicial, although a clear inference could be drawn from the compilation of these new programmes [namely] that he had been responsible for killing the motorcyclist."

[33] *The Taiwanese judgments:* Full copies and translations of the judgments are attached to the request for extradition.

[34] *The sheriff's conclusions in relation to article 6 of the ECHR* : The sheriff summarises his conclusions relating to article 6 of the ECHR at pages 55 *et seq* of his note of decision as follows:

"... The simple fact is that all of the evidence that I have heard at this hearing indicates that Mr Dean had a very full and fair trial process, that even his own lawyers in Taiwan accept that every available piece of evidence was placed before the court and that the court was fully aware of unavailable pieces of evidence and could thus factor that into their decision ... I have heard nothing in this hearing that suggests that there was any level of unfairness at all in relation to the provision of evidence in Taiwan far less a level of information which would suggest a blatant denial of his rights under article 6 of ECHR ... [The sheriff then noted some aspects of the appellant's evidence which he did not accept, for example, the appellant's allegations of police corruption relating *inter alia* to the suppression of CCTV footage, a corruption apparently acquiesced in by the judiciary]."

[35] At page 57 of his note, the sheriff refers to the argument about judicial corruption, bias, and racial prejudice. He dismisses the suggestion that a bench of judges could be influenced by hostile publicity at the time of the accident and be "so overcome by bias against [the appellant] as a foreigner that they returned an unfair decision". In relation to judicial corruption, the sheriff refers (at page 58) to the evidence of Mr Chen, and states:

"... [Mr Chen] has made allegations of judicial corruption to me in his evidence [set out in pages 36-37 of the note], but I do not accept these as either credible or reliable, since he has not given any example nor is he talking from personal experience and I take no account of that area of his evidence since [Mr Chen] concedes that no such corruption is evident in Mr Dean's trial. He is effectively spreading rumour and speculation, and to that extent he is a completely unreliable witness on that matter."

[36] In relation to the appellant's evidence about judicial corruption, the sheriff notes:

"... I think ... that [Mr Dean] has been given some information since his own difficulties in this matter have arisen [set out at page 41 of the note], and he has chosen to believe it and to conclude that it may, by some remote possibility, apply to his case. I am clear that I cannot find that such information as he has applies to this trial, and I have to find that he is grasping at straws in that connection and is doing a disservice to the Taiwanese justice system in putting forward an entirely unsubstantiated allegation about one or more or all of the judges in his case being corruptly influenced – effectively he is saying to me that they accepted money or favours from the mafia to have him wrongly convicted and there is absolutely no basis for such a belief."

[37] The sheriff's views in relation to the newspaper cuttings and DVD are noted in paragraphs [31] and [32] above. In summary, the sheriff rejects allegations of xenophobia or hostility arising from race or nationality or wealth.

[38] As for the Taiwanese judgments, the sheriff concluded that they:

"… disclose a full and careful assessment of the evidence and a reasoned conclusion that [the appellant] was indeed the driver of the vehicle at the time of the fatal crash."

Submissions for the appellant in the appeal to the High Court

[39] Before us, senior counsel for the appellant submitted that a flagrant denial of justice contrary to article 6 took place where the tribunal was not impartial (*Brown* v *The Government of Rwanda* [2009] EWHC 770 (Admin), paragraphs 20 *et seq.*) As Lord Justice Laws pointed out at paragraph 23:

"23. Clearly the kind of bias contemplated by section 81(b) [of the Extradition Act 2003, viz in the present case, race and/or nationality], at least so far as it affects the trial process, might readily also constitute a denial of the right to a 'fair and public hearing within a reasonable time by an independent and impartial tribunal' pursuant to article 6; and to that extent there is a potential overlap between the provisions …"

Reference was also made to *Othman (Abu Qatada)* v *United Kingdom* (2012) 55 EHRR 1; *Kapri* v *Lord Advocate* 2013 SC (UKSC) 311 paragraphs 30-32.

[40] In the present case, the tribunal had not been impartial, and as a result the appellant had not received a fair trial. The appellant, being a rich foreigner (a British national of India origin perceived to be very wealthy) had been subjected to considerable and sustained hostile press coverage. That press coverage must have influenced the judges in the trial and the appeal court. The sheriff had heard both the appellant and Mr Chen giving evidence to that effect. No coherent reason had been given for rejecting the evidence of Mr Chen (a lawyer who lived in Taiwan). The appellant should not have been convicted, as he was not the driver at the time of the accident. Even if convicted, he should have received a lesser sentence. The sheriff had therefore erred in concluding that there had been no breach of article 6.

Submissions for the first respondent in the appeal to the High Court

[41] The solicitor advocate for the first respondent submitted that, on the evidence, the trial had been fair and in accordance with Taiwanese law. There was no evidence of corruption or of a corrupt criminal justice system. There was nothing to suggest that there was undisclosed CCTV footage. Nor was there anything to suggest that the judges had been influenced by media coverage. The press articles described the appellant as a rich foreigner and accused him of causing the death, but that did not amount to xenophobia. The sheriff was correct to conclude that the evidence did not establish that there had been a breach of article 6.

Discussion and decision: whether the sheriff erred in his assessment of the case in terms of article 6 of the ECHR

[42] As noted in paragraph [22] above, the onus is upon the appellant to prove that he has suffered a flagrant denial of justice (*Soering* v *UK* (1989) 11 EHRR 439 at paragraph 113; *R (Ullah)* v *Special Adjudicator* [2004] 2 AC 323 at paragraphs 17 and 24).

[43] In this appeal, the appellant does not contend that the justice system in Taiwan is flawed to such an extent as to permit an argument under extradition law (sheriff's note page 43, and the submissions before us). The

submission is that the evidence led before the sheriff established that the judges had been afraid to deliver a true verdict because of the strength and vitriolic nature of the media coverage due to the fact that the appellant was a foreigner. Thus the appellant did not receive a fair trial in his particular case, and the sheriff erred in concluding that there had been no breach of article 6 of the ECHR.

[44]   We agree with the sheriff that the appellant's trial in Taiwan

"hinged on the straightforward issue of identification of the driver of the offending motor vehicle which was owned by [the appellant]" (sheriff's note page 26).

[45]   The evidence led before the sheriff in relation to what took place before, during, and after the trial in Taiwan is summarised in paragraphs [23] to [33] above. In relation to the oral evidence, assessment of credibility and reliability of witnesses was, first and foremost, a matter for the sheriff. He was entitled to accept or reject all or part of a witness's evidence, and to give differing weight to different pieces of evidence. Thus he was entitled, for example, to reject parts of the appellant's evidence (see paragraphs [34] and [36] above). He was entitled to accept Mr Chen's evidence that the trial had proceeded entirely properly (page 38 of the sheriff's note) but also to find Mr Chen unreliable in certain material respects (page 4 of the sheriff's supplementary report dated 20 January 2015; page 58 of the sheriff's note). The sheriff was also entitled to compare differing versions of events and to prefer one version to another.

[46]   In relation to evidence about media coverage (in particular the newspaper cuttings and the DVD), the media reports seem to us accurately to record details relating to the appellant, the allegations against him, and related matters (for example, the family's reaction) – all matters which one would normally expect to find in press reports about such an incident. They do not, in our view, substantiate the allegation of press coverage in which hostility is attributable to the race or nationality of the appellant. We therefore agree with the sheriff's views at pages 20 and 57 of his note,

quoted in paragraph [31] above.

[47] In relation to the Taiwanese court judgments, the sheriff's reasoning and conclusions cannot, in our view, be criticised or categorised as decisions which "cannot reasonably be explained or justified" (*Henderson* v *Foxworth Investments Ltd,* 2014 SC (UKSC) 203, 2014 SLT 775 paragraphs 66 and 67).

[48] In the result, we have been unable to identify any error in the sheriff's assessment of the evidence, his reasoning, or his conclusion that no breach of article 6 in connection with the appellant's trial in Taiwan was established. We are not therefore persuaded that there is any merit in this ground of appeal.

(3) Section 81 of the 2003 Act: extraneous considerations

[49] Section 81 of the Extradition Act 2003 provides:

"Extraneous considerations

A person's extradition to a category 2 territory is barred by reason of extraneous considerations if (and only if) it appears that –

(a) the request for his extradition (though purporting to be made on account of the extradition offence) is in fact made for the purpose of prosecuting or punishing him on account of his race, nationality, gender, sexual orientation or political opinions, or

(b) if extradited he might be prejudiced at his trial or punished, detained or restricted in his personal liberty by reason of his race, religion, nationality, gender, sexual orientation or political opinions."

[50] Before us, it was agreed that the test to be applied in the context of section 81(b) was whether, on the evidence, there was a "reasonable chance" or a "serious possibility" that the appellant, if extradited, might be punished, detained, or restricted in his personal liberty by reason of his race, religion, nationality, gender, sexual orientation or political opinions (*Tamarevichute* v *The Government of the Russian Federation* [2008] EWHC

534 (Admin) paragraphs 12 and 112). Accordingly both senior counsel for the appellant and the solicitor advocate for the first respondent submitted that the sheriff had erred when, at the foot of page 20 of his note, he stated:

> "The terms of section 81 make it clear that this is a section specifically designed to deal with a situation where it is argued that the extraneous considerations detailed in the 2 sub-sections play *a major role* in the extradition request and the terms of section 81(a) make that very clear. Section 81(b) which is the one argued here is also a section which would require *a high level of certainty* on the part of the requested state that there may be prejudice at any future procedure by reason of race or nationality before it would be proper to refuse extradition [italics added]."

[51] We accept that the test to be applied in respect of the appellant is whether, on the evidence, there is a "reasonable chance" or a "serious possibility" that the appellant, if extradited, might be punished, detained or restricted in his personal liberty by reason of his nationality and/or race. As the sheriff applied a different and stricter test, we propose to reconsider the matter in the light of the evidence available to the sheriff.

Submissions for the appellant in the appeal to the High Court

[52] Senior counsel for the appellant submitted that the appellant's conviction rested

upon a subjective assessment of credibility and reliability (the evidence of the appellant as against the evidence of the club driver), an assessment which (a) had been skewed by the vitriolic media coverage because the appellant was a foreigner and the judges were afraid to deliver a true verdict, and (b) was not susceptible to substantive review, being a decision at first instance. In the context of xenophobia due to race and nationality, the sheriff had failed properly to assess Mr Chen's evidence in relation to the powerful effect of the media coverage. Mr Chen had expressly stated that there was "an anti-foreigner mentality in Taiwan" which might affect the appellant if he were to be returned. The sheriff had not suggested that Mr Chen was lying or confused, and yet had preferred his own view of Taiwan to that of Mr Chen, despite the latter being resident in Taiwan. It would be unfair in this case to apply the evidential standards advocated in *Kapri* v *Lord Advocate* 2015 JC 30. Thus the evidence, including that of the appellant and Mr Chen, established that there was a reasonable chance or a serious possibility that the appellant, if extradited, might be punished, detained or restricted in his personal liberty by reason of his race or nationality. As the sheriff had applied the wrong test, this appeal court should make its own decision.

Submissions for the first respondent in the appeal to the High Court

[53] The solicitor advocate for the first respondent submitted that the media coverage simply described the appellant as a rich foreigner, and blamed him for the death. That did not demonstrate xenophobia. There was no evidence that the judges had been affected by the media, or that they had been influenced in reaching their verdict by issues of race or nationality. It had not therefore been proved that there was a reasonable chance or a serious possibility that the appellant, if extradited, might be punished, detained, or restricted in his personal liberty by reason of his race or nationality.

Discussion and decision: whether the evidence established that there was a reasonable chance or a serious possibility that the appellant, if extradited, might be punished, detained, or restricted in his personal liberty by reason of his race or nationality

[54] We refer to the summary of the evidence available to the sheriff, the assessment of the credibility and reliability of witnesses, the nature of the media coverage, and the content of the Taiwanese judgments, all as set out in paragraphs [23] to [33] above. Focusing initially upon the media reports, it is our opinion that those reports simply recorded details relating to the appellant, the allegations against him, the reaction of the deceased's family, and other similar matters – all issues which one would normally expect to find in press reports about such an incident. Even if the most recent production of media extracts (number 17 of process) were to be taken

into account, the media coverage does not, in our view, substantiate the allegation of press coverage in which hostility is attributable to the race or nationality of the appellant.

[55] As for the three judgments of the Taiwanese courts, these do not, in our opinion, disclose any suggestion of xenophobia, or any evidence which might suggest that the authorities and courts in Taiwan, when taking decisions and actions, were in any way guided by xenophobic motives relating to race or nationality. Rather, as the sheriff states, they demonstrate –

> "... a full and careful assessment of the evidence and a reasoned conclusion that [the appellant] was indeed the driver of the vehicle at the time of the fatal crash."

[56] Thus the only evidence of xenophobic hostility arising from race or nationality came, in our opinion, from the evidence of the appellant and his lawyer Mr Chen. As it was for the sheriff to determine matters of credibility and reliability (*Thomas v Thomas* [1947] AC 484), his assessment of their evidence is difficult to contradict. Accordingly we are not persuaded that we may accept the assertions of the appellant and Mr Chen relating to an anti-foreigner mentality in Taiwan, standing the fact that they were disbelieved on those matters by the sheriff (see for example, the sheriff's note pages 20, 46 and 57).

[57] Having reviewed the evidence available to the sheriff, and the submissions made to us, it is our opinion that the evidence does not demonstrate a "reasonable chance" or a "serious possibility" that the appellant "if extradited ... might be ... punished, detained or restricted in his personal liberty by reason of his race ... [or] nationality" (section 81 of the Extradition Act 2003; *Tamarevichute v The Government of the Russian Federation* [2008] EWHC 534 (Admin) paragraphs 12 and 112). We are not persuaded therefore that the sheriff ought to have decided this issue differently (section 104(3) of the 2003 Act) or that this ground of appeal should succeed.

(4) Article 3 of the ECHR: prison conditions

[58]   Article 3 of the ECHR provides:

"Prohibition of torture

No one shall be subjected to torture or to inhuman or degrading treatment or punishment."

The parties' respective positions

[59]   The appellant's argument is that there are substantial grounds for believing that, if extradited, he will face a real risk of being subjected to inhuman and degrading conditions in Taipei prison, contrary to article 3 of the ECHR. In particular he refers to serious overcrowding (with a prisoner's personal space being restricted to anything from 1.6 square metres to 2.3 square metres), an unsatisfactory staff-inmate ratio, and insufficient medical and pharmacy staff. Accordingly the sheriff erred in deciding, at pages 62-63 of his note, that there is no strength in the article 3 argument.

[60]   The first respondent's contention is that the appellant led insufficient evidence in his attempt to establish that risk (*R(Ullah)* v*Special Adjudicator* [2004] 2 AC 323 paragraph 24; *Saadi* v *Italy* (2009) 49 EHRR 30 paragraph 129; *Gaefgen* v *Germany* (2011) 52 EHRR 1 paragraph 92). In any event, the court has assurances from Taiwan, including an e-mail dated 8 May 2014 with certain undertakings about cell space, a bed, hours out of the cell, and toilet facilities.

The evidence led on behalf of the appellant

[61]   In relation to prison conditions, the evidence led before the sheriff for the appellant comprised:

- the appellant's oral evidence (pages 32 to 33 of the sheriff's note).

- Mr Chen's oral evidence (pages 37 to 38 of the note).

- the appellant's girlfriend's oral evidence (page 39 *et seq* of the note).

- the DVD production 22, including a documentary programme focusing on conditions in Taipei North prison, filmed in about September 2013.

- several documentary productions, namely production 23 (described as Taiwanese government figures recording overcapacity in Taipei prison at 47.6% in 2012); productions 1A9, 1A14, and 1A15 (now productions 40, 45, and 46) described as articles compiled by an organisation called Taiwan Action for Prison Reform and downloaded from the internet. These documents indicated *inter alia* a general overcapacity in Taiwan prisons of 30%, and a low guard-to-prisoner ratio.

[62] For reasons which will become clear from the paragraphs below, we do not consider it necessary to examine, rehearse, or analyse that evidence in any detail. It is sufficient to note that the oral evidence concerning prison conditions could not have been of much assistance to the sheriff, as the appellant and his girlfriend had never been in a Taiwanese prison, and Mr Chen spoke from the limited viewpoint of a lawyer. The DVD documentary programme was not, in our view, something that "a judicial body should simply accept as true, and thus proof of fact" (paragraph 128 of *Kapri* v *Lord Advocate* 2015 JC 30), particularly as the sheriff commented at pages 44 and 45 of his note:

> " ... It was not in any sense wide-ranging filming, designed to cover prisoner conditions in any width or depth, and it was very much confined to one part of the prison ... The scenes which were shown were quite limited, and it appears that the sanction to film within the prison was quite restricted, since a number of scenes and images were shown repeatedly, and I only ever saw one communal cell ..."

[63] As for productions 23, 40, 45, and 46, we consider that these were good examples of the sorts of materials referred to in paragraph [128] of *Kapri*. Their provenance was not clear. Their accuracy was unvouched. They had been downloaded from the internet. They were not (so far as we were aware) spoken to by any witness, but were simply referred to during counsel's submissions (sheriff's note of decision page 43).

[64]   Thus neither the DVD nor the documentary productions could, in our view, be treated as equivalent to the evidence of a responsible expert witness seeking to assist the court.

Submissions in the appeal to the High Court

[65]   Against that background, Mr Dickson, on behalf of the Lord Advocate, submitted before us *inter alia* that the evidence led on behalf of the appellant did not satisfy the high tests set in *R(Ullah)* v *Special Adjudicator* [2004] 2 AC 323 at paragraph 24 and *Gaefgen vGermany* (2011) 52 EHRR 1 at paragraph 92, and moreover did not comply with the guidance in *Kapri*. He acknowledged that, by the time the decision in *Kapri* became available on 25 April 2014, the appellant and Mr Chen had already given their evidence (in January and February 2014). However he was also aware that the appellant had obtained two expert reports, yet had not lodged them. In the absence of defence expert reports, the sheriff had wished to be as fair as possible to the appellant. Accordingly the sheriff had allowed a considerable number of documents to be lodged as productions, at the same time warning parties that if a document remained unspoken to, with its provenance unclear, he would attach little weight to it (see paragraph [8] above). Mr Dickson submitted that, as a result of this approach, the sheriff (i) had applied pre-*Kapri* law and practice and had given weight to certain productions which, in terms of *Kapri*, should not perhaps have been relied upon; and (ii) had not made clear what, if anything, he had taken from the Crown's expert report on the Taiwanese justice system (referred to at page 43 of the sheriff's note, and paragraph [24] above). In fact, in an endeavour to be fair to the appellant, the sheriff had gone to lengths which he should perhaps not have done.

[66]   Mr Dickson further submitted that the appellant had had opportunities to obtain more and better evidence. There had been various adjournments and continuations during the sheriff court proceedings. No further time should be contemplated.

[67]   Finally, *esto* the court were persuaded to any extent by the evidence led on behalf of the appellant, the court should have regard to the various

assurances provided by Taiwan, namely productions 26, 28, 31, 32, and 33. In particular, production 32, the e-mail addressed to Mr Dickson dated 8 May 2014, from Pei-Chi Hong, Prosecutor's Investigator, Department of International and Cross-Strait Legal Affairs, Ministry of Justice, gave details about cell space, a bed, hours out of the cell, and toilet facilities, none of which had been challenged by the appellant or his lawyers.

[68] Mr Bovey QC on behalf of the appellant accepted that the evidence criticised, particularly the DVD programme and the articles downloaded from the internet, did not comply with the guidance in *Kapri*. However as the appellant's extradition proceedings had begun on the basis of *R(B)* v *Westminster Magistrates' Court* [2014] 3 WLR 1336, paragraphs 22-23, it would be unfair to change the approach to evidence mid-case, and to exclude material made available to the court in such a way that the appellant's argument about prison conditions was deemed to have failed. Moreover, the more nuanced approach in *HM Advocate* v *Havrilova* 2012 SCCR 351 was preferable (see paragraph [9] above). But if necessary, a further evidential hearing should take place before the appeal court (cf the procedure in *Kapri*). The case should not be remitted back to the sheriff, as the detailed provisions of the 2003 Act did not permit such a step.

[69] In relation to the assurances given by Taiwan, if these assurances were not worth having, then the general level of overcrowding in prisons was crucial and clearly breached article 3 of the ECHR (cf *Orchowski* v *Poland,* ECtHR 22 October 2009 17885/04, paragraph 122; *Florea* v *Judicial Authority, Rumania* [2015] 1WLR 1953, paragraphs 35-37, 39). The assurances, and in particular the e-mail dated 8 May 2014 production 32, did not satisfy the criteria set out in paragraph 189 of *Othman (Abu Qatada)* v *United Kingdom* (2012) 55 EHRR 1.

[70] Accordingly the sheriff had erred in law. He was wrong to conclude that there was no real risk of a violation of article 3 arising from overcrowding and other conditions in prison in Taiwan. He ought to have decided the question differently. He should have ordered the discharge of the appellant.

Discussion and decision: article 3 of the ECHR and prison conditions

[71] First, we note that the decision in *Kapri* v *Lord Advocate* 2015 JC 30 did not become available until 25 April 2014, by which time, as we understand it, the oral evidence in this case had been completed. The sheriff's decision in this case was issued on 11 June 2014, some six weeks later. It is perhaps a moot point whether the implications of the decision in *Kapri* should have been appreciated and raised in court once the judgment in that case became available. So far as we are aware, those implications were not debated before the sheriff. The sheriff accordingly proceeded to deal with this case, and issued his judgment on the basis of evidence which did not meet the criteria set out in *Kapri*.

[72] Secondly, we consider that sufficient questions have arisen from the materials and submissions put before the sheriff to suggest the need to hear appropriate evidence in the context of article 3 of the ECHR and the prison conditions in which the appellant will be detained.

[73] As a result we are not persuaded that we should attempt to assess whether or not the sheriff could be said to have erred in relation to article 3 and prison conditions. We consider that it is necessary to allow parties a further opportunity, at an evidential hearing before the appeal court, to lead such evidence on that issue alone (if so advised) as they consider appropriate, bearing in mind *Kapri* and the high tests in *R(Ullah)* v *Special Adjudicator* [2004] 2AC 323 at paragraph 24, *Gaefgen* v *Germany* (2011) 52 EHRR 1, paragraph 92.

[74] It may be that, in preparation for the evidential hearing, the first respondent will wish to consider the nature, terms, and signatory of any assurance sought to be relied upon in this case, in the light of the factors listed in paragraph 189 of *Othman* and the criticisms made by senior counsel for the appellant in his address to us. Moreover in relation to section 202 of the 2003 Act, counsel for the first respondent should be prepared to address the court on the meaning and effect of the phrase "received in evidence in proceedings under this Act if it is duly authenticated".

[75] In conclusion, we shall continue the issue of article 3 and prison conditions (but no other issue) to an evidential hearing before the appeal court of three judges. We shall put the case out for a hearing to discuss procedural details.

B. *Appeal in terms of section 108*

[76] We were fully addressed on the appeal in terms of section 108. We shall reserve our opinion on that matter until the issues outstanding in the appeal in terms of section 103 are dealt with.

CONCLUSION

[77] For the reasons given above, we continue that part of the appeal under section 103 relating to article 3 of the ECHR and prison conditions in Taiwan to an evidential hearing (see paragraph 75 above). We shall arrange a hearing to discuss procedural issues. In these circumstances, it would be premature to give our views on the appeal under section 108. As noted in paragraph [76] above, we were fully addressed on that matter, and meantime we reserve our opinion.

PCA Case N° 2013-19

IN THE MATTER OF THE SOUTH CHINA SEA ARBITRATION

- before -

AN ARBITRAL TRIBUNAL CONSTITUTED UNDER ANNEX VII TO THE
1982 UNITED NATIONS CONVENTION ON THE LAW OF THE SEA

- between -

THE REPUBLIC OF THE PHILIPPINES

- and -

THE PEOPLE'S REPUBLIC OF CHINA

AWARD

Arbitral Tribunal:

Judge Thomas A. Mensah (Presiding Arbitrator)
Judge Jean-Pierre Cot
Judge Stanislaw Pawlak
Professor Alfred H.A. Soons
Judge Rüdiger Wolfrum

Registry:

Permanent Court of Arbitration

12 July 2016

this page intentionally blank

REPRESENTATIVES OF THE PARTIES

REPUBLIC OF THE PHILIPPINES   **PEOPLE'S REPUBLIC OF CHINA**

AGENT

Mr. Jose C. Calida   *No agents or representatives appointed*
Solicitor General of the Philippines
replacing Solicitor General Florin T. Hilbay,
as of 30 June 2016

COUNSEL AND ADVOCATES

Mr. Paul S. Reichler
Mr. Lawrence H. Martin
Mr. Andrew B. Loewenstein
Foley Hoag LLP, Washington and Boston

Professor Bernard H. Oxman
University of Miami School of Law, Miami

Professor Philippe Sands QC
Matrix Chambers, London

Professor Alan Boyle
Essex Court Chambers, London

this page intentionally blank

TABLE OF CONTENTS

TABLE OF MAPS

The maps in this Award are illustrative only. Their use by the Tribunal is not intended to endorse any State's position with respect to matters of land sovereignty or maritime boundaries.

this page intentionally blank

TABLE OF FIGURES

this page intentionally blank

GLOSSARY OF DEFINED TERMS

Term	Definition
1948 Map	The map showing the location of the various islands in the South Sea, published by the Boundary Department of the Ministry of Interior of the Republic of China in 1948
1958 Convention on the Continental Shelf	Convention on the Continental Shelf, Art. 1, 25 April 1958, 499 UNTS 311
1958 Convention on the Territorial Sea and the Contiguous Zone	Convention on the Territorial Sea and the Contiguous Zone, Art. 10, 29 April 1958, 516 UNTS 205
1994 Study	T.C. Huang, et. al., "The Flora of Taipingtao (Itu Aba Island)," *Taiwania*, Vol. 39, No. 1-2 (1994)
2009 Map	The map appended to Notes Verbales from the Permanent Mission of the People's Republic of China to the Secretary-General of the United Nations (7 May 2009)
Affidavit of R.Z. Comandante	Affidavit of Mr. Richard Comandante (12 November 2015)
Affidavit of T.D. Forones	Affidavit of Mr. Tolomeo Forones (12 November 2015)
Affidavit of M.C. Lanog	Affidavit of Mr. Miguel Lanog (12 November 2015)
Affidavit of J.P. Legaspi	Affidavit of Mr. Jowe Legaspi (12 November 2015)
Affidavit of C.D. Talatagod	Affidavit of Mr. Crispen Talatagod (12 November 2015)
Affidavit of C.O. Taneo	Affidavit of Mr. Cecilio Taneo (12 November 2015)
Allen Report	Report of Professor Craig H. Allen (19 March 2014)
Arunco Report of 28 May 2012	Report from A.A. Arunco, et al., FRPLEU-QRT Officers, Bureau of Fisheries and Aquatic Resources, Republic of the Philippines, to the Director, Bureau of Fisheries and Aquatic Resources, Republic of the Philippines (28 May 2012)
Area 3	Offshore petroleum block tendered on 30 June 2011, as part of the Fourth Philippine Energy Contracting Round (PECR 4)
Area 4	Offshore petroleum block tendered on 30 June 2011, as part of the Fourth Philippine Energy Contracting Round (PECR 4)
ASEAN	Association of Southeast Asian Nations

Term	Definition
Award on Jurisdiction	The Tribunal's Award on Jurisdiction and Admissibility, dated 29 October 2015
CBD	Convention on Biological Diversity, 5 June 1992, 1760 UNTS 79
China	The People's Republic of China
China's 2006 Declaration	The Declaration of the People's Republic of China under Article 298 of the Convention, dated 25 August 2006, that China "does not accept any of the procedures provided for in Section 2 of Part XV of the Convention with respect to all the categories of disputes referred to in paragraph 1 (a), (b) and (c) of Article 298 of the Convention."
China's Position Paper	The Position Paper of the Government of the People's Republic of China on the Matter of Jurisdiction in the South China Sea Arbitration Initiated by the Republic of the Philippines, published by China on 7 December 2014
Chinese Embassy	The Embassy of the People's Republic of China in the Kingdom of the Netherlands
CITES	Convention on International Trade in Endangered Species of Wild Fauna and Flora, 3 March 1973, 993 UNTS 243
CLCS	Commission on the Limits of the Continental Shelf
CMS	China Marine Surveillance
CNOOC	China National Offshore Oil Corporation
COLREGS	Convention on the International Regulations for Preventing Collisions at Sea, 20 October 1972, 1050 UNTS 1976
Convention	United Nations Convention on the Law of the Sea, 10 December 1982, 1833 UNTS 3 (or "UNCLOS")
DOC	2002 China–ASEAN Declaration on the Conduct of Parties in the South China Sea, 4 November 2002
EIA	Environmental impact assessment
FAO	Food and Agriculture Organization of the United Nations
Ferse Report	Dr. rer. Nat. Sebastian C.A. Ferse, Professor Peter Mumby, PhD and Dr. Selina Ward, PhD, *Assessment of the Potential Environmental Consequences of Construction Activities on Seven Reefs in the Spratly Islands in the South China Sea* (26 April 2016)
First Bailey Report	Dr. Ryan T. Bailey, *Groundwater Resources Analysis of Itu Aba* (9 March 2016)
First Carpenter Report	Professor Kent E. Carpenter, *Eastern South China Sea Environmental Disturbances and Irresponsible Fishing Practices and their Effects on Coral Reefs and Fisheries* (22 March 2014)

Term	Definition
First Motavalli Report	Dr. Peter P. Motavalli, *Soil Resources and Potential Self-Sustaining Agricultural Production on Itu Aba* (9 March 2016)
FLEC	Fisheries Law Enforcement Command of China
Forum Energy	Forum Energy Plc
GSEC101	Geophysical Survey and Exploration Contract 101 block (a Philippine offshore petroleum block)
Hainan Regulation	People's Republic of China, Hainan Province, Hainan Provincial Regulation on the Control of Coastal Border Security (31 December 2012)
Hearing on Jurisdiction	The Hearing held from 7 to 13 July 2015 to consider the matter of the Tribunal's Jurisdiction and, as necessary, the admissibility of the Philippines' Submissions
Hearing on the Merits	The Hearing held from 24 to 30 to November 2015 to consider any outstanding issues of the Tribunal's jurisdiction and admissibility and the merits of the Philippines' Submissions.
IHO	International Hydrographic Organization
ISA	International Seabed Authority
IUCN	International Union for Conservation of Nature and Natural Resources
IUU	illegal, unreported, and unregulated (fishing)
Malaysia's Communication	Communication from the Ministry of Foreign Affairs of Malaysia to the Tribunal, (23 June 2016)
McManus Report	Professor John W. McManus, *Offshore Coral Reef Damage, Overfishing and Paths to Peace in the South China Sea* (rev. ed., 21 April 2016)
Mora Report	Professor Camilo Mora, Dr. Iain R. Caldwell, Professor Charles Birkeland, and Professor John W. McManus, "Dredging in the Spratly Islands: Gaining Land but Losing Reefs," *PLoS Biology* Vol. 14(3) (31 March 2016)
Memorial	The Memorial of the Philippines, filed on 30 March 2014
Nido	Nido Petroleum Ltd.
Parties	The Republic of the Philippines and the People's Republic of China
PCA	The Permanent Court of Arbitration (or "Registry")
Philippines	The Republic of the Philippines
PNOC	PNOC Exploration Corporation
Registry	The Permanent Court of Arbitration (or "PCA")

Term	Definition
Request for Further Written Argument	The Tribunal's Request for Further Written Argument by the Philippines Pursuant to Article 25(2) of the Rules of Procedure, annexed to Procedural Order No. 3 (16 December 2014)
SARV Coastguard Report of 28 April 2012	Report from Commanding Officer, SARV-003, Philippine Coast Guard, to Commander, Coast Guard District Northwestern Luzon, Philippine Coast Guard (28 April 2012)
SC58	Service Contract 58 (a Philippine offshore petroleum block)
SC72	Service Contract 72 (a Philippine offshore petroleum block)
Schofield Report	Professor Clive Schofield, Professor J.R.V. Prescott, and Mr Robert van de Poll, *An Appraisal of the Geographical Characteristics and Status of Certain Insular Features in the South China Sea* (March 2015)
Second Bailey Report	Dr. Ryan T. Bailey, *Supplemental Report on Groundwater Resources Analysis of Itu Aba* (20 April 2016)
Second Carpenter Report	Professor Kent E. Carpenter and Professor Loke Ming Chou, *Environmental Consequences of Land Reclamation Activities on Various Reefs in the South China Sea* (14 November 2015)
Second Motavalli Report	Dr. Peter P. Motavalli, *Second Supplemental Expert Report on Soil Resources and Potential Self-Sustaining Agricultural Production on Itu Aba* (2 June 2016)
Singhota Report	Captain Gurpreet S. Singhota, *Report of the International Navigational Safety Expert appointed by the Permanent Court of Arbitration, The Hague, The Netherlands* (15 April 2016)
SOA	The State Oceanic Administration of China
SOA Report	Feng Aiping and Wang Yongzhi, First Ocean Research Institution of State Oceanic Administration, "Construction Activities at Nansha Reefs Did Not Affect the Coral Reef Ecosystem" (10 June 2015)
SOA Statement	State Oceanic Administration of China, "Construction Work at Nansha Reefs Will Not Harm Oceanic Ecosystems" (18 June 2015)
Sterling Energy	Sterling Energy Plc
Submissions	The Submissions of the Philippines set out at pp. 271-272 of its Memorial, re-stated during the Hearing on the Merits and in a Letter from the Philippines to the Tribunal on 30 November 2015, as amended with leave of the Tribunal granted on 16 December 2015
Supplemental Written Submission	The Supplemental Written Submission of the Philippines, filed on 16 March 2015, pursuant to Article 25 of the Rules of Procedure and Procedural Order No. 3
Third Carpenter Report	Declaration of Professor K.E. Carpenter, para. 5 (24 April 2016)

Term	Definition
Third UN Conference	Third United Nations Conference on the Law of the Sea
UKHO	United Kingdom Hydrographic Office
UNCLOS	United Nations Convention on the Law of the Sea, 10 December 1982, 1833 UNTS 3 (or "Convention")
UNEP	United Nations Environment Programme
Vienna Convention	Vienna Convention on the Law of Treaties, Art. 33(1), 22 May 1969, 1155 UNTS 331
Viet Nam	Socialist Republic of Viet Nam
Viet Nam's Statement	Statement of the Ministry of Foreign Affairs of Viet Nam for the Attention of the Tribunal in the Proceedings between the Republic of the Philippines and the People's Republic of China (14 December 2014)
Written Responses of the Philippines (23 July 2015)	Written Responses of the Philippines to the Tribunal's 13 July 2015 Questions (23 July 2015)
Written Responses of the Philippines (11 March 2016)	Written Responses of the Philippines to the Tribunal's 5 February 2016 Request for Comments (11 March 2016)
Written Responses of the Philippines on Itu Aba (25 April 2016)	Responses of the Philippines to the Tribunal's 1 April 2016 Request for Comments on Additional Materials regarding the Status of Itu Aba (25 April 2016)
Written Responses of the Philippines on UKHO Materials (28 April 2016)	Responses of the Philippines to the Tribunal's 1 April 2016 Request for Comments on Materials from the Archives of the United Kingdom Hydrographic Office (28 April 2016)
Written Responses of the Philippines on French Archive Materials (3 June 2016)	Responses of the Philippines to the Tribunal's 26 May 2016 Request for Comments on Materials from the French Archives (3 June 2016)

this page intentionally blank

GLOSSARY OF GEOGRAPHIC NAMES MENTIONED IN THIS AWARD

For ease of reference, and without prejudice to any State's claims, the Tribunal uses throughout this Award the common English designation for the following geographic features, the Filipino translations for which come from the Philippine National Mapping and Resource Information Agency, *Philippine Coast Pilot* (6th ed., 1995) (Annex 230) and the Philippines' Submissions, and the Chinese translations for which come from the Navigation Guarantee Department of the Chinese Navy Headquarters, *China Sailing Directions: South China Sea (A103)* (2011) (Annex 232(bis)).

As discussed at paragraph 482 below, the name of a feature as an bank, cay, island, reef, or shoal has no bearing on the Tribunal's determination of the status of those features under the Convention.

English Name	Chinese Name	Filipino Name
Amboyna Cay	Anbo Shazhou 安波沙洲	Kalantiyaw Cay
Cuarteron Reef	Huayang Jiao 华阳礁	Calderon Reef
Fiery Cross Reef	Yongshu Jiao 永暑礁	Kagitingan Reef
Flat Island	Feixin Dao 费信岛	Patag Island
Gaven Reefs	Nanxun Jiao 南薰礁	Burgos Reefs
Hughes Reef	Dongmen Jiao 东门礁	Chigua Reef (the Philippines refers to McKennan and Hughes Reefs as a single feature)
Itu Aba Island	Taiping Dao 太平岛	Ligaw Island
Johnson Reef	Chigua Jiao 赤瓜礁	Mabini Reef
Lankiam Cay	Yangxin Shazhou 杨信沙洲	Panata Island
Loaita Island	Nanyue Dao 南钥岛	Kota Island
Macclesfield Bank	Zhongsha Qundao 中沙群岛	Macclesfield Bank
McKennan Reef	Ximen Jiao 西门礁	Chigua Reef (the Philippines refers to McKennan and Hughes Reefs as a single feature)

English Name	Chinese Name	Filipino Name
Mischief Reef	Meiji Jiao 美济礁	Panganiban Reef
Namyit Island	Hongxiu Dao 鸿庥岛	Binago Island
Nanshan Island	Mahuan Dao 马欢岛	Lawak Island
North-East Cay	Beizi Dao 北子岛	Parola Island
Reed Bank	Liyue Tan 礼乐滩	Recto Bank
Sand Cay	Dunqian Shazhou 敦谦沙洲	Bailan Cay
Scarborough Shoal	Huangyan Dao 黄岩岛	Panatag Shoal or Bajo de Masinloc
Second Thomas Shoal	Ren'ai Jiao 仁爱礁	Ayungin Shoal
Sin Cowe Island	Jinghong Dao 景宏岛	Rurok Island
South China Sea	Nan Hai 南海	West Philippine Sea
South-West Cay	Nanzi Dao 南子岛	Pugad Island
Spratly Island	Nanwei Dao 南威岛	Lagos Island
Spratly Island Group (Spratly Islands or Spratlys)	Nansha Qundao 南沙群岛	Kalayaan Island Group (Kalayaan Islands)
Subi Reef	Zhubi Jiao 渚碧礁	Zamora Reef
Swallow Reef	Danwan Jiao 弹丸礁	Celerio Reef
Thitu Island	Zhongye Dao 中业岛	Pagasa Island
West York Island	Xiyue Dao 西月岛	Likas Island

I.   INTRODUCTION

1.   The Parties to this arbitration are the Republic of the Philippines (the "**Philippines**") and the People's Republic of China ("**China**") (together, the "**Parties**").

2.   This arbitration concerns disputes between the Parties regarding the legal basis of maritime rights and entitlements in the South China Sea, the status of certain geographic features in the South China Sea, and the lawfulness of certain actions taken by China in the South China Sea.

3.   The South China Sea is a semi-enclosed sea in the western Pacific Ocean, spanning an area of almost 3.5 million square kilometres, and is depicted in Map 1 on page 9 below. The South China Sea lies to the south of China; to the west of the Philippines; to the east of Viet Nam; and to the north of Malaysia, Brunei, Singapore, and Indonesia. The South China Sea is a crucial shipping lane, a rich fishing ground, home to a highly biodiverse coral reef ecosystem, and believed to hold substantial oil and gas resources. The southern portion of the South China Sea is also the location of the Spratly Islands, a constellation of small islands and coral reefs, existing just above or below water, that comprise the peaks of undersea mountains rising from the deep ocean floor. Long known principally as a hazard to navigation and identified on nautical charts as the "dangerous ground", the Spratly Islands are the site of longstanding territorial disputes among some of the littoral States of the South China Sea.

4.   The basis for this arbitration is the 1982 United Nations Convention on the Law of the Sea (the "**Convention**" or "**UNCLOS**").[1] Both the Philippines and China are parties to the Convention, the Philippines having ratified it on 8 May 1984, and China on 7 June 1996. The Convention was adopted as a "constitution for the oceans," in order to "settle all issues relating to the law of the sea," and has been ratified by 168 parties. The Convention addresses a wide range of issues and includes as an integral part a system for the peaceful settlement of disputes. This system is set out in Part XV of the Convention, which provides for a variety of dispute settlement procedures, including compulsory arbitration in accordance with a procedure contained in Annex VII to the Convention. It was pursuant to Part XV of, and Annex VII to, the Convention that the Philippines commenced this arbitration against China on 22 January 2013.

5.   The Convention, however, does not address the sovereignty of States over land territory. Accordingly, this Tribunal has not been asked to, and does not purport to, make any ruling as to

---

[1]   United Nations Convention on the Law of the Sea, 10 December 1982, 1833 UNTS 3 (hereinafter "**Convention**"). Throughout this Award, references to particular Articles are to the Convention unless stated otherwise.

which State enjoys sovereignty over any land territory in the South China Sea, in particular with respect to the disputes concerning sovereignty over the Spratly Islands or Scarborough Shoal. None of the Tribunal's decisions in this Award are dependent on a finding of sovereignty, nor should anything in this Award be understood to imply a view with respect to questions of land sovereignty.

6. Similarly, although the Convention does contain provisions concerning the delimitation of maritime boundaries, China made a declaration in 2006 to exclude maritime boundary delimitation from its acceptance of compulsory dispute settlement, something the Convention expressly permits for maritime boundaries and certain other matters. Accordingly, the Tribunal has not been asked to, and does not purport to, delimit any maritime boundary between the Parties or involving any other State bordering on the South China Sea. To the extent that certain of the Philippines' claims relate to events at particular locations in the South China Sea, the Tribunal will address them only insofar as the two Parties' respective rights and obligations are not dependent on any maritime boundary or where no delimitation of a boundary would be necessary because the application of the Convention would not lead to any overlap of the two Parties' respective entitlements.

7. The disputes that the Philippines has placed before the Tribunal fall broadly within four categories. First, the Philippines has asked the Tribunal to resolve a dispute between the Parties concerning the source of maritime rights and entitlements in the South China Sea. Specifically, the Philippines seeks a declaration from the Tribunal that China's rights and entitlements in the South China Sea must be based on the Convention and not on any claim to historic rights. In this respect, the Philippines seeks a declaration that China's claim to rights within the 'nine-dash line' marked on Chinese maps are without lawful effect to the extent that they exceed the entitlements that China would be permitted by the Convention.

8. Second, the Philippines has asked the Tribunal to resolve a dispute between the Parties concerning the entitlements to maritime zones that would be generated under the Convention by Scarborough Shoal and certain maritime features in the Spratly Islands that are claimed by both the Philippines and China. The Convention provides that submerged banks and low-tide elevations are incapable on their own of generating any entitlements to maritime areas and that "[r]ocks which cannot sustain human habitation or economic life of their own" do not generate an entitlement to an exclusive economic zone of 200 nautical miles or to a continental shelf. The Philippines seeks a declaration that all of the features claimed by China in the Spratly Islands, as well as Scarborough Shoal, fall within one or the other of these categories and that

none of these features generates an entitlement to an exclusive economic zone or to a continental shelf.

9.   Third, the Philippines has asked the Tribunal to resolve a series of disputes between the Parties concerning the lawfulness of China's actions in the South China Sea. The Philippines seeks declarations that China has violated the Convention by:

(a)   interfering with the exercise of the Philippines' rights under the Convention, including with respect to fishing, oil exploration, navigation, and the construction of artificial islands and installations;

(b)   failing to protect and preserve the marine environment by tolerating and actively supporting Chinese fishermen in the harvesting of endangered species and the use of harmful fishing methods that damage the fragile coral reef ecosystem in the South China Sea; and

(c)   inflicting severe harm on the marine environment by constructing artificial islands and engaging in extensive land reclamation at seven reefs in the Spratly Islands.

10.   Fourth, the Philippines has asked the Tribunal to find that China has aggravated and extended the disputes between the Parties during the course of this arbitration by restricting access to a detachment of Philippine marines stationed at Second Thomas Shoal and by engaging in the large-scale construction of artificial islands and land reclamation at seven reefs in the Spratly Islands.

11.   China has consistently rejected the Philippines' recourse to arbitration and adhered to a position of neither accepting nor participating in these proceedings. It has articulated this position in public statements and in many diplomatic Notes Verbales, both to the Philippines and to the Permanent Court of Arbitration (the "**PCA**" or the "**Registry**"), which serves as the Registry in this arbitration. China's Foreign Ministry has also highlighted in its statements, press briefings, and interviews that it considers non-participation in the arbitration to be its lawful right under the Convention.

12.   The possibility of a party refraining from participating in dispute resolution proceedings is expressly addressed by the Convention, which provides in Article 9 of its Annex VII that the "[a]bsence of a party or failure of a party to defend its case shall not constitute a bar to the proceedings." The Tribunal has thus held that China's non-participation does not prevent the arbitration from continuing. The Tribunal has also observed that China is still a Party to the arbitration and, pursuant to the terms of Article 296(1) of the Convention and Article 11 of

Annex VII, shall be bound by any award the Tribunal issues. The situation of a non-participating Party, however, imposes a special responsibility on the Tribunal. It cannot, in China's absence, simply accept the Philippines' claims or enter a default judgment. Rather, Article 9 requires the Tribunal, before making its award, to satisfy itself "not only that it has jurisdiction over the dispute but also that the claim is well founded in fact and law."

13.   Despite its decision not to appear formally at any point in these proceedings, China has taken steps to informally make clear its view that the Tribunal lacks jurisdiction to consider any of the Philippines' claims. On 7 December 2014, China's Foreign Ministry published a "Position Paper of the Government of the People's Republic of China on the Matter of Jurisdiction in the South China Sea Arbitration Initiated by the Republic of the Philippines" ("**China's Position Paper**").[2] In its Position Paper, China argued that the Tribunal lacks jurisdiction because (a) "[t]he essence of the subject-matter of the arbitration is the territorial sovereignty over the relevant maritime features in the South China Sea"; (b) "China and the Philippines have agreed, through bilateral instruments and the Declaration on the Conduct of Parties in the South China Sea, to settle their relevant disputes through negotiations"; and (c) the disputes submitted by the Philippines "would constitute an integral part of maritime delimitation between the two countries." The Chinese Ambassador to the Netherlands has also sent several communications to the individual members of the Tribunal, directly and via the Registry, to draw certain statements of Foreign Ministry officials and others to the attention of the arbitrators, while at the same time making clear that such communications should not be interpreted as China's participation in the arbitral proceedings.

14.   The Tribunal decided to treat the Position Paper and communications from China as equivalent to an objection to jurisdiction and to conduct a separate hearing and rule on its jurisdiction as a preliminary question, except insofar as an issue of jurisdiction "does not possess an exclusively preliminary character." The Tribunal issued its Award on Jurisdiction and Admissibility (the "**Award on Jurisdiction**") on 29 October 2015, addressing the objections to jurisdiction set out in China's Position Paper, as well as other questions concerning the scope of the Tribunal's jurisdiction. In its Award on Jurisdiction, the Tribunal reached conclusions with respect to seven of the Philippines' fifteen Submissions while deferring decisions on seven other Submissions for further consideration in conjunction with the merits of the Philippines' claims. The Tribunal also requested the Philippines to clarify one of its Submissions. Those questions

---

2   *Position Paper of the Government of the People's Republic of China on the Matter of Jurisdiction in the South China Sea Arbitration Initiated by the Republic of the Philippines* (7 December 2014), *available at* <www.fmprc.gov.cn/mfa_eng/zxxx_662805/t1217147.shtml> (hereinafter "**China's Position Paper**").

regarding the scope of the Tribunal's jurisdiction that were not decided in the Award on Jurisdiction have all been considered and are addressed in the course of this Award.

15. The Tribunal outlined in its Award on Jurisdiction the steps it took to satisfy itself of its jurisdiction, including treating China's communications as a plea on jurisdiction, bifurcating the dispute to have a separate hearing and exchange of questions and answers on issues of jurisdiction and admissibility, probing the Philippines on jurisdictional questions beyond even those in China's Position Paper, and in relation to the seven matters not decided in the Award on Jurisdiction, deferring for later consideration those jurisdictional issues so intertwined with the merits that they lacked an exclusively preliminary character. In the merits phase of the dispute, as set out in more detail elsewhere in this Award, the Tribunal has been particularly vigilant with respect to establishing whether the Philippines' claims are well founded in fact and law. It has done so, for example, by retaining independent experts on technical matters raised by the Philippines' pleadings; inviting comments from both Parties on materials that were not originally part of the record submitted to the Tribunal by the Philippines; and posing questions to the Philippines' counsel and experts before, during, and after the hearing on the merits that was held in The Hague from 24 to 30 November 2015. While China did not attend the hearing, it was provided with daily transcripts and all documents submitted during the course of the hearing and was given an opportunity to comment thereon. In addition to a large delegation from the Philippines, representatives from Australia, the Republic of Indonesia, Japan, Malaysia, Singapore, the Kingdom of Thailand, and the Socialist Republic of Viet Nam attended the hearing as observers.

16. In this Award, the Tribunal addresses those matters of jurisdiction and admissibility that remained outstanding after the Award on Jurisdiction, as well as the merits of those of the Philippines' claims for which the Tribunal has jurisdiction. The Award is structured as follows.

17. **Chapter II** sets out the procedural history of the arbitration, focusing on the events which postdate the issuance of the Award on Jurisdiction. The Chapter demonstrates that, in line with the Tribunal's duty under Article 5 of Annex VII to "assure each party a full opportunity to be heard and to present its case," the Tribunal has communicated to both Parties all developments in this arbitration and provided them with the opportunity to comment on substance and procedure. The Tribunal has consistently reminded China that it remained open to it to participate at any stage, and has taken note of its Position Paper, public statements, and multiple communications from its Ambassador to the Netherlands. The Tribunal has also taken steps, in line with its duty under Article 10 of the Rules of Procedure, to "avoid unnecessary delay and expense and to provide a fair and efficient process for resolving the Parties' dispute."

18.   **Chapter III** sets out the Philippines' requests for relief, including the fifteen final Submissions as amended on 30 November 2015, with leave from the Tribunal communicated on 16 December 2015.   This Chapter notes that while China has not participated in the proceedings, the Tribunal has sought to discern from China's official statements its position on each of the Philippines' claims.

19.   **Chapter IV** covers preliminary matters.   It details the legal and practical consequences of China's non-participation, summarises and incorporates the findings in the Award on Jurisdiction, and addresses the status and effect of that Award and China's reaction to it.

20.   In **Chapter V**, the Tribunal considers the Philippines' requests for a declaration that the Parties' respective rights and obligations in regard to the waters, seabed, and maritime features of the South China Sea are governed by the Convention (the Philippines' Submission No. 1), and for a declaration that China's claims to sovereign and historic rights with respect to the maritime areas encompassed by the 'nine-dash line' are contrary to the Convention and therefore without lawful effect (the Philippines' Submission No. 2).

21.   In **Chapter VI**, the Tribunal addresses the Philippines' requests concerning the status of, and maritime entitlements generated by, certain maritime features in the South China Sea (the Philippines' Submissions No. 3 to 7), namely Cuarteron Reef, Fiery Cross Reef, the Gaven Reefs, Johnson Reef, Hughes Reef, McKennan Reef, Mischief Reef, Scarborough Shoal, Second Thomas Shoal, and Subi Reef.   In arriving at its decisions on Submissions No. 3, 5 and 7, the Tribunal also addresses in Chapter VI whether any feature in the Spratly Islands constitutes a fully entitled island, capable in its natural condition of sustaining human habitation or an economic life of its own within the meaning of Article 121(3) of the Convention, such as to be entitled to potential maritime zones that could overlap with those of the Philippines.

22.   In **Chapter VII**, the Tribunal considers the various allegations by the Philippines that China has violated provisions of the Convention, including with respect to:

(a)   China's interference with the Philippines' sovereign rights over non-living and living resources (the Philippines' Submission No. 8);

(b)   China's failure to prevent exploitation of the Philippines' living resources by Chinese fishing vessels (the Philippines' Submission No. 9);

(c)   China's interference with the traditional fishing activities of Philippine fishermen at Scarborough Shoal (the Philippines' Submission No. 10);

(d)   China's failure to protect and preserve the marine environment through (a) its tolerance and active support of Chinese fishing vessels harvesting endangered species and engaging in harmful fishing methods; and (b) its extensive land reclamation, artificial island-building, and construction activities at seven coral reefs in the Spratly Islands (the Philippines' Submissions No. 11 and 12(b));

(e)   China's construction of artificial islands, installations, and structures at Mischief Reef without the Philippines' authorisation (the Philippines' Submissions No. 12(a) and 12(c)); and

(f)   China's operation of its law enforcement vessels in such a way as to create serious risk of collision and danger to Philippine vessels in the vicinity of Scarborough Shoal during two incidents in April and May 2012 (the Philippines' Submission No. 13).

23.   In **Chapter VIII**, the Tribunal considers the Philippines' claim that China has, through its activities near Second Thomas Shoal and its artificial island-building activities at seven coral reefs in the Spratly Islands, aggravated and extended the Parties' disputes since the commencement of the arbitration (the Philippines' Submission No. 14).

24.   **Chapter IX** examines the Philippines' Submission No. 15 on the future conduct of the Parties and discusses the obligations on both Parties going forward to resolve their disputes peacefully and to comply with the Convention and this Award in good faith.

25.   **Chapter X** sets out the Tribunal's formal decisions.

*   *   *

this page intentionally blank

this page intentionally blank

II. PROCEDURAL HISTORY

26. The Award on Jurisdiction recounts in detail the procedural history of the arbitration from its commencement up until the date on which the Award on Jurisdiction was issued. In this Award, the Tribunal will focus on procedural events which occurred after the issuance of the Award on Jurisdiction.

27. Article 5 of Annex VII to the Convention provides that the Tribunal has a duty to "assur[e] to each party a full opportunity to be heard and to present its case." In line with this duty, and as the procedural history chapters in both Awards demonstrate, the Tribunal has communicated to the Philippines and China all developments in this arbitration and provided them with the opportunity to comment on substance and procedure. The Tribunal consistently reminded China that it remained open to it to participate in these proceedings at any stage. It has also taken steps to ensure that the Philippines is not disadvantaged by China's non-appearance and has conducted the proceedings in line with its duty under Article 10(1) of the Rules of Procedure, "so as to avoid unnecessary delay and expense and to provide a fair and efficient process for resolving the Parties' dispute."

A. INITIATION OF THE ARBITRATION

28. By Notification and Statement of Claim dated 22 January 2013, the Philippines initiated arbitration proceedings against China pursuant to Articles 286 and 287 of the Convention and in accordance with Article 1 of Annex VII of the Convention. The Philippines stated that it seeks an Award that:

> (1)   declares that the Parties' respective rights and obligations in regard to the waters, seabed and maritime features of the South China Sea are governed by UNCLOS, and that China's claims based on its "nine dash line" are inconsistent with the Convention and therefore invalid;
>
> (2)   determines whether, under Article 121 of UNCLOS, certain of the maritime features claimed by both China and the Philippines are islands, low tide elevations or submerged banks, and whether they are capable of generating entitlement to maritime zones greater than 12 M; and
>
> (3)   enables the Philippines to exercise and enjoy the rights within and beyond its exclusive economic zone and continental shelf that are established in the Convention.[3]

The Philippines stressed that it:

> does not seek in this arbitration a determination of which Party enjoys sovereignty over the islands claimed by both of them. Nor does it request a delimitation of any maritime

---

3   Notification and Statement of Claim of the Republic of the Philippines, 22 January 2013, para. 6 (Annex 1).

boundaries. The Philippines is conscious of China's Declaration of 25 August 2006 under Article 298 of UNCLOS, and has avoided raising subjects or making claims that China has, by virtue of that Declaration, excluded from arbitral jurisdiction.[4]

29. In response, China presented a Note Verbale to the Department of Foreign Affairs of the Philippines on 19 February 2013, rejecting the arbitration and returning the Notification and Statement of Claim to the Philippines.[5] In its Note Verbale, China stated that its position on the South China Sea issues "has been consistent and clear" and that "[a]t the core of the disputes between China and the Philippines in the South China Sea are the territorial disputes over some islands and reefs of the Nansha Islands." China noted that "[t]he two countries also have overlapping jurisdictional claims over parts of the maritime area in the South China Sea" and that both sides had agreed to settle the dispute through bilateral negotiations and friendly consultations.

B.   CONSTITUTION OF THE TRIBUNAL AND APPOINTMENT OF THE PCA AS REGISTRY

30. As detailed in the Award on Jurisdiction, the Philippines appointed Judge Rüdiger Wolfrum, a German national, as a member of the Tribunal in accordance with Article 3(b) of Annex VII to the Convention. As China did not appoint an arbitrator, the President of the International Tribunal for the Law of the Sea, pursuant to Articles 3(c) and 3(e) of Annex VII to the Convention, appointed Judge Stanislaw Pawlak, a national of Poland, as the second arbitrator. In accordance with Articles 3(d) and 3(e) of Annex VII to the Convention, the President of the International Tribunal for the Law of the Sea also appointed the remaining three arbitrators, namely Judge Jean-Pierre Cot, a national of France; Professor Alfred H.A. Soons, a national of the Netherlands; and as the Presiding Arbitrator, Judge Thomas A. Mensah, a national of Ghana. The present Tribunal was constituted on 21 June 2013.

31. On 12 July 2013, the Tribunal issued Administrative Directive No. 1, pursuant to which the Tribunal appointed the Permanent Court of Arbitration as Registry and set in place arrangements for a deposit to cover fees and expenses. On 15 July 2013, the Secretary-General of the PCA informed the Tribunal and the Parties that Ms. Judith Levine, PCA Senior Legal Counsel, had been appointed to serve as Registrar. Copies of Administrative Directive No. 1, as with all subsequent documents issued by the Tribunal and correspondence issued on its behalf by the Registry, were transmitted to the Agent and Counsel for the Philippines, and the Embassy of the People's Republic of China in the Kingdom of the Netherlands (the "**Chinese**

---

[4]   Notification and Statement of Claim of the Republic of the Philippines, 22 January 2013, para. 7 (Annex 1).

[5]   Note Verbale from the Embassy of the People's Republic of China in Manila to the Department of Foreign Affairs, Republic of the Philippines, No. (13) PG-039, 19 February 2013 (Annex 3).

Embassy"). Throughout the proceedings, the Chinese Embassy has returned the communications and reiterated that "it will neither accept nor participate in the arbitration unilaterally initiated by the Philippines."

32. On 27 August 2013, the Tribunal issued Procedural Order No. 1, by which it adopted the Rules of Procedure and fixed 30 March 2014 as the date for the Philippines to submit a Memorial that "shall fully address all issues including matters relating to jurisdiction, admissibility, and the merits of the dispute" (the "**Memorial**").

C. WRITTEN ARGUMENTS

33. On 11 March 2014, the Tribunal granted leave pursuant to Article 19 of the Rules of Procedure for the Philippines to amend its Statement of Claim, which added a request to determine the status of Second Thomas Shoal.[6]

34. On 30 March 2014, pursuant to Procedural Order No. 1, the Philippines submitted its Memorial and accompanying annexes, addressing all aspects of the case including issues of jurisdiction, admissibility, and the merits. The Memorial concluded with 15 specific submissions setting out the relief sought by the Philippines (the "**Submissions**"), which are reproduced in their final and amended version in Chapter III below.[7]

35. On 7 April 2014, the Philippines wrote further to the Tribunal regarding "China's most recent actions in and around Second Thomas (Ayungin) Shoal." This followed an earlier complaint that the Philippines had submitted to the Tribunal on 18 March 2014 concerning "recent actions of China to prevent the rotation and resupply of Philippine personnel stationed at Second Thomas (Ayungin) Shoal." The Philippines wrote again to the Tribunal on 30 July 2014, expressing concern about China's activities at several features in the South China Sea, in particular the land reclamation at McKennan Reef, Hughes Reef, Johnson Reef, the Gaven Reefs, and Cuarteron Reef. These complaints to the Tribunal are set out in more detail at Chapter VIII on aggravation of the dispute.

36. On 5 December 2014, the Vietnamese Embassy sent to the Tribunal a "Statement of the Ministry of Foreign Affairs of the Socialist Republic of Viet Nam Transmitted to the Arbitral Tribunal in the Proceedings between the Republic of the Philippines and the People's Republic

---

[6] *See* Award on Jurisdiction and Admissibility, 29 October 2015, para. 99 (hereinafter "**Award on Jurisdiction**"); Amended Notification and Statement of Claim of the Republic of the Philippines, pp. 17-19 (Annex 5).

[7] *See* Award on Jurisdiction, paras. 100-101; Memorial of the Philippines (30 March 2014), para. 7.157, pp. 271-272 (hereinafter "**Memorial**").

of China" and annexed documents ("**Viet Nam's Statement**"). Viet Nam's Statement requested that the Tribunal give due regard to the position of Viet Nam with respect to: (a) advocating full observance and implementation of all rules and procedures of the Convention, including Viet Nam's position that it has "no doubt that the Tribunal has jurisdiction in these proceedings"; (b) preserving Viet Nam's "rights and interests of a legal nature"; (c) noting that the Philippines does not request this Tribunal to consider issues not subject to its jurisdiction under Article 288 of the Convention (namely questions of sovereignty and maritime delimitation); (d) "resolutely protest[ing] and reject[ing]" any claim by China based on the "nine-dash line"; and (e) supporting the Tribunal's competence to interpret and apply Articles 60, 80, 194(5), 206, 293(1), and 300 of the Convention and other relevant instruments. Viet Nam stated that none of the maritime features referred to by the Philippines in these proceedings can "generate maritime entitlements in excess of 12 nautical miles since they are low-tide elevations or 'rocks which cannot sustain human habitation or economic life of their own' under Article 121(3) of the Convention." Viet Nam reserved "the right to seek to intervene if it seems appropriate and in accordance with the principles and rules of international law, including the relevant provisions of UNCLOS." Viet Nam also asked to receive copies of all relevant documents in the arbitration.[8]

37. On 7 December 2014, the Ministry of Foreign Affairs of the People's Republic of China published a "Position Paper of the Government of the People's Republic of China on the Matter of Jurisdiction in the South China Sea Arbitration Initiated by the Republic of the Philippines," copies of which the Chinese Embassy deposited with the PCA for distribution to members of the Tribunal.[9] The Chinese Embassy expressed in a Note Verbale that "[t]he Chinese Government reiterates that it will neither accept nor participate in the arbitration unilaterally initiated by the Philippines. The Chinese Government hereby makes clear that the forwarding of the aforementioned Position Paper shall not be regarded as China's acceptance of or its participation in the arbitration."

38. The Tribunal conveyed copies of China's Position Paper and Viet Nam's Statement to the Parties on 11 December 2014 and invited their comments.

---

[8]   Socialist Republic of Viet Nam, *Statement of the Ministry of Foreign Affairs of the Socialist Republic of Viet Nam Transmitted to the Arbitral Tribunal in the Proceedings Between the Republic of the Philippines and the People's Republic of China*, pp. 1-3, 5-6 (14 December 2014) (Annex 468) (hereinafter "**Viet Nam's Statement**"). As noted in the Award on Jurisdiction, the Tribunal had granted Viet Nam access to copies of the Memorial, after seeking the views of the Parties, on 24 April 2014.

[9]   By the terms of Procedural Order No. 2, issued by the Tribunal on 2 June 2014, China's Counter-Memorial was due by 15 December 2014.

39.   On 16 December 2014, the Tribunal issued Procedural Order No. 3, which established a timetable for further written submissions from both Parties and annexed a Request for Further Written Argument by the Philippines Pursuant to Article 25(2) of the Rules of Procedure (the "**Request for Further Written Argument**"). The Request for Further Written Argument included specific questions relating to admissibility, jurisdiction, and the merits of the dispute and invited comments on any relevant public statements made by Chinese Government officials or others.

40.   In a letter accompanying Procedural Order No. 3, the Tribunal invited the Parties' comments on certain procedural matters, including (a) the possible bifurcation of the proceedings to address the Tribunal's jurisdiction as a preliminary matter, (b) the possible appointment of an expert hydrographer, (c) the possibility of a site visit as contemplated in Article 22 of the Rules of Procedure, (d) the appropriate procedure with regard to any *amicus curiae* submissions that the Tribunal may receive, and (e) the scheduling of a hearing in July 2015.

41.   On 26 January 2015, the Philippines sent the Tribunal its comments on Viet Nam's requests, supporting Viet Nam having access to documents in the interest of transparency. On the same day, the Philippines also (a) conveyed its position that it opposed bifurcation; (b) supported the appointment of a technical expert and made suggestions as to the appropriate profile for an expert; (c) commented that a site visit "would be useful" provided arrangements were made for it to occur "under secure conditions" but acknowledged the "fact that conducting a site visit in the context of this case would present certain challenges, not least because of China's decision not to participate"; (d) commented that any decision on accepting an *amicus curiae* submission would fall within the Tribunal's inherent power and under Article 1(2) of the Rules of Procedure and suggested "that each *amicus* submission should be evaluated on its own merits, to determine whether there is 'sufficient reason' for it to be accepted," so long as it does not delay or disrupt the proceedings; and (e) commented on the dates and scope of an oral hearing.

42.   On 6 February 2015, the Chinese Ambassador to the Kingdom of the Netherlands wrote individually to the members of the Tribunal, setting out "the Chinese Government's position on issues relating to the South China Sea arbitration initiated by the Philippines." The letter described China's Position Paper as having "comprehensively explain[ed] why the Arbitral Tribunal . . . manifestly has no jurisdiction over the case." The letter also stated that the Chinese Government "holds an omnibus objection to all procedural applications or steps that would require some kind of response from China." The letter further clarified that China's non-participation and non-response to any issue raised by the Tribunal "shall not be understood or interpreted by anyone in any sense as China's acquiescence in or non-objection to any and all

procedural or substantive matters already or might be raised by the Arbitral Tribunal." The letter further expressed China's "firm opposition" to some of the procedural items raised in the Tribunal's correspondence, such as "intervention by other States," "*amicus curiae* submissions," and "site visit[s]". Finally, the letter recalled the commitment of China and countries of the Association of Southeast Asian Nations ("**ASEAN**") to resolving disputes through consultation and negotiation and expressed the hope that "all relevant actors will act in a way that contributes to peaceful settlement of the South China Sea disputes, cooperation among the coastal States of the South China Sea and the maintenance of peace and stability in the South China Sea."

43.   On 17 February 2015, the Tribunal authorised the Registry to provide Viet Nam with a copy of Procedural Order No. 3 and the Tribunal's accompanying Request for Further Written Argument. The Tribunal stated that it would address the permissibility of intervention in these proceedings "only in the event that Viet Nam in fact makes a formal application for such intervention."

44.   The Philippines submitted its Supplemental Written Submission and accompanying annexes (the "**Supplemental Written Submission**") on 16 March 2015.

D.   BIFURCATION OF PROCEEDINGS

45.   On 21 April 2015, the Tribunal issued Procedural Order No. 4, in which it considered the communications of China, including China's Position Paper, effectively to "constitute a plea concerning this Arbitral Tribunal's jurisdiction for the purposes of Article 20 of the Rules of Procedure." The Tribunal thus decided to convene a hearing to consider issues of jurisdiction and admissibility from 7 to 13 July 2015 (the "**Hearing on Jurisdiction**"). In Procedural Order No. 4, the Tribunal stated that if it determined after the Hearing on Jurisdiction "that there are jurisdictional objections that do not possess an exclusively preliminary character, then, in accordance with Article 20(3) of the Rules of Procedure, such matters will be reserved for consideration and decision at a later stage of the proceedings."

46.   On 21 May 2015, the Tribunal received a letter from the Philippines which described China's "current[] engage[ment] in a massive land reclamation project at various features in the South China Sea" as "deeply troubling to the Philippines" and submitted that such actions were in "violation of the Philippines' rights and in disregard of . . . China's duty not to cause serious harm to the marine environment." In light of such developments, the Philippines suggested that a merits hearing be provisionally scheduled at the earliest possible date.

E.   HEARING ON JURISDICTION AND ADMISSIBILITY

47.   On 2 June 2015, the Tribunal confirmed the schedule for the Hearing on Jurisdiction. The Tribunal advised that the hearing would not be open to the general public, but that it would consider allowing representatives of interested States to attend upon receipt of a written request.

48.   No comments had been received from China by 16 June 2015, the date set by Procedural Order No. 3 for China's comments on the Philippines' Supplemental Written Submission.

49.   In line with its duty to satisfy itself that it has jurisdiction, the Tribunal did not limit the hearing to the issues raised in China's Position Paper, and on 23 June 2015, the Tribunal sent the Parties a list of issues as guidance for the Hearing on Jurisdiction.

50.   Throughout June and July 2015, the Tribunal received requests from several States, interested in the arbitration, for copies of relevant documents and for permission to attend the Hearing on Jurisdiction. After seeking the views of the Parties on each occasion, the Tribunal granted such requests from Malaysia, Japan, Viet Nam, Indonesia, Thailand, and Brunei.

51.   On 1 July 2015, the Chinese Ambassador to the Kingdom of the Netherlands sent a second letter to the members of the Tribunal recalling China's "consistent policy and practice of [resolving] the disputes related to territory and maritime rights and interests with States directly concerned through negotiation and consultation" and noting China's "legitimate right" under the Convention not to "accept any imposed solution or any unilateral resorting to a third-party settlement," a right that it considered the Philippines breached by initiating the arbitration. The Ambassador stated that his letters and the Chinese Government's statements "shall by no means be interpreted as China's participation in the arbitral proceeding" and that China "opposes any moves to initiate and push forward the arbitral proceeding, and does not accept any arbitral arrangements, including the hearing procedures."

52.   The Hearing on Jurisdiction took place from 7 to 13 July 2015 at the Peace Palace in The Hague. A list of attendees is contained in the Award on Jurisdiction. Copies of the daily transcripts, questions from the Members of the Tribunal, answers from the Philippines and all materials submitted during the hearing were made available to both Parties. A press release was issued by the Registry at the close of the hearing and the transcripts were subsequently published.

53.   On 23 July 2015, the Philippines filed written responses to questions posed by the Tribunal. China did not respond to the invitation to submit by 17 August 2015, comments on matters raised during or after the Hearing on Jurisdiction. However, on 24 August 2015, China

published "Foreign Ministry Spokesperson Hua Chunying's Remarks on the Release of the Transcript of the Oral Hearing on Jurisdiction by the South China Sea Arbitral Tribunal Established at the Request of the Philippines." The spokesperson recalled that China had "consist[e]ntly expounded its position of neither accepting nor participating in the South China Sea arbitration unilaterally initiated by the Philippines" and that China's Position Paper had "pointed out that the Arbitral Tribunal . . . has no jurisdiction over the case and elaborated on the legal grounds for China's non-acceptance and non-participation in the arbitration."[10]

F. PROVISIONAL SCHEDULING OF HEARING ON THE MERITS AND APPOINTMENT OF EXPERT

54. Article 24(1) of the Arbitral Tribunal's Rules of Procedure provides:

> After seeking the views of the Parties, the Arbitral Tribunal may appoint one or more independent experts. That expert may be called upon to report on specific issues and in the manner to be determined by the Arbitral Tribunal. A copy of the expert's terms of reference, established by the Arbitral Tribunal, shall be communicated to the Parties.

55. Previously, in December 2014, the Tribunal had invited the Parties' views on the utility and timing of appointing an expert hydrographer, as well as the qualifications appropriate for such an expert. The Chinese Ambassador's letter of 6 February 2015 did not expressly address this question. The Philippines considered it desirable for the Tribunal to appoint as soon as convenient a "knowledgeable, independent, and impartial hydrographer" from whose input "many issues in dispute . . . would benefit significantly." The Philippines set out a list of appropriate qualifications.

56. On 21 April 2015, when the Tribunal issued Procedural Order No. 4 bifurcating proceedings, the Tribunal invited the Parties' views as to whether it should, without prejudice to any findings on jurisdiction and admissibility, proceed to: (a) reserve a period of time within the next 6 to 12 months for a subsequent merits hearing should it become necessary; (b) take steps already to ascertain the availability of potential technical experts. In so doing, the Tribunal recalled its duty under Article 10(1) of the Rules of Procedure to "conduct the proceedings so as to avoid unnecessary delay and expense and to provide a fair and efficient process for resolving the Parties' dispute."

57. The Philippines, by letter dated 11 May 2015, noted that the week of 23 to 27 November 2015 would be suitable for a hearing on the merits and considered that engaging a technical expert early would help to avoid unnecessary delay and that no prejudice would be suffered as a result

---

[10] Ministry of Foreign Affairs, People's Republic of China, *Foreign Ministry Spokesperson Hua Chunying's Remarks on the Release of the Transcript of the Oral Hearing on Jurisdiction by the South China Sea Arbitral Tribunal Established at the Request of the Philippines* (24 August 2015), *available at* <www.fmprc.gov.cn/mfa_eng/xwfw_665399/s2510_665401/2535_665405/t1290752.shtml> (Annex 635).

of an interim engagement in the event that the Tribunal found that it lacked jurisdiction. China did not comment on either matter.

58.   The Tribunal informed the Parties on 7 August 2015 that, after reviewing a number of candidates, it proposed to appoint Mr. Grant Boyes (a national of Australia) as the Tribunal's expert hydrographer. The Parties were invited to comment on his *curriculum vitae*, declaration of independence, and draft Terms of Reference. The Philippines reported that it had no objection, but proposed a clarification to the Terms of Reference that "[i]n providing the Arbitral Tribunal with technical assistance . . . the Expert shall respect that it is the Arbitral Tribunal, and not the Expert, that makes any determination as to legal questions, in particular the application of Article 121(3) of the Convention." With this clarification, and having received no comments from China, the Tribunal and Mr. Boyes finalised the appointment.

59.   On 10 September 2015, the Parties were invited to comment on a provisional schedule for a merits hearing to take place between 24 to 30 November 2015 and also on a request from the Embassy of the Republic of Singapore in Brussels seeking observer status at any future hearing. The Philippines agreed with the proposed schedule and, consistent with its position in support of transparency, expressed that it had no objection to the attendance of a Singaporean delegation at any future hearings. China did not comment on the proposals and, consistent with its practice throughout the proceedings, returned the correspondence to the Registry and reiterated its position of non-acceptance and non-participation.

G.   ISSUANCE OF AWARD ON JURISDICTION AND ADMISSIBILITY

60.   On 29 October 2015, the Tribunal issued its Award on Jurisdiction, the key findings of which are summarised in Chapter IV below. The Award, which was unanimous, only addressed matters of jurisdiction and admissibility; it did not address the merits of the Parties' dispute. In the dispositif, the Tribunal:

    A.   FINDS that the Tribunal was properly constituted in accordance with Annex VII to the Convention.

    B.   FINDS that China's non-appearance in these proceedings does not deprive the Tribunal of jurisdiction.

    C.   FINDS that the Philippines' act of initiating this arbitration did not constitute an abuse of process.

    D.   FINDS that there is no indispensable third party whose absence deprives the Tribunal of jurisdiction.

    E.   FINDS that the 2002 China–ASEAN Declaration on Conduct of the Parties in the South China Sea, the joint statements of the Parties referred to in paragraphs 231 to 232 of this Award, the Treaty of Amity and Cooperation in Southeast Asia, and the Convention on Biological Diversity, do not preclude, under Articles 281 or 282 of the Convention, recourse to the compulsory dispute settlement procedures available under Section 2 of Part XV of the Convention.

F. FINDS that the Parties have exchanged views as required by Article 283 of the Convention.

G. FINDS that the Tribunal has jurisdiction to consider the Philippines' Submissions No. 3, 4, 6, 7, 10, 11, and 13, subject to the conditions noted in paragraphs 400, 401, 403, 404, 407, 408, and 410 of this Award.

H. FINDS that a determination of whether the Tribunal has jurisdiction to consider the Philippines' Submissions No. 1, 2, 5, 8, 9, 12, and 14 would involve consideration of issues that do not possess an exclusively preliminary character, and accordingly RESERVES consideration of its jurisdiction to rule on Submissions No. 1, 2, 5, 8, 9, 12, and 14 to the merits phase.

I. DIRECTS the Philippines to clarify the content and narrow the scope of its Submission 15 and RESERVES consideration of its jurisdiction over Submission No. 15 to the merits phase.

J. RESERVES for further consideration and directions all issues not decided in this Award.[11]

61. The Tribunal confirmed that it was ready to proceed in late November with a hearing on the merits and any outstanding questions of jurisdiction and admissibility (the "**Hearing on the Merits**") and stated that it was willing to make appropriate adjustments to the schedule if China decided to participate. The Philippines confirmed the schedule, and China did not comment on it. However, on 30 October 2015, the Chinese Ministry of Foreign Affairs issued a "Statement . . . on the Award on Jurisdiction and Admissibility of the South China Sea Arbitration by the Arbitral Tribunal Established at the Request of the Republic of the Philippines" as follows:

> The award rendered on 29 October 2015 by the Arbitral Tribunal established at the request of the Republic of the Philippines (hereinafter referred to as the "Arbitral Tribunal") on jurisdiction and admissibility of the South China Sea arbitration is null and void, and has no binding effect on China.
>
> I. China has indisputable sovereignty over the South China Sea Islands and the adjacent waters. China's sovereignty and relevant rights in the South China Sea, formed in the long historical course, are upheld by successive Chinese governments, reaffirmed by China's domestic laws on many occasions, and protected under international law including the United Nations Convention on the Law of the Sea (UNCLOS). With regard to the issues of territorial sovereignty and maritime rights and interests, China will not accept any solution imposed on it or any unilateral resort to a third-party dispute settlement.
>
> II. The Philippines' unilateral initiation and obstinate pushing forward of the South China Sea arbitration by abusing the compulsory procedures for dispute settlement under the UNCLOS is a political provocation under the cloak of law. It is in essence not an effort to settle disputes but an attempt to negate China's territorial sovereignty and maritime rights and interests in the South China Sea. In the Position Paper of the Government of the People's Republic of China on the Matter of Jurisdiction in the South China Sea Arbitration Initiated by the Republic of the Philippines, which was released by the Chinese Ministry of Foreign Affairs on 7 December 2014 upon authorization, the Chinese government pointed out that the Arbitral Tribunal manifestly has no jurisdiction over the arbitration initiated by the Philippines, and elaborated on the legal grounds for China's non-acceptance of and non-participation in the arbitration. This position is clear and explicit, and will not change.

---

[11] Award on Jurisdiction, para. 413.

III. As a sovereign state and a State Party to the UNCLOS, China is entitled to choose the means and procedures of dispute settlement of its own will. China has all along been committed to resolving disputes with its neighbors over territory and maritime jurisdiction through negotiations and consultations. Since the 1990s, China and the Philippines have repeatedly reaffirmed in bilateral documents that they shall resolve relevant disputes through negotiations and consultations. The Declaration on the Conduct of Parties in the South China Sea (DOC) explicitly states that the sovereign states directly concerned undertake to resolve their territorial and jurisdictional disputes by peaceful means through friendly consultations and negotiations. All these documents demonstrate that China and the Philippines have chosen, long time ago, to settle their disputes in the South China Sea through negotiations and consultations. The breach of this consensus by the Philippines damages the basis of mutual trust between states.

IV. Disregarding that the essence of this arbitration case is territorial sovereignty and maritime delimitation and related matters, maliciously evading the declaration on optional exceptions made by China in 2006 under Article 298 of the UNCLOS, and negating the consensus between China and the Philippines on resolving relevant disputes through negotiations and consultations, the Philippines and the Arbitral Tribunal have abused relevant procedures and obstinately forced ahead with the arbitration, and as a result, have severely violated the legitimate rights that China enjoys as a State Party to the UNCLOS, completely deviated from the purposes and objectives of the UNCLOS, and eroded the integrity and authority of the UNCLOS. As a State Party to the UNCLOS, China firmly opposes the acts of abusing the compulsory procedures for dispute settlement under the UNCLOS, and calls upon all parties concerned to work together to safeguard the integrity and authority of the UNCLOS.

V. The Philippines' attempt to negate China's territorial sovereignty and maritime rights and interests in the South China Sea through arbitral proceeding will lead to nothing. China urges the Philippines to honor its own commitments, respect China's rights under international law, change its course and return to the right track of resolving relevant disputes in the South China Sea through negotiations and consultations.[12]

62. On 6 November 2015, the observer States that had attended the Hearing on Jurisdiction, as well as Brunei and Singapore, were advised of the schedule for the Hearing on the Merits and that they could send delegations of up to five representatives as observers.

63. As it had done before the Hearing on Jurisdiction, the Tribunal provided on 10 November 2015 an "Annex of Issues the Philippines May Wish to Address" as guidance for the Hearing on the Merits.

64. On 6 November 2015, the Philippines sought leave to present for examination two experts, Professor Clive Schofield and Professor Kent Carpenter; and on 14 November 2015, sought leave to supplement its written pleadings with additional documentary and testimonial evidence and legal authorities which it intended to reference during the Hearing on the Merits. The Tribunal invited China's comments on the requests by 17 November 2015.

---

[12] Ministry of Foreign Affairs, People's Republic of China, *Statement of the Ministry of Foreign Affairs of the People's Republic of China on the Award on Jurisdiction and Admissibility of the South China Sea Arbitration by the Arbitral Tribunal Established at the Request of the Republic of the Philippines* (30 October 2015) (Annex 649).

65.   On 18 November 2015, the Tribunal granted both requests, noting that it had not received comments from China, and that the requests were reasonable. The Tribunal also invited the Parties' comments on whether copies of the 10 November 2015 Annex of Issues could be provided to observer States who had confirmed attendance at the Hearing on the Merits (namely Viet Nam, Malaysia, Thailand, Japan, Indonesia and Singapore). Finally, the Tribunal forwarded to the Parties for their comment a Note Verbale from the Embassy of the United States of America, requesting to send a representative to observe the hearing. The Note Verbale explained that "[a]s a major coastal and maritime State, and as a State that is continuing to pursue its domestic Constitutional processes to accede to the United Nations Convention on the Law of the Sea, the United States has a keen interest in the proceedings in light of the important legal issues relating to the law of the sea that are the subject of the arbitration."

66.   The Philippines wrote on 19 November 2015 that it did not object to the U.S. request, nor to providing the Annex of Issues to observer delegations. The Philippines also submitted the additional documentary and testimonial evidence and legal authorities for which it had been granted leave. Copies were provided to the Chinese Embassy.

67.   On 23 November 2015, the Tribunal communicated to the Parties and the U.S. Embassy that it had decided that "only interested States parties to the United Nations Convention on the Law of the Sea will be admitted as observers" and thus could not accede to the U.S. request. The same day, the Tribunal received a Note Verbale from the United Kingdom's Embassy in the Netherlands applying for "neutral observer status" at the Hearing on the Merits and explaining that "[a]s a State Party to the [Convention], and with a strong interest in the maintenance of peace and stability in the South China Sea, underpinned by respect for, and adherence to, international law, the United Kingdom has been closely following proceedings in the arbitration and has an ongoing interest in developments." The request was forwarded to the Parties for their comment, and the Philippines stated it had no objection to it.

68.   On 24 November 2015, the Tribunal received a request from the Australian Embassy to observe the Hearing on the Merits. The request stated that "Australia has taken a close interest in this case. Australia has the third largest maritime jurisdiction in the world, and a significant proportion of our global seaborne trade passes through the South China Sea. As one of the original States Parties to [the Convention], Australia has an abiding national interest in promoting the rule of law regionally and globally, including through the peaceful settlement of disputes in accordance with international law." The request was forwarded to the Parties for their immediate comment. The Philippines did not object to the Australian request. The Tribunal informed the embassies of Australia and the United Kingdom that their respective

requests to send observer delegations had been granted, and so advised the Parties. The United Kingdom, however, informed the Registry that it would not be attending the proceedings.

H. HEARING ON THE MERITS

69. The Hearing on the Merits took place in two rounds on 24, 25, 26, and 30 November 2015 at the Peace Palace in The Hague, the Netherlands. As with the Hearing on Jurisdiction, it was not open to the general public. A press release was issued upon its commencement.

70. The following were present at the Hearing:

Arbitral Tribunal
Judge Thomas A. Mensah (Presiding)
Judge Jean-Pierre Cot
Judge Stanislaw Pawlak
Professor Alfred H.A. Soons
Judge Rüdiger Wolfrum

The Philippines
Agent
Solicitor General Florin T. Hilbay

Representatives of the Philippines
Secretary of Foreign Affairs Albert F. del Rosario
Mrs. Gretchen V. del Rosario
Secretary Ronaldo M. Llamas
Representative Rodolfo G. Biazon
Justice Francis H. Jardeleza
Justice Antonio T. Carpio
Ambassador Jaime Victor B. Ledda
Mrs. Veredigna M. Ledda
Ambassador Enrique A. Manalo
Ambassador Victoria S. Bataclan
Ambassador Cecilia B. Rebong
Ambassador Melita S. Sta. Maria-Thomeczek
Ambassador Joselito A. Jimeno
Ambassador Carlos C. Salinas
Mrs. Isabelita T. Salinas
Deputy Executive Secretary Menardo I. Guevarra
Deputy Executive Secretary Teofilo S. Pilando, Jr.
Undersecretary Emmanuel T. Bautista
Undersecretary Abigail D. F. Valte
Consul General Henry S. Bensurto, Jr.
Minister Igor G. Bailen
Minister and Consul General Dinno M. Oblena
Director Ana Marie L. Hernando
Second Secretary and Consul Zoilo A. Velasco
Third Secretary and Vice Consul Ma. Theresa M. Alders
Third Secretary and Vice Consul Oliver C. Delfin
Attorney Josel N. Mostajo

Attorney Maximo Paulino T. Sison III
Attorney Ma. Cristina T. Navarro
Associate Solicitor Elvira Joselle R. Castro
Attorney Margaret Faye G. Tañgan
Associate Solicitor Maria Graciela D. Base
Associate Solicitor Melbourne D. Pana
Ms. Ma. Rommin M. Diaz
Mr. Rene Fajardo

Counsel and Advocates
Mr. Paul S. Reichler
Mr. Lawrence H. Martin
Professor Bernard H. Oxman
Professor Philippe Sands QC
Professor Alan E. Boyle
Mr. Andrew B. Loewenstein

Counsel
Mr. Joseph Klingler
Mr. Yuri Parkhomenko
Mr. Nicholas M. Renzler
Mr. Remi Reichhold
Ms. Melissa Stewart

Technical Expert
Mr. Scott Edmonds
Mr. Alex Tait
Dr. Robert W. Smith

Assistants
Ms. Elizabeth Glusman
Ms. Nancy Lopez

Expert Witnesses
Professor Kent E. Carpenter
Professor Clive Schofield

China
No Agent or representatives present

Delegations from Observer States

Australia
Ms. Indra McCormick, Embassy of Australia

Republic of Indonesia
Mr. Ibnu Wahyutomo, Embassy of Indonesia
Dr. iur. Damos Dumoli Agusman, Ministry of Foreign Affairs
Mr. Andy Aron, Ministry of Foreign Affairs
Mr. Andreano Erwin, Office of the Special Envoy to the President
Dr. Haryo Budi Nugroho, Office of the Special Envoy to the President
Ms. Ayodhia G.L. Kalake, Coordinating Ministry of Maritime Affairs
Ms. Sora Lokita, Coordinating Ministry of Maritime Affairs

Ms. Ourina Ritonga, Embassy of Indonesia
Ms. Monica Nila Sari, Embassy of Indonesia

Japan
Mr. Masayoshi Furuya, Embassy of Japan
Mr. Nobuyuki Murai, Embassy of Japan
Ms. Kaori Matsumoto, Embassy of Japan
Ms. Yuri Suzuki, Consular Office of Japan in Hamburg

Malaysia
Ambassador Ahmad Nazri Yusof
Dr. Azfar Mohamad Mustafar, Ministry of Foreign Affairs
Mr. Mohd Helmy Ahmad, Prime Minister's Department
Mr. Kamarul Azam Kamarul Baharin, Department of Survey and Mapping
Mr. Intan Diyana Ahamad, Attorney General's Chambers
Ms. Nor'airin Abd Rashid, Embassy of Malaysia

The Republic of Singapore
Mr. Luke Tang, Attorney-General's Chambers
Ms. Vanessa Lam, Ministry of Foreign Affairs
Ms. Lin Zhiping, Ministry of Foreign Affairs
Mr. John Cheo, Ministry of Foreign Affairs

Kingdom of Thailand
Ambassador Ittiporn Boonpracong
Mr. Sorayut Chasombat, Ministry of Foreign Affairs
Mr. Asi Mamanee, Royal Thai Embassy
Ms. Tanyarat Mungkalarungsi, Ministry of Foreign Affairs
Ms. Kanokwan Ketchaimas, Royal Thai Embassy
Ms. Natsupang Poshyananda, Royal Thai Embassy

Socialist Republic of Viet Nam
Mr. Trinh Duc Hai, National Boundary Commission
Ambassador Nguyen Duy Chien
Mr. Nguyen Minh Vu, Ministry of Foreign Affairs
Mr. Nguyen Dang Thang, National Boundary Commission
Mr. Thomas Grant, Counsel

Expert Appointed to Assist the Tribunal
Mr. Grant Boyes

Permanent Court of Arbitration
Ms. Judith Levine, Registrar
Mr. Garth Schofield
Ms. Nicola Peart
Ms. Julia Solana
Mr. Philipp Kotlaba
Ms. Iuliia Samsonova
Ms. Gaëlle Chevalier

Court Reporter
Mr. Trevor McGowan

71. Oral presentations were made by the then Solicitor General Florin T. Hilbay, then Agent of the Philippines; Secretary Albert F. del Rosario, the then Secretary of Foreign Affairs of the Philippines; Mr. Paul S. Reichler and Mr. Lawrence H. Martin of Foley Hoag LLP, Washington, D.C.; Professor Bernard H. Oxman of the University of Miami; Professor Philippe Sands QC of Matrix Chambers, London; Professor Alan E. Boyle of Essex Court Chambers, London; and Mr. Andrew B. Loewenstein of Foley Hoag LLP, Boston.

72. The Registry delivered daily transcripts to the Philippines' delegation and to the Chinese Embassy, along with copies of all materials submitted by the Philippines during the course of their oral presentations.

73. During the first round of oral argument, several questions were posed by individual arbitrators and answered by the Philippines. On 27 November 2015, the Tribunal circulated to the Parties (a) "Questions for the Philippines to Address in the Second Round," (b) "Questions for Professor Schofield," and (c) "Questions for Professor Carpenter." Copies of the questions were subsequently made available to the observer delegations.

74. On 30 November 2015, during the second round of the hearing, the Philippines responded to the Tribunal's written questions circulated on 27 November 2015, as well as to oral questions posed by individual arbitrators. Professor Schofield and Professor Carpenter also responded to the written questions put to them respectively. The Philippines' then Secretary for Foreign Affairs addressed the Tribunal with concluding remarks, in which he recalled, on the 70th anniversary of the United Nations, that two "centrepieces" of the UN order were the sovereign equality of States and the obligation to settle disputes by peaceful means. He also noted the 40th anniversary of the establishment of diplomatic relations between the Philippines and China and stated that it was for the preservation of the valued friendship between the two States that the Philippines had initiated this arbitration. He expressed his belief that this arbitration "benefits everyone" because for China "it will define and clarify its maritime entitlements," for the Philippines, "it will clarify what is ours, specifically our fishing rights, rights to resources, and rights to enforce our laws within our EEZ" and for the rest of the international community, "it will help ensure peace, security, stability and freedom of navigation and overflight in the South China Sea." He expected the arbitration to "be instructive for other States to consider the dispute settlement mechanism under UNCLOS as an option for resolving disputes in a peaceful manner." He summarised the key legal arguments and expressed hope that this arbitration would help "promote[] peace, security and good neighbourliness" and accord to the rule of law

the "primacy that the founders of the United Nations and the drafters of UNCLOS envisioned."[13]

75.   The Agent for the Philippines formally presented the Philippines' fifteen final Submissions.[14] The Presiding Arbitrator outlined the next steps in the proceeding, including an invitation to both Parties to submit by 9 December 2015 their corrections to the transcript, an invitation to the Philippines to submit by 18 December 2015 any further responses to questions posed during the second round, and an invitation to China to comment in writing by 1 January 2016 on anything said during the Hearing on the Merits or submitted subsequently. The Presiding Arbitrator then declared the Hearing on the Merits closed.

76.   In keeping with its prior practice and in accordance with Article 16 of the Rules of Procedure, the Registry issued a Press Release after the closure of the Hearing on the Merits.

I.   POST-HEARING PROCEEDINGS

77.   The Agent for the Philippines submitted in written form the Final Submissions of the Republic of the Philippines on 30 November 2015.

78.   By letter dated 1 December 2015, the Tribunal noted that the Philippines' final Submissions reflected three amendments—to Submissions No. 11, 14 and 15—requested by the Philippines in the course of the Hearing on the Merits.[15] With respect to Submission No. 11, on failure to protect and preserve the marine environment, the Philippines added references to Cuarteron Reef, Fiery Cross Reef, Gaven Reef, Johnson Reef, Hughes Reef and Subi Reef. With respect to Submission No. 14, on China's alleged aggravation and extension of the dispute, the Philippines added reference to "dredging, artificial island-building and construction activities at Mischief Reef, Cuarteron Reef, Fiery Cross Reef, Gaven Reef, Johnson Reef, Hughes Reef and Subi Reef." In response to the Tribunal's direction in paragraph 413(I) of the Award on Jurisdiction to "clarify the content and narrow the scope of its Submission 15," the Philippines changed the text of Submission No. 15 to seek a declaration that "China shall respect the rights and freedoms of the Philippines under the Convention, shall comply with its duties under the Convention, including those relevant to the protection and preservation of the marine environment in the South China Sea, and shall exercise its rights and freedoms in the South China Sea with due regard to those of the Philippines under the Convention." China was invited to provide any comments on the requested amendments by 9 December 2015.

---

[13]   Merits Hearing Tr. (Day 4), pp. 188-200.

[14]   Merits Hearing Tr. (Day 4), pp. 201-205.

[15]   For earlier versions of the submissions, *see* Award on Jurisdiction, paras. 99-102; Memorial, pp. 271-272.

79. On 14 December 2015, the Philippines submitted documents that had been referenced or requested during the hearing. These included electronic versions of materials displayed by Professor Schofield, additional legal authorities, and observations by Dr. Robert Smith and EOMAP satellite bathymetry analysis pertaining to the nature of certain maritime features located between Thitu and Subi Reef.

80. In accordance with Article 19 of the Rules of Procedure, on 16 December 2015, the Tribunal granted leave to the Philippines to make the amendments incorporated in its final Submissions. It also informed the Parties that the final reviewed and corrected transcripts of the Hearing on the Merits would be published on the PCA's website and reminded China of its opportunity to comment in writing by 1 January 2016 on anything said during the hearing or subsequently filed by the Philippines.

81. On 18 December 2015, the Philippines filed a supplementary response to one of Judge Wolfrum's questions posed during the Hearing on the Merits, referring to additional evidence about the alleged taking of giant clams and sea turtles by Chinese fishermen and alleged environmental damage to reefs.

82. On 21 December 2015, an official spokesperson for the Chinese Ministry of Foreign Affairs commented on the publication of the transcript of the Hearing on the Merits as follows:

> The Chinese side will neither accept nor participate in the South China Sea arbitration unilaterally initiated by the Philippines. This longstanding position is fully supported by international law and subject to no change.
>
> In the hearing, the Philippine side attempted to negate China's sovereignty over the Nansha Islands and deny the validity of the Cairo Declaration and the Potsdam Proclamation in disregard of historical facts, international law and international justice. It testifies to the fact that the South China Sea dispute between China and the Philippines is in essence a territorial dispute over which the arbitral tribunal has no jurisdiction. It also shows that the so-called arbitration is a political provocation under the cloak of law aiming at negating China's sovereignty and maritime rights and interests in the South China Sea instead of resolving the dispute.
>
> It is the Chinese people rather than any other individuals or institutions that master China's territorial sovereignty. When it comes to issues concerning territorial sovereignty and maritime delimitation, China will not accept any dispute settlement approach that resorts to a third party. The Chinese side urges the Philippine side to cast aside illusions, change its course and come back to the right track of resolving disputes through negotiations and consultations.[16]

83. On 11 January 2016, the Tribunal noted that China had not submitted any comments on what was said during the Hearing on the Merits or subsequently filed by the Philippines. The

---

[16]   Ministry of Foreign Affairs, People's Republic of China, *Foreign Ministry Spokesperson Hong Lei's Regular Press Conference* (21 December 2015), *available at* <http://www.fmprc.gov.cn/mfa_eng/xwfw_665399/s2510_665401/t1326449.shtml>.

Tribunal also conveyed a request the Registry had received from the Japanese Embassy for copies of any relevant new documents in relation to the Hearing on the Merits. The Tribunal invited the Parties' views on the documents that it proposed to provide to the observer States. The Philippines had no objection to the proposed items being provided to the observer States.

J.   FURTHER EVIDENCE, EXPERT REPORTS, AND COMMUNICATIONS FROM CHINA AND OTHERS

84.   On 5 February 2016, the Tribunal sent a letter to the Parties informing them that, in reviewing the evidentiary record and pursuing its deliberations, it had decided that it would benefit from further evidence and clarifications from the Parties, and from the views of independent experts. The Tribunal referred to Article 22(2) of the Rules of Procedure, which provides for the Tribunal to "take all appropriate measures in order to establish the facts"; Article 22(4), which provides that the Tribunal may "at any time during the arbitral proceedings, require the Parties to produce documents, exhibits or other evidence"; and Article 24 which provides for the Tribunal to appoint independent experts to report on specific issues. The Tribunal's letter addressed the following matters:

(a)   As indicated during the Hearing on the Merits, the Tribunal remained interested in publications and studies from China or elsewhere concerning the environmental impact of China's island-building activities, [17] especially in light of statements made by public officials and China's State Oceanic Administration ("**SOA**") indicating that such studies had been conducted. [18] The Parties were thus invited to submit comments in respect of those materials, and China was specifically asked to indicate whether it had conducted an environmental impact study per Article 206 of the Convention and, if so, to provide the Tribunal with a copy.

(b)   The Tribunal had decided to appoint an expert to provide an independent opinion on whether the Chinese construction activities in the Spratly Islands have a detrimental effect on the coral reef systems and the anticipated duration of such effects.

(c)   The Tribunal considered it appropriate to appoint an expert to review the available documentary material relevant to the Philippines' Submission No. 13 on navigational safety issues and to draw independent conclusions as to whether there had been a violation of the navigational safety provisions covered by the Convention.

---

[17]   Letter from the Tribunal to the Parties (27 November 2015); Annex A to Letter from the Tribunal to the Parties, Questions 22, 23 (27 November 2015); Annex C to Letter from the Tribunal to the Parties (27 November 2015), Merits Hearing Tr. (Day 4), pp. 148-150.

[18]   See China's public statements at paragraphs 922 to 924 below.

(d)   Recalling that it had previously sought the Parties' comments on new documentation about the status of Itu Aba, the Tribunal sought comments on two further documents in the public domain that had recently come to its attention.

85.   The Tribunal proposed on 26 February 2016 to appoint Captain Gurpreet Singh Singhota, a national of the United Kingdom, as an expert on navigational safety issues and invited the Parties' comments on his qualifications, declaration of independence and draft Terms of Reference. On 29 February 2016, the Tribunal proposed to appoint Dr. Sebastian Ferse, a national of Germany, as an expert on coral reef issues and invited the Parties' comments on his qualifications, declaration of independence and draft Terms of Reference. Noting the size and complexity of the coral reef expert's mandate, the Tribunal mentioned that it was considering the appointment of a second expert on coral reef ecology.

86.   The Philippines reported that it approved of the proposed appointments and had no comments. On 11 March 2016, the Philippines submitted its comments concerning additional materials relating to (a) evidence relevant to Submissions No. 11 and 12(b) on protection of the marine environment, and (b) materials relevant to the status of features that may generate overlapping entitlements. Its comments were accompanied by 30 new annexes, including two new expert reports, by Dr. Ryan T. Bailey on "Groundwater Resources Analysis of Itu Aba" and by Dr. Peter P. Motavalli on "Soil Resources and Potential Self-Sustaining Agricultural Production on Itu Aba."

87.   China did not comment on the proposed appointment of either expert candidate. China did not respond to the Tribunal's invitation to supply information about environmental impact assessments and did not comment on the new materials about Itu Aba.

88.   On 15 March 2016, the Tribunal invited China to comment on the new materials filed by the Philippines and informed the Parties that it was proceeding with the appointments of Captain Singhota and Dr. Ferse as experts under Article 24 of the Rules of Procedure.

89.   On 1 April 2016, the Tribunal sent three letters to the Parties:

(a)   The first letter noted that, in furtherance of its mandate to satisfy itself that the Philippines' claims are well founded in fact, the Tribunal considered it appropriate to have reference, to the greatest extent possible, to original records based on the direct observation of the features in question, prior to them having been subjected to significant human modification. It informed the Parties that, as the most extensive hydrographic survey work in the South China Sea prior to 1945 was carried out by the Royal Navy of the United Kingdom, followed closely by the Imperial Japanese Navy, the Tribunal had undertaken to seek records from the archives of the United Kingdom Hydrographic Office (the "**UKHO**"), which also hold certain Japanese records captured during the Second World War. The Tribunal provided documents and survey materials obtained by the Tribunal from the UKHO archives and invited the Parties' comments by 22 April 2016.

(b)   The second letter conveyed a request from Dr. Ferse for the Philippines to seek clarification from the author of a 2015 report that was put into the record by the Philippines,[19] with respect to the extent of reef damage caused by dredging versus clam shell extraction, in light of some more recent reporting on the matter.[20]

(c)   The third letter invited the Parties' comments on four new documents that had come to the Tribunal's attention, namely a "Position Paper on ROC South China Sea Policy," the comments of the People's Republic of China Foreign Ministry Spokesperson in response to that Position Paper; a document published by the "Chinese (Taiwan) Society of International Law" and some remarks of Mr. Ma Ying-jeou, then President of the Taiwan Authority of China, at an international press conference "regarding Taiping [Itu Aba] Island in Nansha Islands."

90.   On 12 April 2016, the Tribunal informed the Parties that it intended to appoint two additional coral reef experts to collaborate with Dr. Ferse, namely Professor Peter Mumby (a national of the United Kingdom and Australia) and Dr. Selina Ward (a national of Australia). Their *curricula vitae*, declarations of independence, and draft Terms of Reference were sent to the Parties. The Philippines approved of their appointments and China did not respond.

91.   On 18 April 2016, the Tribunal sent to the Parties the expert opinion of Captain Singhota on navigational safety issues and, in accordance with Article 24(4) of the Rules of Procedure, invited the Parties to express any comments on the report in writing. The Philippines expressed that it had no comments, and China did not respond.

92.   On 25 April 2016, the Philippines filed its responses to the Tribunal's request for comments on additional materials regarding the status of Itu Aba. While the Philippines considered that it would have been "within its rights in requesting, and the Tribunal would be well-justified in finding, that these materials should be disregarded," it nevertheless "recognized the exceptional

---

[19]   J.W. McManus, "Offshore Coral Reef Damage, Overfishing and Paths to Peace in the South China Sea," draft as at 20 September 2015 (Annex 850).

[20]   V.R. Lee, "Satellite Imagery Shows Ecocide in the South China Sea," *The Diplomat*, 15 January 2016, *available at* <thediplomat.com/2016/01/satellite-images-show-ecocide-in-the-south-china-sea/>.

difficulties China's non-appearance has created for the Tribunal" and chose "not to object to the Tribunal's consideration of Taiwan's most recent materials should the Tribunal itself find it appropriate to do so."[21] The Philippines' comments were accompanied by two revised translations and 21 new annexes, including supplemental expert reports from Dr. Bailey and Dr. Motavalli. The Philippines submitted that: (a) Taiwan's newest materials "must be treated with caution," (b) "[n]o further attempts by Taiwan to influence the Tribunal's deliberations should be entertained," (c) "[i]n any event, Taiwan's latest submissions only prove that Itu Aba has never supported genuine, sustained human habitation or economic life of its own" as explained in part by the "fact that Itu Aba lacks the freshwater and soil resources to do so," (d) the historical account of China's alleged presence in the South China Sea in "Taiwan's Position Paper only underscores the baseless nature of China's claim to exclusive historical rights to the maritime areas located within the nine-dash line," and (e) the "PRC's Spokesperson's remarks make it clear that Taiwan is alone among the littoral authorities in the South China Sea in claiming that Itu Aba is capable of sustaining human habitation and economic life of its own."

93. On 26 April 2016, the Philippines filed its responses to Dr. Ferse's request for clarification on the issue of reef damage attributable to dredging versus clam shell extraction. This included a letter and updated report from Professor John W. McManus, and a supplementary declaration from Professor Carpenter.

94. On 28 April 2016, the Philippines filed its response to the UKHO materials, and submitted that "the documents and survey materials confirm the Philippines' characterization of the relevant features . . . as a submerged feature, a low-tide elevation, or an Article 121(3) rock."

95. On 29 April 2016, the Tribunal sent the Parties the independent expert opinion of Dr. Ferse, Professor Mumby, and Dr. Ward on the "Assessment of the Potential Environmental Consequences of Construction Activities on Seven Reefs in the Spratly Islands in the South China Sea." Pursuant to Article 24(4) of the Rules of Procedure, the Parties had an opportunity to express in writing their respective comments on the report. The Philippines expressed that it had no comments, and China did not respond.

96. On 12 May 2016, the Director-General of the Chinese Department of Treaty and Law of the Chinese Ministry of Foreign Affairs, Xu Hong, gave a "Briefing on the South China Sea Arbitration Initiated by the Philippines." He made the following overview statement on "the

---

[21] Responses of the Philippines to the Tribunal's 1 April 2016 Request for Comments on Additional Materials regarding the Status of Itu Aba, paras. 7-8 (25 April 2016) (hereinafter "**Written Responses of the Philippines on Itu Aba (25 April 2016)**").

relevant policies and positions of the Chinese Government, especially from the international law perspective," before answering questions from the media:

China has made it clear on multiple occasions that because the Arbitral Tribunal clearly has no jurisdiction over the present Arbitration, the decision to be made by such an institution that lacks the jurisdiction to do so has obviously no legal effect, and consequently there is no such thing as the recognition or implementation of the Award. Some people wonder whether China's position above is consistent with international law. Today, I would like to elaborate on China's positions from the international law perspective. . . .

The first question is what is the scope of the jurisdiction of the Arbitral Tribunal.

. . . to settle international disputes by peaceful means is one of the fundamental principles of international law. However, it should be noted that there are a variety of means to settle disputes peacefully, and compulsory arbitration is merely a new type of procedure established under the UNCLOS. Compulsory arbitration is subsidiary and complementary to negotiation and consultation, and its application is subject to several preconditions. . . .

First, compulsory arbitration can only be applied to settle disputes concerning the interpretation and application of the UNCLOS. If the subject matters are beyond the scope of the UNCLOS, the disputes shall not be settled by compulsory arbitration. The issue of territorial sovereignty is one such case. Consequently, States shall not initiate compulsory arbitration on disputes concerning it; and even if they do, the arbitral tribunal has no jurisdiction over them.

Second, a State Party to the UNCLOS may declare in writing that it does not accept compulsory arbitration with respect to disputes concerning maritime delimitation, historic bays or titles, military and law enforcement activities, etc. Such exclusions are effective to other States Parties. With respect to disputes excluded by one party, other parties to the dispute shall not initiate compulsory arbitration; and even if it does, the arbitral tribunal has no jurisdiction over them.

Third, if parties to a dispute have agreed on other means of settlement of their own choice, no party shall unilaterally initiate compulsory arbitration; and even if it does, the arbitral tribunal has no jurisdiction over the dispute.

Fourth, at the procedural level, parties to a dispute are obliged to first exchange views on the means of dispute settlement. Failing to fulfill this obligation, they shall not initiate compulsory arbitration; and even if they do, the arbitral tribunal has no jurisdiction over the dispute.

The above four preconditions act as the "four bars" for States Parties to initiate compulsory arbitration, and for the arbitral tribunal to establish its jurisdiction. They form a part of the package system of dispute settlement, which shall be interpreted and applied comprehensively and in its entirety.

. . . If we apply the above preconditions to the arbitration unilaterally initiated by the Philippines, it is not difficult to see that the Philippines, by initiating the arbitration, has violated international law in at least four aspects.

First, the essence of the subject-matter of the arbitration is territorial sovereignty over several maritime features in the South China Sea, which is beyond the scope of the UNCLOS. Second, even assuming some of the claims were concerned with the interpretation and application of the UNCLOS, they would still be an integral part of maritime delimitation, which has been excluded by China through its 2006 Declaration and consequently is not subject to compulsory arbitration. Third, given that China and the Philippines have agreed to settle their disputes in the South China Sea through negotiation, the Philippines is precluded from initiating arbitration unilaterally. Fourth, the Philippines failed to fulfill the obligation of exchanging views with China on the means of dispute settlement.

In summary, the Philippines' initiation of the arbitration is a typical abuse of compulsory arbitral procedures stipulated in the UNCLOS. . . . In 2014, the Chinese Government issued a Position Paper to elaborate, from an international law perspective, on the question why the Tribunal lacks jurisdiction over the Arbitration. . . .

However, the Tribunal is not objective or just. On several occasions, it distorts the provisions of the UNCLOS to embrace the claims of the Philippines. In violation of the fundamental principle that the jurisdiction shall be established based on facts and law, the Arbitral Tribunal concluded that it had jurisdiction over the Philippines' claims, which is neither convincing nor valid in international law. For such an award, China certainly has good reasons not to recognize it. The opinions made by the Tribunal, as an institution that manifestly lacks jurisdiction and should not exist in the first place, are personal views of the arbitrators at best and are not legally binding, not to mention its recognition or implementation.[22]

97. On 20 May 2016, representatives from the Chinese Embassy in The Hague presented to the Registry a letter from the new Ambassador, with the request that it be delivered to each member of the Tribunal. The letter enclosed for reference, the "relevant position expounded on 20 May 2016 by the Spokesperson of the Ministry of Foreign Affairs of the People's Republic of China on the Philippines' South China Sea arbitration." The Ambassador reiterated that "China does not accept or participate in the Philippines' South China Sea arbitration. This position is consistent and clear. My letter shall not be considered as China's plea or participation in the Philippines' South China Sea arbitration." The enclosed statement of the Foreign Ministry Spokesperson was a response to a question as follows:

Q: The Philippines claims that it had no alternative but to initiate the arbitration because the bilateral means has been exhausted. However, it is otherwise commented that China and the Philippines have never engaged in any negotiation on the subject-matters the Philippines submitted. What is China's comment on that?

A: The Chinese Government consistently adheres to the position of settling the relevant disputes between China and the Philippines by peaceful means through negotiation and consultation. This is a consensus reached and repeatedly reaffirmed by the two sides, as well as an explicit provision in the *Declaration on the Conduct of Parties in the South China Sea* (DOC). Besides, in 2006, China has, pursuant to the relevant provisions in Article 298 of the *United Nations Convention on the Law of the Sea* (UNCLOS), excluded disputes concerning, among others, sea boundary delimitations, historic bays or titles, military and law enforcement activities from the dispute settlement procedures provided in UNCLOS. Before its unilateral initiation of the arbitration in January 2013, the Philippine Government has not conducted any negotiation or consultation with China on the relevant subject-matters, not to mention that it has exhausted the means of bilateral negotiation for dispute settlement. The unilateral initiation of arbitration by the Philippines has failed to meet the prerequisite for arbitration initiation, and cannot play a role of dispute settlement or lead to anywhere for dispute settlement.

China always stands that, with regard to the relevant disputes between China and the Philippines in the South China Sea, a true solution can only be sought through bilateral negotiation and consultation. All sides should encourage the Philippines to work with

---

22   Ministry of Foreign Affairs, People's Republic of China, *Briefing by Xu Hong, Director-General of the Department of Treaty and Law on the South China Sea Arbitration Initiated by the Philippines* (12 May 2016) *available at* <www.fmprc.gov.cn/mfa_eng/wjdt_665385/zyjh_665391/t1364804.shtml>.

China to resolve peacefully the relevant disputes through negotiation in accordance with the
bilateral consensus, the DOC and international law including UNCLOS.[23]

98. The Registry forwarded the Chinese Ambassador's letter to the members of the Tribunal and to
the Philippines.

99. On 26 May 2016, the Tribunal informed the Parties that it considered it appropriate to consult
French material from the 1930s in order to gain a more complete picture as to the natural
conditions of the South China Sea features at that time. The Tribunal provided the Parties with
documents obtained from the *Bibliothèque Nationale de France* (the National Library of
France) and from the *Archives Nationales d'Outre-Mer* (the National Overseas Archives) and
invited their comments. The Philippines commented on 3 June 2016 and supplied
supplementary materials and a further expert report from Dr. Motavalli with its response. China
was invited to, but did not, comment on the Philippines' response.

100. The new Chinese Ambassador sent a second letter to the individual members of the Tribunal on
3 June 2016, enclosing a statement expounded by a Foreign Ministry Spokesperson in response
to a question about the status of Itu Aba. The Ambassador emphasised again that his letter does
not constitute a plea or participation in the arbitration. The enclosed statement of the Foreign
Ministry Spokesperson was the following:

> Q: As reported by some foreign media, the Philippines and the arbitral tribunal are
> attempting to characterize Taiping Dao of China's Nansha Islands as a "rock" other than an
> "island". However, according to experts and journalists who recently visited Taiping Dao,
> it is an island boasting plenty of fresh water and lush vegetation. The installations and
> facilities for medical care, postal service, energy generation, and scientific research are all
> available and in good working condition. It is vibrant and lively everywhere on this island.
> Do you have any comment on this?
>
> A: China has indisputable sovereignty over the Nansha Islands and its adjacent waters,
> including Taiping Dao. China has, based on the Nansha Islands as a whole, territorial sea,
> exclusive economic zone and continental shelf. Over the history, Chinese fishermen have
> resided on Taiping Dao for years, working and living there, carrying out fishing activities,
> digging wells for fresh water, cultivating land and farming, building huts and temples, and
> raising livestock. The above activities are all manifestly recorded in Geng Lu Bu (Manual
> of Sea Routes) which was passed down from generation to generation among Chinese
> fishermen, as well as in many western navigation logs before the 1930s.
>
> The working and living practice of Chinese people on Taiping Dao fully proves that
> Taiping Dao is an "island" which is completely capable of sustaining human habitation or
> economic life of its own. The Philippines' attempt to characterize Taiping Dao as a "rock"
> exposed that its purpose of initiating the arbitration is to deny China's sovereignty over the

---

[23] Ministry of Foreign Affairs, People's Republic of China, *Foreign Ministry Spokesperson Hua Chunying's
Regular Press Conference* (20 May 2016). A slightly different English translation, published by the
Chinese Ministry of Foreign Affairs is available at <www.fmprc.gov.cn/mfa_eng/xwfw_665399/
s2510_665401/2511_665403/t1365237.shtml>.

Nansha Islands and relevant maritime rights and interests. This violates international law, and is totally unacceptable.[24]

101. In response to an invitation from the Tribunal, the Philippines commented on the Ambassador's letter and accompanying statement on 10 June 2016. The Philippines submitted that there is no basis in the Convention for China's assertion "based on the Nansha Islands as a whole" to a territorial sea, exclusive economic zone and continental shelf. With respect to the *Geng Lu Bu*, the Philippines observed that this "Manual of Sea Routes" is reported to be a navigation guide for "Hainan fishermen" consistent with evidence that China's fishermen "did no more than sojourn temporarily" at Itu Aba, and that in any event China had failed to demonstrate any evidence by citation to specific text or supporting documentation that would constitute proof as to the characterisation of Itu Aba.

102. On 8 June 2016, representatives from the Chinese Embassy delivered to the Registry a third letter from the Chinese Ambassador to the individual members of the Tribunal. The letter, which was said not to constitute a plea or participation in the arbitration, enclosed a "Statement of the Ministry of Foreign Affairs of the People's Republic of China on Settling Disputes Between China and the Philippines in the South China Sea through Bilateral Negotiation." The statement laid out jurisdictional points previously made by China in other statements, including the Position Paper, under the following headings:

   I.   It is the common agreement and commitment of China and the Philippines to settle their relevant disputes in the South China Sea through negotiation.

      . . .

   II.   China and the Philippines have never conducted any negotiation on the subject-matters of the arbitration initiated by the Philippines.

      . . .

   III.   The Philippines' unilateral initiation of arbitration goes against the bilateral agreement on settling the disputes through negotiation and violates the provisions of UNCLOS.

      . . .

   IV.   China will adhere to the position of settling the relevant disputes with the Philippines in the South China Sea through negotiation.[25]

---

[24]   Ministry of Foreign Affairs, People's Republic of China, *Foreign Ministry Spokesperson Hua Chunying's Remarks on Relevant Issue about Taiping Dao* (3 June 2016), *available at* <www.fmprc.gov.cn/mfa_eng/xwfw_665399/s2510_665401/2535_665405/t1369189.shtml>.

[25]   Ministry of Foreign Affairs, People's Republic of China, *Statement of the Ministry of Foreign Affairs of the People's Republic of China on Settling Disputes Between China and the Philippines in the South China Sea Through Bilateral Negotiation* (8 June 2016), *available at* <http://www.fmprc.gov.cn/mfa_eng/wjdt_665385/2649_665393/t1370476.shtml>.

103. On 10 June 2016, a fourth letter from the Chinese Ambassador was delivered to the Registry, addressed to the individual members of the Tribunal, enclosing a statement by the Chinese Society of International Law, entitled "The Tribunal's Award in the 'South China Sea Arbitration' Initiated by the Philippines is Null and Void." The statement repeated many of the same jurisdictional points that were covered in the Position Paper and dealt with in the Award on Jurisdiction. Copies of the Chinese Ambassador's correspondence of 8 and 10 June 2016 were forwarded to the Philippines for information.

104. During the same period that the Tribunal received the four most recent letters from the Chinese Ambassador, the Registry received copies or was made aware of various unsolicited statements and commentaries from Chinese associations and organisations pertaining to issues covered in the Award on Jurisdiction. These statements, however, were not provided to the Tribunal by the Chinese Government or any Party to the Convention. The statements were concerned with matters of jurisdiction already decided by the Tribunal and did not offer to assist the Tribunal on issues in dispute in the present phase of the proceedings.

105. On 23 June 2016, the Embassy of Malaysia in the Netherlands sent to the Tribunal two Notes Verbales, drawing attention to an issue with certain maps contained in the Award on Jurisdiction (which had been extracted, for illustrative purposes, from the Philippines' Memorial), and requesting that the Tribunal show due regard to the rights of Malaysia ("**Malaysia's Communication**"). The Malaysian Embassy emphasised that it was not seeking to intervene in the proceedings. The Tribunal sent copies of Malaysia's Communication to the Parties and requested any comments by 28 June 2016. The Philippines commented on 28 June 2016. With respect to the maps, the Philippines noted that it had presented the maps in such a way as to preserve its own claim but would leave the issue to the Tribunal's discretion. With respect to Malaysia's assertions that issues in dispute may directly or indirectly affect its rights and interests, the Philippines noted that this question had already been dealt with by the Tribunal. The Philippines considered Malaysia's Communication therefore to be "without merit" and also pointed out that it was "untimely", in light of the fact that Malaysia had been an observer since 10 June 2015 and until now made no effort to raise its concerns. China did not comment on Malaysia's Communication. On 29 June 2016, the Tribunal forwarded the Philippines' comments to China and acknowledged to Malaysia that it had received and taken note of its Communication.[26]

---

[26] The Tribunal recalls with respect to the maps published at pp. 3 and 9 of the Award on Jurisdiction that it had stated at p. iv of the Award on Jurisdiction: "The figures in this Award have been taken from the Philippines' Memorial and are included for illustrative purposes only. Their use in this Award is not an indication that the Tribunal endorses the figures or adopts any associated arguments from the Philippines." The Tribunal notes that the maps contained in the present Award are likewise for

K.   NOTIFICATION, PUBLICATION, AND TRANSLATION OF AWARD

106.   By advance notification that was published on the PCA's website and sent directly to the Parties, observer States and interested media, the Tribunal advised on 29 June 2016, that it would be issuing this Award on 12 July 2016.

107.   On 1 July 2016, the Philippines informed the Tribunal, in accordance with Article 4(2) of the Rules of Procedure, that as of 30 June 2016 Mr. Jose C. Calida had been appointed Solicitor General of the Philippines and had also been appointed to serve as Agent in the arbitration. The Philippines requested that future correspondence be directed to him and Attorney Anne Marie L. Corominas. A copy of the Philippines' letter was forwarded to China for information.

108.   The Tribunal has authorised the Registry to publish a press release in English (official version), French, and Chinese at the same time as the issuance of the present Award.

109.   In accordance with Article 15(2) of the Rules of Procedure, the Tribunal has instructed that, in due course, the Registry shall arrange for the translation of the Award on Jurisdiction and the present Award into Chinese, to be made available to the public. The English version of the Awards, however, shall remain the only authentic version.

L.   DEPOSITS FOR COSTS OF THE ARBITRATION

110.   Article 33 of the Rules of Procedure states that the PCA may from time to time request the Parties to deposit equal amounts as advances for the costs of the arbitration. Should either Party fail to make the requested deposit within 45 days, the Tribunal may so inform the Parties in order that one of them may make the payment. The Parties have been requested to make payments toward the deposit on three occasions. While the Philippines paid its share of the deposit within the time limit granted on each occasion, China has made no payments toward the deposit. Having been informed of China's failure to pay, the Philippines paid China's share of the deposit.

110.   The deposit has covered the fees and expenses of members of the Tribunal, Registry, and experts appointed to assist the Tribunal, as well as all other expenses including for hearings and meetings, information technology support, catering, court reporters, deposit administration, archiving, translations, couriers, communications, correspondence, and publishing of the Awards. Article 7 of Annex VII to the Convention provides that "[u]nless the arbitral tribunal

illustrative purposes only. The fact that the maps are not identical to the maps used in the Award on Jurisdiction does not reflect any decision taken by the Tribunal with respect to the status of any land territory or any decision taken by the Tribunal with respect to any non-party to the present arbitration.

decides otherwise because of the particular circumstances of the case, the expenses of the tribunal, including the remuneration of its members, shall be borne by the parties to the dispute in equal shares."[27]

111. In accordance with Article 33(4) of the Rules of Procedure, the Registry will "render an accounting to the Parties of the deposits received and return any unexpended balance to the Parties" after the issuance of this Award.

*　　*　　*

---

[27]   *See also* Rules of Procedure, art. 31(1).

this page intentionally blank

III.   RELIEF REQUESTED AND SUBMISSIONS

112. On 30 November 2015, the Agent for the Philippines presented the Philippines' Final Submissions, requesting the Tribunal to adjudge and declare that:

A.   The Tribunal has jurisdiction over the claims set out in Section B of these Submissions, which are fully admissible, to the extent not already determined to be within the Tribunal's jurisdiction and admissible in the Award on Jurisdiction and Admissibility of 29 October 2015.

B.   (1)   China's maritime entitlements in the South China Sea, like those of the Philippines, may not extend beyond those expressly permitted by the United Nations Convention on the Law of the Sea ("UNCLOS" or the "Convention");

(2)   China's claims to sovereign rights jurisdiction, and to "historic rights", with respect to the maritime areas of the South China Sea encompassed by the so-called "nine-dash line" are contrary to the Convention and without lawful effect to the extent that they exceed the geographic and substantive limits of China's maritime entitlements expressly permitted by UNCLOS;

(3)   Scarborough Shoal generates no entitlement to an exclusive economic zone or continental shelf;

(4)   Mischief Reef, Second Thomas Shoal and Subi Reef are low-tide elevations that do not generate entitlement to a territorial sea, exclusive economic zone or continental shelf, and are not features that are capable of appropriation by occupation or otherwise;

(5)   Mischief Reef and Second Thomas Shoal are part of the exclusive economic zone and continental shelf of the Philippines;

(6)   Gaven Reef and McKennan Reef (including Hughes Reef) are low-tide elevations that do not generate entitlement to a territorial sea, exclusive economic zone or continental shelf, but their low-water line may be used to determine the baseline from which the breadth of the territorial sea of Namyit and Sin Cowe, respectively, is measured;

(7)   Johnson Reef, Cuarteron Reef and Fiery Cross Reef generate no entitlement to an exclusive economic zone or continental shelf;

(8)   China has unlawfully interfered with the enjoyment and exercise of the sovereign rights of the Philippines with respect to the living and non-living resources of its exclusive economic zone and continental shelf;

(9)   China has unlawfully failed to prevent its nationals and vessels from exploiting the living resources in the exclusive economic zone of the Philippines;

(10)   China has unlawfully prevented Philippine fishermen from pursuing their livelihoods by interfering with traditional fishing activities at Scarborough Shoal;

(11)   China has violated its obligations under the Convention to protect and preserve the marine environment at Scarborough Shoal, Second Thomas Shoal, Cuarteron Reef, Fiery Cross Reef, Gaven Reef, Johnson Reef, Hughes Reef and Subi Reef;

(12)   China's occupation of and construction activities on Mischief Reef

      (a)   violate the provisions of the Convention concerning artificial islands, installations and structures;

      (b)   violate China's duties to protect and preserve the marine environment under the Convention; and

      (c)   constitute unlawful acts of attempted appropriation in violation of the Convention;

(13)   China has breached its obligations under the Convention by operating its law enforcement vessels in a dangerous manner causing serious risk of collision to Philippine vessels navigating in the vicinity of Scarborough Shoal;

(14)   Since the commencement of this arbitration in January 2013, China has unlawfully aggravated and extended the dispute by, among other things:

      (a)   interfering with the Philippines' rights of navigation in the waters at, and adjacent to, Second Thomas Shoal;

      (b)   preventing the rotation and resupply of Philippine personnel stationed at Second Thomas Shoal;

      (c)   endangering the health and well-being of Philippine personnel stationed at Second Thomas Shoal; and

      (d)   conducting dredging, artificial island-building and construction activities at Mischief Reef, Cuarteron Reef, Fiery Cross Reef, Gaven Reef, Johnson Reef, Hughes Reef and Subi Reef; and

(15)   China shall respect the rights and freedoms of the Philippines under the Convention, shall comply with its duties under the Convention, including those relevant to the protection and preservation of the marine environment in the South China Sea, and shall exercise its rights and freedoms in the South China Sea with due regard to those of the Philippines under the Convention.[28]

113.   As described above at paragraphs 78 and 80, on 16 December 2015 in accordance with Article 19 of the Rules of Procedure, having sought the views of China, the Tribunal granted leave to the Philippines to make the amendments incorporated in its final Submissions.

114.   While China does not accept and is not participating in this arbitration, it has stated its position that the Tribunal "does not have jurisdiction over this case."[29]

115.   In accordance with its decision not to participate, China did not file a Counter-Memorial, has not stated its position on the particular Submissions of the Philippines, and has not commented on specific substantive issues when given the opportunity to do so. China pointed out that its Position Paper "does not express any position on the substantive issues related to the

---

28   Letter from the Philippines to the Tribunal (30 November 2015); *see also* Merits Hearing Tr. (Day 4), pp. 201-205.

29   China's Position Paper, para. 2; *see also* Letter from the Ambassador of the People's Republic of China to the Kingdom of the Netherlands to the individual members of the Tribunal (6 February 2015); Letter from the Ambassador of the People's Republic of China to the Kingdom of the Netherlands to the individual members of the Tribunal (1 July 2015).

subject-matter of the arbitration initiated by the Philippines."[30] Nevertheless, as described in relevant portions of the Award, in proceeding to assess the merits of the respective Submissions, the Tribunal has sought to take into account China's position to the extent it is discernible from China's official statements and conduct.

* * *

---

[30] China's Position Paper, para. 2.

this page intentionally blank

IV. PRELIMINARY MATTERS

A. THE LEGAL AND PRACTICAL CONSEQUENCES OF CHINA'S NON-PARTICIPATION

116. As is evident from the procedural history recounted in Chapter II, China has consistently rejected the Philippines' recourse to arbitration and has adhered to a position of non-acceptance and non-participation in the proceedings. China did not participate in the constitution of the Tribunal, it did not submit a Counter-Memorial in response to the Philippines' Memorial, it did not attend the Hearings on Jurisdiction or on the Merits, it did not reply to the Tribunal's invitations to comment on specific issues of substance or procedure, and it has not advanced any of the funds requested by the Tribunal toward the costs of the arbitration. Throughout the proceedings, China has rejected and returned correspondence from the Tribunal sent by the Registry, reiterating on each occasion "that it does not accept the arbitration initiated by the Philippines."

117. The Convention, however, expressly acknowledges the possibility of non-participation by one of the parties to a dispute and confirms that such non-participation does not constitute a bar to the proceedings. Article 9 of Annex VII provides:

> *Article 9*
> *Default of Appearance*
>
> If one of the parties to the dispute does not appear before the arbitral tribunal or fails to defend its case, the other party may request the tribunal to continue the proceedings and to make its award. Absence of a party or failure of a party to defend its case shall not constitute a bar to the proceedings. Before making its award, the arbitral tribunal must satisfy itself not only that it has jurisdiction over the dispute but also that the claim is well founded in fact and law.

118. Pursuant to Article 9, the Philippines expressly requested that these proceedings continue.[31] The Tribunal has continued the proceedings, confirming that despite its non-appearance, China remains a party to the arbitration, with the ensuing rights and obligations, including that it will be bound under international law by any decision of the Tribunal.[32]

---

[31] Memorial, paras. 1.21, 7.39; Award on Jurisdiction, para. 114.

[32] Convention, art. 296(1) (providing that any decision rendered by a tribunal having jurisdiction under Section 2 of Part XV "shall be final and shall be complied with by all the parties to the dispute."). Article 11 of Annex VII similarly provides that "[t]he award shall be final and without appeal" and "shall be complied with by the parties to the dispute." *See* Award on Jurisdiction, para. 114, *citing Military and Paramilitary Activities in and against Nicaragua (Nicaragua v. United States), Merits, Judgment, ICJ Reports 1986*, p. 14 at p. 24, para. 28; *Arctic Sunrise (Kingdom of the Netherlands v. Russian Federation), Provisional Measures, Order of 22 November 2013, ITLOS Reports 2013*, p. 230 at p. 242, para. 51; *Arctic Sunrise Arbitration (Kingdom of the Netherlands v. Russian Federation)*, Award on Jurisdiction of 26 November 2014, para. 60; *Arctic Sunrise Arbitration (Kingdom of the Netherlands v. Russian Federation)*, Award on the Merits of 14 August 2015, para. 10.

1.   Steps Taken to Ensure Procedural Fairness to Both Parties

119. Article 9 of Annex VII seeks to balance the risks of prejudice that could be suffered by either party in a situation of non-participation. First, it protects the participating party by ensuring that proceedings will not be frustrated by the decision of the other party not to participate. Second, it protects the rights of the non-participating party by ensuring that a tribunal will not simply accept the evidence and claims of the participating party by default.[33]

120. The respective procedural rights of the parties are further articulated in Article 5 of Annex VII, which provides that "the arbitral tribunal shall determine its own procedure, assuring to each party a full opportunity to be heard and to present its case."[34]

121. The Tribunal has taken a number of measures to safeguard the procedural rights of China. For example, it has:

(a)   ensured that all communications and materials in the arbitration have been promptly delivered, both electronically and physically, to the Ambassador of China to the Kingdom of the Netherlands in The Hague;

(b)   granted China adequate and equal time to submit written responses to the pleadings submitted by the Philippines;

(c)   invited China (as with the Philippines) to comment on procedural steps taken throughout the proceedings;

(d)   provided China (as with the Philippines) with adequate notice of hearings and multiple opportunities to comment on the setting and scheduling of both the Hearing on Jurisdiction and Hearing on the Merits, as described at paragraphs 47 to 53, 54 to 59 and 61 to 76 above;

(e)   promptly provided to China (as with the Philippines) copies of transcripts of the Hearing on Jurisdiction and Hearing on the Merits;

(f)   invited China to comment on anything said during the Hearing on Jurisdiction and Hearing on the Merits;

---

[33]   Award on Jurisdiction, para. 115.

[34]   This duty is mirrored in the Rules of Procedure, art. 10(1) ("the Arbitral Tribunal may conduct the arbitration in such manner as it considers appropriate, provided that the Parties are treated with equality and that at any stage of the proceedings each Party is given a full opportunity to be heard and to present its case.") and art. 1 (providing for modification or additions to the Rules of Procedure, or novel questions of procedure, to be addressed "after seeking the views of the Parties.").

(g)   invited China (as with the Philippines) to comment on the proposed candidates and terms of reference for independent experts appointed by the Tribunal;

(h)   invited China (as with the Philippines) to comment on certain materials in the public domain, but not already in the case record;

(i)   made the Registry staff available to Chinese Embassy personnel to answer informal questions of an administrative or procedural nature;

(j)   had the Registry convey written communications from the Chinese Embassy to the individual members of the Tribunal; and

(k)   reiterated that it remains open to China to participate in the proceedings at any stage.

122. The Tribunal has also taken measures to safeguard the Philippines' procedural rights. As noted by the International Tribunal for the Law of the Sea in *Arctic Sunrise*, a participating party "should not be put at a disadvantage because of the non-appearance of the [non-participating party] in the proceedings."[35]

123. One possible disadvantage of non-participation is delay. While ensuring equality of opportunity, the Tribunal has also complied with the obligation in Article 10 of the Rules of Procedure to "conduct the proceedings so as to avoid unnecessary delay and expense and to provide a fair and efficient process for resolving the Parties' dispute."

124. A second possible disadvantage about which the Philippines expressed concern was that China's non-appearance might deprive it of "an opportunity to address any specific issues that the Arbitral Tribunal considers not to have been canvassed, or to have been canvassed inadequately."[36] The Tribunal has taken various steps to ensure both Parties the opportunity to address specific issues of concern to the Tribunal's decision-making. For example, the Tribunal introduced the following process into Article 25(2) of its Rules of Procedure:

> In the event that a Party does not appear before the Arbitral Tribunal or fails to defend its case, the Arbitral Tribunal shall invite written arguments from the appearing Party on, or pose questions regarding, specific issues which the Arbitral Tribunal considers have not been canvassed, or have been inadequately canvassed, in the pleadings submitted by the appearing Party. The appearing Party shall make a supplemental written submission in relation to the matters identified by the Arbitral Tribunal within three months of the Arbitral Tribunal's invitation. The supplemental submission of the appearing Party shall be communicated to the non-appearing Party for its comments which shall be submitted within three months of the communication of the supplemental submission. The Arbitral Tribunal may take whatever other steps it may consider necessary, within the scope of its powers

---

[35]   *Arctic Sunrise (Kingdom of the Netherlands v. Russian Federation), Provisional Measures, Order of 22 November 2013, ITLOS Reports 2013*, p. 230 at p. 243, para. 56.

[36]   Letter from the Philippines to the Tribunal (31 July 2013) (commenting on draft Rules of Procedure).

under the Convention, its Annex VII, and these Rules, to afford to each of the Parties a full opportunity to present its case.[37]

125. The Tribunal implemented the above procedure by issuing a Request for Further Written Argument on 16 December 2014, containing 26 questions pertaining to jurisdiction and the merits. Further, on 23 June 2015, in advance of the Hearing on Jurisdiction, and on 23 November 2015, in advance of the Hearing on the Merits, the Tribunal sent to the Parties lists of specific issues which it wished to be addressed. During both hearings, following the first round of arguments, the Tribunal circulated lists of questions to be addressed during the second round.

126. A third perceived disadvantage that the participating party may face as a result of non-participation is being put in the "position of having to guess" what the non-participating party's arguments might be and to "formulate arguments for both States."[38] The Philippines suggested that the Tribunal could discern China's position on the issues raised by the Philippines' Submissions by consulting communications from China's officials, statements of those associated with the Government of China, and academic literature by individuals closely associated with Chinese authorities.[39] The Tribunal has done so, cognisant of the practice of international courts and tribunals of taking notice of public statements or informal communications made by non-appearing Parties.[40]

127. Concerns about the Philippines "having to guess what China's arguments might be" were to some extent alleviated, at least with respect to jurisdiction, by China's decision to make public its Position Paper in December 2014. The Position Paper was followed by two letters from the former Chinese Ambassador, addressed to the members of the Tribunal, and four more-recent letters from the current Chinese Ambassador. The latter directed the Tribunal's attention to statements of the Chinese Ministry of Foreign Affairs Spokespersons and other public statements and materials. Indeed, the Tribunal has taken note of the regular press briefings of the Chinese Ministry of Foreign Affairs, which frequently touch on issues before the Tribunal, and occasionally contain statements exclusively dedicated to aspects of the arbitration. On the

---

[37] The provision contains some elements of Article 3 of the 1991 Resolution on Non-Appearing States before the International Court of Justice, drafted by the *Institut du Droit International*.

[38] Award on Jurisdiction, para. 119; Memorial, para. 7.42.

[39] Award on Jurisdiction, para. 119; Memorial, para. 1.23.

[40] *See* Procedural Order No. 4, p. 5 (21 April 2015), citing as examples *Arctic Sunrise (Kingdom of the Netherlands v. Russian Federation), Provisional Measures, Order of 22 November 2013, ITLOS Reports 2013*, p. 230 at p. 243, para. 54; *Arctic Sunrise Arbitration (Kingdom of the Netherlands v. Russian Federation)*, Award on Jurisdiction of 26 November 2014, para. 44; *Fisheries Jurisdiction (United Kingdom v. Iceland), Merits, Judgment, ICJ Reports 1974*, p. 3; *Nuclear Tests (Australia v. France), Judgment, ICJ Reports 1974*, p. 253; *Aegean Sea Continental Shelf (Greece v. Turkey), Judgment, ICJ Reports 1978*, p. 3.

very question of China's non-participation, the Director-General of the Department of Treaty and Law at the Chinese Ministry of Foreign Affairs gave the following remarks in response to questions about why China did not participate and whether, having renounced the opportunity to appear before the Tribunal to contest jurisdiction, China should "bear the consequences":

> First, not accepting or participating in arbitral proceedings is a right enjoyed by a sovereign State. That is fully in conformity with international law. And certainly, China is not the first State to do so. For such a proceeding that is deliberately provocative, China has neither the obligation nor the necessity to accept or participate in it. The Philippines' initiation of the Arbitration lacks basic grounds in international law. Such an act can neither generate any validity in international law, nor create any obligation on China.
>
> Second, by not accepting or participating in the arbitral proceedings, we aim to safeguard the solemnity and integrity of international law, including the UNCLOS, to oppose the abuse of the compulsory arbitration procedures, and to fulfill our commitments with the Philippines to settle relevant disputes through negotiations. The commitments were breached by the Philippines, but China remains committed to them.
>
> Third, the actual objective of the Philippines to initiate the Arbitration and that of some other States to fuel the fire are not to genuinely resolve disputes. The Philippines was fully aware that the Arbitral Tribunal has no jurisdiction over disputes concerning territorial sovereignty and maritime delimitation between the two States; it was fully aware that it was absolutely not possible that China would accept the compulsory arbitration; and it was also fully aware that such a means would not help resolve the problem. With full awareness of the above, the Philippines still decided to abuse the provisions of the UNCLOS by unilaterally initiating and then pushing forward the arbitral proceedings. Some other States, who were making every effort to echo it, apparently have their ulterior motives. For such a game, there is no point for China to humor it.
>
> Fourth, whether or not China accepts and participates in the arbitral proceedings, the Arbitral Tribunal has the obligation under international law to establish that it does have jurisdiction over the disputes. But from what we have seen, it apparently has failed to fulfill the obligation and the ruling would certainly be invalid. So there is no such thing of China's taking the consequence of the arbitration. If anything, it is the Philippines that should bear all the consequences of abusing the UNCLOS.[41]

128. It is in relation to the fourth point above, "the Tribunal's obligation under international law to establish that it does have jurisdiction over the disputes" to which the Tribunal next turns.

2. Steps Taken by the Tribunal to Satisfy Itself that It Has Jurisdiction and that the Claim is Well Founded in Fact and Law

129. China's non-participation imposes a special responsibility on the Tribunal. There is no system of default judgment under the Convention. As will be apparent in the course of this Award, the Tribunal does not simply adopt the Philippines' arguments or accept its assertions untested. Rather, under the terms of Article 9 of Annex VII, the Tribunal "must satisfy itself not only that it has jurisdiction over the dispute but also that the claim is well founded in fact and law" before making any award.

---

[41] *See* Ministry of Foreign Affairs, People's Republic of China, *Briefing by Xu Hong, Director-General of the Department of Treaty and Law on the South China Sea Arbitration Initiated by the Philippines* (12 May 2016), *available at* <www.fmprc.gov.cn/mfa_eng/wjdt_665385/zyjh_665391/t1364804.shtml>.

130. The Tribunal has actively sought to satisfy itself as to whether it has jurisdiction over the dispute. Following China's decision not to file a Counter-Memorial, the Tribunal requested the Philippines under Article 25 of the Rules of Procedure to provide further written argument on certain jurisdictional questions and posed questions to the Philippines both prior to and during the Hearing on Jurisdiction. China's Position Paper in December 2014 expounded three main reasons why it considers that the Tribunal "does not have jurisdiction over this case."[42] The Tribunal decided to treat the Position Paper and certain communications from China as constituting, in effect, a plea concerning jurisdiction, which under the Rules of Procedure meant conducting a hearing and issuing a preliminary ruling dedicated to jurisdiction.[43] However, in line with its duty to satisfy itself that it has jurisdiction, the Tribunal did not limit the hearing to the three issues raised by China. It also considered, and invited the Parties to address, other possible jurisdictional questions. These procedures led to the Tribunal's Award on Jurisdiction, issued on 29 October 2015 (a summary of which appears at paragraphs 145 to 164 below).

131. With respect to the duty to satisfy itself that the Philippines' claims are well founded in fact and law, the Tribunal notes that Article 9 of Annex VII does not operate to change the burden of proof or to raise or lower the standard of proof normally expected of a party to make out its claims or defences.[44] However, as a practical matter, Article 9 has led the Tribunal to take steps to test the evidence provided by the Philippines and to augment the record by seeking additional evidence, expert input, and Party submissions relevant to questions arising in this merits phase, including as to the status of features in the South China Sea, the allegations concerning violations of maritime safety obligations, and claims about damage to the marine environment. These steps are described below.

132. First, pursuant to the procedure established in Article 25 of the Rules of Procedure, in the Tribunal's Request for Further Written Argument of 16 December 2014, the Tribunal noted the Philippines' argument that "none of the features in the Spratlys—not even the largest among them—is capable of generating entitlement to an EEZ or a continental shelf."[45] The Tribunal invited the Philippines to "provide additional historical and anthropological information, as well as detailed geographic and hydrographic information regarding" Itu Aba, Thitu, and West York."[46] The Tribunal also invited the Philippines to provide written argument on the status of

---

[42] China's Position Paper, para. 2

[43] *See* Procedural Order No. 4 (21 April 2015).

[44] *See* Rules of Procedure, art. 22.

[45] Memorial, para. 5.96.

[46] The Tribunal's *Request for Further Written Argument by the Philippines Pursuant to Article 25(2) of the Rules of Procedure*, Request No. 20, annexed to Procedural Order No. 3 (16 December 2014) (hereinafter **"Request for Further Written Argument"**).

any maritime feature claimed by China—"whether or not occupied by China"—that could potentially give rise to an entitlement to an exclusive economic zone or continental shelf extending to any of Mischief Reef, Second Thomas Shoal, Subi Reef, Scarborough Shoal, Reed Bank, or the areas designated as Philippine oil blocks "Area 3" and "Area 4". In so doing, the Philippines was invited to provide "historical and anthropological information, as well as detailed geographic and hydrographic information" regarding the following features: Spratly Island, North-East Cay (North Danger Reef); South-West Cay (North Danger Reef); Nanshan Island; Sand Cay; Loaita Island; Swallow Reef; Amboyna Cay; Flat Island; Lankiam Cay; Great Discovery Reef; Tizard Bank reefs; and Union Bank reefs.[47] In response to this request, the Philippines submitted with its Supplemental Written Submission an atlas and an expert report by Professor Clive Schofield, Professor J.R.V. Prescott, and Mr. Robert van der Poll entitled "An Appraisal of the Geographical Characteristics and Status of Certain Insular Feature in the South China Sea" (the **Schofield Report**"). The atlas provided for each feature: a geographic and hydrographic description, a satellite image, photographs, excerpts from various sailing directions and nautical charts, and a summation of the pertinent geographic and hydrographic information by geographer Dr. Robert W. Smith.[48]

133. Second, in accordance with Article 24 of the Rules of Procedure, and after seeking the views of the Parties, the Tribunal retained an independent technical expert—Mr. Grant Boyes—to assist it in "reviewing and analysing geographic and hydrographic information, photographs, satellite imagery and other technical data in order to enable the Arbitral Tribunal to assess the status (as a submerged feature, low-tide elevation, or island)" of the features named in the Philippines' Submissions or any other such feature determined to be relevant during the course of the reference. While the appointment of hydrographic experts is common practice in Annex VII arbitrations,[49] in light of China's non-participation, Mr. Boyes was also tasked with assisting with a "critical assessment of relevant expert advice and opinions submitted by the Philippines."[50]

---

[47] Request for Further Written Argument, Request No. 22.

[48] Supplemental Written Submission of the Philippines, Vol. II (16 March 2015) (hereinafter "**Supplemental Written Submission**").

[49] *See, e.g.*, *Guyana v. Suriname*, Award of 17 September 2007, PCA Award Series at pp. 52-54, RIAA Vol. XXX, p. 1, at pp. 27-29, para. 108; *Barbados v. Trinidad and Tobago*, Award of 11 April 2006, PCA Award Series at p. 33, RIAA Vol. XXVII, p. 147 at p. 160, para. 37; *Bay of Bengal Maritime Boundary Arbitration (Bangladesh v. India)*, Award of 7 July 2014, paras. 15-17.

[50] Terms of Reference for Expert, Mr. Grant Boyes, para. 3.1.1 (10 September 2015). As mentioned at paragraph 3.2, it was noted that in providing the Tribunal with technical assistance, the expert "shall respect that it is the Arbitral Tribunal, and not the Expert, that makes any determination as to legal questions, in particular the application of Article 121(3) of the Convention."

134. Third, the Tribunal posed to Professor Schofield a series of written and oral questions during the Hearing on the Merits, about his testimony, his earlier writings, and specific points in the Schofield Report.[51]

135. Fourth, the Tribunal similarly posed written and oral questions to Professor Kent Carpenter, who submitted two expert reports for the Philippines about the environmental consequences of China's conduct in the South China Sea.[52] Professor Carpenter's second report was submitted, *inter alia*, to adequately address the issues identified by the Tribunal in its "Annex of Issues" circulated in advance of the Hearing on the Merits.[53]

136. Fifth, in light of China's non-participation, the Tribunal decided to appoint coral reef ecology experts to provide their independent opinion on the impact of Chinese construction activities on the coral reef systems in the Spratly Islands. A team composed of Dr. Sebastian Ferse, Professor Peter Mumby, and Dr. Selina Ward prepared a report (the "**Ferse Report**"), on which both sides were invited to comment. In the course of preparing the report, some follow-up questions were put to the Philippines about sources relied on in the Carpenter Report, a process through which the Tribunal gained yet further information.[54]

137. Sixth, the Tribunal has made efforts to understand China's stance on environmental issues, including having (a) asked the Philippines and Professor Carpenter to identify any statements made by Chinese Government officials that suggest China had taken into account issues of ecological preservation and followed environmental protection standards in connection with its construction work;[55] (b) presented to the Parties for their comment a number of official Chinese statements and reports from Chinese State-sponsored scientific institutes concerning the ecological impact of the construction work;[56] (c) specifically and directly asked China whether

---

[51]   Letter from the Tribunal to the Parties with Annex of Questions (10 November 2015); Letter from the Tribunal to the Parties, Annex B: Questions for Prof. Schofield (27 November 2015); Merits Hearing Tr. (Day 3), pp. 3-10; Merits Hearing Tr. (Day 4), pp. 43-66.

[52]   K.E. Carpenter, *Eastern South China Sea Environmental Disturbances and Irresponsible Fishing Practices and their Effects on Coral Reefs and Fisheries* (22 March 2014) (Annex 240) (hereinafter "**First Carpenter Report**"); K.E. Carpenter & L.M. Chou, *Environmental Consequences of Land Reclamation Activities on Various Reefs in the South China Sea* (14 November 2015) (Annex 699) (hereinafter "**Second Carpenter Report**"); Letter from the Tribunal to the Parties with Annex of Questions (10 November 2015); Letter from the Tribunal to the Parties, Annex C: Questions for Prof. Carpenter (27 November 2015); Merits Hearing Tr. (Day 3), pp. 48-54; Merits Hearing Tr. (Day 4), pp. 138-162. *See also* Supplemental Response to Question from Judge Wolfrum (18 December 2016); Declaration of Prof. Kent E. Carpenter, Ph.D. (24 April 2016).

[53]   Letter from the Philippines to the Tribunal (14 November 2016).

[54]   Letter from the Tribunal to Parties (1 April 2016); Letter from the Philippines to the Tribunal (26 April 2016).

[55]   Letter from the Tribunal to Parties, Annex A: Questions for the Philippines, Annex C: Questions for Prof. Carpenter (27 November 2015); Hearing Tr. (Day 3), p. 198.

[56]   Letter from the Tribunal to Parties (5 February 2016).

it had undertaken an environmental impact study and if so, for the Tribunal to be provided with a copy.[57] While China declined to comment, the Tribunal has taken note of its recent official statements to the effect that "[a]s owners of the Nansha Islands, China cares about protecting the ecological environment of relevant islands, reefs and waters more than any other country, organization or people of the world" and that "[b]ased on thorough studies and scientific proof, China adopts dynamic protection measures along the whole process so as to combine construction with ecological environmental protection and realize sustainable development of islands and reefs."[58] As noted below in Chapter VII.D, neither the Tribunal nor its experts, however, have managed to retrieve copies of such studies.

138. Seventh, in relation to the Philippines' Submission No. 13, alleging dangerous manoeuvring by Chinese law enforcement vessels in breach of the Convention's maritime safety obligations, the Tribunal considered it appropriate to appoint an expert to review the available documentary material and draw independent conclusions. In accordance with Article 24 of the Rules of Procedure and having consulted the Parties, the Tribunal commissioned a report by Captain Gurpreet Singhota (the "**Singhota Report**").

139. Eighth, in accordance with Article 22 of the Rules of Procedure, which provides that the Tribunal may "take all appropriate measures in order to establish the facts," and Article 25, which states that the Tribunal "may take whatever other steps it may consider necessary . . . to afford to each of the Parties a full opportunity to present its case," the Tribunal has on several occasions invited the Parties to comment on various sources concerning the prevailing conditions on features in the South China Sea, including some materials in the public domain emanating from the Taiwan Authority of China.[59] The Philippines has responded with comments both during the hearings and in written submissions after the hearings.[60] On 11 March 2016, the Philippines submitted written comments, accompanied by two new expert reports on soil and water quality at Itu Aba.[61] On 25 April 2016, the Philippines responded to

---

[57]   Letter from the Tribunal to Parties (5 February 2016).

[58]   Ministry of Foreign Affairs, People's Republic of China, *Foreign Ministry Spokesperson Hong Lei's Regular Press Conference* (6 May 2015), *available at* <www.fmprc.gov.cn/mfa_eng/xwfw_665399/ s2510_665401/2511_665403/t1361284.shtml>.

[59]   *See, e.g.*, Letter from the Tribunal to the Parties (10 November 2015); Letter from the Tribunal to the Parties (5 February 2016); Letter from the Tribunal to the Parties (1 April 2016).

[60]   *See, e.g.*, Merits Hearing Tr. (Day 1), p. 87, n. 123, p. 94, n. 141; Merits Hearing Tr. (Day 2), pp.114, 120-21; Merits Hearing Tr. (Day 4), pp. 46-50; Request for Further Written Argument, pp. 3-7; Supplemental Written Submission, Vols. I and II.

[61]   Written Responses of the Philippines to the Tribunal's 5 February 2016 Request for Comments (11 March 2016) (hereinafter "**Written Responses of the Philippines (11 March 2016)**"); R.T. Bailey, *Groundwater Resources Analysis of Itu Aba* (9 March 2016) (Annex 878) (hereinafter "**First Bailey Report**"); P.P. Motavalli, *Expert Report on Soil Resources and Potential Self-Sustaining Agricultural*

an invitation to comment further on additional Taiwanese materials. While the Philippines considered that it would have been "within its rights in requesting, and the Tribunal would be well-justified in finding, that these materials should be disregarded," it nevertheless "recognize[d] the exceptional difficulties China's non-appearance has created for the Tribunal" and chose "not to object to the Tribunal's consideration of Taiwan's most recent materials."[62] Accordingly, the Philippines provided comments, translations and exhibits, and supplementary expert reports. China did not submit comments to the Tribunal in response to these materials, though its public statements on relevant questions have been noted.[63]

140. Ninth, the Tribunal sought the Parties' views on records obtained from the UKHO. Prior to the Hearing on the Merits, the Tribunal had requested the Philippines to confirm "whether it has sought and been able to obtain copies of hydrographic survey plans (fair charts), relating in particular to those surveys undertaken by the United Kingdom in the Nineteenth Century and by Japan in the period leading up to the Second World War."[64] The Philippines replied that it had not and explained that it considered it unnecessary to do so.[65] On 1 April 2016, the Tribunal informed the Parties that it considered it appropriate to have reference, to the greatest extent possible, to original records based on the direct observation of the features in question, prior to them having been subjected to significant human modification. As the most extensive hydrographic survey work in the South China Sea prior to 1945 was carried out by the Royal Navy of the United Kingdom, followed closely by the Imperial Japanese Navy, the Tribunal advised that it had undertaken to seek records from the archives of the UKHO, which also hold certain Japanese records captured during the Second World War. The Tribunal provided copies of records to the Parties and invited their comments, which the Philippines provided on 28 April 2016.

141. Tenth, the Tribunal also considered it appropriate to consult French material from the 1930s in light of France's occupation of the Spratly Islands announced in 1933[66] and in order to gain a more complete picture as to the natural conditions of the South China Sea features. Accordingly, the Tribunal sought records from the online database of the *Bibliothèque Nationale de France* and from the *Archives Nationales d'Outre-Mer*. On 26 May 2016, the

---

Production on Itu Aba (Expert Report, 9 March 2016) (Annex 879) (hereinafter "**First Motavalli Report**").

[62] Written Responses of the Philippines on Itu Aba (25 April 2016), paras. 7-8.

[63] Letter from the Tribunal to the Parties (1 April 2016).

[64] Letter from the Tribunal to the Parties (10 November 2015).

[65] *See* Merits Hearing Tr. (Day 2), p. 38.

[66] Republic of France, Ministry of Foreign Affairs, "Notice Relating to the Occupation of Certain Island by French Naval Unites, 1933," *Official Journal of the French Republic*, p. 7837 (26 July 1933) (Annex 159).

Tribunal provided the Parties with the most pertinent documents obtained from those sources and allowed them an opportunity to comment. The Philippines sent its comments, with supplementary materials, on 3 June 2016.

142. As explained in the Tribunal's communications to the Parties, the Tribunal considered historical records concerning conditions on features in the Spratly Islands, prior to them having been subjected to significant human modification, to be more relevant than evidence of the situation currently prevailing, which reflects the efforts of the various littoral States to improve the habitability of features under their control. Accordingly, although the Tribunal has fully considered the contemporary evidence provided by the Philippines, as well as certain materials made public by the Taiwan Authority of China, the Tribunal has not itself sought additional materials on contemporary conditions on any feature in the Spratlys. The Tribunal has, for the same reason, not sought to take advantage of the Taiwan Authority of China's public offer to arrange a site visit to Itu Aba. In this respect the Tribunal notes that China, through its Ambassador's letter of 6 February 2015, objected strongly to the possibility of any site visit to the South China Sea by the Tribunal.[67]

3. Conclusion on the Legal and Practical Consequences of China's Non-Participation

143. For reasons set out above, despite its non-participation in the proceedings, China is a Party to the arbitration and is bound under international law by any awards rendered by the Tribunal.

144. In line with its duties under Annex VII to the Convention, in the circumstances of China's non-participation, the Tribunal has taken steps to ensure procedural fairness to both Parties without compromising the efficiency of the proceedings. The Tribunal has also taken steps to ascertain China's position on the issues for decision, based on statements made by Chinese officials publicly and in communications to the members of the Tribunal. In addition to its thorough review of the materials placed before it by the Philippines, the Tribunal has also taken steps to satisfy itself of its jurisdiction and the legal and factual foundations of the Philippines' claims through obtaining independent expert input, reviewing other materials in the public domain, and inviting further comments from the Parties on those sources.

---

[67] Letter from the Ambassador of the People's Republic of China to the Netherlands to the individual members of the Tribunal (6 February 2015) ("The Chinese Government underlines that China opposes the initiation of the arbitration and any measures to push forward the arbitral proceeding, holds an omnibus objection to all procedural applications or steps that would require some kind of response from China, such as 'intervention by other States', '*amicus curiae* submissions' and 'site visit'."). The Philippines also noted that a site visit "would present certain challenges." Letter from the Philippines to the Tribunal (26 January 2015).

B.   **SUMMARY OF THE TRIBUNAL'S AWARD ON JURISDICTION**

145.   Pursuant to Article 288(4) of the Convention, "[i]n the event of a dispute as to whether a court or tribunal has jurisdiction, the matter shall be settled by decision of that court or tribunal." As set out above, where a Party does not appear before the Tribunal, Article 9 of Annex VII to the Convention requires that "the arbitral tribunal must satisfy itself not only that it has jurisdiction over the dispute but also that the claim is well founded in fact and law." Additionally, the Rules of Procedure adopted by the Tribunal provide at Article 20(3) as follows:

> The Arbitral Tribunal shall rule on any plea concerning its jurisdiction as a preliminary question, unless the Arbitral Tribunal determines, after seeking the views of the Parties, that the objection to its jurisdiction does not possess an exclusively preliminary character, in which case it shall rule on such a plea in conjunction with the merits.[68]

146.   China's Position Paper was said by the Chinese Ambassador to have "comprehensively explain[ed] why the Arbitral Tribunal . . . manifestly has no jurisdiction over the case."[69] In its Procedural Order No. 4 of 21 April 2015, the Tribunal recalled the practice of international courts and tribunals in interstate disputes of (a) taking note of public statements or informal communications made by non-appearing Parties, (b) treating such statements and communications as equivalent to or as constituting preliminary objections, and (c) bifurcating proceedings to address some or all of such objections as preliminary questions.[70] The Tribunal considered that:

> the communications by China, including notably its Position Paper of 7 December 2015 and the Letter of 6 February 2015 from the Ambassador of the People's Republic of China to the Netherlands, effectively constitute a plea concerning this Arbitral Tribunal's jurisdiction for the purposes of Article 20 of the Rules of Procedure and will be treated as such for the purposes of this arbitration.[71]

147.   Accordingly, the Tribunal decided:

> in light of the circumstances and its duty to "assure to each Party a full opportunity to be heard and to present its case," it is appropriate to bifurcate the proceedings and to convene a

---

[68]   Rules of Procedure, art. 20(3).

[69]   Letter from the Ambassador of China to the Netherlands to the individual members of the Tribunal (6 February 2015).

[70]   *See, e.g., Arctic Sunrise (Kingdom of the Netherlands v. Russian Federation), Provisional Measures, Order of 22 November 2013, ITLOS Reports 2013*, para. 54; *Arctic Sunrise Arbitration (Kingdom of the Netherlands v. Russian Federation)*, Award on Jurisdiction of 26 November 2014, para. 44 (referring to Procedural Order No. 4, 21 November 2004); *Fisheries Jurisdiction (United Kingdom v. Iceland), Jurisdiction of the Court, Judgment, ICJ Reports 1973*, p. 3 at pp. 5-8, paras. 3, 5, 10-12; *Fisheries Jurisdiction (Federal Republic of Germany v. Iceland), Jurisdiction of the Court, Judgment, ICJ Reports 1973*, p. 49 at pp. 50-54, paras. 3, 5, 10-11, 13; *Nuclear Tests (Australia v. France), Judgment, ICJ Reports 1974*, p. 253 at pp. 255-257, paras. 4, 6, 13-15; *Nuclear Tests (New Zealand v. France), Judgment, ICJ Reports 1974*, p. 457 at pp. 458-461, paras. 4, 6, 13-15; *Aegean Sea Continental Shelf (Greece v. Turkey), Judgment, ICJ Reports 1978*, p. 3 at pp. 19-20, paras. 44-47.

[71]   Procedural Order No. 4, para. 1.1 (21 April 2015).

hearing to consider the matter of the Arbitral Tribunal's jurisdiction and, as necessary, the admissibility of the Philippines' submissions."[72]

148. The Tribunal also noted that it would not limit itself to hearing only the questions raised in China's Position Paper.[73] The Tribunal accordingly convened the Hearing on Jurisdiction in The Hague on 7, 8, and 13 July 2015 and issued its Award on Jurisdiction on 29 October 2015. The principal findings of that decision are recalled herein.

1.   Preliminary Matters

149. In its Award on Jurisdiction, the Tribunal noted that "both the Philippines and China are parties to the Convention"[74] and that the provisions for the settlement of disputes, including through arbitration, form an integral part of the Convention.[75] Although the Convention specifies certain limitations and exceptions to the subject matter of the disputes that may be submitted to compulsory settlement, it does not permit other reservations, and a State may not except itself generally from the Convention's mechanism for the resolution of disputes.[76]

150. The Tribunal also noted China's non-participation and held that this fact does not deprive the Tribunal of jurisdiction. In this respect, the Tribunal recalled the provisions of Article 9 of Annex VII to the Convention.

151. Although China did not participate in the constitution of the Tribunal, the Tribunal held that it had been properly constituted pursuant to the provisions of Annex VII to the Convention.[77] The Tribunal detailed the steps it had taken to satisfy itself regarding its jurisdiction, including through questions posed to the Philippines and through the Hearing on Jurisdiction in July 2015.[78] The Tribunal also recalled the steps it had taken to safeguard the procedural rights of both Parties in the circumstances of China's non-participation.[79]

152. Finally, the Tribunal considered the argument set out in China's Position Paper that the Philippines' unilateral resort to arbitration constituted an abuse of the dispute settlement

---

[72]   Procedural Order No. 4, para. 1.3 (21 April 2015).

[73]   Procedural Order No. 4, para. 1.4 (21 April 2015).

[74]   Award on Jurisdiction, para. 106.

[75]   Award on Jurisdiction, para. 2.

[76]   Award on Jurisdiction, para. 107

[77]   Award on Jurisdiction, para. 413(A).

[78]   Award on Jurisdiction, paras. 26-97, 112-123.

[79]   Award on Jurisdiction, paras. 117-120.

provisions of the Convention.[80] The Tribunal noted that, although certain provisions of the Convention address the abuse of rights and provide a preliminary procedure to dismiss claims that are facially unfounded, it was more appropriate to consider China's concerns about the Tribunal's jurisdiction as a preliminary objection.[81] The Tribunal also noted that "the mere act of unilaterally initiating an arbitration under Part XV in itself cannot constitute an abuse" of the Convention.[82]

2. Existence of a Dispute concerning Interpretation and Application of the Convention

153. The Tribunal next considered whether there is a dispute between the Parties concerning the interpretation or application of the Convention, which is the basis for the dispute settlement mechanisms of the Convention.[83] In so doing, the Tribunal considered two objections set out in China's Position Paper: first, that the Parties' dispute is actually about sovereignty over the islands of the South China Sea and therefore not a matter concerning the Convention, and second, that the Parties' dispute is actually about the delimitation of the maritime boundary between them and therefore excluded from dispute settlement by an exception set out in the Convention that States may activate by declaration. China activated the exception for disputes concerning sea boundary delimitations when it made a declaration in 2006.

154. With respect to the former objection, the Tribunal noted that there is a dispute between the Parties regarding sovereignty over islands, but held that the matters submitted to arbitration by the Philippines do not concern sovereignty.[84] The Tribunal considered it to be expected that the Philippines and China would have disputes regarding multiple subjects, but emphasised that the Tribunal did not accept that "it follows from the existence of a dispute over sovereignty that sovereignty is also the appropriate characterisation of the claims the Philippines has submitted in these proceedings."[85] The Tribunal also emphasised that "[t]he Philippines has not asked the Tribunal to rule on sovereignty and, indeed, has expressly and repeatedly requested that the Tribunal refrain from so doing."[86] The Tribunal emphasised that it did "not see that any of the Philippines' Submissions require an implicit determination of sovereignty."[87] Finally, the

---

[80] Award on Jurisdiction, paras. 124-129.

[81] Award on Jurisdiction, para. 128.

[82] Award on Jurisdiction, para. 126.

[83] Award on Jurisdiction, paras. 148-178.

[84] Award on Jurisdiction, paras. 152-154.

[85] Award on Jurisdiction, para. 152.

[86] Award on Jurisdiction, para. 153.

[87] Award on Jurisdiction, para. 153.

Tribunal observed that it was "fully conscious of the limits on the claims submitted to it and, to the extent that it reaches the merits of any of the Philippines' Submissions, intends to ensure that its decision neither advances nor detracts from either Party's claims to land sovereignty in the South China Sea."[88]

155. With respect to the latter objection, the Tribunal noted that a dispute concerning whether a State possesses an entitlement to a maritime zone is a distinct matter from the delimitation of maritime zones in an area in which they overlap.[89] While a wide variety of issues are commonly considered in the course of delimiting a maritime boundary, it does not follow that a dispute over each of these issues is necessarily a dispute over boundary delimitation. In particular, the Tribunal emphasised that:

> A maritime boundary may be delimited only between States with opposite or adjacent coasts and overlapping entitlements. In contrast, a dispute over claimed entitlements may exist even without overlap, where—for instance—a State claims maritime zones in an area understood by other States to form part of the high seas or the Area for the purposes of the Convention.[90]

Accordingly, the Tribunal held that the claims presented by the Philippines do not concern sea boundary delimitation and are not, therefore, subject to the exception to the dispute settlement provisions of the Convention.[91] The Tribunal also emphasised that the Philippines had not asked it to delimit any boundary.[92]

156. Turning to the matters raised in the Philippines' Submissions, the Tribunal reviewed the record to determine whether disputes existed between the Parties at the time the Philippines commenced this arbitration and whether such disputes concerned the interpretation and application of the Convention.[93] In so doing, the Tribunal noted that it was necessary to address some ambiguity regarding China's position on the matters before it and recalled that the existence of a dispute may be inferred from the conduct of a State, or from silence, and is a matter to be determined objectively.[94] The Tribunal considered that each of the Philippines' claims reflected a dispute concerning the Convention[95] and noted in particular that a dispute

---

[88] Award on Jurisdiction, para. 153.

[89] Award on Jurisdiction, paras. 155-157.

[90] Award on Jurisdiction, para. 156.

[91] Award on Jurisdiction, para. 157.

[92] Award on Jurisdiction, para. 157.

[93] Award on Jurisdiction, paras. 158-178.

[94] Award on Jurisdiction, paras. 159-163.

[95] Award on Jurisdiction, paras. 164-178.

concerning the interaction between the Convention and other rights (including any Chinese historic rights) is a dispute concerning the Convention.[96]

3.   Involvement of Indispensable Third Parties

157. Having identified the disputes presented by the Philippines' Submissions, the Tribunal considered whether the absence from this arbitration of other States, such as Viet Nam, that have claims to the islands of the South China Sea would be a bar to the Tribunal's jurisdiction.[97] The Tribunal noted that this arbitration differs from past cases in which a court or tribunal has found the involvement of a third party to be indispensable.[98] The Tribunal recalled that "the determination of the nature of and entitlements generated by the maritime features in the South China Sea does not require a decision on issues of territorial sovereignty" and held accordingly that "[t]he legal rights and obligations of Viet Nam therefore do not need to be determined as a prerequisite to the determination of the merits of the case."[99] The Tribunal also recalled that, in December 2014, Viet Nam submitted a "Statement of the Ministry of Foreign Affairs of Viet Nam" for the Tribunal's attention, in which Viet Nam asserted that it has "no doubt that the Tribunal has jurisdiction in these proceedings."[100]

4.   Preconditions to Jurisdiction

158. The Tribunal then considered the preconditions to jurisdiction set out in the Convention. Although the dispute settlement mechanism of the Convention provides for compulsory settlement, including through arbitration, it also permits parties to agree on the settlement of disputes through alternative means of their own choosing. Articles 281 and 282 of the Convention may prevent a State from making use of the mechanisms under the Convention if they have already agreed to another means of dispute resolution. Article 283 also requires the Parties to exchange views regarding the settlement of their dispute before beginning arbitration.

159. The Tribunal considered the applicability of Articles 281 and 282 to the following instruments to determine whether the Parties had agreed to another means of dispute settlement: (a) the 2002 China–ASEAN Declaration on the Conduct of Parties in the South China Sea (the "**DOC**"), (b) a series of joint statements issued by the Philippines and China referring to the

---

[96]   Award on Jurisdiction, para. 168.

[97]   Award on Jurisdiction, paras. 179-188.

[98]   Award on Jurisdiction, para. 181.

[99]   Award on Jurisdiction, para. 180.

[100]   Award on Jurisdiction, para. 183.

resolution of disputes through negotiations, (c) the Treaty of Amity and Cooperation in Southeast Asia, and (d) the Convention on Biological Diversity (the "**CBD**"). The Tribunal held that the DOC is a political agreement and "was not intended to be a legally binding agreement with respect to dispute resolution,"[101] does not provide a mechanism for binding settlement,[102] and does not exclude other means of settlement.[103] The Tribunal reached the same conclusion with respect to the joint statements identified in China's Position Paper.[104] With respect to the Treaty of Amity and Cooperation in Southeast Asia and the CBD, the Tribunal noted that both are legally binding agreements with their own procedures for disputes, but that neither provides a binding mechanism and neither excludes other procedures.[105] Additionally, the Tribunal noted that although there is overlap between the environmental provisions of the UN Convention on the Law of the Sea and the CBD, this does not mean that a dispute concerning one instrument is necessarily a dispute concerning the other or that the environmental claims brought by the Philippines should instead be considered under the framework of the CBD.[106] Accordingly, the Tribunal concluded that none of these instruments prevent the Philippines from bringing its claims to arbitration.

160. With respect to the exchange of views on the settlement of the dispute, the Tribunal held that Article 283 requires parties to exchange views on the means of settling their dispute, not the substance of that dispute.[107] The Tribunal held that this requirement was met in the record of diplomatic communications between the Philippines and China, in which the Philippines expressed a clear preference for multilateral negotiations involving the other States surrounding the South China Sea while China insisted that only bilateral talks could be considered.[108] The Tribunal also considered whether, independently of Article 283, the Philippines was under an obligation to pursue negotiations before resorting to arbitration.[109] In this respect, the Tribunal held that the Philippines had sought to negotiate with China[110] and noted that it is well

---

[101] Award on Jurisdiction, para. 217.

[102] Award on Jurisdiction, para. 300.

[103] Award on Jurisdiction, para. 222.

[104] Award on Jurisdiction, paras. 241-251, 301.

[105] Award on Jurisdiction, paras. 265-269, 281-289, 307-310, 317-321.

[106] Award on Jurisdiction, paras. 284-285.

[107] Award on Jurisdiction, para. 333.

[108] Award on Jurisdiction, paras. 337-342.

[109] Award on Jurisdiction, paras. 344-351.

[110] Award on Jurisdiction, para. 347.

established that international law does not require a State to continue negotiations when it concludes that the possibility of a negotiated solution has been exhausted.[111]

5.   Exceptions and Limitations to Jurisdiction

161.   Finally, the Tribunal examined the subject matter limitations to its jurisdiction set out in Articles 297 and 298 of the Convention. Article 297 automatically limits the jurisdiction a tribunal may exercise over disputes concerning marine scientific research or the living resources of the exclusive economic zone. Article 298 provides for further exceptions from compulsory settlement that a State may activate by declaration for disputes concerning (a) sea boundary delimitations, (b) historic bays and titles, (c) law enforcement activities, and (d) military activities. By declaration on 25 August 2006, China activated all of these exceptions.

162.   The Tribunal considered that the applicability of these limitations and exceptions may depend upon certain aspects of the merits of the Philippines' claims:

(a)   First, the Tribunal noted that its jurisdiction may depend on the nature and validity of any claim by China to historic rights in the South China Sea and whether such rights are covered by the exclusion from jurisdiction of "historic bays or titles."[112]

(b)   Second, the Tribunal noted that its jurisdiction may depend on the status of certain maritime features in the South China Sea and whether the Philippines and China possess overlapping entitlements to maritime zones in the South China Sea. If so, the Tribunal may not be able to reach the merits of certain claims because they would first require a delimitation of the overlapping zones (which the Tribunal is not empowered to do).[113]

(c)   Third, the Tribunal noted that its jurisdiction may depend on the maritime zone in which alleged Chinese law enforcement activities in fact took place.[114]

(d)   Fourth, the Tribunal noted that its jurisdiction may depend on whether certain Chinese activities are military in nature.[115]

163.   The Tribunal recalled that its Rules of Procedure call for it to rule on objections to jurisdiction as a preliminary matter, but permitted it to rule on such objections in conjunction with the

---

[111]   Award on Jurisdiction, para. 350.

[112]   Award on Jurisdiction, para. 393.

[113]   Award on Jurisdiction, para. 394.

[114]   Award on Jurisdiction, para. 395.

[115]   Award on Jurisdiction, para. 396.

merits if the objection "does not possess an exclusively preliminary character." For the foregoing reasons, the Tribunal concluded that it was able, at that time, to rule that it has jurisdiction over certain of the claims brought by the Philippines, but that others were not exclusively preliminary and would be deferred for further consideration in conjunction with the merits.[116]

6. Decisions of the Tribunal

164. In its Award, the Tribunal unanimously concluded that it:

A. FINDS that the Tribunal was properly constituted in accordance with Annex VII to the Convention.

B. FINDS that China's non-appearance in these proceedings does not deprive the Tribunal of jurisdiction.

C. FINDS that the Philippines' act of initiating this arbitration did not constitute an abuse of process.

D. FINDS that there is no indispensable third party whose absence deprives the Tribunal of jurisdiction.

E. FINDS that the 2002 China–ASEAN Declaration on Conduct of the Parties in the South China Sea, the joint statements of the Parties referred to in paragraphs 231 to 232 of this Award, the Treaty of Amity and Cooperation in Southeast Asia, and the Convention on Biological Diversity, do not preclude, under Articles 281 or 282 of the Convention, recourse to the compulsory dispute settlement procedures available under Section 2 of Part XV of the Convention.

F. FINDS that the Parties have exchanged views as required by Article 283 of the Convention.

G. FINDS that the Tribunal has jurisdiction to consider the Philippines' Submissions No. 3, 4, 6, 7, 10, 11, and 13, subject to the conditions noted in paragraphs 400, 401, 403, 404, 407, 408, and 410 of this Award.

H. FINDS that a determination of whether the Tribunal has jurisdiction to consider the Philippines' Submissions No. 1, 2, 5, 8, 9, 12, and 14 would involve consideration of issues that do not possess an exclusively preliminary character, and accordingly RESERVES consideration of its jurisdiction to rule on Submissions No. 1, 2, 5, 8, 9, 12, and 14 to the merits phase.

I. DIRECTS the Philippines to clarify the content and narrow the scope of its Submission 15 and RESERVES consideration of its jurisdiction over Submission No. 15 to the merits phase.

J. RESERVES for further consideration and directions all issues not decided in this Award.[117]

---

[116]   Award on Jurisdiction, paras. 397-412.

[117]   Award on Jurisdiction, para. 413.

C.   THE STATUS AND EFFECT OF THE TRIBUNAL'S AWARD ON JURISDICTION

165.   The Tribunal's Award on Jurisdiction is an "award of the arbitral tribunal" for the purposes of Article 10 of Annex VII to the Convention.[118] Pursuant to Article 11 of Annex VII to the Convention, "[t]he award shall be final and without appeal, unless the parties to the dispute have agreed in advance to an appellate procedure.   It shall be complied with by the parties to the dispute."[119]

166.   The Tribunal is conscious that China has not, to date, accepted the decisions in the Tribunal's Award on Jurisdiction and has stated that the Award "is null and void, and has no binding effect on China."[120]   The Tribunal is also conscious that China has continued to assert publicly that the Tribunal lacks jurisdiction for the same reasons set out in China's Position Paper of 7 December 2014, specifically that:

(a)   "First, the essence of the subject-matter of the arbitration is territorial sovereignty over several maritime features in the South China Sea, which is beyond the scope of the UNCLOS."[121]

(b)   "Second, even assuming some of the claims were concerned with the interpretation and application of the UNCLOS, they would still be an integral part of maritime delimitation, which has been excluded by China through its 2006 Declaration and consequently is not subject to compulsory arbitration."[122]

(c)   "Third, given that China and the Philippines have agreed to settle their disputes in the South China Sea through negotiation, the Philippines is precluded from initiating arbitration unilaterally."[123]

---

[118]   Convention, Annex VII, art. 10.

[119]   Convention, Annex VII, art. 11.

[120]   Ministry of Foreign Affairs, People's Republic of China, *Statement of the Ministry of Foreign Affairs of the People's Republic of China on the Award on Jurisdiction and Admissibility of the South China Sea Arbitration by the Arbitral Tribunal Established at the Request of the Republic of the Philippines* (30 October 2015) (Annex 649).

[121]   Ministry of Foreign Affairs, People's Republic of China, *Briefing by Xu Hong, Director-General of the Department of Treaty and Law on the South China Sea Arbitration Initiated by the Philippines* (12 May 2016), *available at* <www.fmprc.gov.cn/mfa_eng/wjdt_665385/zyjh_665391/t1364804.shtml>.

[122]   Ministry of Foreign Affairs, People's Republic of China, *Briefing by Xu Hong, Director-General of the Department of Treaty and Law on the South China Sea Arbitration Initiated by the Philippines* (12 May 2016), *available at* <www.fmprc.gov.cn/mfa_eng/wjdt_665385/zyjh_665391/t1364804.shtml>.

[123]   Ministry of Foreign Affairs, People's Republic of China, *Briefing by Xu Hong, Director-General of the Department of Treaty and Law on the South China Sea Arbitration Initiated by the Philippines* (12 May 2016), *available at* <www.fmprc.gov.cn/mfa_eng/wjdt_665385/zyjh_665391/t1364804.shtml>.

(d)   "Fourth, the Philippines failed to fulfill the obligation of exchanging views with China on the means of dispute settlement."[124]

China has also continued to assert its view that (e) "the Philippines' initiation of the arbitration is a typical abuse of compulsory arbitral procedures stipulated in the UNCLOS."[125]

167.   The Tribunal considers that each of these objections—concerning (a) the link between sovereignty and the Philippines' claims,[126] (b) the link between maritime delimitation and the Philippines' claims,[127] (c) the effect of the DOC,[128] (d) the Parties' exchange of views on the settlement of the dispute prior to the commencement of the arbitration, [129] and (e) the appropriateness of the Philippines' recourse to arbitration[130]—has been fully addressed and decided in the Tribunal's Award on Jurisdiction, in keeping with the Tribunal's power pursuant to Article 288(4) to decide any dispute concerning the scope of its own jurisdiction.

168.   For the avoidance of doubt, the Tribunal hereby reaffirms in full, and incorporates by reference, the conclusions and reasoning set out in its Award on Jurisdiction.

*   *   *

---

[124]   Ministry of Foreign Affairs, People's Republic of China, *Briefing by Xu Hong, Director-General of the Department of Treaty and Law on the South China Sea Arbitration Initiated by the Philippines* (12 May 2016), *available at* <www.fmprc.gov.cn/mfa_eng/wjdt_665385/zyjh_665391/t1364804.shtml>.

[125]   Ministry of Foreign Affairs, People's Republic of China, *Briefing by Xu Hong, Director-General of the Department of Treaty and Law on the South China Sea Arbitration Initiated by the Philippines* (12 May 2016), *available at* <www.fmprc.gov.cn/mfa_eng/wjdt_665385/zyjh_665391/t1364804.shtml>.

[126]   *See* Award on Jurisdiction, paras. 152-154.

[127]   *See* Award on Jurisdiction, paras. 155-157.

[128]   *See* Award on Jurisdiction, paras. 212-229, 299-300.

[129]   *See* Award on Jurisdiction, paras. 332-352.

[130]   *See* Award on Jurisdiction, paras. 124-129.

this page intentionally blank

V. THE 'NINE-DASH LINE' AND CHINA'S CLAIM TO HISTORIC RIGHTS IN THE MARITIME AREAS OF THE SOUTH CHINA SEA (SUBMISSIONS NO. 1 AND 2)

A. INTRODUCTION

169. In this Chapter, the Tribunal addresses the Parties' dispute reflected in the Philippines' Submissions No. 1 and 2, which request the Tribunal to hold that China is entitled only to those rights provided for by the Convention and that these rights are not supplemented or modified by any historic rights, including within the area marked by the 'nine-dash line' on Chinese maps.[131] Submissions No. 1 and 2 are expressed as follows:

> (1) China's maritime entitlements in the South China Sea, like those of the Philippines, may not extend beyond those expressly permitted by the United Nations Convention on the Law of the Sea ("UNCLOS" or the "Convention");
>
> (2) China's claims to sovereign rights jurisdiction, and to "historic rights" with respect to the maritime areas of the South China Sea encompassed by the so called "nine dash line" are contrary to the Convention and without lawful effect to the extent that they exceed the geographic and substantive limits of China's maritime entitlements expressly permitted by UNCLOS;

170. In its Award on Jurisdiction, the Tribunal held that these Submissions reflect a dispute concerning the source of maritime entitlements in the South China Sea and the interaction of China's claimed historic rights with the provisions of the Convention.[132] This dispute does not concern sovereignty, insofar as the Philippines has asked the Tribunal to determine the source of rights to maritime areas, and not to decide sovereignty over any land features within the South China Sea.[133] The Tribunal also held that this dispute does not concern maritime boundary delimitation.[134] Finally, the Tribunal emphasised that "[a] dispute concerning the interaction of the Convention with another instrument or body of law, including the question of whether rights

---

[131] As noted in the Award on Jurisdiction at p. 62, n.121, the 'nine-dash line' refers to the dashed line depicted on maps accompanying the Note Verbale from the Permanent Mission of the People's Republic of China to the United Nations to the Secretary-General of the United Nations, No. CML/17/2009 (7 May 2009) (Annex 191); Note Verbale from the Permanent Mission of the People's Republic of China to the United Nations to the Secretary-General of the United Nations, No. CML/18/2009 (7 May 2009) (Annex 192). The Tribunal's use of the term 'nine-dash line' is not to be understood as recognising any particular nomenclature or map as correct or authoritative. The Tribunal observes that different terms have been used at different times and by different entities to refer to this line. For example, China refers to "China's dotted line in the South China Sea" (China's Position Paper, para. 8); Viet Nam refers to the "nine-dash line" (Viet Nam's Statement, paras. 2(iii)-(iv), 4(i)); Indonesia has referred to the "so called 'nine-dotted-lines map' (Note Verbale from the Permanent Mission of the Republic of Indonesia to the United Nations to the Secretary-General of the United Nations, No. 480/POL-703/VII/10 (8 July 2010) (Annex 197); and some commentators have referred to it as the "Cow's Tongue" and "U-Shaped Line." As noted below at paragraph 181, the Tribunal observes that the number of dashes varies, depending on the date and version of the map consulted.

[132] Award on Jurisdiction, paras. 164-168.

[133] Award on Jurisdiction, paras. 152-154.

[134] Award on Jurisdiction, paras. 155-157.

arising under another body of law were or were not preserved by the Convention, is unequivocally a dispute concerning the interpretation and application of the Convention."[135]

171. However, the Tribunal held that a final determination on its jurisdiction with respect to the Parties' dispute is dependent on the nature of any historic rights claimed by China and whether they are covered by the exclusion from jurisdiction in Article 298 of the Convention for disputes concerning "historic bays or titles." Accordingly, the Tribunal deferred a decision on its jurisdiction for consideration in conjunction with the merits of the Philippines' claims.[136]

B. **CHINA'S DECLARATIONS AND LEGISLATION CONCERNING ENTITLEMENTS TO MARITIME ZONES**

172. China has set out its claims to maritime zones in legislation and a series of declarations.

173. When China was under the control of its Republican Government in the 1930s, it issued a decree declaring a territorial sea of three nautical miles.[137] Prior to that declaration China appears to have distinguished between the "inner ocean" and the "outer ocean" in its domestic laws, and to have included references to a territorial sea in a number of international agreements, but never to have fixed the extent or boundaries of that zone.[138]

174. On 4 September 1958, China issued a Declaration of the Government of the People's Republic of China on China's Territorial Sea, which provided in relevant part as follows:

> The Government of the People's Republic of China declares:
>
> 1. The breadth of the territorial sea of the People's Republic of China shall be twelve nautical miles. This provision applies to all territories of the People's Republic of China, including the Chinese mainland and its coastal islands, as well as Taiwan and its surrounding islands, the Penghu Islands, the Dongsha Islands, the Xisha Islands, the Zhongsha Islands, the Nansha Islands and all other islands belonging to China which are separated from the mainland and its coastal islands by the high seas.
>
> 2. China's territorial sea along the mainland and its coastal islands takes as its baseline the line composed of the straight lines connecting base-points on the mainland coast and on the outermost of the coastal islands; the water area extending twelve nautical miles outward from this baseline is China's territorial sea. The water areas inside the baseline, including Bohai Bay and the Chiungchow Straits, are Chinese inland waters. The islands inside the baseline, including Tungyin Island, Kaoteng Island, the Matsu Islands, the Paichuan Islands, Wuchiu Island, the Greater and Lesser Quemoy Islands, Tatan Island, Erhtan Island and Tungting Island, are islands of the Chinese inland waters.

---

[135]   Award on Jurisdiction, para. 168.

[136]   Award on Jurisdiction, paras. 398-399.

[137]   See K.H. Wang, "The ROC's Maritime Claims and Practices with Special Reference to the South China Sea," *Ocean Development & International Law*, Vol. 41, No. 3, p. 237 at p. 238 (2010).

[138]   See generally H. Chiu, "China and the Question of Territorial Sea," *Maryland Journal of International Law*, Vol. 1(1), p. 29 at pp. 33-36 (1975).

3. No foreign vessels for military use and no foreign aircraft may enter China's territorial sea and the air space above it without the permission of the Government of the People's Republic of China.

While navigating Chinese territorial sea, every foreign vessel must observe the relevant laws and regulations laid down by the Government of the People's Republic of China.

4. The principles provided in paragraphs (2) and (3) likewise apply to Taiwan and its surrounding Islands, the Penghu Islands, the Dongsha islands, the Xisha Islands, the Zhongsha Islands, the Nansha Islands, and all other islands belonging to China.[139]

175. On 25 February 1992, China enacted a *Law on the Territorial Sea and the Contiguous Zone*, which provided in relevant part as follows:

Article 2

The territorial sea of the People's Republic of China is the sea belt adjacent to the land territory and the internal waters of the People's Republic of China.

The land territory of the People's Republic of China includes the mainland of the People's Republic of China and its coastal islands; Taiwan and all islands appertaining thereto including the Diaoyu Islands; the Penghu Islands; the Dongsha Islands; the Xisha Islands; the Zhongsha Islands and the Nansha Islands; as well as all the other islands belonging to the People's Republic of China.

The waters on the landward side of the baselines of the territorial sea of the People's Republic of China constitute the internal waters of the People's Republic of China.

Article 3

The breadth of the territorial sea of the People's Republic of China is twelve nautical miles, measured from the baselines of the territorial sea.

The method of straight baselines composed of all the straight lines joining the adjacent base points shall be employed in drawing the baselines of the territorial sea of the People's Republic of China.

The outer limit of the territorial sea of the People's Republic of China is the line every point of which is at a distance equal to twelve nautical miles from the nearest point of the baseline of the territorial sea.

Article 4

The contiguous zone of the People's Republic of China is the sea belt adjacent to and beyond the territorial sea. The breadth of the contiguous zone is twelve nautical miles.

The outer limit of the contiguous zone of the People's Republic of China is the line every point of which is at a distance equal to twenty four nautical miles from the nearest point of the baseline of the territorial sea.

Article 5

The sovereignty of the People's Republic of China over its territorial sea extends to the air space over the territorial sea as well as to the bed and subsoil of the territorial sea.[140]

---

[139] People's Republic of China, "Declaration of the Government of the People's Republic of China on China's Territorial Sea" (4 September 1958), *in Collection of the Sea Laws and Regulations of the People's Republic of China* (3rd ed., 2001).

176. On 15 May 1996, China issued a *Declaration of the Government of the People's Republic of China on the Baselines of the Territorial Sea*, setting out certain coordinates for the baselines from which its territorial sea would be measured.[141]

177. On 7 June 1996, in conjunction with its ratification of the Convention, China declared an exclusive economic zone in the following terms:

> 1. In accordance with the provisions of the United Nations Convention on the Law of the Sea, the People's Republic of China shall enjoy sovereign rights and jurisdiction over an exclusive economic zone of 200 nautical miles and the continental shelf.
>
> 2. The People's Republic of China will effect, through consultations, the delimitation of boundary of the maritime jurisdiction with the states with coasts opposite or adjacent to China respectively on the basis of international law and in accordance with the equitable principle.
>
> 3. The People's Republic of China reaffirms its sovereignty over all its archipelagoes and islands as listed in article 2 of the Law of the People's Republic of China on the Territorial Sea and Contiguous Zone which was promulgated on 25 February 1992.
>
> 4. The People's Republic of China reaffirms that the provisions of the United Nations Convention on the Law of the Sea concerning innocent passage through the territorial sea shall not prejudice the right of a coastal state to request, in accordance with its laws and regulations, a foreign state to obtain advance approval from or give prior notification to the coastal state for the passage of its warships through the territorial sea of the coastal state.[142]

178. On 26 June 1998, China enacted a *Law on the Exclusive Economic Zone and the Continental Shelf*, which described the extent of China's exclusive economic zone and continental shelf as follows:

> *Article 2*
>
> The exclusive economic zone of the People's Republic of China covers the area beyond and adjacent to the territorial sea of the People's Republic of China, extending to 200 nautical miles from the baselines from which the breadth of the territorial sea is measured.
>
> The continental shelf of the People's Republic of China comprises the sea-bed and subsoil of the submarine areas that extend beyond its territorial sea throughout the natural prolongation of its land territory to the outer edge of the continental margin, or to a distance of 200 nautical miles from the baselines from which the breadth of the territorial sea is measured where the outer edge of the continental margin does not extend up to that distance.
>
> The People's Republic of China shall determine the delimitation of its exclusive economic zone and continental shelf in respect of the overlapping claims by agreement with the states

---

[140]   People's Republic of China, Law on the Territorial Sea and the Contiguous Zone (25 February 1992), *available at* <www.npc.gov.cn/englishnpc/Law/2007-12/12/content_1383846.htm> *also available at* <www.un.org/depts/los/legislationandtreaties/pdffiles/chn_1992_law.pdf>.

[141]   *See* United Nations, Office of Legal Affairs, Division of Ocean Affairs and the Law of the Sea, *Law of the Sea Bulletin No. 32*, pp. 37-40 (1996).

[142]   United Nations, Secretary-General, *Multilateral Treaties Deposited with the Secretary-General*, Vol. III, Part I, Chapters XXII to XXIX, and Part II, UN Doc. ST/LEG/SER.E/26 (2009).

with opposite or adjacent coasts, in accordance with the equitable principle and on the basis of international law.[143]

179. Article 14 of the *Exclusive Economic Zone and Continental Shelf Act* provides further that "[t]he provisions in this Law shall not affect the rights that the People's Republic of China has been enjoying ever since the days of the past."[144]

C.   CHINA'S CLAIMS TO HISTORIC RIGHTS

180. As the Tribunal noted in its Award on Jurisdiction, the resolution of the Parties' dispute in relation to Submissions No. 1 and 2 is complicated by some ambiguity in China's position. As far as the Tribunal is aware, China has never expressly clarified the nature or scope of its claimed historic rights. Nor has it ever clarified its understanding of the meaning of the 'nine-dash line'.[145] Certain facts can, however, be established.

181. What has become known as the 'nine-dash line' first appeared on an official Chinese map in 1948. In that year, the Ministry of the Interior of the then Republican Government of China published a "Map Showing the Location of the Various Islands in the South Sea" (the "**1948 Map**").[146] A similar line had also appeared in privately produced cartography as early as 1933.[147] The 1948 Map is reproduced as Figure 1 on page 75 below. In this original form, the map featured 11 dashes. The two dashes in the Gulf of Tonkin were removed in 1953,[148] rendering it a 'nine-dash line', and the line has appeared consistently in that nine-dash form in

---

[143]   People's Republic of China, Exclusive Economic Zone and Continental Shelf Act (26 June 1998), *available at* <www.npc.gov.cn/englishnpc/Law/2007-12/11/content_1383573.htm> *also available at* <www.un.org/depts/los/legislationandtreaties/pdffiles/chn_1998_eez_act.pdf>.

[144]   People's Republic of China, Exclusive Economic Zone and Continental Shelf Act (26 June 1998), *available at* <www.npc.gov.cn/englishnpc/Law/2007-12/11/content_1383573.htm>. The translation maintained by the UN Department of Ocean Affairs and the Law of the Sea translates Article 14 as follows: "The provisions of this Act shall not affect the historical rights of the People's Republic of China." People's Republic of China, Exclusive Economic Zone and Continental Shelf Act (26 June 1998), *available at* <www.un.org/depts/los/legislationandtreaties/pdffiles/chn_1998_eez_act.pdf>.

[145]   *See* Award on Jurisdiction, para. 160.

[146]   Boundary Department of the Ministry of Interior, Republic of China, "Map Showing the Location of the Various Islands in the South Sea" (1948). Scholarly accounts indicated that the map was prepared in 1947 and published in 1948. *See, e.g.*, K. Zou, "The Chinese Traditional Maritime Boundary Line in the South China Sea and Its Legal Consequences for the Resolution of the Dispute over the Spratly Islands," *International Journal of Marine and Coastal Law*, Vol. 14, No. 27 (1999).

[147]   *See* K. Zou, "The Chinese Traditional Maritime Boundary Line in the South China Sea and Its Legal Consequences for the Resolution of the Dispute over the Spratly Islands," *International Journal of Marine and Coastal Law*, Vol. 14, No. 27 (1999).

[148]   *See* Z. Gao and B.B. Jia, "The Nine-Dash Line in the South China Sea: History, Status, and Implications," *American Journal of International Law*, Vol. 107, No. 1 at p. 2013 (2013).

official Chinese cartography since that date.[149] The length and precise placement of individual dashes, however, do not appear to be entirely consistent among different official depictions of the line.

182. On 7 May 2009, China sent two Notes Verbales to the UN Secretary-General in response to Malaysia and Viet Nam's Joint Submission of the preceding day to the Commission on the Limits of the Continental Shelf (the "**CLCS**"). In its notes, China stated as follows:

> China has indisputable sovereignty over the islands in the South China Sea and the adjacent waters, and enjoys sovereign rights and jurisdiction over the relevant waters as well as the seabed and subsoil thereof (see attached map). The above position is consistently held by the Chinese Government, and is widely known by the international community.[150]

183. Appended to China's notes was a map depicting the 'nine-dash line' (the "**2009 Map**"), which is reproduced as Figure 2 on page 77 below.

184. China's notes prompted immediate objections from Viet Nam and Malaysia,[151] as well as subsequent objections from Indonesia[152] and the Philippines.[153] In addition to claiming sovereignty over the "Kalayaan Island Group (KIG)", the Philippines' objection stated in relevant part:

> On the "Waters Adjacent" to the Islands and other Geological Features
>
> SECOND, the Philippines, under the Roman notion of *dominium maris* and the international law principle of "*la terre domine la mer*" which states that the land dominates the sea, necessarily exercises sovereignty and jurisdiction over the waters around or adjacent to each relevant geological feature in the KIG as provided for under the United Nations Convention on the Law of the Sea (UNCLOS).

---

[149] The Tribunal notes that, in 2013, China issued a new official map of China with a vertical orientation and a tenth dash to the east of Taiwan island. *See* China Cartographic Publishing House, "Map of the People's Republic of China" (2013). The Tribunal understand that this does not reflect a change in the course of the 'nine-dash line', but rather the fact that prior projections using a horizontal orientation and an inset map of the South China Sea had the effect of obscuring the area east of Taiwan island on the inset map. *See, e.g.*, Map of the People's Republic of China, China Cartographic Publishing House (1992).

[150] Note Verbale from the Permanent Mission of the People's Republic of China to the United Nations to the Secretary-General of the United Nations, No. CML/17/2009 (7 May 2009) (Annex 191); Note Verbale from the Permanent Mission of the People's Republic of China to the United Nations to the Secretary-General of the United Nations, No. CML/18/2009 (7 May 2009) (Annex 192).

[151] Note Verbale from the Permanent Mission of the Socialist Republic of Viet Nam to the United Nations to the Secretary-General of the United Nations, No. 86/HC-2009 (8 May 2009) (Annex 193); Note Verbale from the Permanent Mission of Malaysia to the United Nations to the Secretary-General of the United Nations, No. HA 24/09 (20 May 2009) (Annex 194).

[152] Note Verbale from the Permanent Mission of the Republic of Indonesia to the United Nations to the Secretary-General of the United Nations, No. 480/POL-703/VII/10 (8 July 2010) (Annex 197).

[153] Note Verbale from the Permanent Mission of the Republic of the Philippines to the United Nations to the Secretary-General of the United Nations, No. 000228 (5 April 2011) (Annex 200).

At any rate, the extent of the waters that are "adjacent" to the relevant geological features are definite and determinable under UNCLOS, specifically under Article 121 (Regime of Islands) of the said Convention.

On the Other "Relevant Waters, Seabed and Subsoil" in the SCS

THIRD, since the adjacent waters of the relevant geological features are definite and subject to legal and technical measurement, the claim as well by the People's Republic of China on the *"relevant waters as well as the seabed and subsoil thereof"* (as reflected in the so-called 9-dash line map attached to Notes Verbales CML/17/2009 dated 7 May 2009 and CML/18/2009 dated 7 May 2009) outside of the aforementioned relevant geological features in the KIG and their "adjacent waters" would have no basis under international law, specifically UNCLOS. With respect to these areas, sovereignty and jurisdiction or sovereign rights, as the case may be, necessarily appertain or belong to the appropriate coastal or archipelagic state – the Philippines – to which these bodies of waters as well as seabed and subsoil are appurtenant, either in the nature of Territorial Sea, or 200 M Exclusive Economic Zone (EEZ), or Continental Shelf (CS) in accordance with Articles 3, 4, 55, 57, and 76 of UNCLOS.[154]

185. In response to the Philippines, China restated its position as follows:

China has indisputable sovereignty over the islands in the South China Sea and the adjacent waters, and enjoys sovereign rights and jurisdiction over the relevant waters as well as the seabed and subsoil thereof. China's sovereignty and related rights and jurisdiction in the South China Sea are supported by abundant historical and legal evidence. The contents of the Note Verbale No 000228 of the Republic of Philippines are totally unacceptable to the Chinese Government.

. . . Furthermore, under the legal principle of "la terre domine la mer", coastal states' Exclusive Economic Zone (EEZ) and Continental Shelf claims shall not infringe upon the territorial sovereignty of other states.

Since 1930s, the Chinese Government has given publicity several times the geographical scope of China's Nansha Islands and the names of its components. China's Nansha Islands is therefore clearly defined. In addition, under the relevant provisions of the 1982 United Nations Convention on the Law of the Sea, as well as the Law of the People's Republic of China on the Territorial Sea and the Contiguous Zone (1992) and the Law on the Exclusive Economic Zone and the Continental Shelf of the People's Republic of China–(1998), China's Nansha Islands is fully entitled to Territorial Sea, Exclusive Economic Zone (EEZ) and Continental Shelf.[155]

186. China has repeated variations on this formula in its diplomatic correspondence[156] and in the public statements of its official spokespersons,[157] and has expressly linked the 'nine-dash line' to China's claim to rights "formed over a long course of history":

---

[154] Note Verbale from the Permanent Mission of the Republic of the Philippines to the United Nations to the Secretary-General of the United Nations, No. 000228 (5 April 2011) (Annex 200).

[155] Note Verbale from the Permanent Mission of the People's Republic of China to the United Nations to the Secretary-General of the United Nations, No. CML/8/2011 (14 April 2011) (Annex 201).

[156] *See, e.g.*, Note Verbale from the Embassy of the People's Republic of China in Manila to the Department of Foreign Affairs, Republic of the Philippines, No. (12) PG-251 (12 June 2012) (Annex 213); Note Verbale from the Embassy of the People's Republic of China in Manila to the Department of Foreign Affairs, Republic of the Philippines, No. (13) PG-173 (21 June 2013) (Annex 220); Note Verbale from the Embassy of the People's Republic of China in Manila to the Department of Foreign Affairs, Republic of the Philippines, No. 14(PG)-195 (30 June 2014) (Annex 675); Note Verbale from the

> China has indisputable sovereignty over the Nansha Islands and their adjacent waters. And it is an indisputable fact that the Xisha Islands are an integral part of China's territory. As early as 1948, the Chinese government published an official map which displayed "the dotted line" in the South China Sea. China's sovereignty over the South China Sea and its claims to the relevant rights have been formed over a long course of history. They are solidly grounded in international law and have been consistently upheld by successive Chinese governments.[158]

187. China's formal statement, released following the Tribunal's issuance of the Award on Jurisdiction, is representative of China's consistent characterisation of its maritime entitlements in the South China Sea:

> China has indisputable sovereignty over the South China Sea Islands and the adjacent waters. China's sovereignty and relevant rights in the South China Sea, formed in the long historical course, are upheld by successive Chinese governments, reaffirmed by China's domestic laws on many occasions, and protected under international law including the United Nations Convention on the Law of the Sea (UNCLOS). . . .[159]

D.   THE PHILIPPINES' POSITION

188. The Philippines submits that the Tribunal has jurisdiction to consider its Submissions No. 1 and 2. On the merits, the Philippines argues both (a) that any rights that China may have had in the maritime areas of the South China Sea beyond those provided for in the Convention were extinguished by China's accession to the Convention and (b) that China never had historic rights in the waters of the South China Sea.

Ministry of Foreign Affairs, People's Republic of China, to the Embassy of the Republic of the Philippines in Beijing, No. (2015) Bu Bian Zi No. 5 (20 January 2015) (Annex 681).

[157] *See, e.g.*, Ministry of Foreign Affairs, People's Republic of China, *Foreign Ministry Spokesperson Hong Lei's Regular Press Conference* (9 December 2014) (Annex 620); Ministry of Foreign Affairs, People's Republic of China, *Foreign Ministry Spokesperson Hong Lei's Remarks on Vietnam's Statement on the Chinese Government's Position Paper on Rejecting the Jurisdiction of the Arbitral Tribunal Established at the Request of the Philippines for the South China Sea Arbitration* (12 December 2014) (Annex 621); Ministry of Foreign Affairs, People's Republic of China, *Foreign Ministry Spokesperson Hong Lei's Regular Press Conference* (11 March 2015) (Annex 623); Ministry of Foreign Affairs, People's Republic of China, *Foreign Ministry Spokesperson Hua Chunying's Remarks on the Philippines' Playing up and Airing of a Documentary on the South China Sea Issue* (29 June 2015) (Annex 628).

[158] Ministry of Foreign Affairs, People's Republic of China, *Foreign Ministry Spokesperson Hong Lei's Remarks on Vietnam's Statement on the Chinese Government's Position Paper on Rejecting the Jurisdiction of the Arbitral Tribunal Established at the Request of the Philippines for the South China Sea Arbitration* (12 December 2014) (Annex 621).

[159] Ministry of Foreign Affairs, People's Republic of China, *Statement of the Ministry of Foreign Affairs of the People's Republic of China on the Award on Jurisdiction and Admissibility of the South China Sea Arbitration by the Arbitral Tribunal Established at the Request of the Republic of the Philippines* (30 October 2015) (Annex 649).

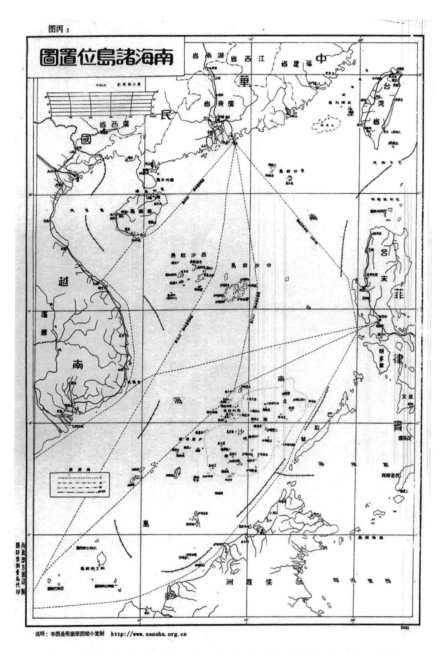

Figure 1: Map showing the "Location of the Various Islands in the South Sea," 1948
Boundary Department of the Ministry of Interior, Republic of China

this page intentionally blank.

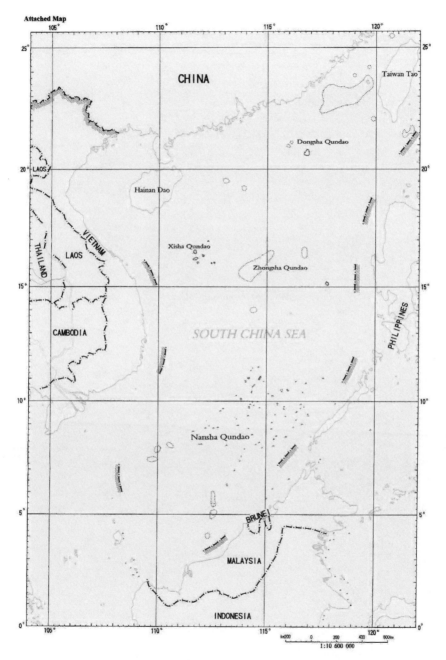

Figure 2: Map attached to China's 7 May 2009 Notes Verbales
Attachment to Note Verbale from the Permanent Mission of the People's Republic of China to the United
Nations to the Secretary-General of the United Nations, No. CML/17/2009 (7 May 2009) (Annex 191); Note
Verbale from the Permanent Mission of the People's Republic of China to the United Nations to the Secretary-
General of the United Nations, No. CML/18/2009 (7 May 2009) (Annex 192).

this page intentionally blank

1.   **Jurisdiction**

189.   With respect to jurisdiction, the Philippines argues that China's statements since May 2009 make a consistent distinction between claims to "sovereignty" and claims to "sovereign rights and jurisdiction," and a further distinction between the "islands in the South China Sea and the adjacent waters" and the "relevant waters". According to the Philippines:

> the most logical way to construe China's language is as an assertion of sovereignty over the islands of the South China Sea and their "adjacent waters", or territorial seas; and a claim of sovereign rights and jurisdiction—short of sovereignty—in the waters that lie between the territorial seas claimed by China and the nine-dash line.[160]

190.   In the Philippines' view, the nature of China's claim as one of sovereign rights and jurisdiction is confirmed by China's conduct in (a) seeking to ban fishing by other States within the 'nine-dash line'; (b) interfering with the Philippines' petroleum exploration activities; and (c) offering concessions to oil blocks in areas within the 'nine-dash line' but beyond the possible limits of China's entitlements under the Convention.[161] At the same time, the Philippines considers that China's conduct makes clear that its claim is not to sovereignty over the entire area within the 'nine-dash line', insofar as China has repeatedly asserted that it respects freedom of navigation and overflight in the South China Sea.[162] The Philippines also notes that this interpretation of China's position has been adopted by numerous Chinese scholars, including those with significant links to the government.[163]

191.   According to the Philippines, the exception to jurisdiction in Article 298 of the Convention is limited to disputes involving "historic bays or titles." Moreover, the Philippines argues, "the concept of 'historic title' as used in Article 298 has a specific and limited meaning: it pertains only to near-shore areas of sea that are susceptible to a claim of sovereignty as such."[164] Because the Philippines understands China's claims to fall short of sovereignty over the maritime areas of the South China Sea (beyond the "islands" and "adjacent waters"), the Philippines considers that China's claim cannot be one of historic title. In this respect, the Philippines argues that there is a consistent distinction—including in the Chinese terminology— between China's use of the term "historical rights" in China's Exclusive Economic Zone and

---

[160]   Merits Hearing Tr. (Day 1), p. 19.

[161]   Merits Hearing Tr. (Day 1), pp. 22-24. See also the Philippines' Position in respect of its Submission No. 8 at paragraphs 681 to 686 below.

[162]   Merits Hearing Tr. (Day 1), pp. 24-27.

[163]   Merits Hearing Tr. (Day 1), pp. 27-28; Memorial, para. 1.23; Z. Gao and B.B. Jia, "The Nine-Dash Line in the South China Sea: History, Status, and Implications," *American Journal of International Law*, Vol. 107, No. 1, p. 98 pp. 123-124 (2013).

[164]   Memorial, para. 7.130.

Continental Shelf Act[165] and the term 'historic title' in Article 298 and elsewhere in the Convention. As such, the Philippines argues, "China's claim of 'historic rights' within the area encompassed by the nine-dash line is not covered by Article 298(1)(a)(i)."[166] Even if China's claim were to a historic title, however, the Philippines submits that Article 298 would nevertheless be inapplicable because the article applies only to disputes over the *delimitation* of historic bays and titles. According to the Philippines, "when Article 298(1)(a)(i) refers to 'those involving historic bays or titles' the 'those' being referred to are not disputes generally but rather disputes concerning delimitation."[167]

2.   China's Claim to Historic Rights

192.   With respect to the merits, the Philippines' argument is two-fold. First, the Philippines submits that international law did not historically permit the type of expansive claim advanced by China's 'nine-dash line' and that, even if China did possess historic rights in the South China Sea, any such rights were extinguished by the adoption of the Convention. Second, the Philippines argues that, on the basis of the historical record of China's activities in the South China Sea, China cannot meet the criteria for having established historic rights within the 'nine-dash line'.

193.   According to the Philippines, international law prior to the adoption of the Convention did not accept "assertions of historic rights over such a vast area" as China now claims.[168] Prior to the Convention, the Philippines argues, "[t]he sea was subject only to two principles: the principle of the freedom of the seas, which prohibits appropriation by any state; and the principle of control over a limited area by the immediately adjacent coastal state, which prohibits appropriation by any other state."[169] In the Philippines' view, "China's claim . . . is inconsistent with both principles."[170]

---

[165]   People's Republic of China, Exclusive Economic Zone and Continental Shelf Act (26 June 1998), *available at* <www.npc.gov.cn/englishnpc/Law/2007-12/11/content_1383573.htm>.   The translation maintained by the UN Department of Ocean Affairs and the Law of the Sea translates Article 14 as follows: "The provisions of this Act shall not affect the historical rights of the People's Republic of China." People's Republic of China, Exclusive Economic Zone and Continental Shelf Act (26 June 1998), *available at* <www.un.org/depts/los/legislationandtreaties/pdffiles/chn_1998_eez_act.pdf>.'

[166]   Memorial, para. 7.128.

[167]   Memorial, para. 7.139.

[168]   Merits Hearing Tr. (Day 1), p. 59.

[169]   Merits Hearing Tr. (Day 1), p. 61.

[170]   Merits Hearing Tr. (Day 1), p. 61.

194. With the adoption of the Convention, the Philippines submits, the States Parties considered "with careful specificity the nature of prior uses [of the sea] that are protected, the nature of the protections, and the areas in which such protections apply."[171] According to the Philippines, where the Convention makes no express exception for prior uses or rights "those historic rights would not have survived as derogations from the sovereignty, sovereign rights and high seas freedoms of other states."[172] Notably, while some protections of prior uses were accepted, the Philippines argues that "distant water fishing states failed to obtain recognition in the exclusive economic zone of historic fishing rights derived from prior high seas fishing."[173] In the course of these debates, the Philippines submits:

> China was a vocal supporter of the demands of developing coastal states for exclusive jurisdiction over the natural resources in the EEZs and continental shelves off their respective coasts, and China was a consistent critic of attempts to limit the content of that jurisdiction. China identified itself as one of those developing coastal states. It made no attempt whatsoever to secure an exception protecting historic claims of maritime rights of the kind that are now at issue.[174]

Accordingly, the Philippines concludes, "[t]he Convention leaves no room for assertions of rights to control activities beyond [the limits fixed in the Convention] in derogation of the sovereign rights of other coastal states or the rights and freedoms of all states."[175]

195. The Philippines also challenges the existence of Chinese historic rights in the maritime areas of the South China Sea. According to the Philippines, China "first claimed the existence of such rights on 7th May 2009."[176] The Philippines submits that Chinese historic maps dating back to 1136, including those purporting to depict the entirety of the Empire of China, consistently show China's territory extending no further south than Hainan.[177] The Philippines also notes that, for periods of the 14th century and for much of the 15th and 16th centuries, the Imperial Chinese Government actively prohibited maritime trade by Chinese subjects.[178] Indeed, the Philippines notes:

> During the mid-15th century, for instance, the Ming authorities suppressed maritime activities, and in 1500 made it a capital offence to build two-masted ships. In 1525, all such

---

[171] Merits Hearing Tr. (Day 1), p. 66.

[172] Merits Hearing Tr. (Day 1), p. 71.

[173] Merits Hearing Tr. (Day 1), p. 67.

[174] Merits Hearing Tr. (Day 1), p. 72 (internal citations omitted).

[175] Merits Hearing Tr. (Day 1), p. 74.

[176] Merits Hearing Tr. (Day 1), p. 77.

[177] Merits Hearing Tr. (Day 1), pp. 79-80.

[178] Merits Hearing Tr. (Day 1), p. 81; Supplemental Written Submission, paras. A13.3-A13.11.

remaining ships were ordered destroyed. In 1551, China defined venturing out to sea in a multi-masted ship to be an act of treason.[179]

196. This ambivalent attitude to seafaring explains, for the Philippines, China's muted reaction to the activities of European States in the South China Sea and its lack of protest to European navigation and the establishment of colonies in Southeast Asia, beginning in the 16th century.

197. Reviewing the published archival records of the Taiwan Authority of China,[180] which the Philippines considers to comprise documents selected to support China's claims, the Philippines emphasises the absence of "any documents evidencing any official Chinese activities in regard to any South China Sea feature prior to the beginning of the 20th century."[181] The Philippines also emphasises a Note Verbale from the Legation of the Chinese Republic in France to the French Ministry of Foreign Affairs in 1932, stating that the Paracel Islands "form the southernmost part of Chinese territory."[182] According to the Philippines, when China "sought to assert its claim to the South China Sea islands,"[183] following the defeat of Japanese forces in the Second World War, the plans included an effort to develop Chinese names for the features, the majority of which were then identified only by Chinese transliterations of their English names.[184] According to the Philippines "Lord Auckland Shoal was thus 'Ao ke lan sha', and Mischief Reef 'Mi-qi fu'. Gaven Reef was 'Ge wen', and Amy Douglas Reef 'A mi de ge la'."[185] Based on this record, the Philippines questions how China could have historic rights in an area "over which it had so little involvement or connection that most of the features had no Chinese names."[186]

---

[179] Merits Hearing Tr. (Day 1), p. 81.

[180] Ministry of Foreign Affairs Research & Planning Committee, Republic of China (ed.), *Archival Compilation on South China Sea Islands by Ministry of Foreign Affairs* (1995); Ministry of the Interior, Republic of China, *Compilation of Historical Archives on the Southern Territories of the Republic of China* (2015).

[181] Merits Hearing Tr. (Day 1), p. 89.

[182] Note Verbale from the Legation of the Republic of China in Paris to the Ministry of Foreign Affairs to France (29 September 1932), *reprinted in* Monique Chemillier-Gendreau, *Sovereignty over the Paracel and Spratly Islands* (2000).

[183] Merits Hearing Tr. (Day 1), p. 94.

[184] Merits Hearing Tr. (Day 1), pp. 94-96; *see also* Letter from the Ministry of Foreign Affairs, Republic of China, to the Ministry of the Interior, Republic of China (1 October 1946), *reprinted in* Republic of China Ministry of Foreign Affairs Research & Planning Committee, ed., *Archival Compilation on South China Sea Islands by Ministry of Foreign Affairs*, Vol. 2, Doc. No. III(1):008 (1995); Letter from the Ministry of the Interior, Republic of China, to the Ministry of Foreign Affairs, Republic of China (9 October 1946), *reprinted in* Republic of China Ministry of Foreign Affairs Research & Planning Committee, ed., *Archival Compilation on South China Sea Islands by Ministry of Foreign Affairs*, Vol. 2, Doc. No. III(1):009 (1995).

[185] Merits Hearing Tr. (Day 1), p. 96.

[186] Merits Hearing Tr. (Day 1), p. 96.

198. According to the Philippines, the absence of any Chinese historic rights in the South China Sea is also apparent in various historical documents obtained by the Tribunal from the *Bibliothèque Nationale de France* and the *Archives Nationales d'Outre-Mer* and provided to the Parties for comment. In the Philippines' view, these documents confirm that "prior to the Second World War France did not consider China to have made a claim in regard to any of the Spratlys, or to the waters of the South China Sea far removed from China's mainland coast."[187] Additionally, "the post-war documents—including France's internal records—make clear that France retained its claim to those features," a position the Philippines considers consistent with its view that the United Kingdom and United States "wished to protect France's sovereignty claim" in connection with the Cairo Declaration and Potsdam Proclamation.[188]

199. In any event, the Philippines argues that any Chinese historical claims to the features of the South China Sea did not, until 2009, "include a claim to the waters beyond their territorial seas."[189] The Philippines notes China's support of the three-mile territorial sea limit during the Second UN Conference on the Law of the Sea in 1960,[190] as well as the fact that China's *Declaration of the Government of the People's Republic of China on China's Territorial Sea* refers to the Spratly Islands as being "separated from the mainland and its coastal islands by the high seas," and not by any maritime area in which China had particular entitlements.[191] The Philippines argues that this has also been the understanding, until recently, of Chinese scholars working from the archives of the People's Republic of China.[192] Finally, when China did make clear in May 2009 that it claims historic rights in the maritime areas within the 'nine-dash line', the Philippines submits that this was promptly objected to by the other littoral States of the South China Sea.[193] As such, the Philippines submits that China has no historic rights within the 'nine-dash line'.

---

[187] Responses of the Philippines to the Tribunal's 26 May 2016 Request for Comments on Materials from the French Archives, para. 30 (3 June 2016) (hereinafter "**Written Responses of the Philippines on French Archive Materials (3 June 2016)**").

[188] Written Responses of the Philippines on French Archive Materials, para. 31 (3 June 2016).

[189] Merits Hearing Tr. (Day 2), p. 2.

[190] Merits Hearing Tr. (Day 2), p. 5.

[191] Merits Hearing Tr. (Day 2), p. 7.

[192] Merits Hearing Tr. (Day 2), pp. 8-9; Z. Gao, "The South China Sea: From Conflict to Cooperation?" *Ocean Development and International Law*, Vol. 25, No. 3, p. 346 (1994).

[193] Merits Hearing Tr. (Day 2), p. 11.

E.   CHINA'S POSITION

200.   China's various statements indicating that it claims historic rights in the South China Sea within the area of the 'nine-dash line' are set out above at paragraphs 180 to 187. On 12 May 2016, when the Director-General of the Department of Treaty and Law at the Chinese Ministry of Foreign Affairs was asked about the 'nine-dash line' in the context of the present arbitration, he responded with the following statement:

> The "nine-dash line" . . . is called by China the dotted line. I want to stress that China's sovereignty and relevant rights in the South China Sea were formed throughout the long course of history and have been maintained by the Chinese Government consistently.
>
> Early in 1948, the dotted line was mapped on China's official map. It was a confirmation of China's rights in the South China Sea formed throughout the history, instead of creation of new claims. For a long time, no State questioned the legitimacy of the dotted line and it also appeared on the official maps of many States.
>
> In recent years, some States started to attack on China's dotted line. The real motive is to intentionally confuse territorial disputes with disputes over maritime delimitation, deny China's sovereignty over the South China Sea Islands and their adjacent waters, and cover up their illegal invasion and occupation of part of the maritime features of China's Nansha Islands.
>
> In the Arbitration, the Philippines requested the Arbitral Tribunal to decide whether maritime entitlements claimed by China in the South China Sea exceeded the limits of the UNCLOS . . . . [T]o answer this question, we need to decide China's territorial sovereignty first. In accordance with international law, territorial sovereignty is the basis of maritime rights. Without first determining China's territorial sovereignty over the maritime f[ea]tures in the South China Sea, it would not be possible to determine maritime entitlements China may claim in it pursuant to the UNCLOS, let alone determine whether China's maritime claims in the South China Sea have exceeded the extent allowed under the UNCLOS.
>
> On the other hand, we have to note that the dotted line came into existence much earlier than the UNCLOS, which does not cover all aspects of the law of the sea. No matter from which lens we look at this, the Tribunal does not have jurisdiction over China's dotted line. As to negotiations, China has reiterated its hope that the relevant parties should resolve the disputes through consultation and negotiation based on historical facts and international law. The door of negotiation remains open.[194]

201.   China has not explained the nature of these claims in the course of these proceedings. The Tribunal will address the nature of China's claims to historic rights in the context of considering its jurisdiction with respect to the Philippines' Submissions No. 1 and 2.

---

[194]   Ministry of Foreign Affairs, People's Republic of China, *Briefing by Xu Hong, Director-General of the Department of Treaty and Law on the South China Sea Arbitration Initiated by the Philippines* (12 May 2016), *available at* <www.fmprc.gov.cn/mfa_eng/wjdt_665385/zyjh_665391/t1364804.shtml>.

F.   THE TRIBUNAL'S CONSIDERATIONS

1.   The Tribunal's Jurisdiction

202. Article 298 of the Convention provides in relevant part as follows:

> *Article 298*
> *Optional exceptions to applicability of section 2*
>
> 1.   When signing, ratifying or acceding to this Convention or at any time thereafter, a State may, without prejudice to the obligations arising under section 1, declare in writing that it does not accept any one or more of the procedures provided for in section 2 with respect to one or more of the following categories of disputes:
>
> (a)   (i)   disputes concerning the interpretation or application of articles 15, 74 and 83 relating to sea boundary delimitations, or those involving historic bays or titles . . . .

203. On 25 August 2006, China issued a declaration pursuant to Article 298, activating all of the optional exceptions to jurisdiction in the following terms: "[t]he Government of the People's Republic of China does not accept any of the procedures provided for in Section 2 of Part XV of the Convention with respect to all the categories of disputes referred to in paragraph 1 (a), (b) and (c) of Article 298 of the Convention."[195]

204. The Tribunal has already addressed the first exception to jurisdiction in Article 298(1)(a)(i) of the Convention, which applies to disputes concerning the interpretation or application of articles 15, 74, and 83 of the Convention relating to sea boundary delimitations, and found it inapplicable in the present case.[196] In brief, a dispute over the source and existence of maritime entitlements does not "concern" sea boundary delimitation merely because the existence of overlapping entitlements is a necessary condition for delimitation. While all sea boundary delimitations will concern entitlements, the converse is not the case: all disputes over entitlements do not concern delimitation. Where, as here, a party denies the existence of an entitlement, a possible outcome may well be the absence of any overlap and any possibility of delimitation. The exception in Article 298(1)(a)(i) of the Convention does not reach so far as to capture a dispute over the existence of entitlements that may—or may not—ultimately require delimitation.

205. What remains for the Tribunal in the present decision is the second exception to jurisdiction in Article 298(1)(a)(i) of the Convention, which applies to disputes involving historic bays or

---

[195]   *See* People's Republic of China, Declaration under Article 298 (25 August 2006), 2834 UNTS 327.
[196]   Award on Jurisdiction, paras. 155-157.

titles. The concept of a historic bay is well understood in international law[197] and, as a matter of plain geography, the South China Sea is not a bay.[198] The question is therefore whether China potentially claims historic title in the South China Sea and, if so, the implications for the Tribunal's jurisdiction.

206. Whether the Parties' dispute involves historic titles, therefore, depends first upon the nature of China's claims in the South China Sea and, second, on the scope of the exception. It is for China to determine the scope of its maritime claims. As far as the Tribunal is aware, however, the most insightful formulation by China of its claims in the South China Sea, beyond its claim to sovereignty over islands and their adjacent waters, is as a claim to "relevant rights in the South China Sea, formed in the long historical course."[199] In the absence of a more specific indication from China itself, it necessarily falls to the Tribunal to ascertain, on the basis of conduct, whether China's claim amounts to 'historic title'.

(a)   The Nature of China's Claimed Rights in the South China Sea

207. Since 1956, China has proclaimed a series of maritime zones—a territorial sea, a contiguous zone, a continental shelf, and an exclusive economic zone—that are, at least in general terms, in line with those anticipated by the Convention. Nevertheless, China's repeated invocation of rights "formed in the long historical course" and its linkage of this concept with the 'nine-dash line' indicates that China understands its rights to extend, in some form, beyond the maritime zones expressly described in the Convention. The Tribunal therefore turns to the rights that China has actually invoked in the South China Sea. Much of the area encompassed by the 'nine-dash line', however, would also fall within a claim to an exclusive economic zone or continental shelf drawn from the various features of the Spratly Islands. Whether or not the Tribunal would agree that the Convention or the features support such entitlements, a matter discussed in Chapter VI below, the mere fact that China asserts rights in the South China Sea does not indicate that China considers those rights to derive from the 'nine-dash line'. Where, however, China has asserted rights in areas beyond the maximum entitlements that could be claimed under the Convention, the Tribunal considers that such assertions indicate a claim to

---

[197]   *See generally* United Nations, *Historic Bays: Memorandum by the Secretariat of the United Nations*, UN Doc. A/CONF.13/1 (30 September 1957); United Nations, *Juridical Regime of Historic Waters, Including Historic Bays*, U.N. Doc A/CN.4/143 (9 March 1962).

[198]   See the definition of a bay in Article 10 of the Convention.

[199]   Ministry of Foreign Affairs, People's Republic of China, *Statement of the Ministry of Foreign Affairs of the People's Republic of China on the Award on Jurisdiction and Admissibility of the South China Sea Arbitration by the Arbitral Tribunal Established at the Request of the Republic of the Philippines* (30 October 2015) (Annex 649).

rights arising independently of the Convention. There are at least three instances when China appears to have asserted such rights.

208. In June 2012, the China National Offshore Oil Corporation ("**CNOOC**") issued a notice of open blocks for petroleum exploration adjacent to the western edge of the 'nine-dash line'.[200] The western portions of at least one of these blocks (Block BS16) lie beyond 200 nautical miles from any feature in the South China Sea claimed by China,[201] and beyond any possible extended continental shelf.[202] The map appended to the CNOOC tender is reproduced as Figure 3 on page 89. The Tribunal acknowledges that the affected area of the 'nine-dash line' is not of direct relevance to the Philippines' own maritime claims, but nevertheless notes that China's 2012 notice assists in understanding the nature of China's claims within the 'nine-dash line'. Thus, with respect to some areas of the blocks, even assuming the maximum possible claim to entitlements that China could make under the Convention, China's authority to issue the petroleum blocks in question cannot be based solely upon entitlements derived from the Convention.

209. China has also objected to the Philippines' award of petroleum blocks within the 'nine-dash line', an issue discussed in greater detail in connection with the Philippines' Submission No. 8. The area of the Philippines' petroleum blocks could be almost covered by entitlements claimed by China under the Convention, if China were understood to claim an exclusive economic zone from all high-tide features in the Spratly Islands, no matter how small, and from Scarborough Shoal. The fact of China's objection is thus not necessarily indicative of the source of China's claimed rights. When, however, China objected to the Philippines' Geophysical Survey and Exploration Contract 101 petroleum block ("**GSEC101**") (depicted in Map 4 on page 269), the Philippines recorded China's Chargé d'Affaires in Manila as stating that "[s]ince ancient times, China has indisputable sovereignty over the Nansha islands and its adjacent waters. The GSEC

---

[200] China National Offshore Oil Corporation, "Notification of Part of Open Blocks in Waters under Jurisdiction of the People's Republic of China Available for Foreign Cooperation in the Year of 2012" (23 June 2012) (Annex 121).

[201] This remains the case even if a full exclusive economic zone were ascribed to the single small rock above water at high tide at Fiery Cross Reef (discussed below at paragraphs 340 to 343 and 563 to 565).

[202] The Tribunal takes note of the Expert Report submitted by Dr. Lindsay Parson and his conclusion that, while China could potentially claim certain areas of continental shelf beyond 200 nautical miles, as a matter of geomorphology, the Spratly Islands would be unlikely to support a claim beyond 200 nautical miles and that the Paracel Islands would be unlikely to significantly extend China's maritime areas beyond a continental shelf that could be claimed from Hainan. Dr. Lindsay Parson, *The Potential for China to Develop a Viable Submission for Continental Shelf Area beyond 200 Nautical Miles in the South China Sea*, pp. 5-6, 9, 37-38 (March 2015) (Annex 514).

101 (SC 72) area is situated in the adjacent waters of the Nansha Islands (Spratlys)." [203] Similarly, when China objected to the Philippines' Service Contract 58 ("**SC58**") block, the Philippines recorded China's Deputy Chief of Mission in Manila as stating that "Service Contract 54, 14, 58, 63, and other nearby service contracts are located 'deep within China's 9-dash line.'"[204] Finally, China objected to the Philippines' Area 3 and Area 4 petroleum blocks by Note Verbale:

> On 30 June 2011 at the launching of Fourth Philippine Energy Contracting Round (PECR4), the Department of Energy of the Philippines offered 15 petroleum blocks to local and international companies for exploration and development. Among the aforesaid blocks, AREA 3 and AREA 4 are situated in the waters of which China has historic titles including sovereign rights and jurisdiction. [205]

Despite the possibility that China's claims were based on a theory of entitlement to continental shelf rights pursuant to the Convention, the framing of China's objections strongly indicates that China considers its rights with respect to petroleum resources to stem from historic rights.

210. A similar conclusion is suggested by China's declaration, in May 2012, of a "Summer Ban on Marine Fishing in the South China Sea Maritime Space," in order to "protect and rationally utilise South China Sea fishery resources."[206] The announcement described the ban and the area in which it would apply as follows:

> All productive activity types, except for using single-layer gill net and line-fishing equipment, shall be prohibited from 16 May 12:00 p.m. until 1 August 12:00 p.m. in the South China Sea areas from 12° north latitude up to the "Common Boundary Line of Fujian-Guangdong Sea Areas" (including the Gulf of Tonkin) under the jurisdiction of the People's Republic of China.[207]

211. This description is not entirely clear with respect to the source of China's claimed right to restrict fishing in the South China Sea areas. That is because first, it applies ultimately only to areas "under the jurisdiction of the People's Republic of China," although a description of the

---

[203] Memorandum from the Acting Assistant Secretary for Asian and Pacific Affairs, Department of Foreign Affairs, Republic of the Philippines, to the Secretary of Foreign Affairs (10 March 2011) (Annex 70).

[204] Memorandum from the Undersecretary for Special and Ocean Concerns, Department of Foreign Affairs, Republic of the Philippines, to the Secretary of Foreign Affairs of the Republic of the Philippines (30 July 2010) (Annex 63).

[205] Note Verbale from the Embassy of the People's Republic of China in Manila to the Department of Foreign Affairs, Republic of the Philippines, No. (11) PG-202 (6 July 2011) (Annex 202).

[206] Fishery Bureau of Nanhai District, Ministry of Agriculture, People's Republic of China, *Announcement on the 2012 Summer Ban on Marine Fishing in the South China Sea Maritime Space* (10 May 2012) (Annex 118).

[207] Fishery Bureau of Nanhai District, Ministry of Agriculture, People's Republic of China, *Announcement on the 2012 Summer Ban on Marine Fishing in the South China Sea Maritime Space* (10 May 2012) (Annex 118).

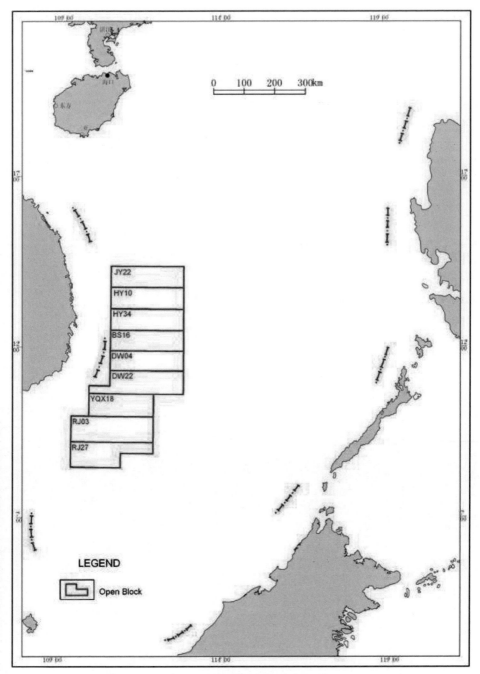

*Figure 3: Map enclosed with China National Offshore Oil Corporation Press Release
Notification of Part of Open Blocks in Waters under Jurisdiction of the People's Republic of China
Available for Foreign Cooperation in the Year of 2012 (23 June 2012) (Annex 121)*

this page intentionally blank

ban by Xinhua, the official press agency of China, noted that it applied "in most parts of the South China Sea . . . including Huangyan Island [Scarborough Shoal]."[208] Second, the area north of 12° north latitude could be almost entirely covered by entitlements claimed from the Convention, if China were understood to claim an exclusive economic zone from the very small rocks of Scarborough Shoal.[209] However, taken together with the conclusion above about the grant of petroleum blocks and China's frequent references to historic rights without further specification, the Tribunal concludes that China does claim rights to petroleum resources and fisheries within the 'nine-dash line' on the basis of historic rights existing independently of the Convention.

212. At the same time, China has unequivocally stated that it respects freedom of navigation and overflight in the South China Sea. On 27 October 2015, China's Vice Foreign Minister stated that "[t]he Chinese side respects and safeguards the freedom of navigation and over-flight in the South China Sea to which all countries are entitled under international law . . . . There has been and will be no obstruction to navigation and over-flight freedom in the South China Sea."[210] The same commitment has been repeated in numerous other statements by Chinese officials and spokespersons.

213. Within the territorial sea, the Convention does not provide for freedom of overflight or for freedom of navigation, beyond a right of innocent passage.[211] Accordingly, the Tribunal considers China's commitment to respect both freedom of navigation and overflight to establish that China does not consider the sea areas within the 'nine-dash line' to be equivalent to its territorial sea or internal waters. The Tribunal also notes that China declared baselines for the territorial sea surrounding Hainan and the Paracel Islands (see paragraph 176 above). In the view of the Tribunal, China would presumably not have done so if the waters both within and beyond 12 nautical miles of those islands already formed part of China's territorial sea (or internal waters) by virtue of a claim to historic rights through the 'nine-dash line'.

214. In sum, on the basis of China's conduct, the Tribunal understands that China claims rights to the living and non-living resources within the 'nine-dash line', but (apart from the territorial sea

---

[208] "Fishing Ban Starts in South China Sea," *Xinhua* (17 May 2012) (Annex 318).

[209] The Tribunal will discuss the entitlements of Scarborough Shoal in detail subsequently (see paragraphs 333 to 334 and 554 to 556 below).

[210] Ministry of Foreign Affairs, People's Republic of China, *Vice Foreign Minister Zhang Yesui Makes Stern Representations to US over US Naval Vessel's Entry into Waters near Relevant Islands and Reefs of China's Nansha Islands* (27 October 2015) (Annex 645).

[211] Convention, art. 17.

generated by any islands) does not consider that those waters form part of its territorial sea or internal waters. The Tribunal will now consider whether a dispute concerning such a claim falls within the exception to compulsory jurisdiction for "historic bays or titles" in Article 298(1)(a)(i) of the Convention.

(b)   The Scope of the Exception in Article 298(1)(a)(i) of the Convention

215.   In assessing the scope of the exception in Article 298(1)(a)(i), the Tribunal notes, as an initial matter, that it disagrees with the Philippines that the exception can be dispensed with on the grounds that, properly interpreted, the exception applies only to "delimitations . . . involving historic bays or titles."[212] The Tribunal considers this interpretation to be contrary to the natural reading of even the English text, but agrees that at least the English text of this Article is potentially ambiguous. The Convention is a multi-lingual instrument, however, and pursuant to Article 320 of the Convention, "the Arabic, Chinese, English, French, Russian and Spanish texts are equally authentic." No comparable ambiguity is to be found in the Chinese, French, Russian, or Spanish versions of the Convention, each of which is structured so as to make clear that the exception extends to "disputes . . . involving historic bays or titles," whether or not such disputes involve delimitation.

216.   Article 33 of the Vienna Convention on the Law of Treaties (the "**Vienna Convention on the Law of Treaties**" or the "**Vienna Convention**") addresses the interpretation of a treaty authenticated in multiple languages and provides that, unless otherwise indicated, "the text is equally authoritative in each language."[213] Article 33 of the Vienna Convention also provides that "when a comparison of the authentic texts discloses a difference of meaning which the application of articles 31 and 32 does not remove, the meaning which best reconciles the texts, having regard to the object and purpose of the treaty, shall be adopted."[214] In the present case, and noting that the Convention is silent on the resolution of differences between its different versions, the Tribunal considers that the broader exception in the non-English texts, for "disputes . . . involving historic bays or titles," best reconciles the different versions.

217.   Article 298(1)(a)(i) of the Convention provides for an exception for disputes involving 'historic titles'. While the ordinary meaning of this term already implies a notion of property, the

---

[212]   Hearing Tr. (Day 1), pp. 51-52.

[213]   Vienna Convention on the Law of Treaties, art. 33(1), 22 May 1969, 1155 UNTS 331 (hereinafter "**Vienna Convention on the Law of Treaties**"). Both the Philippines and China are parties to the Vienna Convention, the Philippines having ratified on 15 November 1972 and China having acceded on 3 September 1997.

[214]   Vienna Convention on the Law of Treaties, art. 33(4).

Tribunal considers that the meaning of the Convention's reference to 'historic titles' should be understood in the particular context of the evolution of the international law of the sea.

218. The genesis of the present Convention dates back at least to the League of Nations Codification Conference which met in The Hague in March and April 1930. The regime of the territorial sea was among the topics considered, and the Preparatory Committee of the Conference recommended that the Conference seek to identify the bays claimed as "historic bays".[215] No convention, however, resulted from the Conference.

219. Efforts at codification next moved to the International Law Commission, which submitted a set of draft articles to the General Assembly in 1956. Article 7 of these draft articles addressed the subject of bays and Article 7(4) provided that "[t]he foregoing provisions shall not apply to so-called 'historic' bays."[216] The commentaries to the draft articles also noted that the breadth of the territorial sea, which was not then agreed upon, could be determined up to 12 nautical miles on the basis of "historic rights".[217]

220. Prior to the First UN Conference on the Law of the Sea, the UN Secretariat prepared an influential memorandum on historic bays which noted as follows:

> the theory of historic bays is of general scope. Historic rights are claimed not only in respect of bays, but also in respect of maritime areas which do not constitute bays, such as the waters of archipelagos and the water area lying between an archipelago and the neighbouring mainland; historic rights are also claimed in respect of straits, estuaries and other similar bodies of water. There is a growing tendency to describe these areas as "historic waters", not as "historic bays".[218]

The report also recalled the observation of the International Court of Justice in *Anglo-Norwegian Fisheries* that "[b]y 'historic waters' are usually meant waters which are treated as internal waters but which would not have that character were it not for the existence

---

[215]   *See* United Nations, *Historic Bays: Memorandum by the Secretariat of the United Nations*, UN Doc. A/CONF.13/1 at paras. 207-208 (30 September 1957).

[216]   Report of the International Law Commission covering the Work of its Eighth Session, 23 April–4 July 1956, UN Doc. A/3159, *Official Records of the General Assembly, Eleventh Session, Supplement No. 9*, *Yearbook of the International Law Commission: 1956*, Vol. II, p. 253 at p. 257.

[217]   Report of the International Law Commission covering the Work of its Eighth Session, 23 April–4 July 1956, UN Doc. A/3159, *Official Records of the General Assembly, Eleventh Session, Supplement No. 9*, *Yearbook of the International Law Commission: 1956*, Vol. II, p. 253 at p. 266.

[218]   United Nations, *Historic Bays: Memorandum by the Secretariat of the United Nations*, UN Doc. A/CONF.13/1, para. 8 (30 September 1957).

of an historic title"[219] and discussed the formation of rights to a historic bay in terms of the formation of historic title.[220]

221. The first reference to historic title in the treaties preceding the present Convention appears in the 1958 Geneva Convention on the Territorial Sea and the Contiguous Zone, Article 12 of which addresses the delimitation of territorial sea, but provides that "[t]he provisions of this paragraph shall not apply, however, where it is necessary by reason of historic title or other special circumstances to delimit the territorial seas of the two States in a way which is at variance with this provision."[221] This provision was introduced by Norway, reflecting its recent experience before the International Court of Justice.[222] As used in Article 12 of the 1958 Convention, 'historic title' was clearly intended to have the same meaning as its usage in *Anglo-Norwegian Fisheries*, namely as an area of sea claimed exceptionally as internal waters (or, possibly, as territorial sea). At the close of the First Conference, a resolution was adopted on the initiative of India and Panama, requesting the General Assembly to "make appropriate arrangements for the study of the juridical regime of historic waters including historic bays, and for the result of these studies to be sent to all Member States of the United Nations."[223] The General Assembly referred the matter to the International Law Commission, which did not, however, take it up.

222. In 1962, following the Second UN Conference on the Law of the Sea, the UN Secretariat produced a memorandum on historic waters, which considered the term as equivalent to historic title. As with historic bays, the UN Secretariat noted that such historic waters "would be internal waters or territorial sea according to whether the sovereignty exercised over them in the course of the development of the historic title was sovereignty as over internal waters or

---

[219] *Anglo-Norwegian Fisheries (United Kingdom v. Norway), Judgment, ICJ Reports 1951*, p. 116 at p. 130.

[220] United Nations, *Historic Bays: Memorandum by the Secretariat of the United Nations*, UN Doc. A/CONF.13/1, paras. 137-198 (30 September 1957).

[221] Convention on the Territorial Sea and the Contiguous Zone, 29 April 1958, 516 UNTS 205 (hereinafter **"1958 Convention on the Territorial Sea and the Contiguous Zone"**).

[222] "Summary Records of the First Committee, 61st to 66th Meetings," UN Doc. A/CONF.13/C.1/SR.61-66 at pp. 190, 192, *Official Records of the United Nations Conference on the Law of The Sea, Volume III (First Committee (Territorial Sea and Contiguous Zone))* (1958); "Certain Legal Aspects Concerning the Delimitation of the Territorial Waters of Archipelagos," UN Doc. A/CONF.13/18, *Official Records of the United Nations Conference on the Law of the Sea, Volume I (Preparatory Documents)*, p. 289 at pp. 300-301 (1958).

[223] India and Panama, "Revised Draft Resolution," UN Doc. A/CONF.13/C.l/L.158/Rev.l (17 April 1958), *Official Records of the United Nations Conference on the Law of the Sea, Volume III (First Committee)*; "Summary Records of the 20th Plenary Meeting," UN Doc. A/CONF.13/38 at p. 68 (27 April 1958), *Official Records of the United Nations Conference on the Law of the Sea, Volume II (Plenary Meetings)*.

sovereignty as over the territorial sea."[224] The memorandum analyses the formation of historic title as a process of acquiring a historic right[225]—a term which is used generally—and concludes that:

> In determining whether or not a title to "historic waters" exists, there are three factors which have to be taken into consideration, namely,
>
> (i)   The authority exercised over the area by the State claiming it as "historic waters";
>
> (ii)   The continuity of such exercise of authority;
>
> (iii)   The attitude of foreign States.[226]

223. During the Third United Nations Conference on the Law of the Sea (the "**Third UN Conference**"), Article 12 of the 1958 Convention was adopted as Article 15 of the 1982 Convention, without significant discussion. The principal proponent of the concept of historic title in the course of the Conference was, in fact, the Philippines, which employed the term with respect to a claim (which it has since abandoned) to a territorial sea within the lines fixed by the Treaty of Paris of 1898 between Spain and the United States that governed the cession of the Philippines.[227]

224. In recent years, the International Court of Justice has twice had the occasion to distinguish between historic fishing rights and historic title that would bear on the entitlement to maritime zones. In *Qatar v. Bahrain*, the Court noted that historic pearl fishing "seems in any event never to have led to the recognition of an exclusive quasi-territorial right to the fishing grounds themselves or to the superjacent waters."[228] Similarly, in *Continental Shelf (Tunisia/Libyan Arab Jamahiriya)*, the Court distinguished the legal basis for historic Tunisian fishing rights—on which it ultimately refrained from ruling—from the regime of the continental shelf.[229]

---

[224]   United Nations, *Juridical Regime of Historic Waters, Including Historic Bays*, UN Doc. A/CN.4/143, para. 167 (9 March 1962).

[225]   United Nations, *Juridical Regime of Historic Waters, Including Historic Bays*, UN Doc. A/CN.4/143, paras. 80-148 (9 March 1962).

[226]   United Nations, *Juridical Regime of Historic Waters, Including Historic Bays*, UN Doc. A/CN.4/143, para. 185 (9 March 1962).

[227]   *See, e.g.*, "Summary Records of Meetings of the Second Committee, 5th Meeting," UN Doc. A/CONF.62/C.2/SR.5 at para. 30 (16 July 1974), *Official Records of the Third United Nations Conference on the Law of the Sea, Volume II (Summary Records of Meetings of the First, Second and Third Committees, Second Session)*.

[228]   *Maritime Delimitation and Territorial Questions between Qatar and Bahrain, Merits, Judgment, ICJ Reports 2001*, p. 40 at pp. 112-113, para. 236.

[229]   *Continental Shelf (Tunisia/Libyan Arab Jamahiriya), Judgment, ICJ Reports 1982*, p. 18 at pp. 73-74, para. 100.

225. The purpose of this extended recitation is to emphasise that there exists, within the context of the law of the sea, a cognizable usage among the various terms for rights deriving from historical processes. The term 'historic rights' is general in nature and can describe any rights that a State may possess that would not normally arise under the general rules of international law, absent particular historical circumstances. Historic rights may include sovereignty, but may equally include more limited rights, such as fishing rights or rights of access, that fall well short of a claim of sovereignty. 'Historic title', in contrast, is used specifically to refer to historic sovereignty to land or maritime areas. 'Historic waters' is simply a term for historic title over maritime areas, typically exercised either as a claim to internal waters or as a claim to the territorial sea, although "general international law . . . does not provide for a single 'régime' for 'historic waters' or 'historic bays', but only for a particular régime for each of the concrete, recognised cases of 'historic waters' or 'historic bays'."[230] Finally, a 'historic bay' is simply a bay in which a State claims historic waters.

226. The Tribunal is of the view that this usage was understood by the drafters of the Convention and that the reference to 'historic titles' in Article 298(1)(a)(i) of the Convention is accordingly a reference to claims of sovereignty over maritime areas derived from historical circumstances. This accords with the only other direct usage of the term, in Article 15 of the Convention, where historical sovereignty would understandably bear on the delimitation of the territorial sea. Other "historic rights", in contrast, are nowhere mentioned in the Convention, and the Tribunal sees nothing to suggest that Article 298(1)(a)(i) was intended to also exclude jurisdiction over a broad and unspecified category of possible claims to historic rights falling short of sovereignty.

227. The terminological distinction outlined above exists also in Chinese, and the Philippines has pressed on the Tribunal the fact that in its public statements, China has invoked its "historic rights" (li shi xing quan li, or 历史性权利) in the South China Sea, rather than historic title (li shi xing suo you quan, or 历史性所有权) as that term appears in the official Chinese text of the Convention.[231] For its part, the Tribunal notes that China's usage has not been entirely consistent, and that at least the English version of China's Note Verbale of 6 July 2011 (of which only the English version is in the record before the Tribunal) refers to "waters of which China has historic titles including sovereign rights and jurisdiction."[232] This instance is at odds with the vast majority of China's statements, however, and the Tribunal considers that it more

---

[230] *Continental Shelf (Tunisia/Libyan Arab Jamahiriya), Judgment, ICJ Reports 1982*, p. 18 at pp. 73-74, para. 100.

[231] Memorial, para. 4.28; Merits Hearing Tr. (Day 1), p. 34.

[232] Note Verbale from the Embassy of the People's Republic of China in Manila to the Department of Foreign Affairs, Republic of the Philippines, No. (11) PG-202 (6 July 2011) (Annex 202).

likely represents an error in translation or an instance of imprecise drafting, rather than a claim by China to sovereignty over the entirety of the South China Sea.

228. More importantly, however, the Tribunal does not see that the absence of a claim to historic title can be inferred from China's use of the broader and less-specific term, as historic title constitutes one form of historic right. For the Tribunal, the dispositive proof that China's claim is not one to historic title lies in China's conduct, which as discussed above (see paragraphs 207 to 214) is incompatible with a claim that the waters of the South China Sea constitute China's territorial sea or internal waters.

229. Having concluded that the exception to jurisdiction in Article 298(1)(a)(i) is limited to disputes involving historic titles and that China does not claim historic title to the waters of South China Sea, but rather a constellation of historic rights short of title, the Tribunal holds that it has jurisdiction to consider the Philippines' Submissions No. 1 and 2. As China has not made such a claim, the Tribunal need not consider whether there would be any limit to the application of Article 298 to expansive claims of historic title extending well beyond those that may have been anticipated when the Convention was concluded in 1982.

2. The Merits of the Philippines' Submissions No. 1 and 2

230. Having determined that it has jurisdiction to consider the Philippines' Submissions No. 1 and 2, the Tribunal now turns to the merits of those claims.

231. Building on prior international law and the 1958 Conventions on the Law of the Sea, the Convention establishes limits for maritime entitlements and sets out the rights and obligations of coastal States—as well as other States—within such maritime zones. Articles 2 through 32 of the Convention govern the rights and obligations of States within the territorial sea and limit the extent of the territorial sea to 12 nautical miles. Articles 55 through 75 of the Convention provide for the creation of an exclusive economic zone and limit its extent to 200 nautical miles. Articles 76 to 85 of the Convention govern the rights and obligations of States to the continental shelf, generally limit the continental shelf to 200 nautical miles, and set out technical criteria according to which some States may claim a continental shelf beyond 200 nautical miles. Articles 86 through 120 and 133 through 191 of the Convention govern the rights and obligations of States in the high seas and in the Area of seabed beyond the limits of national jurisdiction. The Convention thus provides—and defines limits within—a comprehensive system of maritime zones that is capable of encompassing any area of sea or seabed.

232. The Tribunal has already indicated that it understands, on the basis of China's actions, that China claims historic rights to the living and non-living resources in the waters of the South China Sea within the 'nine-dash line', but that China does not consider that those waters form part of its territorial sea or internal waters (other than the territorial sea generated by islands). Such a claim would not be incompatible with the Convention in any areas where China already possesses such rights through the operation of the Convention. This would, in particular, be the case within China's exclusive economic zone and continental shelf. However, to the extent that China's claim to historic rights extends to areas that would be considered to form part of the entitlement of the Philippines to an exclusive economic zone or continental shelf, it would be at least at variance with the Convention.

233. In its Submissions No. 1 and 2, the Philippines requests the Tribunal to declare that China's entitlements in the South China Sea are limited to those provided for in the Convention and that any claim to historic rights, or other sovereign rights and jurisdiction, within the area of the 'nine-dash line' in excess of that provided for in the Convention is prohibited.

234. China's claims to rights and jurisdiction within the 'nine-dash line' and the Philippines' Submissions on this dispute raise three issues that are related, but distinct:

    (a)   First, does the Convention, and in particular its rules for the exclusive economic zone and continental shelf, allow for the preservation of rights to living and non-living resources that are at variance with the provisions of the Convention and which may have been established prior to the Convention's entry into force by agreement or unilateral act?

    (b)   Second, prior to the entry into force of the Convention, did China have historic rights and jurisdiction over living and non-living resources in the waters of the South China Sea beyond the limits of the territorial sea?

    (c)   Third, and independently of the first two considerations, has China in the years since the conclusion of the Convention established rights and jurisdiction over living and non-living resources in the waters of the South China Sea that are at variance with the provisions of the Convention? If so, would such establishment of rights and jurisdiction be compatible with the Convention?

    (a)   The Convention and Prior Claims to Historic Rights and Jurisdiction

235. The Tribunal is faced with the question of whether the Convention allows the preservation of rights to resources which are at variance with the Convention and established anterior to its entry into force. To answer this, it is necessary to examine the relationship between the

Convention and other possible sources of rights under international law. The relationship between the Convention and other international agreements is set out in Article 311 of the Convention. The Tribunal considers that this provision applies equally to the interaction of the Convention with other norms of international law, such as historic rights, that do not take the form of an agreement. Article 311 provides as follows:

Article 311
Relation to other conventions and international agreements

1. This Convention shall prevail, as between States Parties, over the Geneva Conventions on the Law of the Sea of 29 April 1958.

2. This Convention shall not alter the rights and obligations of States Parties which arise from other agreements compatible with this Convention and which do not affect the enjoyment by other States Parties of their rights or the performance of their obligations under this Convention.

3. Two or more States Parties may conclude agreements modifying or suspending the operation of provisions of this Convention, applicable solely to the relations between them, provided that such agreements do not relate to a provision derogation from which is incompatible with the effective execution of the object and purpose of this Convention, and provided further that such agreements shall not affect the application of the basic principles embodied herein, and that the provisions of such agreements do not affect the enjoyment by other States Parties of their rights or the performance of their obligations under this Convention.

4. States Parties intending to conclude an agreement referred to in paragraph 3 shall notify the other States Parties through the depositary of this Convention of their intention to conclude the agreement and of the modification or suspension for which it provides.

5. This article does not affect international agreements expressly permitted or preserved by other articles of this Convention.

6. States Parties agree that there shall be no amendments to the basic principle relating to the common heritage of mankind set forth in article 136 and that they shall not be party to any agreement in derogation thereof.

236. The relationship between the Convention and other rules of international law is also made clear in Article 293(1) of the Convention, which applies to dispute resolution—including these proceedings—and provides that "[a] court or tribunal having jurisdiction under this section shall apply this Convention and other rules of international law not incompatible with this Convention."

237. These provisions mirror the general rules of international law concerning the interaction of different bodies of law, which provide that the intent of the parties to a convention will control its relationship with other instruments. This can be seen, in the case of conflicts between treaties, in Article 30 of the Vienna Convention on the Law of Treaties. Articles 30(2) and 30(3) of the Vienna Convention provide that, as between treaties, the later treaty will prevail to

the extent of any incompatibility, unless either treaty specifies that it is subject to the other, in which case the intent of the parties will prevail.

238. In the case of the Convention, the application of these rules leads to four propositions:

(a) Where the Convention expressly permits or preserves other international agreements, Article 311(5) provides that such agreements shall remain unaffected. The Tribunal considers that this provision applies equally where historic rights, which may not strictly take the form of an agreement, are expressly permitted or preserved, such as in Articles 10 and 15, which expressly refer to historic bays and historic titles.

(b) Where the Convention does not expressly permit or preserve a prior agreement, rule of customary international law, or historic right, such prior norms will not be incompatible with the Convention where their operation does not conflict with any provision of the Convention or to the extent that interpretation indicates that the Convention intended the prior agreements, rules, or rights to continue in operation.

(c) Where rights and obligations arising independently of the Convention are not incompatible with its provisions, Article 311(2) provides that their operation will remain unaltered.

(d) Where independent rights and obligations have arisen prior to the entry into force of the Convention and are incompatible with its provisions, the principles set out in Article 30(3) of the Vienna Convention and Article 293 of the Convention provide that the Convention will prevail over the earlier, incompatible rights or obligations.

239. No article of the Convention expressly provides for or permits the continued existence of historic rights to the living or non-living resources of the exclusive economic zone. Similarly, nothing in the Convention expressly provides for or permits a State to maintain historic rights over the living and non-living resources of the continental shelf, the high seas, or the Area. The question for the Tribunal is therefore whether the Convention nevertheless intended the continued operation of such historic rights, such that China's claims should be considered not incompatible with the Convention.

i.   The Text and Context of the Convention

240. Within the exclusive economic zone, Article 56(1) of the Convention provides for the sovereign rights and jurisdiction of the coastal State in the following terms:

Article 56
Rights, jurisdiction and duties of the coastal State in the exclusive economic zone

1. In the exclusive economic zone, the coastal State has:

    (a) sovereign rights for the purpose of exploring and exploiting, conserving and managing the natural resources, whether living or non-living, of the waters superjacent to the seabed and of the seabed and its subsoil, and with regard to other activities for the economic exploitation and exploration of the zone, such as the production of energy from the water, currents and winds;

    (b) jurisdiction as provided for in the relevant provisions of this Convention with regard to:

        (i) the establishment and use of artificial islands, installations and structures;

        (ii) marine scientific research;

        (iii) the protection and preservation of the marine environment;

    (c) other rights and duties provided for in this Convention.

241. The rights of other States in the exclusive economic zone are then set out in Article 58, which limits them to navigation, overflight, and the laying of submarine cables and pipelines, and other internationally lawful uses of the sea related to these freedoms. High seas rights and freedoms apply in the exclusive economic zone only to the extent they are not incompatible with the provisions of this part of the Convention. Article 58 of the Convention provides as follows:

Article 58
Rights and duties of other States in the exclusive economic zone

1. In the exclusive economic zone, all States, whether coastal or land-locked, enjoy, subject to the relevant provisions of this Convention, the freedoms referred to in article 87 of navigation and overflight and of the laying of submarine cables and pipelines, and other internationally lawful uses of the sea related to these freedoms, such as those associated with the operation of ships, aircraft and submarine cables and pipelines, and compatible with the other provisions of this Convention.

2. Articles 88 to 115 and other pertinent rules of international law apply to the exclusive economic zone in so far as they are not incompatible with this Part.

3. In exercising their rights and performing their duties under this Convention in the exclusive economic zone, States shall have due regard to the rights and duties of the coastal State and shall comply with the laws and regulations adopted by the coastal State in accordance with the provisions of this Convention and other rules of international law in so far as they are not incompatible with this Part.

242. Finally, the rights of other States "whose nationals have habitually fished in the zone" are specifically addressed in Article 62 of the Convention. Under this provision, coastal States are only obliged to permit fishing in the exclusive economic zone by foreign nationals in the event that the coastal State lacks the capacity to harvest the entire allowable catch. Even then, historic fishing in the area is only one of the criteria to be applied in allocating access, and foreign

fishing is subject to the laws and regulation of the coastal State. Article 62 of the Convention provides in relevant part as follows:

Article 62
Utilization of the living resources

1. The coastal State shall promote the objective of optimum utilization of the living resources in the exclusive economic zone without prejudice to article 61.

2. The coastal State shall determine its capacity to harvest the living resources of the exclusive economic zone. Where the coastal State does not have the capacity to harvest the entire allowable catch, it shall, through agreements or other arrangements and pursuant to the terms, conditions, laws and regulations referred to in paragraph 4, give other States access to the surplus of the allowable catch, having particular regard to the provisions of articles 69 and 70, especially in relation to the developing States mentioned therein.

3. In giving access to other States to its exclusive economic zone under this article, the coastal State shall take into account all relevant factors, including, inter alia, the significance of the living resources of the area to the economy of the coastal State concerned and its other national interests, the provisions of articles 69 and 70, the requirements of developing States in the subregion or region in harvesting part of the surplus and the need to minimize economic dislocation in States whose nationals have habitually fished in the zone or which have made substantial efforts in research and identification of stocks.

4. Nationals of other States fishing in the exclusive economic zone shall comply with the conservation measures and with the other terms and conditions established in the laws and regulations of the coastal State. These laws and regulations shall be consistent with this Convention and may relate, inter alia, to the following . . . .

243. As a matter of the text alone, the Tribunal considers that the Convention is clear in according sovereign rights to the living and non-living resources of the exclusive economic zone to the coastal State alone. The notion of *sovereign* rights over living and non-living resources is generally incompatible with another State having historic rights to the same resources, in particular if such historic rights are considered exclusive, as China's claim to historic rights appears to be. Furthermore, the Tribunal considers that, as a matter of ordinary interpretation, the (a) express inclusion of an article setting out the rights of other States and (b) attention given to the rights of other States in the allocation of any excess catch preclude the possibility that the Convention intended for other States to have rights in the exclusive economic zone in excess of those specified.

244. The same considerations apply with respect to the sovereign rights of the continental shelf, which are set out in Article 77 of the Convention. On the continental shelf, the rights of other States are limited to laying cables and pipelines and to the rights and freedoms to which they are otherwise entitled in the superjacent waters. Indeed, the provisions of the Convention concerning the continental shelf are even more explicit that rights to the living and non-living resources pertain to the coastal State *exclusively*. Article 77(2) expressly provides that "[t]he rights referred to in paragraph 1 [relating to natural resources] are exclusive in the sense that if

the coastal State does not explore the continental shelf or exploit its natural resources, no one may undertake these activities without the express consent of the coastal State." Article 81 similarly states that "[t]he coastal State shall have the exclusive right to authorize and regulate drilling on the continental shelf for all purposes."

245. Moving from the text to the context of exclusive economic zone rights, the Tribunal recalls its earlier observation (see paragraph 231 above) that the system of maritime zones created by the Convention was intended to be comprehensive and to cover any area of sea or seabed. The same intention for the Convention to provide a complete basis for the rights and duties of the States Parties is apparent in the Preamble, which notes the intention to settle "all issues relating to the law of the sea" and emphasises the desirability of establishing "a legal order for the seas." The same objective of limiting exceptions to the Convention to the greatest extent possible is also evident in Article 309, which provides that "[n]o reservations or exceptions may be made to this Convention unless expressly permitted by other articles of this Convention."

246. China has stated its view that its "relevant rights in the South China Sea, formed in the long historical course" are "protected under international law including the United Nations Convention on the Law of the Sea (UNCLOS)."[233] Insofar as China's relevant rights comprise a claim to historic rights to living and non-living resources within the 'nine-dash line', partially in areas that would otherwise comprise the exclusive economic zone or continental shelf of the Philippines, the Tribunal cannot agree with this position. The Convention does not include any express provisions preserving or protecting historic rights that are at variance with the Convention. On the contrary, the Convention supersedes earlier rights and agreements to the extent of any incompatibility. The Convention is comprehensive in setting out the nature of the exclusive economic zone and continental shelf and the rights of other States within those zones. China's claim to historic rights is not compatible with these provisions.

247. The Tribunal considers the text and context of the Convention to be clear in superseding any historic rights that a State may once have had in the areas that now form part of the exclusive economic zone and continental shelf of another State. There is no ambiguity here that would call for the Tribunal to have recourse to the supplementary means of interpretation set out in Article 32 of the Vienna Convention. Nevertheless, in light of the sensitivity of the matters at issue in these proceedings, the Tribunal considers it warranted to recall the origin of and purpose behind the Convention's provisions on the exclusive economic zone and continental shelf.

---

[233] Ministry of Foreign Affairs, People's Republic of China, *Statement of the Ministry of Foreign Affairs of the People's Republic of China on the Award on Jurisdiction and Admissibility of the South China Sea Arbitration by the Arbitral Tribunal Established at the Request of the Republic of the Philippines* (30 October 2015) (Annex 649).

>   *ii.   The Negotiation of the Convention and the Creation of the Exclusive
>   Economic Zone*

248. The Tribunal recalls that prior to the adoption of the Convention, the principal failure of the
     First and Second UN Conferences on the Law of the Sea was the lack of agreement on the
     breadth of the territorial sea and the extent of coastal States' jurisdiction over the resources, then
     principally involving fisheries, of the waters adjacent to their coasts. This period coincided with
     the widespread decolonisation of developing States, and many newly independent governments
     sought to secure greater control over the waters adjacent to their coasts. The lack of agreement
     on an international standard and the growing capabilities of the long-distance fishing fleets of
     developed States led to the widespread unilateral declaration of exclusive fishing zones of
     varying breadths and to the declaration, by some States, of a 200-nautical-mile territorial sea.
     Such claims to zones, including the Icelandic exclusive fishing zones considered by the
     International Court of Justice in the *Fisheries Jurisdiction* cases,[234] were generally opposed by
     the traditional maritime States, which sought to limit the scope of national jurisdiction.

249. The creation of the *Ad Hoc* and Permanent Seabed Committees that preceded the Third UN
     Conference on the Law of the Sea was prompted by concern with this unregulated propagation
     of claims to maritime rights and jurisdiction and with the prospect that technological
     developments would rapidly enable the greater exploitation of the resources of the seabed,
     which would fall to those States most capable of claiming them.[235] Latin American and African
     States organised around an assertion of greater control over coastal resources[236] and draft
     articles on the concept of an exclusive economic zone were introduced by Kenya during the
     1972 session of the Seabed Committee.[237] In this form, the exclusive economic zone was a
     compromise proposal: a standardised form of coastal State jurisdiction—exclusive if the coastal
     State so desired—over living and non-living resources that nevertheless stopped short of
     extending the territorial sea beyond 12 nautical miles.

---

[234]   *Fisheries Jurisdiction (United Kingdom v. Iceland), Merits, Judgment, ICJ Reports 1974*, p. 3; *Fisheries
        Jurisdiction (Federal Republic of Germany v. Iceland), Merits, Judgment, ICJ Reports 1974*, p. 175.

[235]   *See, e.g.*, Remarks of the Ambassador of Malta, First Committee, 1515th Meeting,
        UN Doc. A/C.1/PV.1515 (1 November 1967), *Official Records of the UN General Assembly,
        22nd Session.*

[236]   *See, e.g.*, "Conclusions in the General Report of the African States Regional Seminar on the Law of the
        Sea, Held at Yaoundé from 20-30 June 1972," *United Nations Legislative Series, National Legislation
        and Treaties relating to the Law of the Sea*, ST/LEG/SER.B/16, p. 601; "Specialized Conference of
        Caribbean Countries concerning the Problems of the Sea: The Declaration of Santo Domingo"
        (Colombia, Costa Rica, Dominican Republic, Guatemala, Haiti, Honduras, Mexico, Nicaragua, Trinidad
        and Tobago, and Venezuela) (9 June 1972), *reproduced in* 11 ILM 892.

[237]   Report of the Committee on the Peaceful Uses of the Sea-Bed and the Ocean Floor Beyond the Limits of
        National Jurisdiction, UN Doc. A/8721 (1972) at p. 180-182, *Official Records of the UN General
        Assembly, 27th Session, Supplement No. 21.*

250. The Tribunal recalls this history because it frames the debates that took place during the negotiation of the Convention. Japan and the Soviet Union possessed the largest distant sea fishing fleets and sought to preserve the *status quo*, advancing proposals that would have provided only for "preferential rights" for coastal States, while protecting the position of traditional fishing States. As summarised by Japan:

> While according a preferential right of catch to developing coastal States corresponding to their harvesting capacities and a differentiated preferential right to developed coastal States, the proposals also take into consideration the legitimate interests of other States. Thus, they seek to ensure that a gradual accommodation of interests can be brought about in the expanding exploitation and use of fishery resources of the high seas, without causing any abrupt change in the present order in fishing which might result in disturbing the economic and social structures of States.[238]

The Soviet Union, for its part, sought to limit the rights of coastal States to fisheries beyond 12 nautical miles to a preferential right to reserve "such part of the allowable catch of fish as can be taken by vessels navigating under that State's flag."[239] These proposals were ultimately rejected and are not reflected in the text of the Convention, as adopted.

251. In the course of these debates, China actively positioned itself as one of the foremost defenders of the rights of developing States and was resolutely opposed to any suggestion that coastal States could be obliged to share the resources of the exclusive economic zone with other powers that had historically fished in those waters. The Tribunal considers the remarks of Mr. Ling Ching on behalf of China during the 24th meeting of the Second Committee to be representative of the committed position that China repeatedly took during the negotiation of the Convention:

> On the question whether the coastal State should exercise full sovereignty over the renewable and non-renewable resources in its economic zone or merely have preferential rights to them, [Mr. Ling] said that such resources in the off-shore sea areas of a coastal State were an integral part of its natural resources. The super-Powers had for years wantonly plundered the offshore resources of developing coastal States, thereby seriously damaging their interests. Declaration of permanent sovereignty over such resources was a legitimate right, which should be respected by other countries. The super-Powers, however, while giving verbal recognition to the economic zone, were advocating the placing of restrictions on the sovereignty of coastal States over their resources. For example, one of them had proposed that the coastal State should allow foreign fishermen the right to fish within that zone in cases where the State did not harvest 100 per cent of the allowable catch. Such logic made no sense. The suggestion in fact harked back to that super-Power's well-known proposal that coastal States should be allowed only "preferential rights" when fishing their own off-shore areas. Yet, the establishment of exclusive

---

[238] Japan, "Proposals for a Régime of Fisheries on the High Seas," UN Doc. A/AC.138/SC.II/L.12 (1972), *reproduced in* Report of the Committee on the Peaceful Uses of the Sea-Bed and the Ocean Floor Beyond the Limits of National Jurisdiction, UN Doc. A/8721 at p. 188, *Official Records of the UN General Assembly, 27th Session, Supplement No. 21.*

[239] Union of Soviet Socialist Republics, "Draft Article on Fishing (Basic Provisions and Explanatory Note)," UN Doc. A/AC.138/SC.II/L.6 (1972) *reproduced in* Report of the Committee on the Peaceful Uses of the Sea-Bed and the Ocean Floor Beyond the Limits of National Jurisdiction, UN Doc. A/8721 at p. 158, *Official Records of the UN General Assembly, 27th Session, Supplement No. 21.*

economic zones over the resources of which coastal States would exercise permanent sovereignty simply meant that the developing countries were regaining their long-lost rights and in no way implied a sacrifice on the part of the super-Powers. The coastal State should be permitted to decide whether foreign fishermen were allowed to fish in the areas under its jurisdiction by virtue of bilateral or regional agreements, but it should not be obliged to grant other States any such rights.[240]

252. The Tribunal notes these comments not because the remarks of any particular State during the negotiation of a multilateral Convention are indicative of the content of the final treaty, but because China's resolute opposition to any accommodation of historic fishing is largely representative of the position that prevailed in the final text of the Convention. The Tribunal also notes that China's position, as asserted during the negotiation of the Convention, is incompatible with a claim that China would be entitled to historic rights to living and non-living resources in the South China Sea that would take precedence over the exclusive economic zone rights of the other littoral States. China never advanced such a claim during the course of the negotiations, notwithstanding that the South China Sea and the question of sovereignty over the Spratly Islands was raised on several occasions in exchanges between China and the Philippines during the work of the Seabed Committee[241] and between China and Viet Nam during the Third UN Conference.[242]

---

[240] "Summary Records of Meetings of the Second Committee, 24th Meeting," UN Doc. A/CONF.62/C.2/SR.24 at para. 2 (1 August 1974), *Official Records of the Third United Nations Conference on the Law of the Sea, Volume II (Summary Records of Meetings of the First, Second and Third Committees, Second Session)*, p. 187; *see also* "Summary Records of Meetings of the Second Committee, 26th Meeting," UN Doc. A/CONF.62/C.2/SR.26 at para. 108 (5 August 1974), *Official Records of the Third United Nations Conference on the Law of the Sea, Volume II (Summary Records of Meetings of the First, Second and Third Committees, Second Session)*, p. 210; "Summary Records of Meetings of the Second Committee, 30th Meeting," UN Doc. A/CONF.62/C.2/SR.30 at para. 22 (7 August 1974), *Official Records of the Third United Nations Conference on the Law of the Sea, Volume II (Summary Records of Meetings of the First, Second and Third Committees, Second Session)*, p. 228; "Summary Records of the Meetings of the Second Committee, 48th Meeting," UN Doc. A/CONF.62/C.2/SR.48 at para. 29 (2 May 1975), *Official Records of the Third United Nations Conference on the Law of the Sea, Volume IV (Summary Records, Plenary, General Committee, First, Second and Third Committees, as well as Documents of the Conference, Third Session)*, p. 77.

[241] Committee on the Peaceful Uses of the Sea-Bed and the Ocean Floor Beyond the Limits of National Jurisdiction, "Summary Records of the 72nd Meeting," UN Doc. A/AC.138/SR.72 at pp. 13-18, 20 (3 March 1972); Committee on the Peaceful Uses of the Sea-Bed and the Ocean Floor Beyond the Limits of National Jurisdiction, "Summary Records of the 73rd Meeting," UN Doc. A/AC.138/SR.73 at pp. 33-35 (10 March 1972).

[242] "Summary Records of Plenary Meetings, 25th Plenary Meeting," UN Doc. A/CONF.62/SR.25 at para. 21 (5 August 1974), *Official Records of the Third United Nations Conference on the Law of the Sea, Volume I (Summary Records of Plenary Meetings of the First and Second Sessions, and of Meetings of the General Committee, Second Session)*, p. 81; "Summary Records of Plenary Meetings, 191st Plenary Meeting," UN Doc. A/CONF.62/SR.191 at para. 36 (9 December 1982), *Official Records of the Third United Nations Conference on the Law of the Sea, Volume XVII (Plenary Meetings, Summary Records and Verbatim Records, as well as Documents of the Conference, Resumed Eleventh Session and Final Part Eleventh Session and Conclusion)*, p. 103; "Note by the Secretariat," UN Doc. A/CONF.62/WS/37 and Add.1-2 (1983), *Official Records of the Third United Nations Conference on the Law of the Sea, Volume XVII (Plenary Meetings, Summary Records and Verbatim Records, as well as Documents of the Conference, Resumed Eleventh Session and Final Part Eleventh Session and Conclusion)*, p. 240.

253. The Tribunal also considers the negotiating history of the Convention instructive for the light it sheds on the intent for the Convention to serve as a comprehensive text and the importance to that goal of the prohibition on reservations enshrined in Article 309. The Convention was negotiated on the basis of consensus and the final text represented a package deal. A prohibition on reservations was seen as essential to prevent States from clawing back through reservations those portions of the final compromise that they had opposed in negotiations. In this respect the Convention follows the practice of other multilateral treaties considered to be of fundamental importance, including the UN Charter, the Rome Statute of the International Criminal Court, and the UN Framework Convention on Climate Change. The importance of a comprehensive agreement, without reservations, is well expressed in the Conference President's remarks to the Informal Plenary and Group of Legal Experts tasked with preparing the final clauses:

> Our prime concern is the establishment of a completely integrated legal order for the use of the oceans and its resources and potential. All else must be subordinated to and subserve this purpose. This is the function of the Preamble and the Final Clauses. They must not be allowed to create such contention as would obscure and obstruct the overriding objective, hamper the work of the Conference and imperil our chances of success.

> We must seek to preserve intact, and protect, the efficacy and durability of the body of law which we are trying to create in the form of a Convention encompassing all issues and problems relating to the law of the sea as a package comprising certain elements that constitute a single and indivisible entity.

> We must seek to attract the most extensive and representative degree of ratification and the earliest possible entry into force of the new Convention.

> The second objective that I have specified here cannot be achieved if we expose the essential unity and coherence of the new body of law to the danger of impairment through the unrestricted exercise of the right of reservation.[243]

254. On this issue, the Tribunal notes that China and other States were opposed to a complete ban on reservations[244] and that the final approach in the Convention represents a compromise: certain permissible reservations are set out in the text of the Convention while any other reservation is prohibited. Thus China was entitled to, and did, activate the reservations to compulsory dispute settlement in Article 298—that the Tribunal has already determined do not apply to the present dispute—but is not entitled to except itself from the system of compulsory settlement

---

[243] "Note by the President on the Final Clauses," UN Doc. FC/1 (23 July 1979), *reproduced in* Renate Platzöder (ed.), *Third United Nations Conference on the Law of the Sea: Documents, Vol. XII*, p. 349 (1987).

[244] *See* "Summary Records of Plenary Meetings, 135th Plenary Meeting," UN Doc. A/CONF.62/SR.135, paras. 52-53 (25 August 1980), *Official Records of the Third United Nations Conference on the Law of the Sea, Volume XIV (Summary Records, Plenary, General Committee, First and Third Committees, as well as Documents of the Conference, Resumed Ninth Session)*, pp. 23-24; "Summary Records of Plenary Meetings, 161st Plenary Meeting," UN Doc. A/CONF.62/SR.161 at para. 30 (31 March 1982), *Official Records of the Third United Nations Conference on the Law of the Sea, Volume XVI (Summary Records, Plenary, First and Second Committees, as well as Documents of the Conference, Eleventh Session)*, p. 32.

generally.[245] In the Tribunal's view, the prohibition on reservations is informative of the Convention's approach to historic rights. It is simply inconceivable that the drafters of the Convention could have gone to such lengths to forge a consensus text and to prohibit any but a few express reservations while, at the same time, anticipating that the resulting Convention would be subordinate to broad claims of historic rights.

> iii. *Rights in the Exclusive Economic Zone in other Disputes concerning the Law of the Sea*

255. The present dispute is not the first instance in which a State has claimed rights in or to the exclusive economic zone of a neighbouring State. The Tribunal considers it useful, for the purpose of confirming its own reasoning, to briefly canvas the other decisions to have addressed claims involving rights in the exclusive economic zone of another State.

256. In the Tribunal's view, the most relevant instance occurs in the consideration given to historic fishing activities in the delimitation of the *Gulf of Maine* between the United States and Canada by a chamber of the International Court of Justice. The area to be delimited included the Georges Bank, with its abundant fisheries resources, and the United States argued that the delimitation line should take account of the longstanding use of the bank by U.S. fishermen. The Chamber not only rejected this argument for the purposes of the delimitation, but went on to comment on the nature of U.S. fishing rights and the effect on U.S. fishing activities of the adoption by the United States and Canada of exclusive fisheries zones, the case having been instituted prior to the declaration of a full exclusive economic zone by the United States but at a time when States had already begun to declare such zones unilaterally in reflection of the emerging consensus at the Third UN Conference. In this context, the Chamber in *Gulf of Maine* commented as follows:

> The Chamber cannot adopt these positions of the Parties. Concerning that of the United States, it can only confirm its decision not to ascribe any decisive weight, for the purposes of the delimitation it is charged to carry out, to the antiquity or continuity of fishing activities carried on in the past within that part of the delimitation area which lies outside the closing line of the Gulf. Until very recently, as the Chamber has recalled, these expanses were part of the high seas and as such freely open to the fishermen not only of the United States and Canada but also of other countries, and they were indeed fished by very many nationals of the latter. The Chamber of course readily allows that, during that period of free competition, the United States, as the coastal State, may have been able at certain places and times—no matter for how long—to achieve an actual predominance for its fisheries. But after the coastal States had set up exclusive 200-mile fishery zones, the situation radically altered. Third States and their nationals found themselves deprived of any right of access to the sea areas within those zones and of any position of advantage they might have been able to achieve within them. As for the United States, any mere factual predominance which it had been able to secure in the area was transformed into a situation

---

[245] *See* Award on Jurisdiction, para. 107.

of legal monopoly to the extent that the localities in question became legally part of its own exclusive fishery zone. Conversely, to the extent that they had become part of the exclusive fishery zone of the neighbouring State, no reliance could any longer be placed on that predominance. Clearly, whatever preferential situation the United States may previously have enjoyed, this cannot constitute in itself a valid ground for its now claiming the incorporation into its own exclusive fishery zone of any area which, in law, has become part of Canada's.[246]

257. The present case does not, of course, involve delimitation, but the Tribunal considers the Chamber's views on the effect of exclusive fisheries zones, declared as a matter of customary law, to confirm its own interpretation of the provisions of the Convention. The Tribunal has no doubt that Chinese fisherman have long made use of the waters of the South China Sea, including in areas beyond the territorial sea of any feature. If China had historic rights giving it a privileged position with respect to the resources of such waters, the acceptance of the exclusive economic zone as a matter of customary law and China's adherence to the Convention altered that situation. Through the Convention, China gained additional rights in the areas adjacent to its coasts that became part of its exclusive economic zone, including the areas adjacent to any island entitled to such a zone. It necessarily follows, however, that China also relinquished the rights it may have held in the waters allocated by the Convention to the exclusive economic zones of other States.

258. A contrary indication could be ascribed to the decision of the International Court of Justice in the *Fisheries Jurisdiction Cases*.[247] In those disputes, which concerned Iceland's declaration of a 50-nautical-mile exclusive fishing zone, the Court held that the preferential rights asserted by Iceland's fishing zone were not compatible with the exclusion of all fishing by other States and that Iceland could not extinguish the rights of other States to have habitually fished in the area.[248] In the Tribunal's view, however, this decision from 1974 must be understood in the context of the law of the sea as it then was, which differs from the law prevailing under the Convention or in the emergent customary law of the exclusive economic zone in effect at the time of *Gulf of Maine*. As an initial matter, the Tribunal notes that the applicants in *Fisheries Jurisdiction*, the United Kingdom and the Federal Republic of Germany, never asserted that their historical fishing superseded Iceland's declaration of a fisheries zone, but merely claimed a right of access. This thus differs fundamentally from the present proceedings, where the Tribunal understands China to consider that its claimed historic rights to living and non-living

---

[246] *Delimitation of the Maritime Boundary in the Gulf of Maine Area (Canada v. United States), Judgment, ICJ Reports 1984*, p. 246 at pp. 341-342, para. 235.

[247] *Fisheries Jurisdiction (United Kingdom v. Iceland), Merits, Judgment, ICJ Reports 1974*, p. 3; *Fisheries Jurisdiction (Federal Republic of Germany v. Iceland), Merits, Judgment, ICJ Reports 1974*, p. 175.

[248] *Fisheries Jurisdiction (United Kingdom v. Iceland), Merits, Judgment, ICJ Reports 1974*, p. 3 at pp 27-28, para. 62; *Fisheries Jurisdiction (Federal Republic of Germany v. Iceland), Merits, Judgment, ICJ Reports 1974*, p. 175 at pp. 196-197, para. 54.

resources effectively negate the exclusive economic zone rights of other littoral States to the South China Sea. Notwithstanding this difference, the Tribunal also considers the reasoning exhibited in *Fisheries Jurisdiction* to be inapplicable under the present law of the sea. At the time Iceland declared its 50-nautical-mile zone in July 1972, the extension of national jurisdiction over maritime areas beyond the territorial sea was still a hotly contested issue. As the Court read the state of customary law then prevailing, it permitted an exclusive fishing zone of only 12 nautical miles and preferential rights in an undefined area beyond that limit.[249] Only a few short years later, however, the processes at work in the Third UN Conference (described above at paragraph 249 to 252) crystallised into the consensus in favour of the exclusive economic zone. The law applied in *Gulf of Maine* and recorded in the Convention thus differed materially from that considered by the Court in *Fisheries Jurisdiction*.

259. A contrary approach to *Gulf of Maine* might also be identified in the *Eritrea v. Yemen* arbitration, in which the arbitral tribunal emphasised the importance of preserving traditional fishing practices in the Red Sea which had been carried on for centuries, without regard for the specifics of maritime boundaries. The arbitral tribunal also held that "[t]he traditional fishing regime is not limited to the territorial waters of specified islands" but extended also through the exclusive economic zone of Eritrea and Yemen.[250] The Philippines distinguishes this decision[251]—correctly in the Tribunal's view—on the basis of applicable law. *Eritrea v. Yemen* was not an arbitration under Annex VII to the Convention and that arbitral tribunal was not bound by Article 293 to apply only the Convention and rules of law not incompatible therewith. Instead, the Parties' arbitration agreement empowered the arbitral tribunal, in the second stage of the proceedings to render its decision "taking into account the opinion that it will have formed on questions of territorial sovereignty, the United Nations Convention on the Law of the Sea, and any other pertinent factor."[252] The arbitral tribunal in *Eritrea v. Yemen* was thus empowered to—and in the Tribunal's view did—go beyond the law on traditional fishing as it would exist under the Convention. The Tribunal will address below the scope of traditional fishing rights under the current law of the sea in connection with the Philippines' Submission No. 10.

---

[249] *Fisheries Jurisdiction (United Kingdom v. Iceland), Merits, Judgment, ICJ Reports 1974*, p. 3 at p. 23, para. 52; *Fisheries Jurisdiction (Federal Republic of Germany v. Iceland), Merits, Judgment, ICJ Reports 1974*, p. 175 at pp. 191-192, para. 44.

[250] *Eritrea v. Yemen*, Award of 17 December 1999, RIAA Vol. XXII, p. 335 at p. 361, para. 109.

[251] Memorial, paras. 4.65-4.69.

[252] *Eritrea v. Yemen*, Award of 17 December 1999, Annex I – The Arbitration Agreement, art. 2(3), RIAA Vol. XXII, p. 335 at p. 374.

260. Finally, the Tribunal notes that the arbitral tribunal in the *Chagos Marine Protected Area Arbitration* held that Mauritius had rights in the exclusive economic zone declared by the United Kingdom surrounding the British Indian Ocean Territory. These were not fishing rights, in light of the Convention's prohibition in Article 297 on compulsory settlement regarding disputes over sovereign rights with respect to the living resources in the exclusive economic zone, but rather a right to the eventual return of the Chagos Archipelago when no longer needed for defence purposes and a right to the benefit of any oil or minerals discovered in or near the Chagos Archipelago. These rights had their origins in assurances given in 1968 in connection with the detachment of the Chagos Archipelago from the then-colony of Mauritius that were repeated by the United Kingdom thereafter. In that case, however, not only did the United Kingdom not argue that Mauritius's rights were extinguished by the United Kingdom's declaration of an Environmental Protection and Preservation Zone/Fisheries Conservation and Management Zone, but it reiterated its undertakings thereafter[253] and emphasised that the zone it had created was not an exclusive economic zone for purposes beyond fisheries and environmental protection.[254] Article 311 permits States to agree to modify certain aspects of the Convention as between them (an issue the Tribunal will return to below) and the Tribunal considers the United Kingdom's reiteration of its undertakings following the adoption of the Convention to fall within the ambit of that provision.

*

261. For all of the reasons discussed above, the Tribunal concludes that China's claim to historic rights to the living and non-living resources within the 'nine-dash line' is incompatible with the Convention to the extent that it exceeds the limits of China's maritime zones as provided for by the Convention. This is apparent in the text of the Convention which comprehensively addresses the rights of other States within the areas of the exclusive economic zone and continental shelf and leaves no space for an assertion of historic rights. It is also reinforced by the negotiating record of the Convention where the importance of adopting a comprehensive instrument was manifest and where the cause of securing the rights of developing States over their exclusive economic zone and continental shelf was championed, in particular, by China.

262. Accordingly, upon China's accession to the Convention and its entry into force, any historic rights that China may have had to the living and non-living resources within the 'nine-dash line' were superseded, as a matter of law and as between the Philippines and China, by the limits of the maritime zones provided for by the Convention. This should not be considered exceptional

---

[253] *Chagos Marine Protected Area* (*Mauritius v. United Kingdom*), Award of 18 March 2015, para. 430.

[254] *Chagos Marine Protected Area* (*Mauritius v. United Kingdom*), Award of 18 March 2015, para. 124.

or unexpected. The Convention was a package that did not, and could not, fully reflect any State's prior understanding of its maritime rights. Accession to the Convention reflects a commitment to bring incompatible claims into alignment with its provisions, and its continued operation necessarily calls for compromise by those States with prior claims in excess of the Convention's limits.

(b)   China's Claim to Historic Rights in the South China Sea

263.   The Tribunal has held, in the preceding Section, that the entry into force of the Convention had the effect of superseding any claim by China to historic rights to the living and non-living resources within the 'nine-dash line' beyond the limits of China's maritime zones as provided for by the Convention. This conclusion would, in one sense, suffice to decide the dispute presented by the Philippines' Submissions No. 1 and 2. The Tribunal nevertheless considers it important, for the sake of completeness, to distinguish among China's claims to historic rights and to separate those that are, in fact, in excess of and incompatible with the Convention, from those that are not. The Tribunal considers that, in ratifying the Convention, China has, in fact, relinquished far less in terms of its claim to historic rights than the foregoing conclusion might initially suggest. The Tribunal also considers that this is an area where communications between the Parties have been characterised by a high degree of confusion and misunderstanding.

264.   In its public statements, diplomatic correspondence, and in its public Position Paper of 7 December 2014, China has repeatedly asserted its sovereignty over the Spratly Islands and Scarborough Shoal.[255] According to China, its nationals have historically engaged in navigation and trade in the South China Sea and the activities of Chinese fishermen in residing, working, and living among the Spratly Islands "are all manifestly recorded in Geng Lu Bu (Manual of Sea Routes) which was passed down from generation to generation among Chinese fishermen."[256] There is, indeed, much interesting evidence—from all sides—that could be considered by a tribunal empowered to address the question of sovereignty over the Spratly Islands and Scarborough Shoal. This Tribunal, however, is not empowered to address that question. For its part, the Philippines has likewise argued about the historical limits of China's land territory, the degree of China's historical commitment to oceangoing trade and navigation,

---

[255]   *See, e.g.*, China's Position Paper, para. 4.

[256]   Ministry of Foreign Affairs, People's Republic of China, *Foreign Ministry Spokesperson Hua Chunying's Remarks on Relevant Issue about Taiping Dao* (3 June 2016), *available at* <www.fmprc.gov.cn/mfa_eng/xwfw_665399/s2510_665401/t1369189.shtml>; *see also* Letter from the Ambassador of the People's Republic of China to the Netherlands to the individual members of the Tribunal (3 June 2016).

and China's historical knowledge concerning the Spratly Islands. In the Tribunal's view, however, much of this evidence—on both sides—has nothing to do with the question of whether China has historically had rights to living and non-living resources beyond the limits of the territorial sea in the South China Sea and therefore is irrelevant to the matters before this Tribunal.

265. The Tribunal recalls that the process for the formation of historic rights in international law is well summarised in the UN Secretariat's 1962 *Memorandum on the Juridical Regime of Historic Waters, Including Historic Bays* and requires the continuous exercise of the claimed right by the State asserting the claim and acquiescence on the part of other affected States. Although that memorandum discussed the formation of rights to sovereignty over historic waters, as the Tribunal noted above (see paragraph 225), historic waters are merely one form of historic right and the process is the same for claims to rights short of sovereignty.

266. Accordingly, the scope of a claim to historic rights depends upon the scope of the acts that are carried out as the exercise of the claimed right. Evidence that either the Philippines or China had historically made use of the islands of the South China Sea would, at most, support a claim to historic rights to those islands. Evidence of use giving rise to historic rights with respect to the islands, however, would not establish historic rights to the waters beyond the territorial sea. The converse is also true: historic usage of the waters of the South China Sea cannot lead to rights with respect to the islands there. The two domains are distinct.

267. Because the Tribunal is not addressing questions of sovereignty, evidence concerning either Party's historical use of the islands of the South China Sea is of no interest with respect to the formation of historic rights (although, as will be discussed below (see paragraphs 549 to 551), it may bear upon the status of features pursuant to Article 121(3)). The Tribunal does find it relevant, however, to consider what would be required for it to find that China did have historic *maritime* rights to the living and non-living resources within the 'nine-dash line'.

268. On this issue, the Tribunal notes that historic rights are, in most instances, exceptional rights. They accord a right that a State would not otherwise hold, were it not for the operation of the historical process giving rise to the right and the acquiescence of other States in the process. It follows from this, however, that the exercise of freedoms permitted under international law cannot give rise to a historic right; it involves nothing that would call for the acquiescence of other States and can only represent the use of what international law already freely permits.

269. Prior to the introduction of the Convention system—and certainly prior to the Second World War—the international legal regime for the oceans recognised only a narrow belt of territorial

sea and the vast areas of high seas that comprised (and still comprise) the majority of the oceans. Under this regime, nearly all of the South China Sea formed part of the high seas, and indeed China's *Declaration of the Government of the People's Republic of China on China's Territorial Sea* of 4 September 1958 expressly recognises that it applies to "the Dongsha Islands, the Xisha Islands, the Zhongsha Islands, the Nansha Islands and all other islands belonging to China *which are separated from the mainland and its coastal islands by the high seas.*"[257] For much of history, therefore, China's navigation and trade in the South China Sea, as well as fishing beyond the territorial sea, represented the exercise of high seas freedoms. China engaged in activities that were permitted to all States by international law, as did the Philippines and other littoral States surrounding the South China Sea. Before the Second World War, the use of the seabed, beyond the limits of the territorial sea, was likewise a freedom open to any State that wished to do so, although as a practical matter the technological ability to do so effectively has emerged only more recently.

270. Historical navigation and fishing, beyond the territorial sea, cannot therefore form the basis for the emergence of a historic right. As the Chamber in *Gulf of Maine* recognised with respect to historic U.S. fishing on the Georges Bank, such activity was merely the exercise of freedoms already permitted by international law. [258] Evidence that merely points to even very intensive Chinese navigation and fishing in the South China Sea would be insufficient. Instead, in order to establish historic rights in the waters of the South China Sea, it would be necessary to show that China had engaged in activities that deviated from what was permitted under the freedom of the high seas and that other States acquiesced in such a right. In practice, to establish the exclusive historic right to living and non-living resources within the 'nine-dash line', which China now appears to claim, it would be necessary to show that China had historically sought to prohibit or restrict the exploitation of such resources by the nationals of other States and that those States had acquiesced in such restrictions. In the Tribunal's view, such a claim cannot be supported. The Tribunal is unable to identify any evidence that would suggest that China historically regulated or controlled fishing in the South China Sea, beyond the limits of the territorial sea. With respect to the non-living resources of the seabed, the Tribunal does not even see how this would be theoretically possible. Seabed mining was a glimmer of an idea when the Seabed Committee began the negotiations that led to the Convention. Offshore oil extraction was in its infancy and only recently became possible in deep water areas. Indeed, the

---

[257] People's Republic of China, Declaration of the Government of the People's Republic of China on China's Territorial Sea (4 September 1958), in *Collection of the Sea Laws and Regulations of the People's Republic of China* (3rd ed. 2001) (*emphasis added*).

[258] *Delimitation of the Maritime Boundary in the Gulf of Maine Area (Canada v. United States), Judgment, ICJ Reports 1984*, p. 246 at pp. 341-342, para. 235.

China National Offshore Oil Corporation itself was only founded in 1982, the same year that China signed the Convention. With respect to the seabed, the Tribunal does not see any historical activity that could have been restricted or controlled, and correspondingly no basis for a historic right.

271. Accordingly, in the Tribunal's view, China's ratification of the Convention in June 1996 did not extinguish historic rights in the waters of the South China Sea. Rather, China relinquished the freedoms of the high seas that it had previously utilised with respect to the living and non-living resources of certain sea areas which the international community had collectively determined to place within the ambit of the exclusive economic zone of other States. At the same time, China gained a greater degree of control over the maritime zones adjacent to and projecting from its coasts and islands. China's freedom to navigate the South China Sea remains unaffected.

272. Finally, because the Tribunal considers the question of historic rights with respect to maritime areas to be entirely distinct from that of historic rights to land, the Tribunal considers it opportune to note that certain claims remain unaffected by this decision. In particular, the Tribunal emphasises that nothing in this Award should be understood to comment in any way on China's historic claim to the islands of the South China Sea. Nor does the Tribunal's decision that a claim of historic rights to living and non-living resources is not compatible with the Convention limit China's ability to claim maritime zones in accordance with the Convention, on the basis of such islands. The Tribunal will address the question of the entitlements that can be generated by different features in the South China Sea in the following Chapter.

(c) Whether China has Established Exceptional Rights or Jurisdiction since the Adoption of the Convention

273. As a final matter, and for the sake of completeness, the Tribunal considers it appropriate to briefly address whether China has acquired rights or jurisdiction at variance with the Convention in the years since the Convention entered into force in 1996.

274. Paragraphs 3 and 4 of Article 311 of the Convention permit States to agree between them to modify the operation of the Convention between them, provided that such agreements are notified to other States Parties, do not affect the rights of other States, and are in keeping with the object and purpose of the Convention:

> 3. Two or more States Parties may conclude agreements modifying or suspending the operation of provisions of this Convention, applicable solely to the relations between them, provided that such agreements do not relate to a provision derogation from which is incompatible with the effective execution of the object and purpose of this Convention, and provided further that such agreements shall not affect the application of the basic principles embodied herein, and that the provisions of such

> agreements do not affect the enjoyment by other States Parties of their rights or the performance of their obligations under this Convention.
>
> 4.   States Parties intending to conclude an agreement referred to in paragraph 3 shall notify the other States Parties through the depositary of this Convention of their intention to conclude the agreement and of the modification or suspension for which it provides.

Similarly, the subsequent practice of the States parties may bear on the interpretation of a treaty pursuant to Article 31 of the Vienna Convention, or a new rule of customary international law may emerge to modify the provisions of a treaty. International law is not static.

275.   The Tribunal does not consider it necessary here to address in general whether and under which conditions the Convention may be modified by State practice.[259] It is sufficient to say that a unilateral act alone is not sufficient. Such a claim would require the same elements discussed above with respect to historic rights: the assertion by a State of a right at variance with the Convention, acquiescence therein by the other States Parties, and the passage of sufficient time to establish beyond doubt the existence of both the right and a general acquiescence. Here, however, there is no basis for such a claim. Since the adoption of the Convention, historic rights were mentioned in China's *Exclusive Economic Zone and Continental Shelf Act*,[260] but without anything that would enable another State to know the nature or extent of the rights claimed. The extent of the rights asserted within the 'nine-dash line' only became clear with China's Notes Verbales of May 2009. Since that date, China's claims have been clearly objected to by other States. In the Tribunal's view, there is no acquiescence.

(d)   Conclusion

276.   The Philippines' Submissions No. 1 and 2 are linked and represent two aspects of one dispute concerning the source of maritime rights and entitlements in the South China Sea.

277.   With respect to Submission No. 1, for the reasons set out above, the Tribunal concludes that, as between the Philippines and China, the Convention defines the scope of maritime entitlements in the South China Sea, which may not extend beyond the limits imposed therein.

---

[259]   The Tribunal will address the role of State practice in the interpretation of the Convention, in accordance with Article 31 of the Vienna Convention on the Law of Treaties, in relation to the interpretation of Article 121 of the Convention. See paragraphs 552 to 553 below.

[260]   People's Republic of China, Exclusive Economic Zone and Continental Shelf Act (26 June 1998), *available at* <www.npc.gov.cn/englishnpc/Law/2007-12/11/content_1383573.htm> *also available at* <www.un.org/depts/los/legislationandtreaties/pdffiles/chn_1998_eez_act.pdf>.

278.   With respect to Submission No. 2, for the reasons set out above, the Tribunal concludes that, as between the Philippines and China, China's claims to historic rights, or other sovereign rights or jurisdiction, with respect to the maritime areas of the South China Sea encompassed by the relevant part of the 'nine-dash line' are contrary to the Convention and without lawful effect to the extent that they exceed the geographic and substantive limits of China's maritime entitlements under the Convention. The Tribunal concludes that the Convention superseded any historic rights or other sovereign rights or jurisdiction in excess of the limits imposed therein.

*   *   *

this page intentionally blank

VI.   THE STATUS OF FEATURES IN THE SOUTH CHINA SEA (SUBMISSIONS NO. 3 TO 7)

A.   INTRODUCTION

279.   In this Chapter, the Tribunal assesses the status of certain maritime features and the entitlements to maritime zones that they are capable of generating for the purposes of the Convention.

280.   In the terminology of the Convention, a feature that is exposed at low tide but covered with water at high tide is referred to as a 'low-tide elevation'. Features that are above water at high tide are referred to generically as 'islands'. However, the entitlements that an island can generate to maritime zones will depend upon the application of Article 121(3) of the Convention and whether the island has the capacity to "sustain human habitation or economic life of [its] own." Throughout this Chapter, the Tribunal will refer to the generic category of features that meet the definition of an island in Article 121(1) as 'high-tide features'. The Tribunal will use the term 'rocks' for high-tide features that "cannot sustain human habitation or economic life of their own" and which therefore, pursuant to Article 121(3), are disqualified from generating an exclusive economic zone or continental shelf. For high-tide features which are not rocks, and which pursuant to Article 121(2) enjoy the same entitlements as other land territory under the Convention, the Tribunal will use the term 'fully entitled islands'. 'Rocks' and 'fully entitled islands' are thus both sub-sets of the broader category of 'high-tide features'. Finally, the Tribunal will refer to features that are fully submerged, even at low tide, as 'submerged features'.

B.   THE STATUS OF FEATURES AS ABOVE/BELOW WATER AT HIGH TIDE (SUBMISSIONS NO. 4 AND 6)

1.   Introduction

281.   In this Section, the Tribunal addresses the Parties' dispute concerning the status of the maritime features and the source of maritime entitlements in the South China Sea. This dispute is reflected in the Philippines' Submissions No. 4 and 6, which request the Tribunal to hold that certain specified features are low-tide elevations and do not generate any independent entitlement to maritime zones. Submissions No. 4 and 6 provide as follows:

> (4)   Mischief Reef, Second Thomas Shoal and Subi Reef are low-tide elevations that do not generate entitlement to a territorial sea, exclusive economic zone or continental shelf, and are not features that are capable of appropriation by occupation or otherwise;
>
> . . .

(6)   Gaven Reef and McKennan Reef (including Hughes Reef) are low-tide elevations that do not generate entitlement to a territorial sea, exclusive economic zone or continental shelf, but their low-water line may be used to determine the baseline from which the breadth of the territorial sea of Namyit and Sin Cowe, respectively, is measured;

282.   The question of whether features are above or below water at high tide is also implicated by the Philippines' Submissions No. 3 and 7, which are predicated on the Philippines' view that Scarborough Shoal, Johnson Reef, Cuarteron Reef, and Fiery Cross Reef are high-tide features with rocks that remain above water at high tide. For the sake of completeness, and in keeping with its duty under Article 9 of Annex VII to the Convention to satisfy itself that the Philippines' Submissions are well founded in fact, the Tribunal will examine the status, as above or below water at high tide, of all ten features identified in the Philippines' Submissions.

283.   In its Award on Jurisdiction, the Tribunal held that these Submissions reflect a dispute concerning the status of maritime features in the South China Sea and not a dispute concerning sovereignty over such features. The Tribunal also held that this is not a dispute concerning sea boundary delimitation, insofar as "the status of a feature as a 'low-tide elevation', 'island', or a 'rock' relates to the entitlement to maritime zones generated by that feature, not to the delimitation of such entitlements in the event that they overlap." [261]   The Tribunal noted, however, that the possible existence of overlapping entitlements to an exclusive economic zone or continental shelf could have "practical considerations for the selection of the vertical datum and tidal model against which the status of the features is to be assessed." [262]

2.   Factual Background

284.   Scarborough Shoal is known as "Huangyan Dao" (黄岩岛) in China and "Panatag Shoal" or "Bajo de Masinloc" in the Philippines and is a coral reef located at 15° 09′ 16″ N, 117° 45′ 58″ E. Scarborough Shoal is 116.2 nautical miles from the archipelagic baseline of the Philippine island of Luzon and 448.2 nautical miles from China's baseline point 29 (Jiapengliedao) near Hong Kong. [263] The general location of Scarborough Shoal is depicted in Map 2 on page 123 below.

---

[261]   Award on Jurisdiction, paras. 401, 403.

[262]   Award on Jurisdiction, paras. 401, 403.

[263]   All calculations use geographic coordinates expressed in terms of the World Geodetic System (WGS84), and distance measurement is along the geodesic between two points. Geodetic calculations were done using Vincenty's inverse solution. *See* T. Vincenty, "Direct and Inverse Solutions on the Ellipsoid with Application of Nested Equations," *Survey Review*, Vol. 23, No. 176, p. 88 (1975).

285. Cuarteron Reef is known as "Huayang Jiao" (华阳礁) in China and "Calderon Reef" in the Philippines. It is a coral reef located at 08° 51′ 41″ N, 112° 50′ 08″ E and is the easternmost of four maritime features known collectively as the London Reefs that are located on the western edge of the Spratly Islands. Cuarteron Reef is 245.3 nautical miles from the archipelagic baseline of the Philippine island of Palawan and 585.3 nautical miles from China's baseline point 39 (Dongzhou (2)) adjacent to the island of Hainan. The general location of Cuarteron Reef, along with the other maritime features in the Spratly Islands, is depicted in Map 3 on page 125 below.

286. Fiery Cross Reef is known as "Yongshu Jiao" (永暑礁) in China and "Kagitingan Reef" in the Philippines. It is a coral reef located at 09° 33′ 00″ N, 112° 53′ 25″ E, to the north of Cuarteron Reef and along the western edge of the Spratly Islands, adjacent to the main shipping routes through the South China Sea. Fiery Cross Reef is 254.2 nautical miles from the archipelagic baseline of the Philippine island of Palawan and 547.7 nautical miles from the China's baseline point 39 (Dongzhou (2)) adjacent to the island of Hainan.

287. Johnson Reef, McKennan Reef, and Hughes Reef are all coral reefs that form part of the larger reef formation in the centre of the Spratly Islands known as Union Bank. Union Bank also includes the high-tide feature of Sin Cowe Island. Johnson Reef (also known as Johnson South Reef) is known as "Chigua Jiao" (赤瓜礁) in China and "Mabini Reef" in the Philippines. It is located at 9° 43′ 00″ N, 114° 16′ 55″ E and is 184.7 nautical miles from the archipelagic baseline of the Philippine island of Palawan and 570.8 nautical miles from China's baseline point 39 (Dongzhou (2)) adjacent to Hainan. Although the Philippines has referred to "McKennan Reef (including Hughes Reef)" in its Submissions, the Tribunal notes that McKennan Reef and Hughes Reef are distinct features, albeit adjacent to one another, and considers it preferable, for the sake of clarity, to address them separately. McKennan Reef is known as "Ximen Jiao" (西门礁) in China and, with Hughes Reef, is known collectively as "Chigua Reef" in the Philippines. It is located at 09° 54′ 13″ N, 114° 27′ 53″ E and is 181.3 nautical miles from the archipelagic baseline of the Philippine island of Palawan and 566.8 nautical miles from China's baseline point 39 (Dongzhou (2)) adjacent to Hainan. Hughes Reef is known as "Dongmen Jiao" (东门礁) in China and, with McKennan Reef, is known collectively as "Chigua Reef" in the Philippines. It is located at 09° 54′ 48″ N 114°29′ 48″ E and is 180.3 nautical miles from the archipelagic baseline of the Philippine island of Palawan and 567.2 nautical miles from China's baseline point 39 (Dongzhou (2)) adjacent to Hainan.

288. The Gaven Reefs are known as "Nanxun Jiao" (南薰礁) in China and "Burgos" in the Philippines. They constitute a pair of coral reefs that forms part of the larger reef formation known as Tizard Bank, located directly to the north of Union Bank. Tizard Bank also includes the high-tide features of Itu Aba Island, Namyit Island, and Sand Cay. Gaven Reef (North) is located at 10° 12′ 27″ N, 114° 13′ 21″ E and is 203.0 nautical miles from the archipelagic baseline of the Philippine island of Palawan and 544.1 nautical miles from China's baseline point 39 (Dongzhou (2)) adjacent to Hainan. Gaven Reef (South) is located at 10° 09′ 42″ N 114° 15′ 09″ E and is 200.5 nautical miles from the archipelagic baseline of the Philippine island of Palawan and 547.4 nautical miles from China's baseline point 39 (Dongzhou (2)) adjacent to Hainan.

289. Subi Reef is known as "Zhubi Jiao" (渚碧礁) in China and "Zamora Reef" in the Philippines. It is a coral reef located to the north of Tizard Bank and a short distance to the south-west of the high-tide feature of Thitu Island and its surrounding Thitu Reefs. Subi Reef is located at 10° 55′ 22″ N, 114° 05′ 04″ E and lies on the north-western edge of the Spratly Islands. Subi Reef is 231.9 nautical miles from the archipelagic baseline of the Philippine island of Palawan and 502.2 nautical miles from China's baseline point 39 (Dongzhou (2)) adjacent to Hainan.

290. Mischief Reef and Second Thomas Shoal are both coral reefs located in the centre of the Spratly Islands, to the east of Union Bank and to the south-east of Tizard Bank. Mischief Reef is known as "Meiji Jiao" (美济礁) in China and "Panganiban" in the Philippines. It is located at 09° 54′ 17″ N, 115° 31′ 59″ E and is 125.4 nautical miles from the archipelagic baseline of the Philippine island of Palawan and 598.1 nautical miles from China's baseline point 39 (Dongzhou (2)) adjacent to Hainan. Second Thomas Shoal is known as "Ren'ai Jiao" (仁爱礁) in China and "Ayungin Shoal" in the Philippines. It is located at 09° 54′ 17″ N, 115° 51′ 49″ E and is 104.0 nautical miles from the archipelagic baseline of the Philippine island of Palawan and 616.2 nautical miles from China's baseline point 39 (Dongzhou (2)) adjacent to Hainan.

3. The Philippines' Position

291. The Philippines recalls that low-tide elevations are defined and governed by Article 13 of the Convention.[264] "[L]ow-tide elevations are not land territory," the Philippines emphasises, and "no measure of occupation or control can establish sovereignty over such features."[265] According to the Philippines, low-tide elevations can be divided into three categories:

---

[264] Merits Hearing Tr. (Day 2), pp. 19-20.

[265] Merits Hearing Tr. (Day 2), p. 20.

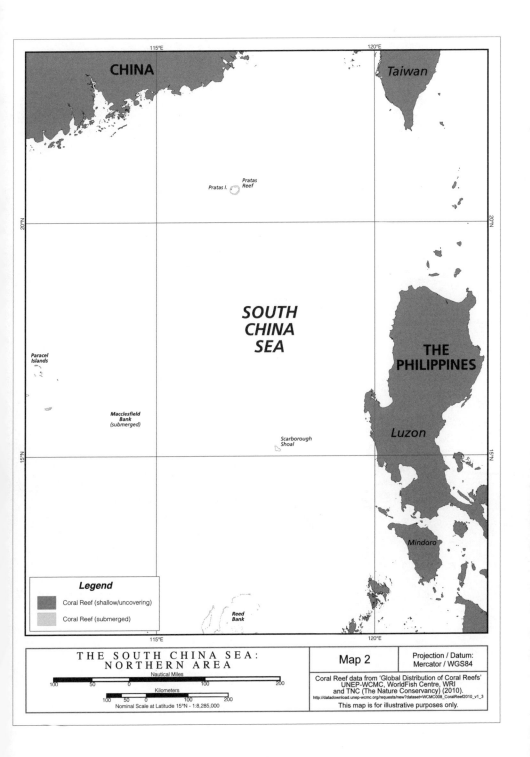

this page intentionally blank

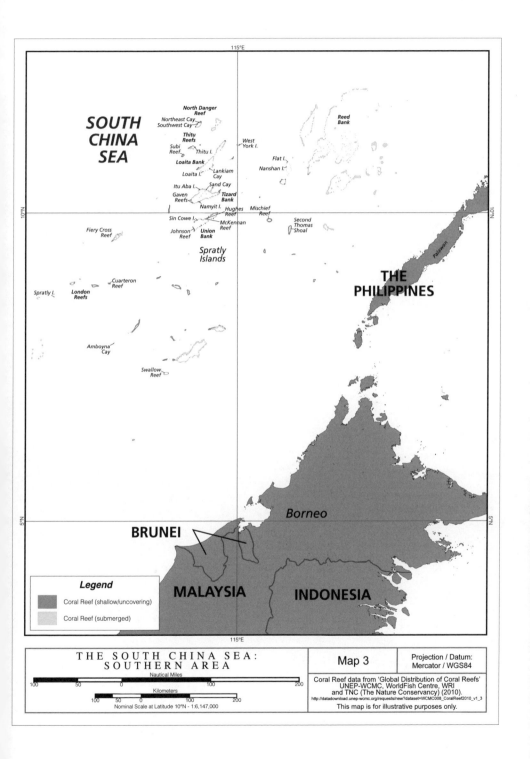

this page intentionally blank

(a)   "[W]here a low-tide elevation is located within 12 miles of a high-tide feature, sovereignty over the low-tide elevation rests with the State by reason of the sovereignty it has over the high-tide feature."[266]

(b)   Where "low-tide elevations . . . lie wholly beyond 12 miles, but within a state's exclusive economic zone or continental shelf . . . , the coastal state enjoys exclusive sovereign rights and jurisdiction with regard to the low-tide elevation in accordance and within the limits of the regime provided for in Articles 56(3) and 77 of the 1982 Convention."[267]

(c)   And where a low-tide elevation would be located "at an even greater distance, beyond areas of national jurisdiction. In such cases, it is part of the deep seabed and subject to Part XI of the Convention, and no state can purport to exercise sovereignty or any sovereign rights over or in respect of it."[268]

The Philippines also notes that, pursuant to Article 13(1), there is a distinction between low-tide elevations falling wholly or partially within the territorial sea of a high-tide feature, which may serve as part of the baseline for the territorial sea of that high-tide feature, and low-tide elevations located beyond the territorial sea, which "have no capacity to generate claims to maritime jurisdiction."[269]

292.   The Philippines submits that each of the five maritime features mentioned in its Submissions No. 4 and 6 is a low-tide elevation: Second Thomas Shoal, Mischief Reef, Subi Reef, "McKennan Reef including Hughes Reef" (which the Philippines treats as single feature), and the Gaven Reefs. The Philippines distinguishes between them, however, and considers that Second Thomas Shoal, Mischief Reef, and Subi Reef lie beyond 12 nautical miles from any high-tide feature. In contrast, the Philippines considers that the Gaven Reefs lie within the 12-nautical-mile territorial sea of Namyit Island and that McKennan Reef lies within the 12-nautical-mile territorial sea of Sin Cowe Island, such that both low-tide elevations can be used to extend the baseline of the territorial sea of the high-tide features.[270]

293.   The Philippines supports its conclusions with two types of satellite imagery. First, the Philippines has provided the Tribunal with what it describes as "multi-band Landsat satellite

---

[266]   Merits Hearing Tr. (Day 2), p. 21.

[267]   Merits Hearing Tr. (Day 2), p. 21.

[268]   Merits Hearing Tr. (Day 2), pp. 21-22.

[269]   Merits Hearing Tr. (Day 2), pp. 22-23.

[270]   Merits Hearing Tr. (Day 2), p. 23.

photographs of each of the five low-tide features."[271] According to the Philippines, this imagery was prepared as follows:

> Two sets of images were produced from different parts of the electromagnetic spectrum resulting in varying wavelengths. The band 1 images correspond to a shorter wavelength of between 0.45 and 0.52 micrometres, and these can penetrate water. The band 4 images correspond to a longer wavelength of between 0.76 and 0.90 micrometres, which are almost entirely absorbed by water. A band 4 image can therefore only show features that are above water.[272]

The Philippines submits that Landsat imagery of each of the five features confirms that none is above water at high tide.[273]

294. Second, the Philippines has provided the Tribunal with satellite imagery analysis prepared by the EOMAP company that depicts the five features bathymetrically at what EOMAP calculates to be Lowest Astronomic Tide, Highest Astronomic Tide, and Mean High Water.[274] The Philippines submits that EOMAP's analysis likewise confirms that all five features are below water at high tide.[275]

295. In addition to satellite analysis, the Philippines relies on what it considers to be the consistent depiction of all five features as low-tide elevations in all published charts and on the corresponding descriptions of the features as submerged at high tide in sailing directions and pilots. The Philippines summarises its conclusions on the available evidence as follows:

> We have collected all the available charts and other evidence we can find. The satellite imagery, including the EOMAP analysis of each of the features, consistently, completely and without the slightest ambiguity demonstrates that all five features are covered by water at high tide. This is simply not an issue and cannot reasonably be disputed.
>
> The charts produced by all the relevant charting agencies—including the Philippines, China, Malaysia, Vietnam, the United Kingdom and the United States—agree that all five features are low-tide elevations. All of the evidence, including the satellite imagery and the Sailing Directions set out in the Atlas, is remarkably—and, we say, gloriously—consistent in its depiction of the features as low-tide elevations.[276]

296. During the hearing, the Philippines was questioned by the Tribunal regarding the depiction of the Gaven Reefs in U.S. Defense Mapping Agency Chart No. 93043 (Tizard Bank South China

---

[271] Merits Hearing Tr. (Day 2), p. 25.

[272] Merits Hearing Tr. (Day 2), p. 25.

[273] Memorial, Figures 5.6, 5.8, 5.10, 5.12.

[274] EOMAP GmbH & Co, *Satellite Derived Bathymetry for Selected Features in the South China Sea* (18 November 2015) (Annex 807).

[275] Merits Hearing Tr. (Day 2), pp. 26-32.

[276] Merits Hearing Tr. (Day 2), p. 25.

Sea)[277] and the description of the feature in the U.S. *Sailing Directions (Enroute), South China Sea and the Gulf of Thailand.*[278] The Philippines responded as follows:

> Taking the U.S. Sailing Directions first, the relevant passage is on your screens. It is true that there is a reference to a white sand dune, and the third sentence says that it is 2 metres high. But the Sailing Directions does not say that the sand dune is "above water at high tide"; in fact, it says the opposite. The first sentence states without ambiguity that both reefs are covered by water at high tide. The white sand dune mentioned in the third sentence is properly read as a reference to its situation at less than high water.

> Both the Philippines and Chinese Sailing Directions support this interpretation. The Philippine Coast Pilot explains that Gaven Reefs "cover at [high water]", and the Chinese Sailing Directions states explicitly that, "these rocks are all submerged by seawater". And these are the words, we say, that dominate.

> I turn to US chart no. 93043, referred to in the Tribunal's question. You can see it on your screens. You can now see the datum for the chart; it is highlighted. This is based on a Japanese survey undertaken in 1936 and 1937. As to the heights—this is significant—these are expressed in "metres above mean sea level". Mean sea level is not the same as high tide; it is a lower level. It cannot therefore be concluded on the basis of this chart—an old chart of about 80 years of age—that any part of Gaven Reef is above water at high tide.[279]

The Philippines also emphasised that the EOMAP imagery of the Gaven Reefs gives no indication of a high-tide feature.[280]

297. During the hearing, the Philippines' expert was also questioned by the Tribunal as to whether or not Subi Reef lies within 12 nautical miles of a high-tide feature on the reefs to the west of Thitu Island. In response, the Philippines submitted additional analysis from EOMAP and the following conclusion:

> Both the U.S. and UK Sailing Directions indicate that a sand cay lies on one of the reefs approximately 3.5 nautical miles from Thitu. However, U.S. chart NGA 93044 (2nd ed. 5/84) has removed the indication of a cay that had been present on the previous U.S. chart of the area, NGA 93061B (4th ed. revised through 9/70). Currently, only British Chart 3483 shows the presence of a tiny cay on one of these reefs. Charts published by the Philippines, China, Vietnam, Japan and Russia give no indication of any feature above water at high tide among these reefs.

> When the satellite imagery used in the EOMap analysis was taken, the tidal level was determined (by EOMap) to be 71 cm below Mean High Water. Even at that relatively low tidal level, the two westernmost reefs were completely submerged.

> On the three easternmost reefs, there are indications of tiny sand spits that had uncovered at that tidal level. While it is likely that these sandy areas cover fully at tidal levels approaching Mean High Water, the EOMap analysis automatically depicts them as small

---

[277] U.S. Defense Mapping Agency Chart No. 93043 (Tizard Bank South China Sea) (Annex NC51).

[278] U.S. National Geospatial-Intelligence Agency, Pub. 161 *Sailing Directions (Enroute), South China Sea and the Gulf of Thailand* (13th ed., 2011) at p. 9 (Annex 233).

[279] Merits Hearing Tr. (Day 4), pp. 74-76.

[280] Merits Hearing Tr. (Day 4), pp. 76-77.

white spots identified as "data flags," because the technology employed only reads the relative heights of features that are covered by water at the time of image capture.[281]

4. China's Position

298. China has not, as far as the Tribunal is aware, specifically set out its position with respect to all of the maritime features at issue in these proceedings. Indeed, the Tribunal recalls that in its public Position Paper of 7 December 2014, China stated that:

> The Philippines asserts that some of the maritime features, about which it has submitted claims for arbitration, are low-tide elevations, thus being incapable of appropriation as territory. As to whether those features are indeed low-tide elevations, this Position Paper will not comment.[282]

299. The Tribunal notes, however, that the record of public statements and diplomatic correspondence before it includes the Chinese statement that "Huangyan Dao [Scarborough Shoal] is not a sand bank but rather an island."[283]

300. The Tribunal also notes China's statement that "China has indisputable sovereignty over Nansha Islands and their adjacent waters, Meiji Jiao [Mischief Reef] and Yongshu Jiao [Fiery Cross Reef] included."[284] This statement is not entirely without ambiguity, but the Tribunal understands it to mean that China considers Mischief Reef and Fiery Cross Reef to be high-tide features, entitled to at least a territorial sea.

301. China has also commented on the entitlements of the maritime features of the Spratly Islands collectively, stating that "China's Nansha Islands is fully entitled to Territorial Sea, Exclusive Economic Zone (EEZ) and Continental Shelf."[285]

302. The Tribunal recalls the statement in its Award on Jurisdiction that "a dispute is not negated by the absence of granular exchanges with respect to each and every individual feature."[286] Where China has not publicly stated its specific view regarding the status of a particular feature, the

---

[281] Geographical Information on Thitu Reefs, pp. 5-8 (Annex 856).

[282] China's Position Paper, para. 24.

[283] Department of Foreign Affairs, Republic of the Philippines, *Record of Proceedings: 10th Philippines–China Foreign Ministry Consultations* (30 July 1998) (Annex 184). *See also* Ministry of Foreign Affairs, People's Republic of China, *Chinese Foreign Ministry Statement Regarding Huangyandao* (22 May 1997) (Annex 106).

[284] Note Verbale from the Embassy of the People's Republic of China in Manila to the Department of Foreign Affairs, Republic of the Philippines, No. 15 (PG)-214 (28 June 2015) (Annex 689).

[285] Note Verbale from the Permanent Mission of the People's Republic of China to the Secretary-General of the United Nations, No. CML/8/2011 (14 April 2011) (Annex 201). *See also* Note Verbale from the Permanent Mission of the People's Republic of China to the Secretary-General of the United Nations, No. CML/12/2009 (13 April 2009).

[286] Award on Jurisdiction, para. 170.

Tribunal will assess the status of the feature on the basis of the best evidence available to it, paying particular attention to the depiction of features on nautical charts or the descriptions in sailing directions issued by China.

5.   **The Tribunal's Considerations**

(a)   **The Interpretation of Article 13 and the Tribunal's Approach to Submissions No. 4 and 6**

303.   The definition and properties of low-tide elevations are set out in Article 13 of the Convention, which provides as follows:

Article 13
Low-tide elevations

1.   A low-tide elevation is a naturally formed area of land which is surrounded by and above water at low tide but submerged at high tide. Where a low-tide elevation is situated wholly or partly at a distance not exceeding the breadth of the territorial sea from the mainland or an island, the low-water line on that elevation may be used as the baseline for measuring the breadth of the territorial sea.

2.   Where a low-tide elevation is wholly situated at a distance exceeding the breadth of the territorial sea from the mainland or an island, it has no territorial sea of its own.

304.   This definition operates in parallel with that of an island in Article 121(1) of the Convention, which provides that "[a]n island is a naturally formed area of land, surrounded by water, which is above water at high tide." The latter Article will be discussed in detail subsequently in connection with the Philippines' Submissions No. 3, 5, and 7 (see paragraphs 473 to 553 below).

i.   Naturally Formed Areas and the Human Modification of Coral Reefs

305.   With respect to low-tide elevations, several points necessarily follow from this pair of definitions. First, the inclusion of the term "naturally formed" in the definition of both a low-tide elevation and an island indicates that the status of a feature is to be evaluated on the basis of its natural condition. As a matter of law, human modification cannot change the seabed into a low-tide elevation or a low-tide elevation into an island. A low-tide elevation will remain a low-tide elevation under the Convention, regardless of the scale of the island or installation built atop it.

306.   This point raises particular considerations in the present case. Many of the features in the South China Sea have been subjected to substantial human modification as large islands with installations and airstrips have been constructed on top of the coral reefs. In some cases, it would likely no longer be possible to directly observe the original status of the feature, as the

contours of the reef platform have been entirely buried by millions of tons of landfill and concrete. In such circumstances, the Tribunal considers that the Convention requires that the status of a feature be ascertained on the basis of its earlier, natural condition, prior to the onset of significant human modification. The Tribunal will therefore reach its decision on the basis of the best available evidence of the *previous* status of what are now heavily modified coral reefs.

ii. The Status and Entitlements of Low-Tide Elevations

307. The Philippines' Submissions request the Tribunal to declare that those features which qualify as low-tide elevations under Article 13 are not entitled to maritime zones and are not capable of appropriation or occupation. These Submissions thus raise the question of the status and entitlements of low-tide elevations.

308. Article 13(2) states that, except where a low-tide elevation falls within the breadth of a territorial sea generated from a high-tide feature or mainland, it generates no territorial sea of its own. Article 13(2) does not expressly state that a low-tide elevation is not entitled to an exclusive economic zone or continental shelf. Nevertheless the Tribunal considers that this restriction is necessarily implied in the Convention. It follows automatically from the operation of Articles 57 and 76, which measure the breadth of the exclusive economic zone and continental shelf from the baseline for the territorial sea. *Ipso facto*, if a low-tide elevation is not entitled to a territorial sea, it is not entitled to an exclusive economic zone or continental shelf. The same restriction follows implicitly from Article 121(3), which provides that even certain high-tide features are deemed to be rocks that are ineligible to generate an exclusive economic zone or continental shelf.

309. With respect to the status of low-tide elevations, the Tribunal considers that notwithstanding the use of the term "land" in the physical description of a low-tide elevation, such low-tide elevations do not form part of the land territory of a State in the legal sense. Rather they form part of the submerged landmass of the State and fall within the legal regimes for the territorial sea or continental shelf, as the case may be. Accordingly, and as distinct from land territory, the Tribunal subscribes to the view that "low-tide elevations cannot be appropriated, although 'a coastal State has sovereignty over low-tide elevations which are situated within its territorial sea, since it has sovereignty over the territorial sea itself'."[287]

---

[287] *Territorial and Maritime Dispute (Nicaragua v. Colombia), Judgment, ICJ Reports 2012*, p. 624 at p. 641, para. 26.

iii. Vertical Datum and the Meaning of "High Tide" in Articles 13 and 121

310. A further consideration is posed by the use of the term "high tide" in the definition of both a low-tide elevation and an island. "High tide" is not a technical term and is potentially subject to a number of different technical interpretations, corresponding with different measurements and water levels. Common datums for measuring high water include Mean High Water (the average height of all high waters at a place over a 19-year period), Mean Higher High Water (the average height of higher high water at a place over a 19-year period), and Mean High Water Springs (the average height of the high waters of spring tides).[288]   The International Hydrographic Organization (the "**IHO**") recommends that a high-water datum be used as the reference datum for heights depicted on nautical charts, but makes no recommendation as between the possibilities.[289] The IHO specifically recommends that Highest Astronomic Tide (the highest tidal level which can be predicted to occur under average meteorological conditions and under any combination of astronomical conditions) be used as the datum for vertical clearances (*i.e.*, bridges), but only for this purpose.[290]

311. The Tribunal sees nothing in the Convention, and no rule of customary international law, that would mandate that the status of low-tide elevations and high-tide features/islands be determined against any particular high-water datum. Accordingly, the Tribunal considers that States are free under the Convention to claim a high-tide feature or island on the basis of any high-water datum that reasonably corresponds to the ordinary meaning of the term "high tide" in Articles 13 and 121. Ordinarily, this would also be the height datum for nautical charts published by that State, above which rocks would be depicted as not covering at high tide.

312. In the present case, the situation is complicated by the fact that the features in question are claimed by multiple States and may or may not lie within one or another State's exclusive economic zone and continental shelf. The Tribunal questioned the Philippines on the issue of vertical datum at several points during the proceedings, and the Philippines responded as follows:

> There is no requirement under the Convention to have regard to any particular charts to determine the status of a feature; and in any event, in this case all the charts point in the same direction. And we have made clear that the Philippines has no objection to this Tribunal

---

[288]   International Hydrographic Organization, *Hydrographic Dictionary*, p. 144 (5th ed., 1994).

[289]   International Hydrographic Organization, *Chart Specifications of the IHO: Medium and Large-scale Charts*, Section B-300, p. 4 (2013) *available at* <www.iho.int/iho_pubs/standard/S-4/S-4_e4.4.0 _EN_Sep13.pdf >.

[290]   International Hydrographic Organization, *Chart Specifications of the IHO: Medium and Large-scale Charts*, Section B-300, p. 4 (2013) *available at* <www.iho.int/iho_pubs/standard/S-4/S-4_e4.4.0 _EN_Sep13.pdf >.

placing reliance upon the Chinese charts which we have referred to in our written pleadings.[291]

The Philippines' elaboration of this answer, however, appeared to be focused on the low-water datum on various charts,[292] against which soundings and baselines would be measured, whereas the determination of the status of a feature would necessarily be measured against a high-water datum.

313. Height datum on modern charts produced by the Philippines is Mean High Water.[293] In contrast, the height datum on modern Chinese charts is China's 1985 National Vertical Datum, which corresponds to Mean Sea Level in the Yellow Sea as observed at Qingdao.[294] Mean sea level is not a high-water datum, and this therefore offers no assistance in determining the appropriate datum for "high tide" for the purposes of Articles 13 and 121. However, the legend to the symbology for standard Chinese cartography indicates that Chinese charts will depict a rock or islet as one which does not cover if it exceeds the level of Mean High Water Springs.[295] Several of the Chinese charts in the record before the Tribunal also include tidal information and reference "high tide" as Mean Higher High Water.[296] The Tribunal considers that either Mean Higher High Water or Mean High Water Springs would be an appropriate approximation of "high tide" if determined on the basis of Chinese nautical charts. The Tribunal is also aware of certain statements in the record before it to the effect that the tidal regime in the South China Sea is complex and unpredictable. The Tribunal will address this issue in the following Section (see paragraphs 314 to 319 below). Ultimately, however, the tidal range in the South China Sea is comparatively small and the selection of a vertical datum will, in most instances, make no difference regarding the status of a feature. The Tribunal need consider this issue further only if

---

[291] Jurisdictional Hearing Tr. (Day 1), p. 85.

[292] Written Responses of the Philippines to the Tribunal's 13 July 2015 Questions, pp. 23-30 (23 July 2015) (hereinafter "**Written Responses of the Philippines (23 July 2015)**").

[293] *See, e.g.*, Chart No. 4803 (Scarborough Shoal) (2006) (Annex NC32); Chart No. 4723 (Kalayaan Island Group) (2008) (Annex NC33).

[294] *See* Letter from the State Council of China to the National Mapping Bureau, 16 May 1987, *available at* <www.gov.cn/xxgk/pub/govpublic/mrlm/201103/t20110330_63783.html>; National Bureau of Surveying and Mapping, "State Height" *available at* <www.sbsm.gov.cn/zszygx/hzzs/chkp/ddcl/201001/t20100115_83615.shtml>.

[295] Navigation Guarantee Department of the Chinese Navy Headquarters, *Symbols Identifying Direction Used on Chinese Charts* (2006) (Annex 231).

[296] *See* Navigation Guarantee Department of the Chinese Navy Headquarters, Chart No. 18400 (Zhenghe Qunjiao to Yongshu Jiao) (2005) (Annex NC17); Navigation Guarantee Department of the Chinese Navy Headquarters, Chart No. 18600 (Yinqing Qunjiao to Nanwei Tan) (2012) (Annex NC24); Navigation Guarantee Department of the Chinese Navy Headquarters, Chart No. 18100 (Shuangzi Qunjiao to Zhenghe Quojiao) (2013) (Annex NC25); Navigation Guarantee Department of the Chinese Navy Headquarters, Chart No. 18300 (Yongshu Jiao to Yinqing Qunjiao) (2013) (Annex NC27).

it appears that a feature is near enough to high water that its status would differ as a result of the datum used.

iv.   Tidal Patterns and Ranges in the Spratly Islands

314. Tides in the South China Sea raise a further consideration: namely, whether the Tribunal has sufficient information to accurately understand tidal patterns in the South China Sea and their effect on the various features at issue in the proceedings. The Tribunal notes that the Royal Navy carried out tidal measurements at Spratly Island in 1864[297] and at North Danger Reef in 1926,[298] in both instances with a series of direct observations that appear long enough to cover at least a fortnight within the lunar cycle. Tidal ranges[299] from these observations are reported in the sailing directions[300] and appear on the 1864 fair chart of Spratly Island[301] and on the 1926 fair chart of North Danger Reef.[302] They indicate a spring tide range of 5¼ feet (1.6 metres) at Spratly Island and a range between Higher High Water and Lower Low Water of 3 feet (0.91 metres).[303] Royal Navy Fleet Charts issued through 1966[304] also indicate the tidal range for North Danger Reef with a range between Higher High Water and Lower Low Water of 2.7 feet (0.82 metres) and range for spring tides of 4.6 feet (1.40 metres).

315. The Chinese charts in the record also record tidal ranges, taken at the Gaven Reefs, Hughes Reef, Fiery Cross Reef, Cuarteron Reef, and Subi Reef. These locations all correspond with current Chinese installations, suggesting that the results are based upon in-person observations over a period of time and may be considered reliable. This Chinese tidal data indicate that mean tidal ranges are quite consistent across the different features in the South China Sea, although some differences in tidal intervals are apparent. Chinese tidal data also provide greater detail on

---

[297]   *See* Letter from Commander Ward, HMS Rifleman, to the Hydrographer of the Admiralty (29 July 1864).

[298]   HMS Iroquois, *Sailing Directions to accompany Chart of North Danger Reef.*

[299]   In tide terminology, the amplitude is the semi-range of the harmonic constituent. *See* International Hydrographic Office, *Hydrographic Dictionary*, Part I, Vol. I, at p. 11 (5th ed., 1994). The tidal range is the difference in height between high tide and low tide. The tidal amplitude is the difference in height between high tide (or low tide) and the level of mean tide. In other words, the amplitude is half the tidal range.

[300]   Admiralty Hydrographic Office, *China Sea Directory*, Vol. II, p. 71 (1st ed., 1868); Admiralty Hydrographic Department, *China Sea Pilot*, Vol. I, p. 120 (1st ed., 1937).

[301]   Survey fair chart of Spratly Island and Amboyna Cay, UKHO Ref. D7446 (1864).

[302]   Survey fair chart of North Danger Reef, UKHO Ref. E1207 (1926).

[303]   The fair chart indicates that the mean rise of Higher High Water is 5 feet, but references soundings to a datum 3.5 feet below mean tide level. Accordingly, the amplitude between Higher High Water and Lower Low Water would be 3 feet.

[304]   *See, e.g.*, Royal Navy Fleet Chart F6064: Reefs in South China Sea (Northern Portion) (1966).

the effect of changes in lunar declination and indicates a range between Higher High Water and Lower Low Water of 0.5 metres (1.64 feet) with minimal lunar declination, increasing to 1.2 metres (3.94 feet) at maximum declination. Tidal data on pre-war Japanese charts of North Danger Reef and Tizard Bank are also available,[305] indicating a maximum tidal range between Higher High Water and Lower Low Water of 1.6 metres at North Danger Reef and 1.8 metres at Itu Aba.

316. The Tribunal notes that the British and Chinese data on tidal ranges are remarkably consistent and that the British range between Higher High Water and Lower Low Water of 0.82 metres nearly matches the average of 0.85 metres of the higher and lower Chinese calculations. Taken as a whole, the Tribunal is comfortable with the conclusion that the average range between Higher High Water and Lower Low Water for tides in the Spratlys is on the order of 0.85 metres, increasing to 1.2 metres during certain periods of the year. The slightly higher ranges indicated from Japanese surveys may be an outlier and can be viewed as an outer limit on the expected tidal range. These are not particularly large tidal ranges, and the differences between different possible high-water datums would be correspondingly small.

317. The Tribunal takes note of the statement in the Schofield Report that "defining tidal levels is likely to be technically challenging in the context of the complex tidal regime of the South China Sea which is variable spatially and temporally and which has not been subject to detailed hydrographic surveys in recent times."[306] In this respect, the Tribunal considers that any complexity with respect to tides concerns the South China Sea as a whole, in particular coastal areas, but does not necessarily pose an issue for the Spratly Islands. The Tribunal notes that tidal regimes tend to be much more complex and variable in shallow-water areas near to the shore of large land masses, or in bays or straits, than in open, deep-water areas or around

---

[305]   Imperial Japanese Navy, Chart No. 521: North Danger Reef (1938); Imperial Japanese Navy, Chart No. 521: Tizard Bank (1938).

[306]   C. Schofield, J.R.V. Prescott & R. van der Poll, *An Appraisal of the Geographical Characteristics and Status of Certain Insular Features in the South China Sea*, p. 7 (March 2015) (Annex 513) (hereinafter **"Schofield Report"**). The authority cited by the Schofield Report for this proposition further states, on the basis of the coastal tidal data of the Philippines and Malaysia, that:

> The tides in the SCS are among the most complex in the world. In addition to a varying bathymetry, bays, gulfs and straits, the ocean circulation system in the SCS crosses the equator. These extraordinary features result, in some locations, in a changing semi-diurnal and diurnal pattern of the tidal cycle in the course of each year or even in the course of one month (a moon cycle) and is not geographically homogeneous. The west side of the basin is generally dominated by a semi-diurnal tidal cycle, whereas the east side is more mixed. The tidal range also varies from close to nil to a predicted 2m during spring tides in the northern part of the Spratlys.

> Y. Lyons, "Prospects for Satellite Imagery of Insular Features and Surrounding Marine Habitats in the South China Sea," *Marine Policy*, Vol. 45, p. 146 at pp. 150-151 (2014).

isolated reefs. Variability in tidal patterns along the coasts of the South China Sea does not indicate similar variability in the central area of the Spratly Islands. The Tribunal, assisted by its expert hydrographer, also recalls that it has before it a substantial amount of information on historical observations of tidal ranges in the Spratly Islands that is remarkably consistent and includes recent tidal observations from the modern Chinese charts, which are consistent with the tidal ranges reported historically.

318. The Tribunal thus considers that it has sufficient evidence to closely estimate the average tidal range at features in the Spratly Islands. The Tribunal also notes that the Royal Navy of the United Kingdom, Japanese Navy, and Chinese Navy all appear to have had a thorough understanding of tides in the Spratly Islands, such that direct observations on features from such sources can be assumed to have been based on an accurate understanding of the tidal conditions at the time the observations were made. This would be particularly true in the case of direct observations made in the course of a survey, where the officers in question would have been present in the area of a feature for days or weeks at a time. Recalling the caveat to its decision with respect to its jurisdiction over Submissions No. 4 and 6, the Tribunal does not consider that "practical considerations for the selection of the vertical datum and tidal model against which the status of the features is to be assessed"[307] pose a hurdle to the assessment of the status of features identified in the Philippines' Submissions.

319. At the same time, although the Tribunal is comfortable that it has a sufficient understanding of the *average* tidal *range* in the Spratly Islands and that this would suffice for interpreting charts or survey data, the Tribunal is not convinced that it is feasible accurately to model the *pattern* and *timing* of tides in the Spratly Islands. The Tribunal notes that Chinese tidal data indicate greater variation in the tidal intervals across different features than it does with respect to ranges. The Tribunal thus does not believe that it is feasible to predict with sufficient certainty the exact tidal state at a particular feature at any precise point in time. This conclusion will have implications for the Tribunal's views (discussed below) on the utility of satellite imagery.

(b)   Evidence on the Status of Features as Above/Below Water at High Tide

320. Before turning to the examination of particular features, the Tribunal considers it appropriate to address certain issues concerning the available evidence on the status of features.

321. As a general matter, the most accurate determination of whether a particular feature is or is not above water at high tide would be based on a combination of methods, including potentially

---

[307]   Award on Jurisdiction, paras. 401, 403.

direct, in-person observation covering an extended period of time across a range of weather and tidal conditions. Such direct observation, however, will often be impractical for remote features or, as in the present case, impossible where human modifications have obscured the original status of a feature or where political considerations restrict in-person observation. The Tribunal considers it important that the absence of full information not be permitted to bar the conclusions that reasonably can be drawn on the basis of other evidence. At the same time, the limitations inherent in other forms of evidence must be acknowledged.

i. Satellite Imagery

322. In attempting to overcome the absence of recent, direct observation of the features in question, the Philippines has placed heavy reliance on remote sensing through satellite imagery. The Tribunal agrees with the general point that satellite imagery may be a very useful tool, but cannot accept the degree of accuracy or certainty that the Philippines would give to such imagery. The Philippines has, for instance, relied upon a spectral analysis of imagery derived from the Landsat 4, 5, 7, and 8 satellites.[308] According to the Philippines, such a comparison of images will establish whether any portion of a reef is above water at high tide, as the ability of different wavelengths of light to penetrate water differs (see paragraph 293 above).[309] Landsat 4 and 5, however, are satellites with a 30-metre ground resolution, meaning that each pixel of the image is equal to a square on the ground of 30 metres on each side.[310] Landsat 7 and 8 include a panchromatic (black and white) band with a ground resolution of 15 metres, but otherwise have the same 30-metre ground resolution for the spectral bands as the earlier Landsat 4 and 5. In the course of the hearing, the Tribunal asked the Philippines' expert to clarify whether the imagery analysed included the use of the panchromatic band (sensitive to all wavelengths of visible light and thus black and white in appearance), which would represent a commonly used process known as pansharpening, in which a higher resolution panchromatic image is used to increase the resolution of a colour image. The Philippines' expert indicated that this had not been done. Whether or not this is the case, however, the maximum resolution that could possibly be derived from the satellite imagery used by the Philippines for this purpose is 15 metres. Small rocks or coral boulders on a reef platform may be a metre or less across and still reach above water at high tide. The resolution of the satellite imagery being used here is insufficient to establish the presence or absence of such features.

---

[308] *See* Schofield Report, pp. 12-13.

[309] Merits Hearing Tr. (Day 2), p. 25.

[310] The technical capabilities of the various Landsat satellites are set out in the *Landsat 8 Data Users Handbook*, p. 3, *available at* <landsat.usgs.gov/documents/Landsat8DataUsersHandbook.pdf>.

323. The Philippines' expert report also makes use of higher resolution imagery from the Worldview family of satellites, with a ground resolution of 0.46 metres (panchromatic).[311] However, this imagery was generally used for high-tide features and not for spectral analysis to detect the coverage of low-tide elevations at high water. Such imagery may be helpful, but as with any satellite imagery, will also suffer from the difficulty that the time of image capture will generally not align with either high or low tide. The precise tidal conditions prevailing at the time the image was taken can only be estimated, unless confirmed by observations on the ground that coincide with the time the images were taken.

324. The analysis provided by the Philippines from EOMAP also suffers from inherent vertical accuracy limitations due to the necessary reliance on predicted tidal information, as well as due to assumptions that are made in the spectral analysis. As an initial matter, the EOMAP materials provide no explanation of the vertical accuracy of their image processing. As a general matter, the Tribunal understands that Landsat satellite-derived bathymetry of this type involves a base error of at least ± one-half metre and a further error of ± 25 percent of the water depth. For WorldView satellites the further error is understood to be less, at ± 10 percent of the water depth. A further difficulty with the EOMAP materials is posed by tidal conditions. The tidal datum used by EOMAP for determining high-tide features is Highest Astronomical Tide, which is normally used to determine clearances for vessels from bridges and other overhead structures and not for the categorisation of features. Additionally, EOMAP has not (and could not have) presented imagery of the features that was actually captured during the tidal conditions represented. Rather, EOMAP has used imagery captured at a single point in time and extrapolated the results for other tidal conditions on the basis of a model of the tidal conditions at the time the image was captured. The accuracy of EOMAP's presentation of any particular tidal state is thus entirely dependent on EOMAP's model of the tidal state on the feature at the precise moment the image was captured. How this fundamental calculation was obtained is nowhere explained to the Tribunal. The Tribunal accepts that it is reasonably possible to predict the general maximum range of tides in an area on the basis of past observations, as well as the normal interval between high and low tides. The tidal range on the particular day that satellite images were taken, however, would necessarily be affected by atmospheric conditions, which would add a further degree of error into the calculation.

325. A final difficulty with the use of EOMAP imagery to determine the status of features is demonstrated by the EOMAP analysis of the Thitu Reefs, provided by the Philippines following

---

[311] The technical capabilities of the Worldview satellites are set out in the Digital Globe *Standard Imagery Data Sheet, available at* <dg-cms-uploads-production.s3.amazonaws.com/uploads/document/file/21/StandardImagery_DS_10-14_forWeb.pdf>.

the Hearing on the Merits. According to the information provided, the imagery was captured at a time when the tide on the Thitu Reefs was "71 cm below Mean High Water."[312] Several areas of the Thitu Reefs were exposed at this time, but EOMAP's imagery does not capture above-water topographic information, and these areas appear simply as white spaces. It is impossible to know whether these areas were barely exposed and likely to cover, or well above water at the time the image was taken. Instead, the areas most relevant to the classification of the feature were rejected as "data flags" from a process that is, ultimately, directed at bathymetric conditions, rather than surface features.

326. As the Philippines correctly notes, satellite imagery is most beneficial when used in conjunction with other evidence,[313] and the Tribunal considers that satellite imagery may be able to disprove the existence of large sand cays or features where the area in question clearly covers with water across a series of images. Additionally, the more far-reaching conclusions advanced by the Philippines regarding the (non-)existence of small sand cays or rocks could perhaps be established with very high-resolution stereoscopic imagery, taken at or near high tide, with in-person observations of tidal conditions taken at a nearby location. Absent such information, however, the Tribunal does not believe that the majority of the conclusions it has been asked to reach concerning the status of features as above or below water at high tide can be drawn on the basis of satellite evidence alone.

ii. Nautical Surveying and Sailing Directions

327. Given the impossibility of direct, contemporary observation and the limitations on what can be achieved with remote sensing, the Tribunal considers that more convincing evidence concerning the status of features in the South China Sea is to be found in nautical charts, records of surveys, and sailing directions. Each of these sources, the Tribunal notes, represents a record of direct observation of the features at a past point in time. Rocks and large coral boulders cemented to the platform of a reef have a high degree of permanence and can reasonably be expected to remain largely unchanged, even over centuries. Older direct observations are thus not *per se* less valuable, provided they are clear in content and obtained from a reliable source. More ephemeral features such as sand cays pose a greater challenge, but can also be consistent over time and will often reform in the same location if dispersed by a storm.

328. The Philippines has introduced a substantial quantity of chart evidence, as well as extracts from a large number of different pilots and sailing directions and emphasises that its conclusions are

---

[312]   Geographical Information on Thitu Reefs, p. 5 (Annex 856).

[313]   Merits Hearing Tr. (Day 4), pp. 54-55.

drawn not from any single source, but from the confirmation of consistent evidence across multiple sources.[314] The Tribunal will address this evidence specifically in the context of particular features, but considers several preliminary observations to be warranted.

329. As an initial matter, the Tribunal considers it more important to focus on the timing of surveys, rather than the publication of charts. There have been many nautical charts of the South China Sea published, but its features have only been surveyed on a few occasions. The details of these surveys are clearly laid out in several publications in the record before the Tribunal.[315] In brief, the first survey work to focus sustained attention on the features in the South China Sea was undertaken by the British Royal Navy between 1862 and 1868. Subsequently, both the Royal Navy and the Imperial Japanese Navy were intensively engaged in surveying the Spratly Islands in the 1920s and 1930s, although much of this information only became public well after the end of the Second World War. The French and American navies also engaged in survey work in the 1930s, although to a lesser degree. More recently, the littoral States surrounding the South China Sea have undertaken their own work, generally in the areas more closely adjacent to their coasts.

330. The majority of the nautical charts of the South China Sea issued by different States, however, are to a greater or lesser extent copies of one another. Often, information is incorporated or outright copied from other, existing charts without express attribution. Where a chain of sources can be established, even very recent charts will often trace the majority of their data to British or Japanese surveys from the 1860s or 1930s. A more recently issued chart may, in fact, include little or no new information regarding a particular feature. Multiple charts depicting a feature in the same way do not, therefore, necessarily provide independent confirmation that this depiction accords with reality. Nor should differences between charts at different scales necessarily be considered significant. Only a few of the nautical charts in the record are large-scale, depicting some of the features addressed by the Philippines at a scale of 1:150,000 or less. This paucity of large-scale charting reflects the remoteness of many of the reefs, the limited amount of detailed survey work in the area, and the lack of a need for more detailed plans, except for military purposes. The Tribunal has identified some relevant evidence in nautical charts up to 1:250,000 scale. Beyond this, however, the Tribunal does not consider that small-scale charts at 1:500,000 or 1:1,000,000 offer meaningful evidence of the absence of tiny

---

[314]   Merits Hearing Tr. (Day 2), p. 35.

[315]   D. Hancox & V. Prescott, "A Geographical Description of the Spratly Islands and an Account of Hydrographic Surveys Amongst Those Islands," *IBRU Maritime Briefing*, Vol. 1, No. 6, p. 40 (1995) (Annex 256); D. Hancox & V. Prescott, *Secret Hydrographic Surveys in the Spratly Islands*, pp. 154-155 (1999).

high-tide features rising above a covering reef. This is particularly the case on recent charts where the trend appears to be to depict less information concerning features on a reef platform as satellite navigation decreases the need for visual orientation.

331. In light of the limitations in the chart evidence before it, the Tribunal questioned the Philippines as to whether it had sought the original fair charts of surveys conducted on the features in the Spratly Islands. The Philippines indicated that it considered the consistent depiction of features in published charts to be sufficient.[316] The Tribunal disagrees and considers that, in any sensitive determination, it will very often be beneficial to have recourse to original survey data, prepared by individuals with direct experience and knowledge of the area in question. The Tribunal takes note of the comments of the International Court of Justice on the probative value of historical surveys in *Nicaragua v. Colombia*,[317] but believes they must be understood in the context of that case. The Convention gives important weight to published nautical charts, and Article 5 provides for States to use the low-water line on large-scale charts as the baseline for the territorial sea. This provision, however, envisages a situation in which a State is presenting information concerning its own coastlines in areas that can be expected to be well surveyed and well charted by that State. Considerations of an altogether different order arise where, as here, a determination involves the status of remote features, subject to the demands of competing States, that have been carefully surveyed only infrequently. The revision of charts may correct errors or introduce new information, but publication also necessarily involves a process of selection and intermediation that may exclude information of particular relevance. Accordingly, the Tribunal has independently sought materials derived from British and Japanese surveys and has provided them to the Parties for comment. Many of the Tribunal's conclusions in this Section are drawn from this material.

332. Finally, the Tribunal notes that sailing directions may offer an alternative source of first-hand observations of the features in question. The record indicates that the descriptions of reefs in the first edition of the British *China Sea Directory* were drafted aboard HMS Rifleman in the course of conducting the survey.[318] Later British surveys in the 1920s and 1930s also sent back amended or supplemental descriptions for direct incorporation into the sailing directions.[319] The

---

[316] Merits Hearing Tr. (Day 2), p. 38.

[317] *Territorial and Maritime Dispute (Nicaragua v. Colombia), Judgment, ICJ Reports 2012*, p. 624 at p. 644, para. 35.

[318] *See* Letter from Commander Reed (on convalescent leave) to the Hydrographer of the Admiralty (26 March 1865); Letter from Commander Reed, HMS Rifleman, to the Hydrographer of the Admiralty (19 June 1868).

[319] HMS Iroquois, *Sailing Directions to accompany Chart of North Danger*; HMS Herald, *Corrections to Sailing Directions for Spratly Island, Amboyna Cay, and Fiery Cross Reef*, UKHO Ref. H3853/1936;

edition of a pilot following survey operations can thus be read more as a first-hand account of the area and features, rather than simply a technical document. In contrast with the British practice, however, the sailing directions of other States appear to be principally derived from the British text, with the exception of the U.S. sailing directions, which appear to have been based on Japanese information, and the Chinese sailing directions, which appear to include independent information. As with published nautical charts, satellite navigation has also caused the more-recent editions of the pilots to become less descriptive of the features on reefs and correspondingly less useful to the particular determination presented to the Tribunal.

(c)   The Status of Particular Features in the South China Sea

       i.   *Scarborough Shoal*

333. Scarborough Shoal was surveyed in detail by HMS Swallow in 1866 and by HMS Herald in 1932. The fair plans of the two surveys indicate between five and seven rocks that are clearly marked as being between one and three feet above high water. The same rocks are depicted in some of the published nautical charts before the Tribunal[320] and are confirmed in all of the relevant sailing directions,[321] including the *China Sailing Directions: South China Sea* published by the Navigation Guarantee Department of the Chinese Navy Headquarters, which describes the reef as follows:

> Huangyan Island (Democracy Reef) Located 340 nautical miles southerly of Yongxing Island, it is the only atoll among these islands to be exposed above sea level. Its shape resembles an isosceles triangle, the west side and south side are each 15 km long, and the surface area is approximately 150 sq. km. The reef basin has a crest width of 1 km - 2 km, and the northern part is 3.3 km at its widest part. In general, the water depth is 0.5 meters - 3.5 meters. Hundreds of large reef segments are distributed along the top surface and are 0.3 meters – 3.5 meters above sea level. The North Rock on the northwest end and the South Rock on the southeast end have a surface area of approximately 10 sq. meters. They are respectively 1.5 meters and 1.8 meters above sea level. The water depth within the lagoon is 10 meters – 20 meters. The east side of South Rock has a 400-meter wide waterway, and boats can come in from the open seas to anchor.[322]

HMS Herald, *Amendments to Sailing Directions for West York, Nanshan, Flat Island, and Mischief Reef*, UKHO Ref. H3911/1938.

[320]   *See, e.g.*, Philippines Chart No. 4803 (Scarborough Shoal) (2006) (Annex NC32); British Admiralty Chart No. 3489 (Manila to Hong Kong) (1998) (Annex NC46).

[321]   Philippine National Mapping and Resource Information Agency, *Philippine Coast Pilot* (6th ed., 1995) (Annex 230); United States National Geospatial-Intelligence Agency, *Pub. 161 Sailing Directions (Enroute), South China Sea and the Gulf of Thailand*, p. 7 (13th ed., 2011) (Annex 233); United Kingdom Hydrographic Office, *Admiralty Sailing Directions: China Sea Pilot (NP31)*, Vol. 2, p. 68 (10th ed., 2012) (Annex 235).

[322]   Navigation Guarantee Department of the Chinese Navy Headquarters, *China Sailing Directions: South China Sea (A103)*, p. 172 (2011) (Annex 232(bis)).

334. The Tribunal concludes that Scarborough Shoal is encumbered by a number of rocks that remain exposed at high tide and is, accordingly, a high-tide feature.

ii.   *Cuarteron Reef*

335. Cuarteron Reef and the other London Reefs were visited by HMS Rifleman in 1864 and 1865, but no comprehensive survey of Cuarteron Reef appears to have been undertaken, likely due to the difficulty in finding any anchorage on the steep slopes of the feature.[323] Cuarteron Reef was visited again in 1938 by HMS Herald in the course of her secret work in the South China Sea, and those observations were incorporated into the 1951 edition of the *China Sea Pilot* which clearly reports a number of rocks above water at high tide:

> Cuarteron reef, about 10 miles eastward of East reef, dries and is encumbered by rocks, especially on its norther side, where some are from 4 to 5 feet (1^m2 to 1^m5) high. Anchorage was obtained by H.M. Surveying Ship *Herald*, in 1938, in a depth of about 15 fathoms (27^m4), about one cable from the northern side; the southern side is steep-to. There is no lagoon.
>
> The tidal streams set eastward and westward along the northern side of Cuarteron reef.
>
> Although considerable depths were found, in 1865, close to all the London reefs, there was generally some slope from the edges on which HMS *Rifleman* found safe anchorage for a short period, but on Cuarteron reef no anchorage could be found.[324]

336. The same general description, albeit with less detail, is repeated in later editions of the *China Sea Pilot*,[325] in the U.S. *Sailing Directions (Enroute): South China Sea and the Gulf of Thailand*,[326] in the Japanese *South China Sea and Malacca Strait Pilot*,[327] and in the *Philippine Coast Pilot*.[328]

337. A slightly different description appears in the *China Sailing Directions: South China Sea* published by the Navigation Guarantee Department of the Chinese Navy Headquarters, which reads as follows:

> Huayang Reef - Approximately 40 nautical miles slightly westerly of due north from the Yongshu Reef is the easternmost part of the Yinqing Reefs. It is an independent table-like

---

[323]   *See* Admiralty Hydrographic Office, *China Sea Directory,* Vol. II, p. 68 (1st ed., 1868).

[324]   *China Sea Pilot*, Vol. I, p. 123 (2nd ed., 1951).

[325]   United Kingdom Hydrographic Office, *Admiralty Sailing Directions: China Sea Pilot (NP31)*, Vol. 2, p. 65 (10th ed., 2012) (Annex 235).

[326]   United States National Geospatial-Intelligence Agency, *Pub. 161 Sailing Directions (Enroute), South China Sea and the Gulf of Thailand*, p. 13 (13th ed., 2011) (Annex 233).

[327]   Japan Coast Guard, *Document No. 204: South China Sea and Malacca Strait Pilot* p. 26 (March 2011) (Annex 234).

[328]   Philippine National Mapping and Resource Information Agency, *Philippine Coast Pilot*, p. 16-72 (6th ed., 1995) (Annex 230).

reef with no lagoon in the center of the reef flat. It appears to be trending toward the east and west. During high tide it is submerged. During spring tide and low tide, it is exposed, and its middle part is low and flat.[329]

338. In the Tribunal's view, the statement that "[d]uring high tide it is submerged" in the Chinese sailing directions is better understood as stating that the reef platform is submerged at high tide, rather than as disproving the existence of particular rocks above water at high tide. In contrast, the references to rocks in the 1938 description of the reef are clear. In light of the purpose of sailing directions in enabling visual navigation, this should be understood as a description of rocks that remain visible at high tide. There is no more recent or more authoritative evidence that would suggest the absence of high-tide rocks on Cuarteron Reef, and the Philippines does not contest the status of Cuarteron Reef as a high-tide feature.

339. The Tribunal concludes that Cuarteron Reef in its natural condition was encumbered by rocks that remain exposed at high tide and is, accordingly, a high-tide feature.

iii.   Fiery Cross Reef

340. Fiery Cross Reef was surveyed by HMS Rifleman in 1866, which produced a detailed fair chart of the feature, which is reproduced as Figure 4 on page 149 below. A prominent rock on the south-west end of the reef is clearly marked on the fair chart, although it is not described in the 1868 edition of the *China Sea Directory*.[330] Fiery Cross Reef was visited again by HMS Herald in 1936, which forwarded the following amended description for the sailing directions:

> The Fiery Cross or N.W. Investigator Reef is a coral reef having several dry patches, upon most of which the sea breaks even in light winds, or with a slight swell. It is 14 miles long, north-east and south-west, and 4 miles wide. The largest dry patch is at its south-west end and has a conspicuous rock, about 2 feet high (0m6), on the south-ease side about 4 cables from the south-west extreme in Lat. 9° 33′ N., Long. 112° 53′ E. Anchorage is obtainable in 13 fathoms (23m7) about 2 cables from the edge of the reef, with this rock bearing 062, distant 7 cables.[331]

341. This description was incorporated into the 1951 edition of the China Sea Pilot, which clarifies that "[a]t high water the whole reef is covered except a prominent rock . . . , about 2 feet (0m6),"[332] and is repeated in later editions of the *China Sea Pilot*,[333] in the U.S. *Sailing*

---

[329]   Navigation Guarantee Department of the Chinese Navy Headquarters, *China Sailing Directions: South China Sea (A103)*, p. 178 (2011) (Annex 232(bis)).

[330]   Admiralty Hydrographic Office, *China Sea Directory*, Vol. II, p. 68 (1st ed., 1868).

[331]   HMS Herald, *Corrections to Sailing Directions for Spratly Island, Amboyna Cay, and Fiery Cross Reef*, UKHO Jacket H3853/1936.

[332]   *China Sea Pilot*, Vol. I, pp. 123-124 (2nd ed., 1951).

[333]   United Kingdom Hydrographic Office, *Admiralty Sailing Directions: China Sea Pilot (NP31)*, Vol. 2, p. 65 (10th ed., 2012) (Annex 235).

Directions (Enroute): South China Sea and the Gulf of Thailand,[334] and in the *Philippine Coast Pilot*.[335] The same rock is also described in the Chinese Navy Headquarters *China Sailing Directions: South China Sea* in the following terms:

> Yongshu Reef - Located at the southeast part of the Nansha Islands and the west end of the Nanhua waterway's south side, the reef is trending from northeast-to-southwest. Most of the atoll is submerged underwater. During high tide, only the western end has 2 sq. meters of natural reef rock exposed. During low tide, there are 7 pieces of reef flat of varying sizes that are exposed.[336]

342. There is no more recent or more authoritative evidence that would suggest the absence of a high-tide rock on Fiery Cross Reef, and the Philippines does not contest the status of Fiery Cross Reef as a high-tide feature. The Tribunal also notes that the Philippines' expert has noted the possible existence of additional small sand cays on Fiery Cross Reef that remain above water at high tide,[337] although the Tribunal recalls its observations on reliance on satellite evidence (see paragraph 326 above).

343. The Tribunal concludes that Fiery Cross Reef, in its natural condition was encumbered by a rock that remained exposed at high tide and is, accordingly, a high-tide feature.

> iv. *Johnson Reef*

344. Union Bank, including Johnson Reef, was not surveyed by HMS Rifleman in the 1860s, and the first Royal Navy survey of the area appears to have been undertaken by HMS Herald in 1931. The fair chart of this survey is extremely accurate with respect to position and shape of features on the Union Bank, as compared to modern imagery. This suggests both that the survey was carefully done and that it benefited from the Royal Navy's use of flying boats and aerial photography in its 1931 survey operations. The fair chart is reproduced as Figure 5 on page 151 below, along with other surveys of Johnson Reef and clearly depicts a high-tide rock in the southern corner of the reef. The corresponding description of Union Bank in the Royal Navy's 1944 sailing directions for the Spratly Islands, however, is vague and adds no detail concerning Johnson Reef.

---

[334] United States National Geospatial-Intelligence Agency, *Pub. 161 Sailing Directions (Enroute), South China Sea and the Gulf of Thailand*, p. 13 (13th ed., 2011) (Annex 233).

[335] Philippine National Mapping and Resource Information Agency, *Philippine Coast Pilot*, p. 16-72 (6th ed., 1995).

[336] Navigation Guarantee Department of the Chinese Navy Headquarters, *China Sailing Directions: South China Sea (A103)*, p. 178 (2011) (Annex 232(bis)).

[337] Schofield Report, p. 66.

345. In addition to the British, the Imperial Japanese Navy was actively involved in surveying the Spratly Islands in the 1930s and published a plan of Union Bank as part of Imperial Japanese Navy Chart No. 525 – Plans in the Southern Archipelago. That chart also clearly depicts a small high-tide feature in the southern extremity of Johnson Reef.

346. The most detailed description of Johnson Reef, however, appears as part of the U.S. survey of what was known as the "Pigeon Passage", a safe route through the Spratlys from Half Moon Shoal in the east to Fiery Cross Reef in the west that was surveyed by USS Pigeon and accompanying vessels in 1935 and 1937. The report of that survey includes plans and descriptions of the principal reefs adjacent to the surveyed route, including a plan for what is incorrectly identified as "Sin Cowe Island". However, from the shape of the reef formation, the coordinates given for it, and its location in the sketch plan of Union Bank, entitled "Shoals Near Sin Cowe Islands," it is apparent that what USS Pigeon identified as Sin Cowe was, in fact, Johnson Reef. The U.S. plan of that feature depicts numerous rocks and notes the coordinates of a "largest rock". The accompanying description of the feature was as follows:

> Sin Cowe Island – Position of the largest rock, which is about 5 feet in diameter and four feet high in S.E. corner is Latitude 9° 42′ 00″ N., Longitude 114° 16′ 30″ E. The reef was sighted 4.7 miles from a height of 70 feet. The island was underwater except for about six rocks at S.E. corner. This is the southernmost of a cluster of about 20 shoals, (see sketches #3 and 4) that extend to the eastward for about 40 miles. These reefs were in two parallel lines, the reefs in pair; one line is at an angle of about 050°T. from Sin Cowe and the second to the northwestward of the first at a distance of about 1.5 miles. The small reef to the northwestward of Sin Cowe bears about 330° true. A coral dune was reported on the southeastern part of this small reef. It was also reported that these reefs were inter-connected below the surface but that the channel between this reef and Sin Cowe Island was probably navigable. The prevailing wind blew directly down the channel from 060° true. Sin Cowe Island is fish-hooked in shape which is caused by a lagoon in its center whose entrance is in the northeast corner of the island. The major axis of this island shoal is about two miles in a north south direction and it varies in width from about one mile at the north end to ½ mile at the south end. It is apparently of volcanic origin with a lining of coral around the lagoon.

> The lagoon is long and narrow; appears deep at its entrance, shoaling gradually toward the head. It might provide anchorage for not more than two submarines but this is doubtful.

> Anchorage space is not recommended here due to the steep banks and large fissures in the coral, although three mine sweepers have been at anchor here at the same time on the southwestern side of the shoal in water ranging from 17 to 30 fathoms.[338]

347. A condensed description, correctly identified as Johnson Reef and describing the same rocks, is set out in later editions of the U.S. sailing directions:

> Johnson Reef (9°42′N., 114°17′E.), of brown volcanic rock with white coral around the inner rim, is located at the SW end of Union Atoll. Johnson Reef partly encloses a shallow lagoon entered from the NE. The largest rock on the reef is about 1.2m high. Several other

---

[338] U.S. Navy Hydrographic Office, *Notes and Sailing Directions: Dangerous Ground in China Sea*, pp. 4-5 (1937).

rocks show above the water on the SE part of the reef; the remainder of the reef is reported to be covered.[339]

348. Although a datum for this 1.2-metre height is not directly given, the definitions section of the U.S. *Sailing Directions* indicates that height references refer to the plane of reference for the chart concerned. Other larger-scale U.S. charts in the area describe the plane of reference as being Mean Sea Level. In light of the tidal ranges identified for the South China Sea (see paragraph 316 above), a rock four feet or 1.2 metres above Mean Sea Level would be exposed at high tide. The U.S. sailing directions also note that "several other rocks show above the water."

349. No such rocks are reported in the Chinese Navy Headquarters *China Sailing Directions: South China Sea*, which describe Johnson Reef as follows:

> Chigua Reef - Located at the edge of the southwest end of the Jiuzhang reef group's large atoll, the reef flat is low-lying, it has no particularly obvious natural markers. During high tide, it is submerged. During low tide, it is exposed and has a shape resembling a horseshoe.[340]

350. Chinese Chart No. 18400, however, depicts a height of "(0.9)" metres above Mean Sea Level in the area of Johnson Reef corresponding with the high-tide elevation depicted in the British and Japanese materials. A 0.9-metre height above Mean Sea Level would be exposed even at Mean High Water Springs and would be exposed by nearly half a metre a Mean Higher High Water.

351. The Tribunal is thus presented with a British survey and Japanese plan that depict a high-tide feature on Johnson Reef, a U.S. survey and sailing directions that describe a rock that would likely be exposed at high water, Chinese sailing directions that are phrased in somewhat general terms and make no mention of any rocks whatsoever, and a published Chinese chart indicating a height above high water on Johnson Reef. Taken together, the weight of the evidence favours the conclusion that Johnson Reef is a high-tide feature, which the Tribunal accordingly reaches.

v.   McKennan Reef

352. Like Johnson Reef and the other features making up Union Bank, McKennan Reef was not surveyed before the 1930s. Also like Johnson Reef, the results of the British and Japanese surveys from that period are consistent. On McKennan Reef, however, they do not show any high-tide feature. Both surveys are reproduced as Figure 6 on page 153 below. Nor is any high

---

[339]   United States National Geospatial-Intelligence Agency, *Pub. 161 Sailing Directions (Enroute), South China Sea and the Gulf of Thailand*, p. 11 (13th ed., 2011) (Annex 233).

[340]   Navigation Guarantee Department of the Chinese Navy Headquarters, *China Sailing Directions: South China Sea (A103)*, p. 178 (2011) (Annex 232(bis)).

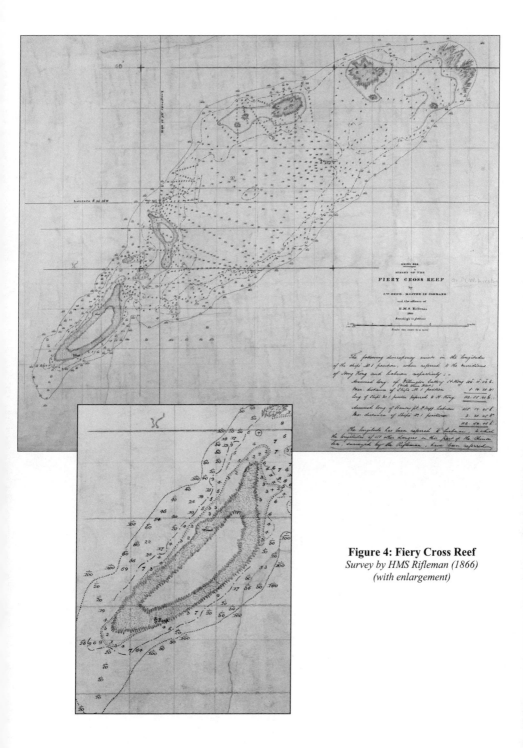

Figure 4: Fiery Cross Reef
Survey by HMS Rifleman (1866)
(with enlargement)

this page intentionally blank

Figure 5: Johnson Reef

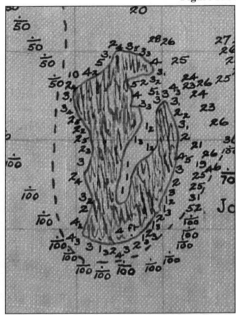

Survey by HMS Herald (1931)
(depicting 4 foot rock in S.E. corner)

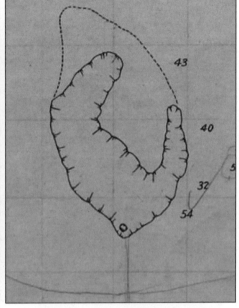

Imperial Japanese Navy Chart No. 525
(depicting high-water feature in S. corner)

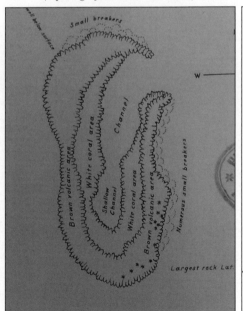

Survey by USS Pigeon (1937)
(depicting multiple rocks in S.E. corner)

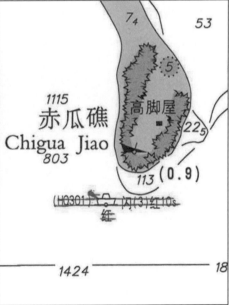

China Chart No. 18400 (2005)
(depicting 0.9 metre height above Mean Sea Level)

this page intentionally blank

Figure 6: McKennan Reef

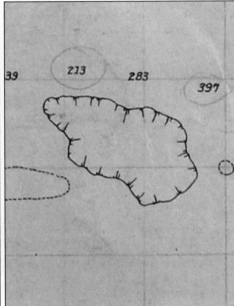

Survey by HMS Herald (1931)
(depicting no high-water feature)

Imperial Japanese Navy Chart No. 525
(depicting no high-water feature)

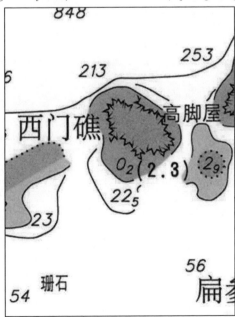

China Chart No. 18400 (2005)
(depicting 2.3 metre height above Mean Sea Level)

153

this page intentionally blank

tide feature evident in U.S. Hydrographic Office Chart No. 5667, published in 1951 on the basis of the earlier Japanese survey.[341] No sailing directions appear to include any description of McKennan Reef and the British *China Sea Pilot* notes that Union Bank as a whole "has not been closely examined."[342]

353. The Philippines argues that the "[c]harts produced by China, the Philippines, the UK and U.S. and Japan all depict McKennan Reef as a low-tide elevation."[343] The Tribunal notes, however, that this statement is not wholly correct. China's Chart No. 18400 depicts Union Bank at 1:250,000 scale, but does not support the position advocated by the Philippines. Although the chart does not include any symbol for a rock or island on the reef platform of McKennan Reef itself, a height of "(2.3)" metres above Mean Sea Level is indicated directly adjacent to McKennan Reef, with a notation that corresponds to that used on Chinese charts for features that do not cover at high water. Such a height would be well above high water against any datum. While the absence of any symbol on the reef platform itself might, at first glance, call this height into question, the Tribunal notes that the same pattern of notation (an apparently bare reef platform with an adjacent height) is used on the same chart to depict Namyit Island on Tizard Bank, where a high-tide feature unequivocally does exist, and also Johnson Reef on Union Bank. The source key to Chart No. 18400 indicates that certain areas of the Chart were surveyed by China between 1989 and 2001 and that the data for Union Bank were derived from "1984, 1982 version of nautical chart."

354. The Philippines also argues that no high-tide feature is apparent in the satellite bathymetry materials prepared by EOMAP, but the Tribunal is unwilling to give weight to this evidence for the reasons discussed above (see paragraph 326). As between the earlier British and Japanese materials depicting no high-tide feature on McKennan Reef and a more recent Chinese chart depicting a height at McKennan Reef, the Tribunal concludes that the Chinese chart is to be preferred as the more recent evidence and that the height indicated for McKennan Reef most likely indicates a coral boulder pushed onto the reef platform and above high water by storm action.

---

[341] The plan of Union Bank from U.S. Hydrographic Office Chart No. 5657 is reproduced (and misnumbered as Chart No. 5667) in D. Hancox and V. Prescott, *Secret Hydrographic Surveys in the Spratly Islands*, p. 215 (1999).

[342] United Kingdom Hydrographic Office, *Admiralty Sailing Directions: China Sea Pilot (NP31)*, Vol. 2, p. 63 (10th ed., 2012) (Annex 235).

[343] Merits Hearing Tr. (Day 2), p. 30.

vi.   *Hughes Reef*

355. Like McKennan Reef and the other features making up Union Bank, Hughes Reef was not surveyed before the 1930s.

356. In contrast to McKennan Reef, however, the British and Japanese surveys of Hughes Reef undertaken in the 1930s suggest different conclusions. No high-tide feature is depicted on Hughes Reef in the British fair chart of Union Bank, whereas Imperial Japanese Navy Chart No. 525 depicts such a feature on the south-west corner of the reef. Both surveys are reproduced as Figure 7 on page 159 below. The same depiction as Imperial Japanese Navy Chart No. 525 also appears in U.S. Hydrographic Office Chart No. 5667, which was based upon the Japanese survey results.[344] No sailing directions appear to include any description of Hughes Reef.

357. The Philippines argues that the "[c]harts produced by China, the Philippines, the UK and US and Japan all depict McKennan Reef as a low-tide elevation"[345] and the Tribunal understands that statement to apply equally to Hughes Reef, in light of the Philippines' conflation of the two features. The Tribunal is reluctant, however, to draw significant conclusions from the comparatively small scale (1:250,000 or smaller) depictions of the features on Union Bank in more recent charts for the reasons outlined above (see paragraph 330). The Tribunal agrees that the U.S. and Philippine charts at 1:250,000 do not depict any feature on the reef platform at Hughes Reef, but notes that the same charts also do not depict any high-tide feature at Sin Cowe, where a high-tide feature unequivocally exists. U.S. Defense Mapping Agency Chart No. 93044 also indicates that its survey data for Union Bank are derived from Taiwan Authority of China Chart No. 477A, which is, in turn, a reproduction of Imperial Japanese Navy Chart No. 525, rather than the product of independent survey work.[346] The Tribunal sees no reason to assume that the removal of any indication of a high-tide feature on Hughes Reef in Chart No. 93044 reflects anything more than a reduction in detail corresponding with the decrease in scale from original 1:100,000 scale of Imperial Japanese Navy Chart No. 525 to the 1:250,000 scale of Chart No. 93044. At the same time, however, China's Chart No. 18400 (the same chart to note a height at McKennan Reef) includes no indication of a height or high-tide feature at Hughes Reef.

---

[344] The plan of Union Bank from U.S. Hydrographic Office Chart No. 5657 is reproduced (and misnumbered as Chart No. 5667) in D. Hancox & V. Prescott, *Secret Hydrographic Surveys in the Spratly Islands*, p. 215 (1999).

[345] Merits Hearing Tr. (Day 2), p. 30.

[346] *See* D. Hancox & V. Prescott, *Secret Hydrographic Surveys in the Spratly Islands*, pp. 154-155 (1999).

358. In light of all of the evidence, the Tribunal concludes that Hughes Reef is a low-tide elevation. Although the Japanese chart does appear to indicate a high-tide feature, no height is given for this feature (in contrast to the depiction of a sand cay on Gaven Reef (North) on the Japanese chart of Tizard Bank) and the observation is not corroborated by any other evidence before the Tribunal. Nor does it appear in the most recent Chinese chart.

      vii.   Gaven Reefs

359. The Gaven Reefs lie on Tizard Bank, which constitutes one of the most-thoroughly surveyed areas of the South China Sea. Tizard Bank was carefully surveyed by HMS Rifleman in 1867 and the large-scale fair chart of that survey does not depict a high-tide feature on the Gaven Reefs. This and other depictions of Gaven Reef (North) are reproduced as Figure 8 on page 161 below. Nor is any high-tide feature mentioned in the original description of Gaven Reef (North) (unnamed at the time) in the 1868 version of the *China Sea Directory*, which reads as follows:

> Two dangerous reefs, covered at high water, lie to the westward of Nam-yit; the first is oval-shaped, three-quarters of a mile long N.N.W. and S.S.E., the island bearing from it E. 7/8 N., distant 6 miles; the second is a mile long North and South, and nearly three-quarters of a mile broad at its northern end, narrowing to a point at the opposite end; this last is the westernmost danger of the Tizard group, and its outer edge is in lat. 10° 13′ 20″ N., long. 114° 13′ 7″ E.[347]

360. The description of the Gaven Reefs appears essentially unchanged throughout the various editions of the *China Sea Directory* and *China Sea Pilot*. A reference to a beacon on Gaven Reef (North) appears in the 1951 edition of the *China Sea Pilot*,[348] but has been removed by the 1964 edition.[349]

361. The Gaven Reefs were also extensively surveyed in the 1930s by the Imperial Japanese Navy, which maintained a presence on Itu Aba Island in Tizard Bank prior to and during the Second World War. The Gaven Reefs were depicted in a large-scale plan of the Tizard Bank, which indicates a sand cay in the north-east corner of Gaven Reef (North) with a survey marker upon it and the words "(height 1.9 metres)" in parentheses adjacent to the sand cay.[350] The accompanying description of Gaven Reef (North) in the Japanese war-time sailing directions for the South China Sea reads as follows:

---

[347]   Admiralty Hydrographic Office, *China Sea Directory*, Vol. II, p. 71 (1st ed., 1868).

[348]   Admiralty Hydrographic Department, *China Sea Pilot*, Vol. I, p. 125 (2nd ed., 1951).

[349]   Admiralty Hydrographic Department, *China Sea Pilot*, Vol. I, pp. 110-111 (3rd ed., 1964).

[350]   Imperial Japanese Navy, Chart No. 523: Tizard Bank (1938).

> Sankaku Shō is a shoal about a mile in extent submerged at H.W. which forms the W. extreme of Chizato Tai; there is a sand cay near its N.E. extremity.[351]

362. The Japanese plan of Tizard Bank was reproduced after the war as U.S. Hydrographic Office Chart No. 5659 in 1950 and reissued in 1974 as Defense Mapping Agency Chart No. 93043, including a magenta overlay with additional details. This chart reproduces the Japanese plan exactly (to the point that the parentheses surrounding the Japanese text on Gaven Reef (North) are printed on the U.S. chart, even though the text itself has been removed) and includes the depiction of the sand cay and survey marker on Gaven Reef (North). The magenta overlay adds the height of "1.9" adjacent to the sand cay, which appears to have been omitted from the 1950 printing. The magenta overlay appears to represent a revision of the plan on the basis of additional, Japanese-language information included in the original Japanese plan, but not transposed to the first edition of the U.S. chart. The accompanying U.S. sailing directions describe the Gaven Reefs in the following terms:

> Gaven Reefs (10°12'N., 114°13'E.) is comprised of two reefs which cover at HW and lie 7 miles W and 8.5 miles WNW, respectively, of Namyit Island. They are the SW dangers of Tizard Bank. The N of the two reefs is marked by a white sand dune about 2m high.[352]

363. During the Hearing on the Merits, the Tribunal questioned the Philippines regarding Chart No. 93043 and the U.S. sailing directions. The Philippines argued that no high-tide feature was indicated insofar as (a) properly interpreted, the sailing directions describe a sand dune that would cover at high water; (b) the feature depicted on Gaven Reef (North) is a Japanese survey marker; (c) the height of 1.9 metres is based on a datum of Mean Sea Level and does not indicate a height above high water; (d) a high-tide feature is not depicted on later U.S. charts, in particular U.S. Defense Mapping Agency Chart No. 93044; and (e) the Chinese sailing directions for the Gaven Reefs indicate that "[d]uring high tide, these reef rocks are all submerged by seawater."[353]

364. The Tribunal, however, reaches a different conclusion on the interpretation of the U.S. and Japanese materials for the following reasons:

---

[351] English translation of Japanese *Pilot for Taiwan and the South-West Islands*, Vol. V, p. 243 (March 1941 ed.), "Sailing Directions for Shinnan Guntao," UKHO Ref. H019893/1944.

[352] United States National Geospatial-Intelligence Agency, *Pub. 161 Sailing Directions (Enroute), South China Sea and the Gulf of Thailand*, p. 9 (13th ed., 2011) (Annex 233).

[353] Navigation Guarantee Department of the Chinese Navy Headquarters, *China Sailing Directions: South China Sea (A103)*, p. 177 (2011) (Annex 232(bis)).

Figure 7: Hughes Reef

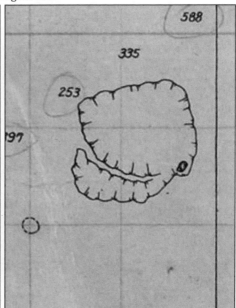

Survey by HMS Herald (1931)
(depicting no high-water feature)

Imperial Japanese Navy Chart No. 525
(depicting a high-water feature in S.E. corner)

China Chart 18400 (2005)
(depicting no high-water feature)

this page intentionally blank

Figure 8: Gaven Reef (North)

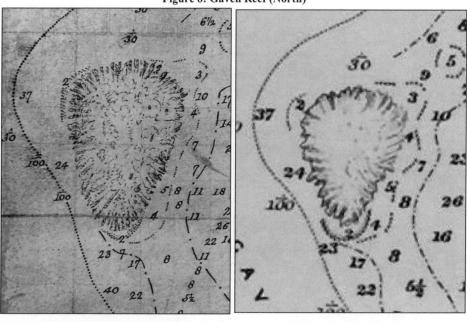

Survey by HMS Rifleman (1867)
(depicting no high-water feature)

British Admiralty Chart No. 1201 (2000)
(depicting no high-water feature)

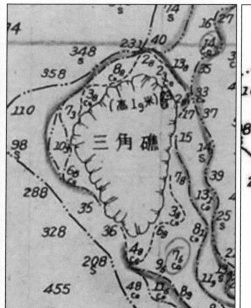

Imperial Japanese Navy Chart No. 523
(depicting sand cay with height of 1.9 metres
above Mean Sea Level)

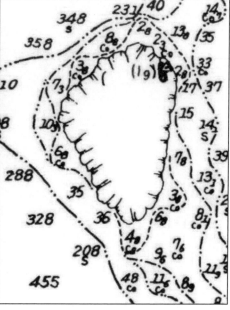

U.S. Chart No. 93043 (1967)
(depicting sand cay with height of 1.9 metres
above Mean Sea Level)

this page intentionally blank

(a)   It is certainly true that both the U.S. and Japanese sailing directions describe Gaven Reef (North) as submerged at high water and also describe a sand cay on the reef. In the Tribunal's view, the proper interpretation of these descriptions is that the reef platform is submerged at high water, while the sand cay remains exposed. Given that the purpose of sailing directions is to facilitate visual navigation, references to particular rocks or cays on a reef will generally describe features that remain visible points of reference at high tide when the reef itself is covered. In the absence of an indication that a rock or cay covers at high water, the Tribunal would normally understand such a description to refer to a high-water feature, even in the absence of an express indication of that fact.

(b)   Both the Japanese chart and the U.S. reproduction thereof clearly depict both a high-water sand cay and a Japanese survey marker on the north-east corner of Gaven Reef (North). This is more clearly visible in the Japanese printing, but is also apparent upon close examination of the U.S. chart.

(c)   The height of 1.9 metres on Gaven Reef (North) is referenced to a datum of Mean Sea Level, as the chart itself indicates. In light of tidal ranges in the Spratly Islands indicated by British and Chinese observations (see paragraph 316 above), a height of 1.9 metres would be well above even Mean High Water Springs. Even using the somewhat higher Japanese tidal information on Chart No. 93043 itself would place Highest High Water at 0.9 metres above Mean Sea Level and still a full metre below the height indicated for the sand cay on Gaven Reef (North).

(d)   More recently published U.S. charts that include Tizard Bank do not reflect more recent survey information. Chart No. 93044—which the Philippines considers to dispose of the existence of a cay on Gaven Reef (North)—indicates that its survey data for Tizard Bank are derived from Taiwan Authority of China Chart No. 478. This chart is, in turn, a reproduction of Imperial Japanese Navy Chart No. 523, rather than the product of independent survey work.[354] The "newer" U.S. chart thus reflects the same underlying Japanese survey as the chart depicting a sand cay. The absence of detail on Gaven Reef (North) is a result of the smaller 1:250,000 scale of the later chart, in comparison with the 1:75,000 scale of the earlier plan.

(e)   There appear to be some inaccuracies in the English translation of the Chinese sailing directions for the Gaven Reefs provided by the Philippines, which properly translate as follows:

---

[354]   *See* D. Hancox & V. Prescott, *Secret Hydrographic Surveys in the Spratly Islands*, pp. 154-155 (1999).

> Gaven Reef (Nanxun Reef) - Located at the southwest end of the Tizard Bank
> (Zhenghe reef group), it is comprised of two coral reefs, one in the south and one in
> the north. The relative positions of the two coral reefs appear to be trending from
> northwest to southeast. The reef in the southeast direction is located approximately
> six nautical miles west of Namyit Island (Hongxiu Island). During high tide, these
> reef rocks are all submerged by seawater.[355]

Hongxiu Island is a reference to Namyit Island, which lies well beyond six nautical miles from Gaven Reef (North). Read correctly, the Chinese sailing directions clearly state that the rocks at Gaven Reef (South) are submerged at high water.

365. The Tribunal therefore considers that it is faced not with uniform evidence concerning the status of Gaven Reef (North), but with a 20th century Japanese survey depicting a sand cay on the reef and a 19th century British survey indicating no such feature. As between the two, the Tribunal considers that the Japanese evidence is to be preferred and sees no more recent evidence that would disprove the existence of a sand cay on Gaven Reef (North). Accordingly, the Tribunal concludes that Gaven Reef (North) is a high-tide feature.

366. The Tribunal has seen no evidence in any of the sources discussed above that would suggest the existence of a high-tide feature on Gaven Reef (South) and notes the description to the contrary in the Chinese sailing directions. The Tribunal concludes that Gaven Reef (South) is a low-tide elevation.

viii. Subi Reef

367. Subi Reef was surveyed along with the nearby Thitu Reefs in 1867 by HMS Rifleman. The detailed fair chart of the feature is reproduced as Figure 9 on page 169 below and depicts no high-tide feature on the reef. The corresponding sailing directions from 1868 describe Subi Reef as follows:

> Soubie Reef, the south-west end of which is in lat. 10° 53½' N., long. 114° 4' E., is the
> westernmost danger in this locality. It is an irregular-shaped coral reef, nearly 3½ miles
> long, N.E. and S.W., and 2 miles broad, is dry at low water, and has a lagoon into which
> there appears to be no passage.[356]

368. The same conclusion follows from the depiction of Subi Reef in U.S. Defense Mapping Agency Chart No. 93061, although the Tribunal notes that this chart is a reissued version of U.S. Hydrographic Office Chart No. 2786, which was simply a copy in 1911 of British Admiralty Chart No. 1201, which was in turn based the 1867 survey data.[357] No high-tide feature on Subi

---

[355] Navigation Guarantee Department of the Chinese Navy Headquarters, *China Sailing Directions: South China Sea (A103)*, p. 177 (2011) (Annex 232(bis)) (corrected translation).

[356] Admiralty Hydrographic Office, *China Sea Directory*, Vol. II, p. 72 (1st ed., 1868).

[357] D. Hancox & V. Prescott, *Secret Hydrographic Surveys in the Spratly Islands*, p. 38 (1999).

Reef is depicted on British Admiralty Chart No. 1201 either,[358] and the Tribunal is unable to identify any source suggesting a rock or cay above high water on Subi Reef. Accordingly, the Tribunal concludes that Subi Reef is a low-tide elevation.

369. A more complex question, however, is whether Subi Reef lies within 12 nautical miles of a high-tide feature, such that it would could serve as a baseline for the territorial sea of that high-tide feature pursuant to Article 13(1) of the Convention. Subi Reef lies slightly more than 12 nautical miles from the baseline of Thitu Island, and would not qualify for the purposes of Article 13(1) for a territorial sea drawn from Thitu Island itself. The 1867 fair chart of the Thitu Reefs, however, clearly depicts a high-water "Sandy Cay" on the reefs to the west of Thitu Island. This feature—provided that it, in fact, exists—would lie within 12 nautical miles of Subi Reef, which would be permitted by Article 13(1) to serve as a baseline for the territorial sea drawn from Sandy Cay.

370. When questioned on this feature during the hearing, the Philippines argued that Sandy Cay no longer exists, insofar as it is not depicted in more recent U.S. charts that include the Thitu Reefs and does not appear in the satellite-derived bathymetry prepared by EOMAP.[359]

371. As an initial matter, the Tribunal does not believe that any reliable conclusions can be drawn from the absence of a depiction of Sandy Cay in the 1984 edition of United States Defense Mapping Agency Chart No. 93044. That chart indicates that the area surrounding the Thitu Reefs was drawn from the Taiwan Authority of China's Chart No. 477, which is in turn is drawn from British Admiralty Chart No. 1201 and the same survey of the Thitu Reefs from 1867.[360] The Tribunal sees nothing to suggest that the later U.S. publication reflects new information on the conditions prevailing on the Thitu Reefs, rather than simply a reduction in detail corresponding with the decreased scale of the chart.

372. On the contrary, the Tribunal notes that a sandbar to the west of Thitu Island is mentioned in all of the recent editions of all relevant sailing directions (including that of the United States):

---

[358]   BA Chart 1201 B8 (2000).

[359]   Merits Hearing Tr. (Day 4), p. 62.

[360]   D. Hancox and V. Prescott, "A Geographical Description of the Spratly Islands and an Account of Hydrographic Surveys Amongst Those Islands," *IBRU Maritime Briefing*, Vol. 1, No. 6, p. 40 (1995) (Annex 256).

(a)　In the Philippine *Coast Pilot*:

> Pagasa Island . . . A reef lies 1.5 miles NW; irregular depths from 4.6 meters to 14.6 meters (15 to 48 ft) exist in the channel between them. A drying reef with a sand cay near its center, lies 1.2 miles WSW of the above reef.[361]

(b)　In the Chinese *Sailing Directions*:

> The western side reef basin extends from Zhongye Island to the west approximately six nautical miles. Aside from some exposed reef on all sides of the shoal, it is all shallow shoals with irregular water depths.　The Tiexiandong Reef lies approximately 1.5 nautical miles northwest of Zhongye Island.　The water depth between this reef and Zhongye Island is 4.5 metres　14.6 metres. Approximately 1.3 nautical miles southwest of this coral reef lies Tiexianzhong Reef, and on top of it is a sandbar.[362]

(c)　In the British *China Sea Pilot*:

> A drying reef with a sand cay near its centre 3½ miles WNW. In the middle of the passage, between this reef and the reef 1¼ miles ENE, leading into the lagoon, there is a shoal.[363]

(d)　In the U.S. *Sailing Directions*:

> The W reefs of Thitu Island are composed of several drying reefs and shoal patches. A sand cay lies on one of these drying reefs about 3.5 miles W of the island.[364]

373.　With respect to satellite imagery, the Tribunal remains unconvinced that reliable conclusions can be drawn from EOMAP's satellite-derived bathymetry.　Moreover, in contrast to a rock or coral boulder, it is possible that a sand cay may be dispersed by storm action and reform in the same location after a short while.　The absence of a sand cay at a particular point in time is thus not conclusive evidence of the absence of a high-tide feature.　In this instance, the Tribunal considers that the strong historical evidence of a sand cay on the reefs west of Thitu is to be preferred, even if the presence of Sandy Cay over time is intermittent.　As Subi Reef lies within 12 nautical miles of the reef on which Sandy Cay is located, it could serve as a basepoint for the territorial sea of Sandy Cay.　The Tribunal also notes, however, that even without a high-tide feature in the location of Sandy Cay, Subi Reef would fall within the territorial sea of Thitu as extended by basepoints on the low-tide elevations of the reefs to the west of the island. Accordingly, the significance of Sandy Cay for the status of Subi Reef is minimal.

---

[361]　Philippine National Mapping and Resource Information Agency, *Philippine Coast Pilot*, p. 16-74 (6th ed., 1995) (Annex 230).

[362]　Navigation Guarantee Department of the Chinese Navy Headquarters, *China Sailing Directions: South China Sea (A103)*, p. 176 (2011) (Annex 232(bis)).

[363]　United Kingdom Hydrographic Office, *Admiralty Sailing Directions: China Sea Pilot (NP31)*, Vol. 2, p. 66 (10th ed., 2012) (Annex 235).

[364]　United States National Geospatial-Intelligence Agency, *Pub. 161 Sailing Directions (Enroute), South China Sea and the Gulf of Thailand*, p. 9 (13th ed., 2011) (Annex 233).

ix.   Mischief Reef

374.   Mischief Reef was first surveyed in the 1930s, when it was considered to be of particular
interest as a possible base for flying boats in the event of war. HMS Herald surveyed the reef in
1933 and prepared a fair chart at 1:50,000 scale that shows no indication of any rock or feature
above water at high tide. The detailed fair chart of the feature is reproduced as Figure 10 on
page 171 below. HMS Herald also forwarded the following description of the reef in 1933:

> An oval-shaped reef about 4½ miles long 100°, and 3 ½ miles broad, with a point on
> the southern side.

> This reef is awash at Low Water Springs, and is studded with rocks which dry about
> 2 feet. There is however a rock which dries 5 feet, situated 054°, 1.3 miles from the South
> Point.

> Very Good shelter is afforded in the lagoon which the reef contains, and boats were
> able to work in comparative comfort in spite of a wind force 4. The average depth in the
> lagoon is about 4 fathoms, but it is only clear of dangers in the southern half, the remainder
> having several patches of coral which either dry at Low Water or have less than 6 feet of
> water over them.

> There are three entrances to the lagoon, one on the S.W. side and two on the south.
> These have been styled the SOUTH WESTERN ENTRANCE, the SOUTHERN
> ENTRANCE and the BOAT CHANNEL.

>> (a)   The SOUTH WESTERN ENTRANCE is about .3 cables wide and 2.2 cables
>> long, with depths of 5 fathoms in the middle. It is however rendered entirely useless
>> for anything except small boats by a strip of coral lying across the inside of the
>> entrance, round which there is only a narrow and tortuous channel each side.

>> (b)   The SOUTHERN ENTRANCE is about ½ cable wide and has depths of over
>> 10 fathoms in it. It is almost straight, and only about 1½ cables long. As with the
>> other two entrances there is a strong tidal stream both at the flood and the ebb, and
>> when the channel was examined, even at Neap Tides there was a tide of 1½ knots
>> running S.W. at the buoy in the middle.

>> I studied this entrance from the bridge at a distance of half a cable and though
>> I am of the opinion that I could have taken "HERALD" safely into the lagoon, I did
>> not consider the risk was justified taking into consideration the dangers known to be
>> existing inside the lagoon. Nor do I think that this can be called a suitable entrance
>> for destroyers, since so many factors have to be taken into consideration, i.e.
>> knowledge of coral reefs, visibility to enable the edges of the coral to be seen, slack
>> water and absence of which, which during "HERALD's" visit was across the
>> entrance force 4.

>> (c)   The BOAT CHANNEL as its name implies is very narrow, and as it reaches
>> the lagoon is only 20 yards wide, though having a depth of more than 4 fathoms in
>> it.

> In view of the fact that I did not consider any entrance suitable for ships of destroyer
> size, a sketch survey only of Mischief Reef was carried out.

> A base was measured by masthead angles between buoys anchored in the South
> Western Entrance and Boat Channel, and this was extended to additional buoys in the
> lagoon, while the rock drying 5 feet on the S.E. side was also fixed.

> The lagoon and entrances were sounded by boats, while ship delineated the outside

of the reef. Deep water extends close up to the reef all round, and ship lay off at night, lights being placed on two of the buoys.

Star sights were obtained to fix the position of the buoy anchored in the middle of Southern Entrance, being adjusted by range and bearing from the ship. The following results were obtained: . . .

The mean position of the middle of Southern Entrance was therefore accepted to be Lat. 9° 53′ 42″ N., Long. 115° 30′ 52″ E.[365]

375. HMS Herald then returned to Mischief Reef in 1938, entered the lagoon, and carried out further surveys to establish the portions of the lagoon that were clear of submerged dangers.[366] This was then added to the extremely detailed description of Mischief Reef in the Royal Navy's 1944 *Sailing Direction for the Dangerous Ground*.[367] During the same period, the Imperial Japanese Navy was also active in surveying Mischief Reef and produced a plan of the feature as part of Imperial Japanese Navy Chart No. 525 – Plans in the Southern Archipelago.[368] It likewise shows no feature above water at high tide.

376. The Tribunal also notes the description of Mischief Reef in the Chinese Navy Headquarters sailing directions, which describe only rocks exposed at half tide in the following terms:

Meiji Reef – Located at the northeast part of the Nansha Islands, it is due east of the Jiuzhang Reefs, and it is approximately 62 nautical miles from Dongmen Reef. The reef resembles an elliptical shape, and it is an enclosed, independent atoll. The reef flat is exposed during low tide and is submerged during high tide. The northern part is relatively wide, and the southern part is relatively narrow. There are dozens of reef rocks on the reef flat that range in height from 0.6 meters – 1.3 meters. During half-tide, they can be exposed. The southwest part has three openings to enter the lagoon. The water depth of the lagoon is 10 meters – 28 meters, and there are over 50 points of exposed reef flat scattered throughout. To develop the distant-sea fishing industry, in 1994, China's fishing authorities constructed stilt houses and navigational aid facilities on this reef, set up administrative offices, and created the conditions for distant-sea operations, fishing vessel safety and production, supply, wind protection, and mooring. Anchoring grounds and the safe anchoring zone within the Meiji Reef are located at the southwest part of the lagoon. In the water areas within the joint line connecting the following five points, the water depth is greater than 10 meters, and the area can provide shelter against level 10 strong winds:

(1) 9°53′.1N, 115°30′.6E;
(2) 9°53′.1N, 115°31′.6E;
(3) 9°54′.2N, 115°31′.5E;
(4) 9°55′.0N, 115°30′.5E;
(5) 9°53′.6N, 115°30′.2E.[369]

---

[365]   HMS Herald, *Report of visit to Mischief Reef*, UKHO Ref. H3331/1933.

[366]   *Sailing Direction for the Dangerous Ground*, UKHO Ref. HD384 (1944 ed.).

[367]   *Sailing Direction for the Dangerous Ground*, UKHO Ref. HD384, pp. 5-6 (1944 ed.).

[368]   Imperial Japanese Navy, Chart No. 525.

[369]   Navigation Guarantee Department of the Chinese Navy Headquarters, *China Sailing Directions: South China Sea (A103)*, p. 177 (2011) (Annex 232(bis)).

Figure 9: Subi Reef and Sandy Cay on Thitu Reefs

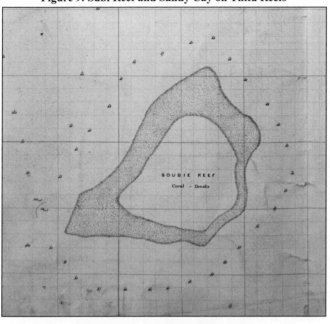

Subi Reef: Survey by HMS Rifleman (1867)
(depicting no high-water feature)

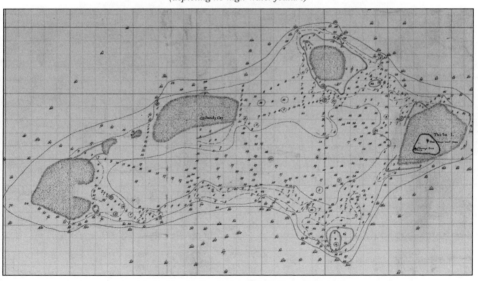

Thitu Reefs: Survey by HMS Rifleman (1867)
(depicting sand cay on reef west of Thitu, within 12 nautical miles of Subi Reef)

this page intentionally blank

Figure 10: Mischief Reef

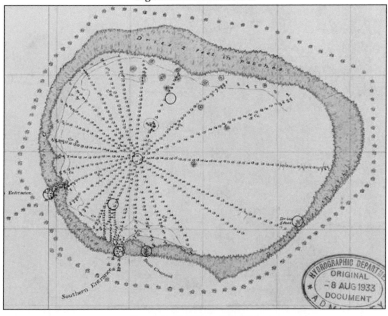

Survey by HMS Herald (1933)
(depicting rock drying to 5 feet in S.E. corner)

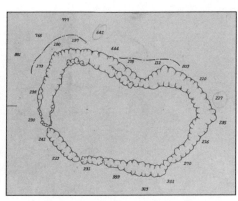

Imperial Japanese Navy Chart No. 525
(depicting no high-water feature)

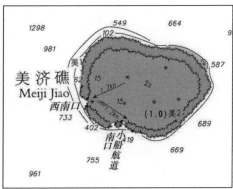

China Chart No. 18500
(depicting height of 1.0 metres above
Mean Sea Level in S.E. corner)

171

this page intentionally blank

377. Despite the absence of any reference to a high-tide feature at Mischief Reef, the Tribunal notes the reference to a drying rock with a height of five feet above Mean Low Water Springs in HMS Herald's description of the reef. China's Chart No. 18500 similarly depicts a height of one metre above Mean Sea Level in the location of that rock. Either measurement would at least be close to the expected level of high water. The Tribunal notes, however, that it does not have direct evidence of tidal conditions at Mischief Reef and concludes that the clear evidence from direct observations—to "drying rocks" by HMS Herald and to rocks exposed "during half-tide" in the Chinese sailing directions—is more convincing. In light, in particular, of the amount of time spent by HMS Herald in surveying Mischief Reef and the knowledge of tidal conditions apparent in the above description, the Tribunal considers it inconceivable that a high-tide rock or feature could have been overlooked or gone unmentioned.

378. Accordingly, the Tribunal concludes that Mischief Reef is a low-tide elevation.

x.   *Second Thomas Shoal*

379. Second Thomas Shoal was also first surveyed in the 1930s, although less intensively than Mischief Reef. Second Thomas Shoal was visited by HMS Iroquois in 1931.[370] No detailed fair plan of the reef appears to have been produced, but it is depicted in medium scale, without any indication of a high-tide feature, on the reporting chart of the combined air/sea survey operations that the Royal Navy undertook in that year to eliminate uncharted dangers and clear safe lanes through the Spratly Islands. Second Thomas Shoal is also described in the Royal Navy's 1944 *Sailing Directions for the Dangerous Ground* in the following terms:

> The northern end of 2nd Thomas shoal lies about 20 miles eastward of Mischief reef; the reef contains a lagoon with depths of about 15 fathoms which may possibly be accessible to vessels of moderate draught, from the eastward. The eastern side of the lagoon has the appearance of having a general depth of about 5 fathoms with a number of isolated drying patches; the most likely looking passages were examined and found to abound with rocks with depths of about 2 fathoms but it is considered that a navigable passage probably exists. The western side of the reef is almost continuous and dries; the only likely passage was found, on examination to be foul. There are two or three large rocks near the southern end which are almost certain to be visible at low water. H.M. Surveying Ship IROQUOIS was unable to find anchorage in the vicinity.[371]

380. The Tribunal notes in particular the description of rocks that "are almost certain to be visible at low water" and takes this as an indication that no rocks on the reef would be visible at high water. The Tribunal is also unaware of any more recent evidence suggesting a high-tide feature

---

[370]   *See* D. Hancox & V. Prescott, *Secret Hydrographic Surveys in the Spratly Islands*, p. 61 (1999).

[371]   *Sailing Direction for the Dangerous Ground*, UKHO Ref. HD384, p. 6 (1944 ed.).

on Second Thomas Shoal, including in Chinese Chart No. 18500 or the Chinese Navy Headquarters sailing directions, which describe the reef in the following terms:

> Ren'ai Reef - Located approximately 25 nautical miles north by west of Xinyi Reef, it is an exposed coral atoll, trending toward south-north, with a distance of approximately 10 nautical miles, the north side is wide while the south side is narrow. The northern half of the atoll is all connected together, while the southern half is divided into several segments. There are several solitary exposed reefs on the atoll. The water of the lagoon inside the atoll is relatively deep, and its south side has several entry-exit points. Slightly larger vessels can enter and exit. On its northeast side, there is an entry-exit point with a water depth of 27 meters.[372]

381. Accordingly, the Tribunal concludes that Second Thomas Shoal is a low-tide elevation.

(d)   Conclusion

382. Based on the considerations outlined above, the Tribunal reaches the following conclusions regarding the status of features in the South China Sea. The following features include, or in their natural condition did include, rocks or sand cays that remain above water at high tide and are, accordingly, high-tide features: (a) Scarborough Shoal, (b) Cuarteron Reef, (c) Fiery Cross Reef, (d) Johnson Reef, (e) McKennan Reef, and (f) Gaven Reef (North).

383. The following features are, or in their natural condition were, exposed at low tide and submerged at high tide and are, accordingly, low-tide elevations: (a) Hughes Reef, (b) Gaven Reef (South), (c) Subi Reef, (d) Mischief Reef, (e) Second Thomas Shoal.

384. The Tribunal additionally records that Hughes Reef lies within 12 nautical miles of the high-tide features on McKennan Reef and Sin Cowe Island, Gaven Reef (South) lies within 12 nautical miles of the high-tide features at Gaven Reef (North) and Namyit Island, and that Subi Reef lies within 12 nautical miles of the high-tide feature of Sandy Cay on the reefs to the west of Thitu.

*   *   *

---

[372] Navigation Guarantee Department of the Chinese Navy Headquarters, *China Sailing Directions: South China Sea (A103)*, p. 180 (2011) (Annex 232(bis)).

C.   THE STATUS OF FEATURES AS ROCKS/ISLANDS (SUBMISSIONS NO. 3, 5, AND 7)

1.   Introduction

385. In this Section, the Tribunal addresses a further aspect of the Parties' dispute concerning the status of the maritime features and the source of maritime entitlements in the South China Sea. This dispute is reflected in the Philippines' Submissions No. 3, 5, and 7, which relate to disputes about the status of maritime features in the South China Sea under Article 121 of the Convention. Submissions No. 3, 5, and 7 provide as follows:

> (3)   Scarborough Shoal generates no entitlement to an exclusive economic zone or continental shelf;
>
> . . .
>
> (5)   Mischief Reef and Second Thomas Shoal are part of the exclusive economic zone and continental shelf of the Philippines;
>
> . . .
>
> (7)   Johnson Reef, Cuarteron Reef and Fiery Cross Reef generate no entitlement to an exclusive economic zone or continental shelf;

386. Article 121 establishes a regime of islands as follows:

> *Article 121*
> *Regime of Islands*
>
> 1.   An island is a naturally formed area of land, surrounded by water, which is above water at high tide.
>
> 2.   Except as provided for in paragraph 3, the territorial sea, the contiguous zone, the exclusive economic zone and the continental shelf of an island are determined in accordance with the provisions of this Convention applicable to other land territory.
>
> 3.   Rocks which cannot sustain human habitation or economic life of their own shall have no exclusive economic zone or continental shelf.

387. Constituting its own Part VIII of the Convention, the "Regime of Islands" in Article 121 presents a definition, a general rule, and an exception to that general rule.

388. Paragraph (1) contains the definition of an "island" as a "naturally formed area of land, surrounded by water, which is above water at high tide." This text is unchanged from the 1958 Convention on the Territorial Sea and the Contiguous Zone.[373]

389. Paragraph (2) contains the general rule that islands generate the same entitlements under the Convention as other land territory. Treating naturally formed islands the same as other land

---

[373]   1958 Convention on the Territorial Sea and the Contiguous Zone, art. 10.

territory was not a new concept, for purposes of generating a territorial sea.[374] Additionally, all islands had previously been treated the same with respect to entitlements to the continental shelf.[375] However, the need to distinguish categories of islands had become apparent after the emergence in the early 1970s of substantially expanded maritime resource zones beyond the territorial sea, in combination with a new regime for the mineral resources of the seabed beyond national jurisdiction, recognised as the "common heritage of mankind." Thus, during the Third UN Conference, an exception to the rule that all natural islands have the same entitlements was accepted and incorporated into paragraph (3).[376]

390. Paragraph (3) acts as a limitation on the general rule in paragraph (2) and provides that "rocks which cannot sustain human habitation or economic life of their own shall have no exclusive economic zone or continental shelf." Article 121 therefore contains a distinction between two categories of naturally formed high-tide features, which the Tribunal refers to as "fully entitled islands" and "rocks" respectively.

391. The interpretation and application of Article 121 arise in two ways as a result of the Philippines' Submissions.

392. First, the Philippines seeks specific determinations that certain features are "rocks" within the meaning of Article 121(3) of the Convention. The Philippines' Submission No. 3 seeks a declaration that "Scarborough Shoal generates no exclusive economic zone or continental shelf." In its Award on Jurisdiction, the Tribunal noted that this Submission reflects a dispute concerning the status of Scarborough Shoal as a fully entitled island or rock within the meaning of Article 121 of the Convention and that the dispute was not barred from the Tribunal's consideration by any requirement of Section 1 of Part XV. The Tribunal noted that this was not a dispute concerning sovereignty over the feature, insofar as the resolution of the Philippines' Submission would not require the Tribunal to render a decision on sovereignty and insofar as the objective of the Philippines' Submission was not to advance its claim to sovereignty over the feature.[377] Accordingly, the question of sovereignty over Scarborough Shoal will remain

---

[374] *See, e.g.,* 1958 Convention on the Territorial Sea and the Contiguous Zone; International Law Commission, *Report of the International Law Commission Covering the Work of its Eighth Session,* UN Doc. A/3159 (4 July 1956).

[375] *See* Convention on the Continental Shelf, art. 1, 25 April 1958, 499 UNTS 311 (hereinafter **"1958 Convention on the Continental Shelf"**).

[376] For a detailed account of the negotiating history of Article 121 of the Convention, see United Nations, Office for Ocean Affairs and the Law of the Sea, *The Law of the Sea: Régime of Islands: Legislative History of Part VIII (Article 121) of the United Nations Convention on the Law of the Sea* (1988).

[377] Award on Jurisdiction, paras. 152-153.

entirely unaffected by the Tribunal's determination.[378] The Tribunal also held that this dispute does not concern sea boundary delimitation, insofar as "a dispute concerning the existence of an entitlement to maritime zones is distinct from a dispute concerning the delimitation of those zones in an area where the entitlements of parties overlap."[379] The Tribunal thus found that it had jurisdiction to consider Submission No. 3.[380] The Tribunal similarly accepted jurisdiction over Submission No. 7, in which the Philippines seeks a declaration that "Johnson Reef, Cuarteron Reef and Fiery Cross Reef generate no entitlement to an exclusive economic zone or continental shelf."[381]

393. Second, by requesting in Submissions No. 5, 8, and 9 declarations about the Philippines' own exclusive economic zone, the Philippines effectively seeks a general determination that all of the high-tide features in the Spratly Islands are "rocks" for purposes of Article 121(3) of the Convention. The Philippines' Submission No. 5 requests a declaration that "Mischief Reef and Second Thomas Shoal are part of the exclusive economic zone and continental shelf of the Philippines." As the Tribunal noted in its Award on Jurisdiction, through Submission No. 5, "the Philippines has in fact presented a dispute concerning the status of every maritime feature claimed by China within 200 nautical miles of Mischief Reef and Second Thomas Shoal," at least as to whether such features are fully entitled islands.[382] The Tribunal held that Submission No. 5 reflects a dispute concerning the sources of maritime entitlements in the South China Sea and whether a situation of overlapping entitlements to an exclusive economic zone or to a continental shelf exists in the area of Mischief Reef and Second Thomas Shoal. The Tribunal found that the dispute was not barred from the Tribunal's consideration by any requirement of Section 1 of Part XV and is not a dispute concerning sovereignty over the features.[383] The Tribunal also held that this dispute does not concern maritime boundary delimitation:

> [T]he premise of the Philippines' Submission is not that the Tribunal will delimit any overlapping entitlements in order to declare that these features form part of the exclusive economic zone and continental shelf of the Philippines, but rather that no overlapping entitlements can exist.[384]

The Tribunal pointed out, however, that if any other maritime feature claimed by China within 200 nautical miles of Mischief Reef or Second Thomas Shoal were found to be a fully entitled

---

[378] Award on Jurisdiction, para. 400.

[379] Award on Jurisdiction, para. 156; *see also* Award on Jurisdiction, paras. 155-157.

[380] Award on Jurisdiction, para. 413(G).

[381] Award on Jurisdiction, paras. 404, 413(G).

[382] Award on Jurisdiction, para. 172.

[383] Award on Jurisdiction, para. 402.

[384] Award on Jurisdiction, para. 402.

island for purposes of Article 121, "the resulting overlap and the exclusion of boundary delimitation from the Tribunal's jurisdiction by Article 298 would prevent the Tribunal from addressing this Submission."[385] Whether this is the case depends on a determination on the status of maritime features in the South China Sea, and accordingly, the Tribunal reserved a decision on its jurisdiction with respect to the Philippines' Submission No. 5 for consideration in this phase of the proceedings.

394. Similarly, the Tribunal reserved for the present Award any decision on its jurisdiction to consider the Philippines' Submissions No. 8 and 9, which seek the following declarations:

> 8) China has unlawfully interfered with the enjoyment and exercise of the sovereign rights of the Philippines with respect to the living and non-living resources of its exclusive economic zone and continental shelf;
>
> 9) China has unlawfully failed to prevent its nationals and vessels from exploiting the living resources in the exclusive economic zone of the Philippines.

395. The Tribunal found in its Award on Jurisdiction that the premise of Submissions No. 8 and 9 is that no overlapping entitlements exist.[386] The Tribunal would only have jurisdiction to consider the Philippines' Submissions if it found that only the Philippines were to possesses an entitlement to an exclusive economic zone and/or continental shelf in the areas where China's allegedly unlawful activities occurred. The Tribunal accepted that if any maritime feature claimed by China within 200 nautical miles of these areas were to be a fully entitled island for purposes of Article 121, "the resulting overlap and the exclusion of boundary delimitation from the Tribunal's jurisdiction by Article 298, would prevent the Tribunal from addressing the submissions."[387] The Tribunal was not prepared to make a decision on the status of features as a preliminary matter and reserved decision on its jurisdiction with respect to Submissions No. 8 and 9 for consideration in this phase of the proceedings.

396. The interpretation and application of Article 121(3) of the Convention is therefore not only required for the features specified by the Philippines in its Submissions No. 3 and 7, but also for all significant high-tide features in the Spratly Islands that could impact the Tribunal's jurisdiction to decide the matters raised in the Philippines' Submissions No. 5, 8, and 9.

2.   Factual Background

397. The location and description of Scarborough Shoal, Johnson Reef, Cuarteron Reef, and Fiery Cross Reef are set out above at paragraphs 284 to 287. The Tribunal recalls that these features,

---

[385]   Award on Jurisdiction, para. 402.

[386]   Award on Jurisdiction, paras. 405-406.

[387]   Award on Jurisdiction, paras. 405-406.

in their natural form, consist of largely submerged reefs, with small protrusions of coral that reach no more than a few metres above water at high tide.

398. At paragraph 365, the Tribunal found that Gaven Reef (North) includes a sand cay that is exposed at high tide, such that Gaven Reef (North) is a high-tide feature. At paragraph 354, the Tribunal also found that McKennan Reef is a high-tide feature.

399. The location and description of Mischief Reef and Second Thomas Shoal are also set out above, at paragraph 290. Both features are located within 200 nautical miles of the Philippines' baselines and fall within the exclusive economic zone claimed by the Philippines under its *Republic Act No. 9522* of 2009.[388] As explained above, whether the Tribunal can make a declaration that the features are indeed "part of the exclusive economic zone and continental shelf of the Philippines" as sought by Submission No. 5, would require the Tribunal to rule out the possibility that any feature claimed by China could generate an entitlement to an exclusive economic zone that would overlap that of the Philippines at either Mischief Reef or Second Thomas Shoal. In practice, this would require a finding that none of the Spratly Islands are fully entitled islands under Article 121 of the Convention.

400. In addition to the foregoing, there are a number of features in the Spratly Islands that are unequivocally above water at high tide and whose classification may impact the Tribunal's decisions with respect to the Philippines' Submissions No. 5, 8, and 9. Set out in the following paragraphs are brief descriptions of the location and geographical characteristics of the six largest features amongst the other high-tide features in the Spratly Islands.

401. Itu Aba is known as "Taiping Dao" (太平岛) in China and "Ligaw" in the Philippines. It is the largest high-tide feature in the Spratly Islands, measuring approximately 1.4 kilometres in length, and almost 400 metres at its widest point. Its surface area is approximately 0.43 square kilometres. It is located at 10° 22′ 38″ N, 114° 21′ 56″ E, lying atop the northern edge of Tizard Bank, 200.6 nautical miles from the archipelagic baseline of the Philippine island of Palawan and 539.6 nautical miles from China's baseline point 39 (Dongzhou (2)) adjacent to the island of Hainan. The general location of Itu Aba, and that of the other major Spratly Island features described in this Section, is depicted in Map 3 on page 125 above. It is surrounded by a coral reef and shallow water. Itu Aba is currently under the control of the Taiwan Authority of China, which stations personnel there. There are multiple buildings, a lighthouse, a runway, and port facilities on Itu Aba.

---

[388] Republic of the Philippines, *Republic Act No. 9522, An Act to Amend Certain Provisions of Republic Act No. 3046, as amended by Republic Act No. 5446, to Define the Archipelagic Baseline of the Philippines and for Other Purposes* (10 March 2009) (Annex 60).

402. Thitu is known as "Zhongye Dao" (中业岛) in China and "Pagasa" in the Philippines. It measures approximately 710 metres in length and 570 metres in width. Its surface area is approximately 0.41 square kilometres. Thitu is located at 11° 03′ 19″ N, 114° 17′ 08″ E, atop the west-side shoal of two adjacent coral reefs separated by a narrow deep channel. It is surrounded by a drying coral reef. Thitu lies 227.4 nautical miles from the archipelagic baseline of the Philippine island of Palawan and 502.1 nautical miles from China's baseline point 39 (Dongzhou (2)) adjacent to the island of Hainan. Thitu is currently under the control of the Philippines, which stations personnel there. There are multiple buildings, a lighthouse, and an airstrip on Thitu.

403. West York Island is known as "Xiyue Dao" (西月岛) in China and "Likas" in the Philippines. It measures approximately 720 metres in length and 440 metres in width. Its surface area is approximately 0.21 square kilometres. It is located atop a coral reef at 11° 05′ 01″ N, 115° 01′ 26″ E, 195.0 nautical miles from the archipelagic baseline of the Philippine island of Palawan and 524.9 nautical miles from China's baseline point 39 (Dongzhou (2)) adjacent to the island of Hainan. It is surrounded by a white sand cay, outside of which there is a coral reef basin. West York Island is currently controlled by the Philippines, which stations a small number of personnel there.

404. Spratly Island is known as "Nanwei Dao" (南威岛) in China and "Lagos" in the Philippines. It measures approximately 390 metres in length and 310 metres in width. Its surface area is approximately 0.17 square kilometres. It is located atop a coral bank at 8° 38′ 41″ N, 111° 55′ 15″E, 298.2 nautical miles from the archipelagic baseline of the Philippine island of Palawan and 584.3 nautical miles from China's baseline point 39 (Dongzhou (2)) adjacent to the island of Hainan. It has a margin of white sand and broken coral and is surrounded by drying rocky ledges. Spratly Island is currently controlled by Viet Nam, which stations personnel there. There are multiple buildings, a lighthouse, sea walls, a runway, and a pier on Spratly Island.

405. North-East Cay is known as "Beizi Dao" (北子岛) in China and "Parola" in the Philippines. It measures approximately 825 metres in length and 244 metres in width. Its surface area is approximately 0.15 square kilometres. It is located in the larger complex of features known as "North Danger Reef" and lies at 11° 27′ 14″ N, 114° 21′ 14″ E, 239.3 nautical miles from the archipelagic baseline of the Philippine island of Palawan and 484.3 nautical miles from China's baseline point 39 (Dongzhou (2)) adjacent to the island of Hainan. It is surrounded by a belt of coral sand and lies on a drying reef. North-East Cay is currently controlled by the Philippines,

which stations a small number of personnel there. There are a few structures, including a lighthouse, on North-East Cay.

406. South-West Cay is known as "Nanzi Dao" (南子岛) in China and "Pugad" in the Philippines. It measures approximately 670 metres in length and 283 metres in width. Its surface area is approximately 0.15 square kilometres. Like North-East Cay, it is located in the larger complex of features known as "North Danger Reef" and lies at 11° 25′ 49″ N, 114° 19′ 52″ E, 239.6 nautical miles from the archipelagic baseline of the Philippine island of Palawan and 484.8 nautical miles from baseline point 39 (Dongzhou (2)) adjacent to the island of Hainan. It is surrounded by a drying reef. South-West Cay is currently controlled by Viet Nam, which stations personnel there. There are multiple buildings, a lighthouse, seawalls, and port facilities on South-West Cay.

407. Other high-tide features claimed by China atop coral reefs in the Spratly Islands are smaller in size than the above-described features, with surface areas of less than 0.14 square kilometres, but present similar characteristics. The Tribunal has examined Amboyna Cay, Flat Island, Loaita Island, Namyit Island, Nanshan Island, Sand Cay, Sin Cowe Island, and Swallow Reef for evidence of human habitation or economic life, but does not consider it necessary to discuss them individually. The Tribunal considers that if the six largest features described above are all to be classified as rocks for purposes of Article 121(3) of the Convention, the same conclusion would also hold true for all other high-tide features in the Spratly Islands.

3.   The Philippines' Position

408. The Philippines submits that Scarborough Shoal and all of the high-tide features in the Spratly Islands are properly characterised as "rocks" under Article 121(3) of the Convention.[389]

(a)   Interpretation of Article 121(3)

409. Based on a review of the origins and negotiating history, the Philippines discerns "certain clear conclusions regarding the object and purpose of the provision."[390] In particular, the Philippines argues that the records of the Third UN Conference reflect overwhelming opposition to the prospect of granting very small, remote, and uninhabited islands extensive maritime zones that would unfairly and inequitably impinge on other States' maritime space and on the area of

---

[389]   Memorial, paras. 5.1-5.114.

[390]   Merits Hearing Tr. (Day 2), p. 62; *see also* Memorial, para. 5.26.

international seabed.[391] The Philippines concludes that Article 121(3) of the Convention was inserted as a result of the drafters' belief "that it would be unjustifiable and inequitable to allow tiny and insignificant features, which just happen to protrude above water at high tide, to generate huge maritime entitlements to the prejudice of other proximate coastal states with lengthy coastlines and significant populations, or to the prejudice of the global commons beyond national jurisdiction."[392] In other words, the object and purpose of Article 121(3) is to "avoid perverse effects of the major extensions of coastal State jurisdiction beyond the territorial sea."[393]

410. The Philippines' makes the following arguments with respect to the interpretation of particular elements of the text of Article 121(3).

411. First, it submits that the meaning of "rock" must not be limited in terms of geological or geomorphological characteristics. Thus, protrusions above water that are composed of coral, mud, sand, or soil may constitute rocks within the meaning of Article 121(3) of the Convention.[394]

412. Second, the Philippines acknowledges that size alone is not determinative of the status of a feature as a rock pursuant to Article 121(3). Nevertheless, it points to the negotiating history and certain State practice to suggest that it would be reasonable to conclude that a high-tide feature with a high-tide area "less that one km^2 could be regarded as sufficiently small to create a presumption that it is not genuinely able to sustain human habitation and economic life of its own."[395] The Philippines' expert, Professor Schofield, states that while size is not dispositive, the physical extent of a feature can be a "pertinent factor" because, in many instances, a "negligible physical dimension will preclude the possibility of a feature being able to sustain human habitation or an economic life associated with it, because of the limited space and resources for habitation and economic life."[396]

413. Third, the Philippines notes that the term "cannot" refers to the capacity or potential of the feature to sustain human habitation or economic life, and not to an enquiry into whether the feature actually does now sustain, or has ever in the past sustained, human habitation or economic life. Even so, the Philippines argues that the fact that a feature has historically been

---

[391] Memorial, paras. 5.16-5.26; Merits Hearing Tr. (Day 2), pp. 62-65.

[392] Merits Hearing Tr. (Day 4), p. 11.

[393] Merits Hearing Tr. (Day 3), pp. 92-93; Written Responses of the Philippines, para. 108 (11 March 2016).

[394] Merits Hearing Tr. (Day 2), pp. 67-69.

[395] Memorial, para. 5.26.

[396] Merits Hearing Tr. (Day 4), p. 44; *see also* Schofield Report, p. 18.

uninhabited and has sustained no economic life would constitute powerful evidence of its lack of capacity to do so.[397]

414. Fourth, the Philippines argues that the words "sustain human habitation" must mean that, in naturally occurring conditions, a feature can "support a stable group of human beings across a significant period of years," by providing fresh water, food and living space and materials for human shelter.[398] Such meaning, the Philippines argues, is supported by the context of the requirement that an island be "naturally formed" in the definition of an island in Article 121(1). The object and purpose of the provision would be undermined if distant States could introduce technology, artificial additions, and external supplies to support human habitation.

415. Fifth, the use of "on their own" in connection with features sustaining an economic life must, according to the Philippines, plainly mean "that the feature itself has the ability to support an independent economic life without infusion from the outside."[399] It would need to be "local and not imported"; "real and not contrived," though "100 percent self-sufficiency is not required."[400]

416. Sixth, "economic life" is not to be equated simply to economic value. Rather it requires some activity that presupposes more than the existence of a resource or the presence of an installation of an economic nature. The feature must, in its naturally formed state, have the capacity to develop sources of production, distribution, and exchange sufficient to support the presence of a stable human population.[401] The Philippines submits that the capacity of a feature to sustain an economic life of its own may be determined by reference to the resources of the territorial sea, but not beyond. According to the Philippines, if resources in the waters beyond the territorial sea could be relied upon, the result would be circular and illogical and entail that the sea dominates the land.[402]

417. The Philippines argues that in order to be a fully entitled island, a feature must be capable both of sustaining human habitation *and* of sustaining an economic life of its own. It submits that the grammatical context of the word "or" in Article 121(3) creates, through a double negative, a cumulative requirement. This cumulativeness is, according to the Philippines, underscored by logic because the concepts of sustained "human habitation" and "economic life" are interrelated,

---

[397] Merits Hearing Tr. (Day 2), pp. 69-70.

[398] Merits Hearing Tr. (Day 2), pp. 73-75, 88; Memorial, para. 5.37.

[399] Merits Hearing Tr. (Day 2), p. 78.

[400] Merits Hearing Tr. (Day 2), p. 81.

[401] Memorial, para. 5.56.

[402] Merits Hearing Tr. (Day 2), p. 82.

and it is difficult to conceive of one without the other.[403] Any alternative reading of Article 121(3) would have undesirable consequences: tiny specks of features incapable of human habitation could generate entitlements to vast ocean spaces merely with the "use [of] factory ships or oil platforms or even casinos built on stilts."[404] That said, the Schofield Report applied a disjunctive test,[405] and both the Philippines and its experts submit that the result in this case would be the same whether the Tribunal required only one or both of the requirements of "human habitation" and "economic life" to be satisfied for a feature to be a fully entitled island.[406]

418. The Philippines points to various commentaries to support its view that installation of a military presence on a rock, serviced from the outside, does not establish that the feature is capable of sustaining human habitation or has an economic life of its own.[407] It cites further support from the practice of Viet Nam and Malaysia, who have externally sustained troops stationed on high-tide features in the Spratly Islands, yet do not claim them as fully entitled islands. The Philippines' expert, Professor Schofield, also explained his view that the lack of an "indigenous" population—meaning a community who decided to settle on a feature of their own accord, as distinct from government or military personnel—may indicate that a feature cannot sustain human habitation.[408]

419. The Philippines argues that the State practice on the interpretation of Article 121(3) is inconsistent, but States generally accept that small, uninhabited, barren outcrops should not generate full maritime zones, citing in particular (a) the United Kingdom's renunciation of its 200-nautical-mile fishery zone around Rockall, in connection with its accession to the

---

[403] Merits Hearing Tr. (Day 2), p. 85.

[404] Merits Hearing Tr. (Day 2), p. 87.

[405] Merits Hearing Tr. (Day 4), p. 45; C. Schofield, et al., *An Appraisal of the Geographical Characteristics and Status of Certain Insular Features in the South China Sea* (March 2015) (Annex 513).

[406] Merits Hearing Tr. (Day 4), pp. 8-9, p. 45.

[407] Merits Hearing Tr. (Day 2), p. 77; (Day 4), pp. 36-37; Memorial, para. 5.106; D. Anderson, "Islands and Rocks in the Modern Law of the Sea," *in United Nations Convention on the Law of the Sea 1982: A Commentary*, Vol. II, p. 313 (M. Nordquist, et. al. eds., 2002); R. Platzöder, *Third United Nations Conference on the Law of the Sea: Documents*, Vol. IV, p. 222 (1987); United Nations, Office for Ocean Affairs and the Law of the Sea, *The Law of the Sea: Régime of Islands: Legislative History of Part VIII (Article 121) of the United Nations Convention on the Law of the Sea*, Part 8, pp. 44-45 (1988); C. Schofield, "What's at Stake in the South China Sea? Geographical and Geopolitical considerations," *in Beyond Territorial Disputes in the South China Sea*, p. 11 at p. 23 (2013); M. Gjetnes, "The Spratlys: Are They Rocks or Islands?," *Ocean Development and International Law*, Vol. 32, No. 2, p. 191 at p. 200 (2001).

[408] Merits Hearing Tr. (Day 4), p. 48.

Convention, and (b) China's own protests at Japan's submission for an extended continental shelf relating to Oki-no-Tori-shima.[409]

420. Recognising that the present case is not one of maritime delimitation, the Philippines also suggests that the Tribunal could seek useful guidance from the approach of international courts and tribunals in the delimitation context.[410] The Philippines notes that features of comparable nature, small size, and remoteness to those in the Spratlys have been "enclaved", that is, given no more than a 12-nautical-mile territorial sea, in a number of cases, including *Maritime Delimitation in the Black Sea, Territorial and Maritime Dispute (Nicaragua v. Colombia),* the *Dubai/Sharjah Border Arbitration, Delimitation of the Continental Shelf Between the United Kingdom of Great Britain and Northern Ireland, and the French Republic* and *Delimitation of the Maritime Boundary Between Bangladesh and Myanmar in the Bay of Bengal.*[411] Such enclaving has been done in order to achieve an "equitable result" in drawing a boundary line, taking into account circumstances that are the same as those that "determine whether an insular feature is a 'rock' under Article 121(3)."[412] According to the Philippines, the jurisprudence "make[s] absolutely clear" that "in any future boundary delimitation in the South China Sea . . . all of the Spratly high-tide features would be enclaved, and in no case given more than a 12-mile territorial sea."[413]

421. The Philippines expresses concern that if any of the Spratly Islands were found to be fully entitled islands and China remained determined to avoid any form of legally binding adjudication or arbitration of the boundary, the dispute could be "frozen". By contrast, the Philippines argues, a determination that the features were only rocks would reduce the incentive to "flex muscles and demonstrate sovereignty over minuscule features" that generate a maximum entitlement of 12 nautical miles, and thus contribute to the "legal order and the maintenance of peace in the South China Sea."[414] The Philippines appealed to the Tribunal's

---

[409] Memorial, paras. 5.28-5.33; Merits Hearing Tr. (Day 2), pp. 58, 89.

[410] Merits Hearing Tr. (Day 2), p. 124.

[411] Memorial, paras. 5.107-5.114; Merits Hearing Tr. (Day 2), p. 124-127; *Maritime Delimitation in the Black Sea (Romania v. Ukraine), Judgment, ICJ Reports 2009,* p. 61; *Territorial and Maritime Dispute (Nicaragua v. Colombia), Judgment, ICJ Reports 2012,* p. 624; *Dubai/Sharjah Border Arbitration,* Award of 19 October 1981, ILR, Vol. 91, p. 543; *Delimitation of the Continental Shelf Between the United Kingdom of Great Britain and Northern Ireland, and the French Republic,* Decision of 30 June 1977, RIAA, Vol. XVIII, p. 3; *Delimitation of the Maritime Boundary Between Bangladesh and Myanmar in the Bay of Bengal (Bangladesh v. Myanmar), Judgment of 14 March 2012, ITLOS Reports 2012.*

[412] Memorial, paras. 5.112-5.113.

[413] Merits Hearing Tr. (Day 2), p. 127; (Day 4), pp. 10-11.

[414] Merits Hearing Tr. (Day 2), p. 129; *see also* Written Responses of the Philippines, paras. 109-115 (11 March 2015).

mandate to "promote the maintenance of legal order in respect of the relevant maritime areas, and the avoidance or reduction of threats to international peace and security that inevitably would emanate from a situation of such legal uncertainty," in accordance with the UN Charter and the Preamble of the Convention.[415]

422. Ultimately, the Philippines submits that the test of whether a feature constitutes a "rock" for the purposes of Article 121(3) involves a "question of appreciation" in light of the natural characteristics of a given feature. It should be an objective test, in the sense that it should not be determined by any State's own subjective assertions, but on the basis of evidence derived from observations by identifiable, authoritative, and credible sources.[416] Beyond the essentials of food, drinkable water, and shelter, certain factors, such as size, prior civilian habitation, and the presence of productive soil, flora, and fauna might all be informative but not determinative.[417] For the Philippines, the interpretation and application of Article 121(3) thus requires "case-by-case determinations on the basis of the available facts, including the particular geographical context."[418]

(b)   Application to Features Identified in Submissions No. 3 and 7

423. The Philippines and its experts submit that all four of the high-tide features identified in its Submissions No. 3 and 7—Scarborough Shoal, Johnson Reef, Cuarteron Reef, and Fiery Cross Reef—are indisputably Article 121(3) rocks.[419] Noting their tiny dimensions and the low height to which they protrude above water, the Philippines draws similarities between these features and Rock No. 32 of Colombia's Quitasueño,[420] which was held by the International Court of Justice in *Territorial and Maritime Dispute (Nicaragua v. Colombia)* to be a rock for the purposes of Article 121(3).[421]

424. Relying largely on aerial and satellite photography, as well as the Philippine, Chinese, UK, and U.S. sailing directions, the Philippines considers all four features to be rocks incapable of supporting human habitation.[422] According to the Philippines, there is no evidence of drinkable

---

[415]   Merits Hearing Tr. (Day 2), p. 129.

[416]   Merits Hearing Tr. (Day 4), p. 33.

[417]   Merits Hearing Tr. (Day 2), p. 88.

[418]   Written Responses of the Philippines, para. 107 (11 March 2016).

[419]   *See* Memorial, paras. 5.137, 7.31, 7.145; Merits Hearing Tr. (Day 2), pp. 17-18, 30-34; (Day 4), pp. 40, 50-52; Schofield Report, p. 18; Supplemental Written Submission, Vol. II, pp. 50, 80, 104, 160.

[420]   Merits Hearing Tr. (Day 2), pp. 91-92.

[421]   *Territorial and Maritime Dispute (Nicaragua v. Colombia), Judgment, ICJ Reports 2012*, p. 624.

[422]   Memorial, paras. 5.89-5.95; Supplemental Written Submission, Vol. II, pp. 48-51, 78-81, 102-105, 158-161.

water, food, or shelter materials on any of the four features.[423] The Philippines observes that other small, barren, and uninhabited protrusions like Quitasueño (Colombia), Rockall (UK), Filfla (Malta), and Jabal al-Tayr and Zubayr (Yemen) have been treated by international courts and tribunals as rocks or features unworthy of being taken into account in delimitations.[424]

425. Finally, the Philippines stresses that neither China's recent island construction nor its earlier installation of small artificial structures atop coral reefs, manned by government personnel sustained entirely with external resources, can convert these features into fully entitled islands.[425]

(c)   Application to Other Maritime Features

426. The Philippines concedes that the three largest features, Itu Aba, Thitu, and West York, "differ from Scarborough Shoal, Johnson Reef, Cuarteron Reef, and Fiery Cross Reef in terms of their area, natural conditions and small population," but submits that these differences are "too minor to elevate such small, insignificant and remote features" to the status of fully entitled islands. According to the Philippines, none of the features in the Spratly Islands is capable, based on its own natural elements, of sustaining both human habitation and economic life of their own.[426]

i.   Itu Aba

427. At the Hearing on the Merits, the Philippines summarised its view of the evidence concerning Itu Aba as follows:

(1) there is no fresh water on Itu Aba suitable for drinking or capable of sustaining a human settlement;

(2) there is no natural source of nourishment on the feature capable of sustaining a human settlement;

(3) there is no soil on Itu Aba capable of facilitating any kind of agricultural production that could sustain human habitation;

(4) there has never been a population on the feature that is indigenous to it;

(5) excluding military garrisons, there has never been human settlement of any kind on Itu Aba;

(6) there was not even a military occupation prior to World War II

---

[423]   Memorial, para. 5.95.

[424]   Memorial, paras. 5.44-5.48.

[425]   Merits Hearing Tr. (Day 2), p. 94.

[426]   Memorial, paras. 5.96-5.114; Supplemental Written Submission, Vol. I, pp. 117-118, paras. 1-4; Schofield Report, p. 18.

(7) the Taiwanese troops that are garrisoned at Itu Aba are entirely dependent for their survival on supplies from Taiwan, and apart from sunlight and air, they derive nothing they need from the feature itself;

(8) no economic activity has been or is performed on Itu Aba.[427]

428. The Philippines points particularly to the lack of drinkable water and the fact that the Taiwan Authority of China has had to compensate for this through construction of desalination plants.[428] The Philippines relies on a 1994 scientific study on "The Flora of Taipingtao (Aba Itu Island)" (the "**1994 Study**"), prepared based on a field inspection by Taiwanese botanists whose work was financed by the Taiwan Authority of China, and submits that its conclusions on water, soil, and vegetation demonstrate the impossibility of sustaining human habitation.[429]

429. The Philippines acknowledges that in the nineteenth century, British vessels observed the presence of fishermen on Itu Aba. But according to the Philippines, the presence of the fishermen is conveyed as "very primitive and temporary" and "short-lived" and the fishermen's "inability to settle on Itu Aba only confirms the feature's uninhabitability."[430] The Philippines notes that the Japanese were the first to use the feature as a military base, during the Second World War, but recalls that military occupation for the sole purpose of asserting sovereignty does not suffice to prove capacity to sustain human habitation or an economic life. The Philippines also observes that all attempts to extract commercial quantities of guano from the Spratlys failed.[431]

430. When asked to comment on certain historical materials obtained by the Tribunal from the archives of the United Kingdom Hydrographic Office that include descriptions and photographs of Itu Aba and other features in the Spratly Islands, the Philippines argued that these materials

---

[427] Merits Hearing Tr. (Day 4), pp. 41-42. *See also* Memorial, paras, 5.96-5.97; Written Responses of the Philippines, para.45 (11 March 2016).

[428] Memorial, para. 5.97; Merits Hearing Tr. (Day 2), pp. 72, 111; (Day 4), pp. 28, 47, 50; *see also* Responses of the Philippines to the Tribunal's 1 April 2016 Request for Comments on Additional Materials regarding the Status of Itu Aba, paras. 42, 51 (25 April 2016) (hereinafter "**Written Responses of the Philippines on Itu Aba (25 April 2016)**").

[429] T.C. Huang, et. al., "The Flora of Taipingtao (Itu Aba Island)," *Taiwania*, Vol. 39, No. 1-2, p. 1 (1994) (Annex 254).

[430] Merits Hearing Tr. (Day 4), p. 22; *see also* Written Responses of the Philippines to the Tribunal's 1 April 2016 Request for Comments, 25 April 2016, paras. 18, 24, 33; Written Responses of the Philippines on Itu Aba, paras. 27, 30 (25 April 2016); Written Responses of the Philippines on French Archive Materials, paras. 10-12 (3 June 2016).

[431] Merits Hearing Tr. (Day 2), p. 113; Supplemental Written Submission, Vol. II, p. 177; *see also* Written Responses of the Philippines on Itu Aba, paras. 19-20 (25 April 2016); Written Responses of the Philippines on French Archive Materials, para. 7 (3 June 2016).

"support [its] conclusion that the feature is a rock as defined in Article 121(3)."[432] The Philippines notes that the 1868 *China Sea Directory* describes Itu Aba as being "almost completely devoid" of natural resources and frequented by fishermen having their permanent residence in Hainan, not on Itu Aba itself.[433] The Philippines considers that the documents obtained by the Tribunal confirm that subsequent Japanese attempts to cultivate or settle the island were either unsuccessful or exclusively "military in nature";[434] that the feature remained uninhabited, excepting a "brief" post-war Taiwanese occupation from 1946 to 1950;[435] and that Itu Aba lacked both fresh water and high-quality soil.[436]

431. The Philippines likewise submits that various historical documents obtained by the Tribunal from the *Bibliothèque Nationale de France* and the *Archives Nationales d'Outre-Mer* and provided to the Parties for comment "confirm that Itu Aba and the other insular features discussed in the French documents . . . lack the natural resources, including fertile soil and freshwater, necessary to sustain human habitation or economic life."[437] The Philippines notes that the *Division Botanique à l'Institut des Recherches Agronomiques de L'Indochine* visited Itu Aba in 1936 and recorded that it was covered only partly with soil, and that the rest was coral sand, guano and natural phosphate, and that the vegetation was very poor.[438] According to the Philippines, "[n]one of the native species cataloged by the visiting botanists are agricultural crops capable of supporting human habitation" as they are "either inedible or have only limited nutritional value."[439] On this basis, the Philippines argues that Itu Aba is "incapable of sustaining agricultural production."[440] The Philippines also points to "the lack of any discussion of freshwater in any of the documents."[441] Furthermore, the Philippines considers that the

---

[432] Responses of the Philippines to the Tribunal's 1 April 2016 Request for Comments on Materials from the Archives of the United Kingdom Hydrographic Office, para. 26 (28 April 2016) (hereinafter "**Written Responses of the Philippines on UKHO Materials (28 April 2016)**").

[433] Written Responses of the Philippines on UKHO Materials, para. 27 (28 April 2016); *China Sea Directory* Vol. II (1st ed. 1868), pp. 70-71.

[434] Written Responses of the Philippines on UKHO Materials, paras. 28-29 (28 April 2016).

[435] Written Responses of the Philippines on UKHO Materials, para. 30 (28 April 2016).

[436] Written Responses of the Philippines on UKHO Materials, paras. 31-32 (28 April 2016).

[437] Written Responses of the Philippines on French Archive Materials, para. 2 (3 June 2016).

[438] Written Responses of the Philippines on French Archive Materials, paras. 14-15 (3 June 2016); Division Botanique à l'Institut des Recherches Agronomiques de l'Indochine, "Visite Botanique au Récif Tizard," *Bulletin Économique de l'Indochine*, pp. 769, 773-774 (September-October 1936).

[439] Written Responses of the Philippines on French Archive Materials, para. 18 (3 June 2016).

[440] Written Responses of the Philippines on French Archive Materials, para. 13 (3 June 2016).

[441] Written Responses of the Philippines on French Archive Materials, para. 20 (3 June 2016).

archival material confirms that Itu Aba "had no permanent human population" and was not recognised as "having any economic value."[442]

432. When asked at the Hearing on the Merits to comment on more recent materials concerning Itu Aba published by the Taiwan Authority, the Philippines noted that two books claimed only the existence of "groundwater wells" without describing the water's drinkability and depicted a "skimming well", which is used to extract relatively fresh water from the upper zone of a fresh-saline aquifer in freshwater lenses.[443] According to the Philippines:

> Taiwan's fancy photographs of a paved airstrip, communications equipment and various buildings change nothing. They amount to no more than a manmade façade, a Potemkin "island". . . whose artifices serve mainly to divert attention from the true nature of the feature: a remote dot of exposed coral that is incapable naturally of sustaining any human habitation or economic life of its own.[444]

433. The Philippines recalls that the Taiwan Authority never claimed maritime entitlement beyond 12 nautical miles from Itu Aba until *after* the Philippines initiated this arbitration.[445]

434. The Philippines suggests that the Taiwan Authority's more recent public declarations and publication of video of conditions on Itu Aba through the internet are attempts by the Taiwan Authority to rebut the Philippines' case and "put its best foot forward" in the context of this arbitration.[446] The Philippines urges the Tribunal to treat with great caution the claims presented by the Taiwan Authority as being unsupported by actual evidence, created specifically for the purpose of litigation, and based on statements by officials with an interest in the outcome of the proceedings. The Philippines asserts that the Taiwan Authority and China's interests are "aligned" in maximising Itu Aba's potential maritime entitlements.[447]

---

[442] Written Responses of the Philippines on French Archive Materials, paras. 5-6, 8-12 (3 June 2016).

[443] Merits Hearing Tr. (Day 4), p. 26. *See* Ministry of the Interior of the Republic of China, *A Frontier in the South China Sea: Biodiversity of Taiping Island, Nansha Islands* (December 2014); Ministry of the Interior of the Republic of China, *Compilation of Historical Archives on the Southern Territories of the Republic of China* (July 2015); Ministry of the Interior of the Republic of China, *Compilation of Historical Archives on the Southern Territories of the Republic of China*, p. 233 (July 2015).

[444] Merits Hearing Tr. (Day 2), p. 114.

[445] Merits Hearing Tr. (Day 4), pp. 38-40; *see also* Written Responses of the Philippines, para. 46 (11 March 2016).

[446] Merits Hearing Tr. (Day 4), p. 25.

[447] Written Responses of the Philippines, paras. 51-53 (11 March 2016); *Armed Activities on the Territory of the Congo (Democratic Republic of the Congo v. Uganda), Judgment, ICJ Reports 2005*, p. 168; *Territorial and Maritime Dispute between Nicaragua and Honduras in the Caribbean Sea (Nicaragua v. Honduras), Judgment, ICJ Reports 2007*, p. 659; *Dispute Concerning Delimitation of the Maritime Boundary Between Bangladesh and Myanmar in the Bay of Bengal (Bangladesh/Myanmar), Judgment of 14 March 2012, ITLOS Reports 2012*.

435. According to the Philippines, earlier statements of Taiwanese officials and academics reference the need for regular external supplies to sustain the garrison and thus undermine the Taiwan Authority's claim that Itu Aba has the natural resources to be self-sufficient.[448] The Philippines observes that the first civilian to register residence on the island only did so in 2016 in the midst of the Taiwan Authority's public relations campaign to "aggrandize" the feature.[449]

436. The Philippines also rejects the Taiwan Authority's claims about "rich supply of groundwater" from five wells on the island. It suggests that the Taiwan Authority's failure to refer to the 1994 Study must "be taken to mean that [it] has no effective response."[450] The Philippines recalls that four of the wells are "skimming wells". According to the Philippines, even the carefully skimmed water from the best well produces limited amounts of water that verges close to minimal potability.[451] The Philippines submits an expert analysis of Itu Aba's groundwater resources by Dr. Ryan T. Bailey.[452] Taking into account the size of the island, its composition, and the annual rainfall, Dr. Bailey concludes that "any freshwater lens on Itu Aba is, at best, a fragile source of freshwater that, if disturbed or affected by periods of low rainfall, would become completely exhausted."[453] The Philippines concludes that "even if Itu Aba does have a marginal freshwater lens beneath it, which is questionable and unsupported by any actual evidence tendered by Taiwan, it requires constant and substantial supplementation by artificial means just to keep Taiwan's few troops alive."[454]

437. The Philippines also takes issue with the Taiwanese claims concerning soil on Itu Aba, which it says are contradicted by the 1994 Study. The Philippines submits from Dr. Peter Motavalli an *Expert Report on Soil Resources and Potential Self-Sustaining Agricultural Production on Itu Aba* and a *Second Supplemental Expert Report on Soil Resources and Potential Self-Sustaining Agricultural Production on Itu Aba*.[455] Dr. Motavalli describes the calcareous soils and highlights several constraints for self-sustaining agricultural production on Itu Aba,[456] queries

---

[448] Written Responses of the Philippines, para. 59 (11 March 2016).

[449] Written Responses of the Philippines, para. 65 (11 March 2016).

[450] Written Responses of the Philippines, para. 69 (11 March 2016).

[451] Written Responses of the Philippines, para. 76 (11 March 2016).

[452] First Bailey Report.

[453] First Bailey Report, p. 10.

[454] Written Responses of the Philippines, para. 86 (11 March 2016).

[455] First Motavalli Report; P.P. Motavalli, *Second Supplemental Expert Report on Soil Resources and Potential Self-Sustaining Agricultural Production on Itu Aba* (2 June 2016) (Annex 934) (hereinafter **"Second Motavalli Report"**).

[456] First Motavalli Report, pp. 3, 7-10; *see also* Dr. L. Xi, "Summary of Land of Guangdong Nansha Islands," *Soil Quarterly* Vol. 6, No. 3 (1947) (Annex 885).

whether the soil for vegetables might have been introduced, and notes the problems of pests and diseases.[457] In his supplemental export report, Dr. Motavalli provides observations on a 1936 report by the *Division Botanique à l'Institut des Recherches Agronomiques de L'Indochine* obtained by the Tribunal from the National Library of France and concludes that:

> the 1936 Report's analysis of an "[a]verage soil sample" on Itu Aba confirms my prior conclusions that the soil is sandy, calcareous, has a high pH, and lacks some major nutrients. In light of these characteristics, I conclude that Itu Aba's soil resources cannot sustain a meaningful level of agricultural production without the use of soil amendments and other major interventions.[458]

The Philippines expresses doubts about the agricultural capability of Itu Aba to even feed a single person.

438. The Philippines considers the Taiwan Authority's submission of additional materials concerning the status of Itu Aba, such as a "Position Paper on ROC South China Sea Policy Republic of China (Taiwan)" and an *"Amicus Curiae* Submission by the Chinese (Taiwan) Society of International Law," similarly unavailing. Even on the basis of the materials submitted by the Taiwan Authority, the Philippines argues that Itu Aba has neither a longstanding history of human habitation nor possesses sufficient fresh water and soil resources to sustain such a population, and notes that any attempts made to carry out "meaningful economic activity" on Itu Aba uniformly "ended in failure."[459] The Philippines attaches a supplemental expert report by Dr. Ryan T. Bailey, who questions the Taiwan Authority's measurements of water quality and salt concentration on Itu Aba's wells.[460] The Philippines considers the historical account presented by the Taiwan Authority relevant insofar as it undermines China's claim to exclusive rights within the 'nine-dash line'.[461]

439. Finally, the Philippines objects to the Taiwan Authority's arguments that if the Tribunal were to find Itu Aba to be a rock, "serious issues could arise, as several nations would no longer be able to claim EEZs of certain islands."[462] The Philippines notes that the Taiwan Authority's position

---

[457] First Motavalli Report, pp. 5, 8; *see also* Dr. L. Xi, "Summary of Land of Guangdong Nansha Islands," *Soil Quarterly* Vol. 6, No. 3 (1947) (Annex 885).

[458] Second Motavalli Report, p. 5.

[459] Written Responses of the Philippines on Itu Aba, para. 11 (25 April 2016); *see also* Written Responses of the Philippines on UKHO Materials, para. 27 (28 April 2016); Written Responses of the Philippines on French Archive Materials, paras. 2-20 (3 June 2016).

[460] Dr. Ryan T. Bailey, *Supplemental Report on Groundwater Resources Analysis of Itu Aba* (20 April 2016) (Annex 911) (hereinafter "**Second Bailey Report**").

[461] Written Responses of the Philippines on Itu Aba, para. 95 (25 April 2016).

[462] Ministry of Foreign Affairs of the Republic of China (Taiwan), *Taiping Island is an Island, not a Rock, and the ROC Possesses Full Rights Associated with an Exclusive Economic Zone and Continental Shelf in accordance with UNCLOS*, Press Release No. 023 (23 January 2016) (Annex 875).

is undermined by China's own stance with respect to Japan's claim to an exclusive economic zone around Oki-no-Tori-shima. It also recalls that restraining excessive State claims is one of the purposes of Article 121(3) and international law in general.[463] The Philippines echoes its appeal to the Tribunal to avoid a situation of dangerous uncertainty:

> Finding that a tiny feature like Itu Aba could generate entitlement to a continental shelf and EEZ would intensify the already dangerous sovereignty disputes in the area (and potentially elsewhere in the world) and encourage further damage to the delicate natural environment of the South China Sea by encouraging States to undertake further efforts to solidify their claims. Such an outcome would be inconsistent with the core objects and purposes of the Convention, namely to 'promote the peaceful uses of the seas and oceans, the equitable and efficient utilization of their resources, the conservation of their living resources, and the study, protection and preservation of the marine environment.' It would be equally inconsistent with the central object of Part XV: the peaceful settlement of disputes.[464]

440. The Philippines submits that there are two ways for the Tribunal to avoid these threats to peace: either find Itu Aba to be a rock, or "enjoin both Parties, pending agreement on delimitation, from exercising any rights in respect of any feature in the Spratly Islands beyond 12 [miles]."[465]

ii.   *Thitu, West York, and Other High-Tide features*

441. The Philippines, which has occupied Thitu since 1970, recalls that it only claims a 12-nautical-mile territorial sea from Thitu and considers it to be a rock for purposes of Article 121(3). The Philippines notes that there is a well on Thitu that contains "brackish but drinkable water," but the water must be filtered for safe consumption. The local population on Thitu was transplanted there and has been maintained by the Philippine Government since 2001. It is only possible to grow vegetables there because soil is continually imported from Palawan and supplies are shipped by naval vessel to personnel monthly.[466] The Philippines argues that without the "umbilical cord" of the Philippines' support, Thitu is—like Itu Aba—incapable of sustaining the habitation of even the small community that the Philippines maintains there.[467] The Philippines' experts take the same view.[468]

442. The Philippines notes that, at 0.21 square kilometres, West York is even smaller than Thitu and Itu Aba. Like Thitu, the Philippines considers West York to be a "rock" unable to sustain human habitation or economic life. According to the Philippines, there is no potable water and

---

[463]   Written Responses of the Philippines, para. 109 (11 March 2016).

[464]   Written Responses of the Philippines, para. 114 (11 March 2016).

[465]   Written Responses of the Philippines, para. 115 (11 March 2016).

[466]   Memorial, para. 5.99.

[467]   Memorial, para. 5.105.

[468]   Schofield Report, p. 28.

agriculture is impossible because the salinity of the water retards growth of introduced plants. There is no population, only a small observation post staffed by a few soldiers sustained by outside supplies.[469]   Accordingly, the Philippines submits that West York does not have conditions sufficient to sustain human habitation or an economic life.

443.   The Philippines and its experts make similar submissions about the status of other high-tide features in the Spratly Islands, including North Danger Reef, South Danger Reef, Nanshan Island, Sand Cay, Loaita Island, and Swallow Reef.[470]

444.   The Philippines considers the materials obtained by the Tribunal from the archives of the UK Hydrographic Agency to confirm that the Philippines has correctly categorised the remaining features as "rock[s] as defined in Article 121(3)."[471] The Philippines notes that the *China Sea Directory* fails to mention the existence of any inhabitants on the features,[472] with other reports describing only the faintest traces of human presence, such as wells with "brackish" water, as on Loaita Island,[473] or foundations of a "small hut", as in the case of Thitu.[474] The Philippines also notes the near-complete lack of vegetation on the features in question.[475]

445.   Finally, the Philippines also considers that documents obtained by the Tribunal from France's National Library and National Overseas Archives confirm that "the other features in the South China Sea are incapable of sustaining human habitation or economic life of their own."[476] In this regard, the Philippines cites a 1949 internal French Government report which states that these "islands have no fixed population and carry only stunted vegetation."[477]

---

[469]   Memorial, para. 5.101.

[470]   Supplemental Written Submission, Vol. I, pp. 117-119; *see generally* Supplemental Written Submission, Vol. II; Schofield Report, pp. 18-68; Merits Hearing Tr. (Day 3), pp. 5-10.

[471]   Written Responses of the Philippines on UKHO Materials, paras. 39 (Loaita Island), 60 (Nanshan Island), 71 (Sand Cay), 91 (Swallow Reef), 95 (Thitu), 98 (West York) (28 April 2016).

[472]   Written Responses of the Philippines on UKHO Materials, para. 96 (28 April 2016); *China Sea Directory*, Vol. II, p. 72 (1st ed. 1868).

[473]   Written Responses of the Philippines on UKHO Materials, para. 62 (28 April 2016); *HMS Herald, Amendments to Sailing Directions for West York, Nanshan, Flat Island, and Mischief Reef*, UKHO Ref. H3911/1938.

[474]   Written Responses of the Philippines on UKHO Materials, para. 97 (28 April 2016); HMS Herald, *Report of 1937 Visit to Thitu and Itu Aba*, UKHO Ref. H2499/1937.

[475]   *See, e.g.*, Written Responses of the Philippines on UKHO Materials, paras. 62, 71, 96 (28 April 2016); *China Sea Directory*, Vol. II, p. 72 (1st ed. 1868); HMS Herald, *Amendments to Sailing Directions for West York, Nanshan, Flat Island, and Mischief Reef*, UKHO Ref. H3911/1938; *Report of the Results of an Examination by the Officers of HMS Rambler of the Slopes and Zoological Condition of Tizard and Macclesfield Banks*, UKHO Ref. HD106, p. 17 (1888).

[476]   Written Responses of the Philippines on French Archive Materials, para. 21 (3 June 2016).

[477]   Written Responses of the Philippines on French Archive Materials, para. 21 (3 June 2016).

4.   China's Position

446.   In connection with the Philippines' Submissions No. 3, 5, and 7, China's Position Paper states that "the Philippines is putting the cart before the horse by requesting the Arbitral Tribunal to determine, even before the matter of sovereignty is dealt with, the issue of compatibility of China's maritime claims with the Convention."[478] China has repeated this position in more recent statements, arguing that

> According to international law, the entity that enjoys maritime entitlements is the State that owns maritime features, rather than the maritime features themselves. Each maritime entitlement is explicitly tied to the State that it belongs to. In its provisions on territorial sea, contiguous zone, exclusive economic zone, and continental shelf, the UNCLOS explicitly grants the maritime entitlements to the "coastal State" of relevant maritime zones in question. It is meaningless to indulge in the empty talk on the legal status and entitlements of maritime features without making a preliminary decision on who is the "coastal State" and in separation from State sovereignty. The legal status and entitlements of maritime features do not constitute actual disputes in themselves, and there is no precedent in international law deciding otherwise.[479]

447.   The Tribunal rejected that argument in its Award on Jurisdiction,[480] holding that it was not necessary to first decide questions of sovereignty and "that it is entirely possible to approach the Philippines' Submissions from the premise . . . that China is correct in its assertion of sovereignty over Scarborough Shoal and the Spratlys."[481]

448.   China also objected that the Philippines had selected to seek specific determinations on the status of only nine maritime features, principally those on which China currently maintains a presence.   China posited that "[i]t is plain that, in order to determine China's maritime entitlements based on the Nansha Islands under the Convention, all maritime features comprising the Nansha Islands must be taken into account."[482] China pointed out that the Philippines had omitted from its requested determinations the "largest island in the Nansha Islands, Taiping Dao, which is currently controlled by the Taiwan authorities of China," as well as features that the Philippines itself occupies.[483]

---

[478]   China's Position Paper, para. 18.

[479]   Ministry of Foreign Affairs, People's Republic of China, *Briefing on the South China Sea Arbitration Initiated by the Philippines: Xu Hong, Director General of Department of Treaty and Law* (19 May 2016).

[480]   Award on Jurisdiction, paras. 400-404.

[481]   Award on Jurisdiction, para. 153.

[482]   China's Position Paper, para. 21.

[483]   China's Position Paper, paras. 19, 22.

449. China considers that it "has, based on the Nansha Islands as a whole, territorial sea, exclusive economic zone, and continental shelf,"[484] but has not explicitly set out its position on the application of Article 121(3) to each of the maritime features identified in the Philippines' Submissions. China's general silence in this regard can be contrasted with (a) the positions of States such as Viet Nam, Indonesia, and the Philippines[485] that high-tide features in the Spratly Islands are "rocks" for purposes of Article 121(3) and should only be entitled to a 12-nautical-mile territorial sea; (b) the position implied in Malaysia and Viet Nam's Joint Submission to the CLCS that sets out official coordinates for the 200-nautical-mile limit of the continental shelves of the two States, drawn only from basepoints adjacent to Borneo and the mainland of Viet Nam and not from any feature in the Spratlys;[486] and (c) recent assertions by the Taiwan Authority that Itu Aba "indisputably qualifies as an 'island' according to the specifications of Article 121 . . . and can sustain human habitation and economic life of its own" and "is thus categorically not a 'rock'."[487]

450. Nevertheless, China's positions on the status of some features, as well as the meaning of Article 121 generally, can be discerned from its own laws, diplomatic exchanges, and public statements.

---

[484] Letter from the Ambassador of the People's Republic of China to the Netherlands to the individual members of the Tribunal (3 June 2016), *enclosing* Ministry of Foreign Affairs, People's Republic of China, *Foreign Ministry Spokesperson Hua Chunying's Remarks on Relevant Issue about Taiping Dao* (3 June 2016), *available at* <www.fmprc.gov.cn/mfa_eng/xwfw_665399/s2510_665401/t1369189.shtml>; *see also* Note Verbale from the People's Republic of China to the Secretary-General of the United Nations, No. CML/8/2011 (14 April 2011) (Annex 201).

[485] Merits Hearing Tr. (Day 2), p. 103; Note Verbale from the Republic of Indonesia to the Secretary-General of the United Nations, No. 480/POL-703/VII/10 (8 July 2010) (Annex 197); Socialist Republic of Viet Nam, *Statement of the Ministry of Foreign Affairs of the Socialist Republic of Viet Nam Transmitted to the Arbitral Tribunal in the Proceedings Between the Republic of the Philippines and the People's Republic of China*, p. 5 (14 December 2014) (Annex 468).

[486] Malaysia and the Socialist Republic of Vietnam, *Joint Submission to the Commission on the Limits of the Continental Shelf, in Respect of the Southern Part of the South China Sea* (6 May 2009) (Annex 223); *see also* Socialist Republic of Vietnam, *Submission to the Commission on the Limits of the Continental Shelf pursuant to Article 76, paragraph 8 of the United Nations Convention on the Law of the Sea: Partial Submission in Respect of Vietnam's Extended Continental Shelf: North Area (VNM-N)* (April 2009) (Annex 222).

[487] Ministry of Foreign Affairs of the Republic of China (Taiwan), *Statement on the South China Sea*, No. 001, para. 3 (7 July 2015) (Annex 656); Ministry of Foreign Affairs of the Republic of China (Taiwan), *ROC Government Reiterates its Position on South China Sea Issues*, No. 240, para. 3 (31 October 2015) (Annex 657); *see also* Republic of China (Taiwan), *Position Paper on ROC South China Sea Policy*, 21 March 2016, *available at* <www.mofa.gov.tw/Upload/RelFile/1112/156185/12467dfc-3b8c-4392-9096-57f84ff31f1c.pdf>; "*Amicus Curiae* Submission by the Chinese (Taiwan) Society of International Law" (23 March 2016), *available at* <csil.org.tw/home/wp-content/uploads/2016/03/SCSTF-Amicus-Curiae-Brief-final.pdf>; Office of the President, Republic of China (Taiwan), *President Ma's Remarks at International Press Conference regarding Taiping Island in Nansha Islands* (23 March 2016), *available at* <english.president.gov.tw/Default.aspx?tabid=491&itemid=36980&rmid=2355>.

(a)   **China's Statements on the Meaning of Article 121(3)**

451.   China has made diplomatic representations that reveal its position and "serious concerns" about the operation of Article 121(3) in practice, notably in the context of protesting Japan's November 2008 claim of an extended continental shelf from Oki-no-Tori-shima.[488] Oki-no-Tori-shima is an atoll, located in the western Pacific Ocean between Okinawa and the Northern Mariana Islands, of which only two small portions naturally protrude above water at high tide.

452.   In a Note Verbale to the UN Secretary-General dated 6 February 2009, submitted in response to Japan's submission to the CLCS concerning the limits of the extended continental shelf, China expressed its view that when States exercise their rights to establish the outer limits of their continental shelf beyond 200 nautical miles, they "shall also have the obligation to ensure respect for the extent of the International Seabed Area . . . which is the common heritage of mankind, and not to affect the overall interests of the international community as a whole."[489] China emphasised that all States "shall implement the Convention in its entirety and ensure the integrity of the Convention, in particular, ensure that the extent of the Area is not subject to any illegal encroachment."[490] With respect specifically to Oki-no-Tori-Shima, China went on to state as follows:

> It is to be noted that the so-called Oki-no-Tori Shima Island is in fact a rock as referred to in Article 121(3) of the Convention. Therefore, the Chinese Government wishes to draw . . . attention . . . to the inconformity with the Convention with regard to the inclusion of the rock of Oki-no-Tori in Japan's Submission.
>
> Article 121(3) of the Convention stipulates that, "Rocks which cannot sustain human habitation or economic life of their own shall have no exclusive economic zone or continental shelf." Available scientific data fully reveal that the rock of Oki-no-Tori, on its natural conditions, obviously cannot sustain human habitation or economic life of its own, and therefore shall have no exclusive economic zone or continental shelf. Even less shall it have the right to the extended continental shelf beyond 200 nautical miles.[491]

453.   A few months later, in advance of the 19th Meeting of States Parties to the Convention in May 2009, China proposed that the agenda include a supplementary item entitled "International Seabed Area as the common heritage of mankind and article 121 of the United Nations

---

[488]   Japan, *Submission to the Commission on the Limits of the Continental Shelf pursuant to Article 76, paragraph 8 of the United Nations Convention on the Law of the Sea: Executive Summary* 12 November 2008) (Annex 228).

[489]   Note Verbale from the People's Republic of China to the Secretary-General of the United Nations, No. CML/2/2009 (6 February 2009) (Annex 189)

[490]   Note Verbale from the People's Republic of China to the Secretary-General of the United Nations, No. CML/2/2009 (6 February 2009) (Annex 189)

[491]   Note Verbale from the People's Republic of China to the Secretary-General of the United Nations, No. CML/2/2009 (6 February 2009) (Annex 189); Note Verbale from the People's Republic of China to the Secretary-General of the United Nations, No. CML/12/2009 (13 April 2009).

Convention on the Law of the Sea."[492] In an explanatory note to its proposal, China recalled the general obligation of good faith in Article 300 of the Convention and stated that in submissions concerning the outer limits of the continental shelf:

> [C]oastal States should comply fully with the Convention, taking into account the overall interests of the international community, and should not interpret the Convention in a biased way, nor put their own interests above the overall interests of the international community, nor encroach upon the Area as the common heritage of mankind.[493]

454. China noted that most States had abided by the provisions of the Convention and made "serious efforts to safeguard the overall interests of the international community when claiming their rights." However, China observed that:

> there is also some case in which the Convention is not abided by, for example, claims on the continental shelf within and beyond 200 nautical miles with an isolated rock in the ocean as base point. Recognition of such claim will set a precedent which may lead to encroachment upon the high seas and the Area on a larger scale. Therefore, the international community should express serious concerns on this issue.[494]

455. China quoted the provisions of Article 121(3) and stated:

> How to implement this provision relates to the interpretation and application of important principles of the Convention, and the overall interests of the international community, and is a key issue for the proper consideration of relevant submission concerning the outer limits of the continental shelf, and the safeguarding of the common heritage of mankind.[495]

China argued that there was a need for "some appropriate guidelines" on the issue of the legal implication of Article 121 on the protection of the common heritage of mankind.

456. During the 15th Session of the International Seabed Authority in June 2009, China raised the issue of rocks under Article 121(3) in the context of particular continental shelf submissions and "argued that the International Seabed Authority was the right forum to discuss matter since it

---

[492]   Note Verbale from the People's Republic of China to the Secretary-General of the United Nations (21 May 2009), *reproduced in* United Nations Convention on the Law of the Sea, Meeting of States Parties, *Proposal for the Inclusion of a Supplementary Item in the Agenda of the Nineteenth Meeting of States Parties*, UN Doc. SPLOS/196, (22 May 2009) (Annex 668).

[493]   Note Verbale from the People's Republic of China to the Secretary-General of the United Nations (21 May 2009), *reproduced in* United Nations Convention on the Law of the Sea, Meeting of States Parties, *Proposal for the Inclusion of a Supplementary Item in the Agenda of the Nineteenth Meeting of States Parties*, UN Doc. SPLOS/196, (22 May 2009) (Annex 668).

[494]   Note Verbale from the People's Republic of China to the Secretary-General of the United Nations (21 May 2009), *reproduced in* United Nations Convention on the Law of the Sea, Meeting of States Parties, *Proposal for the Inclusion of a Supplementary Item in the Agenda of the Nineteenth Meeting of States Parties*, UN Doc. SPLOS/196, p. 2, para. 3 (22 May 2009) (Annex 668).

[495]   Note Verbale from the People's Republic of China to the Secretary-General of the United Nations (21 May 2009), *reproduced in* United Nations Convention on the Law of the Sea, Meeting of States Parties, *Proposal for the Inclusion of a Supplementary Item in the Agenda of the Nineteenth Meeting of States Parties*, UN Doc. SPLOS/196 (22 May 2009) (Annex 668).

had the mandate to protect the common heritage of mankind."[496] Referring to Article 121(3), the Chinese representative "urged member States to be guided by the letter and spirit of the Convention to avoid any encroachment on the common heritage of mankind."[497]

457. China reiterated its position on Oki-no-Tori-shima in a 3 August 2011 Note Verbale to the UN Secretary General, after Korea had also registered protest. China stated that it "consistently maintains that, the rock of Oki-no-Tori, on its natural conditions, obviously cannot sustain human habitation or economic life of its own" and therefore under Article 121(3), the rock of Oki-no-Tori "shall have no exclusive economic zone or continental shelf." [498] China went on to state that:

> the application of Article 121(3) of the Convention relates to the extent of the International Seabed Area as the common heritage of mankind, relates to the overall interests of the international community, and is an important legal issue of general nature. To claim continental shelf from the rock of Oki-no-Tori will seriously encroach upon the Area as the common heritage of mankind.[499]

458. Through the statements recounted above, China has demonstrated a robust stance on the importance of Article 121(3). It has repeatedly alluded to the risks to "the common heritage of mankind" and "overall interests of the international community" if Article 121(3) is not properly applied to small features that on their "natural conditions" obviously cannot sustain human habitation or economic life of their own. China has not, however, assessed those factors in any specific analysis of most of the individual features in the South China Sea, as discussed below.

(b)   China's Position on the Status of Scarborough Shoal

459. China claims sovereignty over Scarborough Shoal, which in China is known as "Huangyan Dao" and treated as part of the Zhongsha Islands.[500]

---

[496]   Delegation of the People's Republic of China, *Statement at the 15th Session of the International Seabed Authority* (June 2009), *summarised in* International Seabed Authority, Press Release, UN Doc. SB/15/14, p. 3 (4 June 2009), *available at* <www.isa.org.jm/sites/default/files/files/documents/sb-15-14.pdf>.

[497]   Delegation of the People's Republic of China, *Statement at the 15th Session of the International Seabed Authority* (June 2009), *summarised in* International Seabed Authority, Press Release, UN Doc. SB/15/14, p. 3 (4 June 2009), *available at* <www.isa.org.jm/sites/default/files/files/documents/sb-15-14.pdf>.

[498]   *See* Note Verbale from the People's Republic of China to the Secretary-General of the United Nations, No. CML/59/2011 (3 August 2011) (Annex 203).

[499]   Note Verbale from the People's Republic of China to the Secretary-General of the United Nations, No. CML/59/2011 (3 August 2011) (Annex 203). China also expressed concern that, were the CLCS to make recommendations on an extended continental shelf claim from Oki-no-Tori before its legal status was been made clear, there would be "adverse impact on the maintenance of an equal and reasonable order for oceans."

[500]   China's Position Paper, para.6

460. In China's 1958 *Declaration of the Government of the People's Republic of China on China's Territorial Sea*, China declared a twelve mile nautical sea from "all territories . . . including . . . the Zhongsha Islands."[501] China's 1992 *Law on the Territorial Sea and the Contiguous Zone* also included the Zhongsha Islands in China's territorial land which generated a 12-nautical-mile territorial sea.[502]

461. In conjunction with its ratification of the Convention, on 7 June 1996, China declared an exclusive economic zone of 200 nautical miles and a continental shelf in accordance with the provisions of the Convention and reaffirmed its sovereignty over the islands listed in Article 2 of its 1992 *Law on the Territorial Sea and the Contiguous Zone*.[503] According to China's 1998 Exclusive Economic Zone and Continental Shelf Act, China's exclusive economic zone and continental shelf are to be measured 200 nautical miles from "the baselines from which the breadth of the territorial sea is measured."[504] China has not, however, published "the baselines from which the breadth of the territorial sea" for Scarborough Shoal is measured. While China has stated that it is entitled to an exclusive economic zone and continental shelf from the Spratly Islands, under the relevant provisions of the Convention and the above-referenced legislation, it has made no such claim specifically with respect to Scarborough Shoal.[505]

462. Various statements of Chinese Foreign Ministry officials, however, indicate that China considers Scarborough Shoal to be at least a high-tide feature within the definition of "island" under Article 121(1) of the Convention. For example, on 22 May 1997, a press briefing entitled "Chinese Foreign Ministry Statement regarding Huangyandao" stated:

---

[501] People's Republic of China, *Declaration of the Government of the People's Republic of China on China's Territorial Sea*, para. 1 (4 September 1958), *reproduced in Collection of the Sea Laws and Regulations of the People's Republic of China* (3rd ed., 2001).

[502] People's Republic of China, *Law on the Territorial Sea and the Contiguous Zone*, Article 2 (25 February 1992) *available at* <www.npc.gov.cn/englishnpc/Law/2007-12/12/content_1383846.htm>.

[503] United Nations, *Multilateral Treaties Deposited with the Secretary-General*, Vol. III, Part 1, Chapters XXII-XXIX, and Part 2, UN Doc. ST/LEG/SER.E/26, p. 450 (1 April 2009).

[504] People's Republic of China, *Law on the Exclusive Economic Zone and the Continental Shelf*, art. 2 (26 June 1998) *available at* < www.npc.gov.cn/englishnpc/Law/2007-12/11/content_1383573.htm>. On 15 May 1996, China issued a *Declaration of the Government of the People's Republic of China on the Baselines of the Territorial Sea*, setting out coordinates for the baselines from which its territorial sea would be measured, but this did not include baselines from Scarborough Shoal's territorial sea. *See* United Nations, Office of Legal Affairs, Division of Ocean Affairs and the Law of the Sea, *Law of the Sea Bulletin No. 32*, pp. 37-40 (1996). China has also subsequently promulgated the coordinates for the baselines from its claim to a territorial sea from Diaoyu Dao and its Affiliated Islands. *See* United Nations, Office of Legal Affairs, Division of Ocean Affairs and the Law of the Sea, *Law of the Sea Bulletin No. 80*, pp. 30-31 (2013).

[505] *Cf.* Note Verbale from the People's Republic of China to the Secretary-General of the United Nations, No. CML/8/2011 (14 April 2011) (Annex 201).

> Huangyan Dao has always been Chinese territory and its legal position has been long determined. According to Article 121 of the UNCLOS, Huangyandao is surrounded by water on all sides and is a natural dry land area that is higher than the water level during high tide; it is not a shoal or submerged reef that does not rise above the water all year round.
>
> . . .
>
> The Philippines has never challenged the position that Huangyandao is China's territory. Recently, the Philippine side suddenly claims that it has maritime jurisdiction over Huangyandao because the island is in the 200 nm EEZ of the Philippines. This position violates the principles of international law and the UNCLOS. . . . The issue of Huangyandao is an issue of territorial sovereignty; the development and exploitation of the EEZ is a question of maritime jurisdiction, the nature of the two issues are different . . . . According to international law, under a situation where is an overlapping of EEZ's among concerned countries, the act of a country to unilaterally proclaim its 200 EEZ is null and void. The scope of the EEZ's of the Philippines and China should be resolved through negotiations based on the principles and regulations of international laws.[506]

463. The above statement expresses China's view that Scarborough Shoal is an island, without engaging in an analysis of whether it might be a rock for purposes of Article 121(3) of the Convention. China does, however, allude to a situation of two "overlapping EEZ[]s" rather than a situation of an exclusive economic zone overlapping only with a territorial sea. As Scarborough Shoal lies more than 200 nautical miles from any other high-tide feature claimed by China, the reference to "overlapping EEZ[]s" suggests that China may consider Scarborough Shoal to be entitled to an exclusive economic zone.

464. In July 1998, according to a record of the "10th Philippines-China Foreign Ministry Consultations" held in Manila on 30 July 1998, the Chinese Foreign Minister expressed the view that "the Huangyan Dao is not a sand bank but rather an island,"[507] in apparent correction of a view expressed earlier by the Philippine Undersecretary of Foreign Affairs that Scarborough Shoal was a shoal, "not an island susceptible of sovereign territorial claim."[508] Again, this statement only reveals China's position with respect to the classification of the feature as a high-tide feature for purposes of Article 121(1) as distinct from a low-tide elevation or submerged shoal. It does not address whether the feature falls into the "rocks" exception of Article 121(3).

465. China has, however, taken certain actions that suggest to the Tribunal that China considers Scarborough Shoal to be a fully entitled island. As discussed above in connection with China's claim to historic rights (see paragraphs 209 to 211), in 2012 China banned some fishing in the

---

[506] Ministry of Foreign Affairs, People's Republic of China, *Chinese Foreign Ministry Statement Regarding Huangyandao* (22 May 1997) (Annex 106).

[507] Department of Foreign Affairs, Republic of the Philippines, *Record of Proceedings: 10th Philippines–China Foreign Ministry Consultations*, p. 23 (30 July 1998) (Annex 184).

[508] Memorandum from the Undersecretary for Policy, Department of Foreign Affairs, Republic of the Philippines, to the President of the Republic of the Philippines, p. 4 (27 May 1997) (Annex 25).

South China Sea north of 12° north latitude. China has also objected to the Philippines' grant of petroleum concessions in the West Calamian Block (SC-58) adjacent to the coast of Palawan, much of which lies beyond 200 nautical miles from any high-tide feature claimed by China, except for Scarborough Shoal. China did not elaborate the basis for these actions, which may have been based either on a theory of historic rights or on a claim to an exclusive economic zone from Scarborough Shoal.

(c)   China's Position on the Status of Itu Aba

466.   According to China, Itu Aba is a fully entitled island, entitled to an exclusive economic zone and continental shelf. On 3 June 2016, China's Foreign Ministry Spokesperson stated as follows:

> Over the history, Chinese fishermen have resided on Taiping Dao for years, working and living there, carrying out fishing activities, digging wells for fresh water, cultivating land and farming, building huts and temples, and raising livestock. The above activities are all manifestly recorded in Geng Lu Bu (Manual of Sea Routes) which was passed down from generation to generation among Chinese fishermen, as well as in many western navigation logs before the 1930s.
>
> The working and living practice of Chinese people on Taiping Dao fully proves that Taiping Dao is an "island" which is completely capable of sustaining human habitation or economic life of its own. The Philippines' attempt to characterize Taiping Dao as a "rock" exposed that its purpose of initiating the arbitration is to deny China's sovereignty over the Nansha Islands and relevant maritime rights and interests.[509]

467.   This express position was previously also suggested by China's comments on the Taiwan Authority's statements "stressing that Taiping Dao [Itu Aba] meets the definition of island according to UNCLOS and is therefore eligible for possessing exclusive economic zone, continental shelf and other maritime rights and interests." When asked to comment, China's Foreign Ministry Spokesperson responded with the following remarks:

> The Nansha Islands including Taiping Dao have been China's territory since ancient times. Chinese people have long been living and working there continuously. China takes the Nansha Islands as a whole when claiming maritime rights and interests, and Chinese people across the Strait all have the responsibility to safeguard the property handed down from our ancestors. China is firmly against attempts of the Philippines to unilaterally deny China's territorial sovereignty and maritime rights and interests in the South China Sea through arbitration.[510]

---

[509]   Letter from the Ambassador of the People's Republic of China to the Netherlands to the individual members of the Tribunal (3 June 2016), *enclosing* Ministry of Foreign Affairs, People's Republic of China, *Foreign Ministry Spokesperson Hua Chunying's Remarks on Relevant Issue about Taiping Dao* (3 June 2016) *available at* <www.fmprc.gov.cn/mfa_eng/xwfw_665399/s2510_665401/t1369189.shtml>.

[510]   *See* Ministry of Foreign Affairs, People's Republic of China, *Foreign Ministry Spokesperson Hua Chunying's Regular Press Conference* (24 March 2016), <www.fmprc.gov.cn/mfa_eng/ xwfw_665399/s2510_665401/2511_665403/t1350552.shtml>; Ministry of Foreign Affairs, People's Republic of China, *Foreign Ministry Spokesperson Hua Chunying's Regular Press Conference* (23 March 2016) *available at* <http://www.fmprc.gov.cn/mfa_eng/xwfw_665399/s2510_665401/

468. In this statement, China did not contradict the characterisation by the Taiwan Authority of Itu
      Aba as a fully entitled island, but rather asserted that its people have lived and worked on Itu
      Aba continuously, which mirrors the elements of "human habitation" and "economic life" in
      Article 121(3) of the Convention.

(d)   China's Position on the Status of Other Features in the Spratly Islands

469. While China has not made statements on the Article 121 status of other specific features in the
      Spratly Islands, it has made general statements that the Spratly Island group as a whole generate
      full maritime entitlements. In its Position Paper, China argued that the Philippines' selection of
      particular features was "an attempt at denying China's sovereignty over the Nansha Islands as a
      whole."[511]

470. In a Note Verbale to the Secretary-General of the United Nations on 14 April 2011, China
      reiterated its sovereignty claims to "the islands in the South China Sea and the adjacent waters"
      and stated that it "enjoys sovereign rights and jurisdiction over relevant waters as well as the
      seabed and subsoil thereof."[512] China added that:

> under the relevant provisions of the 1982 United Nations Convention on the Law of the
> Sea, as well as the Law of the People's Republic of China on the Territorial Sea and the
> Contiguous Zone (1992) and the Law on the Exclusive Economic Zone and the Continental
> Shelf of the People's Republic of China (1998), China's Nansha Islands is fully entitled to
> Territorial Sea, Exclusive Economic Zone (EEZ) and Continental Shelf.[513]

471. China repeated this statement verbatim in its Position Paper.[514] However, given that the
      Position Paper "does not express any position on the substantive issues related to the
      subject-matter of the arbitration,"[515] no further insights on China's position on the application of
      Article 121 to specific features in the Spratly Islands can be gleaned from it.

472. As far as the Tribunal is aware, China has not made specific statements about the status of
      Johnson Reef, Cuarteron Reef, Fiery Cross Reef, Gaven Reef (North), or McKennan Reef for
      purposes of Article 121(3) of the Convention. There are no press briefings about those features

---

t1350212.shtml>; Ministry of Foreign Affairs, People's Republic of China, *Foreign Ministry
Spokesperson Hua Chunying's Regular Press Conference* (28 January 2016), *available at*
<www.fmprc.gov.cn/mfa_eng/xwfw_665399/s2510_665401/t1336013.shtml>.

[511]   China's Position Paper, para. 19.

[512]   Note Verbale from the People's Republic of China to the Secretary-General of the United Nations,
        No. CML/8/2011 (14 April 2011) (Annex 201).

[513]   Note Verbale from the People's Republic of China to the Secretary-General of the United Nations,
        No. CML/8/2011 (14 April 2011) (Annex 201).

[514]   China's Position Paper, para. 21.

[515]   China's Position Paper, para. 2.

comparable to the 1997 statement about Scarborough Shoal[516] or China's recent statement concerning Itu Aba.[517] Nor has China made any comparable statements regarding the other, more significant high-tide features in the Spratlys, with the exception of Itu Aba.

5.   The Tribunal's Considerations

473.   The Tribunal must interpret and apply Article 121 of the Convention in order to make decisions with respect to the Philippines' Submissions No. 3, 5, and 7, as well as to determine its jurisdiction with respect to the Philippines' Submissions No. 8 and 9.

474.   Article 121 has not previously been the subject of significant consideration by courts or arbitral tribunals[518] and has been accorded a wide range of different interpretations in scholarly literature.[519] As has been apparent in the course of these proceedings, the scope of application of its paragraph (3) is not clearly established. Accordingly, the Tribunal will consider the interpretation of this provision before turning to its application to the maritime features in the South China Sea.

(a)   Interpretation of Article 121 of the Convention

475.   The critical element of Article 121 for the Tribunal is its paragraph (3), which provides that "[r]ocks which cannot sustain human habitation or economic life of their own shall have no exclusive economic zone or continental shelf."

---

[516]   Ministry of Foreign Affairs, People's Republic of China, *Chinese Foreign Ministry Statement Regarding Huangyandao* (22 May 1997) (Annex 106).

[517]   Letter from the Ambassador of the People's Republic of China to the Netherlands to the individual members of the Tribunal (3 June 2016), *enclosing* Ministry of Foreign Affairs, People's Republic of China, *Foreign Ministry Spokesperson Hua Chunying's Remarks on Relevant Issue about Taiping Dao* (3 June 2016), *available at* <www.fmprc.gov.cn/mfa_eng/xwfw_665399/s2510_665401/ t1369189.shtml>.

[518]   *See, e.g., Territorial and Maritime Dispute (Nicaragua v. Colombia), Judgment, ICJ Reports 2012,* p. 624.

[519]   *See, e.g.,* D.W. Bowett, *The Legal Regime of Islands in International Law* (1979); E.D. Brown, "Rockall and the Limits of National Jurisdiction of the UK: Part 1," *Marine Policy* Vol. 2, p. 181 at pp. 206-207 (1978); J.M. Van Dyke & R.A. Brooks, "Uninhabited Islands: Their Impact on the Ownership of the Oceans' Resources," *Ocean Development and International Law*, Vol. 12, Nos. 3-4, p. 265 (1983); R. Kolb, "The Interpretation of Article 121, Paragraph 3 of the United Nations Convention on the Law of the Sea: Rocks Which Cannot Sustain Human Habitation or Economic Life of Their Own," *French Yearbook of International Law*, Vol. 40, p. 899 (1994); D. Anderson, "Islands and Rocks in the Modern Law of the Sea," in *United Nations Convention on the Law of the Sea 1982: A Commentary*, Vol. VI, pp. 307-21 (M. Nordquist, gen. ed., 2002); J.L. Jesus, "Rocks, New-born Islands, Sea Level Rise, and Maritime Space," *in* J. Frowein, et al., eds., *Negotiating for Peace*, p. 579 (2003).

476. In order to interpret this provision, the Tribunal must apply the provisions of the Vienna Convention on the Law of Treaties.[520] The general rule of interpretation is set out in Article 31 of the Vienna Convention and provides that a treaty "shall be interpreted in good faith in accordance with the ordinary meaning to be given to the terms of the treaty in their context and in the light of its object and purpose."[521] Further, "any subsequent practice in the application of the treaty which establishes the agreement of the parties regarding its interpretation" shall be taken into account. Pursuant to Article 32 of the Vienna Convention, as supplementary means of interpretation, recourse may be had to the preparatory work of the treaty to confirm its meaning, or determine the meaning when it is otherwise ambiguous, obscure, or leads to a manifestly absurd or unreasonable result.[522]

477. In approaching the interpretation of Article 121, the Tribunal will separately review the text, its context, the object and purpose of the Convention, and the *travaux préparatoires*, before setting out the conclusions that, in the Tribunal's view, follow with respect to the meaning of the provision.

i. The Text of Article 121(3)

478. Article 121(3) contains several textual elements that merit consideration, including the terms (a) "rocks", (b) "cannot", (c) "sustain", (d) "human habitation", (e) "or", and (f) "economic life of their own." Other aspects of the meaning of Article 121(3) arise from its context in the Convention and are discussed subsequently (see paragraphs 507 to 520 below).

(a) "Rocks"

479. The use in Article 121(3) of the term "rocks" raises the question of whether any geological or geomorphological criteria were intended. In other words, was Article 121(3) intended to apply only to features that are composed of solid rock or that are otherwise rock-like in nature?

480. In the Tribunal's view, no such restriction necessarily follows from the use of the term in Article 121(3). The dictionary meaning of "rock" does not confine the term so strictly, and rocks may "consist of aggregates of minerals . . . and occasionally also organic matter . . . . They vary in hardness, and include soft materials such as clays."[523] This was also the conclusion

---

[520]   Vienna Convention on the Law of Treaties, art. 31(1).

[521]   Vienna Convention on the Law of Treaties, art. 31(1).

[522]   Vienna Convention on the Law of Treaties, art. 32.

[523]   "Rock," *Oxford English Dictionary* (Annex 818).

reached by the International Court of Justice in *Territorial and Maritime Dispute (Nicaragua v. Colombia)* when it held Colombia's Quitasueño, a "minuscule" protrusion of coral, to be an Article 121(3) rock:

> International law defines an island by reference to whether it is 'naturally formed' and whether it is above water at high tide, not by reference to its geological composition . . . The fact that the feature is composed of coral is irrelevant.[524]

481. Moreover, any contrary interpretation imposing a geological criteria on Article 121(3) would lead to an absurd result. Within Article 121, rocks are a category of island. An island is defined as a "naturally formed area of land," without any geological or geomorphological qualification. Introducing a geological qualification in paragraph (3) would mean that any high-tide features formed by sand, mud, gravel, or coral—irrespective of their other characteristics—would always generate extended maritime entitlements, even if they were incapable of sustaining human habitation or an economic life of their own. Such features are more ephemeral than a geological rock and may shift location or appear and disappear above high water as a result of conditions over time. A geological criterion would thus accord greater entitlements to less stable and less permanent features. This cannot have been the intent of the Article.

482. The result of this interpretation is that "rocks" for the purposes of Article 121(3) will not necessarily be composed of rock. The Tribunal takes the opportunity to note that the name of a feature will likewise have no bearing on whether it qualifies as a rock for purposes of Article 121(3). A feature may have "Island" or "Rock" in its name and nevertheless be entirely submerged. Conversely a feature with "Reef" or "Shoal" in its name may have protrusions that remain exposed at high tide. In any event, the name of a feature provides no guidance as to whether it can sustain human habitation or an economic life of its own.

        (b)   *"cannot"*

483. The use of the word "cannot" in Article 121(3) indicates a concept of capacity. Does the feature in its natural form have the capability of sustaining human habitation or an economic life? If not, it is a rock. This enquiry is not concerned with whether the feature actually does sustain human habitation or an economic life. It is concerned with whether, objectively, the feature is apt, able to, or lends itself to human habitation or economic life.[525] That is, the fact that a

---

[524] *Territorial and Maritime Dispute (Nicaragua v. Colombia), Merits Judgment, ICJ Reports 2012*, p. 624 at p. 645, para. 37.

[525] According to the Philippines, "the other authentic texts [of Article 121] reflect the same meaning as the English term "cannot": Merits Hearing Tr. (Day 2), p. 70. The Philippines notes that "[i]n Chinese, 'cannot' is 'bu neng', which means 'not able' or 'unable'. Also, for example, the Spanish text uses the phrase 'no aptas'; again, 'not able', 'unable.'" Merits Hearing Tr. (Day 2), p. 71.

feature is currently not inhabited does not prove that it is uninhabitable. The fact that it has no economic life does not prove that it cannot sustain an economic life.

484. Nevertheless, historical evidence of human habitation and economic life in the past may be relevant for establishing a feature's capacity. If a known feature proximate to a populated land mass was never inhabited and never sustained an economic life, this may be consistent with an explanation that it is uninhabitable. Conversely, positive evidence that humans historically lived on a feature or that the feature was the site of economic activity could constitute relevant evidence of a feature's capacity.

(c)   "sustain"

485. The ordinary meaning of sustain generally means to "support, maintain, uphold." The Oxford English Dictionary defines it as "to keep in existence, maintain; spec. to cause to continue in a certain state for an extended period or without interruption; to keep or maintain at the proper level, standard, or rate; to preserve the status of."[526]

486. When used in respect "of land, a place, etc.," to sustain means "to provide or be the source of the food, drink, etc., necessary to keep (a person) alive and healthy); (of food, drink, etc.) to give essential nourishment to (a person)."[527] Stated otherwise, it means "to support or maintain (life) by providing food, drink, and other necessities."[528] When used in connection with sustaining a person, sustain means to "maintain . . . in life and health; to provide with food, drink and other substances necessary for remaining alive; to feed, to keep."[529] When used in connection with sustaining an activity, "sustain" is defined to mean "To keep in existence, maintain; spec. to cause to continue in a certain state for an extended period or without interruption."[530]

487. The Tribunal considers that the ordinary meaning of "sustain" has three components. The first is the concept of the support and provision of essentials. The second is a temporal concept: the support and provision must be over a period of time and not one-off or short-lived. The third is a qualitative concept, entailing at least a minimal "proper standard". Thus, in connection with sustaining human habitation, to "sustain" means to provide that which is necessary to keep

---

[526]   "Sustain," *Oxford English Dictionary* (Annex 819).

[527]   "Sustain," *Oxford English Dictionary* (Annex 333).

[528]   "Sustain," *Oxford English Dictionary* (Annex 333).

[529]   "Sustain," *Oxford English Dictionary* (Annex 819).

[530]   "Sustain," *Oxford English Dictionary* (Annex 819).

humans alive and healthy over a continuous period of time, according to a proper standard. In connection with an economic life, to "sustain" means to provide that which is necessary not just to commence, but also to continue, an activity over a period of time in a way that remains viable on an ongoing basis.

(d)   "human habitation"

488.   The ordinary meaning of "human habitation" is the "action of dwelling in or inhabiting as a place of residence; occupancy by inhabitants" or "a settlement".[531] "Inhabit" is defined as meaning "to dwell in, occupy as an abode, to live permanently or habitually in (a region, element, etc.); to reside in (a country, town, dwelling, etc.)."[532]

489.   In the Tribunal's view, the use in Article 121(3) of the term "habitation" includes a qualitative element that is reflected particularly in the notions of settlement and residence that are inherent in that term. The mere presence of a small number of persons on a feature does not constitute permanent or habitual residence there and does not equate to habitation. Rather, the term habitation implies a non-transient presence of persons who have chosen to stay and reside on the feature in a settled manner. Human habitation would thus require all of the elements necessary to keep people alive on the feature, but would also require conditions sufficiently conducive to human life and livelihood for people to inhabit, rather than merely survive on, the feature.

490.   Forms of human habitation and livelihood vary greatly, and in an international instrument such as the Convention, no particular culture or mode of habitation should be assumed for the purpose of Article 121(3). Certain factors, however, remain constant wherever habitation by humans is concerned. At a minimum, sustained human habitation would require that a feature be able to support, maintain, and provide food, drink, and shelter to some humans to enable them to reside there permanently or habitually over an extended period of time.

491.   In the Tribunal's view, the term "habitation" also generally implies the habitation of the feature by a group or community of persons. No precise number of persons is specified in the Article, but providing the basic necessities for a sole individual would not typically fall within the ordinary understanding of human habitation: humans need company and community over sustained periods of time.

492.   Beyond these basic requirements—necessary to provide for the daily subsistence and survival of a number of people for an indefinite time—the Tribunal considers that the text of Article 121(3)

---

[531]   "Habitation," *Oxford English Dictionary* (Annex 815).

[532]   "Inhabit," *Shorter Oxford English Dictionary* (5th ed., 2002).

does not directly indicate the threshold that would separate settled human habitation from the mere presence of humans. Nor does the text of Article 121(3) elucidate the physical characteristics of a feature that would be necessary to sustain the more settled mode of human habitation, rather than merely ensuring human survival.

(e)   "or"

493. Article 121(3) provides that "[r]ocks which cannot sustain human habitation or economic life of their own shall have no exclusive economic zone or continental shelf." The Tribunal must consider whether the criteria of capacity to sustain "human habitation" and an "economic life of [its] own" are *both* required for a feature to be entitled to an exclusive economic zone and continental shelf, or whether *one* will suffice. The Philippines urges the Tribunal to adopt the former interpretation, arguing that:

> As a matter of logic, the combination of a negative verb form with the disjunctive "or" creates a cumulative requirement. It is, in essence, a double negative. It follows that to be entitled to an EEZ and continental shelf, an insular feature must be able both to sustain human habitation and to sustain economic life of its own.[533]

494. The Tribunal agrees with the Philippines regarding the importance of logic in the interpretation of this provision, but not with the conclusion advanced by the Philippines. Applied to the text of Article 121(3), formal logic would hold that "[r]ocks which cannot sustain (human habitation or economic life of their own)" is equal to "[r]ocks which cannot sustain human habitation [and which cannot sustain] economic life of their own." Formal logic would therefore require that a feature fail both criteria before it would be disentitled to an exclusive economic zone and continental shelf. The text creates a cumulative requirement, as the Philippines argues, but the negative overall structure of the sentence means that the cumulative criteria describe the circumstances in which a feature will be *denied* such maritime zones. The logical result therefore is that if a feature is capable of sustaining either human habitation or an economic life of its own, it will qualify as a fully entitled island.

495. The Tribunal is conscious, however, that formal logic accords imperfectly with linguistic usage at the best of times, even among legal drafters, and is hesitant to accord decisive weight to logical construction alone. Here, it could well be argued that a natural reading of the phrase would include an implied second negation, omitted only to reduce the length of an already somewhat cumbersome clause: in other words, that "[r]ocks which cannot sustain human habitation or [which cannot sustain] economic life of their own shall have no exclusive economic zone or continental shelf." In the Tribunal's view, however, this possibility is

---

[533]   Merits Hearing Tr. (Day 2), p. 84.

foreclosed by the remainder of the paragraph. The first clause of Article 121(3) is not the only negation of a disjunction within the provision. The same construction is repeated in the second half of the paragraph where it provides that such rocks "shall have no exclusive economic zone or continental shelf." Here, however, the logical construction is unequivocally correct: the phrase can only be interpreted to mean that a rock which fails to meet the criteria of the paragraph "shall have no exclusive economic zone [and shall have no] continental shelf." The alternative, in which rocks falling short of the Convention's threshold would generate an entitlement to one or the other of an exclusive economic zone or a continental shelf—but not both—is manifestly absurd and contrary to the clear intent of the Article.

496. The formulation of the remainder of Article 121(3) thus serves to resolve any doubt regarding the interpretation of the phrase "[r]ocks which cannot sustain human habitation or economic life of their own." The Tribunal does not consider it plausible that the drafters of the Convention would have employed a strictly logical construction for one clause within the parallel structure of a single sentence and to have departed from such construction for the other. Accordingly, the Tribunal concludes that, properly interpreted, a rock would be disentitled from an exclusive economic zone and continental shelf only if it were to lack *both* the capacity to sustain human habitation *and* the capacity to sustain an economic life of its own. Or, expressed more straightforwardly and in positive terms, an island that is able to sustain *either* human habitation *or* an economic life of its own is entitled to *both* an exclusive economic zone *and* a continental shelf (in accordance with the provisions of the Convention applicable to other land territory).

497. The Tribunal observes, however, that economic activity is carried out by humans and that humans will rarely inhabit areas where no economic activity or livelihood is possible. The two concepts are thus linked in practical terms, regardless of the grammatical construction of Article 121(3). Nevertheless, the text remains open to the possibility that a feature may be able to sustain human habitation but offer no resources to support an economic life, or that a feature may sustain an economic life while lacking the conditions necessary to sustain habitation directly on the feature itself. This may particularly be the case where multiple islands are used in concert to sustain a traditional way of life, as described by the delegate from Micronesia during the Third UN Conference.[534] The Philippines suggests that an interpretation allowing for

---

[534] The Micronesian delegate stated that:

> Small islands which have no land resources to speak of need the benefits of an economic zone and the sea's resources within it more desperately than any other territories. It would not be equity to deny the sea's resources to those who need them most.

> Suggestions have also been made that uninhabited islands should not have a full economic zone. Almost all of our high islands, and almost all of our atolls, made up of low islands, are inhabited. But some islands are inhabited only part of the year, while others are used

such possibilities would detract from the purpose of the exclusive economic zone regime, which is to accord rights and responsibilities to the populations of the lands that generate the zone. A converse risk is also apparent, however, and too strict a definition, developed in the context of particular islands, could well deprive other populations, making use of islands in a different way, of the resources on which they have traditionally depended.

(f)   "economic life of their own"

498.   The final element of the text of Article 121(3) is the phrase "economic life of their own." In the Tribunal's view, two elements of this phrase require consideration. First, the text makes use of the particular term of "economic life". Second, the text makes clear that the features must be capable of sustaining not simply "economic life", but an economic life "of their own".

499.   The ordinary meaning of "economic" is "relating to the development and regulation of the material resources of a community"[535] and may relate to a process or system by which goods and services are produced, sold and bought, or exchanged. The term "life" suggests that the mere presence of resources will be insufficient and that some level of local human activity to exploit, develop, and distribute those resources would be required. The Tribunal also recalls that "economic life" must be read bearing in mind the time component of "sustain". A one-off transaction or short-lived venture would not constitute a sustained economic life. The phrase presupposes ongoing economic activity. Although the drafters chose not to import any reference to "value", the need for the economic activity to be sustained over a period of time does presuppose a basic level of viability for the economic activity.

500.   The "of their own" component is essential to the interpretation because it makes clear that a feature itself (or group of related features) must have the ability to support an independent economic life, without relying predominantly on the infusion of outside resources or serving purely as an object for extractive activities, without the involvement of a local population.[536] In

---

not as residences but for fishing or in some functional way other than for permanent habitation. They are all the same as vital a part of our economy and livelihood as some islands that may have permanent dwellings on them, but may have little or no fish resources near them. We do not believe that the criteria of inhabitation or size are practical or equitable.

Statement by the Chairman of the Joint Committee of the Congress of Micronesia submitted on behalf of the Congress by the United States of America, UN Doc. A/CONF.62/L.6 (27 August 1974).

[535]   "Economic," *Shorter Oxford English Dictionary* (5th ed., 2002).

[536]   According to the Philippines: "In Chinese, 'of its own', the phrase used is 'qibenshen de jingji shenghuo', in which the term 'qibenshen' means 'it itself', and it proceeds and modifies the phrase 'economic life', 'jingji shenghuo'. It is therefore clear that whatever 'economic life' means, it must be particular to and localised on the feature itself." Merits Hearing Tr. (Day 2), p. 79.

the Tribunal's view, for economic activity to constitute the economic life of a feature, the resources around which the economic activity revolves must be local, not imported, as must be the benefit of such activity. Economic activity that can be carried on only through the continued injection of external resources is not within the meaning of "an economic life of their own." Such activity would not be the economic life of the feature as "of its own", but an economic life ultimately dependent on support from the outside. Similarly, purely extractive economic activities, which accrue no benefit for the feature or its population, would not amount to an economic life of the feature as "of its own".

501. In this respect, the Tribunal must particularly consider the role of economic activity centred on the sea areas adjacent to the feature. In other words, is economic activity derived from a possible exclusive economic zone, continental shelf, or territorial sea of a feature sufficient to endow it with economic life?

502. In the Tribunal's view, economic activity derived from a possible exclusive economic zone or continental shelf must necessarily be excluded. Article 121(3) is concerned with determining the conditions under which a feature will—or will not—be accorded an exclusive economic zone and continental shelf. It would be circular and absurd if the mere presence of economic activity in the area of the possible exclusive economic zone or continental shelf were sufficient to endow a feature with those very zones.

503. A different calculus applies with respect to the territorial sea. Here, no circularity would result as any high-tide feature, regardless of its status under Article 121(3), will suffice to generate a territorial sea. Nevertheless, Article 121(3) does require that the economic life be linked to the feature as its own. In the Tribunal's view, this phrase requires a link between the economic life and the feature itself, rather than merely its adjacent waters. Accordingly, economic activity in the territorial sea could form part of the economic life of a feature, provided that it is somehow linked to the feature itself, whether through a local population or otherwise. Distant fisherman exploiting the territorial sea surrounding a small rock and making no use of the feature itself, however, would not suffice to give the feature an economic life of its own. Nor would an enterprise devoted to extracting the mineral resources of the seabed adjacent to such a feature and making no use of the feature itself.

(g)   *Conclusions Drawn from the Text of Article 121(3)*

504. Despite the complexity apparent in Article 121(3), the Tribunal considers that a number of propositions follow from the text itself:

(a)   First, the use of the term "rock" does not require that a feature be composed of rock in the geologic sense in order to fall within the scope of the provision.

(b)   Second, the use of the term "cannot" makes clear that the provision concerns the objective capacity of the feature to sustain human habitation or economic life. Actual habitation or economic activity at any particular point in time is not relevant, except to the extent that it indicates the capacity of the feature.

(c)   Third, the use of the term "sustain" indicates both time and qualitative elements. Habitation and economic life must be able to extend over a certain duration and occur to an adequate standard.

(d)   Fourth, the logical interpretation of the use of the term "or" discussed above indicates that a feature that is able to sustain either human habitation or an economic life of its own will be entitled to an exclusive economic zone and continental shelf.

505. At the same time, the Tribunal considers that the text is not specific with respect to the threshold separating human habitation from the mere extended presence of humans. A qualitative aspect is apparent, but the text offers little guidance as to where this line should be drawn. Similarly, the text does not permit an easy distinction between economic activity and an economic life, although the phrase "of their own" does serve to exclude certain forms of activity that are entirely dependent on external resources, devoted to using a feature as an object for extractive activities without the involvement of a local population, or which make use solely of the waters adjacent to a feature.

506. Article 31 of the Vienna Convention calls for the interpretation of "the terms of the treaty in their context and in the light of its object and purpose." It is to those latter elements that the Tribunal now turns.

ii.   *The Context of Article 121(3) and the Object and Purpose of the Convention*

507. In the Tribunal's view, two aspects of the context of Article 121(3) require consideration. First, rocks and fully entitled islands exist in the context of a system of classifying features that includes fully entitled islands, rocks, low-tide elevations, and submerged features. Article 121(3) must accordingly be interpreted in conjunction with the other paragraphs of Article 121 and in conjunction with Article 13 concerning low-tide elevations. Second, as Article 121(3) concerns the circumstances in which a feature will be denied entitlements to an exclusive economic zone and continental shelf, it must be interpreted in the context of those

maritime areas and in light of the purpose behind the introduction of the exclusive economic zone.

(a)   The Context of Islands, Rocks, and Low-Tide Elevations

508. As discussed above in connection with the status of features as above or below water (see paragraphs 305 to 306), Article 13 and Article 121 both apply to a "naturally formed area of land." Just as a low-tide elevation or area of seabed cannot be legally transformed into an island through human efforts, the Tribunal considers that a rock cannot be transformed into a fully entitled island through land reclamation. The status of a feature must be assessed on the basis of its natural condition.

509. In addition to maintaining the structure apparent across Articles 13 and 121, this reading is consistent with the object and purpose of Article 121(3). If States were allowed to convert any rock incapable of sustaining human habitation or an economic life into a fully entitled island simply by the introduction of technology and extraneous materials, then the purpose of Article 121(3) as a provision of limitation would be frustrated. It could no longer be used as a practical restraint to prevent States from claiming for themselves potentially immense maritime space. In this regard, the Tribunal agrees with the Philippines that "[a] contrary rule would create perverse incentives for States to undertake such actions to extend their maritime zones to the detriment of other coastal States and/or the common heritage of mankind."[537] Were a feature's capacity to sustain allowed to be established by technological enhancements, then "every high-tide feature, no matter . . . its natural conditions, could be converted into an island generating a 200-mile entitlement if the State that claims it is willing to devote and regularly supply the resources necessary to sustain a human settlement."[538]

510. Accordingly, the Tribunal understands the phrase "cannot sustain" to mean "cannot, without artificial addition, sustain." This reading is consistent with the "naturally formed" qualification of the definition of "island" and the words "of their own" which qualify "an economic life".

511. As noted above with respect to low-tide elevations, many of the high-tide features in the Spratly Islands have been subjected to substantial human modification as large installations and airstrips have been constructed on them. Desalination facilities have been installed and tillable soil introduced. In some cases, it is now difficult to observe directly the original status of the feature in its natural state. In such circumstances, the Tribunal considers that the Convention requires

---

[537]   Merits Hearing Tr. (Day 2), p. 72.

[538]   Merits Hearing Tr. (Day 2), p. 73.

that the status of a feature be ascertained on the basis of its earlier, natural condition, prior to the onset of significant human modification, taking into account the best available evidence of the previous status of the high-tide features, before intensive modification.

(b) *The Link between Article 121(3) and the Purpose of the Exclusive Economic Zone*

512. As noted above, the Tribunal considers that a close analysis of the text of Article 121(3) sheds some light on what will—and what will not—suffice for the purposes of that provision. Ultimately, however, the Tribunal finds that the plain text of the words "human habitation" and "an economic life of its own" offers limited guidance as to the character or scale of activity that would satisfy the requirements of the Article. Here, the meaning of the text of Article 121(3) is shaped by its context within the Convention and the inherent connection between this provision and the concept of the exclusive economic zone. Under the 1958 Geneva Conventions, the rights and jurisdiction of States were limited to the territorial sea and the continental shelf and nothing akin to Article 121(3) was provided for. The genesis of that Article is inextricably linked with the expansion of coastal State jurisdiction through the exclusive economic zone.

513. As discussed already in connection with the Tribunal's consideration of historic rights in the South China Sea, the purpose of the exclusive economic zone that emerges from the history of the Convention (see paragraphs 248 to 254 above) was to extend the jurisdiction of States over the waters adjacent to their coasts and to preserve the resources of those waters for the benefit of the population of the coastal State.

514. These objectives are apparent in the various regional declarations made prior to the Third UN Conference by the States that were the principal proponents of expanded coastal State jurisdiction:

(a) Within Latin America, the 1952 Santiago Declaration by Chile, Ecuador, and Peru linked the expansion of maritime zones to the obligation of governments "to ensure for their peoples the necessary conditions of subsistence, and to provide them with the resources for their economic development."[539]

(b) Similarly, the 1970 Montevideo and Lima declarations emphasised "that ties of geographic, economic and social nature bind the sea, the land and man who inhabits it,

---

[539] Declaration on the Maritime Zone, signed at Santiago, 18 August 1952, 1976 UNTS 326 (Chile, Ecuador and Peru).

from which there arises a legitimate priority in favor of littoral peoples to benefit from the natural resources offered to them by their maritime environment."[540]

(c)   In Africa, the conclusions adopted at the African States Regional Seminar on the Law of the Sea, held at Yaoundé from 20 to 30 June 1972, emphasised that "African States have equally the right to establish beyond the Territorial Sea an Economic Zone over which they will have an exclusive jurisdiction for the purpose of control regulation and national exploitation of the living resources of the Sea and their reservation for the primary benefit of their peoples and their respective economies . . . ."[541]

(d)   Finally, in 1973, the Organization of African Unity adopted the Addis Ababa declaration, setting out draft articles for various aspects of the law of the sea and recording its conviction "that African countries have a right to exploit the marine resources around the African continent for the economic benefit of African peoples."[542]

515.   These objectives are also apparent in the positions taken by coastal developing States throughout the negotiations of the Seabed Committee and the Third UN Conference, and were emphasised equally by certain developed States with a particular dependence on fisheries.[543] Ultimately, the articles of the Convention concerning the exclusive economic zone were (as with much of the Convention) a compromise and intended to balance the interests of the peoples of coastal developing States with the interests of the traditional maritime States and those States with long-range fishing industries that opposed the expansion of coastal State jurisdiction. The principal impetus for expanding such jurisdiction in the first instance, however, is unequivocally linked with the interest of coastal States in preserving marine resources for the benefit of their people. A particular emphasis on the needs of developing States is also recorded in the Preamble to the Convention, which notes that the achievement of a legal order for the oceans

---

[540]   The Declaration of Montevideo on Law of the Sea, signed at Montevideo, Uruguay, 8 May 1970 (Argentina, Brazil, Chile, Ecuador, El Salvador, Panama, Peru, Nicaragua, and Uruguay), *reproduced in* 9 ILM 1081 (1970); *see also* Declaration of Latin American States on the Law of the Sea, Lima, 4-8 August 1970 (Argentina, Brazil, Colombia, Chile, the Dominican Republic, Ecuador, El Salvador, Guatemala, Honduras, Panama, Peru, Mexico, Nicaragua, and Uruguay), *reproduced in* 10 ILM 207 (1971).

[541]   Conclusions in the General Report of the African States Regional Seminar on the Law of the Sea, held in Yaoundé, 20-30 June 1972, *reproduced in* 12 ILM 210 (1973).

[542]   Declaration of the Organization of African Unity on the issues of the Law of the Sea, 1973, *reproduced as* UN Doc. A/CONF.62/33.

[543]   *See, e.g.*, Committee on the Peaceful Uses of the Sea-Bed and the Ocean Floor Beyond the Limits Of National Jurisdiction, Sub-Committee II, "Summary Record of the Twenty-Seventh Meeting,", UN Doc. A/AC.138/SC.II/SR.27, p. 25 at p. 40 (22 March 1972) (Statement of the Representative of Iceland); Committee on the Peaceful Uses of the Sea-Bed and the Ocean Floor Beyond the Limits Of National Jurisdiction, Sub-Committee II, "Summary Record of the Fortieth Meeting," 4 August 1972, UN Doc. A/AC.138/SC.II/SR.40, p. 43 at p. 44 (Statement of the Representative of Norway).

through the Convention would "contribute to the realization of a just and equitable international economic order which takes into account the interests and needs of mankind as a whole and, in particular, the special interests and needs of developing countries, whether coastal or land-locked."

516. As a counterpoint to the expanded jurisdiction of the exclusive economic zone, Article 121(3) serves to prevent such expansion from going too far. It serves to disable tiny features from unfairly and inequitably generating enormous entitlements to maritime space that would serve not to benefit the local population, but to award a windfall to the (potentially distant) State to have maintained a claim to such a feature. Given this context, the meaning attributed to the terms of Article 121(3) should serve to reinforce, rather than counter, the purposes that the exclusive economic zone and Article 121(3) were respectively intended to serve.

517. In the Tribunal's view, this is best accomplished by recognising the connection between the criteria of "human habitation" and the population of the coastal State for the benefit of whom the resources of the exclusive economic zone were to be preserved. This is not to suggest that the purpose of endowing an inhabited island with an exclusive economic zone would be narrowly intended to preserve the resources of the zone for the population of that island. Rather, it is that without human habitation (or an economic life), the link between a maritime feature and the people of the coastal State becomes increasingly slight.

518. The same connection was recognised during the Seabed Committee and can be seen in the remarks of the representative of Peru, who noted that:

> It was obvious that the 200-mile limit was the maximum limit and not the only one, since there were regions in which it could not be applied; nor should it be applied to more or less uninhabited islands, since its main justification lay not in the existence of a territory but in the presence of the population which inhabited it, whose needs should be satisfied through the use of the resources available in its environs.[544]

519. This point was reiterated during the Third UN Conference by Ambassador Koh of Singapore, who later assumed the Presidency of the Conference, when he observed that:

> The rationale for the proposal that coastal States should have the right to establish an economic zone was essentially based upon the interests of the people and the desire to marshal the resources of ocean space for their development. . . . However, it would be unjust, and the common heritage of mankind would be further diminished, if every island, irrespective of its characteristics, was automatically entitled to claim a uniform economic zone. Such an approach would give inequitable benefits to coastal States with small or uninhabited islands scattered over a wide expanse of the ocean. The economic zone of a

---

[544] Committee on the Peaceful Uses of the Seabed and the Ocean Floor beyond the Limits of National Jurisdiction, Sub-Committee II, "Summary Record of the Fifty-first Meeting," UN Doc. A/AC.138/SC.II/SR.51, p. 43 at p. 46 (9 March 1973) (Statement of the Representative of Peru).

barren rock would be larger than the land territory of many States and larger than the economic zones of many coastal States.[545]

A similar view was expressed at the close of the Conference by the representative of Colombia when he noted that "Rocks are entitled only to a territorial sea since they cannot sustain human habitation or economic life of their own. This is logical. It is a 'package' which results from the view that these maritime spaces have been granted to benefit the inhabitants, with an economic concept."[546]

520. In this context, the Tribunal considers that the human habitation with which the drafters of Article 121(3) were concerned was the habitation by a portion of the population for whose benefit the exclusive economic zone was being introduced. Taken together with notions of settlement and residence and the qualitative aspect inherent in the term habitation, it should be understood to refer to the habitation of a feature by a settled group or community for whom the feature is a home.

iii.   *The Travaux Préparatoires of Article 121(3)*

521. The Tribunal considers that further examination of the circumstances that led to the adoption of Article 121 is warranted for the light it sheds on the purpose of the provision itself.

(a)   *The History of Article 121(3)*

522. An early predecessor definition of "island" was introduced at the Imperial Conference of 1923 in order to harmonise marine policy across the British Empire. Resolution 4 of the Conference clarified that the territorial sea would extend three miles from the coastline of "the mainland and also that of islands. The word 'islands' covers all portions of territory permanently above water in normal circumstances and capable of use or habitation."[547] An explanatory memorandum accompanying the Resolution stated that the phrase "capable of use" had been adopted as a compromise, but was intended to mean "capable, without artificial addition, of being used through all seasons for some definite commercial or defence purpose," and that "capable of

---

[545] "Summary Records of Meetings of the Second Committee, 39th Meeting," UN Doc. A/CONF.62/C.2/SR.39 at p. 285, para. 72 (14 August 1974) (Statement of the Representative of Singapore), *Official Records of the Third United Nations Conference on the Law of the Sea, Volume II (Summary Records of Meetings of the First, Second and Third Committees, Second Session).*

[546] "189th Plenary Meeting," UN Doc. A/CONF.62/SR.189, p. 66 at p. 83, para. 251 (8 December 1982) (Statement of the Representative of Colombia), *Official Records of the Third United Nations Conference on the Law of the Sea, Volume XVI (Summary Records, Plenary, First and Second Committees, as well as Documents of the Conference, Eleventh Session).*

[547] Imperial Conference 1923, *Report of Inter-Departmental Committee on the Limits of Territorial Waters* (27 September 1923).

habitation" should mean "capable, without artificial addition, of permanent human habitation." The explanatory memorandum recognised that "these criteria will in many cases admit of argument, but nothing more definite could be arrived at" and no criteria could be selected without being "open to some form of criticism."[548]

523. The United Kingdom sought to introduce similar criteria for islands at the 1930 League of Nations Hague Codification Conference, when it proposed to limit the category of features entitled to a territorial sea to pieces of "territory surrounded by water and in normal circumstances permanently above high water. It does not include a piece of territory not capable of occupation and use."[549] Another group of States proposed instead that an island be any naturally formed part of the earth's surface above water at low tide, with no requirement of capability for use or occupation. The compromise suggested by the preparatory committee to the conference (although never adopted into any formal instrument) was to "allow[] an island (*i.e.*, an isolated island) to have its own territorial waters only if it is above water at high tide," but to "tak[e] island where are above low-water mark into account when determining the base line for the territorial waters of another island or the mainland, if such islands be within those waters."[550]

524. The International Law Commission adopted a similar definition in its 1956 Articles Concerning the Law of the Sea, which provided that "every island has its own territorial sea" and defined an island as "an area of land surrounded by water, which in normal circumstances is permanently above high water mark."[551] A British proposal to insert that an island be "capable of effective occupation and control" was rejected in the course of the ILC's discussions, due to concerns that any feature could be transformed into an island simply by installing a radio station or weather observation post.[552]

525. A modified version of the ILC's text was included in Article 10 of the 1958 Convention on the Territorial Sea and the Contiguous Zone, which recognised a territorial sea from any island,

[548]   Imperial Conference 1923, *Report of Inter-Departmental Committee on the Limits of Territorial Waters* (27 September 1923).

[549]   League of Nations Conference for the Codification of International Law, *Bases of Discussion for the Conference Drawn up by the Preparatory Committee, Vol. II: Territorial Waters*, League of Nations Doc. C.74.M.39.1929.V, p. 53 (15 May 1929).

[550]   League of Nations Conference for the Codification of International Law, *Bases of Discussion for the Conference Drawn up by the Preparatory Committee, Vol. II: Territorial Waters*, League of Nations Doc. C.74.M.39.1929.V, pp. 52-54 (15 May 1929).

[551]   International Law Commission, Articles concerning the Law of the Sea, art. 10, *Yearbook of the International Law Commission*, Vol. II, p. 256 at p. 257 (1956).

[552]   International Law Commission, "Summary Record of the 260th meeting," UN Doc. A/CN.4/SR.260, *Yearbook of the International Law Commission*, Vol. I, at p. 90 (1954).

defined as "a naturally formed area of land, surrounded by water, which is above water at high tide."[553] In describing islands as "naturally formed", the drafters clearly excluded the possibility of States obtaining a territorial sea through the creation of artificial islands.

526. Before the 1970s, the issue of very small high-tide features generating expansive continental shelves had not yet become urgent, given both the uncertainties surrounding the definition of the limit of the continental shelf in the 1958 Continental Shelf Convention and the limited technical capacity of States to exploit the deep seabed. From 1971, however, the definition of islands and their maritime entitlements took on a new relevance in the context of the emerging regime of expanded maritime entitlements. At the Seabed Committee meeting in 1971, prior to the Third UN Conference, Ambassador Arvid Pardo of Malta expressed the following concerns about the prospect of granting such entitlements to all islands without distinction:

> If a 200 mile limit of jurisdiction could be founded on the possession of uninhabited, remote or very small islands, the effectiveness of international administration of ocean space beyond a national jurisdiction would be gravely impaired.[554]

527. During the meetings of the Seabed Committee, some States preferred to retain the rule that all islands generate the same entitlements and warned of the "dangers inherent in drawing any distinction between islands according to their size, location, population."[555] However, many States submitted texts distinguishing between the entitlements of different types of islands on the basis of precisely these criteria.[556]

---

[553] 1958 Convention on the Territorial Sea and the Contiguous Zone, art. 10.

[554] Committee on the Peaceful Uses of the Seabed and the Ocean Floor beyond the Limits of National Jurisdiction, "Summary Record of the Fifty-Seventh Meeting," UN Doc. A/AC.138/SR.57, p. 163 at p. 167 (23 March 1971) (Statement of the Representative of Malta).

[555] Report of the Committee on the Peaceful Uses of the Seabed and the Ocean Floor beyond the Limits of National Jurisdiction, UN Doc. A/8721, at p. 46, para. 186 (1972), *Official Records of the UN General Assembly, 27th Session, Supplement No. 21*.

[556] For example, Malta proposed different entitlements for land greater or less than one square kilometre. Report of the Committee on the Peaceful Uses of the Seabed and the Ocean Floor beyond the Limits of National Jurisdiction, Vol. III, UN General Assembly, *Official Records*, 28th Session, Supplement No. 21, UN Doc. A/9021, pp. 87 at p. 89 (1973). The Organization of African Unity put forward the text of the Addis Ababa Declaration that would determine maritime spaces of islands by taking into account "all relevant factors and special circumstances," including size, population or absence thereof, contiguity to principal territory, geological configuration, or the special interests of island States and archipelagic States. Report of the Committee on the Peaceful Uses of the Seabed and the Ocean Floor beyond the Limits of National Jurisdiction, Vol. III, UN Doc. A/9021, pp. 35 at p. 37 (1973), *Official Records of the UN General Assembly, 28th Session, Supplement No. 21*.

528. The most extensive negotiations over the provision that became Article 121(3) took place
during the Second Session of the Third UN Conference in Caracas in 1974.[557] The
Representative of Romania expressed the following concerns:

> the question of islands had to be considered within the new parameters of the enlarged
> 12-mile territorial sea, the 200-mile economic zone, and the concept of the common
> heritage of mankind. The régime established for islands would be a contributing factor in
> determining the extent of the international area in which coastal and land-locked States had
> an equal interest. The tremendous diversity among islands with regard to size,
> geographical situation, and economic and social importance gave some idea of the
> complexity of the problem for which generalized solutions along the lines of those adopted
> at the 1958 Geneva Conference would no longer be adequate.[558]

529. It was during this session of the Conference that Ambassador Koh of Singapore linked the
regime of islands and the need for restrictions on the features that would generate an exclusive
economic zone with development and the common heritage of mankind (see paragraph 518
above).

530. Some States opposed the introduction of special distinctions because they believed it was a
"practical impossibility" to arrive at a workable formula.[559] The representative of the United
Kingdom pointed out various practical problems with distinguishing entitlements based on the
size, population, or remoteness or geographical proximity of a feature in relation to the coastal
or other States.[560] The representative of Mexico agreed it would be "difficult, if not
impossible," to draft specific regulations to cover the "immense diversity of island situations"
and therefore suggested that the "basic norm must reflect . . . that the marine space of an island

---

[557] For a general summary of the drafting historic of Article 121, see United Nations, Office for Ocean
Affairs and the Law of the Sea, *The Law of the Sea: Régime of Islands: Legislative History of Part VIII
(Article 121) of the United Nations Convention on the Law of the Sea* (1988).

[558] "Summary Records of Meetings of the Second Committee, 39th Meeting,"
UN Doc. A/CONF.62/C.2/SR.39 p. 279 at p. 281-282, paras. 29-36 (14 August 1974) (Statement of the
Representative of Romania), *Official Records of the Third United Nations Conference on the Law of the
Sea, Volume II (Summary Records of Meetings of the First, Second and Third Committees, Second
Session)*; *See also* Romania, "Draft Articles on Definition of and Regime Applicable to Islets and Islands
Similar to Islets," UN Doc. A/CONF.62/C.2/L.53 (21 August 1974).

[559] "Summary Records of Meetings of the Second Committee, 40th Meeting,"
UN Doc. A/CONF.62/C.2/SR.40, p. 286 at p. 286-287, paras. 6-9 (14 August 1974) (Statement of the
Representative of France), *Official Records of the Third United Nations Conference on the Law of the
Sea, Volume II (Summary Records of Meetings of the First, Second and Third Committees, Second
Session)*.

[560] "Summary Records of Meetings of the Second Committee, 40th Meeting,"
UN Doc. A/CONF.62/C.2/SR.40, p. 286 at p. 288, para. 33 (14 August 1974) (Statement of the
Representative of the United Kingdom), *Official Records of the Third United Nations Conference on the
Law of the Sea, Volume II (Summary Records of Meetings of the First, Second and Third Committees,
Second Session)*.

must be measured in accordance with the same provisions as were applicable to other land territory. However, exceptions based on principles of equity could be accepted."[561]

531. Eventually, at the Third Session of the Third UN Conference in Geneva in 1975, the matter was referred to an informal consultative group which, without leaving records, prepared the "Informal Single Negotiating Text" that presented the exception for "rocks which cannot sustain human habitation or economic life of their own," within a provision identical to what became Article 121(3) of the Convention.[562]

532. The Informal Single Negotiating Text reflected a "compromise".[563] The compromise text received support from some States,[564] but efforts persisted by others, including Japan, Greece, and the United Kingdom, to remove the rocks exception in paragraph (3).[565] Some delegates suggested retaining paragraph (3), but introduced further amendments, such as an explicit link

---

[561] "Summary Records of Meetings of the Second Committee, 40th Meeting," UN Doc. A/CONF.62/C.2/SR.40, at p. 289, paras. 46-47 (14 August 1974) (Statement of the Representative of Mexico), *Official Records of the Third United Nations Conference on the Law of the Sea, Volume II (Summary Records of Meetings of the First, Second and Third Committees, Second Session).*

[562] Informal Single Negotiating Text, Part II, UN Doc. A/CONF.62/WP.8/PartII at pp. 170-171 (7 May 1975), *Official Records of the Third United Nations Conference on the Law of the Sea, Volume IV (Summary Records, Plenary, General Committee, First, Second and Third Committees, as well as Documents of the Conference, Third Session).*

[563] "170th Plenary Meeting," UN Doc. A/CONF.62/SR.170, p. 100 at p. 102, para. 27 (16 April 1982) (Statement of the Representative of the USSR), *Official Records of the Third United Nations Conference on the Law of the Sea, Volume XVI (Summary Records, Plenary, First and Second Committees, as well as Documents of the Conference, Eleventh Session).*

[564] *See, e.g.,* "170th Plenary Meeting," UN Doc. A/CONF.62/SR.170, at p. 105, paras. 68-69 (16 April 1982) (Statement of the Representative of Mozambique), *Official Records of the Third United Nations Conference on the Law of the Sea, Volume XVI (Summary Records, Plenary, First and Second Committees, as well as Documents of the Conference, Eleventh Session);* "171st Plenary Meeting," UN Doc. A/CONF.62/SR.171 p. 106 at p. 106, para. 8 (16 April 1982) (Statement of the Representative of Denmark), *Official Records of the Third United Nations Conference on the Law of the Sea, Volume XVI (Summary Records, Plenary, First and Second Committees, as well as Documents of the Conference, Eleventh Session);* "171st Plenary Meeting," UN Doc. A/CONF.62/SR.171, p. 106 at p. 108, para. 31 (16 April 1982) (Statement of the Representative of Trinidad and Tobago), *Official Records of the Third United Nations Conference on the Law of the Sea, Volume XVI (Summary Records, Plenary, First and Second Committees, as well as Documents of the Conference, Eleventh Session);* "171st Plenary Meeting," UN Doc. A/CONF.62/SR.171, p. 106 at p. 109, para. 38 (16 April 1982) (Statement of the Representative of Tunisia), *Official Records of the Third United Nations Conference on the Law of the Sea, Volume XVI (Summary Records, Plenary, First and Second Committees, as well as Documents of the Conference, Eleventh Session).*

[565] "168th Plenary Meeting," UN Doc. A/CONF.62/SR.168, p. 87 at p. 91, para. 57 (15 April 1982) (Statement of the Representative of the United Kingdom), *Official Records of the Third United Nations Conference on the Law of the Sea, Volume XVI (Summary Records, Plenary, First and Second Committees, as well as Documents of the Conference, Eleventh Session);* United Kingdom of Great Britain and Northern Ireland, "Amendments," UN Doc. A/CONF.62/L.126 (13 April 1982).

to the delimitation provisions in Articles 15, 74, and 83[566] or a specification about "uninhabited islets."[567] Neither was accepted.

533. Even in the final sessions of the Third UN Conference, in 1982, proposals to delete paragraph (3) were introduced and rejected. In defence of the compromise reached, the Danish representative emphasised that without paragraph (3), "tiny and barren islands, looked upon in the past as mere obstacles to navigation, would miraculously become the golden keys to vast maritime zones. That would indeed be an unwarranted and unacceptable consequence of the new law of the sea."[568] The representative of Colombia remarked that Article 121 reflected "a unique and delicate balance and would help to preserve the common heritage in the oceans"[569] and, in the final session, recalled the link between the package compromise and the objective of securing to the people of the coastal State the benefits of the exclusive economic zone (see paragraph 518 above). [570]

(b)   Conclusions Drawn from the Travaux Préparatoires

534. The Tribunal accepts that the *travaux préparatoires* of Article 121 are an imperfect guide in interpreting the meaning of paragraph (3) of that Article. In particular, the key compromise that produced the ultimate formulation for that text was reached through informal consultations in 1975, for which no records were kept. Nevertheless, the Tribunal considers that a number of general conclusions can be drawn from the negotiating history.

---

[566] "140th Plenary Meeting," UN Doc. A/CONF.62/SR.140, p. 75 at p. 79, para. 55 (27 August 1980) (Statement of the Representative of Turkey), *Official Records of the Third United Nations Conference on the Law of the Sea, Volume XIV (Summary Records, Plenary, General Committee, First and Third Committees, as well as Documents of the Conference, Resumed Ninth Session)*.

[567] "169th Plenary Meeting," UN Doc. A/CONF.62/SR.169, p. 93 at p. 97, paras. 52-53 (15 April 1982) (Statement of the Representative of Romania), *Official Records of the Third United Nations Conference on the Law of the Sea, Volume XVI (Summary Records, Plenary, First and Second Committees, as well as Documents of the Conference, Eleventh Session)*; Romania, "Amendment to Article 121," UN Doc. A/CONF.62/L.118 (13 April 1982).

[568] "171st Plenary Meeting," UN Doc. A/CONF.62/SR.171, p. 106 at p. 106, para. 8 (16 April 1982) (Statement of the Representative of Denmark), *Official Records of the Third United Nations Conference on the Law of the Sea, Volume XVI (Summary Records, Plenary, First and Second Committees, as well as Documents of the Conference, Eleventh Session)*.

[569] "172nd Plenary Meeting," UN Doc. A/CONF.62/SR.172, p. 114 at p. 116, para. 29 (16 April 1982) (Statement of the Representative of Colombia), *Official Records of the Third United Nations Conference on the Law of the Sea, Volume XVI (Summary Records, Plenary, First and Second Committees, as well as Documents of the Conference, Eleventh Session)*.

[570] "189th Plenary meeting," UN Doc. A/CONF.62/SR.189, p. 66 at p. 83, para. 251 (8 December 1982) (Statement of the Representative of Colombia), *Official Records of the Third United Nations Conference on the Law of the Sea, Volume XVI (Summary Records, Plenary, First and Second Committees, as well as Documents of the Conference, Eleventh Session)*.

535. First, Article 121(3) is a provision of limitation. It imposes two conditions that can disqualify high-tide features from generating vast maritime spaces. These conditions were introduced with the object and purpose of preventing encroachment on the international seabed reserved for the common heritage of mankind and of avoiding the inequitable distribution of maritime spaces under national jurisdiction. This understanding of the object and purpose of Article 121(3) is consistent with the views of both the Philippines and China as summarised above at paragraphs 409 to 422 and 451 to 458.

536. Second, the definitions in Article 121(3) were not discussed in isolation, but were frequently discussed in the context of other aspects of the Convention. These included: (a) the introduction of an exclusive economic zone,[571] (b) the purpose of the exclusive economic zone in securing the benefit of maritime resources for the population of the coastal State,[572] (c) the question of islands under foreign domination or colonial dependence,[573] (d) the introduction of the international seabed area (the common heritage of mankind),[574] (e) the protection of the interests

---

[571] The "essential link" between Article 121(3) of the Convention and the introduction of the exclusive economic zone was recognized by the International Court of Justice in *Nicaragua v. Colombia*: *Territorial and Maritime Dispute (Nicaragua v. Colombia), Judgment, ICJ Reports 2012*, p. 624 at p. 674, para. 139.

[572] "Summary Records of Meetings of the Second Committee, 39th Meeting," UN Doc. A/CONF.62/C.2/SR.39, p. 279 at p. 285, para. 72 (14 August 1974) (Statement of the Representative of Singapore), *Official Records of the Third United Nations Conference on the Law of the Sea, Volume II (Summary Records of Meetings of the First, Second and Third Committees, Second Session)*; "189th Plenary Meeting," UN Doc. A/CONF.62/SR.189, p. 66 at p. 83, para. 251 (8 December 1982) (Statement of the Representative of Colombia), *Official Records of the Third United Nations Conference on the Law of the Sea, Volume XVI (Summary Records, Plenary, First and Second Committees, as well as Documents of the Conference, Eleventh Session)*.

[573] *See* Fiji, New Zealand, Tonga and Western Samoa, "Draft Articles on Islands and on Territories under Foreign Domination or Control," UN Doc. A/CONF.62/C.2/L.30 (30 July 1974); Argentina, Bolivia, Brazil, Colombia, Costa Rica, Cuba, Dominican Republic, Ecuador, El Salvador, Guatemala, Honduras, Libyan Arab Republic, Mexico, Morocco, Nicaragua, Panama, Paraguay, Peru, Uruguay, "Draft Article on Islands and Other Territories under Colonial Domination or Foreign Occupation," UN Doc. A/CONF.62/C.2/L.58 (13 August 1974); "Summary records of meetings of the Second Committee, 38th Meeting," UN Doc. A/CONF.62/C.2/SR.38, p. 273 at p. 278, para. 69 (13 August 1974) (Statement of the Representative of New Zeeland), *Official Records of the Third United Nations Conference on the Law of the Sea, Volume II (Summary Records of Meetings of the First, Second and Third Committees, Second Session)*; "Summary Records of Meetings of the Second Committee, 24th Meeting," UN Doc. A/CONF.62/C.2/SR.24, p. 187 at p. 190, para. 46 (1 August 1974) (Statement of the Representative of Tonga), *Official Records of the Third United Nations Conference on the Law of the Sea, Volume II (Summary Records of Meetings of the First, Second and Third Committees, Second Session)*; "Summary Records of Meetings of the Second Committee, 39th Meeting," UN Doc. A/CONF.62/C.2/SR.39, p. 279 at pp. 284-285, paras. 64-71 (14 August 1974) (Statement of the Representative of Argentina), *Official Records of the Third United Nations Conference on the Law of the Sea, Volume II (Summary Records of Meetings of the First, Second and Third Committees, Second Session)*.

[574] *See* "Summary Records of Meetings of the Second Committee, 39th Meeting," UN Doc. A/CONF.62/C.2/SR.39, p. 279 at p. 284, paras. 62-63 (14 August 1974) (Statement of the Representative of Turkey), *Official Records of the Third United Nations Conference on the Law of the*

of archipelagic States,[575] (f) the role of islands in maritime delimitation,[576] and (g) concerns about the potential for artificial installations to generate maritime zones.[577]

537. Third, the drafters accepted that there are diverse high-tide features: vast and tiny; barren and lush; rocky and sandy; isolated and proximate; densely and sparsely populated, or not populated at all. Many States considered that criteria such as surface area, population size, and proximity to other land might be useful in deciding whether a high-tide feature should be a fully entitled island. But the negotiating history clearly demonstrates the difficulty in setting, in the abstract, bright-line rules for all cases. Proposals to introduce specific criteria were considered, but consistently rejected.[578] Against such attempts at precision, the drafters clearly favoured the language of the compromise reflected in Article 121(3).

Sea, Volume II (Summary Records of Meetings of the First, Second and Third Committees, Second Session).

[575] *See* "Summary Records of Meetings of the Second Committee," 39th Meeting," UN Doc. A/CONF.62/C.2/SR.39, p. 279 at pp. 285-286, paras. 79-80 (14 August 1974) (Statement of the Representative of Greece), *Official Records of the Third United Nations Conference on the Law of the Sea, Volume II (Summary Records of Meetings of the First, Second and Third Committees, Second Session)*; "Summary Records of Meetings of the Second Committee," 37th Meeting, UN Doc. A/CONF.62/C.2/SR.37, p. 266 at p. 272, paras. 73-75 (12 August 1974) (Statement of the Representative of Tunisia), *Official Records of the Third United Nations Conference on the Law of the Sea, Volume II (Summary Records of Meetings of the First, Second and Third Committees, Second Session).*

[576] *See* "Summary Records of Meetings of the Second Committee," 39th Meeting," UN Doc. A/CONF.62/C.2/SR.39, p. 279 at p. 285, para. 76 (14 August 1974) (Statement of the Representative of Greece), *Official Records of the Third United Nations Conference on the Law of the Sea, Volume II (Summary Records of Meetings of the First, Second and Third Committees, Second Session)*; Summary records of meetings of the Second Committee, 40th meeting, UN Doc. A/CONF.62/C.2/SR.40, p. 286 at p. 288, paras. 26-27 (14 August 1974) (Statement of the Representative of Tunisia), *Official Records of the Third United Nations Conference on the Law of the Sea, Volume II (Summary Records of Meetings of the First, Second and Third Committees, Second Session)*; "140th Plenary Meeting," UN Doc. A/CONF.62/SR.140, p. 75 at p. 79, para. 55 (27 August 1980) (Statement of the Representative of Turkey), *Official Records of the Third United Nations Conference on the Law of the Sea, Volume XIV (Summary Records, Plenary, General Committee, First and Third Committees, as well as Documents of the Conference, Resumed Ninth Session)*; "Summary Records of Meetings of the Second Committee, 40th Meeting," UN Doc. A/CONF.62/C.2/SR.40, at pp. 286-287, para. 9 (14 August 1974) (Statement of the Representative of France), *Official Records of the Third United Nations Conference on the Law of the Sea, Volume II (Summary Records of Meetings of the First, Second and Third Committees, Second Session)*; *see also* Algeria, Dahomey, Guinea, Ivory Coast, Liberia, Madagascar, Mali, Mauritania, Morocco, Sierra Leone, Sudan, Tunisia, Upper Volta and Zambia, "Draft Articles on the Regime of Islands, Draft Art. 3," UN Doc. A/CONF.62/C.2/L.62/Rev.1 (27 August 1974).

[577] *See* "Summary Records of Meetings of the Second Committee," 39th Meeting," UN Doc. A/CONF.62/C.2/SR.39, p. 279 at p. 284, para. 63 (14 August 1974) (Statement of the Representative of Turkey), *Official Records of the Third United Nations Conference on the Law of the Sea, Volume II (Summary Records of Meetings of the First, Second and Third Committees, Second Session).*

[578] Attempts to include "geological configuration" or "geomorphological structure" as relevant factors in Article 121 all failed, confirming the Tribunal's interpretation of that portion of the text. *See, e.g.,* Romania, "Draft Articles on Definition of and Régime Applicable to Islets and Islands Similar to Islets,"

538. In particular, repeated attempts during the Conference to define or categorise islands or rocks by reference to size were all rejected. These included proposals to include "size" on a list of "relevant factors";[579] proposals to categorise islands and islets depending on whether they were "vast" or "smaller";[580] and proposals that made distinctions based on whether the surface area of a feature measured more or less than a particular figure, such as one square kilometre[581] or ten square kilometres.[582] In this respect, the representative of United Kingdom recalled that "there were large islands which were largely or completely uninhabited and small ones with dense populations which depend heavily upon the sea."[583] Representatives of small island States, such as Micronesia, Fiji, Tonga, and Western Samoa, also argued that it was inequitable to deprive features of their maritime entitlements on the basis of size.[584] The Tribunal considers that the

---

UN Doc. A/CONF.62/C.2/L.53 (12 August 1974); Algeria, Dahomey, Guinea, Ivory Coast, Liberia, Madagascar, Mali, Mauritania, Morocco, Sierra Leone, Sudan, Tunisia, Upper Volta and Zambia, "Draft Articles on the Regime of Islands," UN Doc. A/CONF.62/C.2/L.62/Rev. 1 (27 August 1974); "103rd Plenary Meeting," UN Doc. A/CONF.62/SR.103 p. 61 at p. 64, para. 39 (18 May 1978) (Statement of the Representative of Madagascar), *Official Records of the Third United Nations Conference on the Law of the Sea, Volume IX (Summary Records, Plenary, General Committee, First, Second and Third Committees, as well as Documents of the Conference, Seventh and Resumed Seventh Session).*

[579] Algeria, Cameroon, Ghana, Ivory Coast, Kenya, Liberia, Madagascar, Mauritius, Senegal, Sierra Leone, Somalia, Sudan, Tunisia and United Republic of Tanzania, "Draft Articles on Exclusive Economic Zone, Report of the Committee on the Peaceful Uses of the Seabed and the Ocean Floor beyond the Limits of National Jurisdiction," Vol. III, UN Doc. A/9021, pp. 87-89 at p. 89 (1973), *Official Records of the UN General Assembly, 28th Session, Supplement No. 21*; Romania, "Draft Articles on Delimitation of Marine and Ocean Space between Adjacent and Opposite Neighbouring States and Various Aspects Involved," UN Doc. A/CONF.62/C.2/L.18 (23 July 1974).

[580] Algeria, Dahomey, Guinea, Ivory Coast, Liberia, Madagascar, Mali, Mauritania, Morocco, Sierra Leone, Sudan, Tunisia, Upper Volta and Zambia, "Draft Articles on the Regime of Islands," UN Doc. A/CONF.62/C.2/L.62/Rev. 1 (27 August 1974).

[581] Report of the Committee on the Peaceful Uses of the Seabed and the Ocean Floor beyond the Limits of National Jurisdiction, Vol. III, UN Doc. A/9021, pp. 35-70 at p. 37 (1973), *Official Records of the UN General Assembly, 28th Session, Supplement No. 21*; Romania, "Draft Articles on Definition of and Regime Applicable to Islets and Islands Similar to Islets," UN Doc. A/CONF.62/C.2/L.53 (12 August 1974).

[582] Report of the Committee on the Peaceful Uses of the Seabed and the Ocean Floor beyond the Limits of National Jurisdiction, Vol. III, UN Doc. A/9021, pp. 35-70 at p. 41 (1973), *Official Records of the UN General Assembly, 28th Session, Supplement No. 21.*

[583] "Summary Records of Meetings of the Second Committee, 40th Meeting," UN Doc. A/CONF.62/C.2/SR.40, p. 286 at p. 288, para. 37 (14 August 1974) (Statement of the Representative of the United Kingdom), *Official Records of the Third United Nations Conference on the Law of the Sea, Volume II (Summary Records of Meetings of the First, Second and Third Committees, Second Session).*

[584] *See* "Statement by the Chairman of the Joint Committee of the Congress of Micronesia submitted on behalf of the Congress by the United States of America," UN Doc. A/CONF.62/L.6 (27 August 1974); "Summary Records of Meetings of the Second Committee, 24th Meeting," UN Doc. A/CONF.62/C.2/SR.24, p. 187 at p. 190, paras. 40-47 (1 August 1974) (Statement of the Representative of Tonga), *Official Records of the Third United Nations Conference on the Law of the Sea, Volume II (Summary Records of Meetings of the First, Second and Third Committees, Second Session)*; "Summary Records of Meetings of the Second Committee, 39th Meeting," UN Doc. A/CONF.62/C.2/SR.39, p. 279 at p. 281, paras. 22-28 (14 August 1974) (Statement of the

travaux make clear that—although size may correlate to the availability of water, food, living space, and resources for an economic life—size cannot be dispositive of a feature's status as a fully entitled island or rock and is not, on its own, a relevant factor. As noted by the International Court of Justice in *Territorial and Maritime Dispute (Nicaragua v. Colombia)*, "international law does not prescribe any minimum size which a feature must possess in order to be considered an island."[585]

iv. Conclusions on the Interpretation of Article 121(3)

539. Drawing on the foregoing consideration of the text, context, object and purpose, and drafting history of Article 121(3), the Tribunal reaches the following conclusions with respect to the interpretation of that provision.

540. First, for the reasons set out above, the use of the word "rock" does not limit the provision to features composed of solid rock. The geological and geomorphological characteristics of a high-tide feature are not relevant to its classification pursuant to Article 121(3).

541. Second, the status of a feature is to be determined on the basis of its natural capacity, without external additions or modifications intended to increase its capacity to sustain human habitation or an economic life of its own.

542. Third, with respect to "human habitation", the critical factor is the non-transient character of the inhabitation, such that the inhabitants can fairly be said to constitute the natural population of the feature, for whose benefit the resources of the exclusive economic zone were seen to merit protection. The term "human habitation" should be understood to involve the inhabitation of the feature by a stable community of people for whom the feature constitutes a home and on which they can remain. Such a community need not necessarily be large, and in remote atolls a few individuals or family groups could well suffice. Periodic or habitual residence on a feature by a nomadic people could also constitute habitation, and the records of the Third UN

Representative of Western Samoa), *Official Records of the Third United Nations Conference on the Law of the Sea, Volume II (Summary Records of Meetings of the First, Second and Third Committees, Second Session)*; "Summary Records of Meetings of the Second Committee, 39th Meeting," UN Doc. A/CONF.62/C.2/SR.39, p. 279 at p. 283, paras. 48-51 (14 August 1974) (Statement of the Representative of Fiji), *Official Records of the Third United Nations Conference on the Law of the Sea, Volume II (Summary Records of Meetings of the First, Second and Third Committees, Second Session)*; see also "Summary Records of Meetings of the Second Committee, 40th Meeting," UN Doc. A/CONF.62/C.2/SR.40, p. 286 at p. 287, paras. 13-15 (14 August 1974) (Statement of the Representative of Jamaica), *Official Records of the Third United Nations Conference on the Law of the Sea, Volume II (Summary Records of Meetings of the First, Second and Third Committees, Second Session)*.

[585]   *Territorial and Maritime Dispute (Nicaragua v. Colombia), Judgment, ICJ Reports 2012*, p. 624 at p. 645, para. 37.

Conference record a great deal of sensitivity to the livelihoods of the populations of small island nations. An indigenous population would obviously suffice, but also non-indigenous inhabitation could meet this criterion if the intent of the population was truly to reside in and make their lives on the islands in question.

543. Fourth, the term "economic life of their own" is linked to the requirement of human habitation, and the two will in most instances go hand in hand. Article 121(3) does not refer to a feature having economic value, but to sustaining "economic life". The Tribunal considers that the "economic life" in question will ordinarily be the life and livelihoods of the human population inhabiting and making its home on a maritime feature or group of features. Additionally, Article 121(3) makes clear that the economic life in question must pertain to the feature as "of its own". Economic life, therefore, must be oriented around the feature itself and not focused solely on the waters or seabed of the surrounding territorial sea. Economic activity that is entirely dependent on external resources or devoted to using a feature as an object for extractive activities without the involvement of a local population would also fall inherently short with respect to this necessary link to the feature itself. Extractive economic activity to harvest the natural resources of a feature for the benefit of a population elsewhere certainly constitutes the exploitation of resources for economic gain, but it cannot reasonably be considered to constitute the economic life of an island as its own.

544. Fifth, the text of Article 121(3) is disjunctive, such that the ability to sustain either human habitation or an economic life of its own would suffice to entitle a high-tide feature to an exclusive economic zone and continental shelf. However, as a practical matter, the Tribunal considers that a maritime feature will ordinarily only possess an economic life of its own if it is also inhabited by a stable human community. One exception to that view should be noted for the case of populations sustaining themselves through a network of related maritime features. The Tribunal does not believe that maritime features can or should be considered in an atomised fashion. A population that is able to inhabit an area only by making use of multiple maritime features does not fail to inhabit the feature on the grounds that its habitation is not sustained by a single feature individually. Likewise, a population whose livelihood and economic life extends across a constellation of maritime features is not disabled from recognising that such features possess an economic life of their own merely because not all of the features are directly inhabited.

545. Sixth, Article 121(3) is concerned with the *capacity* of a maritime feature to sustain human habitation or an economic life of its own, not with whether the feature is presently, or has been, inhabited or home to economic life. The capacity of a feature is necessarily an objective

criterion. It has no relation to the question of sovereignty over the feature. For this reason, the determination of the objective capacity of a feature is not dependent on any prior decision on sovereignty, and the Tribunal is not prevented from assessing the status of features by the fact that it has not and will not decide the matter of sovereignty over them.

546. Seventh, the capacity of a feature to sustain human habitation or an economic life of its own must be assessed on a case-by-case basis. The drafters of the Convention considered proposals with any number of specific tests and rejected them in favour of the general formula set out in Article 121(3). The Tribunal considers that the principal factors that contribute to the natural capacity of a feature can be identified. These would include the presence of water, food, and shelter in sufficient quantities to enable a group of persons to live on the feature for an indeterminate period of time. Such factors would also include considerations that would bear on the conditions for inhabiting and developing an economic life on a feature, including the prevailing climate, the proximity of the feature to other inhabited areas and populations, and the potential for livelihoods on and around the feature. The relative contribution and importance of these factors to the capacity to sustain human habitation and economic life, however, will vary from one feature to another. While minute, barren features may be obviously uninhabitable (and large, heavily populated features obviously capable of sustaining habitation), the Tribunal does not consider that an abstract test of the objective requirements to sustain human habitation or economic life can or should be formulated. This is particularly the case in light of the Tribunal's conclusion that human habitation entails more than the mere survival of humans on a feature and that economic life entails more than the presence of resources. The absence of an abstract test, however, has particular consequences (that will be discussed below) for the Tribunal's approach to evidence of conditions on, and the capacity of, the features in question.

547. Eighth, the Tribunal considers that the capacity of a feature should be assessed with due regard to the potential for a group of small island features to collectively sustain human habitation and economic life. On the one hand, the requirement in Article 121(3) that the feature itself sustain human habitation or economic life clearly excludes a dependence on external supply. A feature that is only capable of sustaining habitation through the continued delivery of supplies from outside does not meet the requirements of Article 121(3). Nor does economic activity that remains entirely dependent on external resources or that is devoted to using a feature as an object for extractive activities, without the involvement of a local population, constitute a feature's "own" economic life. At the same time, the Tribunal is conscious that remote island populations often make use of a number of islands, sometimes spread over significant distances, for sustenance and livelihoods. An interpretation of Article 121(3) that sought to evaluate each feature individually would be in keeping neither with the realities of life on remote islands nor

with the sensitivity to the lifestyles of small island peoples that was apparent at the Third UN Conference. Accordingly, provided that such islands collectively form part of a network that sustains human habitation in keeping with the traditional lifestyle of the peoples in question, the Tribunal would not equate the role of multiple islands in this manner with external supply. Nor would the local use of nearby resources as part of the livelihood of the community equate to the arrival of distant economic interests aimed at extracting natural resources.

548. Ninth, in light of the Tribunal's conclusions on the interpretation of Article 121(3), evidence of the objective, physical conditions on a particular feature can only take the Tribunal so far in its task. In the Tribunal's view, evidence of physical conditions will ordinarily suffice only to classify features that clearly fall within one category or the other. If a feature is entirely barren of vegetation and lacks drinkable water and the foodstuffs necessary even for basic survival, it will be apparent that it also lacks the capacity to sustain human habitation. The opposite conclusion could likewise be reached where the physical characteristics of a large feature make it definitively habitable. The Tribunal considers, however, that evidence of physical conditions is insufficient for features that fall close to the line. It will be difficult, if not impossible, to determine from the physical characteristics of a feature alone where the capacity merely to keep people alive ends and the capacity to sustain settled habitation by a human community begins. This will particularly be the case as the relevant threshold may differ from one feature to another.

549. In such circumstances, the Tribunal considers that the most reliable evidence of the capacity of a feature will usually be the historical use to which it has been put. Humans have shown no shortage of ingenuity in establishing communities in the far reaches of the world, often in extremely difficult conditions. If the historical record of a feature indicates that nothing resembling a stable community has ever developed there, the most reasonable conclusion would be that the natural conditions are simply too difficult for such a community to form and that the feature is not capable of sustaining such habitation. In such circumstances, the Tribunal should consider whether there is evidence that human habitation has been prevented or ended by forces that are separate from the intrinsic capacity of the feature. War, pollution, and environmental harm could all lead to the depopulation, for a prolonged period, of a feature that, in its natural state, was capable of sustaining human habitation. In the absence of such intervening forces, however, the Tribunal can reasonably conclude that a feature that has never historically sustained a human community lacks the capacity to sustain human habitation.

550. Conversely, if a feature is presently inhabited or has historically been inhabited, the Tribunal should consider whether there is evidence to indicate that habitation was only possible through

outside support. Trade and links with the outside world do not disqualify a feature to the extent that they go to improving the quality of life of its inhabitants. Where outside support is so significant that it constitutes a necessary condition for the inhabitation of a feature, however, it is no longer the feature itself that sustains human habitation. In this respect, the Tribunal notes that a purely official or military population, serviced from the outside, does not constitute evidence that a feature is capable of sustaining human habitation. Bearing in mind that the purpose of Article 121(3) is to place limits on excessive and unfair claims by States, that purpose would be undermined if a population were installed on a feature that, as such, would not be capable of sustaining human habitation, precisely to stake a claim to the territory and the maritime zones generated by it. The Tribunal notes that, as a result, evidence of human habitation that predates the creation of exclusive economic zones may be more significant than contemporary evidence, if the latter is clouded by an apparent attempt to assert a maritime claim.

551. The same mode of analysis would apply equally to the past or current existence of economic life. The Tribunal would first consider evidence of the use to which the feature has historically been put before considering whether there is evidence to suggest that that historical record does not fully reflect the economic life the feature could have sustained in its natural condition.

v.   The Relevance of State Practice in the Implementation of Article 121(3)

552. Finally, the Tribunal recalls that Article 31(3) of the Vienna Convention provides that "any subsequent practice in the application of the treaty which establishes the agreement of the parties regarding its interpretation" shall be taken into account together with the context. This means that the Parties must have acquiesced in such practice so that one can speak of an agreement reached concerning the interpretation of the provision in question. Scrutinising the jurisprudence of the International Court of Justice on this issue, in particular the *Advisory Opinion Concerning the Legality of the Use by a State of Nuclear Weapons in Armed Conflict*[586] and the judgment in *Kasikili/Sedudu Island,*[587] indicates that the threshold the Court establishes for accepting an agreement on the interpretation by State practice is quite high. The threshold is similarly high in the jurisprudence of the World Trade Organisation, which requires "a

---

[586]   *Advisory Opinion Concerning the Legality of the Use by a State of Nuclear Weapons in Armed Conflict, ICJ Reports 1996*, p. 66 at p. 75, 81-82, paras. 19, 27.

[587]   *Kasikili/Sedudu Island (Botswana/Namibia), Judgment, ICJ Reports 1999*, p. 1045 at p. 1075-1087, paras. 48-63. The judgment includes a detailed list of the Court's prior jurisprudence on subsequent practice in paragraph 50.

'concordant, common and consistent' sequence of acts or pronouncements" to establish a pattern implying agreement of the parties regarding a treaty's interpretation.[588]

553. On the basis of the foregoing, the Tribunal comes to the conclusion that as far as the case before it is concerned, there is no evidence for an agreement based upon State practice on the interpretation of Article 121(3) which differs from the interpretation of the Tribunal as outlined in the previous Sections.

      (b)   **Application of Article 121(3) to Scarborough Shoal, Johnson Reef, Cuarteron Reef, Fiery Cross Reef, Gaven Reef (North), and McKennan Reef**

      i.   *Scarborough Shoal*

554. In the Tribunal's view, Scarborough Shoal is a "rock" for purposes of Article 121(3).

555. As discussed at paragraphs 333 to 334 above, the Tribunal finds that Scarborough Shoal includes five to seven rocks that are exposed at high tide and is accordingly a high-tide feature. That those protrusions are composed of coral is immaterial to their classification pursuant to Article 121(3).

556. On any account, the protrusions above high tide at Scarborough Shoal are minuscule. This is confirmed by photographs in the record.[589] They obviously could not sustain human habitation in their naturally formed state; they have no fresh water, vegetation, or living space and are remote from any feature possessing such features. Scarborough Shoal has traditionally been used as a fishing ground by fishermen from different States, but the Tribunal recalls that economic activity in the surrounding waters must have some tangible link to the high-tide feature itself before it could begin to constitute the economic life of the feature (see paragraph 503 above). There is no evidence that the fishermen working on the reef make use of, or have any connection to, the high-tide rocks at Scarborough Shoal. Nor is there any evidence of economic activity beyond fishing. There is, accordingly, no evidence that Scarborough Shoal could independently sustain an economic life of its own.

---

[588]   *Japan - Taxes on Alcoholic Beverages*, Report of the Appellate Body, AB-1996-2, WT/DS8/AB/R, WT/DS10/AB/R, WT/DS11/AB/R, pp. 12-13 (4 October 1996); *Chile - Price Band System and Safeguard Measures relating to Certain Agricultural Products*, Report of the Appellate Body, AB-2002-2, WT/DS207/AB/R, paras. 213-214 (23 September 2002); *United States - Measures Affecting the Cross-Border Supply of Gambling and Betting Services*, Report of the Appellate Body, AB-2005-1, WT/DS285/AB/R, paras. 191-195 (7 April 2005); *European Communities - Customs Classification on Frozen Boneless Chicken Cuts*, Report of the Appellate Body, AB-2005-5, WT/DS269/AB/R, WT/DS286/AB/R, paras. 255-276, 304 (12 September 2005).

[589]   Memorial, Figure 5.1; Supplemental Written Submission, Vol. II, p. 158.

ii.   *Johnson Reef*

557.   In the Tribunal's view, Johnson Reef is also a "rock" for purposes of Article 121(3).

558.   As discussed at paragraphs 344 to 351 above, the Tribunal finds that Johnson Reef, in its natural condition, had at least one rock that reaches as high as 1.2 metres above Mean Sea Level and is accordingly a high-tide feature. Like the rocks at Scarborough Shoal, the high-tide portion of Johnson Reef lacks drinking water, vegetation, and living space. It is a minuscule, barren feature obviously incapable, in its natural condition, of sustaining human habitation or an economic life of its own.

559.   While China has constructed an installation and maintains an official presence on Johnson Reef, this is only possible through construction on the portion of the reef platform that submerges at high tide.[590] China's presence is necessarily dependent on outside supplies, and there is no evidence of any human activity on Johnson Reef prior to the beginning of China's presence in 1988. As discussed above (see paragraphs 508 to 511), the status of a feature for the purpose of Article 121(3) is to be assessed on the basis of its natural condition, prior to human modification. China's construction of an installation on Johnson Reef cannot elevate its status from rock to fully entitled island.

iii.   *Cuarteron Reef*

560.   In the Tribunal's view, Cuarteron Reef is also a "rock" for purposes of Article 121(3).

561.   As discussed at paragraphs 335 to 339 above, the Tribunal finds that Cuarteron Reef, in its natural condition, was encumbered by rocks that remain exposed one to two metres above high tide and is accordingly a high-tide feature. The high-tide portions of Cuarteron Reef are minuscule and barren, and obviously incapable, in their natural condition, of sustaining human habitation or an economic life of their own.

562.   While China has constructed an installation and engaged in significant reclamation work at Cuarteron Reef, this is only possible through dredging and the elevation of the portion of the reef platform that submerges at high tide.[591] China's presence is necessarily dependent on

---

[590]   Photographs of the evolution of the original Chinese installation on Johnson Reef are reproduced in Armed Forces of the Philippines, *Matrix of Events: Johnson (Mabini) Reef* (2013) (Annex 90). Photographs and satellite imagery of China's more recent construction and reclamation activities on Johnson Reef are reproduced in Compilation of Images of Johnson Reef (various sources) (compiled 13 November 2015) (Annex 790).

[591]   Photographs of the evolution of the original Chinese installation on Cuarteron Reef are reproduced in Armed Forces of the Philippines, *Matrix of Events: Cuarteron (Calderon) Reef* (2013) (Annex 87).

outside supplies, and there is no evidence of any human activity on Cuarteron Reef prior to the beginning of China's presence in 1988. As with the other high-tide features that have been the subject of construction and reclamation work, the status of a feature for the purpose of Article 121(3) is to be assessed on the basis of its natural condition, prior to human modification. China's construction on Cuarteron Reef, however extensive, cannot elevate its status from rock to fully entitled island.

iv.   Fiery Cross Reef

563.   In the Tribunal's view, Fiery Cross Reef is also a "rock" for purposes of Article 121(3).

564.   As discussed at paragraphs 340 to 343 above, the Tribunal finds that Fiery Cross Reef, in its natural condition, had one prominent rock, which remains exposed approximately one metre above high tide, and is accordingly a high-tide feature. According to the Chinese sailing directions, the surface area of this rock exposed at high tide amounts to only two square metres. The high-tide portion of Fiery Cross Reef is minuscule and barren, and obviously incapable, in its natural condition, of sustaining human habitation or an economic life of its own.

565.   While China has constructed an installation and engaged in significant land reclamation work at Fiery Cross Reef, this is only possible through dredging and the elevation of the portion of the reef platform that submerges at high tide.[592] China's presence is necessarily dependent on outside supplies, and there is no evidence of any human activity on Fiery Cross Reef prior to the beginning of China's presence in 1988. As with the other high-tide features that have been the subject of construction and reclamation work, the status of a feature for the purpose of Article 121(3) is to be assessed on the basis of its natural condition, prior to human modification. China's construction on Fiery Cross Reef, however extensive, cannot elevate its status from rock to fully entitled island.

v.   Gaven Reef (North)

566.   In the Tribunal's view, Gaven Reef (North) is also a "rock" for purposes of Article 121(3).

Photographs and satellite imagery of China's more recent construction and reclamation activities on Cuarteron Reef are reproduced in Compilation of Images of Cuarteron Reef (various sources) (compiled 13 November 2015) (Annex 787).

[592]   Photographs of the evolution of the original Chinese installation on Fiery Cross Reef are reproduced in Armed Forces of the Philippines, *Matrix of Events: Fiery Cross (Kagitingan) Reef* (2013) (Annex 88). Photographs and satellite imagery of China's more recent construction and reclamation activities on Fiery Cross Reef are reproduced in Compilation of Images of Fiery Cross Reef (various sources) (compiled 13 November 2015) (Annex 788).

567. As discussed at paragraphs 359 to 366 above, the Tribunal finds that Gaven Reef (North), in its natural condition, had a small sand cay in its north-east corner that remains exposed at high tide and is accordingly a high-tide feature. It is a minuscule, barren feature obviously incapable, in its natural condition, of sustaining human habitation or an economic life of its own.

568. While China has constructed an installation and engaged in significant reclamation work at Gaven Reef (North), this is only possible through dredging and the elevation of the portion of the reef platform that submerges at high tide.[593] China's presence is necessarily dependent on outside supplies, and there is no evidence of any human activity on Gaven Reef (North) prior to the beginning of China's presence in 1988. As with the other high-tide features that have been the subject of construction and reclamation work, the status of a feature for the purpose of Article 121(3) is to be assessed on the basis of its natural condition, prior to human modification. China's construction on Gaven Reef (North), however extensive, cannot elevate its status from rock to fully entitled island.

vi. McKennan Reef

569. In the Tribunal's view, McKennan Reef is also a "rock" for purposes of Article 121(3).

570. As discussed at paragraphs 352 to 354 above, the Tribunal finds that McKennan Reef includes a feature that remains exposed at high tide and is accordingly a high-tide feature. There is no indication that this feature is of any significant size, and the Tribunal concludes that the height indicated on the recent Chinese chart most likely refers to a coral boulder pushed above high water by storm activity. Such a feature would be obviously incapable, in its natural conditions, of sustaining human habitation or an economic life of its own. There is no evidence of any human activity on McKennan Reef, nor has any State installed a human presence there.

(c) Application of Article 121 to the Spratly Islands as a Whole

571. Before turning to the status of the more significant high-tide features in the Spratly Islands, the Tribunal takes note of China's statement that "China has, based on the Nansha Islands as a whole, territorial sea, exclusive economic zone and continental shelf."[594] The Tribunal also

---

[593] Photographs of the evolution of the original Chinese installation on Gaven Reef (North) are reproduced in Armed Forces of the Philippines, *Matrix of Events: Gaven (Burgos)* (2013) (Annex 89). Photographs and satellite imagery of China's more recent construction and reclamation activities on Gaven Reef (North) are reproduced in Compilation of Images of Gaven Reef (various sources) (compiled 13 November 2015) (Annex 789).

[594] Letter from the Ambassador of the People's Republic of China to the Netherlands to the individual members of the Tribunal (3 June 2016), *enclosing* Ministry of Foreign Affairs, People's Republic of

recalls that in its public Position Paper of 7 December 2014, China objected that "in respect of the Nansha Islands, the Philippines selects only a few features and requests the Arbitral Tribunal to decide on their maritime entitlements. This is in essence an attempt at denying China's sovereignty over the Nansha Islands as a whole."[595]

572. In the Tribunal's view, these statements can be understood in two different ways. To the extent that China considers that the criteria of human habitation and economic life must be assessed while bearing in mind that a population may sustain itself through the use of a network of closely related maritime features, the Tribunal agrees. As already noted (see paragraph 547 above), the Tribunal is conscious that small island populations will often make use of a group of reefs or atolls to support their livelihood and, where this is the case, does not consider that Article 121(3) can or should be applied in a strictly atomised fashion. Accordingly, the Tribunal has not limited its consideration to the features specifically identified by the Philippines in its Submissions, but requested the Philippines to provide detailed information on all of the significant high-tide features in the Spratly Islands.[596] The Tribunal has taken a similarly broad approach in its own efforts to satisfy itself that the Philippines' claims are well founded in fact.

573. On the other hand, China's statements could also be understood as an assertion that the Spratly Islands should be enclosed within a system of archipelagic or straight baselines, surrounding the high-tide features of the group, and accorded an entitlement to maritime zones as a single unit. With this, the Tribunal cannot agree. The use of archipelagic baselines (a baseline surrounding an archipelago as a whole) is strictly controlled by the Convention, where Article 47(1) limits their use to "archipelagic states".[597] Archipelagic States are defined in Article 46 as States "constituted wholly by one or more archipelagos and may include other islands."[598] The Philippines is an archipelagic State (being constituted wholly by an archipelago), is entitled to employ archipelagic baselines, and does so in promulgating the baselines for its territorial sea. China, however, is constituted principally by territory on the mainland of Asia and cannot meet the definition of an archipelagic State.

China, *Foreign Ministry Spokesperson Hua Chunying's Remarks on Relevant Issue about Taiping Dao* (3 June 2016) *available at* <www.fmprc.gov.cn/mfa_eng/xwfw_665399/s2510_665401/t1369189.shtml>; *see also* Note Verbale from the People's Republic of China to the Secretary-General of the United Nations, No. CML/8/2011 (14 April 2011) (Annex 201).

[595]   China's Position Paper, para. 19.

[596]   Request for Further Written Argument, Request 22.

[597]   Convention, art. 47(1).

[598]   Convention, art. 46.

574. In any event, however, even the Philippines could not declare archipelagic baselines surrounding the Spratly Islands. Article 47 of the Convention limits the use of archipelagic baselines to circumstances where "within such baselines are included the main islands and an area in which the ratio of the area of the water to the area of the land, including atolls, is between 1 to 1 and 9 to 1."[599] The ratio of water to land in the Spratly Islands would greatly exceed 9:1 under any conceivable system of baselines.

575. The Convention also provides, in its Article 7, for States to make use of straight baselines under certain circumstances, and the Tribunal is aware of the practice of some States in employing straight baselines with respect to offshore archipelagos to approximate the effect of archipelagic baselines. In the Tribunal's view, any application of straight baselines to the Spratly Islands in this fashion would be contrary to the Convention. Article 7 provides for the application of straight baselines only "[i]n localities where the coastline is deeply indented and cut into, or if there is a fringe of islands along the coast in its immediate vicinity." These conditions do not include the situation of an offshore archipelago. Although the Convention does not expressly preclude the use of straight baselines in other circumstances, the Tribunal considers that the grant of permission in Article 7 concerning straight baselines generally, together with the conditional permission in Articles 46 and 47 for certain States to draw archipelagic baselines, excludes the possibility of employing straight baselines in other circumstances, in particular with respect to offshore archipelagos not meeting the criteria for archipelagic baselines. Any other interpretation would effectively render the conditions in Articles 7 and 47 meaningless.

576. Notwithstanding the practice of some States to the contrary, the Tribunal sees no evidence that any deviations from this rule have amounted to the formation of a new rule of customary international law that would permit a departure from the express provisions of the Convention.

(d) Application of Article 121 to Other High-Tide Features in the Spratly Islands

i. *Factual Findings concerning High-Tide Features in the Spratly Islands*

577. The Tribunal has reviewed a substantial volume of evidence concerning the conditions on the more significant of the high-tide features in the Spratly Islands. This has included evidence presented by the Philippines, as well as evidence in other publicly available sources and materials obtained by the Tribunal from the archives of the United Kingdom Hydrographic Office and France's *Bibliothèque Nationale de France* and *Archives Nationales d'Outre-Mer*.

---

[599]   Convention, art. 47(1).

578. There is no question that all of the significant high-tide features in the Spratly Islands are presently controlled by one or another of the littoral States, which have constructed installations and installed personnel. This presence, however, is predominantly military or governmental in nature and involves significant outside supply. Moreover, many of the high-tide features have been significantly modified from their natural condition. Additionally, accounts of current conditions and human habitation on the features may reflect deliberate attempts to colour the description in such a way as to enhance or reduce the likelihood of the feature being considered to generate an exclusive economic zone, depending on the interests of the State in question. Accordingly, the Tribunal considers historical evidence of conditions on the features—prior to the advent of the exclusive economic zone as a concept or the beginning of significant human modification—to represent a more reliable guide to the capacity of the features to sustain human habitation or economic life.

579. The Tribunal will review different aspects of conditions on the features in turn.

(a)   The Presence of Potable Fresh Water

580. There are consistent reports, throughout the record, of small wells located on a number of features in the Spratly Islands. The 1868 edition of the *China Sea Directory*, reflecting observations collected in the course of HMS Rifleman's survey work in the area, notes the presence of small wells on Itu Aba, Thitu, and North-East Cay, observing with respect to Itu Aba that "the water found in the well on that island was better than elsewhere." [600] HMS Rambler reported a similar small well on Namyit in 1888;[601] HMS Iroquois described two wells on South-West Cay in 1926;[602] and HMS Herald reported a well on Spratly Island in 1936.[603] Finally, the 1944 British *Sailing Directions for the Dangerous Ground* describe two wells on Nanshan Island.[604]

---

[600]   Admiralty Hydrographic Office, *China Sea Directory,* Vol. II, p. 71 (1st ed., 1868); *see also* Admiralty Hydrographic Office, *China Sea Directory,* Vol. II, pp. 72, 74 (1st ed., 1868); Division Botanique à l'Institut des Recherches Agronomiques de l'Indochine, "Visite Botanique au Récif Tizard," *Bulletin Économique de l'Indochine* (September-October 1936).

[601]   *Report of the Results of an Examination by the Officers of H.M.S. Rambler of the Slopes and Zoological Condition of Tizard and Macclesfield Banks*, UKHO Ref. HD106 at p. 15 (1888).

[602]   HMS Iroquois, *Sailing Directions to accompany Chart of North Danger (North-East Cay and South-West Cay)* at p. 2 (1926).

[603]   HMS Herald, *Corrections to Sailing Directions for Spratly Island, Amboyna Cay, and Fiery Cross Reef*, UKHO Ref. H3853/1936 at p. 1 (1936).

[604]   Sailing Direction for the Dangerous Ground, UKHO Ref. HD384 at p. 7 (1944 ed.).

581. Where water quality is noted, the results appear to be varied. In addition to the previously noted observation that the water on Itu Aba was "better than elsewhere",[605] the water on Thitu was described as "brackish but drinkable" in 1937,[606] the water on South-West Cay was noted to be "slightly tainted" such that it "should be used with caution" in 1926,[607] and the water on Spratly Island was deemed "slightly brackish".[608] The wells on Nanshan Island were described as "brackish".[609]

582. At the same time, a Japanese survey report of Itu Aba from 1939, apparently undertaken for commercial purposes, describes significant quantities of fresh water in the following terms:

> At that time, there were four wells, but only two of them were used. One of the two wells is one meter in diameter, and about five meters deep. There is a large quantity of the outwelling water, and according to the result of a survey, the water is suitable for drinking, and the people staying there also used the water for drinking.
>
> Even if they had collected about 10 tons of water per day from the well, the situation of the well has not changed at all. Since they never collected more water than about 10 tons per day, it is impossible to correctly explain the quantity of the water which the well may supply. However, it is recognized that the well is able to supply considerable quantity of water.
>
> Besides the well mentioned above, the other well of similar size was used for various purposes, and all chores that require water were done using this well. The other two wells were not used at that time and were unattended, although it is said that the water outwelled in the manner explained above in these wells.[610]

583. Another Japanese account of a visit to Itu Aba in 1919 similarly indicates that "[t]he quality of the water was good, and the quantity was abundant."[611] More recent accounts of water quality are mixed. One study by Taiwanese botanists in 1994 indicates that "[t]he underground water is salty and unusable for drinking."[612] Another study from the same year indicates that "[o]n the whole, the two freshwater sites actually had better water quality than in usual rivers or lakes"

---

[605] Admiralty Hydrographic Office, *China Sea Directory,* Vol. II, p. 71 (1st ed., 1868); *see also* Admiralty Hydrographic Office, *China Sea Directory,* Vol. II, pp. 72, 74 (1st ed., 1868).

[606] HMS Herald, *Report of 1937 Visit to Thitu and Itu Aba,* UKHO Ref. H2499/1937 at p. 1 (1937).

[607] HMS Iroquois, *Sailing Directions to accompany Chart of North Danger (North-East Cay and South-West Cay)* at p. 2 (1926).

[608] HMS Herald, *Corrections to Sailing Directions for Spratly Island, Amboyna Cay, and Fiery Cross Reef,* UKHO Ref. H3853/1936 at p. 1 (1936).

[609] *Sailing Direction for the Dangerous Ground,* UKHO Ref. HD384 at p. 7 (1944 ed.).

[610] H. Hiratsuka, "The Extended Base for the Expansion of the Fishery Business to Southern Area: New Southern Archipelago–On-Site Survey Report," *Taiwan Times* (May 1939).

[611] U. Kokura, *The Islands of Storm,* pp. 188, 194 (1940).

[612] T.C. Huang, et. al., "The Flora of Taipingtao (Itu Aba Island)," *Taiwania,* Vol. 39, No. 1-2 (1994) (Annex 254).

and that "the freshwater resources of the island were still in good condition."[613] Media coverage of recent visits to Itu Aba by officials and guests of the Taiwan Authority of China also stress that the well water there is drinkable.

584. In the Tribunal's view, this record is consistent with the presence, historically, of small freshwater lenses under most of the significant high-tide features in the Spratlys. The quality of this water will not necessarily match the standards of modern drinking water and may vary over time, with rainfall, usage, and even tidal conditions affecting salinity levels. Overall, the best sources of water appear to have been on Itu Aba and South-West Cay. The Tribunal notes the expert evidence submitted by the Philippines on the limited capacity to be expected of the freshwater lens at Itu Aba, but also notes that these conclusions are predicated in part on the fact that the construction of the airstrip on the feature would have reduced the soil's capacity to absorb rainwater and regenerate the freshwater lens.[614] Ultimately, the Tribunal notes that the freshwater resources of these features, combined presumably with rainwater collection, evidently have supported small numbers of people in the past (see paragraph 601 below) and concludes that they are therefore able to do so in their natural condition, whether or not that remains the case today.

(b)   Vegetation and Biology

585. The record likewise indicates that the larger features in the Spratly Islands have historically been vegetated. The 1868 edition of the British *China Sea Directory* describes Itu Aba as "covered with small trees and high bushes" and notes the presence of "two or three cocoa-nut and a few plantain trees near a small well, but the most conspicuous object is a single black clump tree."[615] Thitu is similarly described as having a "dark clump tree", as well as "some low bushes and two stunted cocoa-nut trees, near to which is a small well and a few plantain trees."[616] Namyit was described in 1888 as "well covered by small trees and shrubs,"[617] Loaita was "covered with bushes",[618] and both cays on North Danger Reef were "covered with coarse

---

[613]   I.M. Chen, "Water Quality Survey in South China Sea and Taiping Island Sea Region," in L. Fang & K. Lee (eds.), *Policy Guiding Principles: The Report for the Ecological Environment Survey on South Sea*, p. 187 at p. 194 (1994).

[614]   *See generally* First Bailey Report; Second Bailey Report.

[615]   Admiralty Hydrographic Office, *China Sea Directory*, Vol. II, p. 70 (1st ed., 1868).

[616]   Admiralty Hydrographic Office, *China Sea Directory*, Vol. II, p. 72 (1st ed., 1868).

[617]   *Report of the Results of an Examination by the Officers of H.M.S. Rambler of the Slopes and Zoological Condition of Tizard and Macclesfield Banks*, UKHO Ref. HD106 at p. 15 (1888).

[618]   Admiralty Hydrographic Office, *China Sea Directory*, Vol. II, p. 71 (1st ed., 1868).

grass."[619] During the same period, however, Spratly Island is noted as having "not a bush or even a blade of grass."[620] The crew of HMS Rifleman were also noted to have been planting coconut trees on Spratly Island and Amboyna Cay in 1864, in order to increase visibility of the features.[621]

586. Over time, the level of vegetation on the features appears to have increased, with Japanese commercial interests (discussed in paragraph 610 to 611 below) having made a concerted effort to introduce fruit trees on Itu Aba. An account from 1919 notes that "[a] huge number of banana trees grew densely everywhere on the island. Also, wild mice ran on trees everywhere on the island, and almost all the ripe bananas had become food for the mice. In fact, the island was dominated by mice."[622] By 1933, Itu Aba is described as having "a dense forest of papaya. Papaya trees which were originally planted by the Japanese spilled their seeds, and thrifted through the whole island. In addition, there remained fine palm fields, pineapple fields and sugar cane fields."[623]

587. In contrast, the *Division Botanique à l'Institut des Recherches Agronomiques de L'Indochine* recorded a lower level of vegetation on Namyit Island and Sand Cay. The vegetation on Namyit Island is described as being "of poorer quality than that on Itu-Aba."[624] The Report notes that certain plants exist "rather abundantly" but that about 15 coconut trees "are the only trees on the island."[625] The report further notes that Sand Cay had no trees, and describes the vegetation as "herbaceous" but "sickly".[626]

588. The source of the crops recorded on Itu Aba is made clear from a 1939 account of commercial activities during the period of Japanese presence that records as follows:

> The company made an effort to develop the island for settlement, and studied the propagation of palm trees, cultivation of papayas, pineapples and bananas, extraction of copra, utilization of papayas, processing of pineapples, etc., and the company grew vegetables to supply food.

[619]   Admiralty Hydrographic Office, *China Sea Directory,* Vol. II, p. 74 (1st ed., 1868).

[620]   Admiralty Hydrographic Office, *China Sea Directory,* Vol. II, p. 66 (1st ed., 1868).

[621]   Letter from Commander Ward, HMS Rifleman, to the Hydrographer of the Admiralty (29 July 1864).

[622]   U. Kokura, *The Islands of Storm,* pp. 182-183 (1940).

[623]   "Look, Japan Made Significant Marks Everywhere," *Osaka Asahi Shimbum* (6 September 1933).

[624]   "Visite Botanique au Récif Tizard," *Bulletin économique de l'Indo-Chine,* pp. 772 (September-October 1936) (translation from the French original).

[625]   "Visite Botanique au Récif Tizard," *Bulletin économique de l'Indo-Chine,* pp. 772 (September-October 1936) (translation from the French original).

[626]   "Visite Botanique au Récif Tizard," *Bulletin économique de l'Indo-Chine,* pp. 772 (September-October 1936) (translation from the French original).

Papayas grew vigorously everywhere on Long Island, and the island was also called the Island of Papayas.[627]

589. Another Japanese account from 1939 records that:

As for the plants, in addition to the short trees of two or three meters, there are 131 palm trees 7 to 10 meters tall, which bear a lot of fruit every year. In addition, there are 31 hard trees, two meters in circumference and 15 meters tall. Further, there are 80 soft trees, one meter in circumference and about 10 meters tall. Besides, there are many trees, 20 centimeters in circumference and about three meters tall growing densely. Besides these, there are a number of papaya and banana trees.

Considerable portion of the open land mentioned above has started to be used as an agriculture field, and napa and radish are grown there.

As for animals, many chickens and pigs are farmed . . . .[628]

590. The Japanese account is confirmed by the French, in a 1936 report by the *Division Botanique à l'Institut des Recherches Agronomiques de L'Indochine*, which provides the most detailed historical account of vegetation on Itu Aba:

As expected, the vegetation of the island is very poor in species. Besides the imported plants: one hundred coconut (well aligned on a southern part of the island and sufficiently well developed to date already from an earlier time), castor oil and papaya trees scattered around the island, twenty species have been identified.

The east side and south of the island, better protected monsoon is covered with beautiful vegetation, the more luxurious being found in soil rich in phosphates. The north and the west, on the contrary, although having the same botanical species, are covered with tortured vegetation, stripped of leaves, and with a lot of dead plants.

The best trees are *Gordia subcordata* (*Boraginées*) over 20 m. high having trunks up to 2 m. of diameter. They are quite numerous and scattered all over the island, especially towards the center.

Two *Erythrina indica*, also at the center of the island, reach 20 m. tall with trunks of 1 m. in diameter.

From the center and to the east is a stand of young tropical almond (*Terminalia Catappa*) from 5 to 6 meters, most of which are the sprouts of ancient tropical almonds, without a doubt used by the phosphate operators. From this population, only 1 *Calophyllurn inophyllum*, very vigorous, reaches 5-6 meters in height.

To the northeast, twenty *Macaranga*, whose species could not be determined due to lack of flowers and fruit, reach 15 to 20 meters in height. They rub shoulders with some *Ochrosia borbonica* 10 meters high bearing ovoid fruits that exude a white latex.

These are the only trees present in the island. Some shrub species also grow there. One of them, *Scaevola Kocniaii* (*Goode niacée*), reaching 5-6 meters high, forms a belt of vegetation all around the island, leaving nothing beyond it but the beaches of white sand. But while these shrubs are vigorous, very green and covered with their white fruit on the south side – they are dead on the north side, and form no more than a hedge of branches.

---

[627]   Y. Yamamoto, "The Brief History of the Sinnan Islands," *Science of Taiwan*, Vol. 7, No. 3 (1939).

[628]   H. Hiratsuka, "The Extended Base for the Expansion of the Fishery Business to Southern Area: New Southern Archipelago–On-Site Survey Report," *Taiwan Times* (May 1939).

At the center of the island, some *Guettarda speciosa* of 2 to 4 m. high live mixed with *Morinda citrifolia* (variety *bracteata*) that are very vigorous and full of fruit.

In the southwest of the island of *Umlaut volutina* (*Urticaceae*) of *Gapsicum fructicosum* (*Solanaceae*) with red fruits, *Clitoria macrophylla* (*Papilionaceae*) invaded in part by *Capparis pumila*, are mixed with castor probably imported by the phosphate miners. Everywhere, too, there are papaya, probably also introduced.

The live coverage is provided by several herbaceous species. A fern reaching over 1m. high, *Blechnum sp.*, forms an almost impenetrable thicket over a large part of the island. Some sedges, *Mariscus albescens*, grow at the foot of the Cordia and seem to suffer from drought. Some Grasses: *Thuaria sarmentosa* and *Ischoemum sp.* meet here and there along the beach. Finally, to the south and center of the island, probably where the original vegetation has been destroyed for the extraction of phosphate, there is an endless carpet of *Ipomoea biloba* covered with purple or white flowers and fruits. In the North, the ground cover consists of a creeping *Tilliacée*, *Triumfetta radicans*, which is located on the beach and in the interior of the island.

To complete this review of the vegetation, in the southwest of the islands, a few *Pandanus* are loaded with large fruits.

In short, as was to be expected and apart from the introduced plants, the vegetation is very poor since it is reduced to twenty species.

The island is now completely abandoned and the empty areas will probably reforest with similar species to existing ones.[629]

591. By 1947, following the war, Itu Aba was described in the following terms:

There are many tropical plants growing here—the land is covered in distinctly beautiful light purple and red morning glories, which are also common on the beaches of Taiwan. Morning glories are part of the Verbenaceae family (Lippia Nodiflora (L.) L. C. Rich), and its Chinese name is Guojiangteng (Quwucao). There are many Barbados nut (Nyctaginaceae family (Pisoniaalda Spanoghe), Chinese name Bishuang) and Yinye Zidan (Tournefortia ArgenfeaL, F, Boraginaceae family) (generally growing on sand by the beach (AG-12), and these plants grow very thickly. Barbados nut grows very quickly, but the timber is not solid; the trees have diameters over ten centimeters, which can usually be toppled by one person. It cannot be used for anything other than firewood. The islands also have coconut and banana, which taste good, but they are not numerous. Papaya and the castor oil plant also grow very well; these two may be planted in large quantities. The soldiers stationed on the island have cleared land to plant vegetables, which can grow, but there is a great deal of pest damage. The Taiping Island Series [of soil] may be cultivated to provide fruits and vegetables to stationed troops with no problem; but it would not be meaningful to grow grains for consumption.[630]

592. Photos of Itu Aba from 1951 also show it as thickly wooded.[631]

593. The Tribunal considers the record to indicate that Itu Aba and Thitu to have been the most heavily forested features in their natural condition, with other features covered in low bushes, grasses, and heavy scrub. Moreover, at least Itu Aba appears to have been amenable to the

---

[629] "Visite Botanique au Récif Tizard," *Bulletin économique de l'Indo-Chine*, pp. 770-771 (September-October 1936) (translation from the French original).

[630] L. Xi, "Summary of Land of Guangdong Nansha Islands," *Soil Quarterly*, Vol. 6, No. 3, p. 77 at p. 80 (1947) (Annex 885).

[631] HMS Dampier, *Report on Visit to Itu Aba and Spratly Islands*, UKHO Ref. H02716/1951 (1951).

introduction and cultivation of papaya and banana trees, even if such species do not necessarily appear to have been naturally occurring. The features also appear to have suffered from the imbalances common to small islands faced with introduced species, resulting in rapid shifts in the flora and fauna.

(c) Soil and Agricultural Potential

594. The historical record before the Tribunal contains less information concerning soil quality on features in the Spratly Islands, and such details are generally not recorded in historical accounts. HMS Rambler noted in 1888 that on Namyit, "[t]he soil of the island was very brown and earthy at the surface, but below a loose oolitic rock."[632] The *Division Botanique à l'Institut des Recherches Agronomiques de L'Indochine* who visited Itu Aba in 1936 recorded the presence of coral sand, natural phosphate, and guano. The Division also analysed an average sample of soil and determined that 87 percent of it contained sand.[633] Further, a Japanese description of Itu Aba in 1939 notes that it "is covered by black soil."[634] None of these observations is particularly insightful with respect to the agricultural potential of the feature.

595. Recent scientific evidence is varied. A 1947 Chinese study discusses two types of soil on Itu Aba and concludes that the more rich is "lush with morning glories; the coconut and banana trees are doing well, but not many have been planted; the castor oil plant grows very well and is unusually prosperous."[635] The same study notes that "approximately 250 meters to the east of the radio station and slightly to the north, in the Barbados nut shrubs, there is a small vegetable patch of only slightly over 2 mu [1,333 square metres]; the vegetables are growing decently but there is pest damage."[636] Another description from 1994, apparently drawing on scientific accounts, describes the soil on Itu Aba in the following terms:

> Sand layers accumulated in the central area of the island. Layers of bird feces reach 30 centimeters. The lower layers are lithified bird feces. Especially in the western area of the island, layers of bird feces reach 1 meter. In many cases, humus soils are on these layers, and thus people may cultivate crops.[637]

---

[632] *Report of the Results of an Examination by the Officers of H.M.S. Rambler of the Slopes and Zoological Condition of Tizard and Macclesfield Banks*, UKHO Ref. HD106 at p. 15 (1888).

[633] "Visite Botanique au Récif Tizard," *Bulletin économique de l'Indo-Chine*, pp. 773-775 (September-October 1936) (translation from the French original).

[634] "Determination Regarding Jurisdiction of New Southern Archipelago will be Announced Today," *Osaka Asahi Shimbum* (18 April 1939).

[635] L. Xi, "Summary of Land of Guangdong Nansha Islands," *Soil Quarterly*, Vol. 6, No. 3, p. 77 at p. 79 (1947).

[636] L. Xi, "Summary of Land of Guangdong Nansha Islands," *Soil Quarterly*, Vol. 6, No. 3, p. 77 at p. 79 (1947).

[637] N. Fujishima, "Discussions on the names of islands in the Southern China Sea," *The Hokkaido General Education Review of Komazawa University* Vol. 9, p. 56 (1994).

596. The Tribunal also takes note of the Philippines' caution that present-day agriculture may involve the use of imported soil,[638] as well as the expert evidence provided by the Philippines that the capacity of the soil on Itu Aba to sustain extensive cultivation is low, as would be the output of such cultivation.[639] Ultimately, the Tribunal considers the most instructive evidence to be the clear indication that fruit and vegetables were being grown on Itu Aba during the period of Japanese commercial activity (see paragraph 589 above and paragraphs 610 to 611 below). The Tribunal sees no evidence that this would have involved the importation of soil and concludes that it most likely reflects the capacity of the feature in its natural condition. At the same time, the Tribunal accepts the point that the capacity for such cultivation would be limited and that agriculture on Itu Aba would not suffice, on its own, to support a sizable population. The Tribunal also considers that the capacity of other features in the Spratly Islands would be even more limited and that significant cultivation would be difficult beyond the larger and more vegetated features of Itu Aba and Thitu.

(d) Presence of Fishermen

597. The record before the Tribunal indicates the consistent presence of small numbers of fishermen, mostly from Hainan, on the main features in the Spratly Islands. A footnote to the description of Tizard Bank in the 1868 edition of the *China Sea Directory* reads as follows:

> Hainan fisherman, who subsist by collecting trepang and tortoise-shell, were found upon most of these islands, some of whom remain for years amongst the reefs. Junks from Hainan annually visit the islands and reefs of the China Sea with supplies of rice and other necessaries, for which the fishermen give trepang and other articles in exchange, and remit their profits home; the junks leave Hainan in December or January, and return with the first of the S.W. monsoon. The fishermen upon Itu-Aba island were more comfortably established than the others . . . .[640]

598. The same volume likewise indicates that the cays on North Danger Reef "are frequented by Chinese fishermen from Hainan, who collect beche-de-mer, turtle-shell, &c. and supply themselves with water from a well in the centre of the north-eastern cay."[641] HMS Rambler reported conversations with "natives (Chinese)" on Namyit in 1888, and in 1926 on North Danger Reef HMS Iroquois described "four native fishermen, apparently from Hainan, . . . residing on the islets, living in a hut on N.E. Cay and visiting S.W. Cay periodically for water. Their occupation was fishing for beche-de-mer on the reefs. A junk from Hainan spent a week

---

[638]   Written Responses of the Philippines, para. 98 (11 March 2016).

[639]   First Motavalli Report.

[640]   Admiralty Hydrographic Office, *China Sea Directory,* Vol. II, p. 71 (1st ed., 1868).

[641]   Admiralty Hydrographic Office, *China Sea Directory,* Vol. II, p. 74 (1st ed., 1868).

fishing for beche-de-mer on North Reef during this period."[642] The 1951 *China Sea Pilot* likewise reports that "Thi tu island was inhabited by 5 Chinese in 1933."[643]

599. A report of the French arrival on Itu Aba in 1933 recorded "Chinese from Hainan managed to survive on the cays (small rocky islands surrounded by coralliferous reefs) from turtle and sea cucumber fishing, as well as a small area planted with coconut and banana trees and potatoes."[644] A later visit in 1936 by the *Division Botanique à l'Institut des Recherches Agronomiques de L'Indochine* recorded that "[t]he only persons on the island seem to be at present, the Chinese and Japanese fishermen that the ocean-going junks drop off and pick in the course of their seasonal journeys from China–Singapore and from Japan–Singapore and back."[645] Finally, a French Government report from 1939, describing the Spratly Islands, noted that "[t]here is no doubt that since time immemorial, these islands were frequented and even temporarily inhabited by the Chinese, Malay, and Annamite fishermen that haunt these parts."[646]

600. In 1951, HMS Dampier reported on a visit to Itu Aba and described meeting a significant number of Filipinos, as well as individuals who appeared to be from Hainan, although their purpose for being at Itu Aba is reported as being unclear and no fishing gear was observed.[647]

601. Taken as a whole, the Tribunal concludes that the Spratly Islands were historically used by small groups of fishermen. Based on the clear reference from 1868, the Tribunal also accepts that some of these individuals were present in the Spratlys for comparatively long periods of time, with an established network of trade and intermittent supply. At the same time, the overall number of individuals engaged in this livelihood appears to have been significantly constrained.

(e) *Commercial Operations*

602. The 1941 edition of the Japanese *Pilot for Taiwan and the Southwest Islands*, providing sailing directions for the South China Sea, includes a general introduction, covering Japanese commercial activities in the area between 1917 and 1939 in the following terms:

> The group was first explored by MATSUJI HIRADA in June 1917; next the RASASHIMA Phosphate Co. (now the RASASHINA WORKS Co.) made 3 expeditions between the years

---

[642] HMS Iroquois, *Sailing Directions to accompany Chart of North Danger (North-East Cay and South-West Cay)* (1926).

[643] Admiralty Hydrographic Office, *China Sea Pilot*, Vol. I, p. 126 (2nd ed., 1951).

[644] "French Flag over the Unoccupied Islets," *The Illustration* (15 July 1933).

[645] "Visite Botanique au Récif Tizard," *Bulletin économique de l'Indo-Chine*, p. 771 (September-October 1936) (translation from the French original).

[646] "Les Iles Spratly," Document No. 210, p. 7 (5 April 1939).

[647] HMS Dampier, *Report on Visit to Itu Aba and Spratly Islands*, UKHO Ref. H02716/1951 (1951).

1918 to 1923 and although excavations were planned at [Itu Aba] and [Northeast and South-West Cay] operations were suspended in 1929 owing to the business falling off and all personnel were withdrawn. Thereafter in 1937 the Kaiyo Kogyo Kabushiki Kaisha (Ocean Exploration Industrial Co. Ltd.) commenced an investigation of the industrial resources of these islands and at the same time conferred a public benefit generally by weather reports communicating with fishing vessels, replenishing supplies, assisting in shipwrecks, &c. Most recently the Nanyo Kohatsu Kabushiki Kaisha (Southern Ocean Enterprise Co. Ltd.) has commenced plans for the working of phosphates and the Hakuyo Suisan Kabushiki Kaisha (Ocean Exploration Marine Products Co. Ltd.) for marine produce; since then personnel of both companies reside continuously at [Itu Aba] the total number of persons being about 130 including officials.

On the basis of this history the Imperial Government formally proclaimed possession of this group on 30th March, 1939. Nevertheless the French Government in July, 1933, upon the discovery of new islands and islets in the adjacent South China Sea proclaimed possession of the [Southern Archipelago]; at the present time near the E. end of [Itu Aba] there are about 20 persons staying permanently who are said to belong to the French Indo-China Registered Company.[648]

603. In the Tribunal's view, this summary appears to correspond with other evidence in the record concerning Japanese commercial and industrial activities on Itu Aba and South-West Cay. HMS Iroquois' 1926 report on South-West Cay confirms the presence of significant guano mining:

The islet is a breeding place for sea birds, and is covered with guano, the export of which has at some time been carried out on a considerable scale. In this connection a number of low wooden sheds and buildings have been erected on the south side of the island, but in May 1926 it appeared that they had been disused for some time. A trolley way runs from a guano quarry in the centre of the island to a pier on the southern side.

Pier. A wooden pier, 330 feet long in a south-easterly direction, and with a least depth of 1 foot (0.3.M) at low water at its outer end, is situated near the centre of the southeastern side of the islet. It carries the trolley way referred to in the previous paragraph, and in May 1926 was in a poor state of repair.[649]

604. The same infrastructure is clearly visible in the 1926 fair chart of North Danger Reef, reproduced below as Figure 11 on page 248.

605. Although HMS Iroquois described the facility as inactive, a British account from the following year noted that:

In July, 1927, H.M.S. Caradoc visited the reef and found a small Japanese schooner lying close to the pier; there were about 8 persons on board and at least 12 living ashore. The Japanese said that from 3,000 to 5,000 tons of guano were exported annually, a steamer shipping this cargo once a year.[650]

606. A similar mining operation was established on Itu Aba in 1921 and later described as follows:

---

[648] English translation of Japanese *Pilot for Taiwan and the South-West Islands*, Vol. V, p. 243 (March 1941 ed.), "Sailing Directions for Shinnan Guntao," UKHO Ref. H019893/1944.

[649] HMS Iroquois, *Sailing Directions to accompany Chart of North Danger (North-East Cay and South-West Cay)*, p. 1 (1926).

[650] Sailing Direction for the Dangerous Ground, UKHO Ref. HD384, p. 4 (1944 ed.).

The mining of phosphate ore started to operate in 1921 in full swing. On Long Island, which is the base for the mining, various facilities for the mining business were eventually prepared: for example, dormitories, warehouses, offices, a clinic, an analysis room, a weather station, etc. were built; a jetty of 84 KEN length to get goods on board was constructed on the sea; and tracks were made in the mining area. At that time about 200 Japanese people lived there, and it is said that the number reached about 600 by 1927. During this period, the company mined 25,900 tons of guano, and the value of it was about 727,000 yen.[651]

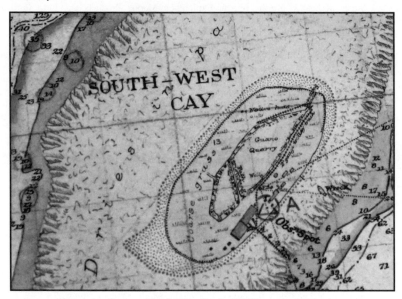

Figure 11: Survey of South-West Cay by HMS Iroquois, 1926

607. Another account from the same year records that:

> Itu Aba Island, which is called the Long Island and which has economic value. The island is the largest island in the New Southern Archipelago, and Rasa Island Phosphate Ore Ltd., of Ministry of Southern Ocean mined phosphate ore there from 1924 to 1926. Offices, dormitories and jetties were constructed on the land, and about 200 employees were engaged in mining.[652]

608. By 1933, however, mining operations had apparently ceased. When the French briefly occupied Itu Aba that year it was deserted, and described as follows:

> The island was deserted, but two occupants had left their mark: cement wells, remains of an iron jetty, rusted rail tracks on the embankment, and a pile of abandoned phosphates bore witness to a Japanese enterprise dating back to 1925; then a hut made out of foliage, a well maintained potato field, a little altar with a votive tea light and stick jars to the Lar gods of the Chinese fishermen. A board hung on a hut, covered with characters which could roughly be translated as "I, Ti Mung, Chief of the Junk, come here in the full moon

---

[651] Y. Yamamoto, "The Brief History of the Sinnan Islands," *Science of Taiwan*, Vol. 7, No. 3 (1939).

[652] "Determination Regarding Jurisdiction of New Southern Archipelago will be Announced Today," *Osaka Asahi Shimbum* (18 April 1939).

of March to bring you food. I found nobody, I left rice in the shelter of the rocks and I left."[653]

609. A Japanese account from the same year records the remnants of the mining operation:

> Over 10,000 tons of phosphate ore were stored here which looked like a castle wall. A Japanese-style protection bank was made on the seashore, and the frames of a big water tank were desolately abandoned: it is said that the iron plates were taken by pirates. All buildings were destroyed, and the area bleakly became a papaya forest. Almost all of the lumber was moved to other places, and only concrete flag stones of tank wells remained; it was done in a more thorough way than that of starving wolves devouring their prey. The weighing machine, located at the place which used to be an analysis room, is only thing protecting Japanese science which had spread to the south.[654]

610. By 1937, however, a new Japanese commercial presence had been established on Itu Aba in the form of the Kaiyo Kogyo Company, engaged in the fishing industry. This is confirmed in the account of HMS Herald's visit to the area in that year, which includes the description that:

> A fishing company also live on the island and engage in the turtle industry. There would appear to be about 40 of these men, mostly Formosans by appearance, who live in large wooden huts. The manager of the company, who only understands a few words of English, Mr. Sadae Chiya, Kaiyokogyo Co. Ltd, Takao Formosa. He lives in an attractive little hut of two rooms.
>
> Also on the island are a generator for electric power, and what looked like a small wireless transmitting and received set."[655]

611. A Japanese account from 1939 confirms the same facts:

> In the early Showa era, the area around the island became the major fishing places for tunas and shellfish based on Kaohsiung City, and the Japanese were active there. They got water in Long Island (the Itu Aba Island) and North Danger (so called the Danger Island). In other words, at that time, the place was considerably developed as a fishery advanced base of Kaohsiung, and thus the fishermen of Kaohsiung feel that it is strange for the government to announce that the place will be incorporated into Kaohsiung after all these years. After that, Kaiyo Kogyo Company was established as suggested by Mr. Sueharu Hirata, who is a resident of Kaohsiung City in 1935. The purposes of the company are fishery and mining phosphate ore. The company is based in the Long Island having employees there and has operated business to date.[656]

612. During the war, Itu Aba was used as a base of operations by Japanese forces and bombed by aircraft of the U.S. Navy in May 1945.[657] HMS Dampier's account of a visit to the island in 1951 records "the remains of what must have been a flourishing concern, before it was

---

[653] "French Flag on the Unoccupied Islands," *Illustration* (1933).

[654] "Look, Japan Made Significant Marks Everywhere," *Osaka Asahi Shimbum* (6 September 1933).

[655] HMS Herald, *Report of 1937 Visit to Thitu and Itu Aba*, UKHO Ref. H2499/1937 at p. 3 (1937).

[656] "Determination Regarding Jurisdiction of New Southern Archipelago will be Announced Today," *Osaka Asahi Shimbum* (18 April 1939). The Shōwa era, referred to in this quotation, began in 1926, corresponding with the ascension of the Emperor Shōwa (Hirohito) to the imperial throne of Japan.

[657] "The Texts of the Day's Communiques on the Fighting in Various War Zones," *New York Times* (4 May 1945); "Australians Widen Borneo Grip; Americans Crash Way into Davao," *New York Times* (4 May 1945).

demolished by shellfire and/or bombing."[658] Photographs taken during the visit also depict a number of large concrete buildings, although whether these were of military construction or the remains of installations built by the Kaiyo Kogyo Company, or another commercial concern, is unclear.

613. Following the war, a Chinese survey of Itu Aba noted the poor mineral content of guano extracted from the Spratly Islands—an issue that may well partially explain the failure of the Rasashima Phosphate Company's operations in the 1920s—and identified fisheries as the mostly likely potential commercial use of the islands:

> The reserve of phosphoric guano is estimated to be over 70,000 tons. However, the content of available phosphoric acid is too low and should not be directly applied. There is greater variation in content and quality is uneven, thus it is not suitable as raw material to produce phosphoric lime. Moreover, sulfuric acid is expensive, which would increase manufacturing costs to the point of being uneconomical. Furthermore, the Nansha Islands are over 600 nautical miles from Yulin Harbor. Transportation is inconvenient and uneconomical, and the phosphoric guano in the Nansha Islands is not very valuable. However, it is possible to transport guano back to Guangdong when ships supplying the island return. We plan to engage in research on usage of the phosphoric guano; if it is possible to improve its fertilizer efficacy, then it would meet the needs of lands in southern China, which are short on phosphate fertilizers.
>
> We believe that in the Nansha Islands, the industry with the best prospects is fishing. The lagoon is calm and a good place to fish. The area is rich in skipjack tuna, abalone, pale fish, shark, sea cucumber, sponge, and kelp. The most valuable are big tortoises and sea turtles, as large as five to six hundred jin [300 to 360 kg]. They lay their eggs on the beach in moonlit nights in the spring and summer; this is the easiest time to catch them. Their meat is edible, tastes like beef, and is highly nutritious. Their eggs can be used to make highly valuable medicines. Since the Japanese have constructed a 30-square meters of fish-drying courtyard and refrigeration facilities on the island, there are great expectations for the fishery industry in this area.[659]

614. There is, however, no evidence of any commercial fishing operation having been established in the Spratly Islands since 1945. Nor, in light of the advances in shipbuilding and fishing technology since that date, does the Tribunal see that a base of operations on a small, isolated feature such as Itu Aba would be economically necessary, or even beneficial. Rather, the historical record indicates only a short period of activity by Thomas Cloma of the Philippines and his associates (who may well have been the Filipinos encountered on Itu Aba in 1951 by the crew of HMS Dampier), who sought to devise a commercial scheme for the islands.[660] There is no evidence, however, that Mr. Cloma or his associates ever took up residence in the Spratlys or succeeded in deriving the least economic benefit from them. Malaysia has also established a

---

[658] HMS Dampier, *Report on Visit to Itu Aba and Spratly Islands*, UKHO Ref. H02716/1951 at para. 10 (21 April 1951).

[659] L. Xi, "Summary of Land of Guangdong Nansha Islands," *Soil Quarterly*, Vol. 6, No. 3, p. 77 at p. 80 (1947).

[660] *See generally* B. Hayton, *The South China Sea*, pp. 65-70 (2014).

small resort and scuba diving enterprise on Swallow Reef, but this operation is only possible due to significant land reclamation activities that have enlarged the small high-tide rocks on the reef; it does not represent the natural capacity of the feature. Otherwise, human activity on the Spratly Islands appears to be entirely governmental in nature.

ii.   *The Application of Article 121 and the Tribunal's Conclusions on the Status of Features*

615.   On the basis of the evidence in the record, it appears to the Tribunal that the principal high-tide features in the Spratly islands are capable of enabling the survival of small groups of people. There is historical evidence of potable water, although of varying quality, that could be combined with rainwater collection and storage. There is also naturally occurring vegetation capable of providing shelter and the possibility of at least limited agriculture to supplement the food resources of the surrounding waters. The record indicates that small numbers of fishermen, mainly from Hainan, have historically been present on Itu Aba and the other more significant features and appear to have survived principally on the basis of the resources at hand (notwithstanding the references to annual deliveries of rice and other sundries).

616.   The principal features of the Spratly Islands are not barren rocks or sand cays, devoid of fresh water, that can be dismissed as uninhabitable on the basis of their physical characteristics alone. At the same time, the features are not obviously habitable, and their capacity even to enable human survival appears to be distinctly limited. In these circumstances, and with features that fall close to the line in terms of their capacity to sustain human habitation, the Tribunal considers that the physical characteristics of the features do not definitively indicate the capacity of the features. Accordingly, the Tribunal is called upon to consider the historical evidence of human habitation and economic life on the Spratly Islands and the implications of such evidence for the natural capacity of the features.

617.   In addition to the presence of fishermen noted above, Itu Aba and South-West Cay were the site of Japanese mining and fishing activities in the 1920s and 1930s. The Spratlys were also the site of the somewhat more adventurous activities of Thomas Cloma and his associates in the 1950s. More recently, many of the features have been transformed by substantial construction efforts and are now the site of installations hosting significant numbers of personnel, generally of a governmental nature. The first question for the Tribunal is whether any of this activity constitutes "human habitation" or an "economic life of its own" for the purposes of Article 121(3). The second is whether there is evidence to suggest that the historical record of human activity on the Spratly Islands is not proof of the natural capacity of the features.

(a)   Historical Human Habitation of the Features of the Spratly Islands

618.   For the Tribunal, the criterion of human habitation is not met by the temporary inhabitation of the Spratly Islands by fishermen, even for extended periods.   As discussed above at paragraph 542, the Tribunal considers human habitation to entail the non-transient inhabitation of a feature by a stable community of people for whom the feature constitutes a home and on which they can remain.   This standard is not met by the historical presence of fishermen that appears in the record before the Tribunal.   Indeed, the very fact that the fishermen are consistently recorded as being "from Hainan", or elsewhere, is evidence for the Tribunal that they do not represent the natural population of the Spratlys.   Nowhere is there any reference to the fishermen "of Itu Aba", "of Thitu", or "of North Danger Reef," nor is there any suggestion that the fishermen were accompanied by their families.   Nor do any of the descriptions of conditions on the features suggest the creation of the shelter and facilities that the Tribunal would expect for a population intending to reside permanently among the islands.   Rather, the record indicates a pattern of temporary residence on the features for economic purposes, with the fishermen remitting their profits, and ultimately returning, to the mainland.

619.   The same conclusion holds true with respect to Japanese commercial activities on Itu Aba and South-West Cay.   A crew of Formosan labourers, brought to the Spratlys to mine guano or capture sea turtles, is inherently transient in nature: their objective was to extract the economic resources of the Spratlys for the benefit of the populations of Formosa and Japan to which they would return.   It was not to make a new life for themselves on the islands.   It may of course occur, and frequently does, that what is initially a remote outpost of an extractive industry will develop over time into a settled community.   This did not, however, occur in the case of either Itu Aba or South-West Cay.   The temporary presence of these persons on the features for a few short years does not suffice to establish a settled community within the meaning of "human habitation" in Article 121(3).

620.   Finally, the Tribunal does not consider that the military or other governmental personnel presently stationed on the features in the Spratly Islands by one or another of the littoral States suffice to constitute "human habitation" for the purposes of Article 121(3).   These groups are heavily dependent on outside supply, and it is difficult to see how their presence on any of the South China Sea features can fairly be said to be sustained by the feature itself, rather than by a continuous lifeline of supply and communication from the mainland.   Military or other governmental personnel are deployed to the Spratly Islands in an effort to support the various claims to sovereignty that have been advanced.   There is no evidence that they choose to inhabit there of their own volition, nor can it be expected that any would remain if the official need for

their presence were to dissipate. Even where the current human presence in the Spratly Islands includes civilians, as is the case on at least Thitu and (very recently) Itu Aba, the Tribunal considers that their presence there is motivated by official considerations and would not have occurred, but for the disputed claims to sovereignty over these features.

621. The Tribunal sees no indication that anything fairly resembling a stable human community has ever formed on the Spratly Islands. Rather, the islands have been a temporary refuge and base of operations for fishermen and a transient residence for labourers engaged in mining and fishing. The introduction of the exclusive economic zone was not intended to grant extensive maritime entitlements to small features whose historical contribution to human settlement is as slight as that. Nor was the exclusive economic zone intended to encourage States to establish artificial populations in the hope of making expansive claims, precisely what has now occurred in the South China Sea. On the contrary, Article 121(3) was intended to prevent such developments and to forestall a provocative and counterproductive effort to manufacture entitlements.

622. The Tribunal sees no evidence that would suggest that the historical absence of human habitation on the Spratly Islands is the product of intervening forces or otherwise does not reflect the limited capacity of the features themselves. Accordingly, the Tribunal concludes that Itu Aba, Thitu, West York, Spratly Island, South-West Cay, and North-East Cay are not capable of sustaining human habitation within the meaning of Article 121(3). The Tribunal has also considered, and reaches the same conclusion with respect to, the other, less significant high-tide features in the Spratly Islands, which are even less capable of sustaining human habitation, but does not consider it necessary to list them individually.

(b) *Historical Economic Life of Their Own of the Features of the Spratly Islands*

623. In the Tribunal's view, all of the economic activity in the Spratly Islands that appears in the historical record has been essentially extractive in nature (*i.e.*, mining for guano, collecting shells, and fishing), aimed to a greater or lesser degree at utilising the resources of the Spratlys for the benefit of the populations of Hainan, Formosa, Japan, the Philippines, Viet Nam, or elsewhere. As set out above at paragraph 543, the Tribunal considers that, to constitute the economic life of the feature, economic activity must be oriented around the feature itself and not be focused solely on the surrounding territorial sea or entirely dependent on external resources. The Tribunal also considers that extractive economic activity, without the presence of a stable local community, necessarily falls short of constituting the economic life of the feature.

624. Applying this standard, the history of extractive economic activity does not constitute, for the features of the Spratly Islands, evidence of an economic life of their own. In reaching this conclusion, however, the Tribunal takes pains to emphasise that the effect of Article 121(3) is not to deny States the benefit of the economic resources of small rocks and maritime features. Such features remain susceptible to a claim of territorial sovereignty and will generate a 12-nautical-mile territorial sea, provided they remain above water at high tide. Rather, the effect of Article 121(3) is to prevent such features—whose economic benefit, if any, to the State which controls them is for resources alone—from generating a further entitlement to a 200-nautical-mile exclusive economic zone and continental shelf that would infringe on the entitlements generated by inhabited territory or on the area reserved for the common heritage of mankind.

625. The Tribunal concludes that Itu Aba, Thitu, West York, Spratly Island, South-West Cay, and North-East Cay are not capable of sustaining an economic life of their own within the meaning of Article 121(3). The Tribunal has also considered, and reaches the same conclusion with respect to, the other, less significant high-tide features in the Spratly Islands, which are even less capable of sustaining economic life, but does not consider it necessary to list them individually.

*

626. The Tribunal having concluded that none of the high-tide features in the Spratly Islands is capable of sustaining human habitation or an economic life of their own, the effect of Article 121(3) is that such features shall have no exclusive economic zone or continental shelf.

(e)   **Decision on the Tribunal's Jurisdiction with respect to Submission No. 5**

627. Having addressed the status of features in the Spratly Islands, the Tribunal can now return to the question of its jurisdiction with respect to the Philippines' Submission No. 5, which requests the Tribunal to declare that "Mischief Reef and Second Thomas Shoal are part of the exclusive economic zone and continental shelf of the Philippines." The Tribunal will consider its jurisdiction both with respect to the exception in Article 298 for disputes concerning sea boundary delimitation and with respect to the effect of States that are not Parties to the present proceedings.

i.   Maritime Boundary Delimitation and the Tribunal's Jurisdiction

628.   In its Award on Jurisdiction, the Tribunal deferred taking a decision on this aspect of its jurisdiction, noting that this was contingent on a determination on the status of the maritime features that the Tribunal was not prepared to make as a preliminary matter. In that decision, the Tribunal noted as follows:

> the Tribunal's jurisdiction to decide on the merits of some of the Philippines' Submissions may depend upon the status of certain maritime features in the South China Sea. Specifically, if (contrary to the Philippines' position) any maritime feature in the Spratly Islands constitutes an "island" within the meaning of Article 121 of the Convention, generating an entitlement to an exclusive economic zone or continental shelf, it may be the case that the Philippines and China possess overlapping entitlements to maritime zones in the relevant areas of the South China Sea. In that case, the Tribunal may not be able to reach the merits of certain of the Philippines' Submissions (Nos. 5, 8, and 9) without first delimiting the Parties' overlapping entitlements, a step that it cannot take in light of Article 298 and China's declaration.[661]

629.   At the same time, the Tribunal emphasised that the Philippines' Submission No. 5 does not itself call for the Tribunal to decide a dispute concerning sea boundary delimitation: "the premise of the Philippines' Submission is not that the Tribunal will delimit any overlapping entitlements in order to declare that these features form part of the exclusive economic zone and continental shelf of the Philippines, but rather that no overlapping entitlements can exist."[662] In other words, nothing in the Convention prevents a Tribunal from recognising the existence of an exclusive economic zone or continental shelf, or of addressing the legal consequence of such zones, in an area where the entitlements of the State claiming an exclusive economic zone or continental shelf are not overlapped by the entitlements of any other State. Doing so does not implicate the delimitation of maritime boundaries or the exclusion from jurisdiction in Article 298(1)(a)(i). In the absence of any possible overlap, there is quite literally nothing to delimit.

630.   The Tribunal went on to note, however, that:

> If, however, another maritime feature claimed by China within 200 nautical miles of Mischief Reef or Second Thomas Shoal were to be an "island" for the purposes of Article 121, capable of generating an entitlement to an exclusive economic zone and continental shelf, the resulting overlap and the exclusion of boundary delimitation from the Tribunal's jurisdiction by Article 298 would prevent the Tribunal from addressing this Submission.[663]

631.   The Tribunal has already held (see paragraphs 277 to 278 above) that there is no legal basis for any Chinese historic rights, or sovereign rights and jurisdiction beyond those provided for in the Convention, in the waters of the South China Sea encompassed by the 'nine-dash line'. The

---

[661]   Award on Jurisdiction, para. 394.

[662]   Award on Jurisdiction, para. 402.

[663]   Award on Jurisdiction, para. 402.

Tribunal sees no evidence that, prior to the Convention, China ever established a historic right to the exclusive use of the living and non-living resources of the waters of the South China Sea, whatever use it may historically have made of the Spratly Islands themselves. In any event, any such right would have been superseded by the adoption of the Convention and the legal creation of the exclusive economic zone. The 'nine-dash line' thus cannot provide a basis for any entitlement by China to maritime zones in the area of Mischief Reef or Second Thomas Shoal that would overlap the entitlement of the Philippines to an exclusive economic zone and continental shelf generated from baselines on the island of Palawan.

632. The Tribunal has now held (see paragraphs 378 and 381 above) that Mischief Reef and Second Thomas Shoal are low-tide elevations and, as such, generate no entitlement to maritime zones of their own. The Tribunal has also now held (see paragraph 626 above) that neither Itu Aba, nor any other high-tide feature in the Spratly Islands, is a fully entitled island for the purposes of Article 121 of the Convention. As such, pursuant to the operation of Article 121(3) of the Convention, these features are legally considered to be "rocks" and to generate no exclusive economic zone or continental shelf. The Tribunal also notes that there is no maritime feature that is above water at high tide in its natural condition and that is located within 12 nautical miles of either Mischief Reef or Second Thomas Shoal.

633. From these conclusions, it follows that there exists no legal basis for any entitlement by China to maritime zones in the area of Mischief Reef or Second Thomas Shoal. Accordingly, there is no situation of overlapping entitlements that would call for the application of Articles 15, 74, or 83 to delimit the overlap. Because no delimitation is required—or, indeed, even possible— there is no possible basis for the application of the exception to jurisdiction in Article 298(1)(a)(i).

ii. Third Parties and the Tribunal's Jurisdiction

634. In its Award on Jurisdiction, the Tribunal considered whether any third parties were indispensable to the proceedings, recalled those cases in which an international court or tribunal had declined to proceed due to the absence of an indispensable party, and concluded that "the absence of other States as parties to the arbitration poses no obstacle."[664] The Tribunal reaffirms and incorporates that decision (see paragraph 157 and 168 above). In light, however, of Malaysia's Communication to the Tribunal of 23 June 2016, the Tribunal considers it

---

[664] Award on Jurisdiction, para. 188.

beneficial to elaborate further on the significance of third parties and the basis for its jurisdiction to reach the conclusions set out in this Award.

635. In its Communication, Malaysia recalls that it claims sovereignty over a number of features in the South China Sea and "may also have overlapping maritime entitlements (including an extended continental shelf) in the areas of some of the features that the Arbitral Tribunal has been asked to classify."[665] Malaysia invokes *Monetary Gold Removed from Rome in 1943*, as well as other cases where courts and tribunals have sought to constrain the effects of maritime boundary delimitation on third parties, and argues that:

> The Arbitral Tribunal must ensure that, in determining whether certain maritime features in the South China Sea are entitled to specific maritime zones under UNCLOS 1982, it does not express any position that might directly or indirectly affect the rights and interests of Malaysia. The Arbitral Tribunal thus cannot purport to decide upon the maritime entitlements pursuant to Articles 13 and 121 of UNCLOS 1982 of any features within the EEZ and Continental Shelf of Malaysia as published in Malaysia's Map of 1979.[666]

636. The Tribunal observes that Malaysia has had observer status in the proceedings since 25 June 2015 and, accordingly, attended the Hearing on Jurisdiction and the Hearing on the Merits and received copies of the full submissions in the case. It has, however, brought its concerns to the Tribunal for the first time in June 2016. Nevertheless, the Tribunal has sought the Parties' comments on Malaysia's Communication and, as set out below, has taken note of Malaysia's concerns.

637. The Tribunal notes that Malaysia is not a party to this arbitration and has not applied to intervene in these proceedings. As Malaysia's Communication correctly notes, as a non-party "Malaysia is not bound by the outcome of the arbitral proceedings or any pronouncement on fact or law to be rendered by the Arbitral Tribunal."[667] This follows generally from the principle that the legal effect of a judicial or arbitral decision is limited to the Parties and from Article 296(2) of the Convention, which expressly provides that "[a]ny such decision shall have no binding force except between the parties and in respect of that particular dispute."

638. The Tribunal further notes that the none of the features specifically identified in the Philippines' Submissions lies within the continental shelf limit claimed by Malaysia in its 1979 Map and that Malaysia has not asserted the position that any maritime feature in the Spratly Islands constitutes a fully entitled island for the purposes of Article 121(3) of the Convention. On the

---

[665] Note Verbale from the Federation of Malaysia to the Tribunal, No. PRMC 5/2016 (23 June 2016), *enclosing* Communication from the Ministry of Foreign Affairs of Malaysia, p. 6 (23 June 2016) (hereinafter "**Malaysia's Communication**").

[666] Malaysia's Communication, p. 6.

[667] Malaysia's Communication, p. 8.

contrary, Malaysia's joint submission (with Viet Nam) to the CLCS sets out official coordinates for the outer limit of Malaysia's 200-nautical-mile continental shelf claim, which is unequivocally drawn from basepoints adjacent to the coast of Borneo, rather than from any feature in the Spratly Islands.

639. The Tribunal observes that—insofar as they involve features not claimed by Malaysia in its 1979 Map—none of its determinations with respect to the Philippines' Submissions No. 4, 6, or 7 bear on the rights or interests that Malaysia has asserted in its Communication. With respect to the Philippines' Submission No. 5, the Tribunal notes that Mischief Reef and Second Thomas Shoal do lie within 200 nautical miles of features claimed by Malaysia, although Malaysia itself has not claimed an exclusive economic zone or continental shelf in the area of either Mischief Reef or Second Thomas Shoal.

640. The Tribunal considers, however, that Malaysia's Communication overstates the *Monetary Gold* principle when it argues expansively that the Tribunal must "avoid deciding any question that requires it to adopt a view that, directly or indirectly, may affect Malaysia's rights and interests."[668] Read correctly, *Monetary Gold* calls for a court or tribunal to refrain from exercising its jurisdiction where the "legal interests [of a third State] would not only be affected by a decision, but would form the very subject-matter of the decision."[669] The circumstances of *Monetary Gold*, however, "represent the limit of the power of the Court to refuse to exercise its jurisdiction,"[670] and any more expansive reading would impermissibly constrain the practical ability of courts and tribunals to carry out their function. The Tribunal considers that, to the extent it has examined certain features claimed by China (that are also claimed by Malaysia) for the purposes of assessing the possible entitlements of China in areas to which Malaysia makes no claim, the legal interests of Malaysia do not form "the very subject-matter of the dispute"[671] and are not implicated by the Tribunal's conclusions.

---

[668] Malaysia's Communication, p. 7.

[669] *Monetary Gold Removed from Rome in 1943 (Preliminary Question), Judgment of 15 June 1954, ICJ Reports 1954*, p. 19 at p. 32.

[670] *Military and Paramilitary Activities in and against Nicaragua (Nicaragua v. United States of America), Jurisdiction and Admissibility, Judgment, ICJ Reports 1984*, p. 392 at p. 431, para. 88.

[671] *Monetary Gold Removed from Rome in 1943 (Preliminary Question), Judgment of 15 June 1954, ICJ Reports 1954*, p. 19 at p. 32.

641. In these circumstances, Malaysia's rights and interests are protected, to the extent they are implicated at all, by its status as a non-party to the proceedings and by Article 296(2), and do not engage the rule in *Monetary Gold*.[672]

*

642. For the foregoing reasons, the Tribunal concludes that it has jurisdiction with respect to the Philippines' Submission No. 5.

(f)   Conclusion

643. Based on the considerations outlined above (see paragraphs 333 to 334), the Tribunal finds with respect to the Philippines' Submission No. 3 that Scarborough Shoal contains, within the meaning of Article 121(1) of the Convention, naturally formed areas of land, surrounded by water, which are above water at high tide. However, under Article 121(3) of the Convention, the high-tide features at Scarborough Shoal are rocks that cannot sustain human habitation or economic life of their own and accordingly shall have no exclusive economic zone or continental shelf.

644. Based on the considerations outlined above (see paragraphs 335 to 351), the Tribunal finds with respect to the Philippines' Submission No. 7 that Johnson Reef, Cuarteron Reef, and Fiery Cross Reef contain, within the meaning of Article 121(1) of the Convention, naturally formed areas of land, surrounded by water, which are above water at high tide. However, for purposes of Article 121(3) of the Convention, the high-tide features at Johnson Reef, Cuarteron Reef, and Fiery Cross Reef are rocks that cannot sustain human habitation or economic life of their own and accordingly shall have no exclusive economic zone or continental shelf.

645. Having found—contrary to the Philippines' Submission No. 6—that Gaven Reef (North) and McKennan Reef are naturally formed areas of land, surrounded by water, which are above water at high tide (see paragraphs 354 and 366 above), the Tribunal finds that for purposes of Article 121(3) of the Convention, the high-tide features at Gaven Reef (North) and McKennan Reef are rocks that cannot sustain human habitation or economic life of their own and accordingly shall have no exclusive economic zone or continental shelf.

646. Based on the considerations outlined above (see paragraphs 374 to 381), the Tribunal concludes that Mischief Reef and Second Thomas Shoal are both low-tide elevations that generate no

---

[672]   See *Military and Paramilitary Activities in and against Nicaragua (Nicaragua v. United States of America), Jurisdiction and Admissibility, Judgment, ICJ Reports 1984*, p. 392 at p. 431, para. 88.

maritime zones of their own. The Tribunal also concludes that none of the high-tide features in the Spratly Islands are capable of sustaining human habitation or an economic life of their own within the meaning of those terms in Article 121(3) of the Convention. All of the high-tide features in the Spratly Islands are therefore legally rocks for purposes of Article 121(3) and do not generate entitlements to an exclusive economic zone or continental shelf. There is, accordingly, no possible entitlement by China to any maritime zone in the area of either Mischief Reef or Second Thomas Shoal and no jurisdictional obstacle to the Tribunal's consideration of the Philippines' Submission No. 5.

647. With respect to the Philippines' Submission No. 5, the Tribunal concludes that both Mischief Reef and Second Thomas Shoal are located within 200 nautical miles of the Philippines' coast on the island of Palawan and are located in an area that is not overlapped by the entitlements generated by any maritime feature claimed by China. It follows, therefore, that, as between the Philippines and China, Mischief Reef and Second Thomas Shoal form part of the exclusive economic zone and continental shelf of the Philippines.

648. The Tribunal now turns to the consideration of the Philippines' Submissions No. 8 through 13, concerning Chinese activities in the South China Sea.

*   *   *

VII. CHINESE ACTIVITIES IN THE SOUTH CHINA SEA (SUBMISSIONS NO. 8 TO 13)

A. ALLEGED INTERFERENCE WITH THE PHILIPPINES' SOVEREIGN RIGHTS IN ITS EEZ AND CONTINENTAL SHELF (SUBMISSION NO. 8)

1. Introduction

649. In this Section, the Tribunal addresses the Parties' dispute concerning the activities of Chinese officials and Chinese vessels with respect to living and non-living resources in the areas of the South China Sea located within the Philippines' exclusive economic zone and continental shelf. This dispute is reflected in the Philippines' Submission No. 8, which requests the Tribunal to declare that:

> (8) China has unlawfully interfered with the enjoyment and exercise of the sovereign rights of the Philippines with respect to the living and non-living resources of its exclusive economic zone and continental shelf;

2. Factual Background

650. Documents adduced by the Philippines record several incidents since 2010 in which China has acted to prevent the Philippines from exploiting the non-living and living resources in the waters that lie within 200 nautical miles of the Philippines' baselines. The following is an overview of these incidents.

(a) Actions regarding Non-Living Resources

651. China has objected to or acted to prevent petroleum exploration by the Philippines in the South China Sea, within 200 nautical miles of the Philippines' baselines, on several occasions.

i. Petroleum Blocks at Reed Bank and the M/V Veritas Voyager Incident

652. In June 2002, the Philippines awarded Sterling Energy Plc ("**Sterling Energy**") a licence to explore oil and gas deposits within the GSEC101 block, located at Reed Bank.[673] The location of the GSEC101 block is depicted in Map 4 on page 269 below.

653. In April 2005, Forum Energy Plc, a UK-based oil and gas exploration and production company ("**Forum Energy**"), acquired the concession from Sterling Energy and became its operator.[674] On 15 February 2010, the Philippines converted the licence into a Service Contract ("**SC72**").[675]

---

[673] Merits Hearing Tr. (Day 2), pp. 140-141.

[674] Forum Energy plc, "SC72 Recto Bank (Formerly GSEC101)" (Annex 342).

654. On 22 February 2010, China delivered to the Philippines a Note Verbale, expressing "its strong objection and indignation" about the award of the Service Contract. China went on to state as follows:

> China has indisputable sovereignty, sovereign rights and jurisdiction over Nansha Islands and its adjacent waters. The so-called "GSEC101" is situated in the waters of China's Nansha Islands. The aforementioned act of the Philippine side has seriously infringed upon China's sovereignty and sovereign rights and goes contrary to its commitments on the South China Sea issue and to the maintenance of peace and stability in the South China Sea. It is illegal, null and void.[676]

655. On 13 May 2010, China reiterated its objections in a further Note Verbale.[677]

656. On 1 March 2011, M/V Veritas Voyager, a Singaporean flagged seismic survey vessel, was engaged in conducting surveys for Forum Energy at Reed Bank, within the GSEC101 area, when it was approached by two China Marine Surveillance ("**CMS**") vessels (Zhongguo 71 and Zhongguo 75). As recorded by the Philippine Navy, the following events were reported by M/V Veritas Voyager:

- O/a 01 0549H March 2011, seven (7) Chinese fishing vessels and two (2) Marine surveillance vessels entered the survey area. These vessels came closer to the survey and chase vessels to have a look at the ongoing survey operations then headed away southward. One of the Veritas Voyager crew who knows how to speak Mandarin communicated with the marine surveillance vessels and was informed that they were on a routine surveillance patrol, and asked who they were and what they were doing.

- O/a 01 0509H March 2011, the two (2) marine surveillance vessels followed the Veritas Voyager for an hour staying in the position at approximately two (2) Nautical Miles off its starboard beam. The two (2) vessels then increased speed and headed off southwest. The mandarin speaking crew onboard MV Veritas Voyager was able to communicate to the surveillance vessel on the details of their towed spread.

- O/a 02 0942H March 2011, the two (2) (Chinese) surveillance vessels approached MV Veritas Voyager again and informed them that they are operating in the territorial waters of China under the UN charter. The Party Manager replied that the Veritas Voyager was operating in the territory of the Philippines with all the required permits. The Marine surveillance vessels then ordered the Veritas Voyager to stop the production and leave the area. After consultation with CGGV senior management, the Party Manager, informed the Chinese Surveillance vessels that they would stop production and proceed to the recovery area.

- O/a 021018H March 2011, MV Veritas Voyager reported that they terminated the operation as of 0936H due to the two Chinese Surveillance vessels that have been tracking them and insisting that they should stop the survey. The Mandarin speaking navigator onboard the Voyager explained what they were working for

---

[675]   Forum Energy plc, "SC72 Recto Bank (Formerly GSEC101)" (Annex 342).

[676]   Note Verbale from the Embassy of the People's Republic of China in Manila to the Department of Foreign Affairs, Republic of the Philippines, No. (10) PG-047 (22 February 2010) (Annex 195).

[677]   Note Verbale from the Embassy of the People's Republic of China in Manila to the Department of Foreign Affairs, Republic of the Philippines, No. (10) PG-137 (13 May 2010) (Annex 196).

Forum Energy on a permitted survey area. However, the Chinese surveillance vessels demanded them to stop immediately and leave the area, stating that according to UN treaty, MV Veritas Voyager is operating in waters belonging to the People's Republic of China. Hence the crew of MV Veritas Voyager told them that they would stop the acquisition. In addition, the Chinese vessels have made aggressive actions against the MV Veritas Voyager by steering at a direct course (Head on) and turning away at the last minute.[678]

657. On 2 March 2011, the Philippines delivered to China a Note Verbale objecting to the incident in the following terms:

At 9:36 a.m. today, 2 March 2011, two Chinese surveillance vessels "Zhongguo 71 and 75" threatened a Philippine-authorized seismic survey vessel operating in Philippine waters around Reed Bank, and demanded that it stop its activities and immediately leave the area.

The area where the incident took place has the following coordinates:

Corner	LAT	LONG
1	10°40'00"N	116°30'00"E
2	10°40'00"N	116°50'00"E
3	10°20'00"N	116°50'00"E
4	10°20'00"N	116°30'00"E

The Philippine Government views the aggressive actions of the Chinese vessels as a serious violation of Philippine sovereignty and maritime jurisdiction.[679]

658. On 9 March 2011, the Chargé d'Affaires of the Chinese Embassy called on the acting Assistant Secretary of Asia and Pacific Affairs of the Philippines. As recorded by the Philippines, the principal points conveyed by China in the conversation were as follows:

1. China has indisputable sovereignty over the waters of Nansha Islands where Reed Bank is situated

Since ancient times, China has indisputable sovereignty over the Nansha islands and its adjacent waters. The GSEC 101 (SC 72) area is situated in the adjacent waters of the Nansha Islands (Spratlys).

On 2 March, Chinese maritime surveillance vessels were in the area. The vessels dissuaded the Forum vessel from further work. This was an action that China had to take to safeguard its sovereignty and sovereign rights as a result of the unilateral action from the Philippine side.

2. [The Philippines] unilateral action in the area is contrary to its commitment to China. [The Philippines] has not given an official reply to Chinese representations on the matter

China has made repeated representations with the Philippines on the GSEC 101 issue since 2002. In 2007, 2009 and February 2010, former Foreign Affairs Secretary Romulo conveyed to China that [the Philippine]Government will not grant to Forum Energy the conversion of the GSEC 101 into a service contract. Secretary Romulo said that GSEC 101 will not be an issue in [Philippines]-China relations.

---

[678] Memorandum from Colonel, Philippine Navy, to Flag Officer in Command, Philippine Navy (March 2011) (Annex 69).

[679] Note Verbale from the Department of Foreign Affairs of the Republic of Philippines to the Embassy of the People's Republic of China in Manila, No. 110526 (2 March 2011) (Annex 198).

However, PH went against its commitment and converted GSEC 101 into a service contract in February 2010. China made repeated representations for the cancellation of the contract, but [the Philippines]declined to reply officially to Chinese representations. Forum is now pursuing activities in the area.

3. In consideration of overall bilateral relations, China has exercised restraint and sincerity on the issue

Looking at the issue from the context of maintaining the overall good relations between [the Philippines]and China, and maintaining peace and stability in the area, China has exercised maximum self-restraint and sincerity on the issue.

Its vessels left the area in order to avoid escalating the issue. This demonstrates China's goodwill and sincerity in wanting to maintain good relations with [the Philippines].

4. China is willing to have cooperation with [the Philippines] following the principle of "setting aside disputes and pursuing joint development"

China expressed willingness to have cooperation in the area by following the principle of "shelving disputes and pursuing joint development" as a prerequisite for cooperation.

5. Is it [the Philippines'] intention to escalate tensions by undertaking high profile unilateral actions?

Since February 2010, [the Philippines] has not replied officially to Chinese representations on the matter but proceeded to undertake unilateral action by sending the seismic survey ship to conduct activities. It even sent military and coast guard vessels to the area. China is perplexed and disappointed with Philippine actions. Does the Philippines want to escalate the issue?

6. [The Philippines] is not handling the issue in a low profile manner. To avoid creating bigger pressures on the options of both governments, [the Philippines] should properly guide media reporting on the 2 March 2011 incident in a positive way

Contrary to [Philippine Department of Foreign Affairs] commitment to handle the GSEC 101 issue in a low profile manner, Wescom Commander General Sabban gave strongly-worded statements to the media. An unidentified [Philippine Department of Foreign Affairs] official also divulged the CDA's meeting with Undersecretary Basilio to the media. These reports have hugged headlines and aroused the attention of both peoples.

Such action is not conducive to the resolution of the issue in a low profile manner and has created bigger pressures from the media on the solutions of both Governments to the problem. It has created unnecessary impediments for both sides to find a way out of the issue. If not handled well, the issue will further escalate and may bring unpleasant results for both sides, which is dangerous.

China requests that [the Philippines]actively guide media reporting in a positive way so that the issue will not be played up.

7. The [South China Sea] issue is the only outstanding issue in [Philippines]China relations. Both countries should look at the issue from a higher and broader Vantage point

The [South China Sea] issue is the only outstanding issue between [the Philippines] and China. It is a difficult issue that could undermine bilateral relations. In handling the issue, both countries should proceed from the overall pursuit of maintaining close and cooperative relations, and maintaining peace and stability in the area.[680]

659. From 22 to 24 March 2011, the Secretary-General of the Philippines' Commission on Maritime and Ocean Affairs Secretariat, visited Beijing for consultations with the Director-General of the Ocean and Boundary Affairs Department of the Chinese Ministry of Foreign Affairs. As recorded by the Philippines, the following views were expressed concerning the Reed Bank incident:

> 2. On the Reed Bank/GSEC 101 Issue
>
> China stated that it has sovereignty over the so-called "Nansha Islands." According to them, "Nansha" is a "comprehensive whole" that includes the Reed Bank. China is concerned with the survey and exploration that are reportedly being undertaken by [the Philippines] in the GSEC 101 area. China cannot and will never accept this. China has always approached the issue from a broader perspective and adopted an attitude of restraint. This however should not be misinterpreted by other countries as a reason to undertake unilateral action on the area. If this happens, China will have reason to do exploration as well on areas it deems as its own. Joint development is the best and most practical way to approach the issue pending the resolution of the disputes. China is open to any [Philippine] proposal on this matter.
>
> [The Philippines] expressed the view that while its relations with China is an important component of [Philippine] foreign policy, the same should be founded on mutual respect for each other's sovereignty and dignity. In this context, [the Philippines] stated the following points:
>
> • [The Philippines] exercises sovereignty and jurisdiction over the Kalayaan Island Group (KIG).
>
> • Even while [the Philippines] exercises sovereignty and jurisdiction over the KIG, nonetheless; the Reed Bank—where GSEC 101/SC 72 is situated—is not part of the "adjacent waters" of the Spratlys (Nansha) islands, using UNCLOS as a standard.
>
> • Reed bank is neither an island nor a rock nor a low tide elevation. It is completely submerged under water and a continental shelf by definition. Indeed, it is part of the continental shelf of Palawan.
>
> • [The Philippines], in the context of friendly relations with China, is open to Chinese investment in the Reed Bank under [Philippine] laws.
>
> • However, with respect to the disputed features (*e.g.*, islands, islets) in the Spratlys, [the Philippines] is open to exploring possible modalities or mechanisms for managing disputes in the said area including ideas on joint cooperation.[681]

660. On 4 April 2011, the Philippines responded formally to China's Notes Verbales of February and May 2010, stating as follows:

---

[680] Memorandum from the Acting Assistant Secretary for Asian and Pacific Affairs, Department of Foreign Affairs, Republic of the Philippines, to the Secretary of Foreign Affairs (10 March 2011) (Annex 70) (emphasis removed from original).

[681] Memorandum from the Secretary General, Commission on Maritime and Ocean Affairs Secretariat, Department of Foreign Affairs, Republic of the Philippines, to the Secretary of Foreign Affairs of the Republic of the Philippines (28 March 2011) (Annex 71) (emphasis removed from original).

FIRST, the Republic of the Philippines has sovereignty and jurisdiction over the Kalayaan Island Group (KIG);

SECOND, even while the Republic of the Philippines has sovereignty and jurisdiction over the KIG, the Reed Bank where GSEC 101 is situated does not form part of the "adjacent waters," specifically the 12 M territorial waters of any relevant geological feature in the KIG either under customary international law or the United Nations Convention on the Law of the Sea (UNCLOS);

THIRD, Reed Bank is not an island, a rock, or a low tide elevation. Rather, Reed Bank is a completely submerged bank that is part of the continental margin of Palawan. Accordingly, Reed Bank, which is about 85 M from the nearest coast of Palawan and about 595 M from the coast of Hainan, forms part of the 200 M continental shelf of the Philippine archipelago under UNCLOS;

FOURTH, Articles 56 and 77 of UNCLOS provides that the coastal or archipelagic State exercises sovereign rights over its 200 M Exclusive Economic Zone and 200 M Continental Shelf. As such, the Philippines exercises exclusive sovereign rights over the Reed Bank.

Therefore, the action of the Philippine Department of Energy is fully consistent with international law. It does not impinge on the sovereignty of the People's Republic of China, or violate the ASEAN-China Declaration of Conduct on the South China Sea (DOC). . . .[682]

ii.   The West Calamian Petroleum Block

661. On 12 January 2006, the Philippine Department of Energy issued Service Contract 58 to PNOC Exploration Corporation ("**PNOC**") in respect of the West Calamian block adjacent to Palawan.[683] The location of SC58 is depicted in Map 4 on page 269 below. PNOC was joined by Nido Petroleum Ltd. ("**Nido**") as operator of the block.[684]

662. On 24 March 2010, Nido announced that it would commence multi beam and sea bed coring in SC58.[685]

663. On 30 July 2010, the Deputy Chief of Mission of the Chinese Embassy called on the Secretary-General of the Philippines' Commission on Maritime and Ocean Affairs Secretariat. As recorded by the Philippines, China made the following representations:

---

[682]   Note Verbale from the Department of Foreign Affairs, Republic of the Philippines, to the Embassy of the People's Republic of China in Manila, No. 110885 (4 April 2011) (Annex 199).

[683]   Department of Energy of the Republic of the Philippines and PNOC Exploration Corporation, West Calamian Block Service Contract No. 58 (12 January 2006) (Annex 335).

[684]   *See* PNOC Exploration Corporation *available at* <pnoc-ec.com.ph/service-contract-no-58-west-calamian/>.

[685]   Letter from Country Representative, Nido Petroleum, to the Office of the Undersecretary, Department of Energy of the Republic of Philippines (7 October 2013) (Annex 340).

Nido Petroleum Ltd. and Service Contract 54

o   Chinese authorities have received reports that Australian company Nido Petroleum
        Ltd. is planning to sell crude oil that it extracted from the Tindalo oil well, which is
        covered by Service Contract 54a. It plans to start selling the oil this August 2010.

o   Mr. Bai Tian [the Deputy Chief of Mission of the Chinese Embassy] further asserted
        that Service Contract 54, 14, 58, 63, and other nearby service contracts are located
        "deep within China's 9-dash line." China considers the Philippines as violating and
        encroaching on China's sovereignty and sovereign rights in these areas.

o   China is requesting for detailed information on these service contracts.

o   China considers this as a very serious matter and that it reserves the right to
        unilaterally act on this matter to protect their interests.

o   China will send the Philippines a Note Verbale on this issue.[686]

664. On 6 August 2010, the First Secretary of the Chinese Embassy, Mr. Yongsheng Li, met with
     Nido's Vice-President, Mr. Leonardo M. Ote. As later memorialised by Nido:

> During the meeting, Mr. Yongsheng showed Mr. Ote a copy of China's 9-dash-line map
> and informed the latter that all areas within that map are being claimed by PRC, including
> those areas covered by Nido's existing service contracts with the Philippine Government.
> Mr. Ote informed Mr. Yongsheng that Nido is a service contractor which derives its
> licenses and permits from the [Philippine Department of Energy]. Mr. Ote suggested that
> Mr. Yongsheng discuss any claims with the [Philippine Department of Energy]. Nido has
> not heard from Mr. Yongsheng since then.[687]

665. In September 2011, according to Nido, COSL, a Chinese service contractor, wrote to Nido's
     Operations Manager for SC 54 "signifying its refusal to conduct any seismic activity in SC54
     and SC58 due to PRC's territorial claims in the said areas."[688]

iii.   The North-West Palawan Petroleum Blocks

666. On 30 June 2011, the Philippine Department of Energy launched the Fourth Philippine Energy
     Contracting Round (PECR 4) and offered 15 petroleum blocks for exploration and development
     by companies, including two blocks in the South China Sea to the north-west of Palawan
     ("**Area 3**" and "**Area 4**"), immediately to seaward of SC58.[689] The locations of Area 3 and
     Area 4 are depicted in Map 4 on page 269 below.

---

[686]   Memorandum from the Undersecretary for Special and Ocean Concerns, Department of Foreign Affairs,
        Republic of the Philippines, to the Secretary of Foreign Affairs of the Republic of the Philippines (30 July
        2010) (Annex 63).

[687]   Letter from Country Representative, Nido Petroleum, to the Office of the Undersecretary, Department of
        Energy of the Republic of Philippines (7 October 2013) (Annex 340).

[688]   Letter from Country Representative, Nido Petroleum, to the Office of the Undersecretary, Department of
        Energy of the Republic of Philippines (7 October 2013) (Annex 340).

[689]   Deloitte LLP, "Fourth Philippine Energy Contracting Round (PECR 4) 2011" (2011) (Annex 336).

667. On 6 July 2011, China delivered to the Philippines a Note Verbale, objecting to the tender in the following terms:

> On 30 June 2011, at the launching of Fourth Philippine Energy Contracting Round (PECR4), the Department of Energy of the Philippines offered 15 petroleum blocks to local and international companies for exploration and development. Among the aforesaid blocks, AREA 3 and AREA 4 are situated in the waters of which China has historic titles including sovereign rights and jurisdiction.
>
> China has indisputable sovereignty, sovereign rights, and jurisdiction over the islands in South China Sea including Nansha Islands and its adjacent waters. The action of the Philippine Government has seriously infringed on China's sovereignty and sovereign rights, violated the Declaration on the Conduct of Parties in the South China Sea (DOC), cannot but complicate the disputes and affect stability in the South China Sea.
>
> The Chinese side urges the Philippine side to immediately withdraw the bidding offer for AREA 3 and AREA 4, refrain from any action that infringes on China's sovereignty and sovereign rights and violates the DOC, and honor its commitment to peace and stability in this region.[690]

(b) Alleged Interference with Living Resources

668. China has also acted to assert its jurisdiction over fisheries in the South China Sea and to restrict fishing by Philippine nationals in areas within 200 nautical miles of the Philippines' baselines.

i. China's Prevention of Fishing by Philippine Vessels at Mischief Reef

669. Beginning in 1995, China undertook the construction of certain elevated structures on the reef platform at Mischief Reef. According to the Philippines, "[i]n relation to Mischief Reef, China has acted to prevent Filipino fishermen from fishing there ever since it took physical control of the reef in 1995."[691]

670. In August 1995, representatives of the Philippines and China held "Bilateral Consultations on the South China Sea Issue," addressing among other issues Mischief Reef. The Agreed Minutes of those consultations record the Philippine representatives' declaration that "previous to the Chinese occupation of Mischief Reef, Filipino fishermen had been freely using the Mischief Reef as shelter."[692]

---

[690] Note Verbale from the Embassy of the People's Republic of China in Manila to the Department of Foreign Affairs, Republic of the Philippines, No. (11) PG-202 (6 July 2011) (Annex 202).

[691] Merits Hearing Tr. (Day 2), p. 156.

[692] Government of the Republic of the Philippines and Government of the People's Republic of China, *Agreed Minutes on the First Philippines-China Bilateral Consultations on the South China Sea Issue* (10 August 1995) (Annex 180).

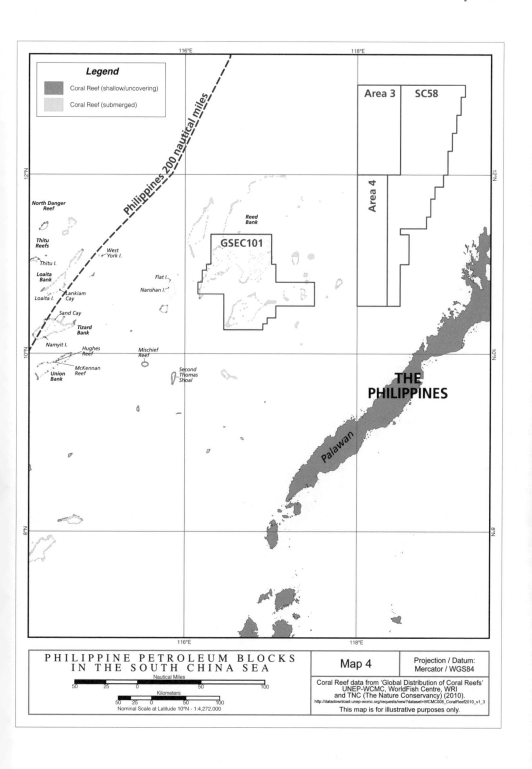

PHILIPPINE PETROLEUM BLOCKS
IN THE SOUTH CHINA SEA

Map 4

Projection / Datum:
Mercator / WGS84

Coral Reef data from 'Global Distribution of Coral Reefs'
UNEP-WCMC, WorldFish Centre, WRI
and TNC (The Nature Conservancy) (2010).
http://datadownload.unep-wcmc.org/requests/new?dataset=WCMC008_CoralReef2010_v1_3
This map is for illustrative purposes only.

this page intentionally blank

ii.   China's Extension of Jurisdiction over Fisheries in the South China Sea

671.   As noted in connection with the Tribunal's consideration of China's claim to historic rights, on 10 May 2012, the Fishery Bureau of Nanhai District under the Chinese Ministry of Agriculture announced a fishing moratorium in the South China Sea.   The announcement provided, in relevant part, as follows:

1.   All productive activity types, except for using single-layer gill net and line-fishing equipment, shall be prohibited from 16 May 12:00 p.m. until 1 August 12:00 p.m. in the South China Sea areas from 12° north latitude up to the "Common Boundary Line of Fujian-Guangdong Sea Areas" (including the Gulf of Tonkin) under the jurisdiction of the People's Republic of China.

2.   During the fishing moratorium, all fishing boats subject to the prohibition shall be moored at harbor with their nets folded without exception.   No unit may supply oil or ice to, or purchase, distribute, freeze or store fish from the fishing boats subject to the fishing moratorium.

3.   During the fishing moratorium, any fishing boat that holds Nansha Special Fishing Permits and goes to conduct fishing production in the sea areas of Nansha Islands south of 12° north latitude must strictly follow the reporting system in its entry and exit of sea ports, and any production activities in the sea area prohibited under the fishing moratorium.

4.   Those who violate the fishing moratorium regulations by carrying out fishing activities shall have their fishing catch and any illegal gains derived therefrom confiscated and a fine of up to 50,000 yuan shall be imposed; if the circumstances are serious, their fishing equipment shall be confiscated and their fishing permit shall be revoked; if the circumstances are especially serious their fishing boat may be confiscated; if it constitutes a crime, their criminal responsibility shall be investigated according to law.[693]

672.   The fishing ban was also announced by Xinhua, the official press agency of China, which stated that the ban applied "in most parts of the South China Sea as part of ongoing efforts to rehabilitate the area's marine resources . . . including Huangyan Island [Scarborough Shoal] but excluding most of the Nansha Islands."[694]   The Xinhua announcement further reported that "[t]he fishing ban is also applicable to foreign ships.   A spokesman from the fishery bureau under the [Ministry of Agriculture] said earlier this week that fishing activity conducted by foreign ships in banned areas will be seen as a 'blatant encroachment on China's fishery resources.'"[695]

---

[693]   People's Republic of China, Ministry of Agriculture, South China Sea Fishery Bureau, *Announcement on the 2012 Summer Ban on Marine Fishing in the South China Sea Maritime Space* (10 May 2012) (Annex 118).

[694]   "Fishing ban starts in South China Sea," *Xinhua* (17 May 2012) (Annex 318).

[695]   "Fishing ban starts in South China Sea," *Xinhua* (17 May 2012) (Annex 318).

673. On 14 May 2012, the Philippines issued the following statement: "Our position is we do not recognize China's fishing ban in as much as portions of the ban encompass our Exclusive Economic Zone (EEZ)."[696]

674. On 27 November 2012, the Standing Committee of Hainan Provincial People's Congress revised "The Hainan Provincial Regulation on the Control of Coastal Border Security" ("the **Hainan Regulation**").[697] As an administrative matter, China considers the Spratly and Paracel Islands, as well as Scarborough Shoal to form part of Hainan Province, since 2012 as part of the city of Sansha.[698] As revised, the Hainan Regulation provides as follows:

> **Article 2** The Regulation is applicable to the border security control in the sea areas and coastal areas within the jurisdiction of the Hainan Province. If any matter is otherwise regulated by other laws or administrative regulations, such laws or administrative regulations shall apply to the matter.
>
> . . .
>
> **Article 31** When entering the sea areas within the jurisdiction of the Hainan Province, all foreign ships and the people on the foreign ships shall obey the laws and regulations of the People's Republic of China, and shall not have the following actions that breach the control of coastal border security:
>
> (1) Illegally stop or anchor when passing the sea areas under the jurisdiction of the Hainan Province, or take provocative acts;
>
> (2) Enter or exit the border without inspection and approval, or change the entry or exit ports without approval;
>
> (3) Illegally board any of the islands and reefs within the jurisdiction of the Hainan Province;
>
> (4) Damage marine defense facilities or production and living facilities on the islands and reefs within the jurisdiction of the Hainan Province;
>
> (5) Engage in propaganda activities that violate national sovereignty or endanger national security; or
>
> (6) Conduct any other actions that breach the control of coastal border security as specified by other laws or regulations.
>
> . . .
>
> **Article 47** If a foreign ship and the people on the foreign ship have one of the following circumstances as specified in Article 31, the authorities of the public security border can legally take such measures as boarding the ship, conducting inspection, detention,

---

[696]   *Philippine Statement on the Inclusion of Bajo de Masinloc and the Philippine Exclusive Economic Zone in China's Fishing Ban* (14 May 2012), *available at* <www.gov.ph/2012/05/14/philippine-statement-on-the-inclusion-of-bajo-de-masinloc-and-the-philippine-exclusive-economic-zone-in-chinas-fishing-ban-may-14-2012/>.

[697]   People's Republic of China, Hainan Province, *Hainan Provincial Regulation on the Control of Coastal Border Security* (31 December 2012) (Annex 123).

[698]   "China establishes Sansha City," *Xinhua*, 24 July 2012, *available at* <en.hainan.gov.cn/englishgov/News/201208/t20120801_734629.html>.

deportation, or ordering to stop sailing, change the route or return the voyage. The involved ship or the auxiliary navigation equipment in the ship may be seized. Prosecution shall be conducted in accordance with relevant laws and regulations such as the *Law of the People's Republic of China on the Penalties for Public Security Administration and the Law of the People's Republic of China on the Control of Exit and Entry of the Border.*[699]

675. In November 2012, the Philippines delivered a Note Verbale to the Chinese Embassy in Manila, seeking clarification of the content the Hainan Regulation:

> The Philippines seeks clarification on the reported law and that foreign vessels illegally entering the waters under the jurisdiction of Hainan Province can be boarded, inspected, detained, confiscated, immobilized, and expelled, among other punitive actions.[700]

676. On 31 December 2012, an official spokesperson of China's Foreign Ministry stated that the Regulation would only be enforced within 12 nautical miles of Hainan's coast.[701]

677. In January 2013, the Philippines reiterated its request for clarification:

> The Philippines seeks clarification anew on the scope of Hainan's rules that there is no change from regulations passed in 1999 limiting enforcement to within 12 nautical miles of Hainan's coast, based on the recent pronouncements of Chinese Foreign Ministry Spokesperson Hua Chunying.
>
> The Philippines further seeks confirmation that the 12 nautical miles enforcement law is absolutely limited to the island of Hainan only.[702]

678. According to the Philippines, China has never formally clarified the intended scope of application of the Hainan Regulation.[703]

> *iii.   China's Prevention of Fishing by Philippine vessels at Second Thomas Shoal*

679. According to the Philippines, "after China took *de facto* control of Second Thomas Shoal in May 2013, it began interfering with Philippine fishing activities in the area."[704]

680. According to the Director of the Bureau of Fisheries and Aquatic Resources of the Philippines, the conduct of and laws enacted by the Chinese Government "have created a deep sense of fear

---

[699]   People's Republic of China, Hainan Province, *Hainan Provincial Regulation on the Control of Coastal Border Security* (31 December 2012) (Annex 123).

[700]   Note Verbale from the Department of Foreign Affairs of the Republic of Philippines to the Embassy of the People's Republic of China in Manila, No. 12-3391 (30 November 2012) (Annex 215).

[701]   "China says 'board and search' sea rules limited to Hainan coast," *Reuters* (31 December 2012) *available at* <in.reuters.com/article/china-seas-idINL4N0A51QH20121231>.

[702]   Note Verbale from the Department of Foreign Affairs of the Republic of Philippines to the Embassy of the People's Republic of China in Manila, No. 13-0011 (2 January 2013) (Annex 216).

[703]   Memorial, para. 6.34.

[704]   Memorial, para. 6.36.

among Filipino fishermen that has significantly curtailed their fishing activities and severely impacted their ability to earn a livelihood."[705]

3. The Philippines' Position

(a) Jurisdiction

681. According to the Philippines, "the only limitation on the Philippines' entitlement to an EEZ and continental shelf is to the extent that any nearby maritime features claimed by China might generate overlapping entitlements."[706] The Philippines submits that there are no maritime features in the South China Sea claimed by China that can generate entitlements to an exclusive economic zone in the areas relevant to its Submission No. 8.[707] For the Philippines, "all of the incidents . . . fall within areas that are indisputably Philippines' EEZ and continental shelf,"[708] and no issue of maritime delimitation is implicated.

682. The Philippines likewise submits that Article 297(3) of the Convention poses no bar to its claims because that Article (concerning jurisdiction over the living resources of the exclusive economic zone) does not restrict compulsory dispute settlement over disputes relating to the exclusive economic zone of the State making the claim. According to the Philippines, "Article 297(3)(a) does not impair the Tribunal's jurisdiction over this Submission in the first instance because China is not 'the coastal State' in those areas."[709] The Philippines also argues that Article 297(3) poses no bar to its claims regarding petroleum activities because "[b]y its terms, the exception applies only to disputes relating to a coastal State's sovereign rights with respect to 'the living resources' in the EEZ. Non-living resources are not covered."[710] Finally, the Philippines submits that the Tribunal's jurisdiction is not barred by the exception in Article 298(1)(b) for law enforcement activities for the same reason that the exception for living resources is not applicable: "In those areas, the Philippines—not China—enjoys the sovereign rights that UNCLOS accords. Submission No. 8 therefore does not implicate China's exercise

---

[705] Affidavit of A.G. Perez, Director, Bureau of Fisheries and Aquatic Resources, Republic of the Philippines (26 March 2014) (Annex 241).

[706] Merits Hearing Tr. (Day 2), p. 133.

[707] Merits Hearing Tr. (Day 2), pp. 96, 130-131.

[708] Merits Hearing Tr. (Day 2), p. 162.

[709] Supplemental Written Submission, para. 5.4.

[710] Supplemental Written Submission, para. 5.6.

of its sovereign rights as 'the coastal State', as Articles 297(3)(a) and 298(1)(b) would require."[711]

(b) The Philippines' Rights in the Exclusive Economic Zone

683. The Philippines submits that "the waters, seabed and subsoil of the South China Sea within 200 M of the Philippine coast, but beyond 12 M from any high-tide feature within the South China Sea, constitute the EEZ and continental shelf of the Philippines" under Articles 57 and 76 of the Convention because none of the maritime features claimed by China "generates entitlement to an EEZ or continental shelf."[712]

684. According to the Philippines, "[b]ecause the sovereign rights and jurisdiction of the coastal State in both the continental shelf and EEZ are exclusive, no other State may interfere with their use or enjoyment."[713] The Philippines submits that "China's interference with oil and gas exploration and exploitation, and the measures adopted to prevent fishing in the Philippines' EEZ and continental shelf, constitute . . . continuing violations of . . . Articles 56, 58, 61, 62, 73, 77 and 81" of the Convention.[714]

i. Interference with Rights to Non-Living Resources

685. The Philippines argues that China's assertiveness in "its claim to 'historic rights' over all the waters, seabed, and subsoil within the so-called 'nine-dash line'" has interfered with the Philippines' enjoyment and exercise of its sovereign rights and jurisdiction under the Convention.[715] The Philippines submits that the following actions by China constitute violations of the Philippines' sovereign rights and jurisdiction:

(a) China's objection to the conversion of the Philippines' contract with Sterling Energy for exploration of oil and gas deposits within the GSEC101 block into a service contract (see paragraphs 652 to 655 above);[716]

(b) The "aggressive manoeuvres" by two CMS vessels towards the MV Veritas Voyager on 2 March 2011 (see paragraphs 656 to 659 above);

---

[711] Supplemental Written Submission, para. 9.11.

[712] Memorial, para. 6.6; Merits Hearing Tr. (Day 2), pp. 132-134.

[713] Memorial, para. 6.14.

[714] Merits Hearing Tr. (Day 2), p. 161.

[715] Memorial, para. 6.15.

[716] *See* Memorial, paras. 6.17-6.19; Merits Hearing Tr. (Day 2), pp. 140-142.

(c)   China's objection to Service Contract 58 in respect of the West Calamian petroleum block and its efforts to dissuade Nido from working in the area (see paragraph 661 to 665 above);

(d)   China's objection to the 2011 tender for the Area 3 and 4 petroleum blocks, north-west of Palawan (see paragraphs 666-667).

ii.   Interference with Rights to Living Resources

686.   The Philippines further argues that China has interfered with the Philippines' sovereign rights and jurisdiction to exploit the living resources of its maritime zones by enacting and enforcing "laws and regulations that purport to extend China's law enforcement jurisdiction, including over fishing resources, throughout the entire area encompassed by the nine-dash line."[717] According to the Philippines, this has created "a cloud of uncertainty which has had a substantial chilling effect on the activities of Philippine fishermen" as well as "an environment of insecurity . . . among all coastal States in the South China Sea."[718] The Philippines objects specifically to:

(a)   China's prevention of fishing by Philippine vessels at Mischief Reef since 1995 (see paragraphs 669 to 670 above);

(b)   The 2012 moratorium on fishing in the South China Sea north of 12°N latitude (see paragraphs 671 to 673 above);

(c)   China's revision of the Hainan Regulation (see paragraphs 674 to 678 above);

(d)   China's prevention of fishing by Philippine vessels at Second Thomas Shoal since 1995 (see paragraphs 679 to 680 above).

4.   China's Position

687.   China has not directly stated its position with respect to the allegations presented in the Philippines' Submission No. 8. Nevertheless, China's position can be discerned from its public statements at the time of the incidents in question.

---

[717]   Memorial, para. 6.29; Merits Hearing Tr. (Day 2), pp. 150, 155-156.

[718]   Memorial, paras. 6.29, 6.35; Merits Hearing Tr. (Day 2), pp. 154, 156, 158.

688. With respect to the Philippines' petroleum exploration, it is apparent that China considers that it—and not the Philippines—has rights in the areas in question:

(a) Regarding the GSEC101 contract at Reed Bank, China stated that "China has indisputable sovereignty, sovereign rights and jurisdiction over Nansha Islands and its adjacent waters. The so-called 'GSEC101' is situated in the waters of China's Nansha Islands."[719]

(b) Regarding the SC58 contract, China is recorded as having stated that "Service Contract 54, 14, 58, 63, and other nearby service contracts are located 'deep within China's 9-dash line.' China considers the Philippines as violating and encroaching on China's sovereignty and sovereign rights in these areas."[720]

(c) And, regarding the Area 3 and Area 4 tender, China stated that "AREA 3 and AREA 4 are situated in the waters of which China has historic titles including sovereign rights and jurisdiction."[721]

689. China's statements with respect to fisheries likewise make clear that China considers that it has sovereign rights in the areas in question. Thus, China's Ministry of Agriculture is reported to have stated that fishing by foreign vessels in the South China Sea north of 12° N latitude constitutes "blatant encroachment on China's fishery resources."[722]

5. The Tribunal's Considerations

(a) The Tribunal's Jurisdiction

690. In its Award on Jurisdiction, the Tribunal held that Submission No. 8 reflects a dispute concerning "China's actions that allegedly interfere with the Philippines' petroleum exploration, seismic surveys, and fishing in what the Philippines claims as its exclusive economic zone."[723] The Tribunal noted that this is not a dispute concerning sovereignty, nor is it barred from the Tribunal's consideration by any requirement of Section 1 of Part XV.[724]

---

[719] Note Verbale from the Embassy of the People's Republic of China in Manila to the Department of Foreign Affairs, Republic of the Philippines, No. (10) PG-047 (22 February 2010) (Annex 195).

[720] Memorandum from the Undersecretary for Special and Ocean Concerns, Department of Foreign Affairs, Republic of the Philippines, to the Secretary of Foreign Affairs of the Republic of the Philippines (30 July 2010) (Annex 63).

[721] Note Verbale from the Embassy of the People's Republic of China in Manila to the Department of Foreign Affairs, Republic of the Philippines, No. (11) PG-202 (6 July 2011) (Annex 202).

[722] "Fishing ban starts in South China Sea," *Xinhua* (17 May 2012) (Annex 318).

[723] Award on Jurisdiction, para. 405.

[724] Award on Jurisdiction, para. 405.

691. The Tribunal also found that the dispute at issue in Submission No. 8 does not concern the delimitation of maritime boundaries. As with Submission No. 5, the Tribunal noted that the premise of Submission No. 8 is "that no overlapping entitlements exist because only the Philippines possesses an entitlement to an exclusive economic zone in the relevant areas."[725] The Tribunal is not asked to delimit overlapping entitlements in the areas in question. Rather, its jurisdiction is contingent on the absence of any possible overlap. Had the Tribunal found that another maritime feature claimed by China within 200 nautical miles of the relevant areas were a fully entitled island for purposes of Article 121 of the Convention and capable of generating an entitlement to an exclusive economic zone and continental shelf, it would necessarily have had to decline jurisdiction over the dispute.

692. The Tribunal has found, however, (see paragraphs 230 to 278 above) that there is no legal basis for any Chinese historic rights, or other sovereign rights and jurisdiction beyond those provided for in the Convention, in the waters of the South China Sea encompassed by the 'nine-dash line' and that none of the high-tide feature in the Spratly Islands is a fully entitled island for the purposes of Article 121 of the Convention (see paragraphs 473 to 626 above). There is thus no maritime feature in the Spratly Islands that is capable of generating an entitlement to an exclusive economic zone or continental shelf in the areas of Mischief Reef or Second Thomas Shoal, or in the areas of the GSEC101 block, Area 3, Area 4, or the SC58 block.

693. The Tribunal has also found (see paragraphs 374 to 381 above) that Mischief Reef and Second Thomas Shoal are low-tide elevations and, as such, generate no entitlement to maritime zones of their own. Additionally, Reed Bank (the area of the GSEC101 block) is an entirely submerged reef formation that cannot give rise to maritime entitlements.[726] Nor is there any high-tide feature claimed by China within 12 nautical miles of Area 3, Area 4, or the SC58 block that could generate an entitlement to a territorial sea in those areas.

694. From these conclusions, it follows that there exists no legal basis for any entitlement by China to maritime zones in the area of Mischief Reef, Second Thomas Shoal, the GSEC101 block, Area 3, Area 4, or the SC58 block. There is thus no situation of overlapping entitlements that would call for the application of Articles 15, 74, or 83 to delimit the overlap and no possible basis for the application of the exception to jurisdiction in Article 298(1)(a)(i).

---

[725] Award on Jurisdiction, para. 405.

[726] *See, e.g.*, Chinese Chart 10019 (Annex NC3), Chinese Chart 18050 (Annex NC21); Navigation Guarantee Department of the Chinese Navy Headquarters, *China Sailing Directions: South China Sea* (A103) (2011) (Annex 232(bis)); United Kingdom Hydrographic Office, *Admiralty Sailing Directions: China Sea Pilot (NP31)*, Vol. 2 (10th ed., 2012) (Annex 235).

695. Because the areas of the South China Sea at issue for Submission No. 8 can only constitute the exclusive economic zone of the Philippines, the Tribunal also considers that Article 297(3)(a) and the law enforcement exception in Article 298(1)(b) of the Convention pose no obstacle to its jurisdiction. These provisions serve to limit compulsory dispute settlement where a claim is brought against a State's exercise of its sovereign rights in respect of living resources in its *own* exclusive economic zone. These provisions do not apply where a State is alleged to have violated the Convention in respect of the exclusive economic zone of another State. The Tribunal therefore concludes that it has jurisdiction with respect to the Philippines' Submission No. 8.

(b) China's Actions and the Philippines' Sovereign Rights

696. In the Tribunal's view, the core of the Parties' dispute with respect to living and non-living resources lies in their differing understandings of their respective rights in the areas of the South China Sea within 200 nautical miles of the Philippines' baselines that are encompassed by the 'nine-dash line'. It is apparent that the Philippines and China have each proceeded on the basis that it, and not the other, has exclusive rights to resources and have acted accordingly.

697. As discussed above, the effect of China's objection to compulsory dispute settlement for maritime delimitation is that the Tribunal could only address this Submission if the respective maritime entitlements of the Parties could be established and if no overlap requiring delimitation were found to exist. Jurisdiction has been established only because the allocation of rights under the Convention is unequivocal. Thus, the Tribunal has found that Mischief Reef, Second Thomas Shoal, the GSEC101 block, Area 3, Area 4, or the SC58 block all fall within areas where only the Philippines possesses possible entitlements to maritime zones under the Convention. The relevant areas can only constitute the exclusive economic zone and continental shelf of the Philippines. Accordingly, the Philippines—and not China—possesses sovereign rights with respect to resources in these areas.

698. The Convention is clear on the allocation of rights within the exclusive economic zone and continental shelf. With respect to non-living resources, Article 77 of the Convention provides that the "coastal State"—which in this case is necessarily the Philippines—"exercises over the continental shelf sovereign rights for the purpose of exploring it and exploiting its natural resources." The Convention goes on to make clear that "[t]he rights referred to . . . are exclusive in the sense that if the coastal State does not explore the continental shelf or exploit its natural resources, no one may undertake these activities without the express consent of the coastal State." These provisions are unequivocal and require no further interpretation. Within

its continental shelf, only the Philippines, or another State acting with its permission, may exploit the resources of the sea-bed.

699. The rights of other States in the waters above the continental shelf and with respect to submarine cables and pipelines are expressly detailed in Articles 78 and 79 of the Convention. Nothing in these Articles permits any State to prevent another State from exercising sovereign rights over its own continental shelf.

700. The same clarity is evident with respect to living resources and the provisions of the exclusive economic zone. Article 56 is clear in allocating to the coastal State—which again is necessarily the Philippines in the areas in question—"sovereign rights for the purpose of exploring and exploiting, conserving and managing the natural resources, whether living or non-living, of the waters superjacent to the seabed and of the seabed and its subsoil, and with regard to other activities for the economic exploitation and exploration of the zone . . . ." The rights of other States in the exclusive economic zone are detailed in Article 58 and are limited to "navigation and overflight and of the laying of submarine cables and pipelines, and other internationally lawful uses of the sea related to these freedoms." The rights of other States do not include restricting a coastal State from exploiting the living resources of its own exclusive economic zone. Indeed, the very notion is incompatible with the concept of sovereign rights and the exclusive jurisdiction over fisheries that was the central objective motivating the introduction of the exclusive economic zone concept (see paragraphs 248 to 254 above).

701. Having established the applicable law and the allocation of rights, the Tribunal now turns to the events underpinning the Philippines' claim.

i.   *Acts in relation to Non-Living Resources*

702. In the case of non-living resources, the Philippines has identified three distinct types of conduct on the part of China that it considers to violate its sovereign rights to the continental shelf: (a) diplomatic statements, in the form of China's objections to the Philippines Government regarding the conversion of the GSEC101 contract, the SC58 contract, and the tender for Area 3 and Area 4; (b) a statement by a Chinese official to a representative of Nido Petroleum Ltd. to the effect that the area of Nido Petroleum's concession from the Philippines was claimed by China; and (c) actions by CMS vessels to order the M/V Veritas Voyager to halt operations and leave the area of Reed Bank.

703. The Tribunal notes that China's diplomatic communications, the statements of its diplomats, and the actions of government-operated ships, such as CMS vessels, are all attributable to China

as such. These actions constitute official acts of China. At the same time, however, the Tribunal reaches different conclusions with respect to the consequences of these actions.

704. As an initial matter, the Tribunal accepts that China has asserted its claim to rights in the waters within 200 nautical miles of the Philippines baselines in good faith. That the Tribunal disagrees with China's understanding of its rights and considers that there is no possible legal basis for China's claimed rights does not mean that China's understanding has not been genuinely held.

705. Correspondingly, the Tribunal does not consider that China's diplomatic communications, asserting China's understanding of its rights in the South China Sea pursuant to the Convention and international law, can themselves constitute breaches of the provisions of the Convention regarding the continental shelf. It is an altogether normal occurrence that States will have different understandings of their respective rights. If the expression of such differences were itself sufficient to place the State whose understanding of the law ultimately proved incorrect in breach of the underlying obligation, it would cast an unacceptable chill on the ordinary conduct of diplomacy. The Tribunal does not exclude that it could reach a different conclusion in the case of diplomatic statements claiming rights in bad faith, or in the case of attempts by one State to induce another to relinquish its rights through repeated statements, veiled threats, or diplomatic coercion. That, however, is not the case on the record before the Tribunal. Accordingly, the Tribunal concludes that China's diplomatic statements to the Philippines regarding their respective rights, although incorrect with respect to the law, do not constitute breaches of the Convention.

706. The Tribunal reaches the same conclusions with respect to the communications of the Chinese Embassy in Manila with Nido Petroleum Company (see paragraph 664 above). Even taking Nido's account of that conversation as fully accurate, the most that can be attributed to the Chinese diplomat in question is the statement that "all areas within [China's '9-dash line'] map are being claimed by PRC, including those areas covered by Nido's existing service contracts with the Philippine Government." [727] There is no evidence before the Tribunal that the conversation included any efforts to induce Nido to cease operations in the SC58 block, any indication of adverse consequences if Nido declined to do so, or even a request that Nido refrain from further operations. On the evidence before the Tribunal, China's representative merely informed Nido of China's claim. When Nido suggested that China take the matter up with the Philippine Department of Energy, China's representative left and did not return. The Tribunal

---

[727] Letter from Country Representative, Nido Petroleum, to the Office of the Undersecretary, Department of Energy of the Republic of Philippines (7 October 2013) (Annex 340).

considers that China's actions in merely informing a private party of its claims in the South China Sea do not, without more,[728] constitute breaches of the Convention.

707. The Tribunal reaches a different conclusion, however, with respect to China's actions in connection with the survey operations of M/V Veritas Voyager. The Tribunal accepts the Philippine Navy's contemporaneous record of events as accurate and notes that the key passage of that account records as follows:

> two (2) (Chinese) surveillance vessels approached MV Veritas Voyager again and informed them that they are operating in the territorial waters of China under the UN charter. The Party Manager replied that the Veritas Voyager was operating in the territory of the Philippines with all the required permits. The Marine surveillance vessels then ordered the Veritas Voyager to stop the production and leave the area. After consultation with CGGV senior management, the Party Manager, informed the Chinese Surveillance vessels that they would stop production and proceed to the recovery area.[729]

708. On these facts, the Tribunal does not consider that China's actions were limited to stating its understanding of the Parties' respective rights. Rather, China acted directly to induce M/V Veritas Voyager to cease operations and to depart from an area that constitutes part of the continental shelf of the Philippines. Prior to this, the Tribunal notes, China was unequivocally aware that there existed a difference of views regarding the Parties' respective entitlements in the South China Sea and, in particular, in the area of Reed Bank. On the account of China's own diplomats (as memorialised at the time by the Philippines), "China has made repeated representations with the Philippines on the GSEC 101 issue since 2002."[730] A dispute on this issue was evident, and the approach called for by the Convention was for the Parties to seek to resolve their differences through negotiations or the other modes of dispute resolution identified in Part XV of the Convention and the UN Charter. Instead, China sought to carry out its own understanding of its rights through the actions of its marine surveillance vessels. China having done so, the Tribunal considers that China's actions amount to a breach of Article 77 of the Convention, which accords sovereign rights to the Philippines with respect to its continental shelf in the area of Reed Bank (the area in question).

---

[728] The Tribunal notes that Nido's account also indicates that, approximately one year later, it was informed by a Chinese subcontractor that the subcontractor would not work in the area of the SC54 and SC58 blocks due to China's territorial claims. This is an action by a private party. There is no evidence before the Tribunal that would suggest that the actions of Nido's subcontractor are attributable to China.

[729] Memorandum from Colonel, Philippine Navy, to Flag Officer in Command, Philippine Navy (March 2011) (Annex 69).

[730] Memorandum from the Acting Assistant Secretary for Asian and Pacific Affairs, Department of Foreign Affairs, Republic of the Philippines, to the Secretary of Foreign Affairs (10 March 2011) (Annex 70).

ii.   Acts in relation to Living Resources

709.   In the case of living resources, the Tribunal notes that the Philippines has, again, identified several distinct types of conduct on the part of China that it considers to violate its sovereign rights in the exclusive economic zone. First, the Philippines objects to China's extension of its jurisdiction over fisheries in the South China Sea through the 2012 moratorium on fishing in the area north of 12° N latitude and through the Hainan Regulation. Second, the Philippines objects to China's prevention of fishing by Philippine vessels at Mischief Reef and Second Thomas Shoal.

710.   With respect to China's assertion of fisheries jurisdiction, the Tribunal asked the Philippines to clarify "[w]hether China has sought to enforce either the May 2012 fishing ban or the Regulations for the Management of Coastal Border Security in Hainan Province against Philippines fishing vessels and the specifics of such enforcement." [731]   In response, the Philippines asserted that China had done so.[732] As evidence of this, the Philippines advanced a Note Verbale from China in which China asserted its right to impose a fishing moratorium in the South China Sea, requested the Philippines to educate its fishermen to comply with the moratorium, and cautioned the Philippines that "Chinese law-enforcing authorities will strengthen their maritime patrols and other law-enforcing actions, investigate and punish the relevant fishing vessels and fishermen who violate the fishing moratorium in accordance with the law."[733] The Philippines also noted that "[s]tatements like that have a deeply chilling effect on Filipino fishermen and their activities."[734]

711.   As an initial matter, the Tribunal notes that the Note Verbale invoked by the Philippines dates from 6 July 2015. To the extent that diplomatic correspondence constitutes evidence of enforcement actions taken by China, the Note Verbale would relate, if at all, to the fishing moratorium imposed by China in the summer of 2015. The Philippines did not invoke any other evidence that would establish that the 2012 fishing moratorium was enforced against any Philippine fishing vessel in any area falling in the Philippines' exclusive economic zone, nor has the Tribunal seen any such indication in the record before it. Accordingly, the Tribunal considers that the relevant question is whether China's 2012 promulgation of the fishing

---

[731]   Letter from the Tribunal to the Parties (10 November 2015).

[732]   Merits Hearing Tr. (Day 2), p. 155.

[733]   Note Verbale from the Embassy of the People's Republic of China in Manila to the Department of Foreign Affairs, Republic of the Philippines, No. (15) PG-229 (6 July 2015) (Annex 580).

[734]   Merits Hearing Tr. (Day 2), p. 156.

moratorium itself, irrespective of whether the moratorium was directly enforced, infringes on the rights of the Philippines and constitutes a breach of the Convention.

712. On this question, the Tribunal considers that the adoption of legislation or the promulgation of the fishing moratorium as a regulation differs from the mere assertion of China's rights in its diplomatic communications with the Philippines. Examining the scope of application specified in the moratorium itself,[735] and noting the public reports to the effect that the ban would apply in "most parts of the South China Sea" and in the "areas north of the 12th parallel, including Huangyan Island [Scarborough Shoal],"[736] the Tribunal concludes that the moratorium was intended to apply to areas of the Philippines' exclusive economic zone north of 12° N latitude and was not limited to Chinese flagged vessels. In contrast to mere statements, the fishing moratorium established a realistic prospect that Filipino fisherman, seeking to exploit the resources of the Philippines' exclusive economic zone, could be exposed to the punitive measures spelled out in the moratorium, including the possible confiscation of the fishing vessel in question. The Tribunal considers that such developments may have a deterring effect on Filipino fishermen and their activities. In effect, the 2012 fishing moratorium constituted an assertion by China of jurisdiction in areas in which jurisdiction over fisheries is reserved to the Philippines through the operation of the provisions of the Convention concerning the exclusive economic zone. The Tribunal considers that such an assertion of jurisdiction amounts to a breach of Article 56 of the Convention, which accords sovereign rights to the Philippines with respect to the living resources of its exclusive economic zone.

713. The Tribunal reaches a different conclusion with respect to the Hainan Regulation. As an initial matter, the Tribunal sees no provision on the face of the Hainan Regulation that would restrict the rights of the Philippines over the resources of its exclusive economic zone. Moreover, the Tribunal notes that China has publicly stated that the regulation applies only within 12 nautical miles of Hainan.[737] The Tribunal does not consider that the Hainan Regulation infringes on the rights of the Philippines or amounts to a breach of the provisions of the Convention concerning the exclusive economic zone.

714. Finally, with respect to China's alleged prevention of Philippine vessels from fishing at Mischief Reef and Second Thomas Shoal, the Tribunal notes that there is a distinct lack of

---

[735] People's Republic of China, Ministry of Agriculture, South China Sea Fishery Bureau, *Announcement on the 2012 Summer Ban on Marine Fishing in the South China Sea Maritime Space* (10 May 2012) (Annex 118).

[736] *See* "Fishing ban starts in South China Sea," *Xinhua* (17 May 2012) (Annex 318).

[737] "China says 'board and search' sea rules limited to Hainan coast," *Reuters* (31 December 2012), *available at* <in.reuters.com/article/china-seas-idINL4N0A51QH20121231>.

evidence on this question in the record before it. Prior to the hearing, the Tribunal invited the Philippines to clarify "the specifics of the actions taken by China" to prevent fishing by Philippines vessels at Mischief Reef and Second Thomas Shoal.[738] The Philippines has stated with respect to Mischief Reef that "China has acted to prevent Filipino fishermen from fishing there ever since it took physical control of the reef in 1995."[739] The Philippines said China's actions to restrict Filipino fishing at Second Thomas Shoal "have also primarily taken place within 12 miles of Second Thomas Shoal ever since China took *de facto* control of that feature in May 2013."[740] The Philippines further stated that "Chinese marine surveillance vessels, navy warships and fishing administration vessels have surrounded the shoal. They have blocked Philippine vessels, including civilian vessels, from approaching Second Thomas Shoal."[741] With respect to evidence of these assertions, however, the Tribunal has reviewed the record identified by the Philippines and is not able to identify a single documented instance in which Chinese Government vessels acted to prevent Filipino fishermen from fishing at either Second Thomas Shoal or Mischief Reef.

715. The Tribunal hastens to emphasise that the absence of evidence on this point in the record before it does not mean that such events did not occur or that China's actions may not otherwise have dissuaded Filipino fishermen from approaching Second Thomas Shoal and Mischief Reef. The Tribunal can readily imagine that the presence of Chinese law enforcement vessels at both locations, combined with China's general claim to fisheries jurisdiction in the South China Sea, could well lead Filipino fishermen to avoid such areas. The Tribunal is not, however, prepared to find a violation of the Convention on this basis. The Tribunal considers that the Philippines has not established that China has prevented Filipino fishermen from fishing at Mischief Reef or Second Thomas Shoal and that, in this respect, the provisions of the Convention concerning fisheries are not implicated.

---

[738]   Letter from the Tribunal to the Parties, 10 November 2015.

[739]   Merits Hearing Tr. (Day 2), p. 156.

[740]   Merits Hearing Tr. (Day 2), p. 158.

[741]   Merits Hearing Tr. (Day 2), p. 158.

(c) Conclusion

716. Based on the considerations outlined above, the Tribunal finds that China has, through the operation of its marine surveillance vessels with respect to M/V Veritas Voyager on 1 to 2 March 2011 breached Article 77 of the Convention with respect to the Philippines' sovereign rights over the non-living resources of its continental shelf in the area of Reed Bank. The Tribunal further finds that China has, by promulgating its 2012 moratorium on fishing in the South China Sea, without exception for areas of the South China Sea falling within the exclusive economic zone of the Philippines and without limiting the moratorium to Chinese flagged vessels, breached Article 56 of the Convention with respect to the Philippines' sovereign rights over the living resources of its exclusive economic zone.

*   *   *

B. **ALLEGED FAILURE TO PREVENT CHINESE NATIONALS FROM EXPLOITING THE
PHILIPPINES' LIVING RESOURCES (SUBMISSION NO. 9)**

1. **Introduction**

717. In this Section, the Tribunal addresses the Parties' dispute concerning China's toleration of
fishing by Chinese vessels in the areas of the South China Sea located within the Philippines'
exclusive economic zone. This dispute is reflected in Submission No. 9 of the Philippines,
which requests the Tribunal to declare that:

> (9)   China has unlawfully failed to prevent its nationals and vessels from exploiting the
> living resources in the exclusive economic zone of the Philippines;

2. **Factual Background**

718. The Philippines' allegations in respect of this Submission concern developments at Mischief
Reef and Second Thomas Shoal, both of which are low-tide elevations lying within 200 nautical
miles of the Philippines' baselines.

719. Since 3 May 2013, China has maintained a significant presence of naval and CMS vessels near
Second Thomas Shoal. As reported by the Armed Forces of the Philippines:

> Starting 03 May 2013, China maintained the presence of at least two (2) vessels at Ayungin
> Shoal [Second Thomas Shoal]. Since then, two (2) PLA Navy frigates (BN 562 and 563)
> and five (5) CMLEA vessels (CMS BN 84, 167, 75, 71 and 8002) have been monitored
> deployed in the shoal and its outlying areas on a rotation basis.[742]

720. These government vessels have been accompanied by a number of fishing vessels. Thus on
4 May 2013, the Philippines' marine detachment maintained on the wreck of the BRP Sierra
Madre on Second Thomas Shoal reported the presence of "1 PLA Navy, 2 CMS, and 1 Chinese
steel-hulled fishing vessels . . . in the vicinity of Ayungin Shoal."[743] On 11 May 2013, the
Armed Forces of the Philippines reported the presence of:

> •   PLA Navy Frigate at vicinity 6 [nautical miles] northwest off Ayungin Detachment.
>
> •   2 CMS vessels at vicinity 7 [nautical miles] southeast off Ayungin Detachment;
>
> •   1 CMS vessel at vicinity 4 [nautical miles] north off Ayungin Detachment.
>
> •   1 Hainan-type Fishing Vessel at vicinity 3 [nautical miles] northeast off Ayungin
>   Detachment. and,

---

[742]   Armed Forces of the Philippines, *Near-occupation of Chinese Vessels of Second Thomas (Ayungin) Shoal
in the Early Weeks of May 2012* (May 2013) (Annex 94).

[743]   Armed Forces of the Philippines, *Near-occupation of Chinese Vessels of Second Thomas (Ayungin) Shoal
in the Early Weeks of May 2012* (May 2013) (Annex 94).

• 1 Hainan-type Fishing Vessel at vicinity 3NM south off Ayungin Detachment[744]

And on 16 May 2013, the Philippines Air Force reported several fishing vessels apparently at work in the vicinity of Second Thomas Shoal:

> PAF Nomad-22 MAS sighted JIANGHU V Missile Frigate 562 (DESIG JIANGMEN), CMS 84 and 167 in the vicinity of Ayungin shoal [Second Thomas Shoal], along with a steel-hulled Hainan fishing vessel and a suspected Hainan fishing vessel with three dinghies believed to be gathering corals and clams and dredging in the shoal.[745]

721. The Philippines' military has likewise reported the presence of Chinese fishing vessels, escorted by Chinese Government ships, at Mischief Reef, where China has maintained a presence since 1995. A Philippines' report from May 2013 notes as follows:

> at least 33 Chinese fishing vessels were said to have been fishing at the Chinese-occupied Mischief Reef and nearby features since 08 May 2013, escorted by a PLA Navy ship and CMS vessels . . . .[746]

3.   The Philippines' Position

722. The Philippines submits that the Tribunal has jurisdiction to consider its Submission No. 9, for the same reasons set out with respect to its Submission No. 8 (see paragraphs 681 to 682 above).

723. On the merits, the Philippines argues that China has violated its obligations under Article 56 of the Convention to respect the sovereign rights and jurisdiction of the Philippines by failing to prevent its nationals and vessels from exploiting the living resources of the Philippines' exclusive economic zone.

724. The Philippines argues that as China has established *de facto* control over areas of the South China Sea, it has acted to prevent fishing by Philippine vessels, while tolerating fishing by Chinese nationals and vessels, including in areas that comprise the Philippines' exclusive economic zone. Thus, according to the Philippines, "since 1995, when China seized and began occupying Mischief Reef, just 126 [nautical miles] off the coast of Palawan, it has prevented Philippines vessels from fishing there. In contrast, Chinese fishing vessels under China's protection have fished freely in the adjacent waters, even though they are part of the Philippines' EEZ."[747] Similarly, the Philippines argues, "after China took *de facto* control of Second Thomas Shoal in May 2013, it began interfering with Philippine fishing activities in the

---

[744] Armed Forces of the Philippines, *Near-occupation of Chinese Vessels of Second Thomas (Ayungin) Shoal in the Early Weeks of May 2012* (May 2013) (Annex 94).

[745] Armed Forces of the Philippines, *Near-occupation of Chinese Vessels of Second Thomas (Ayungin) Shoal in the Early Weeks of May 2012* (May 2013) (Annex 94).

[746] Armed Forces of the Philippines, *Near-occupation of Chinese Vessels of Second Thomas (Ayungin) Shoal in the Early Weeks of May 2012* (May 2013) (Annex 94).

[747] Memorial, para. 6.36.

area, while allowing fishing by Chinese vessels, notwithstanding that Second Thomas Shoal is part of the Philippines' EEZ."[748]

725. Pursuant to Article 56 of the Convention, the Philippines argues, "States have an obligation, acting in good faith, to take the measures necessary to prevent their nationals from exploiting the living resources in the EEZ of another State party."[749] In the Philippines' view, the scope of this duty "extends to such actions as are reasonably necessary to give full effect to the exclusive rights of the coastal State conferred by Article 56."[750]

726. The Philippines relies in particular on the *Fisheries Advisory Opinion* of the International Tribunal for the Law of the Sea,[751] emphasising the portions of that decision that recognise that a State has an obligation to ensure that its nationals and vessels comply with any conditions or regulations imposed by the coastal State when fishing within its exclusive economic zone and to ensure that vessels flying its flag do not engage in illegal, unreported, and unregulated ("**IUU**") fishing.[752] The Philippines also adopts the definition of the "obligation to ensure" set out in the Advisory Opinion, which provides that such an obligation is an obligation "to deploy adequate means, to exercise best possible efforts, to do the utmost."[753]

727. Applying this standard to the activities of Chinese fishermen, the Philippines submits that:

> Instead of adopting measures to prevent fishing, Chinese authorities have actively encouraged illegal and unregulated fishing by Chinese vessels in the Philippines' EEZ. In circumstances in which China has explicitly authorised its own vessels to engage in fishing activities in the EEZ of the Philippines, it simply cannot be said that China has "deployed adequate means" to prevent such fishing activity. Nor can it be said that China has "exercise[d] best possible efforts" to prevent illegal and unregulated fishing activities. And it certainly cannot be said that China has done "the utmost, to obtain [the] result" that its vessels shall not fish in the Philippines' EEZ.[754]

728. The Philippines concludes that "China is not *per se* responsible for the actions of its fishermen, 'but it is responsible for its own failure to control their illegal and damaging activities.'"[755] The

---

[748] Memorial, para. 6.36.

[749] Merits Hearing Tr. (Day 2), p. 160.

[750] Merits Hearing Tr. (Day 2), p. 160.

[751] *Request for Advisory Opinion submitted by the Sub-Regional Fisheries Commission, Advisory Opinion, 2 April 2015, ITLOS Reports 2015.*

[752] Merits Hearing Tr. (Day 4), pp. 85-86.

[753] Merits Hearing Tr. (Day 4), p. 86; *Request for Advisory Opinion submitted by the Sub-Regional Fisheries Commission, Advisory Opinion, 2 April 2015, ITLOS Reports 2015*, para. 129.

[754] Merits Hearing Tr. (Day 4), pp. 87-88.

[755] Merits Hearing Tr. (Day 4), p. 88.

Philippines considers that China's failure to control its fishermen amounts to a breach of the Convention that engages the State responsibility of China.[756]

4.   China's Position

729. As far as the Tribunal is aware, China has never directly addressed the allegation that it has unlawfully permitted its fishermen to fish within the Philippines' exclusive economic zone at Second Thomas Shoal or Mischief Reef.

730. Rather, the position that consistently appears in China's contemporaneous statements is that it does not consider the Philippines to have rights in the area of Second Thomas Shoal and Mischief Reef. Thus, in its diplomatic correspondence with the Philippines, China has stated generally that:

> China possesses indisputable sovereignty over Nansha Islands and its adjacent waters, and the construction, usage and other activities at the relevant islands, reefs, shoals and sands are actions completely within the scope of China's sovereignty, sovereign rights and jurisdiction.[757]

731. China has repeatedly demanded that the Philippines withdraw its personnel from Second Thomas Shoal in the following terms:

> The Chinese side demands the Philippine side withdraw all its personnel and facilities from China's islands and reefs, and honor its commitment to tow away its illegally "grounded" vessel on China's Ren'ai Jiao [Second Thomas Shoal] . . . .[758]

732. Likewise, China has stated that "China has indisputable sovereignty over Nansha Islands and their adjacent waters, Meiji Jiao [Mischief Reef] . . . included."[759]

---

[756]   Merits Hearing Tr. (Day 4), p. 89.

[757]   Note Verbale from the Ministry of Foreign Affairs, People's Republic of China to the Embassy of the Republic of the Philippines in Beijing, No. (2015) Bu Bian Zi No. 5 (20 January 2015) (Annex 681).

[758]   Note Verbale from the Embassy of the People's Republic of China in Manila to the Department of Foreign Affairs, Republic of the Philippines, No. 14 (PG)-195 (30 June 2014) (Annex 675); Note Verbale from the Embassy of the People's Republic of China in Manila to the Department of Foreign Affairs, Republic of the Philippines, No. 14 (PG)-197 (4 July 2014) (Annex 676); Note Verbale from the Embassy of the People's Republic of China in Manila to the Department of Foreign Affairs, Republic of the Philippines, No. 14 (PG)-264 (2 September 2014) (Annex 678); see also Note Verbale from the Embassy of the People's Republic of China in Manila to the Department of Foreign Affairs, Republic of the Philippines, No. 14 (PG)-336 (28 October 2014) (Annex 680); Note Verbale from the Ministry of Foreign Affairs, People's Republic of China to the Embassy of the Republic of the Philippines in Beijing, No. (2015) Bu Bian Zi No. 5 (20 January 2015) (Annex 681); Note Verbale from the Embassy of the People's Republic of China in Manila to the Department of Foreign Affairs, Republic of the Philippines, No. 15 (PG)-068 (4 March 2015) (Annex 685); Note Verbale from the Department of Boundary and Ocean Affairs, Ministry of Foreign Affairs, People's Republic of China, to the Embassy of the Republic of the Philippines in Beijing, No. (2015) Bu Bian Zi No. 22 (30 March 2015) (Annex 686); Note Verbale from the Embassy of the People's Republic of China in Manila to the Department of Foreign Affairs, Republic of the Philippines, No. (2015) PG-329 (29 September 2015) (Annex 692).

5.   The Tribunal's Considerations

(a)   The Tribunal's Jurisdiction

733. In its Award on Jurisdiction, the Tribunal deferred any final decision with respect to its jurisdiction concerning the Philippines' Submission No. 9, for the same reason that it deferred consideration of its jurisdiction with respect to the Philippines' Submission No. 8 (see paragraphs 690 to 691 above). Specifically, the Tribunal considered that its jurisdiction over these Submissions was contingent on whether Mischief Reef and Second Thomas Shoal were low-tide elevations and whether any other feature claimed by China is capable of generating an entitlement to an exclusive economic zone in the area of those features that would overlap the entitlement of the Philippines.

734. Having determined that Mischief Reef and Second Thomas Shoal are both low-tide elevations, and that no high-tide feature in the Spratly Islands is capable of generating an entitlement to an exclusive economic zone, the Tribunal concludes that it has jurisdiction with respect to the Philippines' Submission No. 9 for the same reason already stated with respect to Submission No. 8 (see paragraphs 692 to 695 above).

(b)   The Law Applicable to China's Supervision of its Fishing Vessels

735. The Tribunal has held that Mischief Reef and Second Thomas Shoal are low-tide elevations located within areas where only the Philippines possesses possible entitlements to maritime zones under the Convention. The relevant areas can only constitute the exclusive economic zone of the Philippines. Accordingly, the Philippines—and not China—possesses sovereign rights with respect to resources in these areas, and the law relevant to Chinese fishing activities at these reef formations is the law governing fishing by the vessels of one State in the exclusive economic zone of another.

736. In this respect, Article 61(1) of the Convention provides that "[t]he coastal State shall determine the allowable catch of the living resources in its exclusive economic zone." The remainder of Article 61 concerns the process through which the coastal State will determine the allowable catch.

737. Article 62 of the Convention then outlines the circumstances in which vessels of other States will have access to the fisheries of a State's exclusive economic zone. Article 62(2) provides

---

[759]   Note Verbale from the Embassy of the People's Republic of China in Manila to the Department of Foreign Affairs, Republic of the Philippines, No. 15 (PG)-214 (28 June 2015) (Annex 689).

that "[w]here the coastal State does not have the capacity to harvest the entire allowable catch, it shall, through agreements or other arrangements and pursuant to the terms, conditions, laws and regulations referred to in paragraph 4, give other States access to the surplus of the allowable catch . . . ." Article 62(3) then provides guidance on the factors to be considered in according access to other States.

738. These provisions make clear that it is the Philippines that controls the process of granting and regulating access to the fisheries of its exclusive economic zone, subject to the provisions of the Convention in doing so. It is thus for the Philippines to determine the allowable catch for fisheries within its exclusive economic zone. If after determining the allowable catch, the Philippines also determines that it lacks the capacity to fully harvest the allowable catch, it must allow other States access to the fishery.

739. Article 62(4) then imposes an obligation on nationals of other States fishing in the exclusive economic zone to comply with the laws and regulations of the coastal State and sets out an illustrative list of the areas that may be regulated. Article 62(4) provides in full as follows:

> Nationals of other States fishing in the exclusive economic zone shall comply with the conservation measures and with the other terms and conditions established in the laws and regulations of the coastal State. These laws and regulations shall be consistent with this Convention and may relate, *inter alia*, to the following:
>
> (a) licensing of fishermen, fishing vessels and equipment, including payment of fees and other forms of remuneration, which, in the case of developing coastal States, may consist of adequate compensation in the field of financing, equipment and technology relating to the fishing industry;
>
> (b) determining the species which may be caught, and fixing quotas of catch, whether in relation to particular stocks or groups of stocks or catch per vessel over a period of time or to the catch by nationals of any State during a specified period;
>
> (c) regulating seasons and areas of fishing, the types, sizes and amount of gear, and the types, sizes and number of fishing vessels that may be used;
>
> (d) fixing the age and size of fish and other species that may be caught;
>
> (e) specifying information required of fishing vessels, including catch and effort statistics and vessel position reports;
>
> (f) requiring, under the authorization and control of the coastal State, the conduct of specified fisheries research programmes and regulating the conduct of such research, including the sampling of catches, disposition of samples and reporting of associated scientific data;
>
> (g) the placing of observers or trainees on board such vessels by the coastal State;
>
> (h) the landing of all or any part of the catch by such vessels in the ports of the coastal State;
>
> (i) terms and conditions relating to joint ventures or other cooperative arrangements;

(j)   requirements for the training of personnel and the transfer of fisheries technology, including enhancement of the coastal State's capability of undertaking fisheries research;

(k)   enforcement procedures.

740.   Article 62(4) thus expressly requires Chinese nationals to comply with the licensing and other access procedures of the Philippines within any area forming part of the exclusive economic zone of the Philippines. The Convention imposes an obligation directly on *private* parties engaged in fishing that would apply to Chinese nationals and vessels engaged in fishing at Mischief Reef and Second Thomas Shoal and require them to comply with the terms and conditions of the laws and regulations of the Philippines.

741.   The Convention also imposes obligations on *States* Parties with respect to activities in the exclusive economic zone of other States. Article 58(3) of the Convention provides as follows:

> In exercising their rights and performing their duties under this Convention in the exclusive economic zone, States shall have due regard to the rights and duties of the coastal State and shall comply with the laws and regulations adopted by the coastal State in accordance with the provisions of this Convention and other rules of international law in so far as they are not incompatible with this Part.

742.   The nature of the obligation to have "due regard to the rights and duties" of another State was considered by the tribunal in the *Chagos Marine Protected Area Arbitration* in the context of Article 56(2) (concerning the reversed situation of the regard owed by the coastal State to the rights and duties of other States within its exclusive economic zone). The tribunal in that matter reasoned as follows:

> the ordinary meaning of "due regard" calls for the [first State] to have such regard for the rights of [the second State] as is called for by the circumstances and by the nature of those rights. The Tribunal declines to find in this formulation any universal rule of conduct. The Convention does not impose a uniform obligation to avoid any impairment of [the second State's] rights; nor does it uniformly permit the [first State] to proceed as it wishes, merely noting such rights. Rather, the extent of the regard required by the Convention will depend upon the nature of the rights held by [the second State], their importance, the extent of the anticipated impairment, the nature and importance of the activities contemplated by the [first State], and the availability of alternative approaches.[760]

743.   In the context of the duties of a flag State with respect to fishing by its nationals, the International Tribunal for the Law of the Sea interpreted the obligation of due regard, when read in conjunction with the obligations directly imposed upon nationals by Article 62(4), to extend to a duty "to take the necessary measures to ensure that their nationals and vessels flying their

---

[760]   *Chagos Marine Protected Area Arbitration (Mauritius v. United Kingdom)*, Award of 18 March 2015, para. 519.

flag are not engaged in IUU fishing activities."[761] The *Fisheries Advisory Opinion* goes on to note that:

> the obligation of a flag State . . . to ensure that vessels flying its flag are not involved in IUU fishing is also an obligation "of conduct". . . . as an obligation "of conduct" this is a "due diligence obligation", not an obligation "of result". . . . The flag State is under the "due diligence obligation" to take all necessary measures to ensure compliance and to prevent IUU fishing by fishing vessels flying its flag.[762]

744. The Tribunal agrees with the *Fisheries Advisory Opinion* in this respect. Given the importance of fisheries to the entire concept of the exclusive economic zone, the degree to which the Convention subordinates fishing within the exclusive economic zone to the control of the coastal State, and the obligations expressly placed on the nationals of other States by Article 62(4) of the Convention, the Tribunal considers that anything less than due diligence by a State in preventing its nationals from unlawfully fishing in the exclusive economic zone of another would fall short of the regard due pursuant to Article 58(3) of the Convention.

(c) The Activities of Chinese Fishing Vessels at Mischief Reef and Second Thomas Shoal

745. With respect to Chinese activities at Mischief Reef and Second Thomas Shoal, the Tribunal notes that it has limited evidence before it. The record of Chinese fishing at these features is restricted to reports from the Armed Forces of the Philippines and confined to a single period in May 2013. The most information is available from Second Thomas Shoal, where the Philippines maintains a small marine detachment, but even there it is apparent that the Philippines is able to observe the activities of China's vessels only from a distance and has not sought to enforce its regulations or restrict the activities of Chinese vessels. China's *de facto* control over the waters surrounding both features effectively limits the information available to the Philippines and to this Tribunal.

746. Despite these limitations, the Tribunal is prepared to accept that the account of events provided by the Armed Forces of the Philippines is accurate and that Chinese fishing vessels, accompanied by the ships of CMS, were engaged in fishing at both Mischief Reef and Second Thomas Shoal in May 2013. It does so for two reasons.

747. First, the Tribunal notes that China has asserted sovereign rights and jurisdiction in the South China Sea, generally, and has apparently not accepted these areas as part of the Philippines'

---

[761] *Request for an Advisory Opinion Submitted by the Sub-Regional Fisheries Commission (SRFC)*, Advisory Opinion of 2 April 2015, ITLOS Reports 2015, para. 124.

[762] *Request for an Advisory Opinion Submitted by the Sub-Regional Fisheries Commission (SRFC)*, Advisory Opinion of 2 April 2015, ITLOS Reports 2015, para. 129.

exclusive economic zone (see paragraphs 730 to 732 above). Indeed, the Tribunal notes that China has issued a "Nansha Certification of Fishing Permit" to its nationals,[763] which the Tribunal understands to extend to the area of Mischief Reef and Second Thomas Shoal. The Tribunal considers this assertion of jurisdiction over the activities of (at least) Chinese fishermen in the South China Sea to support the Philippines' evidence that Chinese vessels have indeed been fishing at Mischief Reef and Second Thomas Shoal.

748. Second, the pattern of Chinese fishing activity at Mischief Reef and Second Shoal is consistent with that exhibited at other reef formations for which the Tribunal has information. Thus, in the case of Subi Reef, the Philippines reports as follows:

> a Chinese fishing fleet composed of 30 vessels under a unified command sailed on 06 May 2013 from Hainan province, China to the disputed Spratly Islands in the West Philippine Sea for a "40-day operation." The "40-day operation" is the second of its kind organized by local fishery associations after Sansha City was established by China in June 2012. Each vessel in the fleet, equipped with all-weather communication devices, weighs more than 100 metric tons. Further, a 4,000-ton supply ship and a 1,500-ton transport ship were supplying the fishing vessels with fuel, food, water and other necessities.[764]

749. Meanwhile, in the case of Scarborough Shoal, the Tribunal has ample, corroborated evidence of fishing by Chinese vessels working in apparently close coordination with government vessels from CMS and the Fisheries Law Enforcement Command ("**FLEC**") in the period of April and May 2012.[765] These incidents are discussed in detail in connection with the Philippines' Submissions No. 11 and 13.

750. The Tribunal notes that Subi Reef and Scarborough Shoal are not, as a legal matter, comparable to Mischief Reef and Second Thomas Shoal. Subi Reef lies within the territorial sea of Sandy Cay on the reefs adjacent to Thitu (see paragraphs 367 to 373 above) while Scarborough Shoal is a high-tide feature that would generate its own entitlements to a territorial sea

---

[763] *See* Note Verbale from the Department of Foreign Affairs, Republic of the Philippines, to the Embassy of the People's Republic of China in Manila, No. 15-2341 (16 June 2015) (Annex 690). Details of the Chinese fishing permit system for the Spratly Islands are also evident on the website of the Department of Ocean and Fisheries of Hainan Province, *available at* <dof.hainan.gov.cn/wsbs/bszn/200809/t20080907_993887.html>.

[764] Armed Forces of the Philippines, *Near-occupation of Chinese Vessels of Second Thomas (Ayungin) Shoal in the Early Weeks of May 2012* (May 2013) (Annex 94).

[765] *See, e.g.*, Memorandum from Colonel, Philippine Navy, to Chief of Staff, Armed Forces of the Philippines, No. N2E-0412-008 (11 April 2012) (Annex 77); Report from the Commanding Officer, SARV-003, Philippine Coast Guard, to Commander, Coast Guard District Northwestern Luzon, Philippine Coast Guard (28 April 2012) (Annex 78); Memorandum from the FRPLEU/QRT Chief, Bureau of Fisheries and Aquatic Resources, Republic of the Philippines, to Director, Bureau of Fisheries and Aquatic Resources, Republic of the Philippines (2 May 2012) (Annex 79); Report from FRPLEU/QRT Officers, Bureau of Fisheries and Aquatic Resources, Republic of the Philippines, to Director, Bureau of Fisheries and Aquatic Resources, Republic of the Philippines (2 May 2012) (Annex 80).

(see paragraphs 333 to 334 above). The Tribunal has not addressed—and will not address—the question of which State has sovereignty over Sandy Cay, Thitu, or Scarborough Shoal and would thus have an entitlement to the surrounding territorial sea.

751. In contrast, Mischief Reef and Second Thomas Shoal are not capable of generating entitlements to maritime zones and can only form part of the Philippines' exclusive economic zone. Nevertheless, in light of the fact that China has not accepted these areas as part of the Philippines' exclusive economic zone, the Tribunal considers the similarities in Chinese fishing activities at all of these features to be a significant indication of what has taken place at Mischief Reef and Second Thomas Shoal.

752. The Tribunal expects, from the general positions of the Parties, that Chinese vessels have continued to fish at Mischief Reef and Second Thomas Shoal since May 2013. The Tribunal does not, however, have the direct evidence before it that would enable it to draw such a conclusion for the period subsequent to May 2013.

*

753. Having established that Chinese vessels have been engaged in fishing at Mischief Reef and Second Thomas Shoal in May 2013, the Tribunal considers that China has failed to show the due regard called for by Article 58(3) of the Convention to the Philippines' sovereign rights with respect to fisheries within its exclusive economic zone.

754. In many cases, the precise scope and application of the obligation on a flag State to exercise due diligence in respect of fishing by vessels flying its flag in the exclusive economic zone of another State may be difficult to determine. Often, unlawful fishing will be carried out covertly, far from any official presence, and it will be far from obvious what the flag State could realistically have done to prevent it. That, however, is not the case here.

755. Chinese fishing vessels have in all reported instances been closely escorted by government CMS vessels. The actions of these ships constitute official acts of China and are all attributable to China as such. Indeed, the accounts of officially organised fishing fleets from Hainan at Subi Reef and the close coordination exhibited between fishing vessels and government ships at Scarborough Shoal support an inference that China's fishing vessels are not simply escorted and protected, but organised and coordinated by the Government. In any event, there can be no question that the officers aboard the Chinese Government vessels in question were fully aware of the actions being taken by Chinese fishermen and were able to halt them had they chosen to do so.

756. The obligation to have due regard to the rights of the Philippines is unequivocally breached when vessels under Chinese Government control act to escort and protect Chinese fishing vessels engaged in fishing unlawfully in the Philippines' exclusive economic zone.

(d) Conclusion

757. Based on the considerations outlined above, the Tribunal finds that China has, through the operation of its marine surveillance vessels in tolerating and failing to exercise due diligence to prevent fishing by Chinese flagged vessels at Mischief Reef and Second Thomas Shoal in May 2013, failed to exhibit due regard for the Philippines' sovereign rights with respect to fisheries in its exclusive economic zone. Accordingly, China has breached its obligations under Article 58(3) of the Convention.

*　　*　　*

this page intentionally blank

C.   CHINA'S ACTIONS IN RESPECT OF TRADITIONAL FISHING AT SCARBOROUGH SHOAL
     (SUBMISSION NO. 10)

1.   **Introduction**

758. In this Section, the Tribunal addresses the Parties' dispute concerning China's actions with respect to the traditional fishing activities of Philippine nationals at Scarborough Shoal. This dispute is reflected in the Philippines' Submission No. 10, which provides as follows:

> (10)   China has unlawfully prevented Philippine fishermen from pursuing their livelihoods by interfering with traditional fishing activities at Scarborough Shoal;

759. In its Award on Jurisdiction, the Tribunal held that this Submission reflects a dispute that does not concern maritime boundary delimitation and is not barred from the Tribunal's consideration by any requirement of Section 1 of Part XV.[766] The Tribunal noted that the Philippines had clarified that the activities alleged all occurred within the 12-nautical-mile territorial sea generated by Scarborough Shoal and that, accordingly, determination of Submission No. 10 does not depend on the characterisation of the feature as a rock or an island under Article 121 of the Convention.[767] Nor do Articles 297 and 298 of the Convention apply in the territorial sea to restrict the Tribunal's jurisdiction with respect to fisheries and law enforcement.[768] In addition, the Tribunal noted that traditional fishing rights "may exist even within the territorial waters of another State," and considered that its jurisdiction to address this dispute is not dependent on any prior determination of sovereignty over Scarborough Shoal.[769] In consequence, the Tribunal concluded that it has jurisdiction to address the matters raised in the Philippines' Submission No. 10 "to the extent that the claimed rights and alleged interference occurred within the territorial sea of Scarborough Shoal."[770]

2.   **Factual Background**

760. The facts underlying the present Submission concern the conduct of Chinese Government vessels at Scarborough Shoal since 2012, and in particular their interactions with Philippine fishermen proximate to the feature.

---

[766]   Award on Jurisdiction, para. 407.

[767]   Award on Jurisdiction, para. 407.

[768]   Award on Jurisdiction, para. 407.

[769]   Award on Jurisdiction, para. 407.

[770]   Award on Jurisdiction, para. 407.

(a)   Traditional Fishing by Philippine Fishermen at Scarborough Shoal

761. Even as several States have claimed sovereignty over Scarborough Shoal, there is evidence that the surrounding waters have continued to serve as traditional fishing grounds for fishermen,[771] including those from the Philippines, Viet Nam, and China (including from Taiwan). The background to a Philippine Navy report in the record before the Tribunal describes Scarborough Shoal as "a traditional fishing ground of fishermen from neighbouring Asian countries that have been heading to this area for its rich marine resources. Both foreign and local fishermen are among those who venture to this atoll and they would be fishing there for about a week or more."[772] China's Foreign Ministry Spokesperson has likewise asserted that "[t]he waters surrounding the Huangyan Island [Scarborough Shoal] has been a traditional fishing ground for Chinese fishermen. Since ancient times, Chinese fishermen have been fishing in waters surrounding the Island."[773] Affidavits from Filipino fishermen proffered by the Philippines describe having seen nationals of other States, including Viet Nam and China (including from Taiwan), fishing at Scarborough Shoal.[774]

762. Historical cartography evidences a connection between Scarborough Shoal and the Philippine mainland. A map of the Philippines produced in 1734 included the shoal;[775] another produced in 1784 labelled Scarborough Shoal as "Bajo de Masinloc".[776] Other documents provided by the Philippines—including a 1953 book published by its Bureau of Fisheries—depict

---

[771]   *See, e.g.*, P. Manacop, "The Principal Marine Fisheries" *in* D.V. Villadolid (ed.), *Philippine Fisheries: Handbook Prepared by the Technical Staff of the Bureau of Fisheries*, p. 103 at p. 121 (1953) (Annex 8); A.M. Mane, "Status, Problems and Prospects of the Philippine Fisheries Industry," *Philippine Farmers Journal*, Vol. 2, No. 4, p. 32 at p. 34 (1960) (Annex 244).

[772]   Memorandum from Colonel, Philippine Navy, to Chief of Staff, Armed Forces of the Philippines, No. N2E-0412-008 (April 2012) (Annex 77).

[773]   Ministry of Foreign Affairs, People's Republic of China, *Foreign Ministry Spokesperson Liu Weimin's Regular Press Conference* (18 April 2012), *available at* <nl.china-embassy.org/eng/wjbfyrth/t925289.htm>.

[774]   *See* Affidavit of R.Z. Comandante (12 November 2015), paras. Q38-A38 (Annex 693) (hereinafter "**Affidavit of R.Z. Comandante**"; Affidavit of T.D. Forones (12 November 2015), paras. Q8-A8 (Annex 694) (hereinafter "**Affidavit of T.D. Forones**"); Affidavit of M.C. Lanog (12 November 2015), paras. Q26-A26 (Annex 695) (hereinafter "**Affidavit of M.C. Lanog**"); Affidavit of J.P. Legaspi (12 November 2015), paras. Q-18-A18 (Annex 696) (hereinafter "**Affidavit of J.P. Legaspi**"); Affidavit of Crispen Talatagod (12 November 2015), paras. Q7-A7 (Annex 697) (hereinafter "**Affidavit of C.D. Talatagod**"); Affidavit of C.O. Taneo (12 November 2015), paras. Q18-A18 (Annex 698) (hereinafter "**Affidavit of C.O. Taneo**").

[775]   A.R. Brotons, *Spain in the Philippines (16th-19th Centuries)*, pp. 16, 24 (19 March 2014) (Annex 238).

[776]   Map of Pacific Ocean between the coast of California and Mexico and Japan, Philippines, and the coast of China (Spain, c. 1784) (Annex M113).

Scarborough Shoal as having historically served as one of the "principal fishing areas" for Filipino fishermen.[777]

763. Affidavits of six fishermen interviewed by the Philippines confirm the practice of fishing at Scarborough Shoal in recent generations,[778] providing direct documentation of Philippine fishing activities in the area at least since 1982[779] and indirect evidence from 1972.[780] Fishes caught at the shoal—primarily using spear and net fishing methods[781]—have historically included "[b]onito, talakitok, tanguige and other species of fish found beneath or near rocks."[782]

(b) China's Intermittent Prevention of Fishing by Philippine Vessels at Scarborough Shoal (May 2012 to Present)

764. Beginning in April 2012, a series of incidents occurred between Philippine and Chinese vessels at Scarborough Shoal that heightened tensions between the Parties. Philippine authorities reported increasing numbers of Chinese fishing vessels at Scarborough Shoal and stepped up inspections in response to indications that Chinese vessels were employing destructive fishing methods and harvesting endangered giant clams, corals, and sea turtles. China increased the deployment of its own FLEC and CMS vessels in response, leading to a series of incidents between Chinese and Philippine vessels on 10 April 2012,[783] 28 April 2012,[784] and

---

[777] P. Manacop, "The Principal Marine Fisheries" *in* D.V. Villadolid (ed.), *Philippine Fisheries: A Handbook Prepared by the Technical Staff of the Bureau of Fisheries*, p. 103 at p. 121 (1953) (Annex 8). *See also* A.M. Mane, "Status, Problems and Prospects of the Philippine Fisheries Industry," *Philippine Farmers Journal*, Vol. 2, No. 4 (1960), p. 34 (Annex 244).

[778] *See* Affidavit of R.Z. Comandante, paras. Q7-A8, Q12-A13, Q15-A19, Q35-A35, Q38-A38; Affidavit of T.D. Forones, paras. Q7-A8, Q19-A19; Affidavit of M.C. Lanog, paras. Q13-A13, Q18-A18; Affidavit of J.P. Legaspi, paras. Q2-A4, Q9-A11, Q18-A18; Affidavit of C.D. Talatagod, paras. Q6-A7, Q19-A19; Affidavit of C.O. Taneo, paras. Q6-A9, Q14-A14, Q17-A18.

[779] Affidavit of J.P. Legaspi, paras. Q4-A5; Affidavit of C.D. Talatagod, para. A7.

[780] *See also* Affidavit of R.Z. Comandante, para. A12.

[781] Affidavit of T.D. Forones, paras. A5, A11, A18, A20; Affidavit of J.P. Legaspi, para. Q12-A12, Q15-A15; Affidavit of C.D. Talatagod, para. A4, A9, A20 (Annex 697).

[782] Affidavit of R.Z. Comandante, para. A11.

[783] *See* Memorandum from Colonel, Philippine Navy, to Chief of Staff, Armed Forces of the Philippines, No. N2E-0412-008 (April 2012) (Annex 77); Ministry of Foreign Affairs, People's Republic of China, *Foreign Ministry Spokesperson Liu Weimin's Regular Press Conference* (12 April 2012) (Annex 117); Note Verbale from the Department of Foreign Affairs of the Republic of Philippines to the Embassy of the People's Republic of China in Manila, No. 12-0894 (11 April 2012) (Annex 205); Note Verbale from the Department of Foreign Affairs, Republic of the Philippines, to the Embassy of the People's Republic of China in Manila, No. 12-1137 (26 April 2012) (Annex 207); Note Verbale from the Embassy of the People's Republic of China in Manila to the Department of Foreign Affairs of the Philippines, No. (12) PG-206 (29 April 2012) (Annex 208).

[784] *See* Report from the Commanding Officer, SARV-003, Philippine Coast Guard, to Commander, Coast Guard District Northwestern Luzon, Philippine Coast Guard, paras. 5.44-5.48 (28 April 2012) (Annex 78); Memorandum from the FRPLEU/QRT Chief, Bureau of Fisheries and Aquatic Resources,

26 May 2012.[785] The environmental implications of Chinese fishing are discussed in greater detail with respect to Submission No. 11 (see paragraphs 815 to 993 below). The incidents between Philippine and Chinese vessels are discussed in connection with the Philippines' Submission No. 13 (see paragraphs 1044 to 1109 below).

765. Efforts to negotiate a mutual withdrawal of government vessels were not successful,[786] and by early June 2012, China had "deployed about 28 utility boats across the southeast entrance of the shoal and rigged them together by rope to establish a makeshift boom or barrier," blocking the entrance to the lagoon of Scarborough Shoal.[787]

766. The record indicates that, as tensions intensified, fishermen active in the vicinity of Scarborough Shoal were affected by the Parties' dispute. In a memorandum dated 2 June 2012, the Commander of the Philippines' "Naval Forces Northern Luzon" wrote that China's barrier was "likely designed to discourage if not prevent the ingress/egress of Philippine vessels to the shoal."[788] He also noted that "[t]his recent action poses a danger to safety of life at sea among

---

Republic of the Philippines, to Director, Bureau of Fisheries and Aquatic Resources, Republic of the Philippines (2 May 2012) (Annex 79); Report from FRPLEU/QRT Officers, Bureau of Fisheries and Aquatic Resources, Republic of the Philippines, to the Director, Bureau of Fisheries and Aquatic Resources, Republic of the Philippines (2 May 2012) (Annex 80); Memorandum from the Embassy of the Republic of the Philippines in Beijing to the Secretary of Foreign Affairs of the Republic of the Philippines, No. ZPE-080-2012-S (24 May 2012) (Annex 81); Embassy of the People's Republic of China in the Republic of the Philippines, China's Sovereignty over the Huangyan Island is Indisputable (15 May 2012) (Annex 119); Note Verbale from the Department of Foreign Affairs, Republic of the Philippines, to the Embassy of the People's Republic of China in Manila, No. 12-1222 (30 April 2012) (Annex 209); Note Verbale from the Department of Foreign Affairs, Republic of the Philippines, to the Embassies of ASEAN Member States in Manila, No. 12-1372 (21 May 2012) (Annex 210); Note Verbale from the Embassy of the People's Republic of China in Manila to the Department of Foreign Affairs, Republic of the Philippines, No. (12) PG-239 (25 May 2012) (Annex 211); Note Verbale from the Department of Foreign Affairs of the Republic of Philippines to the Embassy of People's Republic of China in Manila, No. 12-1371 (21 May 2012) (Annex 688).

[785] *See* Report from FRPLEU-QRT Officers, Bureau of Fisheries and Aquatic Resources, Republic of the Philippines, to the Director, Bureau of Fisheries and Aquatic Resources, Republic of the Philippines (28 May 2012) (Annex 82); Note Verbale from the Department of Foreign Affairs of the Republic of Philippines to the Embassy of People's Republic of China in Manila, No. 12-1453 (31 May 2012) (Annex 212); Note Verbale from the Embassy of the People's Republic of China in Manila to the Department of Foreign Affairs, Republic of the Philippines, No. (12) PG-251 (12 June 2012) (Annex 213); Embassy of the People's Republic of China in the Republic of the Philippines, "Ten Questions Regarding Huangyan Island" (15 June 2012) (Annex 120).

[786] Memorandum from the Embassy of the Republic of the Philippines in Beijing to the Secretary of Foreign Affairs of the Republic of the Philippines, No. ZPE-080-2012-S (24 May 2012) (Annex 81); Memorandum from the Embassy of the Republic of the Philippines in Beijing to the Secretary of Foreign Affairs of the Republic of the Philippines, No. ZPE-110-2012-S (26 July 2012) (Annex 84).

[787] Memorandum from the Commander, Naval Forces Northern Luzon, Philippine Navy, to the Flag Officer in Command, Philippine Navy, No. CNFNL Rad Msg Cite NFCC-0612-001 (2 June 2012) (Annex 83).

[788] Memorandum from the Commander, Naval Forces Northern Luzon, Philippine Navy, to the Flag Officer in Command, Philippine Navy, No. CNFNL Rad Msg Cite NFCC-0612-001, para. 5 (2 June 2012) (Annex 83).

Philippine fishermen, who use the shoal as a shelter during the typhoon season to mitigate the effects of the southwest monsoon."[789]

767. Similarly, a memorandum submitted by the Director of the Philippine Bureau of Fisheries and Aquatic Resources states:

> Since April 2012, when the Chinese took control of Scarborough Shoal, Filipinos find it difficult to enter the shoal because the Chinese law enforcement vessels have created a "no fishing zone" around it. Chinese patrol vessels enforce this zone by threatening Filipino fishermen who attempt to fish at Scarborough.
>
> This conduct of the Chinese government, together with its enactment of new laws, such as the 2012 Hainan Regulations and the 2012 fishing ban, have created a deep sense of fear among Filipino fishermen that has significantly curtailed their fishing activities and severely impacted their ability to earn a livelihood.[790]

768. The accounts provided by Filipino fishermen confirm their exclusion from fishing grounds at Scarborough Shoal. Mr. Crispen Talatagod, a retired fisherman from the municipality of Infanta in Pangasinan province, stated:

> I stopped fishing in 2012 because we were prohibited from fishing there by the Chinese. I remember that when my companions and I went to Scarborough Shoal, we were met by an armed member of [the] Chinese Coast Guard. The guard told us that they own Scarborough Shoal and he prevented us from fishing there. We were surprised and afraid at that time. We tried to hide and wait for nighttime before starting to fish, but the Chinese were able to anticipate this. Again, they prohibited us from fishing in Scarborough Shoal. I was not able to return since then.[791]

Similarly, Mr. Tolomeo Forones, a resident of Masinloc, recalled:

> No one fishes there anymore. I tried to go back to Scarborough Shoal last June 2012 and July 2013 with some members of the media. When we arrived only Chinese Coat Guard vessels were there to drive away anyone who attempts to go in.[792]

Additionally, Mr. Cecilio Taneo, of Masinloc, said:

> The Filipinos were prohibited by the Chinese from entering the Scarborough Shoal. While the Filipinos are still far from reaching the Scarborough Shoal, the Chinese already gave a signal not to proceed further. The Chinese used water cannons against the Filipinos.[793]

769. During other periods, however, fishermen were occasionally permitted to continue to fish at the shoal. Opportunities to do so appear to have been limited. Mr. Jowe Legaspi, a fisherman who began fishing at Scarborough Shoal in 1994,[794] reported:

---

[789] Memorandum from the Commander, Naval Forces Northern Luzon, Philippine Navy, to the Flag Officer in Command, Philippine Navy, No. CNFNL Rad Msg Cite NFCC-0612-001 (2 June 2012), para. 5 (Annex 83).

[790] Affidavit of A.G. Perez, Director, Bureau of Fisheries and Aquatic Resources, Republic of the Philippines, paras. 5-6 (26 March 2014) (Annex 241).

[791] Affidavit of C.D. Talatagod, para. A24.

[792] Affidavit of T.D. Forones, para. A25.

[793] Affidavit of C.O. Taneo, para. A30.

> [I]n February to March 2014, they temporarily let fishermen in at Scarborough Shoal. But suddenly in April 2014, they ward us off again. In May or June 2014, they harassed Filipino fishermen through water cannon, sound blare, and there were times that they have a gun when they came near us.[795]

770. Since the introduction of restrictions on Philippine fishing activity at Scarborough Shoal, several of the fishermen interviewed noted a decrease in income,[796] expressed uncertainty about the continued viability of their trade,[797] or have retired.[798]

3. The Philippines' Position

771. The Philippines argues that China violated its obligations under Article 2(3) of the Convention, and considers this conclusion supported indirectly by reference to Articles 51(1) and 62(3) of the Convention.[799] Additionally, the Philippines submits that China has violated Articles 279[800] and 300 of the Convention.[801]

(a) Article 2(3) of the Convention

772. The Philippines maintains that, by preventing Filipino fishermen from fishing in the waters of Scarborough Shoal,[802] China has violated Article 2(3) of the Convention, which provides that "sovereignty over the territorial sea is exercised subject to this Convention and to other rules of international law."[803]

773. As a threshold matter, the Philippines submits that Article 2(3), rather than being merely hortatory, imposes substantive obligations on States. The Philippines recalls the *Chagos*

---

[794] Affidavit of J.P. Legaspi, para. A5.

[795] Affidavit of J.P Legaspi, para. A27.

[796] Affidavit of T.D. Forones, para. Q27-A27; Affidavit of M.C. Lanog, para. Q27-A27; Affidavit of J.P. Legaspi, para. Q28-A28; Affidavit of C.D. Talatagod, para. Q27-A27; Affidavit of C.O. Taneo, para. Q34-A35.

[797] Affidavit of T.D. Forones, para. Q27-A27; Affidavit of C.D. Talatagod, para. Q27-A27.

[798] Affidavit of C.D. Talatagod, para. Q27-A27.

[799] Merits Hearing Tr. (Day 2), pp. 185-186; (Day 4), pp. 108-110.

[800] Memorial, paras. 6.42-6.45; Merits Hearing Tr. (Day 4), pp. 110-111.

[801] Memorial, paras. 6.46-6.47; Merits Hearing Tr. (Day 2), pp. 185-186.

[802] Memorial, paras. 3.51-3.54, 6.36-6.37.

[803] Convention, art. 2(3).

Marine Protected Area Arbitration,[804] in which the tribunal "unanimously rejected" the argument that Article 2(3) was "descriptive" only.[805]

774. In this regard, the Philippines also recalls the individual opinion of Judge Alvarez in the *Anglo-Norwegian Fisheries* case, acknowledging that a State might "determine the extent of its territorial sea," on the condition that such determination "does not infringe on rights acquired by other states." [806]   Finally, the Philippines regards instructive the writings of Sir Gerald Fitzmaurice, who framed traditional fishing rights in the following terms:

> [I]f the fishing vessels of a given country have been accustomed from time immemorial, or over a long period, to fish in a certain area, on the basis of the area being high seas and common to all, it may be said that their country has through them . . . acquired a vested interest that the fisheries of that area should remain available to its fishing vessels (of course on a non-exclusive basis)—so that if another country asserts a claim to that area as territorial waters, which is found to be valid or comes to be recognized, this can only be subject to the acquired rights of the fishery in question, which must continue to be respected.[807]

Accordingly, the Philippines deems Article 2(3) to impose substantive obligations informed by general rules of international law, including the preservation of pre-existing rights.

775. One such rule, the Philippines submits, is the protection of traditional fishing rights of the sort raised in its Submission No. 10; there is, in other words, "a general rule of international law that requires a state to respect long and uninterrupted fishing by the nationals of another state in its territorial sea."[808]

776. In the Philippines' view, the protection of traditional fishing rights is firmly established in national and international jurisprudence. In *The Paquete Habana*, for instance, the Philippines notes that the U.S. Supreme Court recognised, then "adopted and applied the rule of customary international law that exempts fishing vessels from prize capture in wartime."[809]

777. From arbitral practice, the Philippines recalls the holding in the *Eritrea v. Yemen* arbitration, that required Yemen to "ensure that the traditional fishing regime of free access and enjoyment for the fishermen of both Eritrea and Yemen shall be preserved for the benefit of the lives and

---

[804]   *Chagos Marine Protected Area (Mauritius v. United Kingdom)*, Award of 18 March 2015.

[805]   Merits Hearing Tr. (Day 2), p. 164.

[806]   *Anglo-Norwegian Fisheries (United Kingdom v. Norway), Judgment, ICJ Reports 1951*, p. 150.

[807]   G. Fitzmaurice, "The Law and Procedure of the International Court of Justice, 1951-54: General Principles" *British Yearbook of International Law*, Vol. 30, p. 1 at p. 51 (1953).

[808]   Hearing Tr. (Day 2), p. 165.

[809]   Hearing Tr. (Day 2), pp. 165-166, *referring to The Paquete Habana*, 175 U.S. 677 (1900).

livelihoods of this poor and industrious order of men."[810] The Philippines therefore submits that, "provided it has been exercised over a long period of time without interruption or opposition," traditional fishing in the territorial sea of another State is protected by general international law as incorporated through Article 2(3) of the Convention.[811] In this regard, the Philippines notes that, in the *Abyei Arbitration*, the tribunal "applied the same rule even to the delimitation of a land boundary to protect traditional grazing rights."[812]

778. With regard to the scope of traditional fishing rights protected, the Philippines again refers to the *Eritrea v. Yemen* award. The Philippines accordingly argues that a State may restrict fishing rights "only . . . to the extent those activities may go beyond those that have traditionally been conducted."[813] Within the sphere of protected fishing rights, however, the Philippines considers that "any other administrative measure that might impact" traditional fishing rights "must be agreed between the states involved."[814]

779. The Philippines argues that fishing by Philippine nationals at Scarborough Shoal "plainly meets" the threshold required to deem it a protected activity under international law.[815] It characterises Filipino fishing practices in the area as "longstanding",[816] "long",[817] "deep",[818] "peaceful",[819] "uninterrupted",[820] "ancient",[821] and having occurred "since times immemorial".[822] In the Philippines' view, a combination of sources, ranging from (a) colonial maps of the Philippines depicting Scarborough Shoal,[823] (b) twentieth-century publications

---

[810] *Eritrea v. Yemen,* Award of 9 October 1998, RIAA Vol. XXII p 209 at pp. 329-330, para. 526.

[811] Merits Hearing Tr. (Day 2), p. 170; *see also* Merits Hearing Tr. (Day 2), p. 165.

[812] Merits Hearing Tr. (Day 2), p. 170; *Abyei Arbitration (Government of Sudan v. Sudan People's Liberation Movement/Army)*, Final Award of 22 June 2009, RIAA, Vol. XXX, p. 145 at pp. 408-409, 412, paras. 753-754, 766.

[813] Merits Hearing Tr. (Day 2), p. 171.

[814] Merits Hearing Tr. (Day 2), pp. 171-172.

[815] Merits Hearing Tr. (Day 2), p. 170.

[816] Merits Hearing Tr. (Day 2), p. 163.

[817] Merits Hearing Tr. (Day 2), p. 181.

[818] Merits Hearing Tr. (Day 2), p. 174.

[819] Merits Hearing Tr. (Day 2), p. 181.

[820] Merits Hearing Tr. (Day 2), p. 181.

[821] Memorial, para. 6.40.

[822] Memorial, para. 6.41.

[823] Memorial, para. 6.41; Hearing Tr. (Day 2), p. 175.

describing fishing practices there,[824] and (c) testimony of Filipino fishermen,[825] all support the conclusion that the fishing practices it alleges qualify as activities protected under Article 2(3) of the Convention.

780. In the Philippines' view, China has additionally breached its obligations under Article 2(3) of the UN Charter and Article 279 of the Convention to resolve disputes through peaceful means.[826] It suggests that China "rejected" a Philippine proposal to settle the Parties' dispute through recourse to the International Tribunal for the Law of the Sea;[827] instead, the Philippines argues, China "sought to consolidate its hold on Scarborough Shoal by deploying and anchoring Chinese vessels in such manner as to form an effective physical barrier to prevent Philippine vessels from entering the area."[828] The Philippines adds:

> Despite the longstanding use of Scarborough Shoal as a traditional fishing ground by Filipino fishermen, China abruptly acted to prevent them from pursuing their livelihoods in the area in April and May 2012. . . . China has since that date exercised control over Scarborough and only intermittently allowed Filipino fishing vessels to approach the area. These acts violate China's obligations under the Convention.[829]

781. Finally, the Philippines seeks to distinguish its Submissions regarding "historic fishing rights" from "historic rights" as claimed by China. It does so in three ways. First, whereas China allegedly asserts "rights of control", including over "exploration for and exploitation of all the resources within the nine-dash line," the Philippines maintains that it "seeks only access for its fishermen to pursue their traditional livelihood."[830] Second, the Philippines claims that "there is an obvious and significant difference between individual, non-exclusive rights on the one hand," such as those for which it purports to seek protection in this arbitration, and "exclusive sovereign rights on the other," including China's claim to "exclusive sovereign rights to all the resources in areas beyond 12 miles from Scarborough [Shoal]."[831] Third, the Philippines contends that its Submission No. 10 is "limited to the territorial sea"—the regime of which is circumscribed by "other rules of international law" per Article 2(3)— as compared with China's

---

[824] Memorial, para. 6.41; Hearing Tr. (Day 2), pp. 175-176; *see also* A.M. Mane, "Status, Problems and Prospects of the Philippine Fisheries Industry," *Philippine Farmers Journal*, Vol. 2, No. 4 (1960), p. 34 (Annex 244).

[825] Affidavit of R.Z. Comandante; Affidavit of T.D. Forones; Affidavit of M.C. Lanog; Affidavit of J.P. Legaspi; Affidavit of C.D. Talatagod; Affidavit of C.O. Taneo.

[826] Memorial, para. 6.42-6.45, 7.35; Merits Hearing Tr. (Day 2), pp. 185-186; (Day 4), pp. 110-112.

[827] Memorial, para. 3.52; Note Verbale from the Department of Foreign Affairs, Republic of the Philippines, to the Embassy of the People's Republic of China in Manila, No. 12-0894 (11 April 2012). (Annex 205).

[828] Memorial, para. 3.53.

[829] Memorial, para. 6.42.

[830] Merits Hearing Tr. (Day 2), p. 172.

[831] Merits Hearing Tr. (Day 2), p 173.

assertion of "exclusive historic rights . . . beyond the limits of any conceivable entitlement under the Convention."[832]

(b)   Articles 51(1) and 62(3) of the Convention

782. The Philippines considers that Articles 51(1) and 62(3) of the Convention, though not directly applicable to the present case, are nevertheless relevant insofar as they refer to traditional fishing rights.[833]   Article 51(1) provides that "an archipelagic State . . . shall recognize traditional fishing rights and other legitimate activities of the immediately adjacent neighbouring States in certain areas falling within archipelagic waters."   For its part, Article 62(3) provides that, "[i]n giving access to other States to its exclusive economic zone under this article, the coastal State shall take into account all relevant factors, including, inter alia, . . . the need to minimize economic dislocation in States whose nationals have habitually fished in the zone."

783. In the Philippines' view, Articles 51(1) and 62(3) are important for two reasons.   First, they constitute an "express recognition of the existence, and underscore[] the importance, of traditional fishing by the nationals of the immediately adjacent coastal states."[834]   Second, the articles confirm that, where the drafters of the Convention intended to "preserve traditional fishing in the context of the new legal regimes they created," they did so "explicitly" and "made clear to what extent such prior uses were or were not protected."[835]

(c)   China's Obligation to Act in Good Faith and Settle Disputes by Peaceful Means

784. Finally, the Philippines submits that China has "unlawfully endangered justice by exacerbating the dispute between it and the Philippines concerning their maritime rights and entitlements in the vicinity of Scarborough Shoal."[836]   Specifically, the Philippines considers China's conduct to be in breach of its obligations, both under Articles 279 and 300 of the Convention and under general international law, to refrain from "any acts that might aggravate or extend the dispute."[837]   The Philippines' arguments in relation to these issues are elaborated more fully in paragraphs 1130 to 1140 of this Award, relating to its Submission No. 14.

---

[832]   Hearing Tr. (Day 2), p. 173.

[833]   Hearing Tr. (Day 4), pp. 107-110.

[834]   Merits Hearing Tr. (Day 4), pp. 109-110.

[835]   Merits Hearing Tr. (Day 4), p. 110.

[836]   Memorial, para. 6.45.

[837]   Memorial, para. 6.45.

785. In relation to the present Submission, the Philippines observes that China took no actions to disturb traditional fishing by Filipinos in the aftermath of declaring a territorial sea of 12 nautical miles around Scarborough Shoal in 1958.[838] It concludes that, in light of "China's own longstanding practice in what it claims as territorial sea," China has "create[d] an obligation not to endanger justice by abruptly altering the status quo on which local artisanal fishing depends."[839]

4.   China's Position

786. Although China has not responded to the Philippines' Submission in the context of these proceedings, China's position is made clear in its contemporaneous statements from 2012.

787. Like the Philippines, China claims sovereignty over Scarborough Shoal and asserts that its waters constitute a traditional fishing ground for Chinese fishermen. On 12 June 2012, the Embassy of China in Manila published the following statement laying out China's claim:

> Huangyan Island and its surrounding waters have been China's traditional fishing grounds since ancient times. Chinese fishermen have engaged in fishery activities for generations. In addition, they have used Huangyan Island as a safe have in their voyage in the South China Sea. Genglubu, an ancient Chinese navigation log recording trips in the South China Sea, and other ancient documents and literature contain complete records of Chinese fishermen's activities around Huangyan Island. Since the Yuan Dynasty, the Chinese people have never stopped developing and exploiting Huangyan Island and its surrounding waters and the Chinese government has exercised effective management and jurisdiction over their activities all these years. These historical facts are supported by official documents, local chronicles and official maps in the past centuries.[840]

788. China also set out its own account of the events that took place on 10 April 2012:

> When 12 fishing boats from Hainan, China were conducting normal operations in the Huangyan Island lagoon on the morning of April 10, the Philippine Navy warship Gregorio del Pilar blocked the entrance to the lagoon. The Philippine armed personnel boarded four Chinese fishing boats, question the Chinese fishermen, searched the boats and took photos. They were rude and rough, severely violated China's territorial sovereignty and the human rights of Chinese fishermen. On the afternoon of 10 April, upon learning of the incident, the Chinese marine surveillance vessels No.84 and No.75, both performing routine patrol duty nearby, immediately headed to the Island to protect the safety of the Chinese fishermen. On the afternoon of 11 April, the Chinese fishery administration boat No.303 also arrived on the site and instructed the Chinese fishing boats and fishermen to evacuate safely and get rid of the Philippine intimidation. Afterwards, an archaeological ship of the Philippines stayed in the lagoon for illegal operation for a long time, and refused to leave the site until 18 April after China's repeated representations.[841]

---

[838]   Memorial, para. 6.44.

[839]   Memorial, para. 6.44.

[840]   Embassy of the People's Republic of China in the Republic of the Philippines, *Ten Questions Regarding Huangyan Island* (15 June 2012) (Annex 120).

[841]   Embassy of the People's Republic of China in the Republic of the Philippines, *Ten Questions Regarding Huangyan Island* (15 June 2012) (Annex 120).

789. China also elaborated on its actions following April 2012:

> After the occurrence of Huangyan Island Incident, China has consistently adhered to its position of solving the issue through diplomatic consultation. However, the Philippines kept escalating the situation, made erroneous remarks to mislead the public at home and abroad and whip up hostile sentiments. All the above actions have severely damaged the bilateral relations. To prevent further provocations by the Philippines, the Chinese public service ships have continued to keep close watch over Huangyan Island waters, provide administrative and other service to Chinese fishing boats in accordance with China's laws, so as to ensure Chinese fishermen a good environment for operations in their traditional fishing grounds.[842]

790. China has also responded to the Philippines' allegations that China's conduct fell short of its obligation to resolve the Parties' dispute peacefully. On 24 May 2012, the Chargé d'Affaires of the Philippines' Embassy in Beijing met with the Director General of the Department of Boundary and Ocean Affairs of China's Ministry of Foreign Affairs. As recorded by the Philippines, China expressed the following position:

> DG Deng also referred to Article 2.4 of the United Nations Charter, saying that on 10 April, the Philippines used a warship to harass unarmed Chinese fishermen. This is a sign of the use of force. Since April 10, all actions of the Philippines in Huangyan Island are in violation of Chinese territorial sovereignty. The Philippines is now citing Article 2.4. China believes that it is the Philippines that has violated this Article and China deeply regrets this.
>
> . . .
>
> There have been no Chinese words or actions to escalate the situation at the multilateral level; on the diplomatic front or in the media. Nor has China taken any action on the ground in Huangyan Island waters.[843]

791. As far as the Tribunal is aware, China has not made specific statements concerning the status of Filipino fishermen at Scarborough Shoal. Nevertheless, the Tribunal considers the content of China's statements, especially with regard to the presence and conduct of Chinese vessels at the feature, to indicate China's position that its actions at Scarborough Shoal are generally lawful.

5. The Tribunal's Considerations

792. The Tribunal notes at the outset that both the Philippines and China claim sovereignty over Scarborough Shoal and that both the Philippines and China consider Scarborough Shoal to be a traditional fishing ground for their nationals.

793. Consistent with the limitations on its jurisdiction, the Tribunal has refrained from any decision or comment on sovereignty over Scarborough Shoal. The Tribunal also considers it imperative

---

[842] Embassy of the People's Republic of China in the Republic of the Philippines, *Ten Questions Regarding Huangyan Island* (15 June 2012) (Annex 120).

[843] Memorandum from the Embassy of the Republic of the Philippines in Beijing to the Secretary of Foreign Affairs of the Republic of the Philippines, No. ZPE-080-2012-S (24 May 2012) (Annex 81).

to emphasise that the following discussion of fishing rights at Scarborough Shoal is not predicated on any assumption that one Party or the other is sovereign over the feature. Nor is there any need for such assumptions. The international law relevant to traditional fishing would apply equally to fishing by Chinese fishermen in the event that the Philippines were sovereign over Scarborough Shoal as to fishing by Filipino fishermen in the event that China were sovereign. The Tribunal's conclusions with respect to traditional fishing are thus independent of the question of sovereignty.

(a) The Law Applicable to Traditional Fishing

794. The attention paid to traditional fishing rights in international law stems from the recognition that traditional livelihoods and cultural patterns are fragile in the face of development and modern ideas of interstate relations and warrant particular protection.

795. Also referred to as artisanal fishing, traditional fishing was extensively discussed in the *Eritrea v. Yemen* arbitration, which looked to the reports of the Food and Agriculture Organization of the United Nations (the "**FAO**") for guidance on artisanal fishing in the Red Sea. Relying on the FAO's studies of artisanal fishing, that tribunal noted that:

> artisanal vessels and their gear are simple. The vessels are usually canoes fitted with small outboard engines, slightly larger vessels (9-12m) fitted with 40-75 hp engines, or fishing sambuks with inboard engines. Dugout canoes and small rafts (ramas) are also in use. Hand lines, gill nets and long lines are used. In its Report on Fishing in Eritrean waters, the FAO study states that this artisanal fishing gear, which varies according to the boat and the fish, is "simple and efficient".[844]

796. The *Eritrea v. Yemen* tribunal went on, however, to note:

> the term "artisanal" is not to be understood as applying in the future only to a certain type of fishing exactly as it is practised today. "Artisanal fishing" is used in contrast to "industrial fishing". It does not exclude improvements in powering the small boats, in the techniques of navigation, communication or in the techniques of fishing; but the traditional regime of fishing does not extend to large-scale commercial or industrial fishing nor to fishing by nationals of third States in the Red Sea, whether small-scale or industrial.[845]

797. Artisanal fishing has been a matter of concern in a variety of international fora without any common definition having been adopted. Artisanal fishing has been addressed at the World Trade Organization in the context of the Doha Round negotiations on fisheries subsidies,[846]

---

[844] *Eritrea v. Yemen*, Award of 17 December 1999, RIAA Vol. XXII, p. 335 at pp. 359-360, para. 105.

[845] *Eritrea v. Yemen*, Award of 17 December 1999, RIAA Vol. XXII, p. 335 at p. 360, para. 106.

[846] *See* World Trade Organisation, *Ministerial Declaration*, Fourth WTO Ministerial Conference, Doha, Qatar, WT/MIN(01)/DEC/1, paras. 28, 31 (14 November 2001).

where a variety of definitions have been advanced.[847] Traditional, artisanal, and small-scale fishing has also formed part of the work of the FAO,[848] the International Labour Office,[849] and the United Nations Environment Programme ("**UNEP**").[850] Despite this attention, the essential defining element of artisanal fishing remains, as the tribunal in *Eritrea v. Yemen* noted, relative. The specific practice of artisanal fishing will vary from region to region, in keeping with local customs. Its distinguishing characteristic will always be that, in contrast with industrial fishing, artisanal fishing will be simple and carried out on a small scale, using fishing methods that largely approximate those that have historically been used in the region.

798. The legal basis for protecting artisanal fishing stems from the notion of vested rights and the understanding that, having pursued a livelihood through artisanal fishing over an extended period, generations of fishermen have acquired a right, akin to property, in the ability to continue to fish in the manner of their forebears. Thus, traditional fishing rights extend to artisanal fishing that is carried out largely in keeping with the longstanding practice of the community, in other words to "those entitlements that all fishermen have exercised continuously through the ages,"[851] but not to industrial fishing that departs radically from traditional practices. Importantly, artisanal fishing rights attach to the individuals and communities that have traditionally fished in an area. These are not the historic rights of States, as in the case of historic titles, but private rights, as was recognised in *Eritrea v. Yemen*, where the tribunal declined to endorse "the western legal fiction . . . whereby all legal rights, even those in reality held by individuals, were deemed to be those of the State."[852]

799. Where private rights are concerned, international law has long recognised that developments with respect to international boundaries and conceptions of sovereignty should, as much as possible, refrain from modifying individual rights. Thus the Permanent Court of International Justice in its *Settlers of German Origin in Poland* advisory opinion noted that "[p]rivate rights

---

[847]   *See, e.g.*, World Trade Organization, *Definitions Related to Artisanal, Small-Scale And Subsistence Fishing: Note by the Secretariat*, TN/RL/W/197 (24 November 2005).

[848]   *See, e.g.*, Food and Agriculture Organization of the United Nations, *Voluntary Guidelines for Securing Sustainable Small-Scale Fisheries: In the Context of Food Security and Poverty Eradication* (2015).

[849]   *See, e.g.*, M. Ben-Yami, *Risks and Dangers in Small-Scale Fisheries: An overview*, International Labour Office, Sectoral Activities Programme, Doc. SAP 3.6/WP.147 (2000).

[850]   *See, e.g.*, D.K. Schorr, UN Environment Programme, *Artisanal Fishing: Promoting Poverty Reduction and Community Development through New WTO Rules on Fisheries Subsidies: An Issue and Options Paper*, pp. 12-18 (November 2005).

[851]   *Eritrea v. Yemen*, Award of 17 December 1999, RIAA Vol. p. 335 at p. 359, para. 104.

[852]   *Eritrea v. Yemen*, Award of 17 December 1999, RIAA, Vol. XXII, p. 335 at p. 359, para. 101.

acquired under existing law do not cease on a change of sovereignty,"[853] and the tribunal in the *Abyei Arbitration* observed that "traditional rights, in the absence of an explicit agreement to the contrary, have usually been deemed to remain unaffected by any territorial delimitation."[854] The same principle was recognised with respect to rights at sea by the tribunal in the *Bering Sea Arbitration*, when it exempted indigenous peoples from its division of jurisdiction with respect to the hunting of fur seals in the Bering Sea.[855]

800. Before turning to the question of the status of artisanal fishing rights under the Convention, the Tribunal notes that it is conscious of what could be seen as a contradiction in the Philippines' Submissions. On the one hand, the Philippines has asserted (and the Tribunal has agreed) that any historic rights China may have had in the waters of the South China Sea beyond its territorial sea were extinguished by the adoption in the Convention and in customary law of the concept of the exclusive economic zone. On the other hand, the Philippines has argued that its traditional fishing rights at Scarborough Shoal must be protected, even in the event that China has sovereignty over the feature.

801. The Tribunal considers that no contradiction in fact exists between these two positions. Rather, the law reflects the particular circumstances of the creation of the exclusive economic zone.

802. Under the law existing prior to the exclusive economic zone, any expansion of the maritime areas under national jurisdiction functioned essentially as described in paragraph 799 above. The expansion of jurisdiction was considered equivalent to the adjustment of a boundary or a change in sovereignty, and acquired rights, in particular to fisheries, were considered protected. Thus, in the *Fisheries Jurisdiction Cases*, the International Court of Justice held that Iceland's expansion of its fisheries zone could give it only preferential rights vis-à-vis the nationals of States that had habitually fished in the area.[856]

803. With the adoption in the Convention of the exclusive economic zone, however, a different calculus applied. Having reviewed the extensive attention given to the question of fishing by nationals of other States in the exclusive economic zone (see paragraphs 248 to 254 and 522

---

[853] *Questions relating to Settlers of German Origin in Poland*, Advisory Opinion, PCIJ Series B, No. 6, p. 6 at p. 36.

[854] *Abyei Arbitration (Government of Sudan v. Sudan People's Liberation Movement/Army)*, Final Award of 22 June 2009, RIAA, Vol. XXX, p. 145 at p. 412, para. 766.

[855] *Award between the United States and the United Kingdom relating to the Rights of Jurisdiction of United States in the Bering's Sea and the Preservation of Fur Seals (United Kingdom v. United States)*, Award of 15 August 1893, RIAA, Vol. XXVIII, p. 263 at p. 271.

[856] *Fisheries Jurisdiction (United Kingdom v. Iceland), Merits, Judgment, ICJ Reports 1974*, p. 3 at pp. 27-28, para. 62; *Fisheries Jurisdiction (Federal Republic of Germany v. Iceland), Merits, Judgment, ICJ Reports 1974*, p. 175 at pp. 196-197, para. 54.

to 538 above) and the degree of control over fisheries that was ultimately given to the coastal State, the Tribunal does not consider it possible that the drafters of the Convention intended for traditional or artisanal fishing rights to survive the introduction of the exclusive economic zone. In this respect, the Tribunal disagrees with the conclusions of the tribunal in *Eritrea v. Yemen* (which held that the traditional fishing regime in the Red Sea extended throughout the maritime zones of those States) and considers that that tribunal was able to reach the conclusions it did only because it was permitted to apply factors other than the Convention itself under the applicable law provisions of the parties' arbitration agreement (see paragraph 259 above).

804. Under the Convention, therefore, traditional fishing rights are accorded differing treatment across maritime zones:

(a) In archipelagic waters, traditional fishing rights are expressly protected, and Article 51(1) of the Convention provides that "an archipelagic State shall respect existing agreements with other States and shall recognize traditional fishing rights and other legitimate activities of the immediately adjacent neighbouring States in certain areas falling within archipelagic waters."

(b) In the exclusive economic zone, in contrast, traditional fishing rights are extinguished, except insofar as Article 62(3) specifies that "the need to minimize economic dislocation in States whose nationals have habitually fished in the zone" shall constitute one of the factors to be taken into account by the costal State in giving access to any surplus in the allowable catch. The Tribunal considers that the inclusion of this provision—which would be entirely unnecessary if traditional fishing rights were preserved in the exclusive economic zone—confirms that the drafters of the Convention did not intend to preserve such rights. The Convention does not, of course, preclude that States may continue to recognise traditional fishing rights in the exclusive economic zone in their legislation, in bilateral fisheries access agreements, or through regional fisheries management organisations. Such recognition would, in most instances, be commendable, but it is not required by the Convention, except to the extent specified in Article 62(3).

(c) Finally, in the territorial sea, the Convention continued the existing legal regime largely without change. The innovation in the Convention was the adoption of an agreed limit of 12 nautical miles on the breadth of the territorial sea, not the development of its legal content. The Tribunal sees nothing that would suggest that the adoption of the Convention was intended to alter acquired rights in the territorial sea and concludes that within that zone—in contrast to the exclusive economic zone—established traditional fishing rights remain protected by international law. The Tribunal also notes that the vast majority of traditional fishing takes place in close proximity to the coast.

(b)   The Protection of Traditional Fishing at Scarborough Shoal

805.   Based on the record before it, the Tribunal is of the view that Scarborough Shoal has been a traditional fishing ground for fishermen of many nationalities, including the Philippines, China (including from Taiwan), and Viet Nam.   The stories of most of those who have fished at Scarborough Shoal in generations past have not been the subject of written records, and the Tribunal considers that traditional fishing rights constitute an area where matters of evidence should be approached with sensitivity.   That certain livelihoods have not been considered of interest to official record keepers or to the writers of history does not make them less important to those who practise them.   With respect to Scarborough Shoal, the Tribunal accepts that the claims of both the Philippines and China to have traditionally fished at the shoal are accurate and advanced in good faith.

806.   The Tribunal does not have before it extensive details of the fishing methods traditionally used by either Filipino or Chinese fishermen, or of the communities that have traditionally dispatched vessels to Scarborough Shoal.   In keeping with the fact that traditional fishing rights are customary rights, acquired through long usage, the Tribunal notes that the methods of fishing protected under international law would be those that broadly follow the manner of fishing carried out for generations: in other words, artisanal fishing in keeping with the traditions and customs of the region.   The Tribunal is not prepared to specify any precise threshold for the fishing methods that would qualify as artisanal fishing, nor does the Tribunal deem it necessary to consider how and when traditional fishing practices may gradually change with the advent of technology.

807.   Based on the record before it,[857] the Tribunal is of the view that at least some of the fishing carried out at Scarborough Shoal has been of a traditional, artisanal nature.   The Tribunal is also open to the possibility that some of the fishing at Scarborough Shoal may have become sufficiently organised and industrial in character that it can no longer fairly be considered artisanal.

---

[857]   *See* Report from FRPLEU/QRT Officers, Bureau of Fisheries and Aquatic Resources, Republic of the Philippines, to the Director, Bureau of Fisheries and Aquatic Resources, Republic of the Philippines (2 May 2012) (Annex 80); Affidavit of T.D. Forones, para. A5, A8, A11, A18, A20; Affidavit of J.P. Legaspi, para. Q12-A12 Q15-A15; Affidavit of C.D. Talatagod, para. A4, A7, A9, A20.

808. Turning to the Philippines' Submission, the Tribunal notes that Article 2(3) of the Convention provides that "[t]he sovereignty over the territorial sea is exercised subject to this Convention and to other rules of international law." The Tribunal agrees with the finding in the *Chagos Marine Protected Area Arbitration* that, in the territorial sea, "Article 2(3) contains an obligation on States to exercise their sovereignty subject to 'other rules of international law'."[858] Traditional fishing rights constitute a vested right, and the Tribunal considers the rules of international law on the treatment of the vested rights of foreign nationals[859] to fall squarely within the "other rules of international law" applicable in the territorial sea.

809. The Tribunal notes, however, that traditional fishing rights are not absolute or impervious to regulation. Indeed, the careful regulation of traditional fishing may be necessary for conservation and to restrict environmentally harmful practices. Customary international law, in this respect, does not restrict the coastal State from reasonable regulation (a principle recognised with respect to treaty-based fishing rights in *North Atlantic Coast Fisheries*[860]). Nor would it prevent the coastal State from assessing the scope of traditional fishing to determine, in good faith, the threshold of scale and technological development beyond which it would no longer accept that fishing by foreign nationals is traditional in nature.

810. The Tribunal finds as a matter of fact that since May 2012, Chinese Government vessels have acted to prevent entirely fishing by Filipino fishermen at Scarborough Shoal for significant, but not continuous, periods of time. The Philippines has provided evidence of Chinese vessels physically blockading the entrance to Scarborough Shoal,[861] and Filipino fishermen have testified to being driven away by Chinese vessels employing water cannon.[862] During these periods, Chinese fishing vessels have continued to fish at Scarborough Shoal.[863] The actions of Chinese Government vessels constitute official acts of China, and the consequences that follow from them are attributable to China as such.

811. With respect to these actions, the Tribunal considers that the Philippines' Submission No. 10 is based on one of two alternative premises. If, on the one hand, the Philippines is sovereign over

---

[858] *Chagos Marine Protected Area (Mauritius v. United Kingdom)*, Award of 18 March 2015, para. 514.

[859] *See, e.g., Certain German Interests in Polish Upper Silesia*, Merits, Judgment of 25 May 1926, PCIJ, Series A, No.7, p. 4 at p. 42.

[860] *North Atlantic Coast Fisheries (United Kingdom/United States)*, Permanent Court of Arbitration, Award of 7 September 1910, RIAA, Vol. XI, p. 167.

[861] Memorandum from the Commander, Naval Forces Northern Luzon, Philippine Navy, to the Flag Officer in Command, Philippine Navy, No. CNFNL Rad Msg Cite NFCC-0612-001 (2 June 2012) (Annex 83)

[862] Affidavit of T.D. Forones; Affidavit of J.P. Legaspi; Affidavit of C.D Talatagod; Affidavit of C.O. Taneo.

[863] Embassy of the People's Republic of China in the Republic of the Philippines, *Ten Questions Regarding Huangyan Island* (15 June 2012) (Annex 120).

Scarborough Shoal, then the surrounding waters would constitute the territorial sea of the Philippines, with all that follows from it. If, on the other hand, China is sovereign over Scarborough Shoal, the premise of the Philippines' Submission is that China has failed to respect the traditional fishing rights of Filipino fishermen within China's territorial sea.

812. In the Tribunal's view, it is not necessary to explore the limits on the protection due in customary international law to the acquired rights of individuals and communities engaged in traditional fishing. The Tribunal is satisfied that the complete prevention by China of fishing by Filipinos at Scarborough Shoal over significant periods of time after May 2012 is not compatible with the respect due under international law to the traditional fishing rights of Filipino fishermen. This is particularly the case given that China appears to have acted to prevent fishing by Filipinos, specifically, while permitting its own nationals to continue. The Tribunal is cognisant that April and May 2012 represented a period of heightened tensions between the Philippines and China at Scarborough Shoal. China's dispute with the Philippines over sovereignty and law enforcement at Scarborough Shoal, however, was with the Philippine Government. The Tribunal does not see corresponding circumstances that would have justified taking action against Filipino fishermen engaged in their traditional livelihood or that would have warranted continuing to exclude Filipino fishermen from Scarborough Shoal for months after the Philippines had withdrawn its official vessels. The Tribunal notes, however, that it would have reached exactly the same conclusion had the Philippines established control over Scarborough Shoal and acted in a discriminatory manner to exclude Chinese fishermen engaged in traditional fishing.

813. With respect to the Philippines' claim that China's actions at Scarborough Shoal represented a specific failure to fulfil its duties pursuant to Article 2(3) of the UN Charter and Article 279 of the Convention to settle disputes by peaceful means, the Tribunal notes that both Parties found fault with the other in their handling of the standoff and that both found cause to allege breaches of the UN Charter.[864] The Tribunal does not find the record before it sufficient to support such a claim in respect of either Party.

---

[864] *See, e.g.*, Memorandum from the Embassy of the Republic of the Philippines in Beijing to the Secretary of Foreign Affairs of the Republic of the Philippines, No. ZPE-080-2012-S (24 May 2012) (Annex 81).

(c) Conclusion

814. Based on the considerations outlined above, the Tribunal finds that China has, through the operation of its official vessels at Scarborough Shoal from May 2012 onwards, unlawfully prevented Filipino fishermen from engaging in traditional fishing at Scarborough Shoal. The Tribunal records that this decision is entirely without prejudice to the question of sovereignty over Scarborough Shoal.

*   *   *

D.   **ALLEGED FAILURE TO PROTECT AND PRESERVE THE MARINE ENVIRONMENT (SUBMISSIONS NO. 11 AND 12(B))**

1.   **Introduction**

815. This Section addresses the Parties' dispute concerning the protection and preservation of the marine environment. This dispute is reflected in the Philippines' Submission No. 11, which provides (as amended):

> (11)   China has violated its obligations under the Convention to protect and preserve the marine environment at Scarborough Shoal, Second Thomas Shoal, Cuarteron Reef, Fiery Cross Reef, Gaven Reef, Johnson Reef, Hughes Reef and Subi Reef;

816. This dispute is also reflected in the portion of the Philippines' Submission No. 12 concerning environmental harm from China's construction at Mischief Reef:

> (12)   China's occupation of and construction activities on Mischief Reef
>
> (b)   violate China's duties to protect and preserve the marine environment under the Convention; . . .

817. The Philippines' allegations concerning China's environmental violations relate to two general categories of conduct: harmful fishing practices and harmful construction activities.

818. Prior to 30 November 2015, the Philippines' Submission No. 11 had been limited to "the marine environment at Scarborough Shoal and Second Thomas Shoal."[865] The Philippines' Memorial focused on environmentally harmful fishing practices at those two features undertaken by Chinese fishing vessels, allegedly with the toleration and active support of China.[866] The activities complained of included the use of cyanide and explosives and the harvesting of endangered giant clams and sea turtles. The Philippines also introduced evidence of land reclamation and construction by China on a number of features in the Spratly Islands.[867] The Philippines argued, in the context of its Submission No. 12(b) concerning Mischief Reef, that China's construction of artificial islands, installations, and structures had breached its obligations to protect and preserve the marine environment. In support of these allegations, the Philippines filed an expert report by reef ecologist Professor Kent E. Carpenter of Old Dominion University in Norfolk, Virginia, United States (the "**First Carpenter Report**").

---

[865]   Memorial, p. 272; Jurisdictional Hearing Tr. (Day 2), pp. 86-87, 94-95; Merits Hearing Tr. (Day 3), p. 11.

[866]   Memorial, paras. 6.48-6.66.

[867]   Memorial, paras. 6.108-6.111; "Matrix of Events" documents compiled by the Armed Forces of the Philippines for Cuarteron, Gaven, Fiery Cross, Johnson, and Subi Reefs (Annexes 86-91).

819. Subsequent to filing its Memorial, the Philippines periodically expressed to the Tribunal its "deep concerns" about China's "extensive land reclamation" and construction activities at several features in the Spratly Islands and their impact on the "fragile marine environment in the vicinity of these sites"[868] in disregard of China's duty not to cause serious harm to the marine environment."[869] Shortly before the Hearing on the Merits, the Tribunal granted leave to the Philippines to enter into the record new aerial and satellite photography showing China's construction activities in the South China Sea and a second report by Professor Carpenter, co-authored with Dr. Loke Ming Chou of the National University of Singapore, entitled "Environmental Consequences of Land Reclamation Activities on Various Reefs in the South China Sea" (the "**Second Carpenter Report**").

820. During the Hearing on the Merits, the Philippines requested the Tribunal's permission to amend Submission No. 11 so that it would also cover the marine environment at Cuarteron Reef, Fiery Cross Reef, Johnson Reef, Hughes Reef, Gaven Reef and Subi Reef.[870] The Philippines noted that evidence relevant to those features had not been available at the time of drafting the Memorial. The Philippines specified that China's artificial island-building activities at these features breached Articles 123, 192, 194, 197, 205, and 206 of the Convention.[871] The Tribunal granted the Philippines leave to amend its Submissions, noting that the proposed amendment was related to or incidental to the Philippines' original Submissions (which included the environmental effects of island building at Mischief Reef) and did not involve the introduction of a new dispute between the Parties.[872]

821. After seeking the views of the Parties, the Tribunal sought an independent opinion on the environmental impact of China's construction activities. Pursuant to Article 24 of the Rules of Procedure, the Tribunal appointed Dr. Sebastian C.A. Ferse of the Leibniz Center for Tropical Marine Ecology in Bremen, Germany. Dr. Ferse is a coral reef ecologist with over ten years' research experience in Southeast Asia, the Pacific Islands, East Africa, and the Red Sea. His ecological work has focused on coral reef restoration and ecological functioning and the impact of environmental and anthropogenic factors on coral reef benthic communities. Additionally, the Tribunal appointed Dr. Peter J. Mumby, a Professor of coral reef ecology at the School of

---

[868] *See, e.g.*, Letter from the Philippines to the Tribunal (30 July 2014) (Annex 466).

[869] *See, e.g.*, Letter from the Philippines to the Tribunal (27 April 2015).

[870] Merits Hearing Tr. (Day 4), pp. 169, 203. *See also* Letter from the Philippines to the Tribunal (30 November 2015); Letter from the Tribunal to the Parties (1 December 2015); Letter from the Tribunal to the Parties (16 December 2015).

[871] Merits Hearing Tr. (Day 4), pp. 186-187.

[872] Letter from the Tribunal to the Parties (16 December 2015). *See also* Letter from the Tribunal to the Parties (1 December 2015) (inviting China's comments by 9 December 2016).

Biological Sciences at the University of Queensland, Australia, and his colleague, Dr. Selina Ward each with over 20 years' experience. Professor Mumby has advised governments and UN agencies on coral reef and fisheries issues. His work focuses on tropical coastal ecosystems and he is involved in developing ecosystem models to investigate conservation measures in mitigating disturbance on reefs. Dr. Selina Ward is a coral biologist who has conducted research into the responses of corals to environmental stress including elevated nutrients, mechanical damage and elements of climate change. On 26 April 2016, Dr. Ferse, Professor Mumby, and Dr. Ward provided their "Assessment of the Potential Environmental Consequences of Construction Activities on Seven Reefs in the Spratly Islands in the South China Sea."[873] The report is based on an independent review of the factual record, scientific literature, and other publicly available documents, including from China.

822. As discussed further in paragraphs 925 to 938 below, the Tribunal in its Award on Jurisdiction found that it has jurisdiction over Submission No. 11, as involving a dispute over the interpretation and application of Articles 192 and 194 of the Convention (imposing obligations on States to protect and preserve the marine environment).[874] The Tribunal deferred its decision on jurisdiction over all of Submission No. 12 for further consideration in connection with the merits.[875]

2. Factual Background

(a) The Marine Environment of the South China Sea

823. The South China Sea includes highly productive fisheries and extensive coral reef ecosystems, which are among the most biodiverse in the world.[876] The marine environment around Scarborough Shoal and the Spratly Islands has an extremely high level of biodiversity of species, including fishes, corals, echinoderms, mangroves, seagrasses, giant clams, and marine turtles, some of which are recognised as vulnerable or endangered.[877]

---

[873] Dr. rer. nat. S.C.A. Ferse, Professor P. Mumby, PhD and Dr. S. Ward, PhD, *Assessment of the Potential Environmental Consequences of Construction Activities on Seven Reefs in the Spratly Islands in the South China Sea* (26 April 2016) (hereinafter "**Ferse Report**").

[874] Award on Jurisdiction, para. 408.

[875] Award on Jurisdiction, para. 409.

[876] *See, e.g.*, First Carpenter Report, pp. 3-9; Second Carpenter Report, pp. 3, 26-27; J.W. McManus, *Offshore Coral Reef Damage, Overfishing and Paths to Peace in the South China Sea*, pp. 10-11 (rev. ed., 21 April 2016) (hereinafter "**McManus Report**"); Ferse Report, pp. 12-14; Merits Hearing Tr. (Day 3), p. 14.

[877] *See, e.g.*, First Carpenter Report, pp. 4-7; Second Carpenter Report, pp. 3, 26-27; McManus Report, pp. 10-11; Ferse Report, pp. 12-16, Merits Hearing Tr. (Day 3), p. 14. *See also* S. Wells, International Union for Conservation of Nature and Natural Resources (hereinafter "**IUCN**"), "Tridacna gigas,"

824. While coral reefs are amongst the most biodiverse and socioeconomically important ecosystems, they are also fragile and degrade under human pressures.[878] Threats to coral reefs include overfishing, destructive fishing, pollution, human habitation, and construction.[879]

825. In the South China Sea, ocean currents and the life cycles of marine species create a high degree of connectivity between the different ecosystems.[880] This means that the impact of any environmental harm occurring at Scarborough Shoal and in the Spratly Islands may not be limited to the immediate area, but can affect the health and viability of ecosystems elsewhere in the South China Sea.[881]

(b) Harmful Fishing Practices and Harvesting of Endangered Species

826. Documents adduced by the Philippines record a number of instances since the late 1990s in which Chinese fishing vessels have engaged in environmentally harmful fishing practices and the harvesting of endangered or threatened species. The same documents indicate that Chinese Government vessels have been present on some, but not all, of these occasions. The following is an overview of this record.

i. Incidents at Scarborough Shoal in the Period from 1998 to 2006

827. The earliest incidents detailed by the Philippines date from January 1998 when, according to police reports, 22 Chinese fishermen were involved in harvesting corals and marine turtles in the waters of Scarborough Shoal.[882] In March 1998, 29 Chinese fishermen at Scarborough

---

IUCN Red List of Threatened Species (Annex 724); S. Wells, IUCN, "Tridacna maxima," *IUCN Red List of Threatened Species* (Annex 725); S. Wells, IUCN, "Tridacna squamosa," *IUCN Red List of Threatened Species* (Annex 726).

[878]   Ferse Report, p. 7; C. Mora, I.R. Caldwell, C. Birkeland, J.W. McManus, "Dredging in the Spratly Islands: Gaining Land but Losing Reefs," *PLoS Biology* Vol. 14(3), pp. 1-2 (31 March 2016) (Annex 893) (hereinafter "**Mora Report**"); A. Feng & Y. Wang, , First Ocean Research Institution of State Oceanic Administration, "Construction Activities at Nansha Reefs Did Not Affect the Coral Reef Ecosystem," 10 June 2015, *available at* <www.soa.gov.cn/xw/dfdwdt/jgbm_155/201506/t20150610_38318.html> (Annex 872) (hereinafter "**SOA Report**").

[879]   Ferse Report, p. 7; Mora Report, pp. 1-2.

[880]   First Carpenter Report, p. 8; Second Carpenter Report, pp. 3, 26-27; Ferse Report, pp. 12-14.

[881]   First Carpenter Report, pp. 9, 13, 18-19; Second Carpenter Report, pp. 3, 26-27; Ferse Report, pp. 37-39.

[882]   Memorandum from the Fact Finding Committee, National Police Commission, Republic of the Philippines, to the Chairman and Members of the Regional Committee on Illegal Entrants for Region 1, Republic of the Philippines (28 January 1998) (Annex 28); Memorandum from the Assistant Secretary for Asian and Pacific Affairs, Department of Foreign Affairs, Republic of the Philippines, to the Secretary of Foreign Affairs, Republic of the Philippines (23 March 1998) (Annex 29). An even earlier document suggests that 62 Chinese fishermen had been prosecuted in the Philippines in 1995 for illegal fishing in

Shoal were reported to be found in possession of dynamite and corals.[883] Several of the fishermen were prosecuted and convicted under Philippine fisheries laws.[884]

828. Further incidents of unlawful harvesting of coral were reported in a Note Verbale dated 14 January 2000, in which the Philippines asked China to take "resolute action" against fishermen found with corals at Scarborough Shoal, and expressed concern that:

> This illegal activity disturbed the tranquility of the ecosystem and habitat of important species of marine life and, at the same time, caused irreparable damage to the marine environment of the area. It might be noted that the gathering and trade of corals violate the provisions of three (3) international conventions to which China is a signatory, namely, the Convention on Biological Diversity which entered into force on 29 December 1993; the RAMSAR Convention adopted in Iran in 1971, and the Convention on International Trade in Endangered Species of Wild Fauna and Flora (CITES) which entered into force on 01 July 1975.[885]

829. In April 2000, three Chinese fishing vessels were found at Scarborough Shoal by Philippine authorities, loaded with corals, cyanide, blasting caps, detonating cord, and dynamite.[886]

830. On 29 January 2001, Philippine authorities photographed and confiscated the catch of endangered "sharks, eels, turtles and corals" from four Chinese fishing vessels in the vicinity of Scarborough Shoal.[887] The incident led to diplomatic exchanges in which China asserted its sovereignty over Scarborough Shoal and noted that "the Chinese Government attaches great importance to environmental protection and violators are dealt with in accordance with Chinese

---

the Spratlys, Memorandum from the Ambassador of the Republic of the Philippines in Beijing to the Undersecretary of Foreign Affairs of the Republic of the Philippines (10 April 1995) (Annex 21).

[883] Memorandum from the Assistant Secretary for Asian and Pacific Affairs, Department of Foreign Affairs, Republic of the Philippines, to the Secretary of Foreign Affairs, Republic of the Philippines (23 March 1998) (Annex 29).

[884] *People of the Philippines v. Shin Ye Fen, et al.*, Criminal Case No. RTC 2357-I, Decision, Regional Trial Court, Third Judicial Region, Branch 69, Iba, Zambales, Philippines (29 April 1998) (Annex 30); *People of the Philippines v. Wuh Tsu Kai, et al.*, Criminal Case No. RTC 2362-I, Decision, Regional Trial Court, Third Judicial Region, Branch 69, Iba, Zambales, Philippines (29 April 1998) (Annex 31); *People of the Philippines v. Zin Dao Guo, et al.*, Criminal Case No. RTC 2363-I, Decision, Regional Trial Court, Third Judicial Region, Branch 69, Iba, Zambales, Philippines (29 April 1998) (Annex 32).

[885] Note Verbale from the Department of Foreign Affairs, Republic of the Philippines, to the Embassy of the People's Republic of China in Manila, No. 200100 (14 January 2000) (Annex 186). *See also* Convention on Biological Diversity, 5 June 1992, 1760 UNTS 79 (hereinafter "**CBD**"); Convention on Wetlands of International Importance especially as Waterfowl Habitat, 2 February 1971, 996 UNTS 246; the Convention on International Trade in Endangered Species of Wild Fauna and Flora, 3 March 1973, 993 UNTS 243 (hereinafter "**CITES**").

[886] Situation Report the Philippine Navy to the Chief of Staff, Armed Forces of the Philippines, No. 004-18074 (18 April 2000) (Annex 41); Letter from the Vice Admiral, Armed Forces of the Philippines, to the Secretary of National Defense, Republic of the Philippines (27 May 2000) (Annex 42).

[887] Memorandum from the Acting Secretary of Foreign Affairs, Republic of the Philippines, to the President of the Republic of the Philippines (5 February 2001) (Annex 44); Office of Asian and Pacific Affairs, Department of Foreign Affairs, Republic of the Philippines, *Apprehension of Four Chinese Fishing Vessels in the Scarborough Shoal*, pp. 2-3 (23 February 2001) (Annex 46).

laws and regulations."[888] Six weeks later, on 15 March 2001, Philippine authorities again confiscated "endangered marine resources (giant oysters), cyanide and blasting caps" from Chinese fishing vessels.[889]

831. On at least three occasions in 2002, the Philippine Navy confiscated explosives, cyanide, corals, sea shells, and sea clams from Chinese fishing vessels at Scarborough Shoal.[890]

832. On 31 October 2004, Philippine naval vessels again intercepted Chinese fishing vessels at Scarborough Shoal laden with giant clams.[891]

833. On 30 December 2005, during a "routine inspection" at Scarborough Shoal, the Philippine vessel BRP Artemio Ricarte found four Chinese fishing vessels in possession of "assorted corals, live clamshells weighing about 16 tons and illegal fishing gears."[892] The catch was photographed and confiscated and the crew then released. The incident led the Chinese Vice Foreign Minister to summon the Philippine Ambassador in Beijing to convey China's "grave concern and strong opposition" and reiterate China's position that it has "indisputable sovereignty over Scarborough Shoal and adjacent waters."[893] The Philippines in turn expressed "grave concern" about the "harmful illegal fishing and rampant trading of endangered corals and marine species in the South China Sea."[894]

---

[888] Memorandum from the Embassy of the Republic of the Philippines in Beijing to the Secretary of Foreign Affairs, Republic of the Philippines, No. ZPE-06-2001-S (13 February 2001) (Annex 43); see also Memorandum from the Assistant Secretary for Asian and Pacific Affairs, Department of Foreign Affairs, Republic of the Philippines, to the Secretary of Foreign Affairs, Republic of the Philippines, pp. 1-2 (14 February 2001) (Annex 45); Memorandum from the Embassy of the Republic of the Philippines in Beijing to the Secretary of Foreign Affairs, Republic of the Philippines, No. ZPE-09-2001-S (17 March 2001) (Annex 47).

[889] Memorandum from the Embassy of the Republic of the Philippines in Beijing, to the Secretary of Foreign Affairs, Republic of the Philippines, p. 9 (21 May 2001) (Annex 48).

[890] Memorandum from the Director, Naval Operation Center, Philippine Navy to the Flag Officer in Command, Philippine Navy (11 February 2002) (Annex 49); Memorandum from Vice Admiral, Philippine Navy to the Assistant Secretary for Asian and Pacific Affairs, Department of Foreign Affairs, Republic of Philippines (26 March 2002) (Annex 50); Memorandum from the Embassy in the Republic of the Philippines in Beijing to the Secretary of Foreign Affairs, Republic of the Philippines (19 August 2002) (Annex 51); Report from CNS to the Flag Officer in Command, Philippine Navy, File No. N2D-0802-401, (1 September 2002) (Annex 52).

[891] Report from Lt. Commander, Philippine Navy, to Flag Officer in Command, Philippine Navy, No. N2E-F-1104-012 (18 November 2004) (Annex 55).

[892] Letter from the Rear Admiral, Armed Forces of the Philippines, to the Assistant Secretary for Asian and Pacific Affairs, Department of Foreign Affairs, Republic of the Philippines (Annex 57).

[893] Memorandum from the Secretary of Foreign Affairs, Republic of the Philippines, to the President of the Republic of the Philippines (11 January 2006) (Annex 58).

[894] Memorandum from the Secretary of Foreign Affairs, Republic of the Philippines, to the President of the Republic of the Philippines (11 January 2006) (Annex 58).

834. On 8 April 2006, a Philippine naval patrol at Scarborough Shoal located Chinese fishing vessels with "assorted corals and shells" on board that were photographed and then thrown overboard.[895]

        ii.   Incidents at Scarborough Shoal in April 2012

835. On 10 April 2012, the Philippine naval vessel BRP Gregoria del Pilar, and smaller boats launched from it, conducted a "Visit, Board, Search and Seizure Operation" on Chinese fishing vessels inside Scarborough Shoal and reported finding "large amounts of corals and giant clams" inside the first Chinese vessel boarded.[896] A further eight Chinese vessels were boarded throughout the morning, resulting in the documentation and recovery of "assorted endangered species" including "corals and giant clams."[897] Later that afternoon, two CMS vessels moved towards the shoal, "placing themselves between" BRP Gregoria del Pilar and the eight Chinese fishing boats.[898]

836. The incident of 10 April 2012 led to what the Philippine Navy described as a "diplomatic stand-off . . . following the discovery of Chinese fishing vessels . . . harvesting corals and capturing endangered marine species and the subsequent interference by Chinese maritime law enforcement vessels."[899] During the remainder of April 2012, the Philippine Navy and Coast Guard conducted air and sea surveillance missions at Scarborough Shoal and reported sighting three CMS vessels alongside a number of Chinese fishing vessels.[900]

837. A Chinese Ministry of Foreign Affairs Spokesperson confirmed on 12 April 2012 that:

---

[895] Report from the Commanding Officer, NAVSOU-2, Philippine Navy, to the Acting Commander, Naval Task Force 21, Philippine Navy, No. NTF21-0406-011/NTF21 OPPLAN (BANTAY AMIANAN) 01-05 (9 April 2006) (Annex 59).

[896] Memorandum from the Philippine Navy to the Chief of Staff, Armed Forces of the Philippines, No. N2E-0412-008 (11 April 2012) (Annex 77). *See also* Note Verbale from the Department of Foreign Affairs, Republic of Philippines to the Embassy of the People's Republic of China in Manila, No. 12-0894 (11 April 2012) (Annex 205).

[897] Memorandum from the Philippine Navy to the Chief of Staff, Armed Forces of the Philippines, No. N2E-0412-008 (11 April 2012) (Annex 77).

[898] Memorandum from the Philippine Navy to the Chief of Staff, Armed Forces of the Philippines, No. N2E-0412-008 (11 April 2012) (Annex 77).

[899] Memorandum from the Philippine Navy to the Chief of Staff, Armed Forces of the Philippines, No. N2E-0412-008 (11 April 2012) (Annex 77).

[900] Memorandum from the Philippine Navy to the Chief of Staff, Armed Forces of the Philippines, No. N2E-0412-008 (11 April 2012) (Annex 77); *see also* Report from the Commanding Officer, SARV-003, Philippine Coast Guard to the Commander, Coast Guard District Northwestern Luzon, Philippine Coast Guard (28 April 2012) (Annex 78).

> Relevant Chinese authorities have dispatched administrative vessels rather than military vessels to the Huangyan Island waters to protect the safety and legitimate fishing activities of Chinese fishermen and fishing vessels.[901]

838. On 23 April 2012, the Philippine Coast Guard observed two Chinese fishing vessels with stacks of giant clams inside the cargo hold, as well as several Chinese utility boats "dragging something underwater that caused seawater discoloration."[902]

839. On 26 April 2012, the Philippine Coast Guard reported to the Bureau of Fisheries that it had seen a Chinese fishing boat depart Scarborough Shoal "loaded with giant clams and other marine products" but noted that "[a]ll we can do is observe[], we cannot apprehend the poachers because they are being protected by two China Marine Surveillance ships."[903]

840. On 2 May 2012, Philippine Bureau of Fisheries personnel described how, during April 2012, Chinese CMS and FLEC vessels were docking alongside and protecting Chinese fishing vessels in Scarborough Shoal while they undertook trawling, fishing, dredging, and towing.[904]

841. The Philippines expressed its concerns to ASEAN Member States on 21 May 2012, about the issue of "Chinese fishermen poaching in the area" noting that "although these fishermen have already evaded arrests and prosecution for illegal fishing, nevertheless, Chinese Government vessels continue to ply the area in [] much larger numbers now."[905] Simultaneously, the Philippines sent a Note Verbale to the Chinese Embassy in Manila stating that:

> the increase in the number of China's vessels in the area imperils the marine diversity in the Shoal and threatens the marine ecosystem in the whole West Philippine Sea. The Philippines has documented the many instances where Chinese fishermen have unlawfully dredged the area and illegally harvested giant clams and corals.[906]

842. In response, China recalled that after the incident of 10 April 2012, it had urged the Philippines to withdraw all Philippine ships immediately, and once again urged that the Philippines

---

[901]   Ministry of Foreign Affairs, People's Republic of China, *Foreign Ministry Spokesperson Liu Weimin's Regular Press Conference* (12 April 2012) (Annex 117).

[902]   Report from the Commanding Officer, SARV-003, Philippine Coast Guard to the Commander, Coast Guard District Northwestern Luzon, Philippine Coast Guard, para. 5.12(b) (28 April 2012) (Annex 78).

[903]   Memorandum from the FRPLEU/QRT Chief, Bureau of Fisheries and Aquatic Resources, Republic of the Philippines, to the Director, Bureau of Fisheries and Aquatic Resources, Republic of the Philippines (2 May 2012) (Annex 79).

[904]   Report from FRPLEU/QRT Officers, Bureau of Fisheries and Aquatic Resources, Republic of the Philippines, to the Director, Bureau of Fisheries and Aquatic Resources, Republic of the Philippines (2 May 2012) (Annex 80).

[905]   Note Verbale from the Department of Foreign Affairs, Republic of the Philippines, to the Embassies of ASEAN Member States in Manila, No. 12-1372 (21 May 2012) (Annex 210).

[906]   Note Verbale from the Department of Foreign Affairs, Republic of the Philippines, to the Embassy of the People's Republic of China in Manila, No. 12-1371 (21 May 2012) (Annex 688).

"immediately pull out" all remaining ships and "desist from disturbing the operation of Chinese fishing boats and law enforcement activities by China's public service ships."[907]

843. By 2 June 2012, an air reconnaissance mission undertaken by the Philippine Navy reported there were 28 "Chinese fishing vessels trawling alongside each other" at Scarborough Shoal, with flotation devices "believed intended to obstruct the passage to the shoal" and four Chinese FLEC vessels and five CMS ships were sighted in the area.[908]

844. The Philippines has refrained from sending any further vessels to Scarborough Shoal since May 2012 and accordingly its recent monitoring of poaching activities has been limited.[909]

iii. More Recent Incidents in Other Parts of the South China Sea

845. According to reports of the Armed Forces of the Philippines, two fishing vessels "believed to be Chinese were monitored fishing using explosives and sodium cyanide 4 NM SW off LT57" in Second Thomas Shoal on 12 February 2012.[910]

846. A situation report on Second Thomas Shoal prepared by the Armed Forces of the Philippines on 11 May 2013 contains a photograph depicting a Chinese vessel laden with giant clams and corals.[911] A few days later, the Armed Forces of the Philippines also reported sighting various Chinese Government vessels such as "Jianghu V Missile Frigate 562" and China Marine Service vessels, CMS 84 and CMS 167, alongside two Hainan fishing vessels with three dinghies "believed to be gathering corals and clams and dredging in the shoal."[912]

847. During the Hearing on the Merits, one member of the Tribunal asked the Philippines what "hard facts" the Philippines had about the harvesting of giant clams.[913] In addition to referring to

---

[907] Note Verbale from the Embassy of the People's Republic of China in Manila to the Department of Foreign Affairs, Republic of the Philippines, No. (12) PG-239 (25 May 2012) (Annex 211).

[908] Memorandum from the Commander, Naval Forces Northern Luzon, Philippine Navy to the Flag Officer in Command, Philippine Navy, No. CNFNL Rad Msg Cite NFCC-0612-001 (2 June 2012) (Annex 83).

[909] Memorial, para. 3.54; Note Verbale from the Embassy of the People's Republic of China in Manila to the Department of Foreign Affairs, Republic of the Philippines, No. (12) PG-239 (25 May 2012) (Annex 211).

[910] Armed Forces of the Philippines, *Near-occupation of Chinese Vessels of Second Thomas (Ayungin) Shoal in the Early Weeks of May 2013* (May 2013) (Annex 94).

[911] Memorial, para. 6.64, figure 6.7, *extracted from* Armed Forces of the Philippines, *Ayungin Shoal: Situation Update* (11 May 2013) (Annex 95).

[912] Armed Forces of the Philippines, *Near-occupation of Chinese Vessels of Second Thomas (Ayungin) Shoal in the Early Weeks of May 2013*, pp. 3-4 (May 2013) (Annex 94).

[913] Merits Hearing Tr. (Day 3), p. 46.

evidence already in the record,[914] on 18 December 2015, the Philippines submitted a new *BBC* article and video footage reporting that "[a]t least a dozen boats" trailing "plumes of sand and gravel" near Thitu were engaged in harvesting endangered species including hundreds of giant clams.[915] The *BBC* showed the fishermen's method, of breaking up coral with their propellers and described the resultant "complete devastation" of the reefs.[916]

848. The Tribunal-appointed expert, Dr. Ferse, also drew the Tribunal's attention to recent reporting on the damaging use of propellers to break up coral and release giant clams for ultimate sale on lucrative curio markets. One report states "widespread chopping of reefs by fishermen using propellers mounted on small boats in order to poach giant clam shells is visible on recent images of at least 28 reefs in the Spratly and Parcel island groups" and refers to "abundant evidence that China's navy and coast guard have been aware of the Tanmen fishermen's practice of chopping reefs, and tolerated or condoned it."[917]

849. Noting such reports, the Tribunal conveyed a request from Dr. Ferse to seek clarification from a scientist, Professor John McManus of the University of Miami, United States, whose studies had been cited during the Hearing on the Merits.[918] Specifically, the Philippines was invited to find out "what proportion of Professor McManus' estimates on the extent of reef area damaged he would confidently assign to dredging versus clam shell extraction."[919]

850. As a result of this process, Professor McManus provided the Tribunal with a revised version of his unpublished paper[920] and reported that he had conducted further examinations, interviews, studies of satellite imagery, and an underwater inspection at clam extraction sites near Thitu. He stated:

> I confirmed both that the affected areas were very shallow (generally 1-3 m deep) and that the presence of masses of dead broken branching coral, as well as abundant sand on one of the reefs, ruled out dredging as a cause. The thoroughness of the damage to marine life

---

[914] Merits Hearing Tr. (Day 3), pp. 46-47.

[915] R. Wingfield-Hayes, "Why are Chinese fishermen destroying coral reefs in the South China Sea?," *BBC* (15 December 2015), *available at* <www.bbc.com/news/magazine-35106631> (Annex 862). The video accompanying this annex refers to the Philippine arrest and prosecution of Chinese fishermen in November 2014 for poaching up to 500 sea turtles in the Spratlys and is available at <www.fmprc.gov.cn/mfa_eng/xwfw_665399/s2510_665401/2511_665403/t1214543.shtml>.

[916] R. Wingfield-Hayes, "Why are Chinese fishermen destroying coral reefs in the South China Sea?," *BBC*, p. 3 (15 December 2015), *available at* <www.bbc.com/news/magazine-35106631> (Annex 862).

[917] V.R. Lee, "Satellite Imagery Shows Ecocide in the South China Sea," *The Diplomat* (15 January 2016), *available at* <thediplomat.com/2016/01/satellite-images-show-ecocide-in-the-south-china-sea/>.

[918] J.W. McManus, "Offshore Coral Reef Damage, Overfishing and Paths to Peace in the South China Sea," draft as at 20 September 2015 (Annex 850); Merits Hearing Tr. (Day 4), pp. 29-31, 147-150, 157.

[919] Letter from the Tribunal to the Parties (1 April 2016).

[920] Letter from Professor McManus to the Tribunal (22 April 2016), *enclosing* McManus Report.

exceeded anything I had previously seen in four decades of investigating coral reef degradation. Interviews with local fishers, officials and military personnel indicated that this highly destructive PRC harvesting practice was now very widespread across the Spratly area.

. . .

The new results indicate that the People's Republic of China (PRC) is responsible for at least 39 km^2 of damage from shallow dredging and 69 km^2 of damage from giant clam harvest using propellers to dig up the bottom within the Greater Spratly Islands . . . . Vietnam is responsible for shallow dredging covering approximately 0.26 km^2. The overall damage to coral reefs within the Greater Spratly Islands covers at least 124 km^2, of which PRC is responsible for 99%.[921]

851. The Philippines also filed a short additional report from Professor Carpenter commenting on the new material from Professor McManus. Professor Carpenter stated the "extraction methods employed by Chinese fishermen, which are countenanced by the Chinese Government, are extremely destructive to reef habitat and represent unprecedented harm to the marine environment." [922] He recalled having already addressed the environmental impact of giant clam extraction,[923] but at the time he had prepared his reports he had "not appreciated the scale upon which this is occurring." [924] The Tribunal's experts also observe from satellite imagery the presence of tell-tale arc-shaped scars at Cuarteron, Fiery Cross, Gaven, Hughes and Mischief Reefs, indicating extensive propeller damage on the reef flats by boats likely harvesting giant clams.[925]

(c) China's Construction Activities on Seven Reefs in the Spratly Islands

852. The second aspect of the Philippines' environmental submissions relates to Chinese construction activities on seven features in the Spratly Islands: (a) Cuarteron Reef, (b) Fiery Cross Reef, (c) Gaven Reef (North), (d) Johnson Reef, (e) Hughes Reef, (f) Subi Reef, and (g) Mischief Reef.

853. Documents adduced by the Philippines indicate that in the period from the early 1990s until 2013, China undertook some construction and land reclamation on these features, typically starting with basic aluminium, wooden, or fibreglass structures supported by steel bars with

---

[921] Letter from Professor McManus to the Tribunal (22 April 2016).

[922] Declaration of Professor K.E. Carpenter, para. 5 (24 April 2016) (hereinafter "**Third Carpenter Report**").

[923] First Carpenter Report, pp. 14-15; Second Carpenter Report, pp. 29-32; Merits Hearing Tr. (Day 3), pp. 53-54.

[924] Third Carpenter Report, para. 5.

[925] Ferse Report, pp. 17-21, 31.

cement bases.[926] Over time, China installed more sophisticated structures, including concrete multi-storey buildings, wharves, helipads, and weather and communications instruments.[927] The largest of the projects before 2013 was the construction of an artificial island at Fiery Cross Reef of approximately 115 x 80 metres.[928] Other States in the region, including the Philippines and Viet Nam, undertook similar construction activities during the same period.[929] Examples of the pre-2013 structures built by China can be seen below at Figures 13 and 14 on page 333.

854. The massive island-building project that China has embarked on since the end of 2013, however, far exceeds the scale of these earlier construction projects. China has deployed a large fleet of vessels to the seven reefs, primarily using heavy 'cutter-suction dredge' equipment, to create more than 12.8 million square metres of new land in less than three years.[930]

855. The 'cutter-suction dredge' method involves a ship-borne drill which is extended from the dredging vessel into the seabed. The drill's rotating teeth act like picks that chisel away at the seabed or reef, breaking apart and extracting the soil, rock, and reef.[931] This material is then

---

[926]   *See, e.g.*, Armed Forces of the Philippines, *Chronological Development of Artificial Structures on Features* (Annex 96); Armed Forces of the Philippines, *Chronology of Events in the Kalayaan Island Group* (2004) (Annex 53).

[927]   *See* Armed Forces of the Philippines, *Chronological Development of Artificial Structures on Features* (Annex 96).

[928]   Armed Forces of the Philippines, *Matrix of Events: Fiery Cross (Kagitingan) Reef* (2013) (Annex 88).

[929]   *See, e.g.*, Note Verbale from the Embassy of the People's Republic of China in Manila to the Department of Foreign Affairs, Republic of the Philippines, No. 15 (PG)-053 (12 February 2015) (Annex 683); A. Feng & Y. Wang, *State Oceanic Administration*, p. 1 (10 June 2015), *available at* <www.soa.gov.cn/xw/dfdwdt/jgbm_155/201506/t20150610_38318.html> (Annex 872); Ministry of Foreign Affairs, People's Republic of China, *Foreign Ministry Spokesperson Hua Chunying's Remarks on the Philippines' Allegation that China's Construction on Maritime Features of the Nansha Islands Violates the DOC* (5 May 2015), *available at* <www.fmprc.gov.cn/mfa_eng/ xwfw_665399/s2510_665401/t1260672.shtml>. *See also* Asia Maritime Transparency Initiative, "Sandcastles of Their Own: Vietnamese Expansion in the Spratly Islands," *available at* <amti.csis.org/vietnam-island-building/>; J.B. Miller, "Tensions Continue to Boil in South China Sea," *Al Jazeera Centre for Studies*, (29 May 2016), *available at* <studies.aljazeera.net/ mritems/Documents/2016/5/29/4b10b189241a43478b9f862f4d1985a6_100.pdf>.

[930]   *See* Center for Strategic & International Studies, Asia Maritime Transparency Initiative, "Cuarteron Reef Tracker," *available at* <amti.csis.org/cuarteron-reef-tracker/> (Annex 776); Center for Strategic & International Studies, Asia Maritime Transparency Initiative, "Fiery Cross Reef Tracker," *available at* <amti.csis.org/fiery-cross-reef-tracker/> (Annex 777); Center for Strategic & International Studies, Asia Maritime Transparency Initiative, "Gaven Reef Tracker," *available at* <amti.csis.org/gaven-reef-tracker/> (Annex 778); Center for Strategic & International Studies, Asia Maritime Transparency Initiative, "Hughes Reef Tracker," *available at* <amti.csis.org/hughes-reef-tracker/> (Annex 779); Center for Strategic & International Studies, Asia Maritime Transparency Initiative, "Johnson Reef Tracker," *available at* <amti.csis.org/johnson-reef-tracker/> (Annex 780); Center for Strategic & International Studies, Asia Maritime Transparency Initiative, "Subi Reef Tracker," *available at* <amti.csis.org/subi-reef-tracker/> (Annex 781); Center for Strategic & International Studies, Asia Maritime Transparency Initiative, "Mischief Reef Tracker," *available at* <amti.csis.org/mischief-reef-tracker/> (Annex 782).

[931]   Ferse Report, p. 22; Van Oord, *Cutter Suction Dredger Castor*, Video (2012), *available at* <www.vanoord.com/activities/cutter-suction-dredger> (Annex 796).

pumped up through a floating tube pipeline at the stern of the vessel to a reclamation area which can be several kilometres from the dredging location. It is then deposited onto the reef to create dry land, as illustrated in the video by Dutch dredging company Van Oord[932] and the diagram at Figure 12 below, both shown to the Tribunal during the Hearing on the Merits.[933]

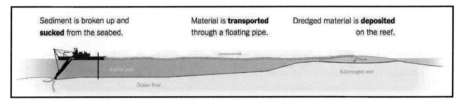

Figure 12: Dredging Operations
Second Carpenter Report, p. 10, reproduced from "What China Has Been
Building in the South China Sea," New York Times (27 October 2015)

856. China's largest suction cutter dredger is the Tian Jing Hao, reportedly capable of extracting 4,500 cubic metres per hour of sand, rock, and other materials from the surrounding seabed.[934] Photographs of the Tian Jing Hao are shown below, and at work, alongside other dredgers in the process of reclamation works at Mischief reef. China has also used "trailing suction hopper dredgers" which collect loose materials from the seabed and shoot material onto the reef, as illustrated in Figures 15 to 17 on page 335 below.

857. The environmental impact of such dredging methods are discussed in the Tribunal's considerations at paragraphs 976 to 983 below. In short, according to the Tribunal's experts, construction and dredging activities can impact reef systems in three ways: (a) direct destruction of reef habitat through burial under sand, gravel and rubble; (b) indirect impacts on benthic organisms such as corals and seagrasses via altered hydrodynamics, increased sedimentation, turbidity, and nutrient enrichment; and (c) indirect impacts on organisms in the water column, such as fishes and larvae, from sediments, chemical and nutrient release, and noise.[935]

---

[932] Van Oord, *Cutter Suction Dredger Castor*, Video (2012), *available at* <www.vanoord.com/activities/cutter-suction-dredger> (Annex 796).

[933] Merits Hearing Tr. (Day 2), p. 198.

[934] CCCC Tianjin Dredging Co., Ltd. "Tian Jing Hao," *available at* </en.tjhdj.com/index.php?mod=product&act=view&cid=46&id=397> (Annex 857); "Tian Jing Hao," *Dredgepoint.org*, *available at* <www.dredgepoint.org/dredging-database/equipment/tian-jing-hao> (Annex 858); *see also* Guangdong TV, "The Magic Dredge Pumping Artifact 'Tianjing Hao', a Great Meritorious Machine in China's Land Reclamation in Nansha," Video (10 April 2015) (Annex 799).

[935] Ferse Report, p. 22.

858. Descriptions of the reef environment and construction activities at each of the seven features identified in the Philippines' Submissions No. 11 and 12(b) are set out in the following Sections.

859. Throughout the course of China's island-building project, in multiple exchanges of diplomatic notes, the Philippines has strongly protested China's activities[936] and China has rejected "the groundless protest and accusation" by the Philippines.[937] China has also pointed out that "the Philippine side has constructed and kept expanding facilities including airports, harbors, stilt houses and schools on some of the illegally occupied islands and reefs."[938]

---

[936] *See* Note Verbale from the Embassy of the Republic of the Philippines to the Embassy of the People's Republic of China in Manila, No. 14-1180 (4 April 2014) (Annex 670); Note Verbale from the Embassy of the Republic of the Philippines to the Embassy of the People's Republic of China in Manila, No. 14-2093 (6 June 2014) (Annex 672); Note Verbale from the Department of Foreign Affairs, Republic of the Philippines, to the Embassy of the People's Republic of China, No. 14-2276 (23 June 2014) (Annex 673); Note Verbale from the Embassy of the Republic of the Philippines to the Embassy of the People's Republic of China in Manila, No. 14-2307 (24 June 2014) (Annex 674); Note Verbale from the Department of Foreign Affairs, Republic of the Philippines, to the Embassy of the People's Republic of China in Manila, No. 14-2889 (18 August 2014) (Annex 677); Note Verbale from the Department of Foreign Affairs, Republic of the Philippines, to the Embassy of the People's Republic of China, No. 14-3504 (10 October 2014) (Annex 679); Note Verbale from the Department of Foreign Affairs, Republic of the Philippines, to the Embassy of the People's Republic of China in Manila, No. 15-0586 (16 February 2015) (Annex 684).

[937] *See Verbatim Text of Response by Deputy Chief of Mission, Embassy of the People's Republic of China in Manila, to Philippine Note Verbale No. 14-1180 dated 04 April 2014* (11 April 2014) (Annex 671); Note Verbale from the Embassy of the People's Republic of China in Manila to the Department of Foreign Affairs, Republic of the Philippines, No. 14 (PG)-195 (30 June 2014) (Annex 675); Note Verbale from the Embassy of the People's Republic of China in Manila to the Department of Foreign Affairs, Republic of the Philippines, No. 14 (PG)-197 (4 July 2014) (Annex 676); Note Verbale from the Embassy of the People's Republic of China in Manila to the Department of Foreign Affairs, Republic of the Philippines, No. 14 (PG)-264 (2 September 2014) (Annex 678); Note Verbale from the Embassy of the People's Republic of China in Manila to the Department of Foreign Affairs, Republic of the Philippines, No. 14 (PG)-336 (28 October 2014) (Annex 680); Note Verbale from the Ministry of Foreign Affairs, People's Republic of China to the Embassy of the Republic of the Philippines in Beijing, No. (2015) Bu Bian Zi No. 5 (20 January 2015) (Annex 681); Note Verbale from the Embassy of the People's Republic of China to the Department of Foreign Affairs, Republic of the Philippines, No. 15 (PG)-068 (4 March 2015) (Annex 685); Note Verbale from the Department of Boundary and Ocean Affairs, Ministry of Foreign Affairs, People's Republic of China, to the Embassy of the Republic of the Philippines in Beijing, No. (2015) Bu Bian Zi No. 22 (30 March 2015) (Annex 686); Note Verbale from the Department of Boundary and Ocean Affairs, Ministry of Foreign Affairs, People's Republic of China, to the Embassy of the Republic of the Philippines in Beijing, No. (2015) Bu Bian Zi No. 23 (30 March 2015) (Annex 687).

[938] Note Verbale from the Embassy of the People's Republic of China in Manila to the Department of Foreign Affairs, Republic of the Philippines, No. 15 (PG)-053 (12 February 2015) (Annex 683).

Figure 13: Fiery Cross Reef Installation circa 2011
Armed Forces of the Philippines, Matrix of Events: Fiery Cross (Kagitingan) Reef (2013) (Annex 88)

Figure 14: Subi Reef Installation circa 2012
Armed Forces of the Philippines, Matrix of Events: Subi (Zamora) (2013) (Annex 91)

this page intentionally blank

Figure 15: Tian Jing Hao, Cutter-Suction Dredge
(Annex 858)

Figure 16: Trailing Suction Hopper Dredge
(Annex 792)

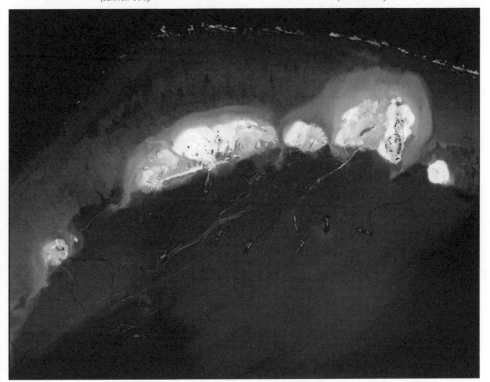

Figure 17: Dredgers at work at Mischief Reef
(Annex 792)

this page intentionally blank

860. While some of these communications have concerned the effect of China's construction work on the present proceedings (an issue discussed further in connection with the Philippines' Submissions concerning the aggravation of the dispute, see Chapter VIII below), the Philippines has also emphasised the environmental impact of China's island-building project. For instance, on 13 April 2015, the Philippine Department of Foreign Affairs released the following statement:

> China's massive reclamation activities are causing irreversible and widespread damage to the biodiversity and ecological balance of the South China Sea/ West Philippine Sea. We cannot accept China's claim that its activities have not caused damage to the ecological environment of the South China Sea.
>
> China has pursued these activities unilaterally, disregarding peoples in the surrounding states who have depended on the sea for their livelihood for generations. . . .
>
> Moreover, we note that China has tolerated environmentally harmful fishing practices by its nationals at Bajo De Masinloc which breaches its obligations under the 1982 United Nations Convention on the Law of the Sea (UNCLOS), the Convention on Biological Diversity, and the Convention on International Trade in Endangered Species of Wild Fauna and Flora (CITES).[939]

861. A more detailed statement was released on 23 April 2015 by the Philippine Bureau of Fisheries and Aquatic Resources, following a comprehensive study by the University of the Philippines on the damage inflicted to marine biodiversity and economic productivity.[940]

862. As detailed below at paragraphs 916 to 924, China maintains that its island-building project "had gone through science-based evaluation and assessment with equal importance given to construction and protection" and that it had taken "full account of issues of ecological preservation and fishery protection" and "followed strict environmental protection standards."[941]

i. Cuarteron Reef

863. Cuarteron Reef is an ellipse-shaped table-like reef extending roughly 5 kilometres west to east, with a shallow reef flat area and no lagoon in the centre.[942] Fishing surveys from the late 1990s recorded an abundance of reef fish resources there, including sharks, parrotfishes, and

---

[939] Department of Foreign Affairs, Republic of the Philippines, "Statement on China's Reclamation Activities and their Impact on the Region's Marine Environment" (13 April 2015) (Annex 608).

[940] Bureau of Fisheries and Aquatic Resources, Republic of the Philippines, "Press Release: DA-BFAR, National Scientist Condemn the Destruction of Marine Resources in the West Philippine Sea" (23 April 2015) (Annex 609).

[941] Embassy of the People's Republic of China in Canada, "An Interview on China's Construction Activities on the Nansha Islands and Reefs 2015/05/27," *available at* <ca.chineseembassy.org/eng/zt/cpot/t1267437.htm> (Annex 820).

[942] See the general geographic description of Cuarteron Reef at paragraph 285 above.

groupers.[943] The Tribunal has found at paragraph 339 above that, in its natural condition, the reef platform at Cuarteron Reef was submerged at high tide, with some rocks remaining exposed. The Tribunal classified Cuarteron Reef as an Article 121(3) rock.

864. Chinese construction activities reportedly commenced at Cuarteron Reef in 1992 with three small buildings.[944] By 1997, further buildings, wharves, and communications facilities were observed.[945] By 2006, Philippine aerial surveys sighted a three-story building, a concrete platform, and a helipad.[946] By October 2013, the Philippines military observed more concrete buildings, solar panels, weather and communications instruments, observation towers, a temporary pier, and the presence of a barge for hauling of construction materials.[947]

865. More substantial land reclamation began in the spring of 2014. Chinese land reclamation intensified throughout 2015,[948] with a permanent pier evident from 9 May 2015.[949] On 26 May 2015, the Chinese Ministry of Transport held a ceremony there to mark the beginning of construction on a 50-metre lighthouse, the main purpose of which, according to the Ministry of Foreign Affairs, is "to better carry out China's international responsibilities and obligations in terms of maritime search and rescue, disaster prevention and relief, maritime scientific research, meteorological observations, protection of the ecology and environment, navigation safety, and fishery and production services."[950] Images from 18 July 2015 showed the presence of large vessels and dredgers at Cuarteron Reef.[951]

866. Aerial and satellite photography demonstrate China's construction efforts. Satellite photography from 23 August 2015, which is reproduced as Figures 18 and 19 on page 341 shows an artificial island approximately 200 times larger than the original installation in 2012, which is barely visible in the photograph from January 2012 reproduced on the same page.

[943] Ferse Report, p. 17.

[944] Armed Forces of the Philippines, *Matrix of Events: Cuarteron (Calderon) Reef* (2013) (Annex 87).

[945] Armed Forces of the Philippines, *Matrix of Events: Cuarteron (Calderon) Reef* (2013) (Annex 87).

[946] Armed Forces of the Philippines, *Matrix of Events: Cuarteron (Calderon) Reef* (2013) (Annex 87).

[947] Armed Forces of the Philippines, *Matrix of Events: Cuarteron (Calderon) Reef* (2013) (Annex 87).

[948] *See* photographs of reclamation works progress at *Compilation of Images of Cuarteron Reef (various sources)* (compiled 13 November 2015) (Annex 787); Bureau of Fisheries and Aquatic Resources, Republic of the Philippines, *Press Release: DA-BFAR, National Scientist Condemn the Destruction of Marine Resources in the West Philippine Sea* (23 April 2015) (Annex 609).

[949] Letter from the Secretary of National Defense, Republic of the Philippines, to the Secretary of Foreign Affairs, Republic of the Philippines (22 June 2015) (Annex 610).

[950] "China to Construct Two 50m Lighthouses in Huayang Jia [Cuarteron] Reef and Chigua Jiao [Johnson South Reef]," *Xinhua* (26 May 2015) (Annex 760).

[951] Letter from the Secretary of National Defense, Republic of the Philippines, to the Secretary of Foreign Affairs, Republic of the Philippines (10 August 2015) (Annex 611).

Calculations presented by the Philippines, estimate that China's construction work as at November 2015 had resulted in the creation of at least 231,000 square metres of new land on Cuarteron Reef.[952] The same report indicates that China built a channel approximately 125 metres wide for large vessels to access and berth within a harbour cut out of the reef platform.

ii. Fiery Cross Reef

867. Fiery Cross Reef is an "open spindle-shaped atoll that extends for about 25 km from northeast to southwest, with a width of about 6 km."[953] An extensive reef flat on the southwest end of the reef surrounds a small closed lagoon in its centre with a maximum depth of 12 metres. According to the Tribunal's coral reef experts, the present coral reef there developed approximately seven to eight thousand years ago.[954] Abundant fisheries were reported in surveys from the late 1990s, and highly biodiverse coral communities were recorded in surveys from 2004 and 2005.[955] The Tribunal has found at paragraph 343 above that, while Fiery Cross Reef was mostly submerged in its natural state, the atoll was encumbered by a rock that remained exposed at high tide. The Tribunal classified Fiery Cross Reef as an Article 121(3) rock.

868. Chinese construction activities reportedly commenced at Fiery Cross reef in 1988 with the building first of a small naval post, followed by an oceanographic observation post, pier, and several other buildings.[956] Subsequent years saw the installation of communications systems and lighthouses, and by 2013 the Philippines Army reported, based on photographic surveys, that "Fiery Cross Reef is now a complete complex of buildings with significant communications and defense and military features."[957] By March 2013, further buildings, including a greenhouse and powerhouse had also been observed.[958]

---

[952] *See* Center for Strategic & International Studies, Asia Maritime Transparency Initiative, "Cuarteron Reef Tracker," *available at* <amti.csis.org/cuarteron-reef-tracker/> (Annex 776).

[953] Ferse Report, p. 17. See the general geographic description of Fiery Cross Reef at paragraph 286 above.

[954] Ferse Report, p. 17.

[955] Ferse Report, pp. 17-18.

[956] Armed Forces of the Philippines, *Matrix of Events: Fiery Cross (Kagitingan) Reef* (2013) (Annex 88).

[957] Armed Forces of the Philippines, *Matrix of Events: Fiery Cross (Kagitingan) Reef* (2013) (Annex 88).

[958] Armed Forces of the Philippines, *Matrix of Events: Fiery Cross (Kagitingan) Reef* (2013) (Annex 88).

869. By November 2014 there were reports that China was building a runway on Fiery Cross Reef.[959] Land reclamation intensified and progressed rapidly throughout 2015.[960] Images from 18 July 2015 showed the presence of at least 18 vessels unloading construction equipment.[961] By November 2015, approximately 2,740,000 square metres of land had been created at Fiery Cross Reef, with sand and rock dredged from the seabed covering virtually the entire platform of the southwestern reef flat.[962] China's recent activities have created an artificial island approximately 300 times larger than the pre-existing installations, which covered an area of approximately 11,000 square metres. The installations now include a three-kilometre runway, a 630,000-square-metre harbour, multiple cement plants, support buildings, temporary loading piers, communication facilities, defence equipment, two lighthouses, a greenhouse, two helipads and a multi-level administrative facility adjacent to the runway.[963]

870. The massive scale of China's construction efforts on Fiery Cross Reef is apparent in aerial and satellite photography. Satellite photography reproduced as Figures 20 and 21 on page 343 shows the reef's progression from its nearly natural state in January 2012 (with China's original installation just visible at the southern end) to an artificial island complex, complete with a large runway, covering the entire reef platform in October 2015.

iii. Gaven Reef (North)

871. Gaven Reef (North) sits on the western end of the largely submerged atoll of Tizard Bank.[964] Its reef flat extends approximately 1.9 kilometres from north to south and 1.2 kilometres from east to west and has no central lagoon.[965] According to surveys conducted between 1998 and 2005, fisheries resources at Gaven Reef (North) were lower than at Fiery Cross Reef, but Gaven Reef

---

[959] *See e.g.*, J. Hardy & S. O'Connor, "China Building Airstrip Capable Island on Fiery Cross Reef," *IHS Jane's Defence Weekly* (20 November 2014) (Annex 720).

[960] *See* Armed Forces of the Philippines, *Aerial Photographs of On-Going Reclamation at Fiery Cross Reef* (2014-2015) (Annex 785).

[961] Letter from the Secretary of National Defense, Republic of the Philippines, to the Secretary of Foreign Affairs, Republic of the Philippines (10 August 2015) (Annex 611).

[962] Asia Maritime Transparency Initiative and Center for Strategic and International Studies, *Fiery Cross Reef Tracker*, *available at* <amti.csis.org/fiery-cross-reef-tracker/> (Annex 777).

[963] J. Perlez, "China Building Aircraft Runway in Disputed Spratly Islands," *New York Times* (16 April 2015) (Annex 756); Asia Maritime Transparency Initiative and Center for Strategic and International Studies, "Fiery Cross Reef Tracker," *available at* <amti.csis.org/fiery-cross-reef-tracker/> (Annex 777); J. Hardy and S. O'Connor, "China Completes Runway on Fiery Cross Reef," *IHS Jane's Defence Weekly* (25 September 2015) (Annex 812).

[964] See the general geographic description of Gaven Reef (North) at paragraph 288 above.

[965] Ferse Report, p. 18.

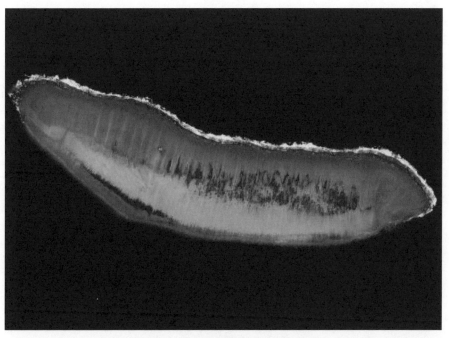

Figure 18: Cuarteron Reef, 14 January 2012
(Annex 787)

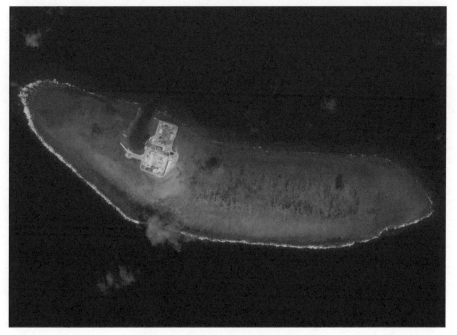

Figure 19: Cuarteron Reef, 23 August 2015
(Annex 787)

this page intentionally blank

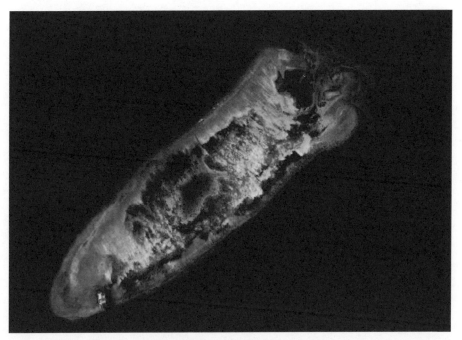

Figure 20: Fiery Cross Reef, 17 January 2012
(Annex 788)

Figure 21: Fiery Cross Reef, 19 October 2015
(Annex 788)

this page intentionally blank

(North) was found to have the highest resources for longlining among the seven reefs.[966] The Tribunal has found at paragraph 366 above that, in its natural state, Gaven Reef (North) included a small sand cay at its north-east end that remained exposed at high tide. The Tribunal classified Gaven Reef (North) as an Article 121(3) rock.

872. China has reportedly had a presence on Gaven Reef (North) since 1988 and, by 1996, had built an outpost with barracks and two octoganal structures.[967] A three-storey concrete building with communications equipment was observed by Philippine surveillance in May 2005, and further enhancements were noted in 2011.[968]

873. Intense reclamation work began at Gaven Reef (North) in the spring of 2014.[969] Philippine surveillance in May 2015 at Gaven Reef (North) observed a new helipad, watch post, and wharf expansion.[970] Within the span of a year, China transformed Gaven Reef (North) from a coral reef to an artificial island measuring approximately 300 by 250 metres, created from 136,000 square metres of materials dredged from the seabed.[971]

874. The change in Gaven Reef (North) is readily visible in aerial and satellite photography. China's original installation, as well as the naturally occurring sand cay, are barely visible at the north end of the reef in satellite imagery from January 2012, reproduced as Figure 22 on page 347. In contrast, a large artificial island in the shape of a sideways "Y" dominates the reef in imagery from November 2015 in Figure 23.

iv. *Johnson Reef*

875. Johnson Reef is a large coral reef platform with a shallow central lagoon located at the south-west end of the Union Bank atoll and measures approximately 4.6 by 2.4 kilometres.[972]

---

[966] Ferse Report, p. 18.

[967] Armed Forces of the Philippines, *Matrix of Events: Gaven (Burgos)* (2013) (Annex 89).

[968] Armed Forces of the Philippines, *Matrix of Events: Gaven (Burgos)* (2013) (Annex 89).

[969] Asia Maritime Transparency Initiative and Center for Strategic and International Studies, "Gaven Reef Tracker," *available at* <amti.csis.org/gaven-reef-tracker/> (Annex 778); Armed Forces of the Philippines, *Aerial Photographs of On-Going Reclamation at Gaven Reef* (2014) (Annex 783).

[970] Letter from the Secretary of National Defense, Republic of the Philippines, to the Secretary of Foreign Affairs, Republic of the Philippines (22 June 2015) (Annex 610); *See also* Asia Maritime Transparency Initiative and Center for Strategic and International Studies, "Gaven Reef Tracker," *available at* <amti.csis.org/gaven-reef-tracker/> (Annex 778).

[971] Asia Maritime Transparency Initiative and Center for Strategic and International Studies, "Gaven Reef Tracker," *available at* <amti.csis.org/gaven-reef-tracker/> (Annex 778).

[972] Ferse Report, p. 18. See also the general geographic description of Johnson Reef at paragraph 287 above.

Its fisheries resources were lower than those recorded at the other reefs, and live coral covered approximately 15 percent of the reef flat.[973] The Tribunal has found at paragraph 351 above that Johnson Reef has been consistently reported as including rocks that remain exposed at high tide and classified Johnson Reef as an Article 121(3) rock.

876. China has reportedly had a presence on Johnson Reef since 1988.[974] By 1992, China had constructed a "heavily fortified area with an observation tower," to which was added, by 2006, a three-storey concrete building, communications eqiupment, solar panels, and a helipad.[975]

877. China began extensive reclamation activities at Johnson Reef in the spring of 2014. Aerial reconnaissance conducted by the Philippines on 9 May 2015 detected further buildings, solar panels, paved roads, and piers.[976] A ceremony was held by the Chinese Ministry of Transport for the construction of a lighthouse on Johnson Reef on 26 May 2015.[977] By November 2015, China had created an artificial island measuring approximately 109,000 square metres, nearly 1,000 times larger than the previous structure.

878. The change in Johnson Reef is readily visible in aerial and satellite photography. China's original installation cannot even be seen without enlargement in satellite imagery from March 2013, reproduced as Figure 24 on page 347. In contrast, a large artificial island, along with a dredged harbour channel into the centre of the reef is readily visible in imagery from November 2015 in Figure 25.

     v.   *Hughes Reef*

879. Hughes Reef also forms part of the rim of the Union Bank atoll and lies to the north-east of Johnson Reef, measuring approximately 2.1 kilometres from north to south, and 2 kilometres from east to west.[978] Hughes Reef features a natural lagoon "meandering across its centre and opening to an adjacent deeper lagoon through a narrow, shallow channel on the eastern side of

---

[973]   Ferse Report, pp. 18-19.

[974]   Armed Forces of the Philippines, *Matrix of Events: Johnson (Mabini) Reef* (2013) (Annex 90).

[975]   Armed Forces of the Philippines, *Matrix of Events: Johnson (Mabini) Reef* (2013) (Annex 90).

[976]   Letter from the Secretary of National Defense, Republic of the Philippines, to the Secretary of Foreign Affairs, Republic of the Philippines, Annex A (22 June 2015) (Annex 610).

[977]   "China to Construct Two 50m Lighthouses in Huayang Jia [Cuarteron] Reef and Chigua Jiao [Johnson South Reef]," *Xinhua* (26 May 2015) (Annex 760).

[978]   See also the general geographic description of Hughes Reef at paragraph 287 above.

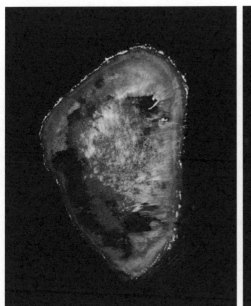

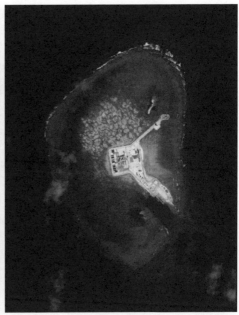

Figure 22: Gaven Reef (North), 15 January 2012
(Annex 789)

Figure 23: Gaven Reef (North), 16 November 2015
(Annex 789)

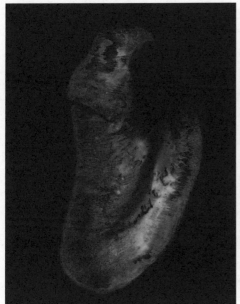

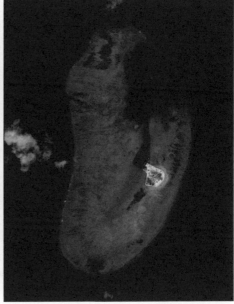

Figure 24: Johnson Reef, 20 March 2013
(Annex 790)

Figure 25: Johnson Reef, 4 November 2015
(Annex 790)

this page intentionally blank

the reef."[979] Fisheries surveys from the late 1990s showed some 'production value' (albeit lower than the other reefs discussed in this Chapter). [980] The Tribunal has found at paragraph 358 above that Hughes Reef is a low-tide elevation.

880. China has reportedly had a presence on Hughes Reef since 1988. By October 2006, China had installed a three-storey concrete building and helipad. [981] By February 2013, there were additional power-houses and communications equipment, but the total land area for these structures was still only approximately 380 square metres. [982]

881. China began large-scale reclamation activities at Hughes Reef in the spring of 2014. Aerial reconnaissance by the Philippines on 9 May 2015 detected a permanent pier, a "massive onshore construction of a 6-storey building," and large cargo vessels transporting sand sediments for "newly reclaimed land". [983] By November 2015, China had created an artificial island on Hughes Reef measuring around 75,000 square metres, on which it has built coastal fortifications, defensive towers, and a multi-level facility.[984] China also enlarged the entrance to the reef to create a 118-metre wide access channel for larger vessels.

882. The change in Hughes Reef is readily visible in aerial and satellite photography. China's original installation cannot even be seen without enlargement in satellite imagery from February 2010, reproduced as Figure 26 on page 351. In contrast, a large artificial island, along with a dredged harbour channel into the centre of the reef is apparent in imagery from September 2015 in Figure 27.

vi.   Subi Reef

883. Subi Reef is coral atoll enclosing a large lagoon that lies to the south-west of Thitu. Subi Reef spans approximately 5.75 kilometres in length and 3.25 kilometres in width and was, originally,

---

[979]   Ferse Report, p. 19.

[980]   Ferse Report, p. 19.

[981]   Armed Forces of the Philippines, *Matrix of Events: Chigua (Kennan) Reef* (2013) (Annex 86). Because the Philippines identified McKennan and Hughes Reefs collectively as "Chigua", a number of materials refer to Hughes Reef as McKennan or discuss the two features together.

[982]   Armed Forces of the Philippines, *Matrix of Events: Chigua (Kennan) Reef* (2013) (Annex 86); Asia Maritime Transparency Initiative and Center for Strategic and International Studies, "Hughes Reef Tracker," *available at* <amti.csis.org/hughes-reef-tracker/> (Annex 779).

[983]   Letter from the Secretary of National Defense, Republic of the Philippines, to the Secretary of Foreign Affairs, Republic of the Philippines, Annex B2 (22 June 2015) (Annex 610).

[984]   Asia Maritime Transparency Initiative and Center for Strategic and International Studies, "Hughes Reef Tracker," *available at* <amti.csis.org/hughes-reef-tracker/> (Annex 779); Armed Forces of the Philippines, *Aerial Photographs of Kennan Reef* (2014-2015) (Annex 784).

a closed atoll, with no passages into the lagoon.[985] According to a 2002 study, Subi Reef was home to a rich variety of over 300 macrobenthic species,[986] although fisheries surveys from the late 1990s indicate that the reef may already have suffered from overfishing. Coral surveys conducted in 2007 recorded between 64 and 74 species of coral at Subi Reef, with live coral cover highest in the inner reef flat and lagoon areas.[987] The Tribunal has found at paragraph 373 above that Subi Reef is submerged at high tide in its natural condition and classified it as a low-tide elevation.

884. According to Philippine military records, China has had a presence on Subi Reef since 1989, and by 1994, "considerable improvements" there included at least five buildings, a wharf and helipad. By October 2006, a four-storey concrete building was present, and by February 2013, there were more concrete structures, a lighthouse, and communications equipment.[988]

885. China began large-scale dredging work at Subi Reef in the summer of 2014,[989] which intensified in early 2015. Photographs taken on 7 July 2015 showed over 80 ships and a dredger at Subi Reef.[990] A few weeks later, two cutter suction dredgers, 44 cargo supply vessels, 22 tugboats, and a floating barge crane were seen reclaiming both sides of Subi Reef.[991] By November 2015, China had created an artificial island measuring approximately 3,950,000 square metres, "covering the majority of the reef."[992] China has built the beginning of what appears to be a three-kilometre runway, a large multi-level facility, reinforced sea walls, towers, and communications facilities. China also created a 230-metre-wide access channel.

886. The massive scale of China's work on Subi Reef and the transformation of nearly the entire atoll into an artificial island is apparent in aerial and satellite photography and can be seen in satellite imagery from July 2012 and November 2015, reproduced as Figures 28 and 29 on page 353.

---

[985] See also the general geographic description of Subi Reef at paragraph 289 above.

[986] Ferse Report, p. 20.

[987] Ferse Report, pp. 20-21.

[988] Armed Forces of the Philippines, *Matrix of Events: Subi (Zamora) Reef* (2013) (Annex 91).

[989] Asia Maritime Transparency Initiative and Center for Strategic and International Studies, "Subi Reef Tracker," *available at* <amti.csis.org/subi-reef-tracker/> (Annex 781); Armed Forces of the Philippines, *Aerial Photographs of On-Going Reclamation at Subi Reef* (February 2015-March 2015) (Annex 786).

[990] Letter from the Secretary of National Defense, Republic of the Philippines, to the Secretary of Foreign Affairs, Republic of the Philippines (10 August 2015) (Annex 611).

[991] Letter from the Secretary of National Defense, Republic of the Philippines, to the Secretary of Foreign Affairs, Republic of the Philippines (10 August 2015) (Annex 612).

[992] Asia Maritime Transparency Initiative and Center for Strategic and International Studies, "Subi Reef Tracker," *available at* <amti.csis.org/subi-reef-tracker/> (Annex 781).

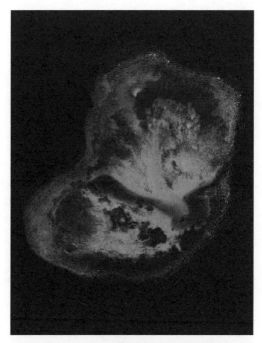

Figure 26: Hughes Reef, 7 February 2010
(Annex 791)

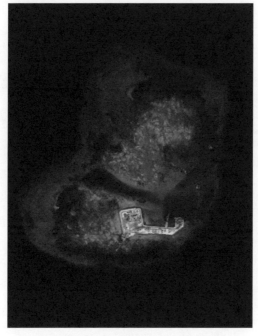

Figure 27: Hughes Reef, 22 September 2015
(Annex 791)

this page intentionally blank

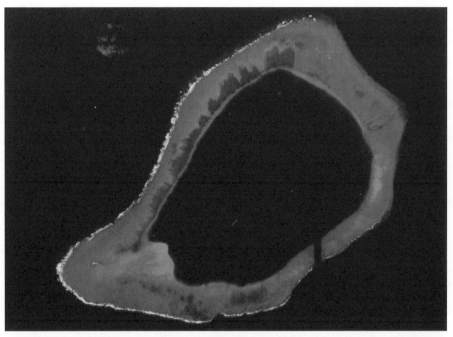

Figure 28: Subi Reef, 27 July 2012
(Annex 795)

Figure 29: Subi Reef, 6 November 2015
(Annex 795)

this page intentionally blank

vii.   *Mischief Reef*

887. Mischief Reef is a large oval-shaped atoll, approximately 6.5 kilometres wide, with three natural entrances into the lagoon.[993] The lagoon featured a number of well-developed patch reefs with massive, foliose, and branching corals.[994] A 2007 survey found 94 species of stony corals there, and live coral cover of 51 percent on the reef slope. Fisheries surveys from the late 1990s described Mischief Reef as having some 'production value,' although the reef appeared to be already under pressure of increased fishing by 2005.[995] The Tribunal has found at paragraph 378 above that, in its natural condition, the highest rocks at Mischief Reef covered at high tide. The Tribunal classified Mischief Reef as a low-tide elevation.

888. China's construction work at Mischief Reef is discussed in greater detail below in connection with the Philippines' Submissions No. 12(a) and 12(c), relating to the lawfulness of constructing artificial islands within the Philippines exclusive economic zone. In brief, Chinese construction activities on Mischief Reef date back at least to January 1995, starting with "typhoon shelters". By 1999, Mischief Reef featured multi-storey structures, communications equipment, wharves and a helipad.

889. Intense land reclamation began at Mischief Reef in January 2015. Progress was rapid, with up to nine dredgers working in the reef simultaneously, according to satellite imagery analysed by the Philippines. By November 2015, the total area of land created by China on Mischief Reef was approximately 5,580,000 square metres.[996] The southern entrance to Mischief Reef was widened from its original 110 metres to 275 metres.

890. The massive scale of China's work at Mischief Reef and the transformation of nearly the entire atoll into an artificial island is apparent in satellite imagery, reproduced as Figures 31 and 32 at page 405 below.

3.   The Philippines' Position

891. The Philippines' submits that China's actions have damaged the diverse and fragile ecosystem of the South China Sea. The Philippines states that "if unchecked [China's] activities will

---

993   See also the general geographic description of Mischief Reef at paragraph 290 above.

994   Ferse Report, p. 20.

995   Ferse Report, p. 20.

996   Asia Maritime Transparency Initiative and Center for Strategic and International Studies, "Mischief Reef Tracker," *available at* <amti.csis.org/mischief-reef-tracker/> (Annex 782).

continue to pose a significant threat to the marine environment of the South China Sea, and of all of the States which border the Sea."[997]

892. The Philippines stresses that China's obligation to protect and preserve the marine environment is "not dependent on deciding which Party, if any, has sovereignty or sovereign rights or jurisdiction over Scarborough Shoal or Second Thomas Shoal or Mischief Reef" or any of the other features named in the amended version of Submission No. 11.[998] What matters, according to the Philippines, is rather whether China has "jurisdiction or control over the harmful fishing practices, the land creation and the construction activities which threaten the marine environment at those locations and elsewhere in the South China Sea."[999]

893. According to the Philippines, China's island-building activities do not fall within the jurisdictional exclusion for "military activities" under Article 298(1)(b).[1000] In this respect, the Philippines notes that China did not invoke the military activities exception, and that in any event China has repeatedly characterised its island-building as being for civilian purposes.[1001] The Philippines also submits that "mixed-use projects" and situations "in which a military unit is used to protect other activities" are not covered by the military activities exception.[1002]

(a) Harmful Fishing Practices and Harvesting of Endangered Species

894. The first component of the Philippines' argument on Submission No. 11 is that China's toleration, encouragement of, and failure to prevent environmentally destructive fishing practices by its nationals violates the "duty to protect and preserve the marine environment" set forth in Articles 192 and 194 of the Convention.[1003] The Philippines complains that China has allowed "its fishermen to harvest coral, giant clams, turtles, sharks and other threatened or endangered species which inhabit the reefs" and "to use dynamite to kill fish and destroy coral, and to use cyanide to harvest live fish."[1004]

---

[997] Merits Hearing Tr. (Day 3), p. 11.

[998] Merits Hearing Tr. (Day 3), p. 12.

[999] Merits Hearing Tr. (Day 3), p. 12.

[1000] *See, e.g.*, Written Responses of the Philippines, paras. 5-6 (11 March 2016); Jurisdictional Hearing Tr. (Day 2), pp. 73-93, (Day 3), pp. 48-57; Merits Hearing Tr. (Day 3), pp. 85-90.

[1001] Jurisdictional Hearing Tr. (Day 2), pp. 74-76; *see also* Merits Hearing Tr. (Day 3), p. 88.

[1002] Merits Hearing Tr. (Day 4), p. 104; *see also* Jurisdictional Hearing Tr. (Day 2), pp. 81-82, (Day 3), p. 57.

[1003] Memorial, paras. 6.66, 7.35; Merits Hearing Tr. (Day 3), pp. 11-12.

[1004] Merits Hearing Tr. (Day 3), p. 12.

895. The Philippines relies principally on the incidents that took place near Scarborough Shoal on 10, 23, and 26 April 2012 (described above at paragraphs 835 to 844), when the Chinese fishing vessels caught with caches of endangered corals and clams were operating under the clear protection of Chinese Government vessels.[1005] The Philippines nevertheless points to incidents from 1998 to 2006 (described above at paragraphs 827 to 834) as evidence of a continued pattern of environmentally destructive activities by Chinese fishing vessels "that had been carried on over many years, with China's full knowledge."[1006]

896. The Philippines explains that the extraction of corals is very damaging to the marine environment because it "reduces the structural complexity of reefs and affects the ability of the reef to support fishes and other animals."[1007] Citing the First Carpenter Report, the Philippines notes that it can take decades for similar numbers of corals to replenish.[1008]

897. The Philippines observes that harvesting of giant clams, sea turtles, and other endangered species compounds environmental impact and reduces biodiversity.[1009] Extracting giant clams is especially problematic because, as Professor Carpenter explains, they are important elements of the coral reef structure and also because the method of harvesting them entails crushing surrounding corals.[1010]

898. With respect to the use of dynamite, the Philippines explains that using explosives pulverises coral, weakens the structure of the reef, and reduces biodiversity by killing fish and destroying their habitat.[1011] As for cyanide, which is used to immobilise fish so that they can be caught live for the aquarium and restaurant trades, the Philippines notes that it can kill or injure non-target species and encourage unsustainable catch levels. Because the stunned fishes may be hidden in coral crevices, the usage of cyanide leads to the coral being broken apart by fishermen to retrieve them.[1012]

[1005] Memorial, para. 6.50.

[1006] Memorial, para. 6.55.

[1007] Memorial, para. 6.56; First Carpenter Report, pp. 5-6.

[1008] Memorial, para. 6.56; First Carpenter Report, pp. 19-21.

[1009] Merits Hearing Tr. (Day 3), p. 22.

[1010] Memorial, para. 6.57; First Carpenter Report, pp. 20-21; Third Carpenter Report, paras. 6-7.

[1011] Memorial, para. 6.59; Merits Hearing Tr. (Day 3), p. 21; First Carpenter Report, p. 15.

[1012] Merits Hearing Tr. (Day 3), pp. 21-22; First Carpenter Report, p. 15.

899. Professor Carpenter explained how these practices impact the highly interconnected and interdependent ecosystem of the South China Sea.[1013] He confirmed the conclusions in his first report, that:[1014]

> These activities not only reduce the potential sustainable fisheries on the reefs themselves, but also can have detrimental effects on biodiversity and fisheries in the greater Philippine archipelago. . . .
>
> With more marine species per unit area than any other region on earth . . . . the Philippines is seen as the 'Amazon River Basin of the Seas'. . . . Because of the connectivity of the eastern South China Sea to the greater Philippine archipelago through prevailing ocean currents, it is important to ensure the sustainable stewardship of Scarborough Shoal and the Spratly Islands.
>
> . . . [C]oral reef degradation of Scarborough Shoal and the Spratly Islands affects the wider marine ecosystem of the South China Sea. Coral reefs provide ecosystem services to the open ocean around these reefs. . . . Coral reef degradation decreases the capacity of reefs to support [visiting foraging species] and . . . reduces the capacity of the reef for . . . cleaner organisms and can impact the health of marine fishes . . . .[1015]

(b) China's Construction Activities on Seven Reefs in the Spratly Islands

900. The Philippines notes that even before the extensive artificial island-building program commenced in late 2013, China's installations on the features in the Spratlys between the early 1990s and 2013 had "inevitably harmed the fragile ecosystem there, and resulted in significant damage to the habitats of vulnerable species."[1016]

901. The Philippines notes, however, that such damage is dwarfed by the "catastrophic" environmental impact of the more recent construction activities,[1017] stating that "the loss of seven major reef features to land creation within 1.5 years will have a huge impact on the ecological integrity of not only the Spratly reefs but also of the South China Sea."[1018] The Philippines observes that with "millions of tons of rock and sand" dredged from the seabed and deposited on shallow reefs, "land creation on this massive scale inevitably destroys that part of the reef."[1019] Separate from the destruction of the reef itself, sedimentation caused by the works smothers coral, depriving it of sunlight and impeding its ability to grow.[1020]

[1013] Merits Hearing Tr. (Day 3), pp. 53-54; First Carpenter Report, p. 1.

[1014] Merits Hearing Tr. (Day 3), pp. 48, 54; First Carpenter Report, p. 1.

[1015] First Carpenter Report, pp. 22-24.

[1016] Memorial, para. 6.110-6.111; First Carpenter Report, p. 18.

[1017] Second Carpenter Report, p. 37.

[1018] Merits Hearing Tr. (Day 3), p. 17; Second Carpenter Report, p. 26.

[1019] Merits Hearing Tr. (Day 3), p. 18; Second Carpenter Report, p. 24.

[1020] Second Carpenter Report, pp. 24-25, 38-39; Merits Hearing Tr. (Day 3), p. 18.

902. The Philippines acknowledges that, for obvious reasons, it was unable to investigate recent conditions at Mischief Reef (and the other features address in Submission No. 11). Nevertheless, the Philippines argues that the Tribunal can use satellite images and scientific reports to "draw the obvious inferences about the harm that large-scale land creation and construction activities will cause."[1021]

903. At the Hearing on the Merits, Professor Carpenter recalled that "abrupt man-made alterations to shallow reef features," such as China's island-building "directly impacts the functioning of these delicate reefs and alters the topography that has taken thousands of years to form."[1022] He summarised the "very significant damage to this complex coral reef ecosystem" as follows:

> The total destruction of a large swathe of reef structures through demolition and burying and landfill is a catastrophic disturbance of the reef. The wholesale removal and destruction of coral reef habitat by the direct destruction and replacement of the shallow portions of the reef ecosystem with man-made structures removes vital components of available reef habitat that have functioned as a single ecosystem for many generations of reef inhabitants. This causes dramatic reductions in populations and local extinction of prominent fishes and invertebrates.
>
> This is of particular concern because there are a number of species listed as threatened with extinction in the South China Sea. . . . The direct ecosystem harm . . . can be multiplied many times over by the wider effects of sediment plumes caused by island building. . . . This sediment cloud covers large areas of the reefs, smothers the coral, and results in widespread destruction of the reef. This in turn dramatically reduces overall primary productivity and topography of the reef, limiting its ability to sustain life.
>
> Recovery from these severe disturbances is uncertain . . . . Here, demolition and burial and landfill has resulted in the total destruction of large swathes of reef structures that destabilise the reef substrate and negatively impact the potential for recovery. Reefs that have been smothered by sedimentation are unlikely to ever recover if unstable sediments remain in place, because reef building requires hard substrate . . . to recruit and thrive.[1023]

904. Professor Carpenter then addressed a variety of questions from the Tribunal, including as to the prospects of replenishment, damage caused by sedimentary plumes and turbidity,[1024] and the reliability of satellite imagery (which he supported by reference to independent studies reaching similar results).[1025] He reported on his efforts to find Chinese statements about the ecological impact of the construction activities and noted that the only report he identified, a 500-word statement[1026] from China's State Oceanic Administration, contains assertions "contrary to

---

[1021] Merits Hearing Tr. (Day 3), p. 19.

[1022] Merits Hearing Tr. (Day 3), pp. 51-52; *see also* Second Carpenter Report, p. 38.

[1023] Merits Hearing Tr. (Day 3), pp. 52-53; *see also* Second Carpenter Report, pp. 37-39.

[1024] Merits Hearing Tr. (Day 4), pp. 151-152.

[1025] Merits Hearing Tr. (Day 4), pp. 147-148.

[1026] State Oceanic Administration of China, "Construction Work at Nansha Reefs Will Not Harm Oceanic Ecosystems" (18 June 2015), *available at* <www.soa.gov.cn/xw/hyyw_90/201506/t20150618 _38598.html> (Annex 821) (hereinafter "**SOA Statement**").

everything that we know about coral reef ecology and conservation."[1027] This statement (the **"SOA Statement"**) did not alter his conclusion that the Chinese activity "constitutes the most rapid nearly permanent loss of coral reef area in human activity."[1028]

905. The Philippines made similar observations about a slightly longer report prepared by SOA scientists (the **"SOA Report"**), which the Tribunal drew to the Parties' attention on 5 February 2016.[1029] According to the Philippines, that report was also "thoroughly contradicted by the evidence,"[1030] contained inaccurate statements about timing, flawed predictions about recovery periods, and misplaced analogies with dredging projects in Australia and other countries.[1031]

(c) Interpretation and Application of Part XII of the Convention

906. In connection with the marine environment, the Philippines alleges China has breached Articles 123, 192, 194, 197, 205, and 206 of the Convention.

907. The Philippines recalls that the general obligation on States under Article 192 to "protect and preserve the marine environment"—which it considers to form part of customary international law [1032] —covers areas within national jurisdiction as well as areas beyond national jurisdiction.[1033] According to the Philippines, this requires States to take "active measures" to prevent harm, to "conserve marine living resources," and to "preserve the ecological balance of the oceans as a whole." [1034]

908. The Philippines notes that the interpretation of Article 192 may be guided by reference to standards in other multilateral environmental instruments, such as CITES and the CBD.[1035] Likewise those instruments provide content for the obligation under Article 194(5) with respect to measures necessary to protect and preserve "rare or fragile ecosystems" and "places that provide habitats for . . . endangered species."[1036]

[1027] Merits Hearing Tr. (Day 4), p. 149.

[1028] Merits Hearing Tr. (Day 4), p. 150.

[1029] SOA Report.

[1030] Written Responses of the Philippines, p. 27 (11 March 2016).

[1031] Written Responses of the Philippines, pp. 26-35 (11 March 2016).

[1032] Merits Hearing Tr. (Day 4), pp. 170-174.

[1033] Merits Hearing Tr. (Day 3), p. 23.

[1034] Memorial, para. 6.68; Merits Hearing Tr. (Day 3), p. 23.

[1035] Memorial, paras. 6.71, 6.73, 6.82-6.83; *see also* Merits Hearing Tr. (Day 3), p. 294, (Day 4), pp. 177-179.

[1036] Memorial, para. 6.78; *see also* Merits Hearing Tr. (Day 3), p. 24.

909. The Philippines notes that States are only required to take appropriate measures and act with due diligence. In this case, however, the Philippines argues that the clear evidence of deliberate and irreparable ecological destruction cannot be squared with China's own laws on environmental protection.[1037] While China's island-building activities at the seven reefs were unquestionably within the control and jurisdiction of China, the Philippines acknowledges that the unlawful harvesting was carried out by non-government Chinese fishing vessels and that "China is not responsible for the actions of its fishermen." China is, however, "responsible for its own failure to control their illegal and damaging activities."[1038] The Philippines argues that China has "not even attempted to do so" but rather has actively "supported, protected and facilitate[ed]" their harmful practices."[1039] The Philippines also observes that as the flag State, China is obliged to monitor and enforce compliance with its laws by all ships flying its flag.[1040]

910. The Philippines highlights five obligations that it considers applicable to States under Part XII of the Convention and relevant in the context of this case:[1041]

   (a) *To protect and preserve marine ecosystems:* The Philippines observes that coral reefs are a fragile and vitally important part of the marine ecosystem and argues that "creating artificial islands out of coral reefs is the worst possible way to treat these fundamental ecological building blocks."[1042]

   (b) *To ensure sustainable use of biological resources:* The Philippines notes that this reflects a long-recognised duty to conserve living resources.[1043] Blast fishing and the use of cyanide are wasteful and unsustainable, and violate Articles 192 and 194 (including as marine pollution),[1044] whether the methods are used in the territorial sea or beyond.[1045]

   (c) *To protect and preserve endangered species:* The Philippines argues that this is implicit in Article 194(5). According to the Philippines, the harvesting of giant clams in April

---

[1037] Merits Hearing Tr. (Day 3), p. 32.

[1038] Merits Hearing Tr. (Day 3), p. 33.

[1039] Merits Hearing Tr. (Day 3), p. 32; *see also* Memorial, para. 6.73.

[1040] Merits Hearing Tr. (Day 3), p. 33.

[1041] Merits Hearing Tr. (Day 3), pp. 22-23; *see also* Jurisdictional Hearing Tr. (Day 2), pp. 96-97.

[1042] Merits Hearing Tr. (Day 3), pp. 25-26; First Carpenter Report, p. 15; Second Carpenter Report, pp. 26-29.

[1043] Merits Hearing Tr. (Day 3), p. 27.

[1044] Memorial, para. 6.76-6.79; Merits Hearing Tr. (Day 3), p. 24.

[1045] Merits Hearing Tr. (Day 3), p. 28; *see also* UN Food and Agriculture Organization, *Code of Conduct for Responsible Fisheries*, para. 8.4.2 (31 October 1995).

2012 under the protection of Chinese authorities constitutes a clear violation of Articles 192 and 194.[1046]

(d) *To apply a precautionary approach in all of these respects:* The Philippines considers this obligation applicable to China, but argues this is not necessary to the Tribunal's findings in the current case because the risks to the marine environment are obvious and there can be no uncertainty.[1047]

(e) *To consult and cooperate with the relevant coastal States:* The Philippines draws this obligation from Articles 197 and 123 of the Convention, the latter of which takes into account the "characteristic regional features" which would include the fundamental biological and ecological importance and fragile nature of the coral reef ecosystem of the South China Sea.[1048] The Philippines submits that there is very little evidence of genuine Chinese cooperation on matters of environmental protection in the South China Sea.[1049] The Philippines considers China's behaviour towards the Philippines and other States bordering the South China Sea to be aggressive rather than cooperative.[1050]

911. Related to the failure to coordinate is, for the Philippines, a failure to assess and communicate. The Philippines argues that China was "fairly and squarely" required to carry out an environmental impact assessment ("**EIA**") within the meaning of Article 206 of the Convention.[1051] At a minimum, the Philippines argues an EIA should have assessed possible effects on the marine ecosystem of the South China Sea, the coral reefs at issue, the biodiversity and sustainability of living resources there and endangered species.[1052] The Philippines argues that there is simply no evidence that China carried out such an EIA and no science-based evaluation has been made public or communicated to the Philippines or to "the competent international organizations" as required by Articles 205 and 206 of the Convention.[1053] According to the Philippines, the 500-word SOA Statement was a "pseudo-evaluation . . . plainly not an EIA."[1054] The (slightly longer) SOA Report also fell short, in its view.[1055] The

---

[1046] Merits Hearing Tr. (Day 3), p. 29.

[1047] Merits Hearing Tr. (Day 3), p. 30.

[1048] Merits Hearing Tr. (Day 3), pp. 39-45.

[1049] Merits Hearing Tr. (Day 3), pp. 42-43.

[1050] Merits Hearing Tr. (Day 3), p. 44.

[1051] Merits Hearing Tr. (Day 3), pp. 34-36.

[1052] Merits Hearing Tr. (Day 3), pp. 38-39.

[1053] Merits Hearing Tr. (Day 4), p. 183; *see also* Merits Hearing Tr. (Day 3), pp. 38-39.

[1054] Merits Hearing Tr. (Day 4), p. 185.

Philippines observed that even without appearing in the arbitration, China could easily have made its evaluation available to the Tribunal and added that China's non-appearance should not exempt it from "the normal burden of proof that attaches to any assertion of fact in inter-State proceedings."[1056]

4. China's Position

912. China has not directly stated its position with respect to the allegations as presented in the Philippines' Submissions No. 11 and 12(b). Nevertheless, China's position can be discerned from contemporaneous official statements.

(a) Harmful Fishing Practices and Harvesting of Endangered Species

913. Statements of Chinese officials relating to the incidents between 1998 and 2006 were primarily focused on asserting Chinese sovereignty over Scarborough Shoal and objecting to interference by Philippine authorities. Nevertheless, on a few occasions Chinese officials did address environmental concerns raised by the Philippines in connection with Scarborough Shoal. For example:

(a) According to a record of a meeting in March 2000, a Chinese Foreign Ministry official expressed to the Philippine Ambassador in Beijing her "particular concern about the practice of dynamite fishing" and that she had "requested the [Ministry of Agriculture] to do something about the situation."[1057]

(b) Following the confiscation of endangered species from Chinese fishing vessels in February 2001, the political counsellor from the Chinese Embassy in Manila reiterated that "Scarborough Shoal is part of Chinese territory and . . . Chinese fishermen have been fishing in the area since ancient times" but reportedly added that "[w]ith regard to the illegal catching of turtles and corals, ... China has a law on this and those who violate the law will be punished." [1058]

[1055] Written Responses of the Philippines, pp. 10-14 (11 March 2016).

[1056] Merits Hearing Tr. (Day 4), pp. 183-184.

[1057] Memorandum from the Embassy of the Republic of the Philippines in Beijing to the Secretary of Foreign Affairs of the Republic of the Philippines, No. ZPE-24-2000-S (14 March 2000) (Annex 40).

[1058] Memorandum from the Assistant Secretary for Asian and Pacific Affairs, Department of Foreign Affairs, Republic of the Philippines, to the Secretary of Foreign Affairs, Republic of the Philippines (14 February 2001) (Annex 45).

(c) In March 2001, the Asian Department Deputy Director-General of the Chinese Foreign Ministry stated to the representative of the Philippine Embassy in Beijing that "the Chinese Government is always against illegal fishing."[1059]

914. By contrast, following poaching incidents in 2005 and 2006, China's Vice Foreign Minister did not mention environmental issues and instead expressed dissatisfaction with the Philippine Navy's continued patrol of vessels in Scarborough Shoal, which he considered to have violated the sovereignty and maritime rights of China.[1060] China's opposition to Philippine interference at Scarborough Shoal persisted through 2012, when in April China confirmed that "relevant Chinese authorities" had been dispatched to "protect the safety and legitimate fishing activities of Chinese fishermen and fishing vessels."[1061]

915. Although a Chinese official stated in May 2015 that, as a State party to the CBD and to CITES, "China will strictly observe provisions of the conventions and honour her obligations in good faith,"[1062] the Tribunal has seen no evidence that Chinese fishermen involved in poaching of endangered species have been prosecuted under Chinese law. China did not respond to reports forwarded by the Tribunal in December 2015 and February 2016 concerning the widespread removal of giant clams by propeller cutting in and around features under Chinese control.[1063]

(b) China's Construction Activities on Seven Reefs in the Spratly Islands

916. The Tribunal has sought to ascertain China's position by reviewing statements by its Foreign Ministry officials, identifying publicly available scientific reports from China,[1064] and tasking

---

[1059] Memorandum from the Embassy of the Republic of the Philippines in Beijing to the Secretary of Foreign Affairs, Republic of the Philippines, No. ZPE-09-2001-S (17 March 2001) (Annex 47).

[1060] Memorandum from the Embassy of the Republic of the Philippines in Beijing to the Secretary of Foreign Affairs, Republic of the Philippines, No. ZPE-61-2005-S (28 October 2005) (Annex 56); Letter from Rear Admiral, Armed Forces of the Philippines, to the Assistant Secretary for Asian and Pacific Affairs, Department of Foreign Affairs, Republic of the Philippines (2006) (Annex 57).

[1061] Ministry of Foreign Affairs, People's Republic of China, *Foreign Ministry Spokesperson Liu Weimin's Regular Press Conference* (12 April 2012) (Annex 117).

[1062] Embassy of the People's Republic of China in Canada, *An Interview on China's Construction Activities on the Nansha Islands and Reefs 2015/05/27, available at* <ca.chineseembassy.org/eng/zt/cpot/t1267437.htm> (Annex 820).

[1063] *See, e.g.*, Letter from the Tribunal to the Parties (18 December 2015) (forwarding BBC reports submitted by the Philippines); Letter from the Tribunal to the Parties (1 April 2016) (forwarding article on giant clam harvesting on behalf of the Tribunal's Expert).

[1064] Letter from the Tribunal to the Parties (5 February 2016).

the independent experts with "analysing any documents concerning China's assessment of the environmental impact of its activities."[1065]

917. On 9 April 2015, a Chinese Foreign Ministry Spokesperson made the following remarks about Chinese construction activities at Mischief Reef:

> China's construction projects on the islands and reefs have gone through scientific assessments and rigorous tests. We put equal emphasis on construction and protection by following a high standard of environmental protection and taking into full consideration the protection of ecological environment and fishing resources. The ecological environment of the South China Sea will not be damaged. We will take further steps in the future to monitor and protect the ecological environment of relevant waters, islands and reefs.[1066]

918. Similar remarks were made by the Director-General of the Department of Boundary and Ocean Affairs of China's Foreign Ministry on 27 May 2015.[1067]

919. A Chinese Foreign Ministry Spokesperson noted, on 16 June 2015, that the "main purpose" of the construction activities is to "meet various civilian demands and better perform China's international obligations and responsibilities in the areas such as . . . ecological environment conservation."[1068]

920. More recently, a Chinese Foreign Ministry Spokesperson provided the following response to a question about whether China's massive land reclamation activities have destroyed coral reefs in the South China Sea "on a large scale":

> The Nansha Islands are China's territory. As owners of the Nansha Islands, China cares about protecting the ecological environment of relevant islands, reefs and waters more than any other country, organization or people in the world.
>
> China's activities on the Nansha Islands strictly follow the principle of conducting green project and building ecological islands and reefs. Based on thorough studies and scientific proof, China adopts dynamic protection measures along the whole process so as to combine construction with ecological environmental protection and realize sustainable development of islands and reefs. To be specific, China takes the approach of "natural simulation" which simulates the natural process of sea storms blowing away and moving biological scraps which gradually evolve into oasis on the sea. The impact on the ecological system of coral reefs is limited. Once China's construction activities are completed, ecological

---

[1065] Terms of Reference for Expert, Dr. Sebastian Ferse, paras. 3.1.2, 3.1.4 (18 March 2016).

[1066] Ministry of Foreign Affairs, People's Republic of China, *Foreign Ministry Spokesperson Hua Chunying's Regular Press Conference* (9 April 2015) (Annex 624).

[1067] Embassy of the People's Republic of China in Canada, *An Interview on China's Construction Activities on the Nansha Islands and Reefs 2015/05/27*, available at <ca.chineseembassy.org/eng/zt/ cpot/t1267437.htm > (Annex 820).

[1068] Ministry of Foreign Affairs, People's Republic of China, *Foreign Ministry Spokesperson Lu Kang's Remarks on Issues Relating to China's Construction Activities on the Nansha Islands and Reefs* (16 June 2015) (Annex 579).

environmental protection on relevant islands and reefs will be notably enhanced and such action stands the test of time.[1069]

921. In light of China's references to "thorough studies", "scientific assessments", and "rigorous tests", the Tribunal has sought further information on environmental studies conducted by China. Thus, during the Hearing on the Merits, the Tribunal asked the Philippines if it was "aware of any experts from China or elsewhere that have published or articulated views about the environmental impact of China's activities or toleration of activities by others within its control that are contrary or different to those of the Philippines."[1070] The Philippines noted "problems of access to the features occupied by China" and the "rather expedited timeframe," and reported that its searches had turned up only "a brief statement from the State Oceanic Administration."[1071]

922. The SOA is an administrative agency under the Chinese Ministry of Land and Resources, responsible for, among other things, the management of sea area uses, the strategic development of the sea, marine environmental protection, and the development of uninhabited islands.[1072] The SOA Statement located by the Philippines was entitled "Construction Work at Nansha Reefs Will Not Harm Oceanic Ecosystems" and included the following:

> The land reclamation work at some of the reefs of China's Nansha Islands will be completed in the near future. In order to ascertain the effects of the construction work on oceanic ecosystems, scientific studies have been conducted by a team of experts and researchers from the fields of civil engineering, marine engineering, marine ecology, environment protection, and hydrogeology.
>
> 1.   The construction work will abide vigorously by the rules of environment protection.
>
> The expansion of the Nansha reefs will abide rigorously by the concept of "Green Construction, Eco-Friendly Reefs" in protecting the ecosystems. . . .
>
> 2.   The construction work employs the method of nature simulation.
>
> The expansion of the Nansha reefs uses the "nature simulation" method as its comprehensive technical concept. This method simulates the displacement of bioclasts such as corals and sands during wind storms and high waves; this biological detritus settles on the combined equilibrium points of the shallow reef flats to form stable supratidal zones which then evolve into oceanic oases. Big cutter suction dredgers are used to collect the loose coral fragments and sands in the lagoon and deposit them on bank-inset reefs to form supratidal platform foundation on which certain kinds of facilities can be built. Through the natural functions of the air, the rain, and the sun, paving it with some quick man-made

---

[1069]   Ministry of Foreign Affairs, People's Republic of China, *Foreign Ministry Spokesperson Hong Lei's Regular Press Conference* (6 May 2016), *available at* <www.fmprc.gov.cn/mfa_eng/xwfw_665399/s2510_665401/2511_665403/t1361284.shtml>.

[1070]   Letter from the Tribunal to the Parties (27 November 2015) (Annex A, Questions 22 and 23 to the Philippines, Annex C, Question 9 to Professor Carpenter); Merits Hearing Tr. (Day 4), pp. 181-182.

[1071]   Merits Hearing Tr. (Day 4), p. 182.

[1072]   State Council of the People's Republic of China, "State Oceanic Administration," *available at* <english.gov.cn/state_council/2014/10/06/content_281474992889983.htm>.

material, the land reclamation area will produce the ecological effects by going from desalination, solidification, efflorescence, to a green coral reef ecological environment.

3.   The construction work adopts the measures of ecological protection.

a.   To plan construction projects on bank-inset reefs made of basically dead corals: use a cutter suction dredger to collect loose coral fragments and sands from flat lagoon basins, which do not constitute hospitable environment for corals . . . .

b.   We used a new "dig, cutter suction, blow, and fill" land reclamation method to integrate digging, transporting, and filling into the construction work; this results in the least ecological impact to the coral reefs.

c.   At the same time that the land reclamation work is in progress, use slope model of concrete to build permanent protective banks and walls around the land area to fend off waves . . . .

d.   The construction embraces the concepts of containment of scope, high efficiency, and sustainability. The duration of construction for every land reclamation project on the reefs will only be about several months.

4.   Conclusion

The construction work on the Nansha reefs stresses ecological protection. Many protection measures were adopted in the stages of planning, design, and construction. Good results have been obtained, and the ecological impact on the coral reefs is partial, temporary, controllable, and recoverable.[1073]

923.   The Tribunal subsequently identified the SOA Report, dated 10 June 2015, by researchers from the First Ocean Research Institution of the SOA. The authors are not State officials, but work for a government-sponsored organisation. The following are extracts from the SOA Report, which was provided to the Parties for comment:

. . . Due to global seawater warming, ocean acidification, overfishing, development of coastal areas and other reasons, modern coral reefs are degenerating rapidly. . . . The site selection, construction and postconstruction monitoring of the construction at Nansha Reefs are in all respects in compliance with domestic laws and regulations. The construction was undertaken with an emphasis on the protection of ecosystem and fishery resources, carried out after scientific assessment and feasibility studies.

1.   There has been abundant global experience in construction in coral reef areas

. . . Nowadays, coral reefs are utilized mainly for four purposes. First, for national defence and military purposes. [e.g., U.S. and Japan] . . . Second, for coastal tourism development. . . . . Third, for the construction of port terminals. [e.g., Bahamas, Sudan, Papua New Guinea and Australia]. . . . Of course, rigorous protection standards must be complied with when carrying out construction in the coral reef areas.

2.   General information on the Coral Reef Ecosystem of Nansha Reefs

Nansha Reefs present typical tropical reef landscape. . . . It is estimated that there are between 127 and 200 species of shallow water reef building corals (hermatypic corals) surrounding the Nansha reefs.

. . . . Research has shown that the South China Sea is not a body of closed waters, therefore nutrients and food organisms can be replenished constantly from surrounding waters . . . . The

---

[1073]   SOA Statement, pp. 1-2.

severe degeneration of coral reefs worldwide has been exacerbated also by human factors such as overfishing, illegal destruction, excessive tourism development activities . . . .

The amount and number of species of coral reefs in China's South China Sea is also showing a tendency of rapid decrease. . . . Such decrease is mainly due to natural factors, with overfishing being the major human factor.

3.   Eco-protection measures implemented during the construction activities

. . . First, enhance the protection through legislation. . . . Second, actively fulfilling obligations under international conventions including the [CBD]. . . . Third, establish marine natural reserves to protect coral reef ecosystems. . . . Fourth, actively conduct research on the restoration of coral reefs. . . .

. . . . The government has evaluated all construction plans available and has chosen the optimal plan while excluded the ones that would have a bigger impact on marine environment. . . .

As to scientific site selection . . . most of the construction sites selected are located in reef flats with the lowest hermatypic coral coverage or where hermatypic corals are mostly dead.

. . . . China had drawn on the construction technology and environmental protection standards implemented in similar projects. . . . The following specific environmental protection measures were implemented to minimise the impact on coral reefs, including:

1)   minimising the extent of the reclamation and dredging areas;

2)   setting trash collecting screens;

3)   timing construction reasonably, trying to avoid spawn periods of red snapper (mid-April), tuna (peak from June to August) and bonito (from March to August);

4)   monitoring the change of grain size of sand sediments regularly . . . to maintain the water quality of coral reef areas;

5)   reducing construction intensity during the peak of growth of Nansha and Xisha coral reefs . . . . ;

6)   monitoring the growth and health of coral reefs in construction areas and indicators such as species . . . in coral reef areas;

7)   centrally collecting the waste water and solid waste produced from life and construction to be sent for treatment at land facilities of harbours;

8)   using newer vessels to ensure no oil spill happens; listening to weather and marine condition forecasts regularly. . . .

4.   Assessment of the environment impact of Nansha construction activities on coral reef systems

. . . The Nansha coral reefs were rated as "sub-healthy" before the construction. After assessing the construction's environmental impact on coral reefs, the health of Nansha coral reefs were still rated "sub-healthy" after the construction was completed. Therefore, the construction activities neither affected the health of . . . nor harmed the coral reef ecosystems. In fact, due to the strong currents and waves . . . the water bodies are updated fairly fast so that little suspended sands are produced from the constructions, leaving the photosynthesis of corals largely unaffected. Because the sites are located in areas where coverage of coral reefs is low, the overall community structure [and] the physical and chemical living environment of coral reefs are not fundamentally changed, therefore their health was not significantly harmed by the construction activities. . . .

> As to the impact of reclamation activities on fishery resources . . . the construction avoided the spawning seasons of the main economic species [including tuna], the impact on fishery resources is reduced to the minimum. . . . [The] South China Sea is not a body of closed waters, therefore nutrients and food organisms can be replenished constantly from surrounding waters. . . .
>
> Research has also shown that coral reefs have strong capability of self-restoration. Generally speaking, coral reefs that have been severely damaged by natural factors or human activities can be restored initially in 5-10 years provided that effective measures are taken, and complex and complete ecosystems can be fully restored in 50-100 years.
>
> . . . [T]he conclusion can be reached that the construction activities did not adversely affect the regional coral reef ecosystems. . . . The assessments are objective. Even so, after the construction is completed, it is important to enhance monitoring of regional ecosystems and implement measures including release, coral restoration and transplantation in order to better protect the coral reefs.[1074]

924. On 5 February 2016, the Tribunal referred the Parties to the above SOA Statement and SOA Report, as well as to a number of general SOA "Communiqués on Marine Environment" and technical guidelines for assessing marine ecosystem health. At the same time, the Tribunal directly invited the Chinese Government "to indicate whether it has conducted an environmental impact study per Article 206 of the Convention and, if so, to provide the Tribunal with a copy." China did not respond to the Tribunal's request.

5. The Tribunal's Considerations

(a) The Tribunal's Jurisdiction

i. Jurisdiction over Submission No. 11 in its Original Form

925. The Tribunal recalls that in its original form, Submission No. 11 sought a declaration that "China has violated its obligations under the Convention to protect and preserve the marine environment at Scarborough Shoal and Second Thomas Shoal."[1075]

926. In its Award on Jurisdiction, the Tribunal held that Submission No. 11 reflects a dispute concerning the protection and preservation of the marine environment at relevant features within the South China Sea and the application of Articles 192 and 194 of the Convention.[1076] The Tribunal found that this is "not a dispute concerning sovereignty or maritime boundary delimitation, nor is it barred from the Tribunal's consideration by any requirement of Section 1 of Part XV."[1077]

[1074] SOA Report, p. 3.

[1075] Memorial, p. 272.

[1076] Award on Jurisdiction, para. 408; *see also* Award on Jurisdiction, para. 173.

[1077] Award on Jurisdiction, para. 408.

927.   The Tribunal noted that because the environmental obligations in Part XII apply to States irrespective of where the alleged harmful activities took place, its jurisdiction is not dependent on the question of sovereignty over any particular feature, on a prior determination of the status of any maritime feature, on the existence of an entitlement by China or the Philippines to an exclusive economic zone in the area, or on the prior delimitation of any overlapping entitlements.[1078]

928.   The Tribunal likewise held that the other possible exceptions in Article 298 of the Convention posed no bar to its jurisdiction over Submission No. 11.[1079] The harmful fishing and harvesting practices complained of in the Submission as originally formulated have no connection with "military activities". To the extent the incidents could be characterised as related to "law enforcement activities", the Tribunal pointed out that the law enforcement activities exception in Article 298(1)(b) would not in any event apply.

929.   First, the law enforcement activities exception concerns a coastal State's rights in its exclusive economic zone and does not apply to incidents in a territorial sea. Thus, the exception could not be relevant to incidents at Scarborough Shoal.[1080]

930.   Second, although the status of Second Thomas Shoal and the question of whether the feature was potentially within the entitlement of either China or the Philippines to an exclusive economic zone were undetermined at the time of the Award on Jurisdiction, the Tribunal noted that Article 297(1)(c) expressly reaffirms the availability of compulsory dispute settlement for disputes concerning "alleged violations of international rules and standards for the protection and preservation of the marine environment."[1081] The Tribunal's decision in this Award that Second Thomas Shoal is a low-tide elevation located in an area that can only form part of the exclusive economic zone of the Philippines (see paragraph 646 to 647 above) further confirms

---

[1078]   Award on Jurisdiction, para. 408.

[1079]   Award on Jurisdiction, para. 408. Article 298, which allows States the option of excluding from compulsory dispute settlement certain categories of disputes, including "(1)(b) disputes concerning military activities, including military activities by government vessels and aircraft engaged in non-commercial service, and disputes concerning law enforcement activities in regard to the exercise of sovereign rights or jurisdiction excluded from the jurisdiction of a court or tribunal under article 297, paragraph 2 or 3." Article 297(2) concerns marine scientific research and Article 297(3) concerns fisheries. Cases under Article 297(1) are therefore not excluded. Article 297(1)(c) includes cases "when it is alleged that a coastal State has acted in contravention of specified international rules and standards for the protection and preservation of the marine environment which are applicable to the coastal State and which have been established by this Convention or through a competent international organization or diplomatic conference in accordance with this Convention."

[1080]   The Tribunal has found Scarborough Shoal to be an Article 121(3) rock, capable of generating a territorial sea, but not an exclusive economic zone. See paragraphs 554 to 556 above.

[1081]   Convention, art. 297(1)(c).

that the law enforcement exception in Article 298(1)(b) has no application in these circumstances.

931. Accordingly, the Tribunal found that it has jurisdiction over the dispute relating to Submission No. 11 in its original form.

ii.   Jurisdiction over Submission No. 12(b) and Submission No. 11 as Amended

932. In its Award on Jurisdiction, the Tribunal noted that Submission No. 12 reflects a dispute concerning China's activities on Mischief Reef and the effects of those activities on the marine environment. The Tribunal noted that this dispute does not concern sovereignty or maritime boundary delimitation, nor is it barred from the Tribunal's consideration by any requirement of Section 1 of Part XV.[1082] However, the Tribunal deferred taking a final decision on jurisdiction over Submission No. 12, in light of factors discussed below at paragraphs 1024 to 1028. The only such factor of relevance to paragraph (b) of Submission No. 12 (relating to the marine environment) was the possible application of the exception in Article 298(1)(b) of the Convention, which excludes disputes concerning military activities from the Tribunal's jurisdiction. The Tribunal considered it preferable to assess the specifics of China's activities on Mischief Reef, and whether such activities are military in nature, in conjunction with the merits.[1083]

933. As already noted, the Tribunal subsequently granted the Philippines leave to amend Submission No. 11 to encompass the marine environment at Cuarteron Reef, Fiery Cross Reef, Johnson Reef, Hughes Reef, Gaven Reef (North), and Subi Reef, in light of the evidence relating to the larger-scale island-building activities at those features which had not been available at the time of the Memorial.[1084] The Tribunal recognised that the amendments were related to, or incidental to the Submissions originally made by the Philippines, and did not involve the introduction of a new dispute between the Parties.[1085] Indeed, the Philippines had already presented evidence of China's gradually increasing construction activities at all seven reefs,[1086] and had already set forth its concerns over the resultant degradation of the marine environment.[1087]

[1082] Award on Jurisdiction, para. 409.

[1083] Award on Jurisdiction, para. 409.

[1084] Merits Hearing Tr. (Day 4), p. 169; Letter from the Tribunal to the Parties (16 December 2015); *see also* Letter from the Tribunal to the Parties (1 December 2015) (inviting China's comments).

[1085] Letter from the Tribunal to the Parties (16 December 2015).

[1086] *See, e.g.*, Armed Forces of the Philippines, *Chronology of Events in the Kalayaan Island Group* (2004) (Annex 53); Armed Forces of the Philippines, *Chronological Development of Artificial Structures on*

934. It thus remains for the Tribunal to decide whether its jurisdiction over the Philippines' Submissions No. 11 and 12(b) is constrained by the military activities exception in Article 298(1)(b) of the Convention.

935. In determining whether Chinese land reclamation activities at the seven reefs are military in nature, the Tribunal takes note of China's repeated statements that its installations and island-building activities are intended to fulfil civilian purposes.

936. On 9 September 2014, a Chinese Foreign Ministry Spokesperson stated that "the construction work China is undertaking on relevant islands is mainly for the purpose of improving the working and living conditions of people stationed on these islands."[1088] The same spokesperson elaborated, in April 2015, that the "main purposes" of the "maintenance and construction work" on the Spratly islands and reefs were:

> optimizing their functions, improving the living and working conditions of personnel stationed there, better safeguarding territorial sovereignty and maritime rights and interests, as well as better performing China's international responsibility and obligation in maritime search and rescue, disaster prevention and mitigation, marine science and research, meteorological observation, environmental protection, navigation safety, fishery production service and other areas.[1089]

937. These same civilian purposes were articulated on 12 June 2015, by the Head of China's delegation to the Meeting of States Parties to the UN Convention on the Law of the Sea.[1090] As noted below with respect to Submission No. 12, China's President Xi Jinping stated in September 2015 that "[r]elevant construction activities that China [is] undertaking in the island of South -- Nansha Islands do not target or impact any country, and China does not intend to pursue militarization."[1091]

Features (Annex 96); "Matrix of Events" documents compiled by the Armed Forces of the Philippines for Cuarteron, Gaven, Fiery Cross, Johnson, and Subi Reefs (Annexes 86-91); Memorial, paras. 5.68-5.75.

[1087] *See* Memorial, paras. 6.108-6.111; *see also* First Carpenter Report, pp.16-18.

[1088] Ministry of Foreign Affairs, People's Republic of China, *Foreign Ministry Spokesperson Hua Chunying's Regular Press Conference* (9 September 2014) (Annex 619).

[1089] Ministry of Foreign Affairs, People's Republic of China, *Foreign Ministry Spokesperson Hua Chunying's Regular Press Conference* (9 April 2015) (Annex 624); *see also* Ministry of Foreign Affairs, People's Republic of China, *Foreign Ministry Spokesperson Lu Kang's Remarks on Issues Relating to China's Construction Activities on the Nansha Islands and Reefs* (16 June 2015) (Annex 579).

[1090] Permanent Mission of the People's Republic of China to the United Nations, *Statement by H.E. Ambassador Wang Min, Head of the Chinese Delegation at the 25th Meeting of States Parties to the UN Convention on the Law of the Sea* (12 June 2014) (Annex 624).

[1091] *See* "China not to pursue militarization of Nansha Islands in South China Sea: Xi," *Xinhua* (25 September 2015), *available at* <news.xinhuanet.com/english/2015-09/26/c_134660930.htm>; United States, The White House, Office of the Press Secretary, "Press Release: Remarks by President Obama and President Xi of the People's Republic of China in Joint Press Conference" (25 September 2015) (Annex 664).

938. The Tribunal will not deem activities to be military in nature when China itself has consistently and officially resisted such classifications and affirmed the opposite at the highest levels. Accordingly, the Tribunal accepts China's repeatedly affirmed position that civilian use compromises the primary (if not the only) motivation underlying the extensive construction activities on the seven reefs in the Spratly Islands. As civilian activity, the Tribunal notes that China's conduct falls outside the scope of Article 298(1)(b) and concludes that it has jurisdiction to consider the Philippines' Submissions No. 11 and 12(b).

(b) Relevant Provisions of the Convention

939. The protection and preservation of the marine environment form a prominent component of the legal regime of the Convention, the importance of which is recognised in the Preamble in the following terms:

> *Recognizing* the desirability of establishing through this Convention, with due regard for the sovereignty of all States, a legal order for the seas and oceans which will facilitate international communication, and will promote the peaceful uses of the seas and oceans, the equitable and efficient utilization of their resources, the conservation of their living resources, and the study, protection and preservation of the marine environment . . .

940. The substantive provisions relevant to the marine environment comprise their own Part XII of the Convention. At the outset, the Tribunal notes that the obligations in Part XII apply to all States with respect to the marine environment in all maritime areas, both inside the national jurisdiction of States and beyond it.[1092] Accordingly, questions of sovereignty are irrelevant to the application of Part XII of the Convention. The Tribunal's findings in this Chapter have no bearing upon, and are not in any way dependent upon, which State is sovereign over features in the South China Sea.

941. Article 192 of the Convention provides that "States have the obligation to protect and preserve the marine environment." Although phrased in general terms, the Tribunal considers it well established that Article 192 does impose a duty on States Parties,[1093] the content of which is informed by the other provisions of Part XII and other applicable rules of international law. This "general obligation" extends both to "protection" of the marine environment from future damage and "preservation" in the sense of maintaining or improving its present condition. Article 192 thus entails the positive obligation to take active measures to protect and preserve

---

[1092] *See, e.g. Request for an Advisory Opinion Submitted by the Sub-Regional Fisheries Commission (SRFC), Advisory Opinion of 2 April 2015, ITLOS Reports 2015*, para. 120.

[1093] *M/V "Louisa" (Saint Vincent and the Grenadines v. Kingdom of Spain), Provisional Measures, Order of 23 December 2010, ITLOS Reports 2008-2010*, p. 58 at p. 70, para. 76; *Dispute Concerning Delimitation of the Maritime Boundary Between Ghana and Côte D'Ivoire in the Atlantic Ocean, Provisional Measures, Order of 25 April 2015, ITLOS Reports 2015*, at para. 69.

the marine environment, and by logical implication, entails the negative obligation not to degrade the marine environment. The corpus of international law relating to the environment, which informs the content of the general obligation in Article 192, requires that States "ensure that activities within their jurisdiction and control respect the environment of other States or of areas beyond national control."[1094] Thus States have a positive "'duty to prevent, or at least mitigate' significant harm to the environment when pursuing large-scale construction activities."[1095] The Tribunal considers this duty informs the scope of the general obligation in Article 192.

942. The content of the general obligation in Article 192 is further detailed in the subsequent provisions of Part XII, including Article 194, as well as by reference to specific obligations set out in other international agreements, as envisaged in Article 237 of the Convention.[1096]

943. Article 194 concerns "pollution of the marine environment," a term which is defined in Article 1 of the Convention to mean "the introduction by man, directly or indirectly, of substances . . . into the marine environment . . . which results or is likely to result in such deleterious effects as harm to living resources and marine life . . . [and] hindrance to . . . legitimate uses of the sea . . . ." The "measures to prevent, reduce and control pollution of the marine environment" are set out in Article 194:

Article 194
Measures to prevent, reduce and control pollution of the marine environment

1. States shall take, individually or jointly as appropriate, all measures consistent with this Convention that are necessary to prevent, reduce and control pollution of the marine environment from any source, using for this purpose the best practicable means at their disposal and in accordance with their capabilities, and they shall endeavour to harmonize their policies in this connection.

[1094] *Legality of the Threat of Use of Nuclear Weapons, Advisory Opinion, ICJ Reports 1996*, p. 226 at pp. 240-242, para. 29.

[1095] *Indus Waters Kishenganga Arbitration (Pakistan v. India)*, Partial Award, 18 February 2013, PCA Award Series (2014), para. 451; *quoting Arbitration Regarding the Iron Rhine ("IJzeren Rijn") Railway between the Kingdom of Belgium and the Kingdom of the Netherlands*, Award of 24 May 2005, PCA Award Series (2007), RIAA Vol. XXVII p. 35 at pp. 66-67, para. 59.

[1096] Article 237, entitled "Obligations under other conventions on the protection and preservation of the marine environment," provides as follows:

1. The provisions of this Part are without prejudice to the specific obligations assumed by States under special conventions and agreements concluded previously which relate to the protection and preservation of the marine environment and to agreements which may be concluded in furtherance of the general principles set forth in this Convention.

2. Specific obligations assumed by States under special conventions with respect to the protection and preservation of the marine environment, should be carried out in a manner consistent with the general principles and objectives of this Convention.

2.   States shall take all measures necessary to ensure that activities under their jurisdiction or control are so conducted as not to cause damage by pollution to other States and their environment, and that pollution arising from incidents or activities under their jurisdiction or control does not spread beyond the areas where they exercise sovereign rights in accordance with this Convention.

3.   The measures taken pursuant to this Part shall deal with all sources of pollution of the marine environment. These measures shall include, inter alia, those designed to minimize to the fullest possible extent:

    (a)   the release of toxic, harmful or noxious substances, especially those which are persistent, from land-based sources, from or through the atmosphere or by dumping;

    (b)   pollution from vessels . . .

    (c)   . . .

    (d)   pollution from other installations and devices operating in the marine environment, in particular measures for . . . regulating the design, construction, equipment, operation and manning of such installations or devices.

    . . .

5.   The measures taken in accordance with this Part shall include those necessary to protect and preserve rare or fragile ecosystems as well as the habitat of depleted, threatened or endangered species and other forms of marine life.

944.   Articles 192 and 194 set forth obligations not only in relation to activities directly taken by States and their organs, but also in relation to ensuring activities within their jurisdiction and control do not harm the marine environment. The *Fisheries Advisory Opinion* of the International Tribunal for the Law of the Sea sheds light on the obligation of a flag State to ensure its fishing vessels not be involved in activities which will undermine a flag State's responsibilities under the Convention in respect of the conservation of living resources and the obligation to protect and preserve the marine environment.[1097] Drawing on decisions of the International Court of Justice in *Pulp Mills on the River Uruguay*[1098] and the Seabed Disputes Chamber advisory opinion,[1099] the International Tribunal for the Law of the Sea noted that the obligation to 'ensure' is an obligation of conduct. It requires "due diligence" in the sense of a flag State not only adopting appropriate rules and measures, but also a "certain level of

---

[1097] *Request for an Advisory Opinion Submitted by the Sub-Regional Fisheries Commission (SRFC), Advisory Opinion of 2 April 2015, ITLOS Reports 2015*, paras. 118-136. *See also Southern Bluefin Tuna (New Zealand v. Japan; Australia v. Japan), Provisional Measures, Order of 27 August 1999, ITLOS Reports 1999*, p. 280, at p. 295, para. 70; *Pulp Mills on the River Uruguay (Argentina v. Uruguay), Judgment, ICJ Reports 2010*, p. 14, at p. 79, para. 197.

[1098] *Pulp Mills on the River Uruguay (Argentina v. Uruguay), Judgment, ICJ Reports 2010*, p. 14.

[1099] *Responsibilities and Obligations of States Sponsoring Persons and Entities with respect to Activities in the Area (Request for Advisory Opinion submitted to the Seabed Disputes Chamber), Advisory Opinion of 1 February 2011, ITLOS Reports 2011*.

vigilance in their enforcement and the exercise of administrative control."[1100] Upon receipt from another State of reports of non-compliance, the flag State "is then under an obligation to investigate the matter and, if appropriate, take any action necessary to remedy the situation as well as inform the reporting State of that action."[1101]

945. The fifth paragraph of Article 194 covers all measures under Part XII of the Convention (whether taken by States or those acting under their jurisdiction and control) that are necessary to protect and preserve "rare or fragile ecosystems" as well as the habitats of endangered species. As observed by the tribunal in *Chagos Marine Protected Area*, the phrasing of Article 194(5) confirms that Part XII is "not limited to measures aimed strictly at controlling marine pollution," which while "certainly an important aspect of environmental protection . . . is by no means the only one."[1102] An 'ecosystem' is not defined in the Convention, but internationally accepted definitions include that in Article 2 of the CBD, which defines ecosystem to mean "a dynamic complex of plant, animal and micro-organism communities and their non-living environment interacting as a functional unit."[1103] The Tribunal has no doubt from the scientific evidence before it that the marine environments where the allegedly harmful activities took place in the present dispute constitute "rare or fragile ecosystems."[1104] They are also the habitats of "depleted, threatened or endangered species," including the giant clam, the hawksbill turtle and certain species of coral and fish.[1105]

946. Part XII of the Convention also includes Article 197 on cooperation, which requires States to cooperate on a global or regional basis, "directly or through competent international organizations, in formulating and elaborating international rules, standards and recommended practices and procedures consistent with this Convention, for the protection and preservation of the marine environment, taking into account characteristic regional features." In its provisional measures order in *MOX Plant*, the International Tribunal for the Law of the Sea emphasised that "the duty to cooperate is a fundamental principle in the prevention of pollution of the marine

---

[1100] *Request for an Advisory Opinion Submitted by the Sub-Regional Fisheries Commission (SRFC), Advisory Opinion of 2 April 2015, ITLOS Reports 2015*, para. 131; *quoting Pulp Mills on the River Uruguay (Argentina v. Uruguay), Judgment, ICJ Reports 2010*, p. 14, at p. 79, para. 197.

[1101] *Request for an Advisory Opinion Submitted by the Sub-Regional Fisheries Commission (SRFC), Advisory Opinion of 2 April 2015, ITLOS Reports 2015*, para. 139.

[1102] *Chagos Marine Protected Area Arbitration (Mauritius v. United Kingdom)*, Award, 18 March 2015, paras. 320, 538.

[1103] CBD, art. 2.

[1104] *See* Ferse Report, p. 7; First Carpenter Report, p.22; Second Carpenter Report, p.8; McManus Report, p. 17; Mora Report, p. 1; *see also* SOA Report (Annex 872).

[1105] First Carpenter Report, pp. 1, 5-7, pp.10-11; Ferse Report, pp. 10-11.

environment under Part XII of the Convention and general international law."[1106] Related to regional cooperation is the provision in Article 123 of the Convention, which covers semi-enclosed seas, such as the South China Sea:

Article 123
Cooperation of States bordering enclosed or semi-enclosed seas

States bordering an enclosed or semi-enclosed sea should cooperate with each other in the exercise of their rights and in the performance of their duties under this Convention. To this end they shall endeavour, directly or through an appropriate regional organization:

(a)   to coordinate the management, conservation, exploration and exploitation of the living resources of the sea;

(b)   to coordinate the implementation of their rights and duties with respect to the protection and preservation of the marine environment;

(c)   to coordinate their scientific research policies and undertake where appropriate joint programmes of scientific research in the area;

(d)   to invite, as appropriate, other interested States or international organizations to cooperate with them in furtherance of the provisions of this article.

947. The final provisions of Part XII relevant to the Philippines' Submissions concern monitoring and environmental assessment. Article 204 requires States to endeavour as far as practicable to "observe, measure, evaluate and analyse . . . the risks or effects of pollution on the marine environment" and to keep under surveillance the effects of any activities which they "permit or in which they engage" in order to determine whether they are likely to pollute the marine environment. Article 205 requires State to publish reports of the results from such monitoring to the competent international organisations, which should make them available to all States. Finally, Article 206 relates to environmental impact assessments:

Article 206
Assessment of potential effects of activities

When States have reasonable grounds for believing that planned activities under their jurisdiction or control may cause substantial pollution of or significant and harmful changes to the marine environment, they shall, as far as practicable, assess the potential effects of such activities on the marine environment and shall communicate reports of the results of such assessments in the manner provided in article 205.

948. Article 206 ensures that planned activities with potentially damaging effects may be effectively controlled and that other States are kept informed of their potential risks. In respect of Article 206, the International Tribunal for the Law of the Sea emphasised that "the obligation to conduct an environmental impact assessment is a direct obligation under the Convention and a general obligation under customary international law."[1107] As such, Article 206 has been

---

[1106]   *MOX Plant (Ireland v. United Kingdom) Provisional Measures, Order of 3 December 2001, ITLOS Reports 2001*, para. 82.

[1107]   *Responsibilities and Obligations of States with respect to Activities in the Area, Advisory Opinion, 1 February 2011, ITLOS Reports 2011*, p. 10 at p. 50, para. 145.

described as an "essential part of a comprehensive environmental management system" and as a "particular application of the obligation on states, enunciated in Article 194(2)."[1108] While the terms "reasonable" and "as far as practicable" contain an element of discretion for the State concerned, the obligation to communicate reports of the results of the assessments is absolute.

949. In applying the provisions of Part XII to the Philippines' Submissions No. 11 and 12(b), the Tribunal will consider first the actions of harmful harvesting and fishing by Chinese fishermen, and second the construction activities by China on the seven coral reefs.

(c) Harmful Fishing Practices and Harvesting of Endangered Species

i. *Harvesting of Vulnerable, Threatened and Endangered Species*

950. Based on contemporaneous reports of naval, coastguard and fisheries authorities, diplomatic exchanges and photographic evidence presented in the record, the Tribunal is satisfied that Chinese fishing vessels have been involved in harvesting of threatened or endangered species on the following occasions at or in the waters of Scarborough Shoal:

(a)   In January and March 1998, Chinese fishermen were found in possession of corals and marine turtles.[1109]

(b)   In April 2000, Chinese fishing vessels were found with four tons of corals on board.[1110]

(c)   In January 2001, Chinese fishing vessels were found with endangered sea turtles, sharks, and corals.[1111]

[1108]   S. Rosenne & A. Yankov (eds.), *United Nations Convention on the Law of the Sea 1982: A Commentary*, Vol. IV, para. 206.6(b) (M. Nordquist, gen. ed., 2002).

[1109]   Memorandum from the Assistant Secretary for Asian and Pacific Affairs, Department of Foreign Affairs, Republic of the Philippines, to the Secretary of Foreign Affairs of the Republic of the Philippines (23 March 1998) (Annex 29); *People of the Philippines v. Shin Ye Fen, et al.*, Criminal Case No. RTC 2357-I, Decision, Regional Trial Court, Third Judicial Region, Branch 69, Iba, Zambales, Philippines (29 April 1998) (Annex 30); *People of the Philippines v. Wuh Tsu Kai, et al*, Criminal Case No. RTC 2362-I, Decision, Regional Trial Court, Third Judicial Region, Branch 69, Iba, Zambales, Philippines (29 April 1998) (Annex 31); *People of the Philippines v. Zin Dao Guo, et al*, Criminal Case No. RTC 2363-I, Decision, Regional Trial Court, Third Judicial Region, Branch 69, Iba, Zambales, Philippines (29 April 1998) (Annex 32).

[1110]   Situation Report from Colonel, Philippine Navy, to Chief of Staff, Armed Forces of the Philippines, No. 004-18074 (18 April 2000) (Annex 41).

[1111]   Memorandum from the Embassy of the Republic of the Philippines in Beijing to the Secretary of Foreign Affairs of the Republic of the Philippines, No. ZPE-06-2001-S (13 February 2001) (Annex 43), Memorandum from the Acting Secretary of Foreign Affairs of the Republic of the Philippines to the President of the Republic of the Philippines (5 February 2001) (Annex 44).

(d)   Tons of corals as well as clams were confiscated from Chinese fishing vessels in February, March and September of 2002.[1112]

(e)   In October 2004, Chinese fishing vessels loaded and photographed with giant clams were intercepted by the Philippine Navy.[1113]

(f)   In December 2005, four Chinese fishing vessels were found and photographed in possession of "assorted corals and live clamshells weighing about 16 tons."[1114]

(g)   In April 2006, Chinese fishing vessels were found and photographed with corals.[1115]

(h)   On 10 April 2012, large amounts of corals and giant claims were found and photographed on board Chinese fishing vessels that were later joined by Chinese Government vessels.[1116]

(i)   On 23 and 26 April 2012, at least two Chinese fishing vessels, operating under the protection of CMS vessels were observed to have giant clams inside the cargo hold.[1117]

951.   In addition to the above events at Scarborough Shoal, the Tribunal has reviewed reports of an incident in the vicinity of Second Thomas Shoal in May 2013, in which fishing vessels from Hainan, accompanied by a Chinese naval ship and two CMS ships, were sighted by Philippine

---

[1112]   Memorandum from the Director, Naval Operation Center, Philippine Navy, to The Flag Officer in Command, Philippine Navy (11 February 2002) (Annex 49), Letter from Vice Admiral, Philippine Navy, to the Assistant Secretary for Asian and Pacific Affairs, Department of Foreign Affairs, Republic of the Philippines (26 March 2002) (Annex 50), Report from CNS to Flag Officer in Command, Philippine Navy, File No. N2D-0802-401 (1 September 2002) (Annex 52).

[1113]   Report from Lt. Commander, Philippine Navy, to Flag Officer in Command, Philippine Navy, No. N2E-F-1104-012 (18 November 2004) (Annex 55).

[1114]   Letter from Rear Admiral, Armed Forces of the Philippines, to the Assistant Secretary for Asian and Pacific Affairs, Department of Foreign Affairs, Republic of the Philippines (2006) (Annex 57).

[1115]   Report from the Commanding Officer, NAVSOU-2, Philippine Navy, to the Acting Commander, Naval Task Force 21, Philippine Navy, No. NTF21-0406-011/NTF21 OPLAN (BANTAY AMIANAN) 01-05 (9 April 2006) (Annex 59).

[1116]   Memorandum from Colonel, Philippine Navy, to Chief of Staff, Armed Forces of the Philippines, No. N2E-0412-008 (11 April 2012) (Annex 77).

[1117]   Memorandum from Colonel, Philippine Navy, to Chief of Staff, Armed Forces of the Philippines, No. N2E-0412-008 (11 April 2012) (Annex 77), Report from the Commanding Officer, SARV-003, Philippine Coast Guard, to Commander, Coast Guard District Northwestern Luzon, Philippine Coast Guard (28 April 2012) (Annex 78).

armed forces and "believed to be gathering corals and clams and dredging in the shoal."[1118] Photographs from the incident show the harvesting of giant claims.[1119]

952. Recent evidence also indicates the large-scale harvest of endangered hawksbill sea turtles by Chinese fishermen, whose arrest by Philippine authorities led to protests by China.[1120]

953. Finally, in addition to the occurrence of the above events recounted in the Philippines' Memorial, the Tribunal is satisfied based on its review of satellite imagery, photographic and video evidence, contemporaneous press reports, scientific studies and the materials from Professor McManus, that in recent years, Chinese fishing vessels have been engaged in widespread harvesting of giant clams through the use of boat propellers to break through the coral substrate in search of buried clam shells.

954. The Tribunal turns now to the harmful impact of the above-described activities and then addresses the extent to which China may be held responsible for breach of the Convention in connection with those activities.

955. Many of the above-listed incidents involved the harvesting of coral species. The Ferse Report describes the impact on the marine environment from the harvesting of coral as follows:

> stony corals are frequently harvested as construction material, or for sale in the curio trade, *e.g.* to tourists. The repeated, targeted removal of coral colonies can modify the community structure – branching species are preferably targeted for the curio trade, and their removal leads to an overall loss of structural complexity. Decreased live coral cover and structural complexity severely affects the reef fish community, as a large proportion of the species on the reef utilise live corals at some point in their life history.[1121]

956. All of the sea turtles (*Cheloniidae*) found on board Chinese fishing vessels are listed under Appendix I to the CITES Convention as species threatened with extinction and subject to the strictest level of international controls on trade. [1122] CITES is the subject of nearly universal adherence, including by the Philippines and China, and in the Tribunal's view forms part of the general corpus of international law that informs the content of Article 192 and 194(5) of the

---

[1118] Armed Forces of the Philippines, *Near-occupation of Chinese Vessels of Second Thomas (Ayungin) Shoal in the Early Weeks of May 2012* (May 2013) (Annex 94).

[1119] Armed Forces of the Philippines, *Near-occupation of Chinese Vessels of Second Thomas (Ayungin) Shoal in the Early Weeks of May 2012* (May 2013) (Annex 94). *See* photographs at Armed Forces of the Philippines, *Ayungin Shoal: Situation Update* (11 May 2013) (Annex 95).

[1120] R. Wingfield-Hayes, "Why are Chinese fishermen destroying coral reefs in the South China Sea?," *BBC* (15 December 2015), *available at* <www.bbc.com/news/magazine-35106631> (Annex 862); Ministry of Foreign Affairs, People's Republic of China, *Foreign Ministry Spokesperson Hua Chunying's Regular Press Conference* (25 November 2014), *available at* <www.fmprc.gov.cn/mfa_eng/xwfw_665399/ s2510_665401/2511_665403/t1214543.shtml>.

[1121] Ferse Report, p. 10 and coral studies cited therein.

[1122] CITES, Appendix I, *available at* <cites.org/eng/app/appendices.php>.

Convention. "[T]he conservation of the living resources of the sea is an element in the protection and preservation of the marine environment,"[1123] and the Tribunal considers that the general obligation to "protect and preserve the marine environment" in Article 192 includes a due diligence obligation to prevent the harvesting of species that are recognised internationally as being at risk of extinction and requiring international protection.

957. The Tribunal is particularly troubled by the evidence with respect to giant clams, tons of which were harvested by Chinese fishing vessels from Scarborough Shoal, and in recent years, elsewhere in the Spratly Islands. Giant clams (*Tridacnidae*) and many of the corals found in the Spratly Islands are listed in Appendix II to CITES and are unequivocally threatened, even if they are not subject to the same level of international controls as Appendix I species. Equally important, however, giant clams play a significant role in the overall growth and maintenance of the reef structure.[1124] The Ferse Report describes the effects of harvesting them as follows:

> Giant clams have historically been harvested widely throughout Southeast Asia and beyond, both for their meat and their shells. The larger species can reach considerable sizes (the largest species, *Tridacna gigas*, can reach almost 1.5m in size and a weight of over 300kg), but they grow slowly. Thus, large individuals have become rare on most reefs. As their shells are highly coveted, collectors have begun to target fossil shells buried in the reef flat (the shallow, extensive habitat on top of reefs). Excavation is highly destructive, with early reports showing a drop in coral cover by 95% from its original value. More recently, fishermen in the South China Sea are reported to utilise the propellers of their boats to excavate shells from reef flats in the Spratly Islands on an industrial scale, leading to near-complete destruction of the affected reef areas.[1125]

958. The Tribunal recalls in particular the very recent examinations conducted by Professor McManus, which led him to estimate that China is responsible for almost 70 square kilometres of coral reef damage from giant clam harvesting using propellers,[1126] a practice he described as more thoroughly damaging to marine life than anything he had seen in four decades of investigating coral reef degradation.[1127]

959. The Tribunal has noted that it considers the duty to prevent the harvest of endangered species follows from Article 192, read against the background of other applicable international law. The Tribunal considers that this general obligation is given particular shape in the context of fragile ecosystems by Article 194(5). Read in this context, the Tribunal thus considers that Article 192 imposes a due diligence obligation to take those measures "necessary to protect and

---

[1123] *Southern Bluefin Tuna (New Zealand v. Japan; Australia v. Japan), Provisional Measures, Order of 27 August 1999, ITLOS Reports 1999*, p. 280, at p. 295, para. 70.

[1124] Merits Hearing Tr. (Day 4), pp. 144-145.

[1125] Ferse Report, p. 10, and studies and reports cited therein.

[1126] McManus Report, p. 66.

[1127] Letter from Professor McManus to the Tribunal (22 April 2016).

preserve rare or fragile ecosystems as well as the habitat of depleted, threatened or endangered species and other forms of marine life." Therefore, in addition to preventing the direct harvesting of species recognised internationally as being threatened with extinction, Article 192 extends to the prevention of harms that would affect depleted, threatened, or endangered species indirectly through the destruction of their habitat.

960. The Tribunal thus considers the harvesting of sea turtles, species threatened with extinction, to constitute a harm to the marine environment as such. The Tribunal further has no doubt that the harvesting of corals and giant clams from the waters surrounding Scarborough Shoal and features in the Spratly Islands, on the scale that appears in the record before it, has a harmful impact on the fragile marine environment. The Tribunal therefore considers that a failure to take measures to prevent these practices would constitute a breach of Articles 192 and 194(5) of the Convention, and turns now to consider China's responsibility for such breaches.

961. The vessels involved in the incidents described above were all Chinese flag vessels, under the jurisdiction and control of China. In the Tribunal's view, where a State is aware that vessels flying its flag are engaged in the harvest of species recognised internationally as being threatened with extinction or are inflicting significant damage on rare or fragile ecosystems or the habitat of depleted, threatened, or endangered species, its obligations under the Convention include a duty to adopt rules and measures to prevent such acts and to maintain a level of vigilance in enforcing those rules and measures.

962. On the question of awareness, it is clear from the record that the Philippines had brought its concerns about poaching of endangered species to the attention of China as early as January 2000, when it stated to the Chinese Embassy that unlawful harvesting "disturbed the tranquillity of the ecosystem and habitat of important species of marine life and . . . caused irreparable damage to the marine environment of the area."[1128] The Philippines also recalled that the gathering and trade of corals violates the provisions of three international conventions to which China is a signatory, including the CBD and CITES. In 2001, China assured the Philippines that it "attaches great importance to environmental protection and violators are dealt with in accordance with Chinese laws and regulations."[1129] After finding 16 tons of clams and corals

---

[1128] Note Verbale from the Department of Foreign Affairs, Republic of the Philippines, to the Embassy of the People's Republic of China in Manila, No. 2000100 (14 January 2000) (Annex 186).

[1129] Memorandum from the Embassy of the Republic of the Philippines in Beijing to the Secretary of Foreign Affairs of the Republic of the Philippines, No. ZPE-06-2001-S (13 February 2001) (Annex 43).

aboard Chinese fishing vessels in 2005, the Philippines expressed its grave concern to China over the "rampant trading of endangered corals and marine species in the South China Sea."[1130]

963. China was therefore, certainly by 2005, on notice of poaching practices of Chinese fishing vessels in Scarborough Shoal and aware of the Philippines' concerns. The poaching, however, has persisted, despite (a) China's earlier statements that it would deal with violators, (b) China being party to CITES since 1981, and (c) China having enacted in 1989 a Law of the Protection of Wildlife, which prohibits the catching or killing of two classes of special state protected wildlife,[1131] and specifically lists among them sea turtles and giant clams.[1132]

964. As the Tribunal has noted above, adopting appropriate rules and measures to prohibit a harmful practice is only one component of the due diligence required by States pursuant to the general obligation of Article 192, read in the context of Article 194(5) and the international law applicable to endangered species. There is no evidence in the record that would indicate that China has taken any steps to enforce those rules and measures against fishermen engaged in poaching of endangered species. Indeed, at least with respect to the April 2012 incidents, the evidence points directly to the contrary. China was aware of the harvesting of giant clams. It did not merely turn a blind eye to this practice. Rather, it provided armed government vessels to protect the fishing boats.[1133] The Chinese Ministry of Foreign Affairs Spokesperson confirmed on 12 April 2012 that it had "dispatched administrative vessels . . . to protect the safety and legitimate fishing activities of Chinese fishermen and fishing vessels."[1134] Despite the reference

---

[1130] Memorandum from the Secretary of Foreign Affairs, Republic of the Philippines, to the President of the Republic of the Philippines, (11 January 2006) (Annex 58).

[1131] Standing Committee of the National People's Congress, Law of the People's Republic of China on the Protection of Wildlife, amended 27 August 2009, Article 9, *available at* <www.china.org.cn/english/environment/34349.htm>. *See also* Regulations of the People's Republic of China for the Implementation of Wild Aquatic Animal Protection, amended on 7 December 2013, Article 12, *available at* <http://www.eduzhai.net/yingyu/615/763/yingyu_246269.html>; Ministry of Agriculture, Measures of the People's Republic of China for Special Licenses for Exploitation of Aquatic Wild Animals, *available at* <http://www.moa.gov.cn/zwllm/zcfg/nybgz/201401/t20140113_3737659.htm>.

[1132] Directory of the People's Republic of China on Special State Protection of Wildlife, Ministry of Forestry and Ministry of Agriculture, 14 January 1989, *available at* <www.unodc.org/res/cld/document/directory-of-the-peoples-republic-of-china-on-special-state-protection-of-wildlife_html/Directory_of_the_Peoples_Republic_of_China_on_Special_State_Protection_of_Wildlife.pdf> (both sea turtles (*Cheloniidae,* 海龟科) and giant clams (*Tridaonidae,* 砗磲科) are expressly protected).

[1133] Memorandum from the Philippine Navy to the Chief of Staff, Armed Forces of the Philippines, No. N2E-0412-008 (11 April 2012) (Annex 77); Report from the Commanding Officer, SARV-003, Philippine Coast Guard to the Commander, Coast Guard District Northwestern Luzon, Philippine Coast Guard (28 April 2012) (Annex 78); Memorandum from the FRPLEU/QRT Chief, Bureau of Fisheries and Aquatic Resources, Republic of the Philippines, to the Director, Bureau of Fisheries and Aquatic Resources, Republic of the Philippines (2 May 2012) (Annex 79).

[1134] Ministry of Foreign Affairs, People's Republic of China, *Foreign Ministry Spokesperson Liu Weimin's Regular Press Conference* (12 April 2012) (Annex 117).

to "legitimate fishing activities", the photographic evidence of endangered species, including giant clams and sharks, on board the vessels in question indicates China must have known of, and deliberately tolerated, and protected the harmful acts. Similarly, with respect to the May 2013 incident in the vicinity of Second Thomas Shoal, the Tribunal accepts, on the basis of the photographic and contemporaneous documentary evidence, that Chinese naval and CMS vessels were escorting Chinese fishing vessels in gathering clams.[1135] The Tribunal therefore has no hesitation in finding that China breached its obligations under Articles 192 and 194(5) of the Convention, to take necessary measures to protect and preserve the marine environment, with respect to the harvesting of endangered species from the fragile ecosystems at Scarborough Shoal and Second Thomas Shoal.

965. There remains the question of China's responsibility for the more recent and widespread environmental degradation caused by propeller chopping for giant clams across the Spratlys. From satellite imagery showing scarring from this practice, it appears the harvesting took place in areas under control of Chinese authorities, at a time and in locations where Chinese authorities were engaged in planning and implementing China's island-building activities. The Tribunal considers that the small propeller vessels involved in harvesting the giant clams were within China's jurisdiction and control. The Tribunal finds that China, despite its rules on the protection of giant clams, and on the preservation of the coral reef environment generally,[1136] was fully aware of the practice and has actively tolerated it as a means to exploit the living resources of the reefs in the months prior to those reefs succumbing to the near permanent destruction brought about by the island-building activities discussed in Section 4.[1137]

966. Accordingly, the Tribunal finds that China has also breached its obligation to protect and preserve the marine environment in respect of its toleration and protection of the harvesting of giant clams by the propeller chopping method.

[1135] Armed Forces of the Philippines, *Near-occupation of Chinese Vessels of Second Thomas (Ayungin) Shoal in the Early Weeks of May 2012* (May 2013) (Annex 94); Armed Forces of the Philippines, *Ayungin Shoal: Situation Update* (11 May 2013) (Annex 95).

[1136] People's Republic of China, Marine Environment Protection Law of the People's Republic of China, art. 9 (25 December 1999) (Annex 614).

[1137] The Tribunal notes that China is not alone in conducting this practice, but estimates suggest that China is responsible for over 99 percent of the destruction of reef in the South China Sea brought about by this method. *See* V.R. Lee, "Satellite Imagery Shows Ecocide in the South China Sea," *The Diplomat* (15 January 2016), *available at* <http://thediplomat.com/2016/satellite-images-show-ecocide-in-the-south-china-sea/>; Ferse Report, pp. 59-60; McManus Report; Letter from Professor McManus to the Tribunal (22 April 2016).

ii.   Use of Cyanide and Dynamite

967. The Tribunal next examines the complaints that China has breached the Convention in relation to Chinese fishermen who used cyanide and explosives at Scarborough Shoal and Second Thomas Shoal.

968. Based on contemporaneous reports from the Philippine navy, coast guard, and police, and photographic evidence presented in the record, the Tribunal is satisfied that Chinese fishing vessels were engaged in the use of dynamite or cyanide on the following occasions:

(a)   As early as 1995, 62 Chinese fishermen in the Spratly Islands were arrested by Philippine authorities after being found in possession of explosives and cyanide.[1138]

(b)   In March 1998, 29 Chinese fishermen at Scarborough Shoal were found in possession of dynamite and convicted under Philippine fisheries law banning it.[1139]

(c)   In April 2000, three Chinese vessels were found at Scarborough Shoal with blasting caps, detonating cord, and dynamite.[1140]

(d)   On three occasions in 2002 Chinese vessels in Scarborough Shoal were found with blasting caps, detonating cord, plastic explosives, cyanide, and cyanide tubes.[1141]

(e)   Cyanide pumps were found aboard Chinese vessels at Scarborough Shoal in December 2005[1142] and April 2006.[1143]

[1138]   Memorandum from the Ambassador of the Republic of the Philippines in Beijing to the Undersecretary of Foreign Affairs of the Republic of the Philippines (10 April 1995) (Annex 21).

[1139]   Memorandum from the Assistant Secretary for Asian and Pacific Affairs, Department of Foreign Affairs, Republic of the Philippines, to the Secretary of Foreign Affairs of the Republic of the Philippines (23 March 1998) (Annex 29); *People of the Philippines v. Shin Ye Fen, et al.*, Criminal Case No. RTC 2357-I, Decision, Regional Trial Court, Third Judicial Region, Branch 69, Iba, Zambales, Philippines (29 April 1998) (Annex 30); *People of the Philippines v. Wuh Tsu Kai, et al*, Criminal Case No. RTC 2362-I, Decision, Regional Trial Court, Third Judicial Region, Branch 69, Iba, Zambales, Philippines (29 April 1998) (Annex 31); *People of the Philippines v. Zin Dao Guo, et al*, Criminal Case No. RTC 2363-I, Decision, Regional Trial Court, Third Judicial Region, Branch 69, Iba, Zambales, Philippines (29 April 1998) (Annex 32).

[1140]   Situation Report the Philippine Navy to the Chief of Staff, Armed Forces of the Philippines, No. 004-18074 (18 April 2000) (Annex 41); Letter from the Vice Admiral, Armed Forces of the Philippines, to the Secretary of National Defense, Republic of the Philippines (27 May 2000) (Annex 42).

[1141]   Memorandum from the Director, Naval Operation Center, Philippine Navy, to The Flag Officer in Command, Philippine Navy (11 February 2002) (Annex 49); Letter from Vice Admiral, Philippine Navy, to the Assistant Secretary for Asian and Pacific Affairs, Department of Foreign Affairs, Republic of the Philippines (26 March 2002) (Annex 50); Report from CNS to Flag Officer in Command, Philippine Navy, File No. N2D-0802-401 (1 September 2002) (Annex 52).

[1142]   Letter from Rear Admiral, Armed Forces of the Philippines, to the Assistant Secretary for Asian and Pacific Affairs, Department of Foreign Affairs, Republic of the Philippines (2006) (Annex 57).

969. After 2006, the only mention in the record of use by Chinese fishing vessels of explosives is a historical entry in a military briefing of May 2013, which recounts that on 12 February 2012 "2 fishing vessels believed to be Chinese were monitored fishing using explosives and sodium cyanide 4 NM SW off LT57 in Ayungin Shoal."[1144] The Tribunal notes that this reference is uncertain as to the provenance of the vessels and, unlike the above-listed incidents, is unsupported by contemporaneous reports, inventories, and photographs. Accordingly, the Tribunal does not include this incident in its further consideration of breach of Part XII of the Convention.

970. The Tribunal accepts the observation in the Ferse Report that cyanide and blast fishing are "highly destructive methods" that have been used in the Spratly Islands in the past decades.[1145] It takes note of the studies referred to by Professor Carpenter which found "both dynamite and cyanide fishing . . . among the most highly destructive of all fishing methods" and that both methods are considered irresponsible and unsustainable according to the FAO Code of Conduct for Responsible Fisheries.[1146] Because explosives shatter coral and cyanide can kill or injure non-target species, the Tribunal considers the use of both dynamite and cyanide to be "pollution" of the marine environment within the meaning of the Convention—they are substances introduced by man that "result in such deleterious effects as to harm living resources and marine life."[1147] They also threaten the fragile ecosystem of the coral reefs and the habitats of endangered species at Scarborough Shoal. The Tribunal therefore considers that failure to take measures against the use of dynamite and cyanide would constitute breach of Articles 192, 194(2) and 194(5) of the Convention.

971. The Tribunal must, however, address whether there is sufficient evidence that China should be held responsible now for the failure to prevent the incidents listed in paragraph 968 above. The Tribunal recalls that while Chinese fishing vessels are within China's jurisdiction and control as the flag State, the obligation to ensure that those fishing vessels do not take measures to pollute the marine environment is one of due diligence.

[1143] Report from the Commanding Officer, NAVSOU-2, Philippine Navy, to the Acting Commander, Naval Task Force 21, Philippine Navy (9 April 2006) (Annex 59)

[1144] Armed Forces of the Philippines, *Near-occupation of Chinese Vessels of Second Thomas (Ayungin) Shoal in the Early Weeks of May 2012* (May 2013) (Annex 94).

[1145] Ferse Report, p. 10.

[1146] First Carpenter Report p. 12; *see also* Merits Hearing Tr. (Day 3), p. 28, UN Food and Agriculture Organization, *Code of Conduct for Responsible Fisheries* (31 October 1995), para. 8.4.2.

[1147] Convention, Arts. 1, 194.

972. In contrast to the poaching of endangered species, there is little evidence in the record with respect to Philippine complaints to China about the use of cyanide and blasting specifically. In a memorandum about a meeting with China's Assistant Foreign Minister in April 1995, the Philippine Ambassador in Beijing recorded raising the issue of 62 Chinese fishermen found in possession of explosives and cyanide. He noted that this is "harmful to the marine environment and thus, illegal. When coral reefs are destroyed, it takes generations before they can be rebuilt. And the poisoning of the marine environment . . . is a matter of grave concern to the Philippine Government."[1148]

973. The Tribunal notes that the above statement pre-dates the introduction in 1999 of the Marine Environment Protection Law of the People's Republic of China.[1149] Indeed in March 2000, the same Philippine Ambassador to Beijing reported that a Chinese diplomat had expressed to him her "particular concern about the practice of dynamite fishing" and had requested the Ministry of Agriculture to do something about the situation.[1150] A year later, the new Philippine Ambassador in Beijing recalled that "local fishing authorities imposed a penalty on the fishermen caught blasting coral reefs near Scarborough Shoal in early 2000." He was also told by a Chinese Foreign Ministry official that "the Chinese Government attaches great importance to environmental protection and violators are dealt with in accordance with Chinese laws and regulations."[1151]

974. In 2000, the People's Republic of China updated its Fisheries Law, Article 30 of which prohibits the "use of explosives, poisons, electricity and any other means in fishing that impairs the fishery resources."[1152] Adopting appropriate rules and measures is one component of the due diligence required by States under the Convention. States are also required to adopt a certain level of vigilance in the enforcement and control of the rules, but there is little in the record to suggest that China has failed to do so with respect to dynamite and cyanide fishing.

[1148] Memorandum from the Ambassador of the Republic of the Philippines in Beijing to the Undersecretary of Foreign Affairs of the Republic of the Philippines (10 April 1995) (Annex 21).

[1149] People's Republic of China, Marine Environment Protection Law of The People's Republic of China (25 December 1999) (Annex 614).

[1150] Memorandum from the Embassy of the Republic of the Philippines in Beijing to the Secretary of Foreign Affairs of the Republic of the Philippines, No. ZPE-24-2000-S (14 March 2000) (Annex 40).

[1151] Memorandum from the Embassy of the Republic of the Philippines in Beijing to the Secretary of Foreign Affairs of the Republic of the Philippines, No. ZPE-06-2001-S (13 February 2001) (Annex 43). See also, Memorandum from the Embassy of the Republic of the Philippines in Beijing to the Secretary of Foreign Affairs of the Republic of the Philippines, No. ZPE-09-2001-S (17 March 2001) (Annex 47).

[1152] People's Republic of China, Fisheries Law, Article 30, *available at* <www.npc.gov.cn/englishnpc/ Law/2007-12/12/content_1383934.htm>.

975. In contrast to the situations of harvesting of endangered species and harmful construction activities, there is scant evidence in the case record about the use of explosives and cyanide over the last decade or Philippine complaints about its use. This suggests China may have taken measures to prevent such practices in the Spratly Islands. In any event, the Tribunal is not prepared to make a finding on the evidence available, under Submission No. 11 with respect to cyanide and explosives.

(d) China's Construction Activities on Seven Reefs in the Spratly Islands

    i.   China's Construction Activities and the Obligation to Protect and Preserve the Marine Environment

976. The Tribunal turns now to the environmental impact of China's extensive island-building project at seven reefs in the Spratly Islands, the nature and extent of which is described in paragraphs 852 to 890 above. In summary, the record shows that since the end of 2013, China has created on top of the coral reefs approximately 12.8 million square metres of land, from millions of tons of dredged coral, rocks and sand. There is no question that the artificial island-building program is part of an official Chinese policy and program implemented by organs of the Chinese State.

977. Before turning to the impact of China's recent island-building activities, the Tribunal recalls that during the preceding two decades, China, as well as the Philippines and other States in the region, undertook some more modest construction and land reclamation work on features in the Spratly Islands, which has included the installation of buildings, wharves, helipads, and weather and communications instruments.[1153] The Tribunal notes Professor Carpenter's observation that most of the construction during this period was "limited to building discrete structures with a minimal footprint on the natural form and structure of existing coral reefs."[1154] Nevertheless, he opined in his first report that the earlier generation of concrete structures (including those built by other States) reduced the coral reefs on which they were installed, displaced the organisms that inhabited them, and made the reefs' structural integrity vulnerable to wave action and

---

[1153] *See, e.g.*, Armed Forces of the Philippines, *Chronological Development of Artificial Structures on Features* (Annex 96); Armed Forces of the Philippines, *Chronology of Events in the Kalayaan Island Group* (2004) (Annex 53); Second Carpenter Report, pp. 6-8; Merits Hearing Tr. (Day 2), pp. 193-194; Note Verbale from the Department of Boundary and Ocean Affairs, Ministry of Foreign Affairs, People's Republic of China, to the Embassy of the Republic of the Philippines in Beijing, No. (2015) Bu Bian Zi No. 22 (30 March 2015) (Annex 686); J. Page & J.E. Barnes, "China Expands Island Construction in Dispute South China Sea," *Wall Street Journal* (19 February 2015) (Annex 748).

[1154] Second Carpenter Report, p. 6.

storms.[1155] Human presence on the features also entails the disposal of waste, and waste water, which promotes algal growth that can detrimentally affect fisheries.[1156] The Ferse Report also acknowledged that while the Spratly Islands are an area of high diversity and among the least impacted reefs in the South China Sea, the "area is not pristine" and had already been affected by the impacts of human activity, such as overfishing and destructive fishing, construction activities and human habitation "for several decades prior to commencement of large-scale construction in 2013."[1157] The Ferse Report concluded however, that "[t]he scale of these previous impacts generally cannot be compared with the environmental harm caused by the construction activities, both in terms of spatial extent and duration."[1158]

978. The conclusions of the Tribunal-appointed independent experts are unequivocal with respect to the more recent construction activities, which they say have "impacted reefs on a scale unprecedented in the region."[1159] They cite a 2016 study analysing satellite imagery that found up to 60 percent of the shallow reef habitat at the seven reefs has been directly destroyed.[1160] Construction-related sedimentation and turbidity have affected large portions of the reefs beyond the immediate area of construction. The Ferse Report states:

> The effects of these impacts on the reefs, together with altered hydrodynamics and released nutrients, are likely to have wide-ranging and long-lasting ecological consequences for the affected reefs and the wider ecosystem of the Spratly Islands, and possibly beyond. Reefs subjected to direct land reclamation have disappeared entirely. Reefs subjected to dredging in order to create landfill will have lost their complex structure that was built over centuries to millennia. This structure will take decades to centuries to recover. Reefs that did not experience dredging directly but were impacted by the associated sedimentation and nutrient release will likely have experienced severe coral mortality and recovery will take place more slowly than in natural settings, likely taking decades. The capacity for ongoing . . . carbonate production is severely diminished on several of the reefs, and their capacity to keep up with increasing sea level rise is impaired. [1161]

979. The Tribunal accepts the conclusion in the Ferse Report that "China's recent construction activities have and will cause environmental harm to coral reefs at Cuarteron Reef, Fiery Cross Reef, Gaven Reef, Johnson Reef, Hughes Reef, Mischief Reef, and Subi Reef; beyond the pre-existing damage to reefs that resulted from destructive fishing and the collection of corals and clams, storm damage, Crown-of-Thorns starfish, and the human presence on small garrisons

---

[1155] First Carpenter Report, pp. 14, 16-17.

[1156] Memorial, para. 6.110-6.111; First Carpenter Report, pp. 16-18.

[1157] Ferse Report, p. 3.

[1158] Ferse Report, p. 59.

[1159] Ferse Report, p. 3.

[1160] Ferse Report, p. 3; Mora Report.

[1161] Ferse Report, p. 3.

on the reefs." The Ferse Report also arrives at the following conclusions as to the extent and likely duration of the harm.

- The harm caused by direct burial of reef habitat during the construction of artificial islands is near-permanent. The duration of harm to areas affected by dredging and dredging-related release of sediments and nutrients and the prospects and likely rates for rejuvenation differ depending on the environmental setting of each particular affected habitat area. We expect that the harm to areas affected by dredging for navigable channels and basins will likely be near-permanent and that the prospects for rejuvenation are low, particularly as long as maintenance dredging for the use of the artificial islands continues. Second, where major geomorphological structures have been removed through dredging, such as large coral 'bommies' (accumulations of corals that typically stand several metres above the substrate), there is little prospect for recovery on ecological time scales. These structures constitute accumulated reef growth on geological time scales of centuries to millennia. This statement applies to much of the lagoon and deeper parts of the reef flat where these features (bommies or patch reefs) have been described in the Spratly Islands. Harm to areas affected by smothering of sediments and increased turbidity, which includes most of the lagoons at Mischief and Subi Reefs and parts of the outer reef slopes of all seven reefs, is likely to endure for years to decades within the lagoons (due to limited water exchange), and for weeks to months on the outer reef slopes. Rejuvenation of these areas is possible (provided chronic stressors such as sedimentation are removed and recurrent stressors such as bleaching events are infrequent), but will take several decades, and it will likely take centuries for large massive colonies to regrow.

- China's construction activities have led to reduced productivity and complexity of the affected reefs, with significant reductions of nursery habitat for a number of fish species. Therefore, not only will the reefs affected by construction have a greatly reduced capacity to sustain local fisheries but their ability to help replenish the fisheries of neighbouring jurisdictions will also be vastly diminished – at least threefold. The construction activities thus will have a broader impact on the marine ecosystem in and around the South China Sea and on fisheries resources. However, the magnitude of this impact will depend on the relative role of the seven affected reefs as critical habitat and source of larvae for fisheries resources compared to other reefs in the Spratly Islands, which is difficult to quantify due to a lack of empirical studies. On the basis of available information, cascading effects cannot be ruled out.[1162]

980. The conclusions in the Ferse Report largely confirm the conclusions reached in the First and Second Carpenter Reports. However, Dr. Ferse and his colleagues noted in Part IX of their report, that in some respects they consider Professor Carpenter may have overstated or understated particular aspects of the damage.[1163]

981. The Tribunal is conscious that the conclusions reached in the Ferse Report and those by Professor Carpenter and in other recent scientific studies,[1164] are at odds with China's stated position that its construction activities have followed a "high standard of environmental protection" and that the marine environment end ecosystem of the South China Sea "will not be

---

[1162] Ferse Report, pp. 59-60.

[1163] Ferse Report, pp. 42-46.

[1164] *See, e.g.*, McManus Report; Mora Report.

damaged."[1165] The Tribunal has accordingly sought out China's position on the environmental impact of its construction activities, by reviewing statements of Chinese officials and scientists, by asking the Philippines and the Tribunal-appointed experts to locate and assess the claims by Chinese officials and scientists, and by directly requesting China to comment on a range of materials and questions about the alleged impact of the construction.

982. The Ferse Report noted that several ecological studies of the area by Chinese researchers actually emphasise the need for conservation of the seven reefs,[1166] and "available satellite and aerial imagery provides little indication of effective mitigation measures."[1167] As to the general claim that the construction activity "does not damage the environment on the reefs," the Ferse Report stated it "is contradicted by the facts."[1168] While the Ferse Report noted that the Chinese statements contained "accurate descriptions of the environmental conditions at the reefs," the Chinese assessments of the nature and extent of impacts from construction were "largely in disagreement with the available information."[1169] The following are examples of specific claims made by Chinese scientists that were addressed in the Ferse Report:

(a) *Replenishment:* Chinese scientists claimed that in the South China Sea "the nutrients and food organisms can be replenished constantly from surrounding waters." The Ferse Report noted there is "very limited support" for the potential for replenishment from outside the Spratly Islands, in light of larval connectivity patterns within the South China Sea.[1170]

(b) *Timing of works:* In relation to the claim by Chinese scientists that the construction was timed "reasonably, trying to avoid spawn periods of red snapper (mid-April), tuna (peak from June to August) and bonito (from March to August)," the Ferse Report analysed satellite and aerial imagery to conclude that land construction had indeed occurred in

---

[1165] *See, e.g.*, Permanent Mission of the People's Republic of China to the United Nations, *Statement by Head of the Chinese Delegation at the 25th Meeting of States Parties to the UN Convention on the Law of the Sea* (12 June 2014) (Annex 617), Ministry of Foreign Affairs, People's Republic of China, *Foreign Ministry Spokesperson Hua Chunying's Regular Press Conference* (9 April 2015) (Annex 624), Ministry of Foreign Affairs, People's Republic of China, *Foreign Ministry Spokesperson Hong Lei's Regular Press Conference* (28 April 2015) (Annex 625), Note Verbale from the Embassy of the People's Republic of China in Manila to the Department of Foreign Affairs, Republic of the Philippines, No. 14 (PG)-336 (28 October 2014) (Annex 680).

[1166] Ferse Report, p. 48, fn. 279; *see also* SOA Report, pp. 1-2.

[1167] Ferse Report, p. 48.

[1168] Ferse Report, p. 48.

[1169] Ferse Report, p. 2.

[1170] SOA Report, p. 3; Ferse Report, p. 49.

months during those spawning periods.[1171] The Ferse Report noted that construction activity occurred during the suspected spawning time of reef corals.

(c) *Water quality:* Chinese scientists claimed that China avoided "fine sands from going into reclamation areas to maintain the water quality of coral reef areas." The Ferse Report stated that satellite and aerial imagery clearly shows water quality in the vicinity of each construction site was affected by increased sediment and turbidity from dredging.[1172]

(d) *Restoration and Transplantation:* Chinese scientists claimed that "the restoration of coral reef communities could be realized should effective measures be taken" and that "coral reefs that have been severely damaged . . . can be restored initially in 5-10 years provided that effective measures are taken, and complex and complete ecosystems can be fully restored in 50-100 years." They also suggested implementing measures like "transplantation" to better protect the coral reefs. The Ferse Report explained that restoration is not likely to succeed if stressors persist and if ecological connectivity and larval supply are disturbed. The Ferse Report noted the uncertainty of restoration science. It further noted "large parts of the seven reefs have been permanently destroyed by construction, and for the remaining areas, recovery is uncertain and, if it occurs, it will take more than a century until the large massive coral colonies have regrown." Further, restorative activities are "extremely expensive" and have only ever been attempted on far smaller scales. Transplantation is unlikely to be suitable on the scale of the impacts from construction, as it could risk impacting other reefs in the region, and involves "prohibitive" labour and costs.[1173]

(e) *Impact on reef structure:* Chinese scientists claimed that due to strong currents and waves, "the photosynthesis of corals" was left "largely unaffected" and because the sites are located in areas where coverage of coral reefs is low, "the overall community structure of coral reefs" and the "physical and chemical living environment of coral reefs" have not fundamentally changed. The Ferse Report pointed to the sediment plumes generated by dredging and notes they are "very likely to have altered the community structure of the affected coral reefs." The Ferse Report recalled that the construction has permanently altered the hydrodynamics of the affected reefs, and elevated level of sediments are likely, "from months to years in those parts of the reefs that are

---

[1171] SOA Report, p. 2; Ferse Report, pp. 50-51, 53.

[1172] SOA Report, p. 2; Ferse Report, pp. 50-51.

[1173] SOA Report, p. 3; Ferse Report, pp. 52-55.

well-flushed by open ocean waters, and from years to decades in areas with less flushing, such as the lagoons of Mischief and Subi Reef."[1174]

(f) *Impact on reef health:* Chinese scientists claimed that in light of the status of the reefs as "sub-healthy" both before and after the construction activities, it can be concluded that the "construction activities neither affected the health of the ecosystems of Nansha nor harmed the coral reef ecosystems." The Ferse Report noted the lack of available information on post-construction monitoring but recalls that "the available evidence leaves little doubt that the coral reef ecosystems of the seven affected reefs have suffered significant and extensive harm as a result of construction activities."[1175]

(g) *Selection of sites containing dead coral:* The SOA and other Chinese scientists claim that the construction sites contained dead coral. The Ferse Report noted that even deep lagoon basins containing less live corals than other reef habitats constitute a vital habitat for molluscs, echinoderms and crustaceans. On the reefs lacking a deep lagoon (Cuarteron, Hughes, Gaven, and Johnson), material for land reclamation was gathered from the shallow reef habitat. In any event, sediment plumes affected both lagoon and outer reef slope habitats.

(h) *Use of "nature simulation" method:* China embraces the "nature simulation" as its "comprehensive technical concept" in the Nansha reef expansion project. It claims the land reclamation area will "produce the ecological effects by going from desalination, solidification, efflorescence, to a green coral reef ecological environment."[1176] The Ferse Report observed that this statement overlooks the importance of biogenic sediment production. "Rather than simulating the natural process of island development, the construction process increases the erosion of the reefs by shifting the balance between carbonate accretion and erosion, and thus increases the risk of drowning the reef as sea levels continue to rise."[1177]

(i) *Recovery:* China's SOA has claimed that "[g]ood results have been obtained and the ecological impact on the coral reefs is partial, temporary, controllable, and

---

[1174] SOA Report, p. 3; Ferse Report, p. 53.

[1175] SOA Report, p. 3; Ferse Report, pp. 50-51.

[1176] SOA Statement, p. 1.

[1177] Ferse Report, p. 56.

recoverable." [1178]   The Ferse Report summed up its responses to this and previous statements as follows:

> Ecological impacts from the construction activities affected large parts of the reefs and include permanent (for reclaimed reef flats and excavated channels) and long-lasting (for sediment resuspension in lagoons) effects. The extensive sediment plumes visible from aerial and satellite imagery that remained near the construction areas for several weeks to months render the amount of control over potential impacts doubtful. For large areas of reef affected by the construction activities, recovery is unlikely, or may take decades to centuries. [1179]

983. Based on the compelling evidence, expert reports, and critical assessment of Chinese claims described above, the Tribunal has no doubt that China's artificial island-building activities on the seven reefs in the Spratly Islands have caused devastating and long-lasting damage to the marine environment. The Tribunal accordingly finds that through its construction activities, China has breached its obligation under Article 192 to protect and preserve the marine environment, has conducted dredging in such a way as to pollute the marine environment with sediment in breach of Article 194(1), and has violated its duty under Article 194(5) to take measures necessary to protect and preserve rare or fragile ecosystems as well as the habitat of depleted, threatened or endangered species and other forms of marine life.

ii.   China's Construction Activities and the Obligation to Cooperate

984. The Tribunal further notes that China's construction activities at the seven coral reefs have been met with protest from the Philippines and other neighbouring States. [1180]   Article 197 of the Convention requires States to cooperate on a regional basis to formulate standards and practices for the protection and preservation of the marine environment. In relation to semi-enclosed seas, the Convention further specifies in Article 123 that States shall endeavour to coordinate the implementation of their rights and duties with respect to the protection and preservation of the marine environment.

985. The importance of cooperation to marine protection and preservation has been recognised by the International Tribunal for the Law of the Sea on multiple occasions. [1181]   The International Court

---

[1178]   SOA Statement, p. 2.

[1179]   Ferse Report, p. 57.

[1180]   *See, e.g.,* Department of Foreign Affairs, Republic of the Philippines, "Statement on China's Reclamation Activities and their Impact on the Region's Marine Environment" (13 April 2015) (Annex 608); Joint Communiqué 48th ASEAN Foreign Ministers Meeting Kuala Lumpur, 4 August 2015, *available at* <www.asean.org/storage/images/2015/August/48th_amm/joint%20communique%20of%20the%2048th%20 amm-final.pdf>.

[1181]   *The MOX Plant Case (Ireland v. United Kingdom), Provisional Measures, Order of 3 December 2001, ITLOS Reports 2001,* para. 82; *Case concerning Land Reclamation by Singapore in and around the Straits of Johor (Malaysia v. Singapore), Provisional Measures, Order of 8 October 2003, ITLOS Reports*

of Justice, also recognised, in *Pulp Mills on the River Uruguay*, that "by co-operating . . . the States concerned can manage the risks of damage to the environment that might be created by the plans initiated by one or [the] other of them, so as to prevent the damage in question."[1182]

986. With respect to China's island-building program, the Tribunal has before it no convincing evidence of China attempting to cooperate or coordinate with the other States bordering the South China Sea. This lack of coordination is not unrelated to China's lack of communication, discussed below.

iii. China's Construction Activities and the Obligation to Monitor and Assess

987. Article 206 requires that when States have "reasonable grounds for believing that planned activities under their jurisdiction or control may cause significant and harmful changes to the marine environment" they shall as far as practicable assess the potential effects of such activities on the marine environment" and also "shall communicate reports of the results of such assessments."

988. The Tribunal considers that given the scale and impact of the island-building activities described in this Chapter, China could not reasonably have held any belief other than that the construction "may cause significant and harmful changes to the marine environment." Accordingly, China was required, "as far as practicable" to prepare an environmental impact assessment. It was also under an obligation to communicate the results of the assessment.

989. In *Construction of a Road (Nicaragua v. Costa Rica)*,[1183] the International Court of Justice found that Costa Rica's simple assertions as to the existence of a preliminary assessment did not equate to having "adduced any evidence that it actually carried out such a preliminary assessment."[1184] Despite China's repeated assertions by officials at different levels, that it has

---

2003, para. 92; *Request for an Advisory Opinion Submitted by the Sub-Regional Fisheries Commission (SRFC), Advisory Opinion of 2 April 2015, ITLOS Reports 2015*, para. 140; *see also* Merits Hearing, Tr. (Day 4), pp. 40-41.

[1182]   *Pulp Mills on the River Uruguay (Argentina v. Uruguay), Judgment, ICJ Reports 2010*, p.14, p.49, para. 77; *see also* "Consequences Arising Out Of Acts Not Prohibited By International Law (Prevention of Transboundary Harm From Hazardous Activities)," in *Report of the International Law Commission on the work of its Fifty-third session (23 April-1 June and 2 July-10 August 2001)*, UN Doc. GAOR A/56/10 (2001).

[1183]   *Certain Activities Carried out by Nicaragua in the Border Area (Costa Rica v. Nicaragua: Construction of a Road in Costa Rica Along the San Juan River (Nicaragua v. Costa Rica), Merits Judgment, ICJ Reports 2015*, para. 154.

[1184]   *Certain Activities Carried out by Nicaragua in the Border Area (Costa Rica v. Nicaragua: Construction of a Road in Costa Rica Along the San Juan River (Nicaragua v. Costa Rica), Merits Judgment, ICJ Reports 2015*, para. 154.

undertaken thorough environmental studies, neither the Tribunal, the Tribunal-appointed experts, the Philippines, nor the Philippines' experts have been able to identify any report that would resemble an environmental impact assessment that meets the requirements of Article 206 of the Convention, or indeed under China's own Environmental Impact Assessment Law of 2002.[1185]

990. By China's own legislative standards, an EIA must be "objective, open and impartial, comprehensively consider impacts on various environmental factors and the ecosystem they form after the implementation of the plan or construction project, and thus provide scientific basis for the decision-making."[1186] Additionally, the "state shall encourage all relevant units, experts and the public to participate in the EIA in proper ways." [1187] With respect to construction projects, Chinese law requires an EIA to include, *inter alia*, analysis, projection and evaluation on the potential environmental impacts of the project, and suggestions on implementation of environmental monitoring.[1188] The SOA Statement and the SOA Report which the Tribunal did manage to locate both fall short of these criteria, and are far less comprehensive than EIAs reviewed by other international courts and tribunals, or those filed in the foreign construction projects to which the SOA scientists referred in their report.[1189]

991. The Tribunal cannot make a definitive finding that China has prepared an environmental impact assessment, but nor can it definitely find that it has failed to do so in light of the repeated assertions by Chinese officials and scientists that China has undertaken thorough studies. Such a finding, however, is not necessary in order to find a breach of Article 206. To fulfil the obligations of Article 206, a State must not only prepare an EIA but also must communicate it. The Tribunal directly asked China for a copy of any EIA it had prepared; China did not provide one.[1190] While acknowledging that China is not participating in the arbitration, China has

---

[1185] People's Republic of China, *Law of the People's Republic of China on Evaluation of Environmental Effects* (28 October 2002) (Annex 615).

[1186] People's Republic of China, *Law of the People's Republic of China on Evaluation of Environmental Effects* (28 October 2002) (Annex 615).

[1187] People's Republic of China, *Law of the People's Republic of China on Evaluation of Environmental Effects* (28 October 2002) (Annex 615).

[1188] People's Republic of China, *Law of the People's Republic of China on Evaluation of Environmental Effects* (28 October 2002), Article 17 (Annex 615).

[1189] The Philippines' March 2016 Written Comments, p. 14; Merits Hearing Tr. (Day 4), p. 184, *Pulp Mills on the River Uruguay (Argentina v. Uruguay),* Merits, Counter-Memorial of Uruguay (20 July 2007), Vols. VI and VII; Commonwealth of Australia, Queensland Government, Department of State Development, *Final Environmental Impact Statement for the proposed Abbot Point Growth Gateway Project, available at* <www.statedevelopment.qld.gov.au/abbotpoint-eis> (Annex 892).

[1190] Letter from the Tribunal to the Parties (5 February 2016); Letter from the Tribunal to the Parties 15 March 2016 (inviting China's comments).

nevertheless found occasions and means to communicate statements by its own officials, or by others writing in line with China's interests.[1191] Therefore had it wished to draw attention to the existence and content of an EIA, the Tribunal has no doubt it could have done so. In any event, the obligation to communicate is, by the terms of Article 205, to "competent international organizations, which should make them available to all States." Although China's representatives have assured the States parties to the Convention that its "construction activities followed a high standard of environmental protection," it has delivered no assessment in writing to that forum or any other international body as far as the Tribunal is aware.[1192] Accordingly, the Tribunal finds that China has not fulfilled its duties under Article 206 of the Convention.

(e) Conclusion

992. Based on the considerations outlined above, the Tribunal finds that China has, through its toleration and protection of, and failure to prevent Chinese fishing vessels engaging in harmful harvesting activities of endangered species at Scarborough Shoal, Second Thomas Shoal and other features in the Spratly Islands, breached Articles 192 and 194(5) of the Convention.

993. The Tribunal further finds that China has, through its island-building activities at Cuarteron Reef, Fiery Cross Reef, Gaven Reef (North), Johnson Reef, Hughes Reef, Subi Reef and Mischief Reef, breached Articles 192, 194(1), 194(5), 197, 123, and 206 of the Convention.

*   *   *

[1191]   See paragraph 127 above.

[1192]   Permanent Mission of the People's Republic of China to the United Nations, *Statement by H.E. Ambassador Wang Min, Head of the Chinese Delegation at the 25th Meeting of States Parties to the UN Convention on the Law of the Sea* (12 June 2014) (Annex 617).

this page intentionally blank

E.   OCCUPATION AND CONSTRUCTION ACTIVITIES ON MISCHIEF REEF (SUBMISSION NO. 12)

1.   **Introduction**

994.   In this Section, the Tribunal addresses the Parties' dispute concerning China's activities on Mischief Reef and its construction there of installations and artificial islands. This dispute is reflected in parts (a) and (c) of the Philippines' Submission No. 12, which provides as follows:

>   (12)   China's occupation of and construction activities on Mischief Reef
>
>   (a)   violate the provisions of the Convention concerning artificial islands, installations and structures;
>
>   . . .
>
>   (c)   constitute unlawful acts of attempted appropriation in violation of the Convention;

995.   To avoid duplication, the Tribunal has addressed the matters raised in the Philippines' Submission No. 12(b)—asserting that China has violated its "duties to protect and preserve the marine environment"—in connection with Submission No. 11 (at paragraphs 815 to 993 above).

2.   **Factual Background**

(a)   **China's Initial Activities on Mischief Reef (1995 to 2013)**

996.   Chinese construction activities on Mischief Reef reportedly date back at least to January 1995, when fiberglass structures flying the Chinese flag were observed at four separate locations on the reef platform.[1193] Fishermen from the Philippines reported the presence of "an estimated 1,000 uniformed men" aboard eleven Chinese vessels anchored there and in the structures on the reef.[1194]

997.   On 6 February 1995, the Philippines submitted an Aide Memoire[1195] to the Chinese Ambassador in Manila. According to Philippine records, China had denied[1196] that it was building a base on the feature. The Philippines expressed "serious concern" over Chinese activities on Mischief Reef, including:

[1193]   Letter from Captain, Philippine Navy, to the Assistant Secretary for Asian and Pacific Affairs, Department of Foreign Affairs, Republic of the Philippines (13 November 2004) (Annex 54); Armed Forces of the Philippines, *Chronology of Events in the Kalayaan Island Group* (2004) (Annex 53).

[1194]   Armed Forces of the Philippines, *Chronology of Events in the Kalayaan Island Group* (2004) (Annex 53).

[1195]   Memorandum from the Undersecretary of Foreign Affairs of the Republic of the Philippines to the Ambassador of the People's Republic of China in Manila (6 February 1995) (Annex 17).

[1196]   Armed Forces of the Philippines, *Chronology of Events in the Kalayaan Island Group* (2004) (Annex 53).

1.   The presence of three large warships and five smaller vessels belonging to the People's Republic of China on or around Panganiban Reef, otherwise known as Mischief Reef;

2.   The construction by the People's Republic of China of certain structures on Panganiban Reef; and

3.   The detention of Filipino fishermen by military elements of the People's Republic of China deployed on and around Panganiban Reef.[1197]

The Philippines added that China's actions violated "the spirit of the 1992 ASEAN Declaration on the South China Sea" and requested the immediate removal of Chinese vessels from the reef.

998.   On 10 March 1995, China's Vice Premier and Minister of Foreign Affairs reportedly described the structures on Mischief Reef as "typhoon shelters" constructed by Chinese fishing authorities "for the purpose of protecting the lives of Chinese fishermen and their production."[1198] The Minister reiterated that the structures were civilian in nature and did "not pose threat to any country."[1199]

999.   In the period from October 1998 to February 1999, China substantially enlarged two of the structures on Mischief Reef while removing the other two.[1200] On 15 October 1998, according to Philippine diplomatic archives, China informed the Philippine Ambassador in Beijing of "plans to renovate and reinforce the structures it [China] constructed on Mischief Reef back in 1995."[1201] According to the Philippines' then-Undersecretary for Policy in the Department of Foreign Affairs, the Philippine Ambassador was informed by the Chinese Ministry of Foreign Affairs that:

> Chinese local fishing authorities will undertake "soon" the renovation and reinforcement works which have become necessary because the structures have deteriorated over the years due to exposure to the elements. Furthermore, the Chinese have stated that they will give positive consideration to the use of the facilities by other countries, including the Philippines, after the renovation and reinforcement works have been completed and when the conditions are ripe.[1202]

[1197] Memorandum from the Undersecretary of Foreign Affairs of the Republic of the Philippines to the Ambassador of the People's Republic of China in Manila (6 February 1995) (Annex 17).

[1198] Memorandum from the Ambassador of the Republic of the Philippines in Beijing to the Undersecretary of Foreign Affairs of the Republic of the Philippines (10 March 1995) (Annex 18).

[1199] Memorandum from the Ambassador of the Republic of the Philippines in Beijing to the Undersecretary of Foreign Affairs of the Republic of the Philippines (10 March 1995) (Annex 18).

[1200] Letter from Captain, Philippine Navy, to the Assistant Secretary for Asian and Pacific Affairs, Department of Foreign Affairs, Republic of the Philippines (13 November 2004) (Annex 54).

[1201] Memorandum from the Undersecretary for Policy, Department of Foreign Affairs, Republic of the Philippines, to all Philippine Embassies (11 November 1998) (Annex 35).

[1202] Memorandum from the Undersecretary for Policy, Department of Foreign Affairs, Republic of the Philippines, to all Philippine Embassies (11 November 1998) (Annex 35).

1000. Philippine records indicate that, in addition to reinforcing two of the existing structures, China added a concrete platform supporting a three-storey building at each site.[1203] A report by the Armed Forces of the Philippines described the construction activities as involving "[a]bout 100-150 personnel working on site laying foundations for rectangular structure."[1204]

1001. On 5 November 1998, the Philippines sent China a Note Verbale in which it demanded from China that it:

> immediately cease and desist from doing further improvements over the illegal structures it has built in [Mischief] Reef and to dismantle any repair works, renovations, reinforcements, fortifications and/or improvements made therein.[1205]

1002. On 9 November 1998, the Philippine Ambassador in Beijing met the Deputy Director General of the Asia Department of the Chinese Ministry of Foreign Affairs. At the meeting, the Deputy Director General characterised the activities as "the work of the local fishing authorities undertaking repair and renovation." [1206] On 14 November 1998, China's Minister of Foreign Affairs explained that "the structures are solely for shelter of fishermen . . . . The scale of work is small and there is no change in the civilian nature of the facilities."[1207]

1003. By February 1999, the two sites at Mischief Reef were equipped with a helipad, new communications equipment, and wharves.[1208] An oblique photograph taken by the Philippines and reproduced as Figure 30 on page 402 below depicts the smaller of China's two structures following these improvements:

[1203] Letter from Captain, Philippine Navy, to the Assistant Secretary for Asian and Pacific Affairs, Department of Foreign Affairs, Republic of the Philippines (13 November 2004) (Annex 54).

[1204] Armed Forces of the Philippines, *Chronological Development of Artificial Structures on Features* (Annex 96).

[1205] Note Verbale from the Department of Foreign Affairs, Republic of the Philippines, to the Embassy of the People's Republic of China in Manila, No. 983577 (5 November 1998) (Annex 185).

[1206] Memorandum from the Ambassador of the Republic of Philippines in Beijing to the Secretary of Foreign Affairs of the Republic of the Philippines, No. ZPE-77-98-S (9 November 1998) (Annex 34). *See also* Memorandum from the Ambassador of the Republic of Philippines in Beijing to the Secretary of Foreign Affairs of the Republic of the Philippines, No. ZPE-76-98-S (6 November 1998) (Annex 33).

[1207] Memorandum from the Secretary of Foreign Affairs of the Republic of the Philippines to the President of the Republic of the Philippines (14 November 1998) (Annex 36).

[1208] Letter from Captain, Philippine Navy, to the Assistant Secretary for Asian and Pacific Affairs, Department of Foreign Affairs, Republic of the Philippines (13 November 2004) (Annex 54).

Figure 30: Aerial Photograph of Structure on Mischief Reef
Supplemental Written Submission, Vol. II, p. 126.

(b)   Island-Building Activities on Mischief Reef (Post-2013)

1004. Construction on Mischief Reef between 1999 and 2013 appears to have been relatively limited. China's intensive construction of artificial islands on seven coral reefs commenced in 2014, with construction on Mischief Reef resuming from January 2015.[1209] On 28 May 2015, for instance, the Philippine Secretary of National Defense, identified "around 32 dredger vessels, 32 cargo ships and three (3) ocean tugs" deployed at the reef.[1210]

1005. On 3 February 2015, in response to the commencement of substantial construction on Mischief Reef that year, the Philippines delivered to China a Note Verbale "to strongly protest China's land reclamation activities at Panganiban (Mischief) Reef."[1211] The Philippines went on to assert as follows:

> Panganiban [Mischief] Reef is a low-tide elevation located in the exclusive economic zone of the Philippines and on its continental shelf. Pursuant to Articles 60 and 80 of the 1982 United Nations Convention on the Law of the Sea (UNCLOS), the Philippines has the *exclusive* right to authorize the construction of artificial islands, installations or other

---

[1209]   See Note Verbale from the Department of Foreign Affairs, Republic of the Philippines, to the Embassy of the People's Republic of China in Manila, No. 15-0359 (3 February 2015) (Annex 682).

[1210]   Letter from the Secretary of National Defense, Republic of the Philippines, to the Secretary of Foreign Affairs, Republic of the Philippines (22 June 2015) (Annex 610).

[1211]   Note Verbale from the Department of Foreign Affairs, Republic of the Philippines, to the Embassy of the People's Republic of China in Manila, No. 15-0359 (3 February 2015) (Annex 682).

structures in the vicinity of Panganiban [Mischief] Reef. China's reclamation activities constitute a flagrant violation of these rights.[1212]

The Philippines concluded by requesting that China "desist from its reclamation activities."[1213]

1006. On 12 February 2015, China replied that "China has indisputable sovereignty over the Nansha Islands and its adjacent waters. The development of any facility in the Nansha Islands falls within the scope of China's sovereignty."[1214]

1007. Aerial and satellite photography up to and over the course of 2015 details China's construction of an artificial island on Mischief Reef and is reproduced at Figures 31 and 32 on page 405 below. The latter photograph from October 2015 shows an artificial island covering the entire northern half of the reef.

1008. Calculations presented by the Philippines estimate that China's construction work has resulted in the creation of 5,580,000 square metres of new land on Mischief Reef as of November 2015.[1215]

1009. China's activities on Mischief Reef are not limited to the creation of new land alone. Chinese construction on the feature has added fortified seawalls, temporary loading piers, cement plants, and a 250-metre-wide channel to allow transit into the lagoon by large vessels.[1216] Additionally, one analysis has noted that an area of approximately 3,000 metres in length has "been cleared and flattened along the northern rim of the reef,"[1217] a development that, according to media reports, may indicate the intention to build an airstrip.[1218] A Chinese Foreign Ministry Spokesperson was questioned regarding the construction of an airstrip on Mischief Reef and did not deny this, noting instead that "[c]onstruction activities taken by the Chinese side on some

---

[1212] Note Verbale from the Department of Foreign Affairs, Republic of the Philippines, to the Embassy of the People's Republic of China in Manila, No. 15-0359 (3 February 2015) (Annex 682) (emphasis in original).

[1213] Note Verbale from the Department of Foreign Affairs, Republic of the Philippines, to the Embassy of the People's Republic of China in Manila, No. 15-0359 (3 February 2015) (Annex 682).

[1214] Note Verbale from the Embassy of the People's Republic of China in Manila to the Department of Foreign Affairs, Republic of the Philippines, No. 15 (PG)-053 (12 February 2015) (Annex 683) (emphasis added).

[1215] See Center for Strategic & International Studies, Asia Maritime Transparency Initiative, Mischief Reef Tracker, available at <amti.csis.org/mischief-reef-tracker/#> (accessed 1 November 2015) (Annex 782).

[1216] "Third South China Sea airstrip being built, says expert, citing satellite photos," The Guardian (15 September 2015) (Annex 770).

[1217] G. Poling, "Spratly Airstrip Update: Is Mischief Reef Next?," Center for Strategic & International Studies (16 September 2015) (Annex 835).

[1218] "Third South China Sea Airstrip Being Built, Says Expert, Citing Satellite Photos," The Guardian (15 September 2015) (Annex 770).

stationed islands and reefs in the Nansha Islands are completely lawful, reasonable and justified."[1219]

3.   The Philippines' Position

1010. The Philippines submits that China's activities at Mischief Reef violate Articles 60 and 80 of the Convention, relating to artificial islands, installations. and structures. and constitute unlawful acts of attempted appropriation under the Convention.

(a)   Military Activities and the Tribunal's Jurisdiction

1011. The Philippines submits that the Tribunal has jurisdiction to consider the matters raised in its Submission No. 12, and that the Tribunal's jurisdiction is not constrained by the exception for military activities in Article 298(1)(b).[1220]

1012. The Philippines notes that China did not invoke the military activities exception in its Position Paper of 7 December 2014.[1221] In the Philippines' view, the Tribunal should accept China's own characterisation of its activities. According to the Philippines, "[t]he decision by a State to characterise its own actions as military activities is not one that is taken lightly. The political, legal and other consequences may extend well beyond Article 298, or indeed the Law of the Sea Convention as a whole."[1222] Far from China having invoked the exception, the Philippines notes that "China repeatedly told the Philippines that the facilities at Mischief Reef were being built for civilian use" and argues that any "fleeting intimation of a concurrent defence purpose falls far short of a characterisation of the activities as military."[1223] The Philippines also recalls that China's President Xi Jinping has stated that China does not intend to militarise the features.[1224]

[1219]   Ministry of Foreign Affairs, People's Republic of China, *Foreign Ministry Spokesperson Hong Lei's Regular Press Conference* (14 September 2015), *available at* <www.fmprc.gov.cn/mfa_eng/xwfw_665399/s2510_665401/2511_665403/t1296485.shtml>.

[1220]   Jurisdictional Hearing Tr. (Day 3), pp. 48-53.

[1221]   Jurisdictional Hearing Tr. (Day 2), p. 73.

[1222]   Jurisdictional Hearing Tr. (Day 2), pp. 74-75.

[1223]   Jurisdictional Hearing Tr. (Day 2), pp. 75-76.

[1224]   Merits Hearing Tr. (Day 3), p. 88; "China not to pursue militarization of Nansha Islands in South China Sea: Xi," *Xinhua* (25 September 2015), *available at* <news.xinhuanet.com/english/2015-09/26/c_134660930.htm>; United States, The White House, Office of the Press Secretary, "Press Release: Remarks by President Obama and President Xi of the People's Republic of China in Joint Press Conference" (25 September 2015) (Annex 664).

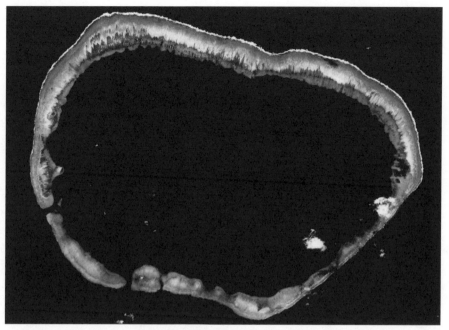

Figure 31: Mischief Reef, 24 January 2012
(Annex 792)

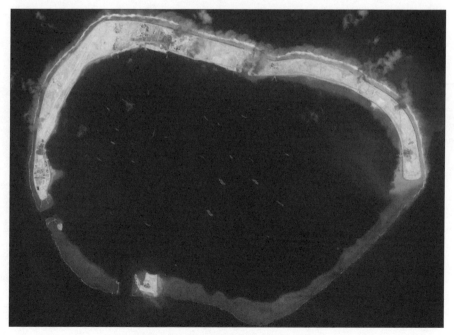

Figure 32: Mischief Reef, 19 October 2015
(Annex 792)

this page intentionally blank

1013. According to the Philippines, "the context [of the military activities exception] requires that the nature and purpose of the activity be military, to the exclusion of other activities or purposes that are more than purely incidental."[1225] With this in mind, the Philippines argues that "mixed-use projects" and situations "in which a military unit is used to protect other activities" are not covered by the exception to jurisdiction.[1226] With respect to land reclamation in particular, the Philippines submits that "the involvement of military personnel in construction or land reclamation activities does not necessarily mean that the purpose of the activities is military. The logistical capabilities of the armed forces are at times engaged for civilian purposes in different parts of the world."[1227] The Philippines also notes that "[t]he Chinese People's Liberation Army is expressly tasked by the constitution to 'participate in national reconstruction', and has an extensive record of civil projects."[1228]

1014. Finally, the Philippines argues that subsequent Chinese statements cannot change the nature of the activities it has undertaken. According to the Philippines, "[t]he nature of the activity complained of is determined as of the time that activity occurred. The respondent cannot thereafter unilaterally change the jurisdictional facts regarding its past conduct, especially two-and-a-half years after the proceedings were commenced."[1229]

(b)   Articles 60 and 80 of the Convention

1015. The Philippines develops its Submissions from the position that Article 56(1) provides coastal States the "exclusive right to regulate the establishment and use" of such structures within its exclusive economic zone.[1230] On this basis, the Philippines submits that China's construction of artificial islands, installations, and structures on Mischief Reef violate Articles 60 and 80 of the Convention.[1231] Specifically, the Philippines argues that, under Article 60, coastal States enjoy the "exclusive right" to authorise or regulate the construction of structures, a principle that is extended to the continental shelf by virtue of Article 80.[1232]

[1225]   Merits Hearing Tr. (Day 4), p. 103.

[1226]   Merits Hearing Tr. (Day 4), p. 104.

[1227]   Jurisdictional Hearing Tr. (Day 2), pp. 81-82.

[1228]   Jurisdictional Hearing Tr. (Day 2), p. 82.

[1229]   Jurisdictional Hearing Tr. (Day 3), p. 57.

[1230]   Memorial, para. 6.100.

[1231]   Memorial, para. 6.100.

[1232]   Memorial, para. 6.101.

1016. In this connection, the Philippines notes that Mischief Reef "is located within 200 M" of Palawan and "not within 200 M of any other feature claimed by China that is capable of generating an EEZ or a continental shelf."[1233] In its view, therefore, the Philippines remains the only possible beneficiary of the effects of Articles 60 and 80 of the Convention with respect to Mischief Reef.[1234] Accordingly, because China did not "seek and receive authorization from the Philippines,"[1235] it violated Articles 56(1)(b)(i), 60(1), and 80 of the Convention.[1236] Because the Philippines considers the Convention to require similar authorisation for the "operation and use" of structures already built (in addition to their construction in the first instance), moreover, it submits that China's violation is a "continuing" one, at least so long as its activities on Mischief Reef persist.[1237]

(c) Attempted Appropriation under the Convention

1017. The Philippines also considers China's construction of artificial islands, installations, and other structures to constitute acts of attempted and unlawful appropriation.[1238] Taking into account China's assertions of sovereignty over the reef, as well as the presence of China's flag, the Philippines considers that it is "beyond dispute" that China claims to have appropriated Mischief Reef.[1239]

1018. In the Philippines' view, low-tide elevations are incapable of being "fully assimilated with islands or other land territory" such as to extend a State's sovereignty over such features (see also paragraphs 307 to 309 above).[1240] Drawing on guidance provided by the International Court of Justice in *Maritime Delimitation and Territorial Questions between Qatar and Bahrain* and *Sovereignty over Pedra Branca/Pulau Batu Puteh, Middle Rocks and South Ledge (Malaysia/Singapore)*, the Philippines considers that "sovereignty and other rights" in relation to low-tide elevations are determined "by the maritime zone in which they are located."[1241] As a result, and to the extent such features lie within the territorial sea of an island or other land

---

[1233] Memorial, para. 6.103.

[1234] Memorial, para. 6.103.

[1235] Memorial, para. 6.103.

[1236] Memorial, para. 6.103.

[1237] Memorial, para. 6.104.

[1238] Memorial, paras. 6.105-6.107.

[1239] Merits Hearing Tr. (Day 2), p. 211.

[1240] Memorial, paras. 5.86, 6.105, *quoting Maritime Delimitation and Territorial Questions between Qatar and Bahrain, Merits, Judgment, ICJ Reports 2001*, p. 40 at p. 102, para. 206.

[1241] Memorial, para. 6.105.

territory, the Philippines submits that low-tide elevations fall under the sovereignty of the coastal State in whose territorial sea those features are located.[1242] In this case, because it considers Mischief Reef to lie within its exclusive economic zone and continental shelf, the Philippines deems Mischief Reef to be "subject to [its] sovereign rights."[1243] Those rights, it suggests, do not depend on occupation or express proclamation.[1244]

4. China's Position

1019. Although China is not participating in these proceedings, its statements relating to the nature and purpose of its actions at Mischief Reef provide an indication of China's position regarding its activities on the reef.

1020. In bilateral meetings from 20 to 21 March 1995, the Chinese Vice Minister for Foreign Affairs informed his Philippine counterpart that the reef's structures "are not military [structures], they are wind shelters and Chinese fishermen have long used Mischief [Reef] as wind shelter."[1245] China reiterated its position throughout 1995.[1246] During bilateral talks on 10 August 1995, for instance, China emphasised the economic character of its activities and explained that the construction was intended to provide shelter for fishermen from local winds:

> It is nothing serious for the Chinese side to construct some windsheltering facilities for peaceful purposes. Some people just exaggerated this and they said that the Chinese side is constructing a military facility. This does not square with the fact[s].[1247]

1021. Further statements by China have largely reflected its previous assertions as to the structures' purpose, continuing throughout the 1990s to characterise its activities on Mischief Reef as civilian in nature.[1248] On 15 March 1999, China informed the Philippines that the facilities were

---

[1242]   Memorial, para. 6.105-6.106.

[1243]   Memorial, para. 6.107.

[1244]   Merits Hearing Tr. (Day 2), pp. 207-208.

[1245]   Government of the Republic of the Philippines and Government of the People's Republic of China, *Philippine–China Bilateral Consultations: Summary of Proceedings* (20-21 March 1995) (Annex 175).

[1246]   *See, e.g.*, Memorandum from the Ambassador of the Republic of the Philippines in Beijing to the Secretary of Foreign Affairs of the Republic of the Philippines, No. ZPE-231-95 (20 April 1995) (Annex 22); Memorandum from the Ambassador of the Republic of the Philippines in Beijing to the Undersecretary of Foreign Affairs of the Republic of the Philippines (10 April 1995) (Annex 21).

[1247]   Government of the Republic of the Philippines, *Transcript of Proceedings: Republic of the Philippines– People's Republic of China Bilateral Talks* (10 August 1995) (Annex 181).

[1248]   Memorandum from the Ambassador of the Republic of the Philippines in Beijing to the Undersecretary of Foreign Affairs of the Republic of the Philippines (10 March 1995) (Annex 18); Memorandum from the Ambassador of the Republic of the Philippines in Beijing to the Secretary of Foreign Affairs of the Republic of the Philippines, No. ZPE-231-95 (20 April 1995) (Annex 22); Memorandum from the Ambassador of the Republic of Philippines in Beijing to the Secretary of Foreign Affairs of the Republic of the Philippines, No. ZPE-76-98-S (6 November 1998) (Annex 33); Memorandum from the

"meant for civilian use and not for military purposes," and stated that, "[b]y repairing the structures, China's actual intention to use them as fishermen shelters will be supported."[1249] China explained, further, that the "so-called radar facilities" on the reef were "nothing but dish-type television satellite antennae to enable the personnel on the reef to watch ordinary TV programs."[1250] At a bilateral meeting the following month, China reiterated that its facilities would "remain for civilian purposes."[1251]

1022. In keeping with its earlier pronouncements, more recent Chinese statements have continued to characterise China's activities on Mischief Reef as intended for civilian purposes. On 9 April 2015, for example, a Spokesperson for China's Foreign Ministry stated:

> The Chinese government has been carrying out maintenance and construction work on some of the garrisoned Nansha Islands and reefs with the main purposes of optimizing their functions, improving the living and working conditions of personnel stationed there, better safeguarding territorial sovereignty and maritime rights and interests, as well as better performing China's international responsibility and obligation in marine search and rescue, disaster prevention and mitigation, marine science and research, meteorological observation, environmental protection, navigation safety, fishery production service and other areas. The relevant construction, which is reasonable, justified and lawful, is well within China's sovereignty. It does not impact or target any country, and is thus beyond reproach.
>
> After the construction, the islands and reefs will be able to provide all-round and comprehensive services to meet various civilian demands besides satisfying the need of necessary military defense. The maritime areas in the South China Sea, where shipping lanes criss-cross and fishing grounds scatter around, are far away from the landmass. These areas are prone to marine accidents due to the influence of typhoon and monsoon. Civilian functions and facilities will be included in the construction for ships to take shelter, and for navigation aid, search and rescue, marine meteorological observation and forecast, fishery service and administration, so as to provide services to ships of China, neighboring countries and other countries that sail across the South China Sea.[1252]

1023. On 16 June 2015, China's Foreign Ministry Spokesperson reiterated that "the main purpose of China's construction activities is to meet various civilian demands."[1253] The statement was

---

Ambassador of the Republic of Philippines in Beijing to the Secretary of Foreign Affairs of the Republic of the Philippines, No. ZPE-18-99-S (15 March 1999) (Annex 38); Government of the Republic of the Philippines and Government of the People's Republic of China, *Philippine–China Bilateral Consultations: Summary of Proceedings* (20-21 March 1995) (Annex 175).

[1249] Memorandum from the Ambassador of the Republic of Philippines in Beijing to the Secretary of Foreign Affairs of the Republic of the Philippines, No. ZPE-18-99-S (15 March 1999) (Annex 38).

[1250] Memorandum from the Ambassador of the Republic of Philippines in Beijing to the Secretary of Foreign Affairs of the Republic of the Philippines, No. ZPE-18-99-S (15 March 1999) (Annex 38).

[1251] Government of the Republic of the Philippines and Government of the People's Republic of China, Joint Statement: Philippine-China Experts Group Meeting on Confidence Building Measures (23 March 1995) (Annex 178(bis)).

[1252] Ministry of Foreign Affairs, People's Republic of China, *Foreign Ministry Spokesperson Hua Chunying's Regular Press Conference* (9 April 2015) (Annex 624).

[1253] Ministry of Foreign Affairs, People's Republic of China, *Foreign Ministry Spokesperson Lu Kang's Remarks on Issues Relating to China's Construction Activities on the Nansha Islands and Reefs* (16 June

mirrored in remarks by the Chinese Foreign Minister at an ASEAN Regional Forum on 6 August 2015:

> At the end of June, China announced the completion of land reclamation. Next, we will build facilities mainly for public good purposes, including multi-functional lighthouse, search and rescue facilities for maritime emergencies, meteorological observatory station, maritime scientific and research center, as well as medical and first aid facilities.[1254]

5. The Tribunal's Considerations

(a) The Tribunal's Jurisdiction

1024. In its Award on Jurisdiction, the Tribunal held that Submission No. 12 reflects a dispute concerning "China's activities on Mischief Reef and their effects on the marine environment."[1255] It determined that this is not a dispute concerning sovereignty or maritime boundary delimitation, nor is it barred from the Tribunal's consideration by any requirement of Section 1 of Part XV.[1256] The Tribunal warned, however, that its jurisdiction to address the questions raised in Submission No. 12 "is dependent on the status of Mischief Reef as an 'island', 'rock', or 'low-tide elevation'."[1257] Had the Tribunal found—contrary to the premise of the Philippines' Submission—that Mischief Reef is a fully entitled island or rock and thus constitutes land territory, it would necessarily lack jurisdiction to consider the lawfulness of China's construction activities on Mischief Reef (at least in terms of the provisions of the Convention concerning artificial islands) or the appropriation of the feature.[1258] Accordingly, the Tribunal deferred taking any final decision with respect to its jurisdiction over this Submission.[1259]

1025. The Tribunal has now found, however, that Mischief Reef is a low-tide elevation and not a rock or fully entitled island (see paragraphs 374 to 378 above) and, as such, generates no entitlement to maritime zones of its own. The Tribunal has also found that none of the high-tide features in the Spratly Islands is a fully entitled island for the purposes of Article 121 of the Convention

---

2015), *available at* <www.fmprc.gov.cn/mfa_eng/xwfw_665399/s2510_665401/t1273370.shtml>. The following week, China protested Philippine overflight over the reef. Note Verbale from the Embassy of the People's Republic of China in Manila to the Department of Foreign Affairs, Republic of the Philippines, No. 15 (PG)-214 (28 June 2015) (Annex 689).

[1254] Ministry of Foreign Affairs, People's Republic of China, *Wang Yi on the South China Sea Issue At the ASEAN Regional Forum* (6 August 2015) (Annex 634).

[1255] Award on Jurisdiction, para. 409.

[1256] Award on Jurisdiction, para. 409.

[1257] Award on Jurisdiction, para. 409.

[1258] Award on Jurisdiction, para. 409.

[1259] Award on Jurisdiction, para. 413(H).

(see paragraphs 473 to 647 above). From these conclusions, it follows that there exists no legal basis for any entitlement by China to maritime zones in the area of Mischief Reef and no situation of overlapping entitlements that would call for the application of Articles 15, 74, or 83 to delimit the overlap. Mischief Reef is necessarily a low-tide elevation located within the exclusive economic zone of the Philippines.

1026. In its Award on Jurisdiction, the Tribunal also reserved for the merits the question of whether Chinese activities at Mischief Reef constitute "military activities" within the scope of Article 298(1)(b) of the Convention.[1260] Article 298(1)(b) excludes disputes concerning military activities from compulsory dispute settlement under the Convention.

1027. In determining whether Chinese activities at Mischief Reef are military in nature, the Tribunal takes note of China's repeated statements that its installations and island construction are intended to fulfil civilian purposes.[1261] The Tribunal also takes note of the public statement of China's President Xi Jinping that "[r]elevant construction activities that China are undertaking in the island of South – Nansha Islands do not target or impact any country, and China does not intend to pursue militarization."[1262]

[1260] Award on Jurisdiction, paras. 372, 396, 409.

[1261] *See* Ministry of Foreign Affairs, People's Republic of China, *Wang Yi on the South China Sea Issue At the ASEAN Regional Forum* (6 August 2015) (Annex 634); Ministry of Foreign Affairs, People's Republic of China, *Foreign Ministry Spokesperson Lu Kang's Remarks on Issues Relating to China's Construction Activities on the Nansha Islands and Reefs* (16 June 2015), *available at* <www.fmprc.gov.cn/mfa_eng/xwfw_665399/s2510_665401/t1273370.shtml>; Ministry of Foreign Affairs, People's Republic of China, *Foreign Ministry Spokesperson Hua Chunying's Regular Press Conference* (9 April 2015) (Annex 624).

China has also made the same point frequently in its diplomatic communications and conversations with officials of the Philippines. As recorded by the Philippines, these include at least the following: Memorandum from the Ambassador of the Republic of Philippines in Beijing to the Secretary of Foreign Affairs of the Republic of the Philippines, No. ZPE-18-99-S (15 March 1999) (Annex 38); Memorandum from the Ambassador of the Republic of Philippines in Beijing to the Secretary of Foreign Affairs of the Republic of the Philippines, No. ZPE-76-98-S (6 November 1998) (Annex 33); Memorandum from the Ambassador of the Republic of the Philippines in Beijing to the Secretary of Foreign Affairs of the Republic of the Philippines, No. ZPE-231-95 (20 April 1995) (Annex 22); Government of the Republic of the Philippines, *Transcript of Proceedings: Republic of the Philippines–People's Republic of China Bilateral Talks* (10 August 1995) (Annex 181); Government of the Republic of the Philippines and Government of the People's Republic of China, *Philippine–China Bilateral Consultations: Summary of Proceedings* (20-21 March 1995) (Annex 175); Memorandum from the Ambassador of the Republic of the Philippines in Beijing to the Undersecretary of Foreign Affairs of the Republic of the Philippines (10 March 1995) (Annex 18).

[1262] "China not to pursue militarization of Nansha Islands in South China Sea: Xi," *Xinhua* (25 September 2015), *available at* <news.xinhuanet.com/english/2015-09/26/c_134660930.htm>; United States, The White House, Office of the Press Secretary, "Press Release: Remarks by President Obama and President Xi of the People's Republic of China in Joint Press Conference" (25 September 2015) (Annex 664).

1028. The Tribunal will not deem activities to be military in nature when China itself has consistently resisted such classifications and affirmed the opposite at the highest level. Accordingly, the Tribunal accepts China's repeatedly affirmed position that civilian use comprises the primary (if not the only) motivation underlying the dramatic alterations on Mischief Reef. As civilian activity, the Tribunal notes that China's conduct falls outside the scope of Article 298(1)(b) and concludes that it has jurisdiction to consider the Philippines' Submission.

(b) China's Actions at Mischief Reef and the Philippines' Sovereign Rights

1029. As a preliminary matter, and as noted previously in this Award (see paragraph 696 above), the Tribunal is of the view that the Parties' dispute in relation to the Philippines' Submission No. 12 appears to stem from divergent understandings of their respective rights in the areas of the South China Sea within 200 nautical miles of the Philippines' baselines that are encompassed by the 'nine-dash line', including Mischief Reef. Each Party, in other words, has conducted its affairs from the premise that it, and not the other Party, has sovereign rights over Mischief Reef.

1030. However much these beliefs have been held in good faith, the Tribunal has found that Mischief Reef is a low-tide elevation that falls within an area where only the Philippines possesses possible entitlements to maritime zones under the Convention. Mischief Reef, therefore, can only constitute part of the exclusive economic zone and continental shelf of the Philippines; it does not lie within any entitlement that could be generated by any feature claimed by China (or another State).

i. Acts in Relation to the Installations and the Construction of Islands at Mischief Reef

1031. Having found that Mischief Reef lies within the exclusive economic zone and continental shelf of the Philippines, the Tribunal notes that the Convention is clear with respect to the law governing artificial islands, installations, and structures.

1032. Article 56(1)(b) of the Convention provides that, within the exclusive economic zone, the coastal State enjoys "jurisdiction as provided for in the relevant provisions of this Convention with regard to: (i) the establishment and use of artificial islands, installations and structures."

1033. Article 60 then elaborates on this provision. Paragraphs (1) and (2) provide as follows:

> 1.   In the exclusive economic zone, the coastal State shall have the exclusive right to construct and to authorize and regulate the construction, operation and use of:
>
> (a)   artificial islands;

(b)   installations and structures for the purposes provided for in article 56 and other economic purposes;

(c)   installations and structures which may interfere with the exercise of the rights of the coastal State in the zone.

2.   The coastal State shall have exclusive jurisdiction over such artificial islands, installations and structures, including jurisdiction with regard to customs, fiscal, health, safety and immigration laws and regulations.

The remaining paragraphs of Article 60 address (a) the notice that must be given regarding the construction of artificial islands, installations, and structures; (b) the procedures with respect to safety zones; and (c) the obligation to remove abandoned or disused installations and structures. Article 60(8) also expressly provides that "[a]rtificial islands, installations and structures do not possess the status of islands. They have no territorial sea of their own, and their presence does not affect the delimitation of the territorial sea, the exclusive economic zone or the continental shelf."

1034. With respect to the continental shelf, Article 80 provides that "Article 60 applies *mutatis mutandis* to artificial islands, installations and structures on the continental shelf."

1035. These provisions speak for themselves. In combination, they endow the coastal State—which in this case is necessarily the Philippines—with exclusive decision-making and regulatory power over the construction and operation of artificial islands, and of installations and structures covered by Article 60(1), on Mischief Reef. Within its exclusive economic zone and continental shelf, only the Philippines, or another authorised State, may construct or operate such artificial islands, installations, or structures.

1036. The Tribunal considers that China's initial structures on Mischief Reef from 1995 onwards constituted installations or structures for the purposes of Article 60(1). The Tribunal takes China at its word that the original purpose of the structures was to provide shelter for fishermen and concludes that this is an economic purpose. The Tribunal also notes that the original structures, which China declined to permit fishermen from the Philippines to use, also had the potential to interfere with the exercise by the Philippines of its rights in the exclusive economic zone. Accordingly, pursuant to Article 60 of the Convention, only the Philippines could construct or authorise such structures.

1037. China's activities at Mischief Reef have since evolved into the creation of an artificial island. China has elevated what was originally a reef platform that submerged at high tide into an island that is permanently exposed. Such an island is undoubtedly "artificial" for the purposes of Article 60. It is equally clear that China has proceeded without receiving, or even seeking, the permission of the Philippines. Indeed, China's conduct has taken place in the face of the

Philippines' protests. Article 60 is unequivocal in permitting only the coastal State to construct or authorise such artificial islands.

1038. In light of these provisions of the Convention, the Tribunal considers China's violation of its obligations to be manifest.

ii.   Acts in Relation to Appropriation

1039. The Tribunal now turns to the Philippines' Submission that China, through its occupation and construction activities, has unlawfully attempted to appropriate Mischief Reef.

1040. The Tribunal recalls, first, that Mischief Reef is incapable of appropriation. As the Tribunal has already concluded at paragraphs 307 to 309 above, low-tide elevations "do not form part of the land territory of a State in the legal sense." Rather, such features form part of the submerged landmass of a State and, in the case of Mischief Reef, fall within the legal regime for the continental shelf. In consequence, low-tide elevations, as distinct from land territory, cannot be appropriated. As the Tribunal has now found, Mischief Reef is a low-tide elevation; it follows from this that it is incapable of appropriation, by occupation or otherwise.

1041. As a low-tide elevation within the Philippines' exclusive economic zone and continental shelf, the legal relevance of Mischief Reef is that it lies within an area in which sovereign rights are vested exclusively in the Philippines and where only the Philippines may construct or authorise artificial islands. The Tribunal has already held in relation to the Philippines' Submissions No. 8 and 9 that China's actions at Mischief Reef have unlawfully interfered with the Philippines' enjoyment of its sovereign rights.

1042. Having established that Mischief Reef is not capable of appropriation and addressed the effect of China's actions on the Philippines' sovereign rights, the Tribunal sees no need to address Submission No. 12(c).

(c)   Conclusion

1043. Based on the considerations outlined above, the Tribunal finds that China has, through its construction of installations and artificial islands at Mischief Reef without the authorisation of the Philippines, breached Articles 60 and 80 of the Convention with respect to the Philippines' sovereign rights in its exclusive economic zone and continental shelf. The Tribunal further finds that, as a low-tide elevation, Mischief Reef is not capable of appropriation.

*   *   *

this page intentionally blank

F.   OPERATION OF LAW ENFORCEMENT VESSELS IN A DANGEROUS MANNER (SUBMISSION
      NO. 13)

1.   Introduction

1044. In this Section, the Tribunal addresses the Parties' dispute concerning China's operation of its
      law enforcement vessels near Scarborough Shoal. This dispute is reflected in the Philippines'
      Submission No. 13, which requests a declaration that:

> (13)   China has breached its obligations under the Convention by operating its law
>   enforcement vessels in a dangerous manner causing serious risk of collision to
>   Philippine vessels navigating in the vicinity of Scarborough Shoal;

1045. In its Award on Jurisdiction, the Tribunal held that Submission No. 13 "reflects a dispute
      concerning the operation of China's law enforcement activities in the vicinity of Scarborough
      Shoal and the application of Articles 21, 24, and 94 of the Convention."[1263] The Tribunal found
      that the Submission did not concern "sovereignty or maritime delimitation."[1264] It determined
      that the dispute was not barred from its consideration by any requirement of Section 1 of Part
      XV of the Convention.[1265] The Tribunal also concluded that Article 298(1)(b) of the
      Convention, which excludes certain disputes concerning "law enforcement activities" from the
      procedures in Section 2, was inapplicable because that exception applies only in the context of
      the exclusive economic zone; the present dispute relates "principally to events that occurred *in
      the territorial sea*" of Scarborough Shoal.[1266] Finally the Tribunal considered its jurisdiction
      "not dependent on a prior determination of sovereignty over Scarborough Shoal."[1267]
      Accordingly, the Tribunal found that it has jurisdiction to address the matters raised in
      Submission No. 13.[1268]

2.   Factual Background

1046. The facts underlying the present Submission concern interactions between Chinese law
      enforcement vessels and Philippine coast guard and surveillance ships on 28 April 2012 and on
      26 May 2012.

[1263]   Award on Jurisdiction, para. 410.

[1264]   Award on Jurisdiction, para. 410.

[1265]   Award on Jurisdiction, para. 410.

[1266]   Award on Jurisdiction, para. 410 (emphasis added).

[1267]   Award on Jurisdiction, para. 410.

[1268]   Award on Jurisdiction, para. 410.

(a)   **Near-Collision of Philippine Vessels BRP Pampanga and BRP Edsa II with
        Chinese Vessel FLEC 310**

1047. On 28 April 2012, BRP Pampanga, a Philippine Coast Guard ship conducting maritime patrol
      and law enforcement activities in the vicinity of Scarborough Shoal, established contact with
      another vessel, BRP Edsa II, in order to be relieved of its duties before returning to port. At
      08:15 local time, the captain and commander of BRP Edsa II boarded the Pampanga for
      "briefing and turnover".[1269]

1048. At 09:00, the Philippine vessels came in contact with FLEC 310, a vessel operated by China's
      Fisheries and Law Enforcement Command.[1270] According to BRP Pampanga's after operations
      report, while the ship was stationary, FLEC 310 approached it "from port to almost dead ahead
      at a distance of about 600 yards with speed of 20.3 knots."[1271]

1049. Fifteen minutes later, at 09:15, FLEC 310 approached BRP Edsa II,[1272] passing from the
      "starboard quarter to the port side" of the ship at a distance of 200 yards and a speed of
      20.6 knots.[1273] BRP Pampanga's after operations report describes the manoeuvre as creating
      two-metre high waves in FLEC 310's wake that "battered" two Philippine rubber boats, which
      were in the water at the time for the purpose of transferring personnel.[1274] At 09:25, BRP
      Pampanga "turned over the area" to BRP Edsa II and began its voyage to Manila, where it
      arrived that night.[1275]

(b)   **Near-Collision of Philippine Vessel MCS 3008 with Several Chinese Vessels
        upon Approach to Scarborough Shoal**

1050. On 26 May 2012, MCS 3008, a Philippines Bureau of Fisheries and Aquatic Resources vessel,
      approached Scarborough Shoal for the purpose of resupplying BRP Corregidor, a ship of the

---

[1269]   Report from the Commanding Officer, SARV-003, Philippine Coast Guard, to Commander, Coast Guard
         District Northwestern Luzon, Philippine Coast Guard (28 April 2012), para. 5.45 (Annex 78) (hereinafter
         "SARV Coastguard Report of 28 April 2012").

[1270]   SARV Coastguard Report of 28 April 2012, paras. 5.46, 7.1.

[1271]   SARV Coastguard Report of 28 April 2012, paras. 5.46, 7.1.

[1272]   SARV Coastguard Report of 28 April 2012, paras. 5.46, 7.1.

[1273]   SARV Coastguard Report of 28 April 2012, para. 5.46.

[1274]   SARV Coastguard Report of 28 April 2012, paras. 5.46, 7.1.

[1275]   SARV Coastguard Report of 28 April 2012, paras. 5.46-5.48.

Philippine Coast Guard.[1276] At approximately 15:50 local time and having come within seven nautical miles of Scarborough Shoal, MCS 3008 was approached by CMS 71.[1277]

1051. According to the report of the Philippine Coast Guard officers aboard the MCS 3008, CMS 71 "increased speed and at less than 100 yards" from the MCS 3008 and "attempted to cross this unit's port bow."[1278] MCS 3008 "responded by increasing speed to 20 knots and altering course to the starboard" and then passing to the rear of the CMS 71 "in order to evade a possible impact."[1279]

1052. Once it "was able to evade the first dangerous maneuver of CMS 71," MCS 3008 reported, "the same vessel immediately swinged to its starboard and again attempted to cross [the] starboard bow of [MCS 3008]."[1280] In response, and "in order to avoid a possible collision ensued by this second intentional act of CMS 71," MCS 3008 "immediately maneuvered hard port" and "passed through the rear of [CMS 71]."[1281]

1053. After steering clear of the "deliberate maneuvers of CMS 71," MCS 3008 reported that it was approached by another Chinese vessel, FLEC 303, which "steered towards our position and . . . aimed to cross [MCS 3008]'s starboard bow."[1282] MCS 3008 "instantly . . . reacted by increasing speed to 22 knots and swerving towards the rear of FLEC 303" in order to avoid a collision.[1283]

1054. Following these incidents, MCS 3008 continued toward BRP Corregidor. During this time, MCS 3008 was pursued by three Chinese vessels: FLEC 303, CMS 71, and CMS 84 (a third Chinese vessel, also belonging to CMS).[1284] All three Chinese vessels pursued MCS 3008 until the latter approached BRP Corregidor. While MCS 3008 was alongside BRP Corregidor, CMS 84 "passed through starboardside of our position at a distance of less than 100 yards."[1285] According to MCS 3008, CMS 84 "eventually stopped and positioned on the port quarter at a

---

[1276] Report from A.A. Arunco, et al., FRPLEU-QRT Officers, Bureau of Fisheries and Aquatic Resources, Republic of the Philippines, to the Director, Bureau of Fisheries and Aquatic Resources, Republic of the Philippines (28 May 2012), para. 1.d (Annex 82) (hereinafter "**Arunco Report of 28 May 2012**").

[1277] Arunco Report of 28 May 2012, para. 1.a.

[1278] Arunco Report of 28 May 2012, para. 1.a.

[1279] Arunco Report of 28 May 2012, para. 1.a.

[1280] Arunco Report of 28 May 2012, para. 1.b.

[1281] Arunco Report of 28 May 2012, para. 1.b.

[1282] Arunco Report of 28 May 2012, para. 1.c.

[1283] Arunco Report of 28 May 2012, para. 1.c.

[1284] Arunco Report of 28 May 2012, para. 1.d.

[1285] Arunco Report of 28 May 2012, para. 1.e.

distance of approx. 500 yards from our position."[1286] At the same time, a fourth Chinese vessel, FLEC 301, "was stationed at the port beam with a distance of about one thousand (1,000) yards."[1287]

1055. After checking the tidal level, MCS 3008 proceeded towards the entrance to the lagoon of Scarborough Shoal.[1288] As MCS 3008 pulled away from BRP Corregidor, CMS 84 again began to chase. According to the officers of MCS 3008, "sensing that CMS 84 was aiming to cross through the bow of this vessel, this unit increased speed which eventually caused the Chinese vessel to be left behind by a few yards."[1289]

1056. As MCS 3008 continued toward the lagoon entrance, three Chinese vessels, FLEC 303, CMS 71, and FLEC 306 approached it. As reported by MCS 3008,

> when FLEC 303 was already about 50 yards from this vessel, said Chinese vessel immediately altered course as if crossing to our starboard bow. However, when FLEC 303 was already dead ahead of this unit, the Chinese vessel decreased speed and established a blocking position. [MCS 3008] right away swerved towards the rear of the Chinese vessel to evade a possible impact.[1290]

1057. Thereafter, MCS 3008 "sighted CMS 71 moving fast towards our position. Again, because of our speed, CMS 71 was only able to get near our position from a distance of approximately 70 yards on our portside."[1291]

1058. At the entrance to the lagoon, MCS 3008 encountered FLEC 306, along with three Chinese fishing vessels. MCS 3008 described this incident as follows:

> On our route towards the basin, this vessel sighted three (3) Chinese fishing vessels and FLEC 306 on a blocking position near the lone entrance inside the shoal. Furthermore, three (3) Chinese service ships were now chasing this unit with CMS 71 joining CMS 84 and FLEC 303.
>
> After being able to position [a] few yards from the entrance of the shoal and reviewing our prepared safe way points, this unit decided to enter the shoal's basin by passing in between the three (3) Chinese fishing vessels (CFV's) and FLEC 306 which was fast moving towards our location. This unit considered such path as the only possible way towards the basin because of our safe distance from the CFV's and FLEC 306 in which, all the while seemed to have given way for the entry of this vessel inside. However, as this unit was on its way towards the basin, ships personnel sighted two (2) mooring lines which was planted by CFV's obviously intended to impede our movement towards the shoal's basin. While this unit stopped engines and then maneuvered backwards to avoid the lines, crew of the CFV's from which the line came from and FLEC 306 suddenly echoed cheers and clapped

---

[1286] Arunco Report of 28 May 2012, para. 1.e.

[1287] Arunco Report of 28 May 2012, para. 1.e.

[1288] Arunco Report of 28 May 2012, para. 1.f.

[1289] Arunco Report of 28 May 2012, para. 1.g.

[1290] Arunco Report of 28 May 2012, para. 1.h.

[1291] Arunco Report of 28 May 2012, para. 1.i.

hands. At this point, FLEC 306 was already on a blocking position [a] few yards dead ahead of this unit.

With the lines planted by the CFV's, FLEC 306 posing a blockade and three (3) Chinese service ships positioned at the rear, it was evident that all efforts by the Chinese vessels were already employed in order to obstruct our entry to the shoal's basin. Nevertheless, with the sheer determination to comply with the directive from higher-ups for this vessel to go inside the shoal's basin coupled with the courage that the officers and crew exuded on such situation, this unit sped up, maneuvered hard to the starboard and swerved toward the astern of FLEC 306.

The scenario went worse this time with FLEC 306 going all engines back and determined to ram our vessel. Nevertheless, this unit continued to employ speed and immediately maneuver[ed] hard left which was just enough to dodge from the deliberate intention of said FLEC which was just about 10 meters away on our portside and at the same time, to keep this vessel safe from a shallow area approximately 25 yards away on the starboardside. . . .

After avoiding the chase, harassment and intended sabotage, finally, this unit was able to enter the shoal basin safely and anchored . . . .[1292]

3. The Philippines' Position

1059. The Philippines alleges that China has operated its law enforcement vessels in a dangerous manner, causing "serious risk[] of collision" to Philippine vessels navigating in the vicinity of Scarborough Shoal.[1293] In consequence, the Philippines submits that China has breached its obligations relating to safe navigation under Articles 94 and 21 of the Convention and related provisions in the Convention on the International Regulations for Preventing of Collisions at Sea, 1972[1294] (the "**COLREGS**").[1295]

(a) The Applicability of the COLREGS to China

1060. The Philippines submits, first, that China's conduct in the territorial sea of Scarborough Shoal is governed and constrained by the general requirements of flag States under the Convention. In this regard, it recalls the *Fisheries Advisory Opinion*, in which the International Tribunal for the Law of the Sea held that the Convention "contains provisions concerning general obligations" which must be met by flag States "in all marine areas regulated by the Convention," including those regulated by Articles 91, 92, and 94 of the Convention.[1296] It follows, in the Philippines'

[1292] Arunco Report of 28 May 2012, paras. 1.j-1.n.

[1293] Memorial, para. 6.114.

[1294] Convention on the International Regulations for Preventing Collisions at Sea, 20 October 1972, 1050 UNTS 1976 (hereinafter "**COLREGS**").

[1295] Memorial, para. 6.114.

[1296] Merits Hearing Tr. (Day 3), pp. 56-57; *Request for an Advisory Opinion Submitted by the Sub-Regional Fisheries Commission (SRFC), Advisory Opinion of 2 April 2015, ITLOS Reports 2015*, para. 111.

view, that China has obligations under the Convention whenever its vessels, "including those operated by CMS and FLEC . . . are operated in the territorial sea of Scarborough Shoal or anywhere else."[1297] In other words, the obligations of a flag State apply "regardless of where the ships were located" at any particular point in time.[1298]

1061. The Philippines recalls that Article 94(3) of the Convention requires flag States to "take such measures . . . as are necessary to ensure safety at sea," including measures concerning "the use of signals, the maintenance of communications and the prevention of collisions."[1299] The Philippines also refers to Article 94(5), which clarifies the scope of the flag State's duties in the following terms:

> In taking the measures called for in paragraphs 3 and 4 each State is required to conform to generally accepted international regulations, procedures and practices and to take any steps which may be necessary to secure their observance.[1300]

1062. Finally, the Philippines notes that Article 21(4) of the Convention also refers to "international regulations relating to the prevention of collisions at sea."[1301]

1063. The correct interpretation of the aforementioned provisions, in the Philippines' view, includes the COLREGS as one of the "generally accepted international regulations" to which flag States are required to conform.[1302] The International Maritime Organisation, for example, recognises the COLREGS as one of its conventions that "may, on account of their world-wide acceptance, be deemed to fulfil the requirement of general acceptance" for the purposes of Article 94(3).[1303]

1064. The Philippines submits that while Article 21(4) technically applies only to foreign ships in innocent passage, if the coastal State fails to ensure its vessels respect COLREGS in the territorial sea and subsequently endangers the navigation of foreign ships in the territorial sea, this would constitute a violation of its duties under Article 24 to refrain from hampering innocent passage and to publicise dangers to navigation.[1304]

[1297] Merits Hearing Tr. (Day 3), pp. 57, 60.

[1298] Merits Hearing Tr. (Day 3), p. 56.

[1299] Convention, art. 94(3)(c).

[1300] Merits Hearing Tr. (Day 1), p. 72.

[1301] Memorial, para. 6.131.

[1302] Memorial, para. 6.131; Merits Hearing Tr. (Day 3), p. 59-60; W. Tetley, *International Maritime and Admiralty Law* (2002), p. 237.

[1303] International Maritime Organization, *Implications of the United Nations Convention on the Law of the Sea for the International Maritime Organization*, Doc. LEG/MISC/3/Rev. 1 (6 January 2003), pp. 10-11.

[1304] Memorial, para. 6.133.

(b)   Exceptions to the COLREGS for Special Circumstances

1065. According to the Philippines, the COLREGS are legally binding rules.[1305] By their terms, they extend to "all vessels upon the high seas and in all waters connected therewith navigable by seagoing vessels"[1306] and apply to "the high seas, the EEZ, the territorial sea, archipelagic waters, [and] straits used for international navigation and archipelagic sea lanes."[1307] They therefore bind China with respect to its vessels operating in the vicinity of Scarborough Shoal.

1066. While the Philippines acknowledges that Rule 2(b) of the COLREGS recognises "special circumstances" in which a departure from the rules may be "necessary to avoid immediate danger," it maintains that the exception "does not undermine the otherwise mandatory nature of the regulations."[1308] It notes the practice of national courts in limiting that exception only to circumstances raising "immediate" danger, rather than "generic special circumstances".[1309] In any event, the Philippines considers the exception in Rule 2(b) to be inapplicable in the present case.[1310]

(c)   Application of the COLREGS to Chinese Vessels at Scarborough Shoal

1067. The Philippines submits that China has violated Rules 2, 6, 7, 8, 15, and 16 of the COLREGS.[1311] In so doing, the Philippines relies on the expert report of Professor Craig H. Allen (the "**Allen Report**").[1312] Professor Allen is a Professor of Law and Adjunct Professor of Marine Affairs at the University of Washington in Seattle, and served for 21 years with the United States Coast Guard. Professor Allen produced his expert report *pro bono*.[1313] Relying on the contemporaneous reports and dispatches provided to him by the Philippines, Professor Allen considers China to have violated Rules 2, 6, 8, and 16 of the COLREGS on both occasions comprising the basis for Submission No. 13.

[1305]   Merits Hearing Tr. (Day 3), pp. 61-62.

[1306]   Memorial, para. 6.133; COLREGS, Rule 1(a).

[1307]   Memorial, para. 6.133 *quoting* S. Rosenne & L. Sohn (eds.), *United Nations Convention on the Law of the Sea 1982: A Commentary*, Vol. V, p. 775 (M. Nordquist, gen. ed. 2012).

[1308]   Merits Hearing Tr. (Day 3), p. 62.

[1309]   Merits Hearing Tr. (Day 3), p. 62; *see, e.g., Crowley Marine Services Inc. v. Maritrans Inc.*, 447 F.3d 719, 725 (9th Cir. 2006).

[1310]   Merits Hearing Tr. (Day 3), p. 62.

[1311]   Memorial, para. 6.140.

[1312]   Report of Craig H. Allen, p. 4 (19 March 2014) (Annex 239) (hereinafter the "**Allen Report**").

[1313]   Allen Report, p. 1.

1068. The Philippines argues first that China is in breach of the general principle of responsibility for the prevention of collisions provided in Rule 2. That provision states:

> *Rule 2.* RESPONSIBILITY
>
> (a) Nothing in these Rules shall exonerate any vessel, or the owner, master or crew thereof, from the consequences of any neglect to comply with these Rules or of the neglect of any precaution which may be required by the ordinary practice of seamen, or by the special circumstances of the case.
>
> (b) In construing and complying with these Rules due regard shall be had to all dangers of navigation and collision and to any special circumstances, including the limitations of the vessels involved, which may make a departure from these Rules necessary to avoid immediate danger.[1314]

1069. The Philippines argues that the conduct of Chinese vessels in both the 28 April and 26 May 2012 incidents place China in breach of Rule 2. Relying on the Allen Report, the Philippines describes the conduct of FLEC 310 (on 28 April 2012) and of CMS 71, FLEC 303, and FLEC 306 (on 26 May 2012) as having "intentionally endanger[ed] another vessel through high speed 'blocking' or harassment maneuvers."[1315] With regard to Rule 2, Professor Allen states that Chinese vessels "demonstrated serious and apparently intentional breaches" of the requirement that ships take "precautions as are required by the ordinary practice of seamen."[1316] Based on an analysis of the vessels' conduct, the Allen Report concludes that the Chinese vessels showed "a flagrant disregard of the tenets of good seamanship"[1317] on both occasions.

1070. Second, the Philippines maintains that the Chinese vessels breached Rule 6 of the COLREGS, requiring vessels to "proceed at a safe speed so that [they] can take proper and effective action to avoid collision."[1318] Professor Allen considers Rule 6 to have been violated when Chinese vessels passed BRP Pampanga and BRP Edsa II at distances of 600 and 200 yards and speeds of over 20 knots.[1319] The Philippines notes that the interpretation of the term "safe speed" is not specified and is thus contingent on the particular facts of each case, but maintains that the circumstances of the two incidents leave little doubt that China failed to ensure that its vessels "proceed[ed] at a safe speed" in accordance with the regulation.[1320] The failure, in the

---

[1314]   Memorial, para. 6.134; COLREGS, Rule 2.

[1315]   Memorial, para. 6.141; Allen Report, p. 4.

[1316]   Allen Report, p. 4.

[1317]   Allen Report, p. 4.

[1318]   Memorial, para. 6.135; Merits Hearing Tr. (Day 3), p. 66; COLREGS, Rule 6.

[1319]   Allen Report, p. 4.

[1320]   Merits Hearing Tr. (Day 3), pp. 66-67; Memorial, para. 6.136; A.N. Cockcroft & J.N.F. Lameijer, *A Guide to the Collision Avoidance Rules: International Regulations for Preventing Collisions at Sea* (7th ed., 2011), p. 18; Allen Report, p. 4.

Philippines' view, was further aggravated by the size of the Chinese vessels and the wake created by the manoeuvres, heightening the threat to the Philippine ships and their crews.[1321]

1071. Third, the Philippines argues that the Chinese vessels breached Rules 7 and 8 of the COLREGS, which set out the principles governing the risk of collision and avoidance of collision, respectively.[1322]

1072. In the Philippines' view, the Chinese vessels failed to take the necessary steps in accordance with Rule 8, which requires evasive action to have "due regard to the observance of good seamanship" and achieve passing at a "safe distance."[1323] Although the COLREGS do not define what constitutes a "safe distance" and the Philippines recognises the determination is context-specific, it submits that the term implies that "the passing distance must be large enough to leave a margin for error and allow for the unexpected," such as to provide for a "margin for human error or mechanical malfunction."[1324] The Philippines submits, supported by the Allen Report, that the Chinese vessels "not only fail[ed] to take actions to avoid collision but [took] actions that made collision substantially more likely."[1325] That no collision actually occurred during the incidents in question does nothing to diminish China's culpability, in the Philippines' view, since it considers both rules to impose an obligation of conduct, rather than result.[1326]

1073. Finally, the Philippines, supported by the Allen Report, alleges breach of Rules 15 and 16 of the COLREGS, both of which it considers to have been violated. Rule 15 states:

> When two power-driven vessels are crossing so as to involve risk of collision, the vessel which has the other on her own starboard side shall keep out of the way and shall, if the circumstances of the case admit, avoid crossing ahead of the other vessel.[1327]

The Philippines' notes that Rule 15 requires that "the vessel on the left . . . turn away"[1328] and submits that, when CMS 71 approached MCS 3008 at speed from the left (*i.e.*, with MCS on the starboardside of CMS 71) on 26 May 2012 "it was the 'give-way vessel' according to Rule 15."[1329] Nevertheless, CMS 71 attempted to cross ahead of the Philippine vessel, rather than avoiding such a manoeuvre as called for by Rule 15. In the context of Rule 15, Professor

---

[1321] Allen Report, p. 4; Merits Hearing Tr. (Day 3), p. 67.

[1322] Memorial, para. 6.137.

[1323] COLREGS, Rules 7-8.

[1324] Allen Report, p. 5.

[1325] Memorial, para. 6.144; *see also* Allen Report, p. 5.

[1326] Merits Hearing Tr. (Day 3), p. 64; Allen Report, p. 4.

[1327] Memorial, para. 6.139; Hearing Tr. (Day 3), p. 67; COLREGS, Rule 15.

[1328] Merits Hearing Tr. (Day 3), p. 67.

[1329] Memorial, para. 6.145; Allen Report, p. 5.

Allen principally notes the failure of CMS 71 to give MSC 3008 right of way by attempting to cut across the latter's bow on 26 May 2012.[1330]

1074. Additionally, as the "give-way vessel", the Philippines submits that CMS violated Rule 16, regarding the obligations of the give-way vessel, insofar as "CMS 71 was . . . under the obligation to 'keep out of the way' of the MCS 3008, which she did not do."[1331] Professor Allen notes that, by "intentionally closing [in] on [the Philippine] vessels" in an attempt to block their progress toward Scarborough Shoal, the Chinese vessels—FLEC 310 in particular—"violated Rule 16's requirement to 'so far as possible, take early and substantial action to *keep well clear*'."[1332] The Philippines likewise argues that "during the incident of 28 April 2012, the FLEC 310's approach toward Philippine vessels made it the 'give-way vessel', requiring that it 'so far as possible, take early and substantial action to keep well clear'."[1333]

1075. Professor Allen recognises that the operational requirements of law enforcement ships (such as intercepting a vessel) may stand in "occasional tension" with the COLREGS. He cautions, however, that Rule 2(b) permits only limited exception from Rule 16, to "avoid immediate danger".[1334] Professor Allen finds no such danger justifying a departure from the regulations. He concludes that the incidents alleged by the Philippines "apparently involved *intentional* violations of the most basic rules for preventing collisions at sea" and would be "condemned by all professional mariners."[1335]

4.   China's Position

1076. China has made no statements as to the specific matters raised in the Philippines' Submission No. 13, concerning the incidents in the vicinity of Scarborough Shoal on 28 April and 26 May 2012. It has, however, made statements concerning the presence of Chinese vessels at Scarborough Shoal, both generally and in response to Philippine diplomatic notes concerning the incidents.

1077. On 30 April 2012, the Department of Foreign Affairs of the Philippines submitted a Note Verbale to the Embassy of the People's Republic of China in Manila expressing the Philippines'

[1330]   Allen Report, p. 5.

[1331]   Memorial, para. 6.145.

[1332]   Allen Report, p. 5 (emphasis in original).

[1333]   Memorial, para. 6.146; Allen Report, p. 5.

[1334]   Allen Report, pp. 5-6; COLREGS, Rule 2(b).

[1335]   Allen Report, p. 6.

"grave concern over the provocative and extremely dangerous maneuvers" committed by Chinese vessels at Scarborough Shoal.[1336] The Philippines referred to the incident on 28 April 2012 and requested China "to instruct its ships to observe the [COLREGS]."[1337]

1078. In response to this and several other Philippine diplomatic notes expressing "grave concern" over the conduct of Chinese vessels in the area,[1338] on 25 May 2012, China replied that it "does not accept the contents" of the Philippines' notes and asserted that the conduct of its vessels was justified. China stated:

> The various jurisdiction measures adopted by the Chinese government over Huangyan Island [Scarborough Shoal] and its waters, and activities by Chinese ships, including government public service ships and fishing boats, in Huangyan Island and its waters are completely within China's sovereignty.
>
> . . .
>
> The Chinese side once again urges the Philippine side to concretely respect China's territorial sovereignty over Huangyan Island, immediately pull out all Philippine ships from the Huangyan Island waters and desist from disturbing the operation of Chinese fishing boats and law enforcement activities by China's public service ships.[1339]

1079. While China has responded to specific Philippine allegations relating to the conduct of Chinese vessels at Scarborough Shoal, it has specifically addressed only an encounter that occurred on 10 April 2012.[1340] For example, in its Position Paper, China maintained that the presence of Philippine naval vessels at Scarborough Shoal on 10 April 2012 constituted "provocations" that "forced [China] to take response measures to safeguard its sovereignty."[1341] More generally, China has stated that "the legality of China's actions in the waters of the Nansha Islands and

---

[1336] Note Verbale from the Department of Foreign Affairs, Republic of the Philippines, to the Embassy of the People's Republic of China in Manila, No. 12-1222 (30 April 2012) (Annex 209).

[1337] Note Verbale from the Department of Foreign Affairs, Republic of the Philippines, to the Embassy of the People's Republic of China in Manila, No. 12-1222 (30 April 2012) (Annex 209).

[1338] Note Verbale from the Department of Foreign Affairs of the Republic of Philippines to the Embassy of People's Republic of China in Manila, No. 12-1371 (21 May 2012) (Annex 688). See also the largely identical Note Verbale from the Department of Foreign Affairs, Republic of the Philippines, to the Embassies of ASEAN Member States in Manila, No. 12-1372 (21 May 2012) (Annex 210). The Philippines submitted several other diplomatic notes in April and May 2012 relating to China's conduct at Scarborough Shoal generally. See, e.g., Note Verbale from the Department of Foreign Affairs of the Republic of Philippines to the Embassy of People's Republic of China in Manila, No. 12-1304 (14 May 2012) (Annex 669);

[1339] Note Verbale from the Embassy of the People's Republic of China in Manila to the Department of Foreign Affairs, Republic of the Philippines, No. (12) PG-239 (25 May 2012) (Annex 211).

[1340] See, e.g., Note Verbale from the Embassy of the People's Republic of China in Manila to the Department of Foreign Affairs, Republic of the Philippines, No. (12) PG-239 (25 May 2012) (Annex 211).

[1341] China's Position Paper, para. 48.

Huangyan Dao rests on both its sovereignty over relevant maritime features and the maritime rights derived therefrom."[1342]

1080. As far as the Tribunal is aware, China has not made specific statements with respect to the incidents of 28 April and 26 May 2012. Accordingly, the Tribunal does not have explicit Chinese statements concerning the incidents alleged by the Philippines in its Submission No. 13. However, the Tribunal considers China's statements described above as indicating that it considers its actions at Scarborough Shoal to have been generally lawful.

5. **The Tribunal's Considerations**

(a) **Background on the COLREGS**

1081. The COLREGS, entered into force on 15 July 1977. With 156 contracting parties representing more than 98 percent of world tonnage, the COLREGS comprise one of the most widely adopted multilateral conventions in force. Both China and the Philippines are parties to the COLREGS.[1343]

1082. Although the Philippines did not become a party to the COLREGS until 2013, in assessing the Philippines' Submission No. 13 the Tribunal considers the COLREGS to bind both Parties relating to the conduct of their respective vessels by virtue of Article 94 of the Convention. Article 94(1) of the Convention requires flag States to effectively exercise their "jurisdiction and control" in administrative, technical, and social matters over ships flying their flag.[1344] Subsection 3 of that article clarifies the scope of flag States' duties, requiring them to "take such measures . . . as are necessary to ensure safety at sea," including measures concerning, *inter alia*, "the use of signals, the maintenance of communications and the prevention of collisions."[1345] The precise scope of those obligations is clarified in Article 94(5):

> In taking the measures called for in paragraph[] 3 . . . each State is required to conform to generally accepted international regulations, procedures and practices and to take any steps which may be necessary to secure their observance.[1346]

1083. In the Tribunal's view, Article 94 incorporates the COLREGS into the Convention, and they are consequently binding on China. It follows that a violation of the COLREGS, as "generally accepted international regulations" concerning measures necessary to ensure maritime safety, constitutes a violation of the Convention itself. With this in mind, the Tribunal turns to the independent expert opinion and factual record regarding the two incidents and to an evaluation of China's conduct in light of the applicable regulations.

(b)   Report of Tribunal-Appointed Independent Expert

1084. In assessing the present Submission, the Tribunal takes into account the Allen Report, submitted by the Philippines, as well as the report of 15 April 2016 by Captain Gurpreet S. Singhota,[1347] who was appointed by the Tribunal in accordance with Article 24 of the Rules of Procedure in order to obtain an independent expert assessment of the Philippines claims. Captain Singhota's experience includes 26 years of service with the International Maritime Organization's Maritime Safety Division, Sub-committee on Safety of Navigation, and other departments, as well as 14 years of seagoing experience. Captain Singhota certified that he "is, and shall remain, impartial and independent with respect of each of the Parties."[1348]

1085. After a review of the factual record, Captain Singhota concludes that China has breached its obligations under Rules 2, 6, 8, 15, and 16 of the COLREGS.

1086. With respect to the alleged incidents of 28 April 2012, Captain Singhota finds that high-speed manoeuvring by FLEC 310 in the vicinity of BRP Pampanga, veering away a distance of approximately 0.32 nautical miles from the Philippine vessel, exemplifies "unprofessional ship handling . . . totally inconsistent with the practice of good seamanship."[1349] In such circumstances, a "momentary decision-making lapse," Captain Singhota suggests, could have resulted in a "catastrophic collision".[1350] He therefore considers FLEC 310's conduct to have violated Rule 2(a) of the COLREGS. Noting FLEC 310's high speed at the time of its encounters with BRP Pampanga and Edsa II (20.3 and 20.6 knots, respectively), the report also identifies a breach of Rule 6 relating to safe speed in the prevailing situations.[1351]

[1347]   Captain Gurpreet S. Singhota, *Report of the International Navigational Safety Expert appointed by the Permanent Court of Arbitration, The Hague, The Netherlands* (15 April 2016) (hereinafter "**Singhota Report**").

[1348]   Terms of Reference for Expert, Captain Gurpreet S. Singhota, 18 March 2016; Declaration of Captain Singhota, 24 February 2016.

[1349]   Singhota Report, p. 4, para. 8.

[1350]   Singhota Report, p. 4, para. 8.

[1351]   Singhota Report, p. 4, para. 12.

1087. Captain Singhota attributes two additional breaches to FLEC 310's conduct under Rules 8 and 16 of the COLREGS. He explains that where risk of collision exists, Rule 8 imposes obligations on give-way vessels to "take timely action to keep clear" and to maintain a safe distance from the other ship. Observing that thresholds for "safe" distances vary and are context-specific, the report concludes that FLEC 310's closing in, within 600 yards (0.296 nautical miles) and 200 yards (0.098 nautical miles), respectively, of the Philippine vessels "certainly" fell short of the requirement of passing at a safe distance.[1352] Because Rule 16 requires give-way vessels to take "early and substantial" action to maintain a safe distance, the report also considers that provision to have been violated over the course of the encounter.[1353]

1088. With respect to the alleged incidents of 26 May 2012, Captain Singhota considers the "high-speed blocking" manoeuvres of FLEC and CMS vessels vis-à-vis MCS 3008 to constitute a "total disregard of good seamanship and neglect of any precaution, which may be required by the ordinary practice of seamen."[1354] In particular, the report deems the conduct of CMS 71, FLEC 303, and FLEC 306, and especially CMS 71's attempt to cut across the bow of MCS 3008 at a distance of fewer than 100 yards (0.049 nautical miles), to have breached Rules 2, 6, and 8 of the COLREGS.[1355] The report considers CMS 71 "unnecessarily" attempting to cut across the bow of MCS 3008 also to violate Rule 15:

> To cross another vessel's bow unnecessarily, where collision is probable, or even only possible, is an unseamanlike manoeuvre, and apart from the regulations would be held to be negligent in fact and in law.[1356]

Finally, Captain Singhota considers that the actions of the Chinese vessels "created situations that required them to assume the role of the give-way vessel."[1357] As such, Rule 16 required them to "so far as possible, take early and substantial action to *keep well clear*."[1358]

1089. Captain Singhota concludes that the Chinese manoeuvres on 26 April and 28 May 2012 "demonstrated a complete disregard for the observance and practice of good

---

[1352]   Singhota Report, p. 5, paras. 13-14.

[1353]   Singhota Report, p. 5, para. 15.

[1354]   Singhota Report, p. 6, para. 17.

[1355]   Singhota Report, pp. 6-7, paras. 19-21.

[1356]   Singhota Report, p. 7, para. 22.

[1357]   Singhota Report, p. 7, para. 23.

[1358]   Singhota Report, p. 7, para. 23.

seamanship including the ordinary practice of seamen but most importantly, a total disregard for the observance of the collision regulations."[1359]

(c)   Application of Article 94 of the Convention and the COLREGS

1090. Having determined that Article 94 of the Convention incorporates the COLREGS into the duties of flag States by reference, the Tribunal must interpret and apply the COLREGS in order to make decisions as to the Philippines' Submission No. 13.

1091. As a preliminary matter, the Tribunal observes that the conduct of each of the Chinese vessels in question—CMS 71, CMS 84, FLEC 303, FLEC 306, and FLEC 310—is attributable to China. All Chinese-flagged vessels involved in the incidents alleged by the Philippines on 28 April and 26 May 2012 belonged to one of two agencies: CMS or the FLEC. Accordingly, because the conduct complained of was committed by vessels falling directly under the command and control of the Chinese Government, the Tribunal considers the vessels' behaviour to constitute official acts of China. Their conduct is automatically attributable to China as such.

1092. Having regard to the entirety of the record before it, the Tribunal determines that the activities of Chinese vessels implicated in Submission No. 13 constituted violations of the COLREGS.

1093. The Tribunal notes that the evidence demonstrates that FLEC 310 passed within 200 yards of BRP Edsa II and within 600 yards of BRP Pampanga, in both cases at a speed of more than 20 knots. Similar conduct occurred on 26 May 2012, during which CMS 71 and FLEC 303 attempted to cut across the bow of MCS 3008 on three occasions, once at a distance of less than 100 yards.[1360]

1094. Such conduct is irreconcilable with an obligation of responsible navigation. In this regard, the Tribunal accepts Captain Singhota's characterisation of the Chinese vessels' conduct as having been in "total disregard of good seamanship and neglect of any precaution."[1361] It follows that Rule 2(a) was breached by each of the aforementioned incidents.

1095. In this connection, moreover, the Tribunal considers the exception posed by Rule 2(b), permitting departure from the COLREGS where "necessary to avoid immediate danger," inapposite to the case at hand. Quite apart from the Philippines' argument that national courts,

---

[1359]   Singhota Report, p. 10, para. 28 (emphasis in original).

[1360]   Arunco Report of 28 May 2012, para. 1.a.

[1361]   Singhota Report, p. 6, para. 17.

such as those in the United States,[1362] construe the exception narrowly, the high threshold established by the exception cannot apply to the facts as presented. If anything, the record suggests that the Chinese manoeuvres themselves created an immediate danger, rather than having been undertaken in response to a pre-existing threat.[1363] Additionally, while the Tribunal is aware that China's statements suggest that its actions were justified as part of general law enforcement activities in the vicinity of a feature which China considers to comprise part of its sovereign territory, the Tribunal also recognises that, where the operational requirements of law enforcement ships stand in tension with the COLREGS, the latter must prevail.[1364] Accordingly, the Tribunal can find no danger justifying a departure from the regulations under Rule 2(b).

1096. The Tribunal turns next to Rule 6 of the COLREGS, which requires ships to preserve the means to avoid collision when circumstances so require. It provides, in relevant part, that:

> Every vessel shall at all times proceed at a safe speed so that she can take proper and effective action to avoid collision and be stopped within a distance appropriate to the prevailing circumstances and conditions.[1365]

1097. On 28 April 2012, FLEC 310 passed by BRP Pampanga at 20.3 knots and Edsa II at 20.6 knots (see paragraphs 1048 to 1049 above). The COLREGS do not define what constitutes a "safe speed", and the meaning and application of the phrase remains dependent on the particular facts of each case, including factors such as the vessels' size and probability of harm. In this instance, however, both Professor Allen and Captain Singhota[1366] consider the incidents described above to have occurred at unsafe speeds. The Tribunal concurs with that view and determines that the Chinese vessels' actions breached Rule 6.

1098. Next, the Tribunal turns to Rules 7 and 8 of the COLREGS. Rule 7(a) provides: "Every vessel shall use all available means appropriate to the prevailing circumstances and conditions to determine if risk of collision exists. If there is any doubt such risk shall be deemed to exist."[1367] Both experts conclude that such a risk existed on 28 April and 26 May 2012. The Allen Report concludes a breach of Rule 7 occurred in each of three instances: (a) FLEC 303 closing at high speed within 600 yards of BRP Pampanga and passing BRP Edsa II within 200 yards;

[1362] See, e.g., Merits Hearing Tr. (Day 3), p. 62; Crowley Marine Services Inc. v. Maritrans Inc., 447 F.3d 719, 725 (9th Cir. 2006).

[1363] See Allen Report, p. 6.

[1364] See, e.g., Allen Report, pp. 5-6; COLREGS, Rule 2(b).

[1365] COLREGS, Rule 6(a).

[1366] Allen Report, p. 4; Singhota Report, pp. 4, 6.

[1367] COLREGS, Rule 7(a).

(b) dangerous manoeuvres undertaken by CMS 71, FLEC 303, and CMS 84, which passed the Philippine vessels at distances of 100 or fewer yards; and (c) FLEC 306 nearly "ramming" MCS 3008.[1368] The Singhota Report reaches a similar conclusion, although its analysis primarily evaluates the incidents under the framework of Rule 8 (which presumes that a risk of collision exists).[1369] Under these circumstances, the Tribunal considers the "risk" identified under Rule 7 to have been clearly established.

1099. Having established that a "risk of collision" existed, the Tribunal turns to Rule 8, which governs the means by which vessels may act to avoid such risks, as follows:

> Any action taken to avoid collision shall be taken in accordance with the Rules of this Part and shall, if the circumstances of the case admit, be positive, made in ample time and with due regard to the observance of good seamanship.
>
> . . .
>
> Action taken to avoid collision with another vessel shall be such as to result in passing at a safe distance. The effectiveness of the action shall be carefully checked until the other vessel is finally past and clear.[1370]

1100. Rule 8 of the COLREGS does not define what constitutes a "safe distance". Professor Allen suggests that the term be read to imply that "the passing distance . . . be large enough to leave a margin for error and allow for the unexpected."[1371] Captain Singhota proposes that a "safe distance" must allow for "human error on the bridge and engine or [for] steering gear failure at a critical phase of the maneuver," as well as for any incidental effects of the "interaction" between passing vessels.[1372] In any event, the Tribunal considers the conduct of FLEC 303, FLEC 306 FLEC 310, and CMS 71 all to fall short of any reasonable definition of a safe distance.

1101. Indeed, far from avoiding a collision, the actions of the Chinese ships made the possibility of a collision substantially more likely.[1373] That fact alone—independent of any question as to whether a collision, whether through the crew's effort or by good fortune, was ultimately averted—suffices to demonstrate a violation of the COLREGS. For the same reasons as those underlying its conclusion with respect to Rule 2(a), the Tribunal considers the other requirement

---

[1368]   Allen Report, p. 5.

[1369]   Singhota Report, p. 5, 7, paras. 13, 21.

[1370]   COLREGS, Rules 8(a), 8(d).

[1371]   Allen Report, p. 5.

[1372]   Singhota Report, p. 5, para. 13; *see also* Singhota Report, p. 4, para. 8.

[1373]   *See* Allen Report, p. 5; Singhota Report, p. 4, para. 8 ("It is quite likely that if there had been any momentary decision-making lapse on part of the bridge team, engine or steering gear failure, a catastrophic collision would have been the inevitable result.").

imposed by Rule 8, namely "due regard to the observance of good seamanship," also to have been violated.

1102. Finally, the Tribunal considers Rules 15 and 16, relating to right-of-way. Rule 15 states that when two power-driven vessels are crossing so as to involve a risk of collision, the vessel "which has the other on her own starboard side shall keep out of the way and shall, if the circumstances of the case admit, avoid crossing ahead of the other vessel."[1374]

1103. Rule 16, in turn, requires that "[e]very vessel which is directed . . . to keep out of the way of another vessel shall, so far as possible, take early and substantial action to keep well clear."[1375]

1104. On 28 April 2012, FLEC 310 approached BRP Pampanga to within 600 yards; fifteen minutes later, it passed BRP Edsa II from the starboard quarter to the port side at a distance of "barely 200 yards".[1376] In other words, rather than abiding by the applicable regulations by "keep[ing] out of the way" and avoiding the other ship, FLEC 310 did the opposite. The attempt by CMS 71, on 26 May 2012, to cut across the bow of MCS 3008 from the port (left) side at a distance of merely 100 yards admits of the same error. Accordingly, both incidents constituted a breach of the Rules of the COLREGS in this respect.

1105. In light of the foregoing analysis, the Tribunal considers China to have repeatedly violated the Rules of the COLREGS over the course of the interactions described by the crew of the Philippine vessels and as credibly assessed in the two expert reports. Where Chinese vessels were under an obligation to yield, they persisted; where the regulations called for a safe distance, they infringed it. The actions are not suggestive of occasional negligence in failing to adhere to the COLREGS, but rather point to a conscious disregard of what the regulations require. The various violations are underscored by factors such as the large disparity in size of the Chinese and Philippine vessels, the shallow waters in which the incidents took place, and the creation of a two metre-high wake causing additional risk to the Philippines' crews.[1377]

1106. The Tribunal notes that, in addition to the COLREGS themselves, the Singhota Report identifies Resolution MSC.303(87) adopted by the International Maritime Organisation's Maritime Safety

---

[1374]   COLREGS, Rule 15.

[1375]   COLREGS, Rule 16.

[1376]   *See* Singhota Report, p. 5, para. 14.

[1377]   Allen Report, p. 4.

Committee Resolution on 17 May 2010, entitled "Assuring safety during demonstrations, protests or confrontations on the high seas."[1378] The resolution calls upon governments to urge:

(1)   persons and entities under their jurisdiction to refrain from actions that intentionally imperil human life, the marine environment, or property during demonstrations, protests or confrontations on the high seas; [and]

. . .

(3)   all vessels, during demonstrations, protests or confrontations on the high seas, to comply with COLREG and SOLAS by taking all steps to avoid collisions and safeguard navigation, security and safety of life at sea.[1379]

While this resolution operates in the context of the high seas, the text is of interest insofar as it confirms the priority of maritime safety even in situations of confrontation.

1107. As the Allen Report makes clear, "operational requirements" of law enforcement vessels such as those of CMS and FLEC occasionally stand in tension with the obligations imposed by the COLREGS, without diminishing the nature or binding force of their provisions.[1380] In this regard, the Tribunal having reviewed the record relevant to Submission No. 13 and having considered possible circumstances precluding wrongfulness has found no convincing evidence that the aforementioned violations are excusable by any mitigating circumstances.

1108. The Tribunal emphasises again that its determinations in Submission No. 13 do not depend upon, and do not involve any finding of sovereignty over Scarborough Shoal and its waters. The same conclusions about violations of the navigational safety provisions of the Convention would be reached irrespective of which State has sovereignty over Scarborough Shoal. The Tribunal does not purport to make a finding on that question.

(d)   Conclusion

1109. Based on the considerations outlined above, the Tribunal finds that China has, by virtue of the conduct of Chinese law enforcement vessels in the vicinity of Scarborough Shoal, created serious risk of collision and danger to Philippine vessels and personnel. The Tribunal finds China to have violated Rules 2, 6, 7, 8, 15, and 16 of the COLREGS and, as a consequence, to be in breach of Article 94 of the Convention.

[1378]   Resolution MSC.303(87), *available at* <www.imo.org/en/knowledgecentre/indexofimoresolutions/ maritime-safety-committee-(msc)/documents/msc.303(87).pdf#search=msc%2e303%2887%29>; *see also* Singhota Report, Annex 5.

[1379]   Resolution MSC.303(87), art. 1/c operative paragraph 3, *available at* <www.imo.org/en/ knowledgecentre/indexofimoresolutions/maritime-safety-committee-(msc)/documents/msc.303(87) .pdf#search=msc%2e303%2887%29>.

[1380]   Allen Report, pp. 5-6; COLREGS, Rule 2(b).

this page intentionally blank

VIII. AGGRAVATION OR EXTENSION OF THE DISPUTE BETWEEN THE PARTIES (SUBMISSION NO. 14)

A. INTRODUCTION

1110. In this Chapter, the Tribunal addresses the Parties' dispute concerning China's actions since the commencement of this arbitration in January 2013, which the Philippines argues have "aggravated and extended the dispute." This dispute is reflected in the Philippines' Submission No. 14, which provides as follows (as amended):

> (14)   Since the commencement of this arbitration in January 2013, China has unlawfully aggravated and extended the dispute by, among other things:
>
> (a)   interfering with the Philippines' rights of navigation in the waters at, and adjacent to, Second Thomas Shoal;
>
> (b)   preventing the rotation and resupply of Philippine personnel stationed at Second Thomas Shoal;
>
> (c)   endangering the health and well-being of Philippine personnel stationed at Second Thomas Shoal; and
>
> (d)   conducting dredging, artificial island-building and construction activities at Mischief Reef, Cuarteron Reef, Fiery Cross Reef, Gaven Reef, Johnson Reef, Hughes Reef and Subi Reef; and

1111. Paragraphs (a) to (c) of Submission No. 14 comprised the initial formulation of this Submission, and concern China's interactions with the Armed Forces of the Philippines at Second Thomas Shoal.[1381] In light of the "extensive land reclamation activities" undertaken by China at many of the disputed features since the commencement of this dispute,[1382] the Philippines sought to amend Submission No. 14 to include paragraph (d), concerning China's dredging, artificial island-building, and construction activities at Mischief Reef, Cuarteron Reef, Fiery Cross Reef, Gaven Reef, Johnson Reef, Hughes Reef, and Subi Reef, when presenting its final Submissions at the end of the Hearing on the Merits.[1383] On 16 December 2015, after having invited China's comments on the requested amendments, the Tribunal gave the Philippines leave to amend its Submissions, noting in this respect that "the requested amendments are related to or incidental to the Submissions originally made by the Philippines and do not involve the introduction of a new dispute between the Parties."[1384]

[1381]   Memorial, p. 272.

[1382]   Letter from the Philippines to the Tribunal (30 July 2014); Letter from the Philippines to the Tribunal (27 April 2015); Merits Hearing Tr. (Day 3), pp. 74-75; Award on Jurisdiction, paras. 53, 72; *see also* supplemental documents of the Philippines filed on 19 November 2015 (Annexes 607-819).

[1383]   Merits Hearing Tr. (Day 4), p. 204.

[1384]   Letter from the Tribunal to the Parties (16 December 2015).

B. FACTUAL BACKGROUND

1112. Reflecting the different factual matters alleged by the Philippines to have aggravated and extended the Parties' dispute, the Tribunal will separately address (a) the events that occurred in and around Second Thomas Shoal, and (b) China's various construction activities at Mischief Reef, Cuarteron Reef, Fiery Cross Reef, Gaven Reef (North), Johnson Reef, Hughes Reef, and Subi Reef.

1. Chinese Actions in and around Second Thomas Shoal

1113. On 7 May 1999, the Philippine Navy grounded BRP Sierra Madre on Second Thomas Shoal, where it has remained to the present day.[1385] BRP Sierra Madre is a tank landing ship designed for offloading tanks and other heavy equipment onto an unimproved beach. She was built by the United States in 1944 and transferred to the Philippines in 1976. Since May 1999, the Philippines has maintained a detachment of approximately seven marines on board BRP Sierra Madre.[1386] This detachment is resupplied at regular intervals and the personnel rotated.[1387]

1114. On 22 January 2013, the Philippines commenced this arbitration by way of a Notification and Statement of Claim served on China. On 19 February 2013, China rejected and returned the Philippines' Notification and Statement of Claim.[1388]

(a) China's Objections to the Presence of BRP Sierra Madre at Second Thomas Shoal

1115. Beginning in February 2013, the Armed Forces of the Philippines reported the repeated presence of Chinese Government vessels and unidentified aircraft in the vicinity of Second Thomas Shoal.[1389]

[1385] Memorandum from the Secretary of Foreign Affairs, Republic of the Philippines, to the President of the Republic of the Philippines (23 April 2013) (Annex 93).

[1386] Memorandum from the Secretary of Foreign Affairs, Republic of the Philippines, to the President of the Republic of the Philippines (23 April 2013) (Annex 93).

[1387] Note Verbale from the Department of Foreign Affairs, Republic of the Philippines, to the Embassy of the People's Republic of China in Manila, No. 13 1882 (10 June 2013) (Annex 219); Letter from the Philippines to the Tribunal (18 March 2014).

[1388] Note Verbale from the Embassy of the People's Republic of China in Manila to the Department of Foreign Affairs, Republic of the Philippines, No. (13) PG-039 (19 February 2013) (Annex 3).

[1389] Armed Forces of the Philippines, *Near-Occupation of Chinese Vessels of Second Thomas (Ayungin) Shoal in the Early Weeks of May 2013* (May 2013) (Annex 94).

1116. In April 2013, China objected to the continued presence of BRP Sierra Madre on at least three occasions. As recorded by the Philippines, these objections were made on 11 April 2013, when the Philippine Ambassador to China met with the Special Representative of the Department of Boundary and Ocean Affairs of the Chinese Ministry of Foreign Affairs, on 16 April 2013 when the Chinese Ambassador to the Philippines met with an Undersecretary of the Philippine Ministry of Foreign Affairs, and on 17 April 2013, when the Philippine Ambassador to China met with the Chinese Vice Foreign Minister.[1390] As recorded by the Philippines, China objected that "the Philippine Navy vessel BRP Sierra Madre (LST 57), on the pretext of being stranded, was 'illegally grounded' on Second Thomas Shoal" and that "Philippine authorities promised China that they would immediately remove the stranded vessel but they have not done so up to this day."[1391] At the first of these meetings, the Chinese representative was also recorded as saying that China "would not allow the continuous stranding of the vessel."[1392]

1117. Beginning on 3 May 2013, the Armed Forces of the Philippines reported a significant increase in the presence of Chinese Government vessels at Second Thomas Shoal, including two Chinese Navy frigates and five Civilian Maritime Law Enforcement Agency vessels on a rotation basis.[1393]

1118. On 9 May 2013, the Philippines delivered a Note Verbale to China, objecting to the presence of Chinese vessels in the area of Second Thomas Shoal. After asserting that Second Thomas Shoal forms part of the continental shelf of the Philippines, the Note Verbale went on to state as follows:

> The Philippines notes that under UNCLOS, State Parties are obliged to "refrain from any threat or use of force against the territorial integrity or political independence of any State," or conduct any activities that are in "any manner inconsistent with the principles of international law embodied in the UN Charter." In this context, the Philippines protests the provocative and illegal presence of the following Chinese vessels in the vicinity of Ayungin [Second Thomas] Shoal:
>
> • Two (2) China Marine Surveillance (CMS) ships located at 0720H 04 May 2013 at vicinity three nautical miles East of Ayungin Shoal in the West Philippine Sea; and
>
> • One (1) Chinese warship believed to be a Type 053H1G (Jianghu-V Class) Missile Frigate with bow number 563 between Ayungin Shoal and Rajah Solaiman Reef also in the WPS.

[1390] Memorandum from the Secretary of Foreign Affairs, Republic of the Philippines, to the President of the Republic of the Philippines (23 April 2013) (Annex 93).

[1391] Memorandum from the Secretary of Foreign Affairs, Republic of the Philippines, to the President of the Republic of the Philippines (23 April 2013) (Annex 93).

[1392] Memorandum from the Secretary of Foreign Affairs, Republic of the Philippines, to the President of the Republic of the Philippines (23 April 2013) (Annex 93).

[1393] Armed Forces of the Philippines, *Near-Occupation of Chinese Vessels of Second Thomas (Ayungin) Shoal in the Early Weeks of May 2013* (May 2013) (Annex 94).

. . .

> The Philippines notes that it has filed a third-party adjudication under Annex VII of
> UNCLOS for the peaceful and durable solution of disputes in the South China Sea. In this
> connection, the Philippines respectfully reiterates its call for China to participate in this
> peaceful endeavor.[1394]

1119. On 22 May 2013, a spokesperson of the Chinese Foreign Ministry responded publicly to a
question concerning the Philippines' protest, noting as follows:

> Second Thomas Shoal is part of the Nansha Islands. China's possession of the islands and
> the surrounding waters is indisputable. Official Chinese vessels have conducted normal
> patrols in these waters, this cannot be questioned. China urges the countries involved to
> thoroughly implement the *Declaration of Conduct of Parties in the South China Sea,* and
> admonishes these countries not to take actions which would exacerbate or complicate the
> dispute or to take any actions which would affect the peace and stability of the South China
> Sea.[1395]

1120. On 28 May 2013, Major General Zhang Zhaozhong of the Chinese People's Liberation Army
gave an interview on Chinese State television and made the following comments regarding
China's strategy at features in the South China Sea:

> we have begun to take measures to seal and control the areas around the Huangyan Island
> [Scarborough Shoal], seal and control continuously up till now. In the over one year period
> since then, there have been fishermen in the inside. Our fishermen are often there because
> there is lot of fish there. Fishermen go there in large ships and then sail small boats in the
> lagoon to fish. They can have shelter in the lagoon when there is a typhoon.
>
> The fishermen conduct normal production there. In the area around the island, fishing
> administration ships and marine surveillance ships are conducting normal patrols while in
> the outer ring there are navy warships. The island is thus wrapped layer by layer like a
> cabbage. As a result, a cabbage strategy has taken shape.
>
> If the Philippines wants to go in, in the outermost area, it has first to ask whether our navy
> will allow it. Then it has to ask whether our fishery administration ships and marine
> surveillance ships will allow it. Therefore, our fishermen can carry out their production
> safely while our country's marine rights and interests as well as sovereignty are·
> safeguarded. Is that not satisfactory?
>
> . . .
>
> We should do more such things in the future. For those small islands, only a few troopers
> are able to station on each of them, but there is no food or even drinking water there. If we
> carry out the "cabbage" strategy, you will not be able to send food and drinking water onto
> the islands. Without the supply for one or two weeks, the troopers stationed there will
> leave the islands on their own. Once they have left, they will never be able to come back.
>
> For many things, we have to grab the right timing to do them. Over the past few years, we
> have made a series of achievements at the Nansha Islands (the Spratly Islands}, the greatest
> of which I think have been on the Huangyan Island [Scarborough Shoal], Meiji Reef
> (Mischief Reef) and Ren'ai Shoal (Second Thomas Shoal).

[1394]   Note Verbale from the Department of Foreign Affairs, Republic of the Philippines, to the Embassy of the
People's Republic of China in Manila, No. 13-1585 (9 May 2013) (Annex 217).

[1395]   Ministry of Foreign Affairs, People's Republic of China, *Foreign Ministry Spokesperson Hong Lei's
Regular Press Conference* (22 May 2013) (Annex 584).

We have gained quite satisfactory experience about the ways to recover the islands and reefs and defend them.[1396]

1121. On 10 June 2013, the Philippines responded to these comments by Note Verbale, reiterating its earlier position on Second Thomas Shoal and stating further that:

> The Philippines protests these statements, which it cannot help but regard as threats to use force to prevent the Philippines from delivering essential supplies to its personnel at Ayungin Shoal, in violation of Article 2 of the UN Charter, and Article 301 of UNCLOS, which provides that "States Parties shall refrain from any threat or use of force against the territorial integrity or political independence of any State, or in any other manner inconsistent with the principles of international law embodied in the UN Charter."
>
> The Philippines has no obligation to notify China of its naval or other maritime activities in the vicinity of Ayungin Shoal, or in any other area over which the Philippine is sovereign or has sovereign rights. However, in the interests of avoiding conflict, and so that its peaceful intentions cannot be misunderstood, the Philippines hereby voluntarily notifies China: that it will deliver essential supplies to its personnel at Ayungin Shoal this week; that, in this instance, these supplies will be delivered by a Philippine flag ship; that the only mission of this vessel is to deliver the essential supplies to the personnel presently situated at Ayungin Shoal; and that this vessel has no hostile intent or purpose, and will seek to avoid contact with any Chinese vessels that may be in the vicinity.
>
> The Philippines urges China to refrain from any hostile action to interfere with this sovereign act of the Philippine Government.
>
> Finally, the Philippines reminds China that both States are obligated by the UN Charter and UNCLOS to settle all disputes peacefully, and that, to this end, the Philippines has initiated arbitration proceedings under Annex VII of UNCLOS, to obtain a peaceful, lawful and durable settlement of the competing claims in the West Philippine Sea/South China Sea. The Philippines, which has pledged to accept and comply with the results of these proceedings, whatever they might be, calls upon China once again to actively participate in these peaceful dispute settlement proceedings.[1397]

(b) China's Interference in the Rotation and Resupply of Philippine Personnel at Second Thomas Shoal

1122. On 7 March 2014, representatives of the Philippines' Embassy in Beijing were invited to a meeting with the Representative of the Department of Boundary and Ocean Affairs of China's Foreign Ministry. As recorded by the Philippines, China's representative conveyed the following:

> a) The Chinese side heard that the Philippine plans to carry out "large scale construction" in Ayungin Shoal /Second Thomas shoal, "(which is) in Chinese Nansha Islands." (Mr. Xiao referred to Ayungin by Its Chinese name Ren'ai Reef throughout the meeting). China expresses grave concern, and seeks some clarification. If this is true, he said, China opposes and resolutely objects such course of action.

[1396] "China Boasts of Strategy to 'Recover' Islands Occupied by Philippines," *China Daily Mail* (28 May 2013) (Annex 325).

[1397] Note Verbale from the Department of Foreign Affairs, Republic of the Philippines, to the Embassy of the People's Republic of China in Manila, No. 13-1882 (10 June 2013) (Annex 219).

b)   In 1999, the Philippines illegally run aground a warship in Ayungin and immediately China made representations and "repeatedly made representations" to the Philippines to tow away the ship as soon as possible. The Philippines promised China that it would tow away this ship, but it has not done so. The Philippines "has no intention of removing this warship" and even engaged in construction. The Philippines "has failed on its promise and has engaged in constant illegal activities." Last year's "piling" and this year's "planned construction and reinforcement" are "cases in point."

c)   The Philippines has also "distorted the fact, misguided the public and covered up the truth." "We believe such actions blatantly over-turned the promise of the Philippines." "The rhetoric and behavior of the Philippines is provocative to China's sovereignty and sovereign rights and China will not tolerate such." It is also a "severe violation of the DOC". "China has indisputable sovereignty over the Nansha Islands and adjacent waters."

d)   The Chinese side is asking the Philippines to respect China's sovereignty and sovereign rights, tow away the grounded vessel and "put an end to any construction work or plans" and observe its commitments. "China would never accept the Philippines occupying Ren-ai Reef under any circumstance and in any form."

e)   "If the Philippines chooses to ignore China's major concerns and resolute objections, insists on construction, this would severely violate China's sovereign rights, push China's bottom line, and severely undermine DOC, the peace and stability in the SCS, China will not sit idly by and tolerate. We will take resolute measures and actions. There will be further damage to relations. All consequences will borne by the Philippines side.[1398]

1123. On 9 March 2014, two China Coast Guard vessels intercepted two Philippine vessels, which had been dispatched by the Philippines to conduct rotation and resupply operations for personnel stationed aboard BRP Sierra Madre, and prevented the Philippine vessels from entering Second Thomas Shoal. As reported by the Armed Forces of the Philippines:

> [O]n 9:30 AM of March 9, 2014, while en route to Ayungin Shoal at the area 7.2 NM NE off Bulig Shoal on course 055 degrees true, two (2) Chinese Coast Guard (CCG) vessels with bow numbers 3112 and 3113 suddenly appeared and trailed them at a distance of 1,400 yards.
>
> Thirty (30) minutes later, CCG 3113 approached the port quarter of AM700 at a distance of 400 yards while CCG 3112 approached the port beam of the civilian-contracted vessel at a distance of 200 yards. Both CCG vessels were blocking and preventing AM700 and the civilian-contracted watercraft from proceeding to Ayungin Shoal.
>
> At 12:40 PM, in the area NW off Hasa-Hasa Shoal at latitude 09.223 degrees North longitude 116.05 degrees true, CCG 3112 relayed to our vessels through digital signboard, sirens and megaphones at a distance of 1,000 yards that the CCG vessels were carrying out routine patrols in the area, which is under the jurisdiction of the People's Republic of China. Furthermore, they warned that our ships have to leave the area and should bear full responsibility of the consequences resulting therefrom.
>
> At 2:30PM, while the civilian-contracted vessel was avoiding contact with the CCG vessel, the former's engine suffered a mechanical breakdown, leaving her stranded in the water. The AM700 provided assistance to the civilian-contracted vessel and towed her back to

---

[1398]   Memorandum from the Embassy of the Republic of the Philippines in Beijing to the Secretary of Foreign Affairs, Republic of the Philippines, No. ZPE-070-2014-S (7 March 2014) (Annex 98).

Balabac, Palawan. The planned resupply and personnel rotation operations at Ayungin Shoal were aborted due to the said incident.[1399]

1124. On 11 March 2014, the Philippines conveyed its protest against these actions by Note Verbale, noting in relevant part as follows:

> The Department understands that China has purported to justify its actions by claiming that the Philippine vessels were carrying "construction materials" to Ayungin Shoal. The Philippines rejects this false accusation. Ayungin is part of the continental shelf of the Philippines. It is, therefore, entitled to exercise sovereign rights and jurisdiction in the area without the permission of other States. Nevertheless, in the interests of easing tensions, the Philippines wishes to make it perfectly clear that its chartered vessels were not carrying construction materials. To the contrary, they were merely delivering essential supplies to the Philippine personnel stationed there and to conduct rotation of personnel.
>
> . . .
>
> China's recent actions therefore represent a dramatic and dangerous departure from the *status quo*. As such, they constitute a flagrant, willful and material breach of Paragraph 5 of the 2002 ASEAN-China Declaration on the Conduct of Parties in the South China Sea (the "DOC"), pursuant to which the signatory States, including China, specifically undertook
>
> > "to exercise self-restraint in the conduct of activities that would complicate or escalate disputes and affect peace and stability including, among others, refraining from action of inhabiting on the presently uninhabited islands, reefs, shoals, cays, and other features and to handle their differences in a constructive manner."
>
> In addition, China's actions constitute a clear and urgent threat to the rights and interests of the Philippines under the 1982 United Nations Convention on the Law of the Sea (the "UNCLOS"), which are currently the subject of arbitration under Annex VII of UNCLOS. In accordance with Articles 76 and 77 of UNCLOS, only the Philippines has sovereign rights over the continental shelf in the area where Ayungin Shoal is located. No other State is lawfully entitled to assert sovereign rights or jurisdiction over said area. In this respect, the Philippines observes that there are no insular features claimed by China in the South China Sea capable of generating any potential entitlement in the area where Ayungin Shoal is located.
>
> China's actions also constitute a grave and imminent threat to the Philippines' right to have its maritime dispute with China settled peacefully and in good faith, as well as its right not to have the dispute aggravated or extended pending the outcome of the arbitration.
>
> The Department takes note of the fact that China's actions come just three weeks before the Philippines is due to submit its Memorial in the aforementioned arbitration. Under the, circumstances, the Department is, regrettably, compelled to conclude that China's conduct at Ayungin Shoal is intended as retaliation for the Philippines' initiative in seeking the resolution of its maritime dispute with China in accordance with international law, something the Philippines and China were unable to achieve despite years of negotiation.[1400]

[1399] Letter from Major General, Armed Forces of the Philippines, to the Secretary of Foreign Affairs, Republic of the Philippines, (10 March 2014) (Annex 99); *see also* "China expels Philippine vessels from Ren'ai Reef," *Xinhua* (10 March 2014) (Annex 331); Memorandum from the Embassy of the Republic of the Philippines in Beijing to the Secretary of Foreign Affairs of the Republic of the Philippines, No. ZPE 075 2014-S, (11 March 2014) (Annex 102); Letter from the Philippines to the Tribunal (18 March 2014).

[1400] Note Verbale from the Department of Foreign Affairs, Republic of the Philippines, to the Embassy of the People's Republic of China in Manila, No. 140711 (11 March 2014) (Annex 221).

1125. Upon receipt of the Philippines' Note, the Chargé d'Affaires of the Chinese Embassy in Manila responded as follows:

> The Chinese side does not accept the protest from the Philippine side. The Ren'ai reef is part of the Nansha islands and China has indisputable sovereignty over the Nansha islands and their adjacent waters. The Philippines grounding its warship on China's Ren'ai reef in 1999 due to so-called malfunction. The Philippines refused to honor its commitment of pulling away the ship on the excuse of technical problems despite China's persistent request.
>
> The Philippines violated the Declaration on the Conduct of Parties in the South China Sea and severely infringed China's sovereignty and jurisdiction over Ren'ai reef. It should be pointed out that the grounding of the Philippine ship does not constitute its occupation of the Ren'ai reef.
>
> China is resolute and firm in safeguarding its national sovereignty and never accepts the Philippines' illegal occupation of the Ren'ai reef in any form.[1401]

1126. Several days later, as reported by the Philippines to the Tribunal, "the Philippines was able to provide some essential food and water to its personnel aboard the *Sierra Madre* by means of an airdrop."[1402] The Philippines noted, however, that this "is an interim solution at best, as the Philippines still has not been able to rotate its personnel (a step which can be accomplished only by sea), and its capacity to deliver supplies by air is limited."[1403]

1127. A similar incident occurred when the Philippines attempted to resupply the BRP Sierra Madre on 29 March 2014. As reported by the Philippines to the Tribunal:

> On 29 March 2014, the Philippines sent a vessel to Second Thomas Shoal to carry out the supply and rotation of personnel aboard the BRP *Sierra Madre*, which has been grounded at the Shoal since 1999. The supply vessel is in the service of the Bureau of Fisheries and Aquatic Resources ("BFAR") and was selected to make the peaceful nature of its mission clear. Nevertheless, China attempted to interdict the vessel and prevent it from carrying out its humanitarian mission.
>
> China's actions on 29 March followed the same pattern as its actions on 9 March, which were reported in my letter dated 18 March. . . .
>
> About an hour from the shoal, the BFAR ship was spotted by a China Coast Guard vessel, which accelerated to approach the port side of the Philippine vessel, sounding its whistle at least three times in the process. Very shortly thereafter, a second, larger China Coast Guard vessel emerged, moving fast to block the path of the BFAR vessel and demanding that it turn around or "take full responsibility" for its actions. The maneuvers of the Chinese vessels created a grave risk of collision, in violation of the Convention on the International Regulations for Preventing Collisions at Sea, and Article 94 of the United Nations Convention on the Law of the Sea.
>
> . . .

[1401] Memorandum from the Assistant Secretary for Asian and Pacific Affairs, Department of Foreign Affairs, Republic of the Philippines, to the Secretary of Foreign Affairs, Republic of the Philippines (11 March 2014) (Annex 101).

[1402] Letter from the Philippines to the Tribunal (18 March 2014).

[1403] Letter from the Philippines to the Tribunal (18 March 2014).

In the face of these threatening actions, the smaller BF AR vessel changed course and increased the ship's speed to avoid the Chinese vessels. Ultimately, it was able to evade them by navigating into the shallow water of the Shoal where the deeper-draft Chinese ships were unable to follow. Once it had done so, the BFAR vessel completed its rotation and resupply mission.[1404]

2. China's Dredging, Artificial Island-Building and Construction Activities

1128. Since the commencement of the arbitration, China has greatly intensified its programme of building artificial islands and installations at Mischief Reef, Cuarteron Reef, Fiery Cross Reef, Gaven Reef (North), Johnson Reef, Hughes Reef, and Subi Reef. The factual background to China's construction activities is set out in detail with respect to the Philippines' Submission No. 11 (see paragraphs 823 to 852 to 890 above) and Submission No. 12 (see paragraphs 996 to 1009 above). Furthermore, the environmental impacts of these activities as outlined in the First and Second Carpenter Reports and the Ferse Report and the Tribunal's conclusions thereon are set out at paragraphs 976 to 993 above.

1129. For the purposes of the present Submission, the Tribunal recalls that these Chinese activities commenced, intensified, and were brought to the Tribunal's attention in the period following the commencement of the arbitration. For example on 30 July 2014, the Philippines brought to the Tribunal's attention the "extensive land reclamation activities" being undertaken by the Chinese at Hughes Reef, Johnson Reef, Gaven Reef (North) and Cuarteron Reef, involving the use of dredgers to pile sand around the reefs and expand the size of the artificial islands previously constructed, and the addition of a landing strip at Hughes Reef.[1405] On 27 April 2015, the Philippines advised the Tribunal that "China has recently extended its reclamation activities to two new features: Subi Reef and Mischief Reef."[1406]

C. THE PHILIPPINES' POSITION

1. Jurisdiction

1130. The Philippines submits that the Tribunal has jurisdiction to consider its Submission No. 14. It argues that Articles 297 and 298 of the Convention do not exclude the Tribunal's jurisdiction to consider this Submission. In the alternative, the Philippines argues that these exceptions do not apply to conduct that aggravates a dispute pending arbitration.[1407]

[1404] Letter from the Philippines to the Tribunal (7 April 2014).

[1405] Letter from the Philippines to the Tribunal (30 July 2014).

[1406] Letter from the Philippines to the Tribunal (27 April 2015).

[1407] Jurisdictional Hearing Tr. (Day 2), p. 91.

1131. According to the Philippines, the military activities exception in Article 298(1)(b) of the Convention does not exclude jurisdiction because the conduct relevant to paragraphs (a) to (c) of this Submission is not military in nature; rather, the activities are more appropriately considered law enforcement activities.[1408] The Philippines notes that China's conduct at Second Thomas Shoal "was largely carried out by CCG [China Coast Guard] and CMS vessels seeking to enforce China's purported 'jurisdiction'," and that where military vessels were used, they were used for civilian or law enforcement purposes.[1409] With regard to construction activities, the Philippines submits that China has repeatedly stated that "their purpose was civilian, not military," and that there is no basis to conclude that they are military activities.[1410] Based on its argument that the nature and purpose of the activity must be exclusively military, to the exclusion of all other incidental activities and purposes, the Philippines submits that the "involvement of military units in construction projects does not change their nature or purpose."[1411]

1132. The Philippines likewise argues that the exception in Article 298(1)(b) of the Convention for law enforcement activities does not apply. According to the Philippines, pursuant to Article 297(2) and (3), "the exception applies only to claims involving marine scientific research or fishing in the EEZ" and Submission No. 14 "addresses neither subject",[1412] and because:

> Second Thomas Shoal is a low-tide elevation substantially more than 12 M from any high-tide feature. It is subject to the sovereign rights of the Philippines in respect of the EEZ and the continental shelf. As a result, China is not "the coastal State" entitled to invoke the law enforcement activities exception in the area of Second Thomas Shoal.[1413]

1133. In the alternative, and in the event that the Tribunal considers the activities could be characterised as military in nature, the Philippines submits that the Tribunal's jurisdiction would remain unaffected. The Philippines argues that China's activities in and around Second Thomas Shoal "give[] rise to a distinct legal dispute under, *inter alia*, Article 300 of the Convention, which establishes obligations regarding good faith and abuse of rights, and out of the inherent obligation of a party to a dispute to refrain from aggravating or extending a dispute that is

---

[1408] Supplemental Written Submission, para. 9.25; Jurisdictional Hearing Tr. (Day 2), pp. 84-85.

[1409] Supplemental Written Submission, para. 9.25; Jurisdictional Hearing Tr. (Day 2), pp. 80-84, 92; Merits Hearing Tr. (Day 3), p. 84; (Day 4), pp. 103-104.

[1410] *See* Jurisdictional Hearing Tr. (Day 2), pp. 75-76; (Day 3), pp. 48-57; Merits Hearing Tr. (Day 2), pp. 213-215; (Day 4), p. 105-106.

[1411] Merits Hearing Tr. (Day 4), p. 104.

[1412] Supplemental Written Submission, para. 9.29; Jurisdictional Hearing Tr. (Day 2), pp. 78-79, 92.

[1413] Supplemental Written Submission, para. 9.28.

sub judice."[1414] According to the Philippines, "the act that constitutes an aggravation or extension of the dispute need not arise from a breach of any substantive duty under the Convention."[1415] Accordingly, "restrictions on jurisdiction over disputes arising from those duties are irrelevant," including the exceptions set out in Articles 297 and 298 of the Convention.[1416] Nor is the issue of the status and entitlements, if any, that are generated by features "relevant to the question of the Tribunal's jurisdiction to determine whether China's activities at that feature aggravated or extended the dispute."[1417]

2. The Philippines' Rights to Have this Dispute Settled Peacefully

1134. With respect to the merits of Submission No. 14, the Philippines submits that it has a right to have a dispute settled peacefully, and that China is under a corresponding obligation not to aggravate or extend a dispute pending its resolution. The Philippines argues that China has engaged in acts that have aggravated and extended the dispute.

(a) Obligation Not to Engage in Acts that Might Aggravate a Dispute

1135. The Philippines argues that China and the Philippines are required under Article 279 of the Convention to "settle any dispute between them concerning the interpretation or application of this Convention by peaceful means in accordance with Article 2, paragraph 3, of the Charter of the United Nations."[1418] According to the Philippines, a "long-recognized corollary" of this obligation "is the prohibition of any acts that might aggravate or extend the dispute."[1419] The Philippines elaborates this obligation by reference to the "basic principles of good faith and abuse of rights" in Article 300 of the Convention, and the requirement that States Parties "behave with restraint with a view to narrowing, not widening, the differences between them."[1420] It argues that aggravation and extension of the dispute are inconsistent with Articles 279 and 300 of the Convention.[1421] Furthermore, it argues that aggravation or extension of the

---

[1414] Jurisdictional Hearing Tr. (Day 2), pp. 144-145 *See also* Supplemental Written Submission, para. 9.26; Jurisdictional Hearing Tr. (Day 2), p. 91; *Southern Bluefin Tuna Cases (New Zealand v. Japan; Australia v. Japan)*, Award on Jurisdiction and Admissibility of 4 August 2000, RIAA, Vol. XXIII, p. 1 at p. 46, para. 64.

[1415] Merits Hearing Tr. (Day 3), pp. 78, 84.

[1416] Merits Hearing Tr. (Day 3), p. 78.

[1417] Merits Hearing Tr. (Day 3), p. 78.

[1418] Memorial, para. 6.43; Merits Hearing Tr. (Day 3), p. 76.

[1419] Memorial, para. 6.45.

[1420] Memorial, para. 6.46; Merits Hearing Tr. (Day 3), p. 76.

[1421] Merits Hearing Tr. (Day 3), p. 76.

dispute prejudices "the integrity of the adjudicative process and the ability of the Tribunal to render effective relief."[1422]

1136. In support of this proposition, the Philippines cites the Permanent Court of International Justice's decision on provisional measures in *Electricity Company of Sofia and Bulgaria*,[1423] which recognised the "universally accepted" principle that parties in a case must refrain from aggravating the dispute. [1424] The Philippines acknowledges that this principle was articulated in connection with a decision on provisional measures, and that this principle "is commonly invoked in the context of provisional measures."[1425] Nonetheless, it submits that:

> there is nothing in the Law of the Sea Convention or international law that limits the principle's application to provisional measures, that requires a party to seek provisional measures in order to invoke the principle, or that restricts application of the principle only to the limited circumstances in which it may be appropriate to prescribe provisional measures.[1426]

1137. In further support of the obligation to refrain from aggravation, the Philippines relies on the decision of the International Court of Justice in *United States Diplomatic and Consular Staff in Tehran*, [1427] the UN General Assembly's Friendly Relations Declaration of 1970, [1428] and paragraph 5 of the DOC.[1429]

(b) China's Conduct in relation to the Dispute

1138. The Philippines submits that China's actions in and around Second Thomas Shoal and its construction activities "violate the right of the Philippines under Article 279 of the Convention to have this dispute settled peacefully in accordance with Article 2(3) of the U.N. Charter" as well as the right not to have the dispute aggravated or extended.[1430]

[1422] Merits Hearing Tr. (Day 3), p. 77.

[1423] *Electricity Company of Sofia and Bulgaria (Belgium v. Bulgaria), Interim Measures of Protection, Order of 5 December 1939, PCIJ Series A/B, No. 79*, p. 199 (5 December 1939).

[1424] Memorial, para. 6.45; Merits Hearing Tr. (Day 3), p. 75.

[1425] Memorial, para. 6.46; Merits Hearing Tr. (Day 3), p. 75.

[1426] Merits Hearing Tr. (Day 3), pp. 75-76.

[1427] *United States Diplomatic and Consular Staff in Tehran (United States v. Iran), Judgment, ICJ Reports 1980*, p. 3 at p. 43, para. 93

[1428] UN General Assembly, *Declaration on Principles of International Law concerning Friendly Relations and Co-operation among States in accordance with the Charter of the United Nations*, UN Doc. A/RES/25/2625 (24 October 1970).

[1429] Merits Hearing Tr. (Day 3), p. 76; *Declaration on the Conduct of Parties in South China Sea*, para. 5 (4 November 2002).

[1430] Memorial, para. 6.151.

1139. With respect to Second Thomas Shoal, the Philippines argues that "China has dramatically and dangerously altered the *status quo pendente lite*" since the commencement of this arbitration, by aggressively challenging "the long-standing presence of the Philippines at Second Thomas Shoal" and "unlawfully preventing" the routine rotation and resupply missions "that the Philippines has been conducting consistently since 1999."[1431] According to the Philippines, these actions stem from a violation of the Convention, insofar as China's "interdiction of Philippine vessels navigating in the area [of Second Thomas Shoal] violates the exclusive rights and jurisdiction appertaining to the Philippines under Articles 56 and 77 of the Convention."[1432] The Philippines also considers that China's actions at Second Thomas Shoal were "intended as a reprisal for the Philippines' decision to move forward with this arbitration."[1433]

1140. With respect to construction activities, the Philippines submits that China has "greatly intensified its programme of building artificial islands and installations since the commencement of the arbitration."[1434] The Philippines refers to satellite imagery of the seven features addressed in this part of Submission No. 14, to official government statements, and to the findings of the expert reports referred to above which highlight the impact of these construction activities on the ecological integrity of the South China Sea. "[A]fter thousands of years of development," the Philippines notes, "these coral reefs are no longer in the condition in which they were found at the time this dispute was submitted to arbitration."[1435] Additionally, "[t]he direct evidence of the natural state of these features, which is relevant to several issues in this case, has been destroyed or covered over, and this following China's rejection of a site visit by the Tribunal."[1436] As a result, the Philippines argues, "[t]he Tribunal's capacity to render effective relief has been prejudiced," and "China has presented the Tribunal with a *fait accompli* of unprecedented proportions."[1437]

[1431] Memorial, paras. 6.148, 6.152.

[1432] Memorial, para. 6.150.

[1433] Letter from the Philippines to the Tribunal (18 March 2014); Note Verbale from the Department of Foreign Affairs, Republic of the Philippines, to the Embassy of the People's Republic of China in Manila, No. 140711, (11 March 2014) (Annex 221).

[1434] Merits Hearing Tr. (Day 3), pp. 82-83.

[1435] Merits Hearing Tr. (Day 3), p. 84.

[1436] Merits Hearing Tr. (Day 3), p. 84.

[1437] Merits Hearing Tr. (Day 3), p. 84.

D.   CHINA'S POSITION

1.   Obligation Not to Engage in Acts that Might Aggravate a Dispute

1141. In the course of these proceedings, China has on a number of occasions commented on the importance of good faith and the duties incumbent on States Parties pursuant to the Convention. In a letter to the individual members of the Tribunal dated 6 February 2015, the Chinese Ambassador to the Netherlands wrote that:

> China has made consistent and steadfast efforts to uphold and contribute to the international rule of law. To uphold the international rule of law, it is essential to adhere to the fundamental principles of international law, including the principle of respecting state sovereignty and territorial integrity, which are also enshrined in the *Charter of the United Nations*. On that basis, efforts should be made to maintain peace and stability in the international community, and promote cooperation, development and win-win results among all countries, rather than to instigate or even exacerbate disagreements and disputes in the name of "international rule of law", consequently disturbing regional peace and stability.[1438]

1142. In its Position Paper, China recalled the principle of good faith, stating that it:

> would call attention to Article 300 of the Convention, which provides that, "States Parties shall fulfil in good faith the obligations assumed under this Convention and shall exercise the rights, jurisdiction and freedoms recognized in this Convention in a manner which would not constitute an abuse of right." While being fully aware that its claims essentially deal with territorial sovereignty, that China has never accepted any compulsory procedures in respect of those claims, and that there has been an agreement existing between the two States to settle their relevant disputes by negotiations, the Philippines has nevertheless initiated, by unilateral action, the present arbitration. This surely contravenes the relevant provisions of the Convention, and does no service to the peaceful settlement of the disputes.[1439]

1143. China also argued in its Position Paper that the Philippines has violated the principle of good faith in relation to the DOC:

> [T]he Philippines recently called on the parties to the DOC to comply with Paragraph 5 of the DOC and to provide "the full and effective implementation of the DOC," in a proposal made in its Department of Foreign Affairs statement dated 1 August 2014. This selective and self-contradictory tactic clearly violates the principle of good faith in international law.
>
> The principle of good faith requires all States to honestly interpret agreements they enter into with others, not to misinterpret them in disregard of their authentic meaning in order to obtain an unfair advantage. This principle is of overriding importance and is incorporated in Article 2(2) of the Charter of the United Nations. It touches every aspect of international law (*Cf.* Sir Robert Jennings and Sir Arthur Watts (eds.), *Oppenheim's International Law*, 9th ed., 1992, vol. 1, p. 38). In the *Nuclear Tests Case*, the ICJ held that, "One of the basic principles governing the creation and performance of legal obligations, whatever their source, is the principle of good faith. Trust and confidence are inherent in international

---

[1438]   Letter from Ambassador of the People's Republic of China to the Kingdom of the Netherlands to the individual members of the Tribunal, para. 7 (6 February 2015) (Annex 470).

[1439]   China's Position Paper, para. 84.

co-operation" (*Nuclear Tests Case (Australia v. France)*, Judgment of 20 December 1974, ICJ Reports 1974, p. 268, para. 46).[1440]

2. China's Conduct in relation to the Dispute

(a) Chinese Activities in and around Second Thomas Shoal

1144. The Tribunal notes that China has expressed its position on Second Thomas Shoal in public statements and diplomatic correspondence in the record. China has consistently asserted that it:

> has indisputable sovereignty over the Nansha Islands, which include the Ren'ai Jiao, and the adjacent waters. China hereby strongly protests and firmly opposes to the Philippines' reinforcement of a military vessel illegally 'grounded' on the Ren'ai Jiao."[1441]

1145. In its Position Paper, China provides a more detailed explanation of its position on, and conduct in, Second Thomas Shoal. Describing it as a "constituent part of China's Nansha Islands," China asserts that:

> the Philippines illegally ran a naval ship aground in May 1999 at that feature on the pretext of 'technical difficulties'. China has made repeated representations to the Philippines, demanding that the latter immediately tow away the vessel. The Philippines, for its part, had on numerous occasions made explicit undertaking to China to tow away the vessel . . . . However, for over 15 years, instead of fulfilling that undertaking, the Philippines has attempted to construct permanent installations on Ren'ai Jiao. On 14 March 2014, the Philippines even openly declared that the vessel was deployed as a permanent installation on Ren'ai Jiao in 1999. China has been forced to take necessary measures in response to such provocative conduct.[1442]

1146. China has expressed two principal objections to the conduct of the Philippines in Second Thomas Shoal. First, it objects to the Philippines' refusal "to fulfill its commitment of towing away the vessel."[1443] Second, China alleges that the Philippines has "aggravate[d] the situation by carrying out illegal activities in an attempt to permanently occupy the Ren'ai Jiao."[1444] As it states in its Position Paper:

> In recent years, the Philippines has repeatedly taken new provocative actions in respect of . . . Ren'ai Jiao. Such actions have gravely hindered mutual political trust between China and the Philippines.[1445]

[1440] China's Position Paper, paras. 52-53.

[1441] Ministry of Foreign Affairs, People's Republic of China, *Foreign Ministry Spokesperson Hua Chunying's Remarks on the Philippines' Reinforcing a Military Vessel Illegally "Grounded" on China's Ren'ai Jiao* (15 July 2015) (Annex 630).

[1442] China's Position Paper, para. 51.

[1443] Memorandum from the Secretary of Foreign Affairs, Republic of the Philippines, to the President of the Republic of the Philippines (23 April 2013) (Annex 93).

[1444] Ministry of Foreign Affairs, People's Republic of China, *Foreign Ministry Spokesperson Hua Chunying's Remarks on the Philippines' Reinforcing a Military Vessel Illegally "Grounded" on China's Ren'ai Jiao* (15 July 2015) (Annex 630).

[1445] China's Position Paper, para. 91.

(b) China's Dredging and Construction Activities

1147. In relation to what a spokesperson of China's Foreign Ministry has referred to as "the land reclamation project of China's construction on some stationed islands and reefs of the Nansha Islands," China has consistently argued that its activities are "reasonable, justified and lawful," and within its sovereignty.[1446] China notes that its "indisputable sovereignty over Nansha Islands and their adjacent waters" includes Mischief Reef and Fiery Cross Reef, among others.[1447]

1148. In June 2015, the Foreign Ministry Spokesperson noted that:

> [t]he construction activities . . . are not targeted at any other country, do not affect the freedom of navigation and overflight enjoyed by all countries in accordance with international law in the South China Sea, nor have they caused or will they cause damage to the marine ecological system and environment in the South China Sea. . . .[1448]

1149. As discussed above in relation to the Philippines' Submissions No. 11 and 12, China has repeatedly stated publicly that the predominant purpose of its construction activities is civilian in nature.[1449] China's Foreign Ministry Spokesperson described the "main purpose" of the activities as:

> meet[ing] various civilian demands and better perform[ing] China's international obligations and responsibilities in the areas such as maritime search and rescue, disaster prevention and mitigation, marine scientific research, meteorological observation, ecological environment conservation, navigation safety as well as fishery production service. After the land reclamation, we will start the building of facilities to meet relevant functional requirements.[1450]

E. THE TRIBUNAL'S CONSIDERATIONS

1. The Tribunal's Jurisdiction

1150. The Tribunal must first address whether it has jurisdiction in respect of Submission No. 14.

[1446] Ministry of Foreign Affairs, People's Republic of China, *Foreign Ministry Spokesperson Lu Kang's Remarks on Issues relating to China's Construction Activities on the Nansha Islands and Reefs* (16 June 2015) (Annex 579). Ministry of Foreign Affairs, People's Republic of China, *Foreign Ministry Spokesperson Hong Lei's Regular Press Conference* (27 April 2015) (Annex 589).

[1447] Note Verbale from the Embassy of the People's Republic of China in Manila to the Department of Foreign Affairs, Republic of the Philippines, No. 15 (PG)-214, (28 June 2015) (Annex 689).

[1448] Ministry of Foreign Affairs, People's Republic of China, *Foreign Ministry Spokesperson Lu Kang's Remarks on Issues Relating to China's Construction Activities on the Nansha Islands and Reefs* (16 June 2015) (Annex 579).

[1449] *See e.g.*, Ministry of Foreign Affairs, People's Republic of China, *Foreign Ministry Spokesperson Hong Lei's Regular Press Conference on April 27, 2015*, (27 April 2015) (Annex 589).

[1450] Ministry of Foreign Affairs, People's Republic of China, *Foreign Ministry Spokesperson Lu Kang's Remarks on Issues Relating to China's Construction Activities on the Nansha Islands and Reefs* (16 June 2015) (Annex 579).

1151. In its Award on Jurisdiction, the Tribunal held that Submission No. 14, then in its unamended form, reflected a dispute concerning "China's activities in and around Second Thomas Shoal and China's interaction with the Philippine military forces stationed on the Shoal." [1451] According to the Tribunal, "[t]his is not a dispute concerning sovereignty or maritime boundary delimitation, nor is it barred from the Tribunal's consideration by any requirement of Section 1 of Part XV." [1452] However, the Tribunal noted that its jurisdiction to address the questions relating to Submission No. 14 "may depend on the status of Second Thomas Shoal as an 'island', 'rock', or 'low-tide elevation'." [1453] The Tribunal also noted the exclusion in Article 298(1)(b) for disputes concerning military activities and considered that "the specifics of China's activities in and around Second Thomas Shoal and whether such activities are military in nature to be a matter best assessed in conjunction with the merits."

1152. The Tribunal thus reserved any final decision on its jurisdiction with respect to Submission No. 14 for further consideration in this Award. [1454] The Tribunal also notes that the Philippines' amendment of its claims to include Submission No. 14(d) took place following the Tribunal's Award on Jurisdiction and that the Tribunal has not yet considered its jurisdiction in respect of the Philippines' amended claim.

(a) China's Actions in and around Second Thomas Shoal

1153. As set out above, the Tribunal has now found that Second Thomas Shoal is a low-tide elevation (see paragraphs 379 to 381) and, as such, generates no entitlement to maritime zones of its own. The Tribunal has also found that none of the high-tide features in the Spratly Islands is a fully entitled island for the purposes of Article 121 of the Convention (see paragraphs 473 to 647 above). The Tribunal has also found that there are no high-tide features within 12 nautical miles of Second Thomas Shoal (see paragraph 632 above). From these conclusions, it follows that there exists no legal basis for any entitlement by China to maritime zones in the area of Second Thomas Shoal. There is as a result no situation of overlapping entitlements that would call for the application of Articles 15, 74, or 83 to delimit the overlap. Nor is there any need to address sovereignty over Second Thomas Shoal before the Tribunal may consider China's actions there. Second Thomas Shoal is a low-tide elevation located within the exclusive economic zone of the Philippines.

[1451] Award on Jurisdiction, para. 411.

[1452] Award on Jurisdiction, para. 411.

[1453] Award on Jurisdiction, para. 411.

[1454] Award on Jurisdiction, paras. 411, 413(H).

1154. However, the Tribunal's jurisdiction is still contingent on the application of the military activities exception in Article 298(1)(b) of the Convention. That exception provides as follows:

> When signing, ratifying or acceding to this Convention or at any time thereafter, a State may, without prejudice to the obligations arising under section 1, declare in writing that it does not accept any one or more of the procedures provided for in section 2 with respect to one or more of the following categories of disputes:
>
> . . .
>
> (b)   disputes concerning military activities, including military activities by government vessels and aircraft engaged in non-commercial service . . . .

China activated this exception through its August 2006 Declaration.[1455]

1155. On its face, Article 298(1)(b) excludes the consent of any State Party making such a declaration in respect of any dispute concerning military activities. The Tribunal notes, however, that the Philippines has advanced two limitations that it considers to restrict the scope of Article 298(1)(b) and render it inapplicable in the present proceedings.

1156. First, the Philippines argues that "[t]he decision to rely on those options is a matter of choice, both at the declaration stage and thereafter. A respondent is not required to insist on a jurisdiction exception covered by a declaration."[1456] The Tribunal understands the Philippines' position to be that if China has not specifically invoked Article 298(1)(b) in the course of these proceedings, the Tribunal need look no further into the application of this provision. The Tribunal, however, cannot agree with this proposition. Article 298(1) provides for a State Party to "declare in writing that it does not accept" a form of compulsory dispute resolution with respect to one or more of the enumerated categories of disputes. This formulation stands in stark contrast to the more optional formulation employed in Article 297(2) and 297(3), which provide that a State Party "shall not be obliged to accept the submission" of a dispute to compulsory settlement. In contrast to an objection under Article 297, the Tribunal sees nothing to suggest that a provision of Article 298(1) must be specifically invoked. Once made, a declaration under Article 298(1) excludes the consent of the declaring State to compulsory settlement with respect to the specified categories of disputes. Article 299(1) then expressly provides in unequivocal terms that "[a] dispute . . . excepted by a declaration made under article 298 from the dispute settlement procedures provided for in section 2 may be submitted to such procedures only by agreement of the parties to the dispute." Such a declaration stands until modified or withdrawn. The absence of any mention of Article 298(1)(b) from China's

---

[1455]   People's Republic of China, Declaration under Article 298 (25 August 2006), 2834 UNTS 327.

[1456]   Jurisdiction Hearing Tr. (Day 2), p. 74.

Position Paper and public statements does not obviate the Tribunal's need to consider the applicability of this provision.

1157. Second, the Philippines argues that "Articles 297 and 298 do not apply to aggravation and extension of the dispute."[1457] According to the Philippines, "Submission 14 addresses only breaches of [China's] obligation [to refrain from aggravating or extending the dispute] that occurred after the dispute was submitted to this Tribunal. Jurisdiction over the dispute originally submitted to the Tribunal is the only requirement for jurisdiction over this submission. Articles 297 and 298 are inapplicable."[1458] The Tribunal understands this argument to be that, insofar as any obligation not to aggravate the dispute concerns events subsequent to the commencement of proceedings, it is not separately subject to the limitations on dispute resolution set out in the Convention. Rather, these limitations apply to the dispute that is alleged to have been aggravated.

1158. In this respect, the Tribunal notes that Article 298(1)(b) applies to "*disputes concerning* military activities" and not to "military activities" as such. Accordingly, the Tribunal considers the relevant question to be whether the dispute itself concerns military activities, rather than whether a party has employed its military in some manner in relation to the dispute. Where a State Party has initiated compulsory dispute settlement under the Convention in respect of a dispute that does not concern military activities, Article 298(1)(b) would not come into play if the other Party were later to begin employing its military in relation to the dispute in the course of proceedings. Nor does the Tribunal see that Article 298(1)(b) would limit its ancillary jurisdiction to prescribe provisional measures in respect of military activities taking place in relation to a dispute that does not, itself, concern military activities.

1159. Where the aggravation of the dispute is alleged not in connection with a request for provisional measures, but—as in the present case—as a substantive claim, the Tribunal finds it necessary to consider whether the claim of aggravation remains dependent on an underlying dispute, or whether it constitutes itself a distinct dispute to which the military activities exception would be applicable. The Tribunal notes that the Philippines has never clearly identified the dispute that it considers to have been aggravated by China's actions at Second Thomas Shoal. Rather, when pressed to elaborate on the existence of a dispute, the Philippines argued that China's interference with navigation and prevention of the rotation and resupply of Philippines troops "gives rise to a distinct legal dispute under, *inter alia*, Article 300 of the Convention, which establishes obligations regarding good faith and abuse of rights, and out of the inherent

---

[1457] Merits Hearing Tr. (Day 3), p. 84.

[1458] Jurisdictional Hearing Tr. (Day 2), p. 91.

obligation of a party to a dispute to refrain from aggravating or extending a dispute that is *sub judice*."[1459] The Tribunal likewise held in its Award on Jurisdiction that "Submission No. 14 reflects a dispute concerning China's activities in and around Second Thomas Shoal and China's interaction with the Philippine military forces stationed on the Shoal."[1460]

1160. It follows that China's actions in and around Second Thomas Shoal and its interaction with the Philippine military forces stationed there constitute a distinct matter, irrespective of their effect in potentially aggravating other disputes before the Tribunal. The Tribunal considers that it must evaluate whether this dispute concerns military activities for the purposes of Article 298(1)(b).

1161. On the basis of the record set out above, the Tribunal finds that the essential facts at Second Thomas Shoal concern the deployment of a detachment of the Philippines' armed forces that is engaged in a stand-off with a combination of ships from China's Navy and from China's Coast Guard and other government agencies. In connection with this stand-off, Chinese Government vessels have attempted to prevent the resupply and rotation of the Philippine troops on at least two occasions. Although, as far as the Tribunal is aware, these vessels were not military vessels, China's military vessels have been reported to have been in the vicinity. In the Tribunal's view, this represents a quintessentially military situation, involving the military forces of one side and a combination of military and paramilitary forces on the other, arrayed in opposition to one another. As these facts fall well within the exception, the Tribunal does not consider it necessary to explore the outer bounds of what would or would not constitute military activities for the purposes of Article 298(1)(b).

1162. Accordingly, the Tribunal finds that it lacks jurisdiction to consider the Philippines' Submissions No. 14(a) to (c).

(b)   China's Dredging and Construction Activities

1163. The Tribunal has already discussed its jurisdiction with respect to China's dredging, artificial island-building, and construction activities at Cuarteron Reef, Fiery Cross Reef, Johnson Reef, Hughes Reef, Gaven Reef (North), Subi Reef, and Mischief Reef in connection with the matters raised in the Philippines' Submissions No. 11 and 12 (see paragraphs 925 to 938 and 1024 to 1028 above).

[1459]   Jurisdictional Hearing Tr. (Day 2), pp. 144-145.

[1460]   Award on Jurisdiction, para. 411.

1164. For the reasons already set out, the Tribunal will not find activities to be military in nature when China itself has consistently resisted such classification and affirmed the opposite at the highest level. Accordingly, the Tribunal accepts China's repeatedly affirmed position that civilian use comprises the primary (if not the only) motivation underlying its works on the aforementioned features. As civilian activity, the Tribunal notes that China's conduct falls outside the scope of Article 298(1)(b) in any event. Accordingly, for the purposes of its jurisdictional analysis, the Tribunal need not engage with the question of whether the Philippines' Submission No 14(d) constitutes a distinct dispute from those the Philippines alleges to have been aggravated or extended.

1165. The Tribunal concludes that it has jurisdiction with respect to the matters raised in the Philippines' Submission No. 14(d). The Tribunal now turns to the activities underpinning this portion of the Philippines' claim.

2. The Law Applicable to Conduct in the Course of Dispute Resolution Proceedings

1166. The Philippines' claim that China, through its dredging, artificial island-building, and construction activities, has acted to aggravate and extend the dispute between the Parties, requires the Tribunal to consider the law applicable to the conduct of parties in the course of dispute resolution proceedings.

1167. In this respect, the Tribunal recalls the point made by the Permanent Court of International Justice in *Electricity Company of Sofia and Bulgaria*. In that matter, the Court was requested by Belgium to indicate provisional measures pursuant to Article 41 of its Statute to order that certain municipal court proceedings be suspended pending the resolution of the international case. The Court noted that Article 41 of its Statute:

> applies the principle universally accepted by international tribunals and likewise laid down in many conventions . . . to the effect that the parties to a case must abstain from any measure capable of exercising a prejudicial effect in regard to the execution of the decision to be given and, in general, not allow any step of any kind to be taken which might aggravate or extend the dispute.[1461]

The Court then went on to direct Bulgaria to "ensure that no step of any kind is taken capable of prejudicing the rights claimed by the Belgian Government or of aggravating or extending the dispute submitted to the Court."[1462]

[1461] *Electricity Company of Sofia and Bulgaria (Belgium v. Bulgaria), Interim Measures of Protection, Order of 5 December 1939, PCIJ Series A/B, No. 79*, p. 194 at p. 199.

[1462] *Electricity Company of Sofia and Bulgaria (Belgium v. Bulgaria), Interim Measures of Protection, Order of 5 December 1939, PCIJ Series A/B, No. 79*, p. 194 at p. 199.

1168. The same principle was recognised by the International Court of Justice in *LaGrand* as underpinning its power to indicate provisional measures and as evidence of the binding character of orders issued pursuant to Article 41 of the Court's Statute.[1463] Additionally, the International Court of Justice has frequently issued provisional measures directing the parties to refrain from any actions which could aggravate or extend the dispute[1464] and has done so notwithstanding that Article 41 of its Statute expressly refers only to measures "to preserve the respective rights of either party."[1465] In so doing, the Court has indicated that "independently of the requests for the indication of provisional measures submitted by the Parties to preserve specific rights, the Court possesses by virtue of Article 41 of the Statute the power to indicate provisional measures with a view to preventing the aggravation or extension of the dispute whenever it considers that circumstances so require."[1466] The International Tribunal for the Law of the Sea has likewise directed parties to "pursue cooperation and refrain from any unilateral action that might lead to aggravating the dispute" when ordering provisional measures under Article 290(1) of the Convention.[1467]

1169. In the Tribunal's view, the proper understanding of this extensive jurisprudence on provisional measures is that there exists a duty on parties engaged in a dispute settlement procedure to refrain from aggravating or extending the dispute or disputes at issue during the pendency of the

---

[1463] *LaGrand (Germany v. United States of America), Judgment, ICJ Reports 2001*, p. 466 at p. 503, paras. 102-103.

[1464] *Nuclear Tests (Australia v. France), Interim Protection, Order of 22 June 1973, ICJ Reports 1973*, p. 99 at p. 106; *Nuclear Tests (New Zealand v. France), Interim Protection, Order of 22 June 1973, ICJ Reports 1973*, p. 135 at p.142; *Frontier Dispute (Burkina Faso/Republic of Mali), Provisional Measures, Order of 10 January 1986, ICJ Reports 1986*, p3 at p. 9, para. 18, and p. 11, para. 32, point 1A; *United States Diplomatic and Consular Staff in Tehran, Provisional Measures, Order of 15 December 1979, ICJ Reports 1979*, p.7 at p. 21, para. 47(B); *Application of the Convention on the Prevention and Punishment of the Crime of Genocide (Bosnia and Herzegovina v. Yugoslavia (Serbia and Montenegro)), Provisional Measures, Order of 8 April 1993, ICJ Reports 1993*, p. 3 at p. 24, para. 52(B); *Land and Maritime Boundary between Cameroon and Nigeria (Cameroon v. Nigeria), Provisional Measures, Order of 15 March 1996, ICJ Reports 1996*, p. 13 at p. 24, para. 49(1); *Armed Activities on the Territory of the Congo (Democratic Republic of the Congo v. Uganda), Provisional Measures, Order of 3 July 2000, ICJ Reports 2000*, p. 129, para. 47(1).

[1465] Statute of the International Court of Justice, art. 41.

[1466] *Land and Maritime Boundary between Cameroon and Nigeria (Cameroon v. Nigeria), Provisional Measures, Order of 15 March 1996, ICJ Reports 1996*, p. 13 at pp. 22-23, para. 41. In its more recent jurisprudence, however, the Court has noted that it has consistently indicated measures directing the parties to refrain from actions that would aggravate or extend the dispute in conjunction with other provisional measures and found no need to address potential aggravation when it found that other measures were not warranted. *Pulp Mills on the River Uruguay (Argentina v. Uruguay), Provisional Measures, Order of 23 January 2007, ICJ Reports 2007*, p. 3 at p. 16, paras. 49-50; *see also Pulp Mills on the River Uruguay (Argentina v. Uruguay), Provisional Measures, Declaration of Judge Buergenthal, ICJ Reports 2007*, p. 21.

[1467] *Delimitation of the Maritime Boundary between Ghana and Côte D'Ivoire in the Atlantic Ocean, Provisional Measures, Order of 25 April 2015, ITLOS Reports 2015*, para. 108(1)(e).

settlement process. This duty exists independently of any order from a court or tribunal to refrain from aggravating or extending the dispute and stems from the purpose of dispute settlement and the status of the States in question as parties in such a proceeding. Indeed, when a court or tribunal issues provisional measures directing a party to refrain from actions that would aggravate or extend the dispute, it is not imposing a new obligation on the parties, but rather recalling to the parties an obligation that already exists by virtue of their involvement in the proceedings.

1170. Recognition of a duty to refrain from aggravating or extending a dispute during settlement proceedings is also apparent in the widespread inclusion of express provisions to such effect in multilateral conventions providing for the settlement of disputes[1468] and its nearly routine inclusion in bilateral arbitration and conciliation treaties.[1469] Such a duty has also been underlined by the General Assembly of the United Nations in its Friendly Relations Declaration, which provides:

> States parties to an international dispute, as well as other States shall refrain from any action which may aggravate the Situation so as to endanger the maintenance of international peace and security, and shall act in accordance with the purposes and principles of the United Nations.[1470]

1171. In the Tribunal's view, such a duty is inherent in the central role of good faith in the international legal relations between States. Article 26 of the Vienna Convention on the Law of Treaties recognises this when it provides that "[e]very treaty in force is binding upon the parties to it and must be performed by them in good faith."[1471] This obligation is no less applicable to the provisions of a treaty relating to dispute settlement. Where a treaty provides for the

---

[1468] See, e.g., Convention on Conciliation and Arbitration within the Conference on Security and Co-operation in Europe, art. 16, 15 December 1992, 1842 UNTS 150; European Convention for the Peaceful Settlement of Disputes, art. 31, 29 April 1957, 320 UNTS 243; Revised General Act for the Pacific Settlement of International Disputes, art. 33(3), 28 April 1949, 71 UNTS 101.

[1469] The Tribunal notes the inclusion of such a provision in well over 50 bilateral arbitration conventions concluded between a variety of different States. See, e.g., Treaty for Conciliation, Judicial Settlement and Arbitration between the United Kingdom of Great Britain and Northern Ireland and Switzerland, art. 31, 7 July 1965, 605 UNTS 205; Treaty between Brazil and Venezuela for the Pacific Settlement of Disputes, art. XXII, 30 March 1940, 51 UNTS 306; Treaty for the Pacific Settlement of Disputes between the Kingdom of Iraq and the Empire of Iran, art. 19, 24 July 1937, 190 UNTS 270; Treaty of Arbitration, Judicial Settlement and Conciliation between Denmark and the United States of Venezuela, art. 20, 19 December 1933, 158 UNTS 250; Treaty of Friendship, Non-Aggression, Judicial Settlement, Arbitration and Conciliation between the Turkish Republic and the Kingdom of Yugoslavia, art. 21, 27 November 1933, 161 UNTS 230; Arbitration Treaty between France and Netherlands, 10 March 1928, art. 20, 102 UNTS 110; Arbitration Convention between Germany and France, art. 19, 16 October 1925, 54 UNTS 316.

[1470] UN General Assembly, Declaration on Principles of International Law concerning Friendly Relations and Co-operation among States in accordance with the Charter of the United Nations, UN Doc. A/RES/25/2625 (24 October 1970).

[1471] Vienna Convention on the Law of Treaties, art. 26.

compulsory settlement of disputes, the good faith performance of the treaty requires the cooperation of the parties with the applicable procedure. Compulsory settlement is also premised on the notion that the final result will be binding on the parties and implemented by them as a resolution of their dispute. The very purpose of dispute settlement procedures would be frustrated by actions by any party that had the effect of aggravating or extending the dispute, thereby rendering it less amenable to settlement.

1172. Within the Convention, the same principles find expression in Article 279, which provides that:

> States Parties shall settle any dispute between them concerning the interpretation or application of this Convention by peaceful means in accordance with Article 2, paragraph 3, of the Charter of the United Nations and, to this end, shall seek a solution by the means indicated in Article 33, paragraph 1, of the Charter.

In carrying out the dispute settlement procedures of the Convention, the Parties are also under an obligation, pursuant to Article 300, to "fulfil in good faith the obligations assumed under this Convention and . . . exercise the rights, jurisdiction and freedoms recognized in this Convention in a manner which would not constitute an abuse of right."[1472] Finally, the Tribunal considers that the final and binding nature of the Award has an impact on the permissible conduct of the parties in the course of proceedings. Article 296 of the Convention provides that "[a]ny decision rendered by a court or tribunal having jurisdiction under this section shall be final and shall be complied with by all the parties to the dispute"; Article 11 of Annex VII to the Convention provides that "[t]he award shall be final and without appeal, unless the parties to the dispute have agreed in advance to an appellate procedure. It shall be complied with by the parties to the dispute." The Tribunal concludes that actions by either Party to aggravate or extend the dispute would be incompatible with the recognition and performance in good faith of these obligations.

1173. In the Tribunal's view, there is no need to reach beyond the text of the Convention to identify the source of the law applicable to the conduct of parties in the course of dispute settlement proceedings under Part XV. To the extent that it were necessary to do so, however, the Tribunal considers, for the reasons set out above, that the duty to "abstain from any measure capable of exercising a prejudicial effect in regard to the execution of the decision to be given and, in general, not allow any step of any kind to be taken which might aggravate or extend the dispute"[1473] constitutes a principle of international law that is applicable to States engaged in dispute settlement as such. Pursuant to Article 293 of the Convention, this principle constitutes

---

[1472]   Convention, art. 300.

[1473]   *Electricity Company of Sofia and Bulgaria (Belgium v. Bulgaria), Interim Measures of Protection, Order of 5 December 1939, PCIJ Series A/B, No. 79*, p. 194 at p. 199.

one of the "other rules of international law not incompatible with this Convention" to which the Tribunal may have recourse.[1474]

3. The Effect of China's Dredging and Construction Activities on the Parties' Disputes

1174. Having found that the Convention and other rules of international law binding on the Parties impose a duty to refrain from aggravating or extending the dispute pending the completion of dispute resolution proceedings, the Tribunal considers that a necessary first step is to identify clearly the dispute that is alleged to have been aggravated or extended. Neither the Convention, nor international law, go so far as to impose a legal duty on a State to refrain from aggravating generally their relations with one another, however desirable it might be for States to do so. Actions must have a specific nexus with the rights and claims making up the parties' dispute in order to fall foul of the limits applicable to parties engaged in the conduct of dispute resolution proceedings.

1175. In the Tribunal's view, China's dredging, artificial island-building, and construction activities at Cuarteron Reef, Fiery Cross Reef, Johnson Reef, Hughes Reef, Gaven Reef (North), Subi Reef, and Mischief Reef bear on a number of the disputes submitted by the Philippines for resolution in these proceedings:

(a) First, the Philippines has put before this Tribunal a dispute concerning the status and entitlements of a number of features in the South China Sea that are presently under the control of China. This is reflected in the Philippines' Submissions No. 4, 6, and 7. As discussed in connection with the Tribunal's consideration of those Submissions (see paragraphs 305 to 306, 321, 511, 541, and 578 above), China's dredging, artificial island-building, and construction activities has had the effect of obscuring evidence of the natural status of those features.

(b) Second, the Philippines has put before the Tribunal a series of disputes concerning the Parties' respective entitlements to maritime zones and corresponding rights under the Convention in the area of Mischief Reef. These disputes are reflected in the Philippines' Submissions No. 5, 8, 9, and 12. China's dredging, artificial island-building, and construction activities have had the effect of obscuring evidence of the natural status of Mischief Reef, which is in turn determinative of the Parties' potential rights in the area. Additionally, as the Tribunal has found that Mischief Reef is a low-tide elevation located on the continental shelf of the Philippines, China's construction there of a very large

---

[1474] Convention, art. 293.

artificial island has an effect on the implementation of the Tribunal's decision and the Philippines' future exercise of its sovereign rights in the area of Mischief Reef.

(c)   Third, the Philippines has put before the Tribunal a dispute concerning the protection and preservation of the marine environment at Scarborough Shoal, Second Thomas Shoal, Cuarteron Reef, Fiery Cross Reef, Gaven Reef (North), Johnson Reef, Hughes Reef, Subi Reef, and Mischief Reef. China's construction at seven of these features of large artificial islands, covering significant portions of the reef platform, has an effect on the implementation of the Tribunal's decision and the practical possibility of avoiding harm to the marine environment.

1176. In the course of dispute resolution proceedings, the conduct of either party may aggravate a dispute where that party continues during the pendency of the proceedings with actions that are alleged to violate the rights of the other, in such a way as to render the alleged violation more serious. A party may also aggravate a dispute by taking actions that would frustrate the effectiveness of a potential decision, or render its implementation by the parties significantly more difficult. Finally, a party may aggravate a dispute by undermining the integrity of the dispute resolution proceedings themselves, including by rendering the work of a court or tribunal significantly more onerous or taking other actions that decrease the likelihood of the proceedings in fact leading to the resolution of the parties' dispute.

1177. The Tribunal considers that China's intensified construction of artificial islands on seven features in the Spratly Islands during the course of these proceedings has unequivocally aggravated the disputes between the Parties identified above. First, China has effectively created a *fait accompli* at Mischief Reef by constructing a large artificial island on a low-tide elevation located within the Philippines' exclusive economic zone and continental shelf, an area in which only the Philippines has sovereign rights with respect to living and non-living resources and where only the Philippines may construct or authorise artificial islands. In practical terms, the implementation of the Tribunal's decision will be significantly more difficult for the Parties, and Mischief Reef cannot be returned to its original state, before China's construction work was begun.

1178. Second, China has aggravated the Parties' dispute with respect to the protection and preservation of the marine environment by causing irreparable harm to the coral reef habitat at Cuarteron Reef, Fiery Cross Reef, Gaven Reef (North), Johnson Reef, Hughes Reef, Subi Reef, and Mischief Reef. The Tribunal has already found that China has seriously violated its obligation to preserve and protect the marine environment in the South China Sea (see paragraphs 950 to 993 above). Whatever other States have done within the South China Sea, it pales in comparison to China's recent construction. In practical terms, neither this decision nor any action that either Party may take in response can undo the permanent damage that has been done to the coral reef habitats of the South China Sea. In this respect, the Tribunal is conscious that the marine environment at Cuarteron Reef, Fiery Cross Reef, Gaven Reef (North), Johnson Reef, Hughes Reef, and Subi Reef did not form part of the Philippines' claims in these proceedings prior to the close of the November 2015 hearing. In the Tribunal's view, China's actions have aggravated the dispute between the Parties with respect to the marine environment at Mischief Reef and extended that dispute to encompass additional features that became the sites of large-scale construction work while this arbitration was ongoing.

1179. Finally, China has undermined the integrity of these proceedings and rendered the task before the Tribunal more difficult. At the same time that the Tribunal was called upon to determine the status of features in the Spratly Islands and the entitlements that such features were capable of generating, China has permanently destroyed evidence of the natural status of those same features (see paragraphs 305 to 306, 321, 511, 541, and 578 above). The small rocks and sand cays that determine whether a feature constitutes a low-tide elevation or a high-tide feature capable of generating an entitlement to a territorial sea are now literally buried under millions of tons of sand and concrete. Despite this, the Tribunal has reached a decision on the status of features in the South China Sea using the best evidence available to it and drawing heavily on historical sources. The Tribunal is satisfied that its decisions regarding the status of features are well founded in fact, but records that they were rendered significantly more difficult by China's works at the features in question.

1180. The Tribunal notes China's consistent position that it will not participate in these proceedings and its view that "non-participation in the present arbitration is solidly grounded in international law."[1475] China has also continued to reject the jurisdiction of this Tribunal, notwithstanding the decisions reached in the Tribunal's Award on Jurisdiction.[1476] The Tribunal recalls that Article 9 of Annex VII to the Convention anticipates the possibility that a party may not appear before the arbitral tribunal. However, the Convention also provides that "[i]n the event of a dispute as to whether a court or tribunal has jurisdiction, the matter shall be settled by decision

---

[1475] China's Position Paper, paras. 76-85.

[1476] *See, e.g.*, Ministry of Foreign Affairs, People's Republic of China, *Statement of the Ministry of Foreign Affairs of the People's Republic of China on the Award on Jurisdiction and Admissibility of the South China Sea Arbitration by the Arbitral Tribunal Established at the Request of the Republic of the Philippines* (30 October 2015); Ministry of Foreign Affairs, People's Republic of China, *Briefing by Xu Hong, Director-General of the Department of Treaty and Law on the South China Sea Arbitration Initiated by the Philippines* (12 May 2016) *available at* <www.fmprc.gov.cn/mfa_eng/wjdt_665385/zyjh_665391/t1364804.shtml>.

of that court or tribunal"[1477] and that "[a]ny decision rendered by a court or tribunal having jurisdiction under this section shall be final and shall be complied with by all the parties to the dispute."[1478] China has been free to represent itself in these proceedings in the manner it considered most appropriate, including by refraining from any formal appearance, as it has in fact done. The decision of how best to represent China's position is a matter for China, not the Tribunal. China is not free, however, to act to undermine the integrity of these proceedings or to frustrate the effectiveness of the Tribunal's decisions. The Convention and general international law limit the actions a party may take in the course of ongoing dispute resolution proceedings. China has fallen short of its obligations in this respect.

4. Conclusion

1181. Based on the considerations outlined above, the Tribunal finds that China has in the course of these proceedings aggravated and extended the disputes between the Parties through its dredging, artificial island-building, and construction activities. In particular, while these proceedings were ongoing:

(a) China has aggravated the Parties' dispute concerning their respective rights and entitlements in the area of Mischief Reef by building a large artificial island on a low-tide elevation located in the exclusive economic zone of the Philippines.

(b) China has aggravated the Parties' dispute concerning the protection and preservation of the marine environment at Mischief Reef by inflicting permanent, irreparable harm to the coral reef habitat of that feature.

(c) China has extended the Parties' dispute concerning the protection and preservation of the marine environment by commencing large-scale island-building and construction works at Cuarteron Reef, Fiery Cross Reef, Gaven Reef (North), Johnson Reef, Hughes Reef, and Subi Reef.

(d) China has aggravated the Parties' dispute concerning the status of maritime features in the Spratly Islands and their capacity to generate entitlements to maritime zones by permanently destroying evidence of the natural condition of Mischief Reef, Cuarteron Reef, Fiery Cross Reef, Gaven Reef (North), Johnson Reef, Hughes Reef, and Subi Reef.

*   *   *

[1477] Convention, art. 288(4).

[1478] Convention, art. 296(1).

IX. THE FUTURE CONDUCT OF THE PARTIES (SUBMISSION NO. 15)

1182. In this Chapter, the Tribunal addresses the Philippines' Submission No. 15, which requests the Tribunal to adjudge and declare that:

> (15) China shall respect the rights and freedoms of the Philippines under the Convention, shall comply with its duties under the Convention, including those relevant to the protection and preservation of the marine environment in the South China Sea, and shall exercise its rights and freedoms in the South China Sea with due regard to those of the Philippines under the Convention.

1183. As originally framed, the Philippines' Submission No. 15 requested a declaration that "China shall desist from further unlawful claims and activities."[1479] In its Award on Jurisdiction, the Tribunal noted that the claims and activities to which the original Submission could potentially relate were unclear. Thus the Tribunal held that it was unable at the time to determine whether a dispute existed "between the Parties concerning the interpretation or application of the Convention or to assess the scope of the Tribunal's jurisdiction in this respect."[1480] Accordingly, the Tribunal directed the Philippines "to clarify the content and narrow the scope of its Submission No. 15" and reserved the question of its jurisdiction in relation to Submission No. 15 for consideration in conjunction with the merits of the Philippines' claims.[1481]

1184. The Philippines reframed its Submission at the Hearing on the Merits and in subsequent correspondence. The Tribunal granted leave to the Philippines to amend its Submission accordingly, noting that the proposed amendment was related to or incidental to the Philippines' original Submission and did not involve the introduction of a new dispute between the Parties.[1482]

A. THE PHILIPPINES' POSITION

1185. The Philippines observes that "[t]he focus of this submission is prospective."[1483] According to the Philippines, the record of China's "significant, persistent and continuing violations" of the Philippines' rights under the Convention, and China's "statements and conduct in this regard provide ample justification for ordering China to respect the rights and freedoms of the Philippines in the future, and to honour its environmental obligations."[1484]

[1479] Memorial, p. 272.

[1480] Award on Jurisdiction, para. 412.

[1481] Award on Jurisdiction, paras. 412, 413(I).

[1482] Letter from the Tribunal to the Parties (16 December 2015).

[1483] Merits Hearing Tr. (Day 3), p. 90.

[1484] Merits Hearing Tr. (Day 3), p. 91.

1186. The Philippines links its Submission No. 15 to the requirement of "due regard", which it argues is "one of the basic organising principles" of the Convention and should be given "broad application."[1485] The Philippines provides as examples of China's failure to show due regard to the Philippines' rights China's attempts to prevent Philippine fishing or hydrocarbon activities in areas within 200 miles of the Philippines, as well as the conduct by China of its own activities within that area.[1486]

1187. The Philippines concentrated its arguments about Submission No. 15 on the hypothetical situation that would result from the Tribunal finding any of the Spratly features to be fully entitled islands under Article 121 of the Convention, and the uncertainty, tension and "perverse effects" that would potentially result from such a finding.[1487] It reflected on the "chaos and insecurity" that had resulted in the past year and a half from "unilateral actions in the absence of a precisely defined legal order."[1488]

1188. With respect to the Tribunal's jurisdiction to address the issues described in connection with Submission No. 15, the Philippines argued there are "no obstacles". It acknowledges that due to China's invocation of Article 298's exclusion for sea boundary delimitation, "the Tribunal could not proceed to delimit any areas of overlapping entitlements." However, the Philippines states that "the Tribunal would retain jurisdiction in respect of the rights and obligations of the parties in the area of overlap pending such a delimitation."[1489] The Philippines explains:

> [P]aragraph 3 of Articles 74 and 83 is not a delimitation provision to which Article 298(1)(a) applies. Rather, the paragraph invites the structuring of a binding code of conduct pending delimitation of overlapping entitlements. As such, that paragraph 3 is a specific manifestation of the obligation to settle disputes peacefully, set forth in Article 279, and of the prohibition on abuse of rights set forth in Article 300. Paragraph 1(a) of Article 298 does not apply to those articles either; they are not specifically mentioned, and they are not delimitation provisions.[1490]

B. CHINA'S POSITION

1189. China has not directly stated its position with respect to Submission No. 15 as amended.

1190. The Tribunal has already noted however, in respect of Submission No. 14, that in the course of these proceedings, Chinese officials have made a number of statements on the importance of

---

[1485] Merits Hearing Tr. (Day 3), pp. 90-91.

[1486] Merits Hearing Tr. (Day 3), pp. 91-92.

[1487] Merits Hearing Tr. (Day 3), pp. 92-101.

[1488] Merits Hearing Tr. (Day 3), pp. 97-98.

[1489] Merits Hearing, p. 96.

[1490] Merits Hearing, pp. 96-97.

good faith and the duties incumbent on States pursuant to the Convention.[1491] For example, the Position Paper emphasised that, pursuant to Article 300 of the Convention, States Parties shall "exercise the rights, jurisdiction and freedoms recognized in this Convention in a manner which would not constitute an abuse of right."[1492] More recently, on 19 May 2016, China's Foreign Minister Wang Yi spoke of China acting in accordance with law and "safeguarding the sanctity of the UNCLOS."[1493]

C. THE TRIBUNAL'S CONSIDERATIONS

1191. There are three components to the Philippines' Submission No. 15 as amended.

1192. First, the Tribunal is asked to adjudge and declare that China shall respect the rights and freedoms of the Philippines under the Convention.

1193. Second, the Tribunal is asked to adjudge and declare that China shall comply with its duties under the Convention, including those relevant to the protection and preservation of the marine environment in the South China Sea.

1194. Third, the Tribunal is asked to adjudge and declare that China shall exercise its rights and freedoms in the South China Sea with due regard to those of the Philippines under the Convention.

1195. All of these propositions fall within the basic rule of "*pacta sunt servanda*", expressed in Article 26 of the Vienna Convention on the Law of Treaties as: "Every treaty in force is binding upon the parties to it and must be performed by them in good faith." In essence, what the Philippines is requesting is a declaration from the Tribunal that China shall do what it is already obliged by the Convention to do.

1196. As both Parties have pointed out, the Convention itself expresses in Article 300 that:

> States Parties shall fulfil in good faith the obligations assumed under this Convention and shall exercise the rights, jurisdiction and freedoms recognized in this Convention in a manner which would not constitute an abuse of right.

[1491] See paragraphs 1141 to 1143 above.

[1492] China's Position Paper, para. 84.

[1493] Ministry of Foreign Affairs, People's Republic of China, *Transcript of Foreign Minister Wang Yi's Interview With Belahodood of Al Jazeera* (19 May 2016), *available at* <www.fmprc.gov.cn/mfa_eng/zxxx_662805/t1364778.shtml>.

1197. The Tribunal accepts that various provisions of the Convention make clear that States are under a duty to resolve their disputes peacefully,[1494] and that States are under a general duty to have "due regard" to the rights and obligations of other States.[1495]

1198. There is, however, no dispute between the Parties that these general obligations define and regulate their conduct. The root of the disputes presented by the Philippines in this arbitration lies not in any intention on the part of China or the Philippines to infringe on the legal rights of the other, but rather—as has been apparent throughout these proceedings—in fundamentally different understandings of their respective rights under the Convention in the waters of the South China Sea. In such circumstances, the purpose of dispute resolution proceedings is to clarify the Parties' respective rights and obligations and thereby to facilitate their future relations in accordance with the general obligations of good faith that both governments unequivocally recognise.

1199. To the extent that the matters presented by the Philippines have fallen within its jurisdiction, the Tribunal has already acted, through this Award, to clarify the Parties' respective rights and obligations in the South China Sea. The Tribunal notes that much of the Philippines' concern reflected in Submission No. 15 that "chaos and insecurity" will result from "unilateral actions in the absence of a precisely defined legal order"[1496] is connected with the hypothetical situation of potentially overlapping entitlements to maritime zones and the absence of an interim regime pending the delimitation of a maritime boundary. The Tribunal's findings with respect to Submissions No. 3, 5, and 7, however, and its conclusion that there is no possible overlap of entitlements that would require delimitation, render that concern purely hypothetical and no basis for further action by the Tribunal.

1200. Going forward, it is a fundamental principle of international law that "bad faith is not presumed,"[1497] and Article 11 of Annex VII provides that the "award . . . shall be complied with by the parties to the dispute."[1498] It goes without saying that both Parties are obliged to resolve their disputes peacefully and to comply with the Convention and this Award in good faith.

[1494] Convention, art. 279.

[1495] *See Dispute Concerning Delimitation of the Maritime Boundary Between Bangladesh and Myanmar in the Bay of Bengal (Bangladesh/Myanmar), Judgment of 14 March 2012, ITLOS Reports 2012*, paras. 475-476.

[1496] Merits Hearing Tr. (Day 3), p. 98.

[1497] *Chagos Marine Protected Area Arbitration (Mauritius v. United Kingdom)*, Award, 18 March 2015, para. 447; *quoting Affaire du lac Lanoux (Spain/France)*, Award of 16 November 1957, RIAA, Vol. XII, p. 281 at p. 305.

[1498] Convention, Annex VII, art. 11. The same obligation arises from Article 296 of the Convention itself.

D.   CONCLUSION

1201. The Tribunal considers it beyond dispute that both Parties are obliged to comply with the Convention, including its provisions regarding the resolution of disputes, and to respect the rights and freedoms of other States under the Convention. Neither Party contests this, and the Tribunal is therefore not persuaded that it is necessary or appropriate for it to make any further declaration.

*   *   *

this page intentionally blank

X. DISPOSITIF

1202. The Tribunal recalls and incorporates the following findings reached unanimously in its Award on Jurisdiction and Admissibility of 29 October 2015:

A. that the Tribunal was properly constituted in accordance with Annex VII to the Convention.

B. that China's non-appearance in these proceedings does not deprive the Tribunal of jurisdiction.

C. that the Philippines' act of initiating this arbitration did not constitute an abuse of process.

D. that there is no indispensable third party whose absence deprives the Tribunal of jurisdiction.

E. that the 2002 China–ASEAN Declaration on Conduct of the Parties in the South China Sea, the joint statements of the Parties referred to in paragraphs 231 to 232 of the Tribunal's Award on Jurisdiction and Admissibility of 29 October 2015, the Treaty of Amity and Cooperation in Southeast Asia, and the Convention on Biological Diversity, do not preclude, under Articles 281 or 282 of the Convention, recourse to the compulsory dispute settlement procedures available under Section 2 of Part XV of the Convention.

F. that the Parties have exchanged views as required by Article 283 of the Convention.

G. that the Tribunal has jurisdiction to consider the Philippines' Submissions No. 3, 4, 6, 7, 10, 11, and 13, subject to the conditions noted in paragraphs 400, 401, 403, 404, 407, 408, and 410 of the Tribunal's Award on Jurisdiction and Admissibility of 29 October 2015.

1203. For the reasons set out in this Award, the Tribunal unanimously, and without prejudice to any questions of sovereignty or maritime boundary delimitation, decides as follows:

A. **In relation to its jurisdiction, the Tribunal:**

(1) FINDS that China's claims in the South China Sea do not include a claim to 'historic title', within the meaning of Article 298(1)(a)(i) of the Convention, over the waters of the South China Sea and that the Tribunal, therefore, has jurisdiction to consider the Philippines' Submissions No. 1 and 2;

(2) FINDS, with respect to the Philippines' Submission No. 5:

a. that no maritime feature claimed by China within 200 nautical miles of Mischief Reef or Second Thomas Shoal constitutes a fully entitled island for the purposes of Article 121 of the Convention and therefore that no maritime feature claimed by China within 200 nautical miles of Mischief Reef or Second Thomas Shoal has the capacity to generate an entitlement to an exclusive economic zone or continental shelf;

b. that Mischief Reef and Second Thomas Shoal are low-tide elevations and, as such, generate no entitlement to maritime zones of their own;

c. that there are no overlapping entitlements to an exclusive economic zone or continental shelf in the areas of Mischief Reef or Second Thomas Shoal; and

d.   that the Tribunal has jurisdiction to consider the Philippines' Submission No. 5;

(3) FINDS, with respect to the Philippines' Submissions No. 8 and 9:

a.   that no maritime feature claimed by China within 200 nautical miles of Mischief Reef or Second Thomas Shoal constitutes a fully entitled island for the purposes of Article 121 of the Convention and therefore that no maritime feature claimed by China within 200 nautical miles of Mischief Reef or Second Thomas Shoal has the capacity to generate an entitlement to an exclusive economic zone or continental shelf;

b.   that Mischief Reef and Second Thomas Shoal are low-tide elevations and, as such, generate no entitlement to maritime zones of their own;

c.   that Reed Bank is an entirely submerged reef formation that cannot give rise to maritime entitlements;

d.   that there are no overlapping entitlements to an exclusive economic zone or continental shelf in the areas of Mischief Reef or Second Thomas Shoal or in the areas of the Philippines' GSEC101, Area 3, Area 4, or SC58 petroleum blocks;

e.   that Article 297(3)(a) of the Convention and the law enforcement exception in Article 298(1)(b) of the Convention are not applicable to this dispute; and

f.   that the Tribunal has jurisdiction to consider the Philippines' Submissions No. 8 and 9;

(4) FINDS that China's land reclamation and/or construction of artificial islands, installations, and structures at Cuarteron Reef, Fiery Cross Reef, Gaven Reef (North), Johnson Reef, Hughes Reef, Subi Reef, and Mischief Reef do not constitute "military activities", within the meaning of Article 298(1)(b) of the Convention, and that the Tribunal has jurisdiction to consider the Philippines' Submissions No. 11 and 12(b);

(5) FINDS, with respect to the Philippines' Submissions No. 12(a) and 12(c):

a.   that no maritime feature claimed by China within 200 nautical miles of Mischief Reef or Second Thomas Shoal constitutes a fully entitled island for the purposes of Article 121 of the Convention and therefore that no maritime feature claimed by China within 200 nautical miles of Mischief Reef or Second Thomas Shoal has the capacity to generate an entitlement to an exclusive economic zone or continental shelf;

b.   that Mischief Reef and Second Thomas Shoal are low-tide elevations and, as such, generate no entitlement to maritime zones of their own;

c.   that there are no overlapping entitlements to an exclusive economic zone or continental shelf in the areas of Mischief Reef or Second Thomas Shoal; and

d.   that the Tribunal has jurisdiction to consider the Philippines' Submissions No. 12(a) and 12(c);

(6) FINDS with respect to the Philippines' Submission No. 14:

    a.   that the dispute between China and the Philippines concerning the stand-off between the Philippines' marine detachment on Second Thomas Shoal and Chinese military and paramilitary vessels involves "military activities", within the meaning of Article 298(1)(b) of the Convention, and that the Tribunal has no jurisdiction to consider the Philippines' Submissions No. 14(a) to (c); and

    b.   that China's land reclamation and/or construction of artificial islands, installations, and structures at Cuarteron Reef, Fiery Cross Reef, Gaven Reef (North), Johnson Reef, Hughes Reef, Subi Reef, and Mischief Reef do not constitute "military activities", within the meaning of Article 298(1)(b) of the Convention, and that the Tribunal has jurisdiction to consider the Philippines' Submission No. 14(d);

(7) FINDS, with respect to the Philippines' Submission No. 15, that there is not a dispute between the Parties such as would call for the Tribunal to exercise jurisdiction; and

(8) DECLARES that it has jurisdiction to consider the matters raised in the Philippines' Submissions No. 1, 2, 3, 4, 5, 6, 7, 8, 9, 10, 11, 12, 13, and 14(d) and that such claims are admissible.

B.   In relation to the merits of the Parties' disputes, the Tribunal:

(1) DECLARES that, as between the Philippines and China, the Convention defines the scope of maritime entitlements in the South China Sea, which may not extend beyond the limits imposed therein;

(2) DECLARES that, as between the Philippines and China, China's claims to historic rights, or other sovereign rights or jurisdiction, with respect to the maritime areas of the South China Sea encompassed by the relevant part of the 'nine-dash line' are contrary to the Convention and without lawful effect to the extent that they exceed the geographic and substantive limits of China's maritime entitlements under the Convention; and further DECLARES that the Convention superseded any historic rights, or other sovereign rights or jurisdiction, in excess of the limits imposed therein;

(3) FINDS, with respect to the status of features in the South China Sea:

    a.   that it has sufficient information concerning tidal conditions in the South China Sea such that the practical considerations concerning the selection of the vertical datum and tidal model referenced in paragraphs 401 and 403 of the Tribunal's Award on Jurisdiction and Admissibility of 29 October 2015 do not pose an impediment to the identification of the status of features;

    b.   that Scarborough Shoal, Gaven Reef (North), McKennan Reef, Johnson Reef, Cuarteron Reef, and Fiery Cross Reef include, or in their natural condition did include, naturally formed areas of land, surrounded by water, which are above water at high tide, within the meaning of Article 121(1) of the Convention;

    c.   that Subi Reef, Gaven Reef (South), Hughes Reef, Mischief Reef, and Second Thomas Shoal, are low-tide elevations, within the meaning of Article 13 of the Convention;

d.   that Subi Reef lies within 12 nautical miles of the high-tide feature of Sandy Cay on the reefs to the west of Thitu;

e.   that Gaven Reef (South) lies within 12 nautical miles of the high-tide features of Gaven Reef (North) and Namyit Island; and

f.   that Hughes Reef lies within 12 nautical miles of the high-tide features of McKennan Reef and Sin Cowe Island;

(4)   DECLARES that, as low-tide elevations, Mischief Reef and Second Thomas Shoal do not generate entitlements to a territorial sea, exclusive economic zone, or continental shelf and are not features that are capable of appropriation;

(5)   DECLARES that, as low-tide elevations, Subi Reef, Gaven Reef (South), and Hughes Reef do not generate entitlements to a territorial sea, exclusive economic zone, or continental shelf and are not features that are capable of appropriation, but may be used as the baseline for measuring the breadth of the territorial sea of high-tide features situated at a distance not exceeding the breadth of the territorial sea;

(6)   DECLARES that Scarborough Shoal, Gaven Reef (North), McKennan Reef, Johnson Reef, Cuarteron Reef, and Fiery Cross Reef, in their natural condition, are rocks that cannot sustain human habitation or economic life of their own, within the meaning of Article 121(3) of the Convention and accordingly that Scarborough Shoal, Gaven Reef (North), McKennan Reef, Johnson Reef, Cuarteron Reef, and Fiery Cross Reef generate no entitlement to an exclusive economic zone or continental shelf;

(7)   FINDS with respect to the status of other features in the South China Sea:

a.   that none of the high-tide features in the Spratly Islands, in their natural condition, are capable of sustaining human habitation or economic life of their own within the meaning of Article 121(3) of the Convention;

b.   that none of the high-tide features in the Spratly Islands generate entitlements to an exclusive economic zone or continental shelf; and

c.   that therefore there is no entitlement to an exclusive economic zone or continental shelf generated by any feature claimed by China that would overlap the entitlements of the Philippines in the area of Mischief Reef and Second Thomas Shoal; and

DECLARES that Mischief Reef and Second Thomas Shoal are within the exclusive economic zone and continental shelf of the Philippines;

(8)   DECLARES that China has, through the operation of its marine surveillance vessels in relation to M/V Veritas Voyager on 1 and 2 March 2011 breached its obligations under Article 77 of the Convention with respect to the Philippines' sovereign rights over the non-living resources of its continental shelf in the area of Reed Bank;

(9)   DECLARES that China has, by promulgating its 2012 moratorium on fishing in the South China Sea, without exception for areas of the South China Sea falling within the exclusive economic zone of the Philippines and without limiting the moratorium to Chinese flagged vessels, breached its obligations under Article 56 of

the Convention with respect to the Philippines' sovereign rights over the living resources of its exclusive economic zone;

(10)   FINDS, with respect to fishing by Chinese vessels at Mischief Reef and Second Thomas Shoal:

a.   that, in May 2013, fishermen from Chinese flagged vessels engaged in fishing within the Philippines' exclusive economic zone at Mischief Reef and Second Thomas Shoal; and

b.   that China, through the operation of its marine surveillance vessels, was aware of, tolerated, and failed to exercise due diligence to prevent such fishing by Chinese flagged vessels; and

c.   that therefore China has failed to exhibit due regard for the Philippines' sovereign rights with respect to fisheries in its exclusive economic zone; and

DECLARES that China has breached its obligations under Article 58(3) of the Convention;

(11)   FINDS that Scarborough Shoal has been a traditional fishing ground for fishermen of many nationalities and DECLARES that China has, through the operation of its official vessels at Scarborough Shoal from May 2012 onwards, unlawfully prevented fishermen from the Philippines from engaging in traditional fishing at Scarborough Shoal;

(12)   FINDS, with respect to the protection and preservation of the marine environment in the South China Sea:

a.   that fishermen from Chinese flagged vessels have engaged in the harvesting of endangered species on a significant scale;

b.   that fishermen from Chinese flagged vessels have engaged in the harvesting of giant clams in a manner that is severely destructive of the coral reef ecosystem; and

c.   that China was aware of, tolerated, protected, and failed to prevent the afore-mentioned harmful activities; and

DECLARES that China has breached its obligations under Articles 192 and 194(5) of the Convention;

(13)   FINDS further, with respect to the protection and preservation of the marine environment in the South China Sea:

a.   that China's land reclamation and construction of artificial islands, installations, and structures at Cuarteron Reef, Fiery Cross Reef, Gaven Reef (North), Johnson Reef, Hughes Reef, Subi Reef, and Mischief Reef has caused severe, irreparable harm to the coral reef ecosystem;

b.   that China has not cooperated or coordinated with the other States bordering the South China Sea concerning the protection and preservation of the marine environment concerning such activities; and

c.   that China has failed to communicate an assessment of the potential effects of such activities on the marine environment, within the meaning of Article 206 of the Convention; and

DECLARES that China has breached its obligations under Articles 123, 192, 194(1), 194(5), 197, and 206 of the Convention;

(14) With respect to China's construction of artificial islands, installations, and structures at Mischief Reef:

    a.   FINDS that China has engaged in the construction of artificial islands, installations, and structures at Mischief Reef without the authorisation of the Philippines;

    b.   RECALLS (i) its finding that Mischief Reef is a low-tide elevation, (ii) its declaration that low-tide elevations are not capable of appropriation, and (iii) its declaration that Mischief Reef is within the exclusive economic zone and continental shelf of the Philippines; and

    c.   DECLARES that China has breached Articles 60 and 80 of the Convention with respect to the Philippines' sovereign rights in its exclusive economic zone and continental shelf;

(15) FINDS, with respect to the operation of Chinese law enforcement vessels in the vicinity of Scarborough Shoal:

    a.   that China's operation of its law enforcement vessels on 28 April 2012 and 26 May 2012 created serious risk of collision and danger to Philippine ships and personnel; and

    b.   that China's operation of its law enforcement vessels on 28 April 2012 and 26 May 2012 violated Rules 2, 6, 7, 8, 15, and 16 of the Convention on the International Regulations for Preventing Collisions at Sea, 1972; and

DECLARES that China has breached its obligations under Article 94 of the Convention; and

(16) FINDS that, during the time in which these dispute resolution proceedings were ongoing, China:

    a.   has built a large artificial island on Mischief Reef, a low-tide elevation located in the exclusive economic zone of the Philippines;

    b.   has caused—through its land reclamation and construction of artificial islands, installations, and structures—severe, irreparable harm to the coral reef ecosystem at Mischief Reef, Cuarteron Reef, Fiery Cross Reef, Gaven Reef (North), Johnson Reef, Hughes Reef, and Subi Reef; and

    c.   has permanently destroyed—through its land reclamation and construction of artificial islands, installations, and structures—evidence of the natural condition of Mischief Reef, Cuarteron Reef, Fiery Cross Reef, Gaven Reef (North), Johnson Reef, Hughes Reef, and Subi Reef; and

FINDS further that China:

    d.   has aggravated the Parties' dispute concerning their respective rights and entitlements in the area of Mischief Reef;

    e.   has aggravated the Parties' dispute concerning the protection and preservation of the marine environment at Mischief Reef;

f.   has extended the scope of the Parties' dispute concerning the protection and preservation of the marine environment to Cuarteron Reef, Fiery Cross Reef, Gaven Reef (North), Johnson Reef, Hughes Reef, and Subi Reef; and

g.   has aggravated the Parties' dispute concerning the status of maritime features in the Spratly Islands and their capacity to generate entitlements to maritime zones; and

DECLARES that China has breached its obligations pursuant to Articles 279, 296, and 300 of the Convention, as well as pursuant to general international law, to abstain from any measure capable of exercising a prejudicial effect in regard to the execution of the decisions to be given and in general, not to allow any step of any kind to be taken which might aggravate or extend the dispute during such time as dispute resolution proceedings were ongoing.

*   *   *

this page intentionally blank

Done at The Hague, this 12ᵗʰ day of ___July___ 2016,

_____
Judge Rüdiger Wolfrum

_____
Judge Stanislaw Pawlak

_____
Judge Jean-Pierre Cot

_____
Professor Alfred H.A. Soons

_____
Judge Thomas A. Mensah
Presiding Arbitrator

_____
Ms. Judith Levine
Registrar

THE TAIWANESE YEAR BOOK OF INTERNATIONAL LAW 2016

作　　者：彭明敏 (Ming-Min Peng)、顏慶章 (Ching-Chang Yen)、
　　　　　卜睿哲 (Richard Bush)、艾瑞璽 (Charles R. Irish)、
　　　　　淺田正彥 (Masahiko Asada)、鄔楓 (Lutz-Christian Wolff)、
　　　　　顏維婷 (Wei-Ting Yen)

出 版 者：台灣國際法學會
　　　　　Taiwanese Society of International Law

地　　址：台北市中山區南京東路二段 125 號 14 樓－1

電　　話：(02)2515-4932

傳　　真：(02)2517-3558

網　　址：www.tsil.org.tw

E M A I L：tsilorg@ms78.hinet.net

出版日期：2017 年 11 月

I S B N：978-986-81291-5-3

定　　價：新台幣 1500 元整

訂書匯款資料：

銀行帳號：101-10-0062001 華南銀行儲蓄分行

戶　　名：社團法人台灣國際法學會